DATE DUE

DEC 2 0 1991		
JUN 2 2 1993		
AUG 0 8 1994		
JUN 0 1 1995		
JUN 0 5 1997		
MAR 2 9 1999		
DEC 0 6 2000		

DEMCO 38-297

Investments

GARY SMITH

Pomona College

SCOTT, FORESMAN/LITTLE, BROWN HIGHER EDUCATION
A Division of Scott, Foresman and Company
Glenview, Illinois   London, England

To James Tobin
For those who know him, no explanation is necessary.
For those who don't, no explanation could be sufficient.

"Goodness is the only investment that never fails."
Henry David Thoreau, *Walden*, 1854

Library of Congress Cataloging-in-Publication Data
Smith, Gary
  Investments/Gary Smith.
    p. cm.
  Includes bibliographical references.
  ISBN 0-673-39858-7
  1. Investments. I. Title.
HG4521.S6815 1989
332.6—dc20   89-29556
              CIP

Artwork, illustrations, and other materials supplied by the publisher.
Copyright © 1990 Scott, Foresman and Company.
1 2 3 4 5 6—WKK—94 93 92 91 90 89

TO THE INSTRUCTOR

Financial markets are continually evolving in new and sometimes complex ways, as innovative people develop new products and services. Underneath the seeming complexity of these innovations are some recurrent general principles—such as present value, leverage, hedging, efficient markets, and the conservation of value—that are explained and illustrated in *Investments*. These concepts can be stated in plain English and easily understood. Instead of temporarily memorizing facts and formulas for the next test, students are encouraged to learn these basic principles that can be applied to all investments.

These principles are illustrated again and again in *Investments* by actual applications to interesting topics, including junk bonds, leveraged buyouts, insider trading, speculative bubbles, global diversification, term structure bets that bankrupted some savings and loan associations, and strategies that have helped others survive. *Investments* has numerous real-world examples and exercises—far more than competing textbooks—that give students opportunities to apply the general principles they have learned. Many of the exercises contain quotations from the financial press for students to interpret and critique; these too are practice for life after the classroom—samples of the opportunities that will confront students and the advice they will be offered.

OPTIONAL MATERIAL

This book can be adapted to a variety of interests and time constraints. Those chapter sections that can be easily skipped have been labeled optional, both in the table of contents and in the text itself. Later chapters do not assume that these optional sections have been covered. Chapter 3 ("Amortized Loans") and Chapter 12 ("The Human Factor in Investment") can also be omitted with no loss of continuity. The essential ideas of mean-variance analysis are discussed in the last section ("Diversified Portfolios") of Chapter 13; the details are given in Chapter 14. This organization allows Chapter 14 to be omitted by those with insufficient time to cover the details. Those who assign Chapter 14 may want to skip the last section of Chapter 13.

SUPPLEMENTS

Robert Brooks has prepared a student study guide and accompanying computer software. The user-friendly software runs on IBM and IBM-compatible PCs and enables students to do the computations required in the text's exercises (and in many situations they will encounter after the course is over). The study guide contains additional explanations of the text material and exercises that can be assigned as homework or done for practice—including exercises designed specifically for the course software. Adopters can also obtain an instructor's manual that I have written which contains lecture examples, detailed answers to all of the text exercises, and additional exercises for class discussion or tests. Ninety transparencies of important figures and tables are also available.

ACKNOWLEDGMENTS

Many reviewers read my repeated drafts carefully and made thoughtful, detailed suggestions. They really should be considered coauthors:

Wayne Boyet, Nicholls State University
W. Ken Farr, Georgia College
John A. Haslem, University of Maryland, College Park
John Howe, Louisiana State University, Baton Rouge
Michael Kuehlwein, Pomona College
Linda Martin, Arizona State University
Michael McBain, Marquette University
George A. Racette, University of Oregon
Louis O. Scott, University of Georgia, Athens
Neal Stoughton, University of California, Irvine
Paul Tatsch, University of the Pacific
William C. Wood, James Madison University, Harrisonburg, Va.
Terry Zivney, University of Tennessee, Chattanooga

I have learned much from the thousands of students who have taken courses from me during the past eighteen years. At the risk of offending others, I will single out Chris Lalli and Reza Zefari, now at Goldman Sachs, for supplying useful data; Ed Yardeni, the Director of Economics & Fixed Income Research at Prudential-Bache, for his insights; and Dave Swensen, Associate Vice President in Yale University's Investments Office, for his detailed comments on my manuscript.

Gary Smith

TO THE STUDENT

To the casual observer, financial markets may appear to be little more than national casinos, sideshows that have little or nothing to do with real economic activity. After all, investment analysts, brokers, and bankers don't produce anything tangible like cars and houses, do they? This cynical belief is ill-informed. Financial markets are central to modern economies, offering attractive investments to savers who want to provide for the future, and plentiful opportunities to those who need funds to buy a house, build a factory, or start a new business. This bringing together of savers and borrowers benefits both groups.

Financial markets transform the small savings of cautious households into large investments by bold entrepreneurs. They allow workers to be capitalists, sharing in the profits of industrial giants. They manufacture liquidity and reduce all sorts of risks. Although none of these effects are tangible, they help make possible the cars, houses, and other products of modern economies.

Fluctuations in the prices of bonds, stocks, and other assets reflect the changing state of the economy and also affect peoples' economic lives, enriching or impoverishing participants and making it easier or more difficult for entrepreneurs to obtain financing. It is no coincidence that financial markets and economic activity collapsed together in the Great Depression. Every U.S. recession in the past 30 years has been preceded by a tightening of financial markets—what participants call "credit crunches." It was an easing of financial markets that brought the economy out of the 1981-1982 recession and fueled the subsequent economic recovery. No wonder that financial events are front-page news.

Educated citizens need to understand financial markets—to see why some economists use the stock market to help predict economic booms and recessions; why low interest rates are good for bond and stock prices; and how speculative bubbles sometimes emerge, and then burst. Why are junk bonds called "junk" and why do some investors find them appealing? What motivates takeover bids and the "shark repellents" used to resist unwanted offers? What is insider trading and why is it illegal?

How can a company's stock sell for more or less than the value shown on the company's own books? What does it mean when a nation's corporations, as a whole, are valued by financial markets at less than the cost of their land, buildings, and other assets? Why are the interest rates on one-year bonds often lower than the rates on longer-term bonds? Why was there a flip-flop in 1989, when short-term bonds offered the highest rates?

You will learn the answers to these questions and many more in this book. You will see how stock exchanges operate, how the Dow Jones Industrial Average is calculated, and how investment professionals predict whether stock prices will rise or fall. You will see why many savings and loan associations were bankrupted by a policy of using short-term deposits to finance long-term mortgages, and how those that survived have switched to less risky strategies. You will learn about options, futures, and program trading strategies, and see why the popularity of these strategies caused the chairman of the New York Stock Exchange to warn of a financial meltdown shortly before October 19, 1987—a day when stock prices fell by more than 20% and stockholders suffered an aggregate loss of $500 billion.

Financial markets are not only in the news; they also affect your pocketbooks. The market crash on October 19, 1987 is an obvious example. But there are hundreds of less frightening, everyday examples, too. Borrowers must decide whether to borrow a lot or a little, long-term or short-term, fixed-rate or variable-rate. Savers must choose among thousands of competing assets. This textbook is not intended to make you rich overnight, but it should help you make rational decisions and avoid wasting money on get-rich-quick schemes.

You may believe that if one company is more profitable than another, then its stock must be a better investment. You will see the error in this reasoning. You will see why there is an inherent conflict of interest between stockbrokers and their customers. You will learn about the growth trap, regression towards the mean, and other statistical pitfalls. You will understand why apparent patterns in asset prices are often illusions, temporary coincidences that are of no use in predicting the future course of prices. You will see why it is hard to distinguish investment skill from luck and, hence, why past investment success does not guarantee future success. You will see how some people bear unnecessary risks and how others are too cautious, foregoing the extra return made possible by prudent risk taking. You will learn of some who have done well by not following the crowd, indeed, by purposely doing the opposite of what others are doing.

In this book, you will see the surprising power of compound interest and some commonplace financial mistakes that lead people to choose the wrong car loan, to borrow too much (or, in some cases, too little), and to agree to disastrous creative financing deals. You will read about the downfall of the no-money-down gurus, and the recurring popularity of Ponzi schemes, multi-level distribution plans, and other investments that are literally too good to be true. You will learn of historical episodes in which contagious dreams of quick-and-easy riches led to speculative booms and panic.

Investments are extremely interesting and will provide a rewarding career for some readers. Many of the most successful investors do it not for the money, though money is certainly a nice consequence, but because it is fun—a challenging, exciting, ever-evolving game of wits, in which money is used to keep score. It is a profession worth considering and a game worth winning.

CONTENTS

PART TWO   FIXED-INCOME SECURITIES

PART THREE   COMMON STOCK

PART FOUR MARKET EFFICIENCIES AND INEFFICIENCIES

Chapter 12
The Human Factor in Investments   380

PART FIVE   RISK AND RETURN

Chapter 13
Decision Making Under Uncertainty   406

PART SIX   OTHER INVESTMENTS

Investments

Overview

CHAPTER 1

The Investment Setting

The love of money is the root of all evil. . .
New Testament

Lack of money is the root of all evil. . .
George Bernard Shaw

Throughout our lives we buy food, clothing, and a vast variety of necessities, luxuries, and frivolities. Some purchases, such as a pizza or an ice cream cone, are for immediate consumption, while others, such as a house, a car, or a television set, are investments—capital assets intended to provide many years of shelter, transportation, and entertainment. This book is about the investments that people make to provide for future consumption, either for themselves or for their heirs.

This introductory chapter provides an overview of topics we will cover. We will look first at some of the variety of investments that are available and then at the markets in which investments are bought and sold.

TYPES OF INVESTMENTS

It is clear that a house and car are investments that provide years of valuable service. However, the returns from some other investments are difficult to see, let alone value, and they get left out of the books of myopic accountants. There may be little or no financial reward from taking a course in English literature or U.S. history; but an introduction to great writers may yield years of pleasurable reading, and historical knowledge can provide an invaluable understanding of the world about you. A trip to the Grand Canyon, the High Sierras, or Tokyo is entered in the accountant's books as a consumption expense, even though it yields a lifetime of memories.

While the investments mentioned so far in this chapter provide services directly, other investments function more as means to an end. We may buy distant land, precious metals, and questionable art not to use, but to sell later in order to buy the pizza, blankets, and other things that we may wish to enjoy at some future time. No matter. These purchases too are considered investments because they are intended to provide for future consumption. The return from such investments depends on the prices received when they are sold. Thus, while a television is valued for the many years of pleasurable viewing it gives, gold bullion is appreciated for the handsome profit it is expected one day to provide. Some investments, such as a house or a Mercedes automobile, may yield both useful services and a satisfying resale value.

Financial Versus Real Assets

Some investments are **real assets**—tangible physical assets such as land, houses, livestock, and precious metals. In the United States and other countries with well-developed financial markets, people also hold a vast variety of **financial assets**—paper claims such as bank deposits, bonds, and stocks. There are many different ways to invest—to provide for future consumption—and in this book we will look at how rational investors choose among the many alternatives.

People also borrow, and, indeed, most financial assets are the financial liabilities of others. Say that Joshua has $2000 and Joanna needs a car to get to her job each day. If Joshua loans Joanna $2000 to buy a used car, he may get an IOU from her, promising to repay this loan plus interest. This IOU is an asset for Joshua and a liability for Joanna because part of her paycheck will go to him, allowing him to buy food with her wages. This financial arrangement is appealing to both: it allows Joshua to invest without stockpiling cars and other real assets, and it allows Joanna to buy a car so that she can get to work. If we consolidate their accounts, Joshua's IOU asset and Joanna's IOU liability cancel each other out, and their aggregate net worth is the car. In the very same way, for society as a whole (neglecting debts to or from other countries), financial assets and liabilities cancel each other out, and a nation's aggregate wealth is its tangible assets.

The federal government periodically estimates the total amount of private tangible assets in the United States; its figures for 1987 are shown in Table 1–1 on p. 4. These estimates do not take into account the nation's most important tangible asset—the citizens themselves. With brawn and brains, or what economists call **human capital,** people grow food, build roads, and heal the sick. Both kinds of capital, human and nonhuman, are important, as people could produce little without machines and machines could do little without people.

The value of human capital cannot be measured by market prices, since people, unlike land, buildings, and machines, are not bought and sold. However, we can get a very rough idea of the relative importance of human

real assets
Real assets are tangible physical assets, such as land, houses, livestock, and precious metals.

financial assets
Financial assets are paper claims, such as bank deposits, bonds, and stocks.

human capital
Human capital refers to the fact that a person's brains and brawn produce income.

TABLE 1–1 U.S. Tangible Assets in 1987

Asset	1987 Value (Trillions of Dollars)
Land	$ 5.2
Residential structures	6.3
Consumer durables	3.3
Business structures	3.7
Business equipment	3.6
Government structures	3.3
Government equipment	0.9
Total assets	**$26.3**

Source: Survey of Current Business, August 1988: Federal Reserve Board, "Balance Sheets of the U.S.," 1988.

capital by comparing how much of the nation's aggregate annual income is paid to labor with how much goes to owners of machines and other nonhuman capital: In the United States, about three-quarters of the nation's income goes to workers. If we infer that human capital is three times the $26.3 trillion in nonhuman capital reported in Table 1–1, the value of human capital in 1987 was $78.9 trillion. Total capital, human plus nonhuman, amounted to $105.2 trillion—nearly $500,000 per person. If that seems like a lot, you're underestimating the value of your human capital. In a later chapter, you will learn how to estimate your human capital in another way and come up with a comparable answer.

We cannot buy or sell humans, but we can invest in our own human capital by eating properly, exercising, and improving our minds. As for nonhuman capital, we do buy and sell land, houses, and consumer durables, either directly or, else, indirectly through financial claims. Instead of buying a farm, we deposit money in a bank, which then loans money to a farmer who buys land and equipment. The farmer hopes to produce a profitable crop, repay the bank loan plus interest, and keep some reward for hard work. The bank, in turn, uses the money it receives from the farmer to repay our deposit plus interest, and it keeps a little to pay its bills and earn a profit. Thus, implicitly, we and the bank have invested in the farm because we have a claim to part of the profits that it will make. If the crop fails, the bank may foreclose and sell the farm to repay our investment.

These arrangements involve the assets of some and the liabilities of others, and in this book we will look at both assets and liabilities. Figure 1–1 is an overly simplified sketch, showing three different routes by which the savings of investors are channeled into the acquisition of tangible assets. People can buy houses and other real assets directly; they can buy securities

FIGURE 1–1   Three routes to the purchase of tangible assets

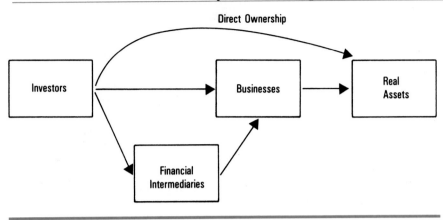

issued by others who acquire tangible assets; or they can deposit funds in banks and other financial intermediaries, which lend to those acquiring tangible assets. This sketch is oversimplified because people, businesses, and governments are both borrowers and lenders. A household borrows money from a bank to buy a house and also buys corporate bonds, lending money to businesses. Businesses borrow money by issuing corporate bonds and also buy U.S. government bonds. The federal government issues bonds and also buys household mortgage notes. Nonetheless, it is important to remember that what lies behind financial claims—the assets of some and the liabilities of others—are real, tangible assets and that the reason financial claims exist is to allow investors to own tangible assets indirectly.

Financial Assets and Liabilities

Table 1–2 on p. 6 shows the Federal Reserve Board's estimates of household financial and tangible wealth in 1988. The first four items are easily recognized as real assets. The items listed in the rest of this table are financial and form the outline for the following brief introduction to some of the financial assets and liabilities that are discussed more fully in later chapters.

Bank deposits include checking accounts, saving accounts, certificates of deposit, money-market shares, and all the other myriad ways of depositing money in financial intermediaries. A financial intermediary borrows from some to lend to others. Commercial banks are the most familiar example. When you deposit money in a bank, the bank is borrowing from you and will, in turn, lend this money to households—to buy houses and cars—and to businesses—to buy plant and equipment. If all goes as planned, the bank will earn enough interest on its loans to pay you the promised interest on your deposit and still make a profit.

TABLE 1–2 Financial and Tangible Wealth of U.S. Households in December 1988 (billions of dollars)

Assets		Liabilities	
Land	1.3	Mortgages	2.1
Residential structures	3.1	Consumer credit	0.7
Consumer durables	1.8	Other loans	0.3
Nonresidential plant and equipment	0.3		
Deposits in banks and other intermediaries	3.1		
Treasury bonds	0.8		
State and local bonds	0.3		
Corporate bonds	0.3		
Corporate stock	2.2		
Unincorporated businesses	2.3		
Pension funds	2.9		
Total	18.4		3.1

Source: Board of Governors of the Federal Reserve System, "Household Net Worth," March 1989.

At the end of World War II, 70 percent of bank funds came from depositor checking accounts. Now, less than 25 percent does. In part, this change reflects the growth of time and savings accounts—from 20 percent of bank funds in 1945 to around 50 percent today. But there has also been a dramatic increase in bank borrowing in ways that were virtually unknown not very many years ago. A bank certificate of deposit (CD) involves a deposit in a bank in return for a receipt stating the amount of interest to be paid after a specified period, typically between three months and five years. Large CDs ($100,000 and up) are actively traded in the short-term bond market until they mature. Banks also borrow a considerable amount of money through *repurchase agreements (repos)*, using the government bonds they own as collateral. These deals are called repurchase agreements because, legally, the banks sell these government bonds to investors (usually businesses) with an agreement that the bank will repurchase the bonds after a specified number of days (often just overnight) at a higher, fixed price, the difference representing implicit interest on the loan. Banks also raise money through Eurodollars, (U.S. dollars deposited in banks outside the United States) by encouraging dollar deposits in their foreign branches. The actual transactions may take place in the United States, but (because of regulatory or tax advantages) be recorded as a deposit in a Caribbean branch for a period as brief as one night.

Just as banks now perform many nontraditional services, so there are many other financial intermediaries—"near banks"—that compete vigorously with banks to attract funds for relending. Savings and loans, mutual savings banks, and credit unions are clearly financial intermediaries. So, too, are mutual funds which pool the savings of small investors in order to acquire a large portfolio of investments. (Money-market funds buy short-term securities that mature within a year, while bond and stock funds buy longer-term bonds and corporate stock.) To varying degrees, pension funds and insurance companies are also financial intermediaries in that they invest the savings of others.

In this book you will learn the tax advantages of investing through pension funds, consider the reasons people buy insurance, and evaluate the alleged advantages of mutual funds. You will also analyze the portfolio decisions of these financial institutions (how they select particular stocks and why they might buy bonds rather than stocks, for example) and how their rapid growth has changed financial markets.

Treasury bonds are issued by the federal government to pay for spending that exceeds tax revenue. The president and Congress determine federal expenditures and tax rates, and when the government's outlays exceed its revenue, its budget is in deficit and the U.S. Treasury must sell securities to raise the money needed to pay the government's bills. The Treasury also sells securities regularly to replace old bonds that are maturing. If the government's budget is balanced, so that tax revenue covers government expenses (including interest on maturing debt), then the new securities sold will just offset the old ones maturing, and the government debt, the total amount of Treasury securities outstanding, will be constant. If the government's budget is in deficit, then the amount of new securities sold will exceed the amount maturing and the government debt will increase. During those occasions with a budget surplus, the outstanding debt will decline. In 1987 the federal deficit was $150 billion and the government debt increased from $2100 billion at the beginning of the year to $2250 billion at year-end. Among the important issues explored in this book are why short- and long-term Treasury bonds have different interest rates and how investors can choose among them. (No, the bond with the higher interest rate is not necessarily the most attractive!)

State and local bonds (usually called *municipal bonds,* or *munis*) are issued by state and local governments to finance expenditures that exceed their current tax revenues. Although used for similar purposes, there are some important differences between federal and municipal bonds. The interest on state and local bonds has been exempt from federal income taxes (and the interest on federal bonds excempt from state and local income taxes) ever since an 1819 case (*McCulloch* v. *Maryland*), in which Supreme Court Chief Justice John Marshall declared that "the power to tax involves the power to destroy." The 1913 laws establishing a federal income tax reinforced this principle by specifically exempting municipal bonds. However, the 1986 Tax Reform Act breached this reciprocal immunity by imposing federal income taxes on some state and local bonds that are issued to finance privately owned projects, such as sports arenas and convention centers.

Another difference is that U.S. Treasury securities are completely safe because the federal government has the power to print money to pay its debts. The Federal Reserve Board (Fed) controls the U.S. money supply. The Fed can increase the money supply by using newly printed paper money — Federal Reserve notes — to buy Treasury bonds, and it can reduce the money supply by selling some of its securities and retiring the money received.

The Fed makes its own decisions, but there is no doubt that if the Treasury ever had trouble raising money, the Fed would step in and buy as many securities as needed. Congress also controls the minting of coins and can authorize the printing of U.S. Treasury notes (greenbacks), as it did during the Civil War when there was no Federal Reserve. (Some $300 million in greenbacks are still in circulation today and can be identified by the label *U.S. Treasury note.*) State and local governments do not have the power to print money or the same assurances of support from the Fed, and there are occasional defaults on their bonds.

In Chapter 4, we will look at how the tax advantages and the default risk of municipal bonds have opposite effects on their interest rates. You will see that a choice among municipal and Treasury bonds does not depend solely on their interest rates and, indeed, why some investors have a strong preference for Treasury securities while others choose munis.

Corporate bonds are issued by corporations to help finance their expenditures. (The corporate-bond entry in Table 1–2 shows the bonds held by households; not shown are corporate bank loans or the corporate bonds held by others.) There are more than 15 million businesses in the United States, of which some 3 million are corporations. A corporation is said to be publicly owned when it issues shares that can be purchased by any member of the public. The shareholders are the legal owners of the corporation and elect a board of directors that supervises the company's operations. Businesses that are privately owned can be organized either as a proprietorship or partnership. Some privately owned companies are very large (for example, Levi Strauss, Mars, and United Parcel Service), but most are small so-called mom-and-pop businesses.

A corporation is a legal entity that can borrow money from a bank as you or I would borrow money to buy a car or a house, or issue bonds as the U.S. Treasury does. Most corporations are more creditworthy than you or I, but none are as secure as the U.S. Treasury. In this book, you will learn why different corporate bonds have different interest rates and once again see that the bond with the highest interest rate is not necessarily the best investment (indeed, many experienced investors believe the reverse to be true).

Corporate stock refers to the shares issued by incorporated businesses. These shares are very different from the debts we have discussed so far.

Households, businesses, and governments borrow money using promissory notes, legally binding agreements to repay the loan plus some specified interest. These agreements may be called IOUs, loans, bills, notes, bonds, or something more exotic. What these debts have in common is that they are **fixed-income securities**—notes that specify the amount of money to be repaid. Corporate stock is different because there are no specified payments from one party to another. A person who buys corporate stock acquires partial ownership of the company. While corporate bonds are debt, corporate stock is **equity,** a claim on the company's profits after interest and other fixed expenses have been paid and, in the event of liquidation, a claim on the company's assets after its debts have been settled.

Imagine that you own a small business that has assets worth $100,000 but owes $20,000 to a bank. Your claim is equity and its value is equal to the value of the business in excess of its debts, in this case $80,000. In the same way, if this business were a corporation, the shareholders would be the legal owners and their stock would be equity, not debt.

Just as a small business owner consumes some of the profits and uses the remainder to expand, so a corporation disburses some of its profits to shareholders as dividends and plows back the rest. The size of the dividend is determined by the corporation's directors, who are elected by the shareholders and presumably act in their interest when deciding how to split the company's profits between dividends and reinvestment.

The value of the corporate equity shown in Table 1–2 reflects the market prices of shares as investors buy and sell corporate stock among themselves. In this book we will look at a variety of valuation models that use a firm's assets, profits, and dividends to estimate a rational value for its stock and thereby explain market prices.

Unincorporated businesses are businesses that have not incorporated. The entry in Table 1–2 is an estimate of the value of the debt and equity of such businesses held by households. The value of unincorporated businesses is difficult to estimate because there are no publicly traded shares. Instead, government economists use valuation models similar to those developed to explain the value of corporate stock.

Pension funds represent private retirement savings, which have been invested in various financial and nonfinancial assets. The wealth of many low- to middle-income households consists largely of their human capital, perhaps a house, and a pension fund that implicitly makes them part owner of American businesses.

Mortgages are the loans people take to buy real estate, typically the houses in which they live. The most common mortgage is a thirty-year amortized loan, in which the loan plus interest is repaid with constant monthly payments for thirty years. In Chapter 3 you will see how these monthly payments are determined and learn some creative variations on these conventional loans.

Consumer credit involves loans from a bank, finance company, or other

fixed-income securities
A fixed-income security has specified payments.

equity
Common stock is equity, a claim on the company's profits after interest and other expenses have been paid.

financial intermediary to finance the purchase of cars, dishwashers, personal computers, and other consumer durables. Chapter 3 will show the general mechanics of such loans and expose some expensive mistakes and deceptions that hurt unwary borrowers.

Other loans includes a hodge-podge of miscellaneous loans, including money borrowed from brokerage firms to finance the purchase of stock. In later chapters, you will see why investors buy stock with borrowed money and why this is sometimes financially rewarding and, other times, disastrous.

THE INVESTMENT INDUSTRY: AN OVERVIEW

financial markets
Financial markets are established means for trading bonds, stocks, and other financial assets.

A *market* is a means of bringing together buyers and sellers to make transactions. **Financial markets**—those markets established for trading bonds, stocks, and other financial assets—come in many different forms and involve a variety of agents. We will look first at the types of markets and then at the participants.

Primary Versus Secondary Markets

primary market
Primary markets accommodate the initial issuance of a security.

There is an important distinction between primary and secondary markets. The **primary market** is a market that involves the initial issuance of a security and includes such transactions as these: a household deposits $1000 in its checking account; a bank loans a household $100,000 to buy a house; the U.S. Treasury raises money by selling a $10,000 bond; a business incorporates by issuing stock. In each case, a financial record of the transaction is created, showing the existence of a debt or of equity.

secondary market
The secondary market describes the trading of assets after their initial issuance in the primary market.

A **secondary market** is a market in which debt or equity certificates are resold to others. Examples abound. When a business acquires a certificate of deposit (CD) by depositing $100,000 in a bank (a primary-market transaction), this CD can be sold to someone else (a secondary-market trade) who can either trade it again or hold it until it matures. After a bank loans someone money to buy a house, it can sell the mortgage note to a government agency that packages it with other mortgages and resells it to a pension fund or insurance company, with the mortgage payments forwarded from the bank to the current owner of the mortgage. The investor who buys a Treasury bond can sell it to another investor, who then collects the semiannual interest and maturation value. Stockholders can sell some or all of their shares to others. In each case, the security may pass from hand to hand as one person after another invests for a while and then sells when the investor needs some money or decides that this is no longer an attractive investment.

The primary market refers to the sale of newly created securities. The secondary market is a resale market, where existing securities are bought and sold.

The distinction is important for several reasons. If there were no established secondary market, investors would be reluctant to acquire securities in the first place, knowing how difficult it is to resell them later. It is also important to recognize that the stock exchanges whose prices are reported in the news each day are secondary markets, not primary markets.

Types of Secondary Markets

On the organized exchanges, traders meet face to face and strike deals. Trading is very different off the exchanges, in the over-the-counter market. We will look at each type of market in turn.

Stock Exchanges When you want to sell some furniture you no longer need, you can talk to friends, put a notice on a few bulletin boards, or place an ad in a local paper. If the furniture is valuable, you might use the market created by furniture dealers, swap meets, and auctions.

What if you have some shares of stock to sell? You could use these same haphazard methods, but organized stock exchanges offer a much easier and more efficient way for buyers and sellers to find each other. The most well known, by far, is the New York Stock Exchange (NYSE) where some 1700 stocks, including almost all of the nation's largest and most well-known companies, are traded.

The stock exchanges are physical locations, or trading floors, where securities are bought and sold, usually through a designated specialist who collects buy and sell orders and executes a transaction when someone is willing to sell at a price that another is willing to pay. Charged with maintaining a "fair and orderly" market, the specialist buys for his own account when there is an excess of sell orders and sells when buyers predominate. We will look at the specialist's role more closely in Chapter 6.

A commonplace fiction, sometimes promoted by the exchanges themselves, is that the stock exchanges play a vital role in raising capital to finance the expansion of American business. In fact, the exchanges are not used by corporations to raise cash. Instead, the exchanges are a secondary market where investors trade securities among themselves. When you buy 100 shares of IBM, the company itself has nothing to do with the transaction. You buy shares from Jack, who bought from Jill, and so on and so forth through endless trades back to the time when IBM first issued the stock. And so it is with virtually all stock transactions. When a newly incorporated firm or an occasional mature company sells stock to raise money, this transaction is made through investment bankers rather than on the exchanges.

In 1988, U.S. businesses spent $540 billion on plant and equipment, of which $320 billion was replacement and repair of existing capital and $220 billion was new investment. These expenditures were *not* financed by selling stock. In fact, in 1988 businesses, on balance, repurchased some $110 billion more stock than they sold. Their total spending, $540 billion on capital plus $110 billion to retire stock, was financed by $370 billion in retained profits and $280 billion in bond sales, bank loans, and other debts. Over the five years 1984–1988, US corporations sold $250 billion in new stock and repurchased $650 billion, a net retirement of $400 billion.

The stock exchanges are unquestionably useful. The hundreds of millions of shares traded daily (and the accompanying fees paid to brokers) are ample proof that people value this marketplace. Buyers use the market to find sellers, while sellers find buyers. Undoubtedly, investors would be reluctant to acquire share if they could not count on using the stock exchanges to find buyers when they are ready to sell. But the stock exchanges are not the place where businesses raise money to finance expansion.

Trading Over the Counter Securities that aren't listed on organized exchanges are said to be traded *over the counter (OTC)*, a reference to the practice long ago of dealers literally trading securities over the counters of their shops. Because this trading is now conducted by telephone, telex, and computer links, a more apt label might be the over-the-phone market.

Off the exchanges, in the over-the-counter market, dealers maintain a market in a security by quoting prices at which they are willing to buy or sell for their own accounts. The *bid* price is the price they are willing to pay; the *ask* price is the price at which they will sell. These market makers generally do not intend to accumulate large positions. Instead, they hope to buy at $40 and sell at $42 a short while later, making their profit on the price spread. A pure *broker* brings together a buyer and seller and collects a commission without risking any capital. A *dealer* who maintains a position in a security can lose money if prices move adversely.

Other Secondary Markets Deals can of course be worked out privately between investors without using the exchanges or the over-the-counter market. To facilitate such private deals, large institutions have developed a computerized network called INSTINET in which subscribers can, if they wish, make tentative offers to buy or sell securities. INSTINET is registered with the Securities and Exchange Commission as a stock exchange, but it is quite different from the other stock exchanges and the OTC market in that there is no designated specialist or market maker who will buy or sell as needed (and who extracts a fee for this service).

Some Participants in Financial Markets

Treasury bonds are issued at public auctions, mostly to dealers, and then traded in the over-the-counter market. Municipal bonds, corporate bonds, and stocks, in contrast, are issued through *investment bankers,* such as Morgan Stanley and Salomon Brothers, who, based on their knowledge of financial markets and evaluation of the company's financial condition, recommend a price for the new issue. If it is a large issue, several investment banks will join together to form a syndicate to distribute the securities. The investment banks have regular customers—both individual and institutional investors—who, it is hoped, can be persuaded to buy. Sometimes, the investment banks agree to make their "best effort" to market the new issue, collecting a fee for each sale; in this instance, the firm may end up issuing fewer securities than hoped. More often, investment banks underwrite the issue with a "firm commitment" to buy the securities themselves if necessary. In this arrangement, the investment bank's fee is the difference between the price it pays the issuing firm and the price it receives when it sells the securities, either in the initial offering or later in the secondary market.

Individual investors generally participate in financial markets in two ways. The first is through financial intermediaries such as a bank, savings and loan, insurance company, pension fund, or mutual fund. In each case, the individual sends money to the intermediary, and the institution makes its own investment decisions, covering its expenses with the difference between what it earns on its investments and what it distributes to investors. With a bank deposit, the investor's return is guaranteed in advance, and the bank's profit depends on how well it invests the funds at its disposal. Insurance is similar, but more complicated, because the payoff depends on whether or not the insured event occurs. Mutual funds buy securities on behalf of investors and pass along the investment profits, less the management fee and other expenses; thus, the return to investors depends on the fund's performance, but the fund's profit does not. (Of course, a fund that does dismally will eventually lose investors and, with them, the management fees they pay.)

The second way in which individual investors participate in financial markets is by trading securities for themselves, using the services of a brokerage firm such as Merrill Lynch, PaineWebber, or Charles Schwab. At Merrill Lynch and other full-service brokerage firms, the investor has a specific account executive who gives advice (based on the firm's research and the broker's knowledge of the investor) and is paid out of the commission charged on each transaction. At discount brokerages, commissions are lower because the firm does not do research or offer advice; the customer's transactions are handled by whoever happens to answer the phone.

Either way, the brokerage firm can execute a secondary market transaction for customers on one of the stock exchanges or over the counter. Most full-service brokerage firms also act as investment bankers, and the account executives peddle new issues to their customers, which can be viewed as either an opportunity or a nuisance.

Market Regulation

The slogan *buyer beware* means that in a voluntary transaction, it is ultimately the buyer's responsibility to evaluate what is being purchased and to judge whether it is worth the price. A cornerstone of our free-market system is the belief that voluntary exchanges are mutually beneficial (otherwise, the buyer or seller would not agree to the deal) and should be allowed to flourish. Yet, throughout history greedy merchants have sold defective products, worthless patent medicines, and adulterated foods—ranging from milk containing plaster of paris to sugar containing sand. Because we seldom have the means or experience to recognize the defects and dangers in what we buy, our government tests and inspects many products for us and imposes a variety of regulations on sellers that are intended to insure that we get what we think we are buying.

Similarly, after the stock-market crash in 1929, Congress passed the Securities Act of 1933 and the Securities Exchange Act of 1934 to protect investors from defective securities that are hazardous to their financial health. The underlying philosophy of these laws is that investors should be allowed to make their own decisions about whether a security is worth its price, but that they should have available all the facts needed for an informed decision.

A corporation that sells more than $1.5 million in securities to the public (more than thirty-five investors) must file a registration statement with the Securities and Exchange Commission (SEC) that includes a prospectus disclosing all important financial details relevant to an investor considering the purchase of these securities. The SEC certifies the apparent completeness of the prospectus, but makes no judgment as to whether the securities are fairly priced. State governments also regulate the sale of securities in a variety of ways through what are often called *blue-sky laws,* in reference to speculative schemes based on nothing more substantial than the blue sky.

The SEC requires corporations to file periodic reports that keep investors informed of material changes in the company's financial condition. Each year, corporations must file Form 10–K with the SEC disclosing income, expenses, borrowing, and other aspects of their financial condition. Shareholders receive a glossy, condensed version of this annual report, complete with dazzling charts and stunning photographs. Each quarter, corporations must file a briefer disclosure on Form 10–Q and generally send a condensed version of this on to shareholders, too. Irregular events that may cause an important change in the firm's financial condition must be reported to the SEC on Form 8–K. A corporation's *insiders* (its officers and directors, and any investor controlling more than 5 percent of its stock) must report any purchases or sales of the company's stock to the SEC. All of the various reports required by the SEC are available to the public by request.

Finally, the SEC is empowered to enforce a variety of rules governing mutual funds, the stock exchanges, the over-the-counter market, invest-ment advisers, and virtually all aspects of security markets. The overall intent is to compel the disclosure of pertinent facts and to protect investors from fraud, misrepresentation, and manipulation.

MAKING INVESTMENT DECISIONS

There are essentially two ways of profiting from an investment: income and capital gains. **Income** is composed of the benefits you receive while owning the asset: **capital gains** are the profits when you sell the asset. Income includes the cash flow generated by the investment itself—the interest from a bond, dividends from a stock, rent from an apartment building—of which some is taxable and some, like the interest on most municipal bonds, is not. Income also includes the services provided by an asset—transportation from a car, shelter from a house, and pleasure from fine art.

> **income**
> Income encompasses the cash and services received while owning an asset.

> **capital gains**
> Capital gains are the profit made when an asset is sold for more than the purchase price.

If you own stocks, bonds, or other assets that experience price in-creases, these capital gains are taxable; but you don't have to pay the tax until you "realize" the gain by selling the asset. If, for instance, you buy 100 shares of stock for $20 a share and its price immediately jumps to $30, you do not have to pay a tax on this capital gain unless you sell. Perhaps the price then falls back to $25, and you take your profit while you can. By selling your 100 shares at $25, you realize a $500 profit (less brokerage commissions) and, at year's end, will have to pay income tax on it.

Most investment returns are not known in advance. The promised interest on a bond may disappear with a sudden default. The dividends from a stock may surge or stagnate, depending on the company's fortunes. Rent may grow faster or slower than the expenses of operating an apart-ment building. As John Maynard Keynes, an insightful and successful investor as well as economist, once wrote:

> *The outstanding fact is the extreme precariousness of the basis of knowledge on which our estimates of prospective yield have to be made. Our knowledge of the factors which will govern the yield of an investment some years hence is usually very slight and often negligible. If we speak frankly, we have to admit that our basis of knowledge for estimating the yield ten years hence of a railway, a copper mine, a textile factory, the goodwill of a patent medicine, an Atlantic liner, a building in the city of London amounts to little and sometimes nothing.*[1]

While the income from investments is difficult to estimate, the capital gains are virtually impossible to predict. Market prices today depend on imperfect estimates of the future income from the investment and our hunches, nothing more, about tomorrow's market price—which depend on the same sort of vague, ambiguous considerations.

The Fallacy of Get-Rich-Quick Schemes

People are often lured to investments by the ill-conceived notion that riches are there for the taking. This dream is aided and abetted by the get-rich-quick gurus who peddle shortcuts to success. For instance, a July 1987 letter began "IMAGINE turning $1000 into $34,500 in less than one year!"[2] To aid the imagination, this come-on was highlighted in yellow. The letter said that "no special background or education" was needed and that "It's an investment you can make with *spare cash* that you might ordinarily spend on lottery tickets or the race track." The investment being touted was low-priced stocks and to show the "explosive profit potential" the letter listed the 1985 low prices and 1986 high prices of twenty stocks, noting that $100 invested in each ($2000 in all) would have grown to $26,611. Not only that, but another stock, LKA International, once went from 2 cents to 69 cents a share, which, as the initial come-on said, would have turned $1000 into $34,500. The letter concluded by offering a special $39 report that would allow access to "the carefully guarded territory of a few shrewd 'inner circle' investors."

The first question is why anyone possessing a get-rich-quick system needs to peddle it. If it is so easy to make money, why waste time and energy selling reports, newsletters, and books at a few dollars apiece? Some gurus answer that they have made more than enough money and now want to share their secret with others who are as poor as they once were. But, if so, why don't they send us money instead of asking us to mail them some?

The second issue is the preposterous idea that large amounts of money lie about, for the taking. Financial markets don't give away money. The exchanges are places where investors make voluntary transactions—one buying and the other selling—and it strains credulity to believe that a stock would trade at 2 cents a share if it was clear that the price will be 69 cents a short while later. No one willingly sells for 2 cents what soon can be sold for 69 cents. Even if only a few people know that the price will soon be 69 cents, they will buy millions of shares, driving the price today up to 69 cents.

About 70 percent of all trades on the stock exchange are made by institutions—mutual funds, pension funds, college endowments, and so on—run by intelligent, informed investors. They know at least as much as individual investors, and they have the resources to buy massive amounts of any stock that is an obvious bargain, eliminating the mispricing. As a result, financial markets are fair and efficient in the sense that the current market price is never obviously too high or too low.

When trades of LKA International stock were made at 2 cents a share, there were an equal number of buyers and sellers, neither side knowing for sure whether the price would be higher or lower the next day and the day after that. The optimists bought, the pessimists sold, and, as it turned out, the optimists happened to be right. But to count on being right every time—to expect to always buy stocks at their lowest prices and sell at their highest—is foolish.

Anyone who really knows which direction a stock's price is going has the means to soon make a fortune. In Chapter 11, we will look at how Ivan Boesky admitted in 1986 to having made $50 million using illegal insider information about a handful of impending corporate takeovers. He knew what other investors did not know, and he got very rich, very quickly. The first lesson taught by this episode is that he did not bother peddling newsletters. The second lesson is that no investor makes this kind of money legally, because no one knows for certain which way security prices are headed. Probably the most successful stock-market investor of all time is another man we will look at in Chapter 11: Warren Buffett, who has made about 25 percent a year averaged over nearly forty years. This real-life result is not close to the dreams concocted in newsletters, but it is absolutely spectacular compared to the performance of other investors.

Risk and Uncertainty

If the future market price is uncertain, then an investment is risky. For some, this risk is so nerve-wracking that they avoid bonds and stocks altogether and put their money in a bank. In this book, you will see that they still participate in financial markets in other ways—for instance, through a pension fund or in the purchase and financing of a home. You will also see that even if the bank deposit is insured, there is still considerable risk, of a very different sort, in a bank-account strategy. Further, by avoiding the stock market, they pass up what has, on average, been a very profitable investment; later chapters show that there are ways to manage risks and insure a relatively safe return from stocks.

For other investors, the uncertainty of security markets is the main attraction. Investing is a game, much like poker or backgammon, that blends skill and luck, that is played for high stakes against professionals, and that has its results printed in the daily newspaper. Not only are there thrills and excitement, but, unlike a gambling casino or state lottery, the average investor in stocks and bonds makes money.

Historical Returns as a Guide

Table 1–3 shows the annual percentage returns, income plus capital gains, on a variety of assets over a recent thirty-nine-year period. Short-term Treasury bills mature within a year, while the long-term government and corporate bonds reported here have a maturity of twenty years. The numbers shown are the average returns each year for each type of asset. Within each category, some individual assets did much better than average and some much worse. While some stocks doubled in price in 1988, others went bankrupt.

The data in Table 1–3 demonstrate that asset returns do vary considerably from year to year: 1973 and 1974 were particularly bad years for stocks, while 1958, 1975, and 1985 were unusually good years. The bottom of the table shows the average annual return for each asset since 1926 and the standard deviation, a measure of the volatility of the annual returns about the average (the details of this statistic are explained in an appendix to this chapter).

These data are annual returns, covering the period from the first trading day of each year to the last. Such annual data conceal the fact that asset prices fluctuate considerably month-to-month, week-to-week, and even day-to-day within each year. One of the most dramatic instances occurred on Monday, October 19, 1987, when stock prices fell by more than 20 percent in a single day. For the year 1987 as a whole, the return on stocks was a respectable 5.2 percent. But the unprecedented collapse on this infamous day—dubbed Black Monday—sent many investors to the sidelines, convinced that the stock market is too risky for their tastes. In Chapter 12, we will look at the unsettling October 19 crash in detail.

Figure 1–2 on p. 20 graphs the annual returns for Treasury bills, long-term bonds, and corporate stock back to 1926, confirming visually what the standard deviations tell us numerically—that the annual returns on long-term bonds have varied more than the returns on Treasury bills, and that stock returns have been even more volatile. The returns also seem random in the sense that past returns appear to be of no use in predicting whether the return in any particular year will be relatively high or low. This lack of predictability is consistent with the argument that balance between asset buyers and sellers is impossible if predicting the coming year's return to be exceptionally high, or low, were easy. We will look at more detailed evidence in support of this hypothesis in later chapters.

Notice, too, that Treasury bills have had the lowest average returns and stocks have had the highest. One explanation, which we will return to again and again in later chapters, is that most investors are risk averse and will not hold risky assets with volatile returns unless they expect, on average, to earn more than they would with safe investments. Thus, stocks and other risky assets should have relatively high expected returns.

Of course, there is a big difference between what people expect and what they actually get. By definition, the return on a risky asset is very

TABLE 1–3 Annual Percentage Returns, 1950–1988

	Short-Term Treasury Bills	Long-Term Treasury Bonds	High-Grade Corporate Bonds	NYSE Corporate Stocks
1950	1.2	0.1	2.1	31.7
1951	1.5	− 3.9	− 2.7	24.0
1952	1.7	1.2	3.5	18.3
1953	1.8	3.6	3.4	− 1.0
1954	0.9	7.2	5.4	52.6
1955	1.6	− 1.3	0.5	31.5
1956	2.5	− 5.6	− 6.8	6.6
1957	3.1	7.5	8.7	− 10.8
1958	1.5	− 6.1	− 2.2	43.4
1959	3.0	− 2.3	− 1.0	12.0
1960	2.7	13.8	9.1	0.5
1961	2.1	1.0	4.8	26.9
1962	2.7	6.9	7.9	− 8.7
1963	3.1	1.2	2.2	22.8
1964	3.5	3.5	4.8	16.5
1965	3.9	0.7	− 0.5	12.4
1966	4.8	3.7	0.2	− 10.0
1967	4.2	− 9.2	− 5.0	24.0
1968	5.2	− 0.3	2.6	11.1
1969	6.6	− 5.1	− 8.1	− 8.4
1970	6.5	12.1	18.4	3.9
1971	4.4	13.2	11.0	14.3
1972	3.8	5.7	7.3	19.0
1973	6.9	− 1.1	1.1	− 14.7
1974	8.0	4.4	− 3.1	− 26.4
1975	5.8	9.2	14.6	37.2
1976	5.1	16.8	18.6	23.8
1977	5.1	− 0.7	1.7	− 7.2
1978	7.2	− 1.2	− 0.1	6.6
1979	10.4	− 1.2	− 4.2	18.4
1980	11.2	− 4.0	− 2.6	32.4
1981	14.7	1.9	− 1.0	− 4.9
1982	10.5	40.4	43.8	21.4
1983	8.8	0.7	4.7	22.5
1984	9.9	15.4	16.4	6.3
1985	7.7	31.0	30.9	32.2
1986	6.2	24.4	19.9	18.5
1987	5.5	− 2.7	− 0.3	5.2
1988	6.4	9.7	10.7	16.8
1926–1988:				
Average	3.5	4.8	5.4	12.1
Standard deviation	3.4	8.5	8.5	21.0

Source: Ibbotson, Roger G., and Rex A. Singuefield, *Stocks, Bonds, Bills, and Inflation 1989 Yearbook*™, Ibbotson Associates, Inc., Chicago. All rights reserved.

FIGURE 1–2 Rates of return, 1926-1987

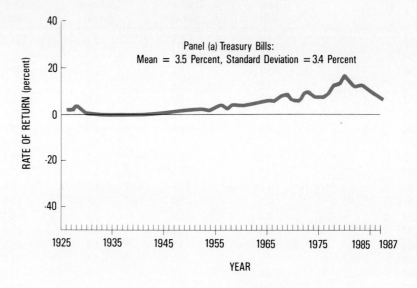

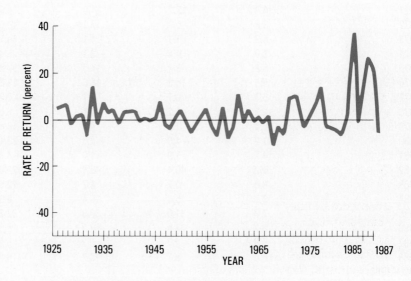

FIGURE 1–2, *cont'd*   Rates of return, 1926-1987

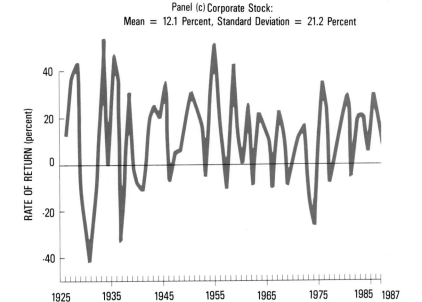

Panel (c) Corporate Stock:
Mean = 12.1 Percent, Standard Deviation = 21.2 Percent

uncertain. The data in Table 1–3 and Figure 1–2 describe in retrospect what happened to investors who bought these various assets. Asset demands and asset prices depend on what people anticipate in the future, the topic we turn to in the next chapter.

SUMMARY

Investments are a means of providing for future consumption. Some investments are real—such as precious metals, machinery, and real estate—while others are financial—such as bank deposits, Treasury bonds, and corporate stock. Fixed-income securities promise to pay specified amounts at stated times. Corporate stock is equity, shares issued by incorporated businesses conveying partial ownership of a company and a claim on a company's profits after interest and other fixed expenses have been paid. The dividends received by shareholders are not contractually fixed, but instead are determined by the firm's directors and, it is hoped, will increase over time as the company prospers.

The total return on an investment includes the income that is received while owning the asset—shelter from a house, interest on a bond, dividends from stock—and any capital gain that is realized when it is sold. Some income is taxable and some, like the interest on most municipal bonds, is not. Capital gains are taxed when they are realized by the sale of the asset.

The labels primary market and secondary market are used to distinguish between the initial issuance of a security and its later resale, from one investor to another. In the primary market for corporate stock, newly incorporated companies (and an occasional existing corporation) use investment bankers to sell shares that have been described in a prospectus required by the Securities and Exchange Commission (SEC). The secondary market encompasses the stock exchanges and the over-the-counter market where investors trade shares among themselves. Shares of most of the nation's largest and most well known corporations are traded on the New York Stock Exchange (NYSE), using designated specialists who collect buy and sell orders, execute transactions, and trade for their own accounts as needed to maintain an orderly market. Off the exchanges, in the over-the-counter market, dealers maintain a market by quoting prices at which they are willing to buy and sell a security.

People naturally hope that their investments will yield a quick and easy fortune. Others prey on these hopes by selling success systems. Caution is suggested by the observation that the system purveyors would not need to sel' books and newsletters if their methods rea.!y worked. In addition, financial markets are where reasonably well-informed investors make voluntary transactions. Thus, if there is a balance between buyers and sellers at $10 a share, it must not be certain that the price will soon be $20, or $2.

Since 1926, the total returns on stock, dividends plus capital gains, have averaged about 12 percent a year. There is considerable, seemingly unpredictable, variation from year to year, with the market sometimes dropping more than 20 percent in a year and other times rising by 40 percent. The returns on long-term bonds have been less volatile than stock returns and lower on average; the returns on short-term Treasury bills have been even more stable and lower still, on average. This relationship between variation and average return is consistent with the presumption that risk-averse investors will not hold risky assets unless they can expect, on average, to earn a relatively high return.

The Mean and Standard Deviation

The arithmetic **mean** is just the simple average value of the data. If there are n values

$$X_1, X_2, \ldots, X_n,$$

then the mean is the sum of these values, divided by n:

$$\text{Mean} = \frac{X_1 + X_2 + \ldots + X_n}{n}$$

The usual mathematical symbol for the mean is $\overline{X}$ (pronounced "X bar") and the conventional shorthand notation is

$$\overline{X} = \frac{\sum\limits_{i=1}^{n} X_i}{n}$$

where the greek letter Σ (capital "sigma") signifies the summation of a set of values $X_1, X_2, \ldots, X_n$ written as X_i for i ranging from 1 to n. If the range is obvious, then the limits can be omitted

$$\overline{X} = \frac{\sum X_i}{n}$$

or even

$$\overline{X} = \frac{\sum X}{n}.$$

mean
The mean of a set of data is the average value of the observations.

23

variance

The statistical variance is the average squared deviation of the outcomes about their mean.

The **variance** is the average squared deviation from the mean, calculated by adding up each of n squared deviations about the mean and dividing by n. (If the data are a small sample, statisticians usually divide by $n-1$ rather than n.)

$$\text{Variance} = \text{average squared deviation from the mean}$$
$$= \frac{\Sigma(X_i - \overline{X})^2}{n-1}$$

The variance gauges whether the data are close to the mean or scattered widely. Because the variance squares each deviation, it has a scale much larger than that of the original data. To offset this, statisticians also compute the

$$\text{standard deviation} = \text{square root of the variance.}$$

To illustrate these computations consider the stock returns shown in Table 1–3 for the ten years for 1970–79. The mean is

$$\overline{X} = \frac{(3.9 + 14.3 + 19.0 + \ldots + 18.4)}{10}$$
$$= \frac{74.9}{10}$$
$$= 7.49$$

The variance is

$$\text{var} = \frac{(3.9-7.49)^2 + (14.3-7.49)^2 + \ldots + (-18.4-7.49)^2}{9}$$
$$= \frac{3316.989}{9}$$
$$= 368.5543,$$

and the standard deviation is

$$\text{std. dev.} = \sqrt{368.5543}$$
$$= 19.20.$$

These compare with a mean of 12.1 percent and a standard deviation of 21.0 percent for the entire period 1926–88. Thus, during the 1970s annual stock returns were lower on average and slightly less volatile than for the period as a whole.

EXERCISES

1. Which of the following are financial assets and which are real assets?
a. Gold coins
b. U.S. savings bonds
c. Shares of General Motors stock
d. A personal computer
e. Canceled postage stamps

2. Most financial assets are also liabilities. For each of the following assets, indicate for which of the identified parties it is an asset and for which a liability.
a. Checking account: depositor, bank
b. Car loan: car buyer, bank
c. Treasury bonds: investor, U.S. government
d. Corporate pension: worker, business

3. Why do you suppose people deposit money in bank savings accounts paying 7 percent interest rather than loaning money, as the bank does, to businesses at 10 percent? Give three reasons.

4. Meaures of wealth inequality in the United States typically consider an individual's wealth to consist of bank accounts, bonds, stocks, and real estate, after mortgages and other debts have been deducted. Name two very important omissions.

5. Critically evaluate the assertion that "the main function of the stock exchanges is . . . to generate funds to be employed in private business ventures."[3]

6. A newly incorporated company wants to sell 5 million shares at $10 apiece to the general public. Under a "best effort" agreement, its investment bank will try to sell all 5 million shares at $10 and charge the company a 4 percent fee, netting it $9.60 per share sold. Alternatively, the investment bank will underwrite the issue by agreeing to buy all 5 million shares for a price P and selling as many as it can at $10 apiece. Explain why you anticipate that P will be equal to, larger, or smaller than $9.60.

7. Louis Rukeyser characterized the stock prospectus that the SEC requires of newly incorporated companies as follows:

> You will encounter a classic of the school of unreadable literature written by lawyers for lawyers. Full disclosure of all possible threats, from technological competition to tapeworms, is the motif—but the morass of figures and cautions is likely to tell you everything but what you really want to know: Is the company going to be a success?[4]

Why do you think a prospectus contains so much, yet doesn't tell you whether the company is going to be a success?

8. An advertisement states:

LOAN SHARKS
If they only knew about rare coins. This typical rare coin appreciated 1460% since 1980.
This coin cost
$52.00 in 1980
$104.50 in 1982
$135.00 in 1983
$170.00 in 1984
$265.00 in 1985
$760.00 in 1986

By the year 2000 this coin in gem quality could send your child to college or buy you a trip around the world.[5]

Why is this example unconvincing? Where are you going to find someone to sell you such an obviously profitable coin?

9. One way of gauging the degree of liquidity provided by a secondary market is to divide (a) the price you would receive today if you started looking for a buyer today by (b) the price you would receive today if you had begun looking for a buyer six months ago. Does a low ratio indicate an asset that is liquid or illiquid? Using this criterion, name three very illiquid assets with poor secondary markets.

10. A house, a car, and many other real assets provide services, which are untaxed income. Imagine that at your college graduation an anonymous benefactor gives you $100,000—enough to allow you to buy a house near your new job. You can either use this $100,000 gift to buy a house or else buy Treasury securities and rent a comparable house for $12,000 a year. If you have to pay a 28 percent tax on the income from your Treasury securities, how much interest do they have to pay each year to provide enough after-tax income to pay your rent?

11. The standard deviation of the annual returns from 1926 through 1986 was 21.2 percent for all stocks and 36.0 percent for small companies.[6] Which category do you guess had the higher average return?

12. Explain how the following quotation misinterprets studies of the historical rates of return from stock, data such as those in Table 1–3:

> An exhaustive computer survey, conducted a few years ago at the University of Chicago, showed that the average annual profit (before taxes) on *any* New York Stock Exchange investment held for one month or longer—regardless of what the company was, when the shares were purchased or when they were sold—was 9.3 percent.[7]

13. The appendix to this chapter shows that the annual returns from stocks during the 1970s had a mean of 7.49 percent and a standard deviation of 19.20 percent. Use the data in Table 1–3 to find the mean and standard deviation for the years 1950–59 and for 1960–69. Based on these results, write a sentence comparing stock returns during these three decades.

14. Table 1-A shows the annual profits (relative to net worth) for five very different companies over the ten-year period 1972–81. Calculate the mean and the standard deviation for each company, and write a brief paragraph summarizing the differences. Investors in a company's stock are interested in the size and stability of the company's profits. Based on these data alone, which of these five companies do you think investors like the most and which do you think they liked the least over this ten-year period (as gauged by a comparison of the stock prices in 1981 with those in 1972)?

15. Each fall, *Forbes* magazine reports the returns for mutual funds and for the stock market as a whole over the preceding twelve months. The stock market returns were −4.8 percent in 1984, 30.9 percent in 1985, and 35.8 percent in 1986; Table 1-B gives the annual percentage returns in these years for twenty-four randomly selected mutual funds. For each of these three years, calculate the average return for these twenty-four funds.

TABLE 1–A   Company Profits as a Percentage of Net Worth

Year	American Water Works	Brown & Sharpe	Campbell Soup	McDonald's	Pan American
1972	7.2	2.1	11.0	17.9	−7.0
1973	6.6	5.8	13.6	19.9	−4.7
1974	6.8	6.5	13.7	20.4	−26.7
1975	7.3	−5.4	13.1	21.0	−18.0
1976	7.8	2.3	14.3	21.0	−2.3
1977	8.0	7.7	13.9	21.3	12.3
1978	7.7	15.2	14.2	20.4	18.3
1979	7.5	18.4	14.8	19.8	10.5
1980	8.7	16.8	14.0	19.4	10.0
1981	8.5	6.8	13.0	19.3	−2.4

TABLE 1–B

Mutual Fund	Percentage Returns		
	1984	1985	1986
State Bond Diversified	−2.2	27.3	34.6
Bull & Bear Capital Growth	−17.9	25.8	29.3
Composite Growth	−13.2	19.8	26.0
Keystone Custodian S-1	−14.8	17.7	34.2
AMEV Capital	−16.8	27.9	47.6
Valley Forge	7.7	10.7	7.0
Keystone International	−11.0	15.4	55.2
Bullock Dividend Shares	−3.1	31.0	39.4
Tri-Continental Corp.	−2.1	31.8	45.3
Hartwell Growth	−24.3	9.7	30.1
Fidelity Puritan	2.6	35.6	26.3
Columbia Growth	−18.0	34.7	28.6
Pennsylvania Mutual	−2.9	23.1	29.3
Vance, Sanders Special	−13.1	8.5	14.7
Value Line Leveraged Growth	−25.3	32.2	39.0
Exchange Fund of Boston	−12.8	30.2	33.9
IDS Progressive	−3.9	17.4	28.8
Smith, Barney Equity	−11.1	22.9	36.0
MidAmerica Mutual	−9.0	32.4	22.2
Vanguard Windsor	2.8	42.6	29.8
Commonwealth Indenture A&B	−4.9	26.1	27.2
Acorn	−9.4	34.8	32.8
Keystone Custodian K-2	−16.5	21.8	39.6
ASA Limited	−9.5	−22.0	1.0

Source: Forbes, August, 27, 1984; September 16, 1985, and September 8, 1986.

CHAPTER 2

Required Returns and Present Value

> *It is a difference of opinion that makes horse races. . .*
>
> Mark Twain

There are a few key ideas that are absolutely essential to an understanding of investments. One is the subject of this chapter—the relationship between an investment's required return and its present value. The rate of return on an investment determines the value that it will grow to in the future. Conversely, the rate of return that investors require from an investment determines how much they are willing to pay today to receive a specified amount in the future. This chapter will explain how that insight can be used to value opportunities, understand market prices, and avoid several commonplace financial errors.

FUTURE VALUE

future value
The future value of an investment is its value after it has earned a specified rate of return for a given number of years.

The **future value** of an investment is its value after it has earned a specified rate of return for a given number of years. If, for example, you invest $1000 and earn a 10 percent annual rate of return, at the end of one year you will have:

$$\text{First year principal} + \text{interest} = \$1000 + 0.10(\$1000)$$
$$= \$1000 + \$100$$
$$= \$1100$$

or, in a slightly different form,

$$\$1000 + 0.10(\$1000) = \$1000(1 + 0.10)$$
$$= \$1000(1.10)$$
$$= \$1100.$$

If you reinvest your money for a second year at 10 percent, you will earn 10 percent interest not only on your original $1000, but also on the $100 interest you earned the first year:

$$\text{Second year principal} + \text{interest} = \$1100 + 0.10(\$1100)$$
$$= \$1100(1.10)$$
$$= \$1000(1.10)^2$$
$$= \$1210.$$

This phenomenon of earning interest on interest is called **compound interest.**

compound interest
Compound interest describes the earning of interest on interest.

If you continue to reinvest your money year after year at 10 percent, after n years you will have $\$1000(1.10)^n$. The general formula is apparent: If you invest an amount P, earning an annual rate of return R for n years, your investment grows to a future value

$$F = P(1 + R)^n. \tag{1}$$

The table in Appendix 1 at the end of the book shows future values for a variety of horizons and rates of return.

If the rate of return varies year by year—say R_1 the first year, R_2 the second, and so on—then your investment grows to

$$F = P(1 + R_1)(1 + R_2) \ldots (1 + R_n) \tag{2}$$

after n years. For instance, $1000 invested for three years at 10 percent has a future value of

$$\$1000(1.10)^3 = \$1331$$

while $1000 invested for three years at 10 percent, 11 percent, and then 12 percent a year respectively has a future value of

$$\$1000(1.10)(1.11)(1.12) = \$1367.52.$$

Table 1-3 in the previous chapter showed that, since 1926, corporate bonds have yielded an average return of 5 percent a year and corporate stock about 12 percent. How much difference does it make if you invest $1000 at 12 percent instead of 5 percent for a year? For ten years? For sixty

TABLE 2–1   Effect of Compounding on Future Value of a $1,000
Investment

	Future Value of $1,000 Investment	
Years	Annual Rate of Return, R = 5 Percent	Annual Rate of Return, R = 12 Percent
1	$1,050	$1,120
10	1,629	3,106
20	2,653	9,646
40	7,040	93,051
60	18,679	897,597

years? The differences, ever larger as the horizon increases, are shown in
Table 2–1. The growth in an investment's future value when interest is
compounded over an even longer period is illustrated in Investment Example 2–1.

PRESENT VALUE

A future-value calculation answers this question: if you invest $1000 at 10
percent, how much will you have after one year? Often, we are interested
in the reverse question: how much money do you have to invest now in
order to have $1100 after one year? The answer can be determined by
solving Equation 1 for P, given a specified future value, F, and rate of
return, R. To attain an amount F = $1100 after one year of earning R = 10
percent, you must invest an amount P such that

$$P(1 + 0.10) = \$1100$$

or

$$P = \frac{\$1100}{1 + 0.10}$$
$$= \$1000.$$

If you want $1100 after two years, the requisite investment is given by

$$P(1 + 0.10)^2 = \$1100$$

or

$$P = \frac{\$1100}{(1 + 0.10)^2}$$
$$= \$909.09.$$

INVESTMENT EXAMPLE
2–1

DID THE INDIANS CHARGE TOO MUCH FOR MANHATTAN?

Peter Minuit purchased Manhattan Island from the Algonquian Indians in 1626 for cloth, beads, and other trinkets worth about $24 at the time, a price that seems a bargain compared to the prices of Manhattan real estate today. Yet the lesson of future value is that $1 today is not the same as $1 tomorrow because $1 today turns into $1 plus interest tomorrow. In the same spirit, $24 nearly 400 years ago is not the same as $24 today because that $24 could have earned some 400 years' worth of interest. What would have happened to that $24 paid in 1626 if it had been invested patiently, year after year, at 6 percent? By 1989, some 363 years later, it would have grown to a remarkable $24(1.06)^{363} = $36.8

billion. Because the area of Manhattan is about 31.2 square miles, this works out to approximately $42 a square foot.

A seemingly modest rate of return that is compounded many, many times eventually turns a small investment into a fortune, a principle often dubbed "the miracle of compound interest." The accompanying table shows a corollary to this principle—that slightly different rates of return, year after year, compound to vastly different future values. It may not appear as if there is much difference between an investment yielding 6 percent a year and one yielding 7 percent. And there really isn't, *if* we don't look too far into the future. But the further ahead we look, the more the power of compounding separates the results.

| | Future Value of $24 Purchase of Manhattan in 1626 | |
Annual Rate of Return (percent)	Future Value, 1989	Future Value per Square Foot, 1989
4	$36.6 million	$ 0.04
5	1.2 billion	1.36
6	36.8 billion	42.35
7	1,113 billion	1,279.68
8	32,586 billion	37,463.82

Calculating Present Value

The future-value formula can also be used to answer another important question. Suppose that you have been offered $1100, to be paid a year from today. How much is this future $1100 worth to you *now;* that is, how much are you willing to pay for it? The amount you are willing to pay should reflect the return you require on such an investment. If you are willing to pay $1000 now for $1100 in one year, then you evidently require a 10 percent return on your investment, since $1000 invested for a year at 10 percent will grow to $1100. If you require a 20 percent return on this investment, then the amount P that you are willing to pay is given by

$$P(1 + 0.20) = \$1100$$

or

$$P = \frac{\$1100}{1 + 0.20}$$
$$= \$916.67.$$

Repeating the logic, if you require a 20 percent return, then you are willing to pay $916.67 today for $1100 a year from now because, at this price, the return is indeed 20 percent.

The amount you are willing to pay today to receive a specified future amount, F, after n years is called the **present value** of this future payment and can be calculated from a rearrangement of Equation 1,

present value
The present value of a cash flow is determined by discounting the cash flow by the investor's required rate of return.

$$P = \frac{F}{(1 + R)^n}. \tag{3}$$

Appendix 2 at the end of the book gives a number of illustrative present value calculations for $F = \$1$ and various values of R and n.

The rate of return, R, used to determine a present value is your **required rate of return**. If the required rate of return varies from year to year, a rearrangement of Equation 2 is appropriate:

required rate of return
The required rate of return is used to determine the present value of a cash flow.

$$P = \frac{F}{[(1 + R_1)(1 + R_2) \ldots (1 + R_n)]} \tag{4}$$

If there is more than one future payment, these payments are called a **cash flow.**

cash flow
A cash flow is a stream of future payments.

The present value of a cash flow is equal to the sum of the present values of the payments.

Suppose, for instance, that you can receive $1100 one year from now and another $1100 two years hence. At a required return R, the present value is

$$P = \frac{\$1100}{(1 + R)} + \frac{\$1100}{(1 + R)^2}.$$

If $R = 10$ percent, then

$$P = \frac{\$1100}{(1 + 0.10)} + \frac{\$1100}{(1 + 0.10)^2}$$
$$= \$1000 + \$909.09$$
$$= \$1909.09.$$

If instead of a 10 percent return, you require $R = 20$ percent,

$$P = \frac{\$1100}{(1 + 0.20)} + \frac{\$1100}{(1 + 0.20)^2}$$
$$= \$916.67 + \$763.89$$
$$= \$1680.56.$$

A more complex situation, involving a professional football contract, is analyzed in Investment Example 2–2 on pp. 34–35.

The Appropriate Required Return

The present value depends critically on your required return. To receive $1100 a year from now, you are willing to pay $1000 if you require a 10 percent return, but only $916.67 if you require a 20 percent return.

> **The higher is the required return, the lower is the present value of a given cash flow.**

What determines the required return and, implicitly, the amount investors are willing to pay for future cash flows? One obvious influence is the rates of return available on other investments. You won't settle for a 5 percent return when banks are paying 10 percent, but you might accept this return when bank deposits are paying only 3 percent.

> **Required returns go up and down with the rates of return available on alternative investments.**

At any point in time, there is not a single required return that applies to all investments, because investments have other characteristics that make them more attractive, or less so. For instance, many people care about an investment's **risk**—the certainty or uncertainty of the promised cash flow. If you can invest your money safely in a bank at 10 percent and the $1100 offer is just a shaky promise from a disreputable stranger, then you may well require 20 percent, 30 percent, or an even higher return and, hence, will pay very little for this $1100 IOU.

risk
Risk exists when the outcomes are uncertain.

> **The less attractive the investment, the higher is your required return and the lower is its present value.**

This rule implies what many find counterintuitive—that the least attractive investments have the highest potential returns. Indeed, it is the requisite low prices and high potential returns that compensate for the otherwise undesirable features of these investments. This rule is one explanation for the historical data presented in the previous chapter, which showed that risky corporate bonds have had higher returns on average than government bonds and that even riskier stocks have had even higher average returns. Similarly, we will see in Chapter 4 that the "junk bonds" issued by shaky companies have lower prices and higher potential returns than the secure bonds issued by strong companies.

34

THE VALUE OF JOE CRIBBS'S CONTRACT

In these days of free agents and creative financing, sports stars often work under very complex and interesting employment contracts. Usually, the details are kept secret; but sometimes they leak into print. One case that did become part of the public record occurred in 1983 when Joe Cribbs, a running back who left the NFL's Buffalo Bills, signed a five-year $2.45 million contract with the USFL's Birmingham Stallions. After signing, Cribbs demanded that the contract be renegotiated because, in his words, it was "not what I thought it was when I signed it."*

The contract included the following provisions:

1. A $650,000 signing bonus, composed of $200,000 to be paid at the time of signing and the remainder paid in installments over seven years.
2. A basic salary of $250,000 a year for 1984, 1985, 1986, with the club having the option in 1986 of hiring Cribbs for two more years at $250,000 a year.
3. A deferred salary of $550,000—$100,000 to be paid in 1989 and the rest later *if* the club decided to exercise its 1986 option.
4. An interest-free loan of $350,000 made over three years, 1984–86, to be repaid over five years, 1986–90.

---

*Robert W. Creamer, "Scorecard," *Sports Illustrated*, May 21, 1984, p. 11.

5. A $125,000 agent's fee to be deducted from Cribbs's income in three installments, $75,000 at the time of signing and $25,000 during each of the next two years.

The total proceeds to Cribbs, before deducting the agent's fee, comes to $2.45 million:

Signing bonus	$ 650,000
Basic salary	1,250,000
Deferred salary	550,000
	$2,450,000

However, $950,000 of this total was contingent on the club deciding three years down the road that it wants to hire Cribbs for another two years, and, for a thirty-two-year-old running back, that outcome was far from certain. On the other side of the ledger, the $2.45 million figure ignores the interest-free loan, which is something of value because Cribbs can invest the money temporarily and keep all of the profits. In this case, though, the loan would be very temporary. The table on p. 35 shows all of the guaranteed cash flows (in thousands of dollars).

Why do you think the club prefers deferred payments? Because money paid later is not as burdensome as money paid today. To figure the true cost of money paid later, we can calculate the present value of these future dollars from the standpoint of either Cribbs or the club, the difference being the agent's fee that the club pays but Cribbs doesn't get. Let's calculate present value from Cribbs's perspective, using the data in the table.

The easiest way to simplify a maze of income and expenses is to calculate the net cash flow, year by

Year	Signing Bonus	Agent's Fee	Basic Salary	Deferred Salary	Interest-Free Loan	Loan Payback	Net Cash Flow
1983	$200	− $75					$125
1984		− 25	$250		$100		325
1985		− 25	250		100		325
1986	50		250		150	− $30	420
1987	100					− 80	20
1988	100					− 80	20
1989	100			$100		− 80	120
1990	100					− 80	20

year. The results are shown in the table's last column. The present value of this cash flow is as follows:

$$P = \$125{,}000$$
$$+ \ \$325{,}000/(1 + R)$$
$$+ \ \$325{,}000/(1 + R)^2$$
$$+ \ \$420{,}000/(1 + R)^3$$
$$+ \ \$20{,}000/(1 + R)^4$$
$$+ \ \$20{,}000/(1 + R)^5$$
$$+ \ \$120{,}000/(1 + R)^6$$
$$+ \ \$20{,}000/(1 + R)^7$$

What value should we use for the required return? In June of 1983, when the contract was signed, U.S. Treasury securities were yielding about 10 percent, and the prime rate banks charged large corporations was 10.5 percent. Since there was considerable risk involved in this deal, Cribbs may well have had a required return of 15 percent, 20 percent, or even higher; not knowing how long the Birmingham Stallions would last, he may have preferred $100,000 in 1983 to a promise of $120,000 in 1984.

Instead of assuming an artificially precise required return to five decimal places, we should calculate the present value for a plausible range of values for the required return. As shown in the second accompanying table, the resulting present value is about $1 million, plus or minus $100,000— not an insignificant amount, to be sure, but considerably less than the advertised $2.45 million.

Required Return, R (percent)	Present Value, P (millions of dollars)
10	$1.11
15	1.01
20	0.93

Other characteristics besides risk may make an investment more or less desirable. For instance, some people may be repulsed by companies doing business in South Africa, by companies manufacturing cigarettes, or by companies operating funeral homes. The squeamish will use high required rates of return to discount the cash flow from such businesses. The degree of aversion varies, of course, from investor to investor. Someone who is less risk averse than average, or less repulsed by investments in South Africa, will use lower required returns and happily buy the investments others shun (just as lobster lovers used to find lobsters a bargain years ago when others considered them unappetizing).

PRESENT VALUE VERSUS MARKET PRICE

The present value is what a cash flow is worth to you—that is, how much you are willing to pay now in order to receive this cash flow later. Others may be willing to pay even more or somewhat less, because they disagree with your estimate of the cash flow or because they have a different required return (perhaps because they are more or less risk averse than you).

Consider, for instance, the opportunity to recover a sunken ship that divers have discovered near Martha's Vineyard, a Massachusetts island. The divers cannot get the necessary equipment in place and secures government approval to begin recovery of the ship before winter sets in. Thus, recovery activity will have to wait for a year, and the sale of the treasure will have to wait for another year after that, until various government claims have been satisfied and buyers located. Strapped for funds, the divers are willing to sell 20 percent of what they will receive two years from now in return for an immediate cash payment that allows them to buy equipment and eat during the winter. Press reports at the time the ship sank indicate that it was carrying silver, jewelry, and collectibles that you estimate will be worth (after giving the state and federal governments their share) around $12 million. How much are you willing to pay now for 20 percent of this potential treasure?

A starting point is the calculation that 20 percent of $12 million is $0.20(\$12 \text{ million}) = \$2.4$ million. Next, we have to recognize that this $2.4 million is two years away (and thus, must be discounted to obtain a present value) and that the actual value of the treasure is far from certain. If you can earn 8 percent on safe bonds, perhaps you require an 18 percent return on something this risky. If so, your present value is

$$\frac{\$2.4 \text{ million}}{(1 + 0.18)^2} = \$1.72 \text{ million.}$$

If the owners are willing to sell a 20 percent stake for $1 million, you leap at the bargain; if they demand $2 million, you refuse politely. Of course, others may step in where you hesitate to invest. Another investor, looking at the same opportunity, may estimate the salvage of the treasure at $20 million and have a required return of only 12 percent. To this person, the present value is

$$\frac{0.20(\$20 \text{ million})}{(1 + 0.12)^2} = \$3.19 \text{ million},$$

and a $2 million price is too good to pass up.

This simple example illustrates a very important principle. Present values can vary from person to person because of different estimates of the cash flow and different required returns. This principle explains why some investors buy assets that others shun. Indeed, for every buyer, there is a seller—for every person who thinks the price is low, there is someone else who believes the price is high.

The next several chapters will apply present-value logic in many different ways. It is used by banks to calculate mortgage payments (the cash flow), given the interest rate and the amount borrowed. It is used in the financial press to calculate bond yields, given the price and cash flow. It is used by corporations to evaluate investment projects, given the cash flow and the required rate of return. And it can be used by investors to calculate either the present value or the implicit rate of return on corporate stock, given an estimate of the cash flow from these shares.

CONSTANT CASH FLOWS

In many cases, the cash flow is the same, period after period—for example, constant monthly mortgage payments, constant semiannual income from a bond, and constant quarterly profits from a small business. If so, the present value is as follows:

$$P = \frac{X}{(1 + R)} + \frac{X}{(1 + R)^2} + \ldots + \frac{X}{(1 + R)^n}$$

where

X = constant cash flow each period
R = required return per period
n = number of periods

The appendix to this chapter shows that this equation simplifies to the following handy formula:

$$P = \left(\frac{X}{R}\right)\left[1 - \frac{1}{(1 + R)^n}\right] \tag{5}$$

Appendix 3 at the end of the book gives the calculated present value of a payment of $1 per period for selected values of n and R.

Equation 5 can be used to determine the present value P of any investment that yields a constant cash flow. For example, a bond, stock, or machine that pays \$100 a year for ten years has, at a 10 percent required return, a present value of

$$P = \frac{\$100}{(1 + 0.10)} + \ldots + \frac{\$100}{(1 + 0.10)^{10}}$$

$$P = \left(\frac{\$100}{0.10}\right)\left[1 - \frac{1}{(1 + 0.10)^{10}}\right]$$

$$= \$1000(1 - 0.38554)$$

$$= \$614.46$$

This answer can also be determined from Appendix 3 at the end of the book. For 10 periods and $R = 10\%$, the present value of a \$1 cash flow is \$6.1446. The present value of a \$100 cash flow is 100(\$6.1446) = \$614.46.

Equation 5 also applies to loans that are repaid in constant installments, since the loan payments X are set so that their present value P at the loan rate R is equal to the amount you borrowed. For instance, using the previous numbers, if you borrow \$614 and repay this loan in ten equal annual installments at a 10 percent interest rate, the size of each payment is \$100—because, as we've just seen, the present value of such a cash flow is equal to \$614. More generally, the appropriate payments can be determined by rearranging Equation 5 as

$$X = \frac{RP}{\left[1 - \dfrac{1}{(1 + R)^n}\right]}. \tag{6}$$

Investment Examples 2–3 and 2–4 apply Equations 5 and 6 to a state-lottery payoff and to a personal-computer loan. A more detailed analysis of loans is given in Chapter 3.

Another application of Equation 5 is a perpetual cash flow, which continues period after period, forever. In 1750, Great Britain consolidated its debts by issuing bonds that never mature, but instead pay a constant amount forever. Such bonds are generically labeled *perpetuities,* and those perpetuities issued by Great Britain are called *British Consols.*

To value a perpetuity, look at Equation 5 and notice that the term $1/(1 + R)^n$ approaches zero as n becomes infinitely large (as long as the required return is positive). Therefore, the present value of a perpetuity is

$$P = \frac{X}{R} \tag{7}$$

For example, if the cash flow is \$100 a year forever and the required return is 10 percent, then the present value is

$$P = \frac{\$100}{0.10} = \$1000$$

INVESTMENT EXAMPLE
2–3

THE VALUE OF A LOTTERY PAYOFF

State lotteries have become an important source of government revenue and news stories. In May 1984, newspaper headlines told how "Thousands Seek Millions as Jackpot Fever Grips New York."* New York's May 12, 1984, Lotto game offered an $18.5-million-plus jackpot and people stood in hour-long lines, beginning at five o'clock in the morning, betting more than a million dollars an hour.

The New York Lotto game is won by matching (not necessarily in order) the six numbers selected by a machine from forty-four ping-pong balls numbered one to forty-four. The probability of picking the winning number is about one in seven million. The amount of money paid out depends on the number of tickets sold, and this money is split evenly if there is more than one winner. On average, the New York Lotto game, like most state lotteries, pays out only 40 percent of what it takes in. In May of 1984, there had been no winner for three straight games and the state accumulated the prize money, giving the May 12 game a prize of at least $18.5 million.

There were $24.1 million in tickets sold for the May 12 game, and the prize ballooned to $22.1 million, a considerably higher payout ratio than usual, since the May 12 prize was swollen with money from those who bought tickets for the three previous drawings and won nothing. As it turned

*John J. Goldman, "Thousands Seek Millions as Jackpot Fever Grips N.Y.," *Los Angeles Times*, May 12, 1984.

out, there were four winning tickets on May 12, and each received $22,100,000/4 = $5,525,000.

The winners of this lottery did not get their money all at once, however, but in twenty-one annual installments, without interest. What is the present value of their annual $5,525,000/21 = $263,095 payments? That is, how much would the state of New York have to deposit in a bank account now in order to pay a winner $263,095 a year for twenty-one years? (Or imagine that a winner goes to a bank with a notarized letter from the state of New York, affirming the lottery winning. How much could this winner borrow to buy a Manhattan apartment, so that the annual mortgage payments come to $263,095 a year for twenty-one years?) The present value is

$$P = \$263{,}095 + \left[\frac{\$263{,}095}{(1+R)} + \cdots + \frac{\$263{,}095}{(1+R)^{20}} \right]$$

or, simplified via Equation 5,

$$P = \$263{,}095 + \frac{\$263{,}095}{R} \left[1 - \frac{1}{(1+R)^{20}} \right]$$

The present value works out to be $1.9 million with a 15 percent interest rate and $2.5 million at a 10 percent interest rate, which (because the prize is spread over twenty-one years) is only 35 percent to 45 percent of the advertised value of $5.525 million! The May 12 Lotto game offered better-than-average odds; but you didn't really think that the state of New York was taking a loss, did you?

This result makes sense, in that a $100 annual return on a $1000 investment does provide the requisite 10 percent return.

HOW SWEET IS A SWEETHEART LOAN?

Employers sometimes loan their employees money at below-market interest rates. Joe Cribbs's contract contains one example (see Investment Example 2–2). Another, somewhat more modest, is the offer by Pomona College, to loan up to $3000 for three years interest-free to any faculty member who purchases a personal computer. This offer is intended to encourage faculty members to participate in the microcomputer revolution. But is this deal really attractive enough to turn a hesitant professor into a eager buyer? From the faculty member's perspective, does an interest-free loan reduce the effective cost of a computer by $5 or by $500? Similarly, from the standpoint of the college, is this an expensive program or just a drop in the endowment bucket?

Each $3000 loan is to be repaid in thirty-six monthly installments of $3000/36 = $83.33. The burden of this loan is the present value of these thirty-six payments:

$$P = \$83.33/(1 + R) + \$83.33/(1 + R)^2 + \ldots + \$83.33/(1 + R)^{36}$$

What required return is appropriate? From a faculty member's standpoint, there are two possibilities come to mind. If the professor would have withdrawn money from a bank or money-market fund to buy the computer, then Pomona College's loan will allow these funds to stay put earning interest. In this case, the rate of return on such investments would be the appropriate required return. If, instead, the professor would have borrowed from a bank or computer store to make

the purchase, then the interest rate charged on such loans would be the correct required rate.

Pomona College's program started in 1983, when many safe investments were paying 10 percent and when loan rates averaged 17 percent on personal bank loans, 19 percent on credit-card purchases, and even higher rates at many computer stores. The present values for required returns ranging from 10 percent to 18 percent are shown in the accompanying table [the data derived by using Equation 5, with the annual rates divided by 12 to give monthly rates]. Notice that, as you have come to expect, the present value drops as the required return increases. Here we are considering the present value of an expense ($83.33 a month for thirty-six months) and, so, the lower the present value, the lighter the burden of these payments.

Required Return (percent)	Present Value	Saving ($3000 minus present value)
10	$2583	$417
12	2509	491
15	2404	596
18	2305	695

Notice, also, that we do not use the Pomona College interest rate charged on the loan—0 percent—as the required return. If we did, we would just go around in a circle, showing that thirty-

six monthly payments of $83.33 do indeed add up to $3000:

$$P = \$83.33/(1 + 0) + \$83.33/(1 + 0)^2 + \ldots + \$83.33/(1 + 0)^{36}$$
$$= 36(\$83.33)$$
$$= \$3000$$

We should not try to measure the present value of these monthly payments by discounting them with an artificial, below-market interest rate; rather, we should gauge the true burden of these payments by taking into account market interest rates. A present-value calculation should always discount the cash flow, no matter how that cash flow is determined, by the required return, which reflects market interest rates (adjusted for risk and other salient characteristics of the cash flow).

The last column in the accompanying table represents the difference between the $3000 the professor receives from Pomona College and the present value burden of the monthly payments. This difference, the implicit value of the interest-free loan, ranges from $400 to $700, a substantial saving on a $3000 computer. Naturally enough, the saving is smaller for someone who would otherwise buy the computer with money that could be earning 10 percent in a money-market fund than for somebody who would otherwise have to borrow the $3000 at 18 percent.

Another way of looking at these savings is to consider how much money the professor could borrow from a bank at 18 percent, with thirty-six monthly payments of $83.33. Since loan payments are figured such that the present value of the monthly payments is equal to the amount borrowed at the quoted rate, the answer is the $2305 shown in the table. Thus, another way to interpret the $695 present-value saving is that in return for these $83.33 monthly payments, the professor can borrow only $2305 from a bank but can borrow $3000 from the college—receiving an extra $695 to spend on a computer.

Yet another way of interpreting the results is to consider the fact that if the professor borrowed $3000 from a bank at 18 percent, the monthly payments, calculated by using Equation 6 with $R = 18\%/12 = 1.5\%$, would be $108.46, which is $25.13 more than the $83.33 that must be paid to Pomona College. What is the value to the professor of saving $25.13 a month for thirty-six months? We cannot just multiply by 36, since $1 tomorrow is not the same as $1 today. Instead, we calculate the present value at 18 percent, using Equation 5,

$$P = \$25.13/(1 + 0.18/12) + \ldots + \$25.13/(1 + 0.18/12)^{36}$$
$$= [\$25.13/(0.18/12)][1 - 1/(1 + 0.18/12)^{36}]$$
$$= \$695$$

All logical roads lead to the present-value conclusion, a $695 savings at an 18 percent required return.

From the standpoint of Pomona College, this loan is an investment of $3000 that yields $83.33 a month, a 0 percent return. To value the loan in present-value terms, we observe that the school could invest its money instead in safe bonds paying 10 percent, and then note that the present value of its receipts of $83.33 a month for thirty-six months, discounted at 10 percent, is $2583. That is, the school is spending $3000 for a cash flow that is worth only $2583, a $417 subsidy per professor. If 100 professors participate, the total cost of these interest-free loans is 100($417) = $41,700.

COMPOUND INTEREST

The sale of Manhattan in 1626, discussed in Investment Example 2–1, is a dramatic example of the power of compound interest, that earning interest on interest causes wealth to grow geometrically. In the 1960s, banks and other financial institutions began using compound interest to relieve some of the pressures they felt during credit crunches. At the time, the maximum interest rates that banks could pay their depositors were set by the Federal Reserve Board, under Regulation Q. This regulation was enacted by Congress in the 1930s, the theory being that banks needed to be protected from ruinous deposit-rate wars, which tempted them into speculative investments, hoping to earn enough to pay what they had promised depositors. In the 1980s, Regulation Q was phased out at the urging of consumer groups (who felt that rate wars are good for depositors) and of banks (who were losing depositors to money-market funds and other investments that did not have rate ceilings).

In the 1960s, whenever market interest rates jumped above the deposit rates allowed by Regulation Q, banks lost deposits—a diversion of funds called *disintermediation*—and could do little more than offer depositors electric blankets, toaster ovens, and other incentives. Then someone somewhere noticed that Regulation Q was phrased in terms of annual percentage rates, which could be turned into higher effective rates by compounding more often than once a year.

Suppose, for example, that the quoted annual rate is 12 percent (more than banks were paying then, but a number easily divisible in the arithmetic to come). If there is no compounding during the year, then $1 grows to $1.12 by year's end. With semiannual compounding, the deposit is credited with $12\%/2 = 6\%$ interest halfway through the year. Then, during the second half of the year, the investment earns another 6 percent interest on both the principal and the first six-months' interest, giving an effective rate of return for the year of 12.36 percent:

$$\$1(1.06)(1.06) = \$1.1236$$

This rate is an effective rate of return in the sense that 12 percent compounded semiannually pays as much as 12.36 percent compounded annually.

With quarterly compounding, $12\%/4 = 3\%$ interest is credited every three months. Thus,

$$\$1(1.03)(1.03)(1.03)(1.03) = \$1.1255,$$

raising the effective rate to 12.55 percent. Monthly compounding, paying $12\%/12 = 1\%$ each month, pushes the effective return up to 12.68 percent.

In general, an amount P invested at an annual percentage rate of return *APR*, compounded m times a year, grows to $P(1 + APR/m)^m$ after 1 year and to $P(1 + APR/m)^{mn}$ after n years.

As the examples have shown, more frequent compounding increases the effective return. If we go from monthly to daily compounding, then 12%/365 in interest is credited daily, and the effective annual return rises to 12.7468 percent. Theoretically, even more frequent compounding is possible; indeed, mathematicians can handle *continuous* compounding, taking the limit of $\$1(1 + APR/m)^m$ as the frequency of compounding becomes infinitely large (and the time between compounding infinitesimally small)

$$\text{limit } (1 + APR/m)^m \rightarrow e^R$$
$$(m \rightarrow \infty)$$

where $e = 2.718 \ldots$ is the base of natural logarithms. In practice, of course, the bank doesn't continuously update the balance in one's account with every last instant's worth of interest. But at some specified interval, perhaps quarterly or annually, the bank can use mathematical formulas of this sort to determine the amount of interest one has earned. In our example, with $APR = 12$ percent, continuous compounding pushes the effective annual rate up to 12.7497 percent. Although advertisements trumpeting "continuous compounding" attempt to convey the feeling that the bank is doing something marvelous for us and our money, the improvement over daily compounding is slight.

AFTER-TAX RETURNS

Cash-flow calculations should take taxes into account. If you receive $100 but have to pay a 30 percent tax on it, then what matters to you is not the $100 you receive *before taxes*, but the $70 you keep *after taxes*. Tax rates vary from person to person (because tax brackets rise with income), from institution to institution (because, for example, banks, nonfinancial corporations, and colleges are treated differently), and from asset to asset (because interest on investments such as corporate and municipal bonds are taxed differently). The taxes for different institutions and assets will be discussed in later chapters, where appropriate. We will concentrate now on individual tax brackets.

Personal-Income-Tax Brackets

The United States has a progressive tax system, in which federal income tax rates rise with income. The historic Tax Reform Act of 1986 compressed fifteen tax brackets (ranging from 11 percent to 50 percent) down to two

TABLE 2–2 Federal Tax Brackets, 1988

Single Individual		Married Couple Filing Joint Return	
Taxable Income	Tax Bracket (percent)	Taxable Income	Tax Bracket (percent)
$0–$17,850	15	$0–$29,750	15
$17,850–$43,150	28	$29,750–$71,900	28
$43,150–$89,560	33	$71,900–$149,250	33
Over $89,560	28	Over $149,250	28

basic rates, 15 percent and 28 percent. As shown in Table 2–2, in 1988 a single individual paid 15 percent tax on the first $17,850 of taxable income; for a married couple filing a joint return, the 15 percent rate applied to the first $29,750 of taxable income. Amounts over these thresholds were taxed at a 28 percent rate, plus a 5 percent surcharge for income in the indicated range. This 5 percent surcharge has the effect of phasing out the 15 percent bracket, so that a single person with $89,560 (and a married couple with $149,250) or more of taxable income pays a 28 percent tax on all of this income.

It is important to recognize that taxes are levied only on taxable income, which excludes some income (such as interest on municipal bonds) and reflects a variety of deductions and adjustments. In calculating taxable income, you are allowed to subtract a personal exemption ($1,950 in 1988, plus exemptions for dependents) and a standard deduction ($3000 for a single individual in 1988, $5000 for a married couple filing a joint return), which makes the first several thousand dollars of income effectively tax free. Many taxpayers are able also to increase their deductions by itemizing such expenses as large medical bills, interest on a home mortgage, state and local income and property taxes, and charitable contributions.

Another important point about the 1986 law is that the tax brackets in Table 2–2 are *marginal* tax rates that apply only to income in that bracket. A single person who earns $20,000 of taxable income is in a 28 percent tax bracket and pays the following tax:

$$\begin{aligned}
\text{Tax on first } \$17,850: 15\% \ (\$17,850) &= \quad \$2,677.50 \\
\text{Tax on } \$20,000 - \$17,850: 28\% \ (\$2,150) &= \quad \underline{602.00} \\
&\quad\ \ \$3,279.50
\end{aligned}$$

The total tax of $3,279.50 is 16.4 percent of total taxable income ($3,279.50/$20,000 = 0.164) and an even smaller percentage of total income, before exclusions and deductions. When this person with $20,000 of taxable income considers an investment yielding $100 in taxable income, the appropriate tax rate is not the 16.4 percent average tax rate, but the 28 percent marginal tax rate. The reason is that out of an additional $100 of taxable income, this person must pay an extra $28 in taxes.

For comparing and evaluating investment decisions, the marginal tax rate (which is generally higher than the average tax rate) is appropriate.

Now consider an investor in a 28 percent tax bracket analyzing an investment that is expected to give an after-tax cash flow of $100 after one year, $200 after two years, and $400 after three years. What required return is appropriate? If a safe Treasury bond pays 10 percent before taxes, this investor would pay a 28 percent tax on the 10 percent return and keep only 7.2 percent after taxes. (For instance, $1000 invested for a year at 10 percent before taxes earns $100 of taxable income, pays a tax of $0.28(\$100) = \$28$, and keeps $72 after taxes, which is a 7.2 percent return on the $1000 investment.)

In general, if the tax rate is t and the before-tax rate of return R, the after-tax rate of return is $(1 - t)R$.

Now we can calculate the present value in our example by discounting the after-tax cash flow by an after-tax required rate of return. If this investment is reasonably safe—and completely safe Treasury bonds yield a 7.2 percent after-tax return—then perhaps this investor's required return is 8 percent. If so,

$$P = \frac{\$100}{(1 + 0.08)} + \frac{\$200}{(1 + 0.08)^2} + \frac{\$400}{(1 + 0.08)^3}$$
$$= \$582.$$

Taxes Do Matter

It has been said that "the power to tax involves the power to destroy," meaning that governments can tax unwanted activities right out of business. If the government were really serious about discouraging cigarette smoking, Congress could levy an annual $50,000-an-acre tax on tobacco farmers and a $10-a-cigarette tax on smokers. Instead, the federal government requires cigarette warning labels and simultaneously gives subsidies to tobacco farmers.

Seemingly slight differences in after-tax returns can, by virtue of the power of compound interest, turn into substantial differences in future wealth. Consider, for instance, a 10 percent before-tax rate of return. A 30

TABLE 2–3 How Varying After-Tax Returns Affect a $10,000 Investment Over Time

	After-Tax Return on a $10,000 Investment Having a 10 Percent Before-Tax Return		
Years	Tax Rate, $t = 0$	Tax Rate, $t = 0.3$	Tax Rate, $t = 0.5$
1	$11,000	$10,700	$10,500
5	16,105	14,026	12,763
10	25,937	19,762	16,289
20	67,275	38,697	26,533
30	174,494	76,123	43,129

percent tax reduces the after-tax return to 7 percent and a 50 percent tax reduces it to 5 percent. Table 2–3 shows how much difference this disparity makes to a $10,000 investment over time.

NOMINAL AND REAL RETURNS

People do not invest solely to accumulate piles of paper dollars. They save now so that they (or their heirs) can spend later. Yet, conventionally reported rates of return keep track of only how many dollars are earned, not how much these dollars can buy. To keep track of purchasing power, we need to take into account the prices of goods and services and, in particular, determine whether the dollar value of our investments is rising faster than prices. This calculation can be made by subtracting the inflation rate from the dollar rate of return, giving a real rate of return.

Suppose, for example, that you put $100 in the bank at 5 percent, giving you $105 at the end of the year. This 5 percent return is called the **nominal rate of return,** which measures the percentage increase in your dollars without adjusting for their purchasing power. To gauge purchasing power, we need to consider the rate of inflation too. Let's say that prices have increased by 5 percent during this year. Now consider some typical product, say cereal, whose price has risen by 5 percent. Perhaps a box of cereal that was $2.00 at the beginning of the year is $2.10 at the end. The $100 you put in the bank at the beginning of the year was enough to buy 50 boxes of cereal. At the end of the year, you have $105 (5 percent more dollars), but now cereal costs $2.10 a box (5 percent more); so you can still only buy 50 boxes of cereal. Your 5 percent nominal rate of return is just enough to keep up with inflation, no more. Your **real rate of return,** which measures the percentage increase in your purchasing power, is in this case 0 percent. If the rate of inflation is instead 3 percent while your nominal

nominal rate of return
The nominal rate of return compares the dollars received from an investment with the dollars invested, without adjusting for the purchasing power of these dollars.

rate of return is 5 percent, then your purchasing power increases by 2 percent. (The cost of cereal rises from $2.00 to $2.06, and your $105 can buy $105/$2.06 = 50.97 boxes, about 2 percent more than at the start of the year.)

In general, if we let R be the nominal return and r be the corresponding real return for a rate of inflation p, then

real rate of return
An asset's real rate of return measures the percentage increase in purchasing power and is approximately equal to the nominal percentage return minus the percentage rate of inflation.

$$r = \frac{\dfrac{(\$ \text{ at end})}{(\text{price at end})}}{\dfrac{(\$ \text{ at beginning})}{(\text{price at beginning})}} - 1$$

$$= \frac{\dfrac{(\$ \text{ at end})}{(\$ \text{ at beginning})}}{\dfrac{(\text{price at end})}{(\text{price at beginning})}} - 1$$

$$= \frac{(1 + R)}{(1 + p)} - 1,$$

which is approximately equal to $R - p$.

> **The real rate of return on an investment, measuring the percentage increase in purchasing power, is approximately equal to the nominal (dollar) percentage return minus the percentage rate of inflation, or $r = R - p$.**

A 10 percent nominal return during a 2 percent inflation is an 8 percent real return, implying that you can buy 8 percent more at the end of the year than you could at the beginning. A 5 percent nominal return during a 12 percent inflation is a -7 percent real return, meaning that you can buy 7 percent less at the end of the year than at the start.

Taking Account of Inflation in Present-Value Calculations

Many people make the mistake of thinking that present-value logic—that a dollar today is worth more than a dollar tomorrow—hinges on inflation. They reason that "a dollar today buys more than a dollar tomorrow, because prices tomorrow will be higher than they are today." It is true that dollars lose purchasing power as prices rise, but present-value logic hinges on something else—that a dollar today can be *invested* to grow to more than a dollar tomorrow.

Imagine a not-so-hypothetical experiment. It is 1982, and safe Treasury

TABLE 2–4   Nominal and Real Cash Flows in a Hypothetical Situation

Year	Nominal Cash Flow	Real Cash Flow with a 4 Percent Inflation Rate
1	$100	$100/(1.04) = $96.15
2	150	150/(1.04)² = 138.68
3	200	200/(1.04)³ = 177.80

bills are yielding a 14.9 percent rate of return, while the rate of inflation is 3.9 percent. To make the conclusion even more obvious, assume the rate of inflation is zero. In such a situation, how much would you pay today for $1000 a year from now? Would you pay $1000 because there is no inflation? Or would you pay closer to $1000/1.149 = $870 because you can invest $870 in Treasury bills for a year and have it grow to $1000? It is rates of return that make current dollars valuable, and it is rates of return, not inflation, that should be used to discount future cash flows.

A more subtle question is whether nominal or real required returns should be used in present-value calculations. The answer is that either return is acceptable, as long as we are consistent with the way the cash flows are measured. If we use nominal cash flows, then we must discount by nominal required rates of return; if we use real cash flows, then real rates of return are appropriate.

Consider the example shown in Table 2–4 of a three-year cash flow— $100, $150, and $200, respectively—with a 7 percent nominal required rate of return, and a 4 percent inflation rate. If we use the nominal cash flow and nominal interest rate in our calculations, the present value is

$$P = \frac{\$100}{(1 + 0.07)} + \frac{\$150}{(1 + 0.07)^2} + \frac{\$200}{(1 + 0.07)^3}$$
$$= \$387.73.$$

Now let's use the real cash-flow data shown in the table. By dividing $100 by 1.04, we determine that $100 a year from now, after a 4 percent inflation, will buy as much as $96.15 buys today. The real required rate of return is $(1.07/1.04) - 1 = 0.028846$, approximately $7\% - 4\% = 3\%$. The present value, using the real cash flow and real required rate, works out to be

$$P = \frac{\$96.15}{(1.028846)} + \frac{\$138.68}{(1.028846)^2} + \frac{\$177.80}{(1.028846)^3}$$
$$= \$387.73,$$

the same as before. As stated earlier, present-value calculations can be done either by discounting a nominal cash flow by a nominal required rate of return or by discounting a real cash flow by a real rate of return. Thus, real rates of return aren't necessary for present-value calculations. They are of more interest for seeing whether investments are keeping ahead of inflation.

The Effect of Inflation Expectations on Nominal Interest Rates

If people can earn a 5 percent rate of return when the inflation rate is 2 percent, their real rate of return is 3 percent. If the rate of inflation rises to 12 percent, they won't be enthusiastic about investing their money at 5 percent, because their real return will be a disheartening −7 percent. Instead, they may try to stockpile some of the commodities whose prices are rising by 12 percent a year. Neglecting storage and other expenses, stockpiling will give a 12 percent nominal return, for a 0 percent real return—not much, but better than −7 percent. For bonds to be competitive, they must offer more than a 5 percent nominal return.

Thus, interest rates tend to increase during inflationary periods because of investor reluctance to hold securities whose anticipated returns are less than the expected rate of inflation. There is not, however, a simple, fixed relationship between the expected inflation rate and nominal interest rates. An increase in the expected inflation rate does not automatically raise nominal interest rates by an equal amount, leaving real interest rates constant. Real interest rates depend on demand, supply, and institutional rigidities (such as Regulation Q).

Nor is it true that all real interest rates are invariably positive. Throughout the 1970s, many people kept funds in savings accounts paying about 5 percent interest while consumer prices increased relentlessly by more than 5 percent a year. These investors accepted negative real returns because they believed that these savings accounts were the best of their alternatives. Stocks, bonds, and other assets that might have earned higher yields were too risky or had brokerage fees too high for small investors. Some investments had stiff minimum requirements. It took $10,000 to buy a Treasury bill. It required millions of dollars to buy a shopping center. And it was not possible to guarantee a 0 percent real rate of return by investing in the Consumer Price Index (CPI). Some people may have stocked up on wine and soup. But it is difficult to stockpile flammable gasoline, perishable food, fashionable clothing, advanced computers, medical services, hair cuts, sales taxes, and other components of the CPI.

Before-tax real interest rates were relatively stable and generally positive in the 1950s and 1960s in the United States, causing many people to assume that real interest rates are almost constant and always positive. But these assumptions were shown to be faulty in the 1970s and 1980s, when real interest rates turned, first, persistently negative and, then, substantially positive, as shown in Figures 2–1 and 2–2 on p. 50. A look in the other direction reveals that real interest rates were not very stable before the 1950s either.

FIGURE 2–1   Interest rates and inflation, 1926-1987

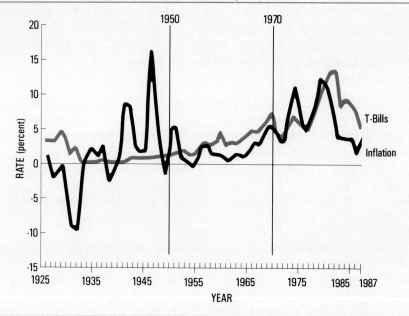

FIGURE 2–2   Real interest rates, 1926-1987

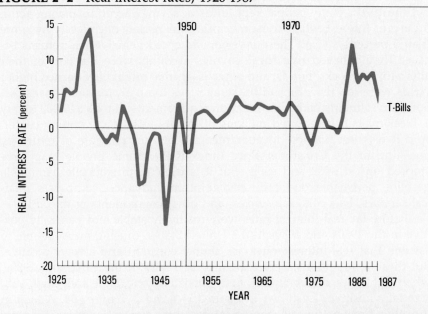

A very specific example of volatile real interest rates occurred in 1985. In January, 462 financial professionals surveyed by Drexel Burnham Lambert forecast a 5.2 percent inflation over the next decade, while at the time the average yield on ten-year Treasury bonds was 11.4 percent. A year later, in February 1986, their consensus inflation forecast was still above 5 percent, while the ten-year Treasury-bond yield had dropped nearly 3 percentage points, to 8.7 percent.[1]

Careful empirical studies seem to confirm these informatl observations. A study of the real returns on corporate bonds all the way back to 1791 found that real interest rates tend to fall during inflation (averaging -7 percent during those 17 years when prices rose by 7.5 percent or more) and to rise during deflations (averaging more than 12 percent during those eleven years when prices fell by 6 percent or more).[2] A more mathematical study, by Lawrence Summers, found that during the years 1860–1940 there was "no tendency for interest rates to increase with movements in expected inflation."[3] In the years since World War II, (Summers found a slight positive relationship, but "in almost every case the data reject quite decisively the hypothesis" that real interest rates are constant.

The Effects of Taxes on Real Returns (optional)

If R is the nominal interest rate and t is the tax rate, then the after-tax real return is $(1 - t)R - p$. Because taxes are paid on nominal rather than real returns, a one-percentage-point increase in the rate of inflation requires more than a one-percentage-point increase in nominal interest rates for after-tax real returns to be constant. For instance, with a 30 percent tax rate, each one-percentage-point increase in R and p reduces the real after-tax return by 0.3 percent:

$$\text{Change in } [(1 - t)R - p] = (1 - t)(\text{change in } R) - (\text{change in } p)$$
$$= (0.7)(1\%) - (1\%)$$
$$= -0.3\%$$

For the real after-tax return to be constant, a 1 percent increase in the inflation rate must be accompanied by a 1.43 percent increase in nominal interest rates.

$$\text{Change in } [(1 - t)R - p] = (1 - t)(\text{change in } R) - (\text{change in } p)$$
$$= (0.7)(1.43\%) - (1\%)$$
$$= 0\%$$

Figure 2–3 on p. 52 shows that nominal Treasury-bill rates did rise during the inflation-filled 1970s, but, with a 30 percent tax rate, not nearly enough to keep after-tax real returns from falling. In the early 1980s, the rate of inflation fell faster than interest rates, and real returns soared.

FIGURE 2–3   Nominal and real returns on one-year Treasury bills, 1950-1987

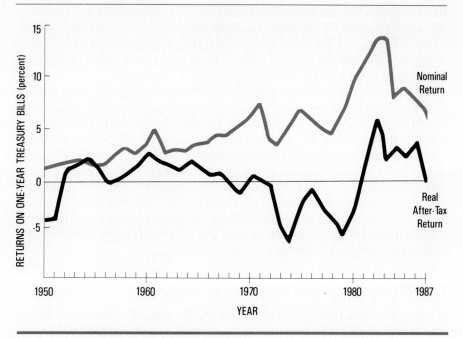

During inflations, real returns fall relatively more for people in high tax brackets, because taxes are paid on nominal rather than real rates of return. Table 2–5 uses three hypothetical situations to illustrate this point. In the first case, there is no inflation, and the nominal return is 5 percent. In the second case, there is 5 percent inflation, and the nominal return is 10 percent. If there were no taxes, the real returns would be 5 percent in each case. Taxes reduce the real returns, particularly for those in high tax brackets during the more rapid inflation. If taxes were paid on real returns, the after-tax returns would be the same in both cases for all taxpayers. But taxes are paid on nominal returns, and, as a consequence, real returns are diminished for those in high tax brackets.

Nominal returns must increase by more than inflation to hold real after-tax returns constant. If, as in the third scenario in Table 2–5, the nominal return increases by 7 percent when inflation increases by 5 percent, those in a 28 percent tax bracket will continue to earn about a 3.6 percent real after-tax return. Those investors in lower tax brackets now earn higher real after-tax returns with the more rapid inflation, while those in higher tax brackets fare better with less inflation. For debtors, the data in Table 2–5 are the real after-tax cost of borrowing, and the conclusions are reversed. Debtors in low tax brackets find inflation more burdensome than debtors

TABLE 2–5   Effect of Inflation on Real After-Tax Returns

Tax Bracket (percent)	Real After-Tax Returns (percent)		
	When Nominal Return, $R = 5$ Percent and Inflation, $p = 0$ Percent	When Nominal Return, $R = 10$ Percent and Inflation, $p = 5$ Percent	When Nominal Return, $R = 12$ Percent and Inflation, $p = 5$ Percent
0	5.00	5.00	7.00
15	4.25	3.50	5.20
28	3.60	2.20	3.64
33	3.35	1.70	3.04

in high tax brackets. These differences were even more pronounced before 1987, when the highest tax bracket was 50 percent, and in the 1970s, when there was a 70 pecent tax bracket.

There are four lessons to be learned from this table. The first is that nominal rates of return have to increase by more than the rate of inflation to keep after-tax real returns from falling. The second is that investors in high tax brackets have very sound personal reasons for disliking inflation. The third is that such people will avidly seek lightly taxed assets during inflations. The fourth lesson is that inflations transfer wealth from high-income creditors and low-income debtors to low-income creditors, high-income debtors, and the tax collector.

SUMMARY

The future value of an investment is the value to which it will grow at a stated date if it earns a specified rate of return. The present value of a cash flow is the amount you are willing to pay for it, and it is determined by discounting the cash flow by your required rate of return. The higher is the required return, the lower is the present value. This required rate of return depends on the returns available on alternative investments and on other characteristics, such as the riskiness of the cash flow, that make this investment relatively attractive or unattractive. An investment that is risky, or otherwise undesirable, has a low present value, implying that risk-averse investors will not acquire risky investments unless the price is low and the potential return is high. Present values can vary from person to person because investors may disagree about the prospective cash flow or have different required returns, perhaps due to different degrees of risk aversion.

Compound interest describes the earning of interest on interest, a powerful arithmetic process that causes seemingly slight differences in annual returns to grow to large differences in wealth after many years. Over short horizons, compound interest—crediting interest monthly, daily, or even continuously—can be used to boost the effective return on a bank deposit or other investment.

Cash flows usually must be adjusted for taxes, and, if so, the required rate of return should also be after taxes, reflecting the after-tax rates of return available on alternative investments. The appropriate tax rate for calculating the after-tax cash flow and required return is the marginal tax rate, which is typically larger than an investor's average tax rate.

The nominal return from an investment compares the dollars received with the dollars invested. The real return measures the percentage increase in purchasing power, and it is approximately equal to the nominal return minus the rate of inflation. Present-value logic, which concludes that a dollar today is worth more than a dollar tomorrow, is based not on the fact that inflation reduces the purchasing power of dollars, but on the fact that money invested today will earn additional dollars. Thus, the required return used to discount nominal cash flows depends on the rates of return available on alternative investment, not on the rate of inflation. Nominal interest rates do tend to increase during inflations, but not invariably by an amount equal to the rate of inflation, and, so, real interest rates do vary from year to year. Present-value calculations can be done either by discounting nominal cash flows by nominal required returns or by discounting real cash flows by real required returns.

The Present Value of a Constant Cash Flow

The present value of a constant cash flow is

$$P = \frac{X}{(1 + R)} + \frac{X}{(1 + R)^2} + \ldots + \frac{X}{(1 + R)^n}$$

If we factor out $\frac{X}{(1 + R)}$ and set $b = \frac{1}{(1 + R)}$ then

$$P = \frac{X}{(1 + R)} (1 + b + b^2 + \ldots + b^{n-1})$$

The series $1 + b + b^2 + \ldots + b^{n-1} = \frac{(1 - b^n)}{(1 - b)}$ so that

$$P = \frac{X}{(1 + R)} \frac{(1 - b^n)}{(1 - b)}$$

Now substituting $\frac{1}{1 + R}$ back in for b, we obtain Equation 5 in the text:

$$P = \frac{X}{1 + R} \frac{1 - \left(\frac{1}{1 + R}\right)^n}{1 - \frac{1}{1 + R}}$$

$$= X \frac{1 - \left(\dfrac{1}{1 + R}\right)^n}{(1 + R) - 1}$$

$$= \frac{X}{R}\left[1 - \frac{1}{(1 + R)^n}\right] \qquad (5)$$

The concept of a perpetuity helps us understand this equation, which can be rewritten as

$$P = \frac{X}{R} - \left(\frac{X}{R}\right)\left[\frac{1}{(1 + R)^n}\right]$$

The first term $\left(\dfrac{X}{R}\right)$ is what the present value would be if the cash flow went on forever; the second term is an adjustment for its finite life. More specifically, we can think of X for n periods (Flow A) as equal to X forever (Flow B) less X after Period n (Flow C):

	Period								
	1	2	3	4	...	n	$n + 1$	$n + 2$	...
Flow B	X	X	X	X	...	X	X	X	...
Flow C	0	0	0	0	...	0	X	X	...
Flow A	X	X	X	X	...	X	0	0	...

Flow A = Flow B − Flow C. Since Flow B is a perpetuity, its present value is X/R. Flow C becomes a perpetuity in Period n with a present value that period equal to X/R; the present value of Flow C today is $(X/R)/(1 + R)^n$. The present value of Flow A is, as Equation 5 shows, the present value of Flow B minus the present value of Flow C.

EXERCISES

1. If $5000 is invested for three years, which of these returns gives the largest future value?
  a. 10 percent each year
  b. 5 percent the first year, 10 percent the second year, and 15 percent the third year
  c. 15 percent the first year, 10 percent the second year, and 5 percent the third year
2. Which investment grows to a larger future value?

  a. $20,000 invested for twenty years at 10 percent
  b. $10,000 invested for twenty years at 20 percent
3. In 1987, an advertisement in the *New Yorker* solicited offers on a 1967 Mercury Cougar XR7 (*Motor Trend*'s 1967 car of the year) that had been mothballed, undriven, in a climate-controlled environment for twenty years.[4] If

TABLE 2–A

Country	Stock Price Index (= 100 in 1967 for each nation)
Canada	357.1
France	484.6
Italy	361.0
Japan	1654.9
United Kingdom	810.9
United States	262.1
West Germany	224.2

Source: Business Conditions Digest, August 1988, p. 96.

the 1967 price was $4000, what price would the original owner have to receive in 1987 to obtain a 10 percent annual return on this investment?

4. Vincent Van Gogh sold only one painting during his lifetime, for a price of about $30. In 1987, a sunflower still life he painted in 1888 sold for $39.85 million, more than three times the highest price paid previously for any work of art. Observers attributed the record price in part to the fact that his other sunflower paintings are all in museums and most likely will never be available for sale. If this painting had been purchased for $30 in 1888 and sold in 1987 for $39.85 million, what would have been the annual rate of return?

5. In 1987 a small company that was issuing stock estimated that a $6600 investment would be worth $106,500 after five and one-third years, a "total percentage return" of 1614 percent and a 303 percent "average percentage return." What is wrong with these percentage-return calculations?

6. In 1924, Computing-Tabulating-Recording Company became International Business Machines (IBM). Its net after-tax profits were $2.15 million that year and $6,582 million in 1984. What was IBM's annual compounded rate of growth of profits during this period?

7. *Business Conditions Digest* monitors stock prices in seven major industrial countries by constructing indexes that are equal to 100 in 1967 for each nation. The index values at the end of 1987 are shown in Table 2–A. What were the annual rates of increase for each country over these twenty years?

8. The world's population was 2.986 billion in 1960 and 4.432 billion in 1980. What was the annual rate of increase during these twenty years? At this rate, what will the world's population be in the year 2000? In 2050?

9. In 1986 the *New York Post* began offering $29.95 automobile classified ads that ran until the car was sold; but the newspaper required that the seller reduce the asking price by 5 percent every three weeks. If a car was offered initially for $5000 and didn't sell, how long did it take for the price to fall to $2500?

10. In 1940 your grandfather invested $1000 in a special trust to be paid to a future grandchild (you) sixty years later. How much will this trust be worth in the year 2000 if it has been earning 8 percent a year?

11. You have $10,000 to invest at an annual rate of return R. How long will it take you to double your money if R is

a. 6 percent? **b.** 9 percent? **c.** 12 percent?

12. "The United States made the Louisiana Purchase in 1808 for $15 million—a bargain at only 2½ cents an acre." What is the future value of 2½ cents invested for 182 years, until 1990, at 4 percent a year? At 6 percent? At 8 percent?

13. What is the implicit rate of return that has been omitted from this letter to the editor of *Barron's*?[5]

> To the editor:
> Re: the Nov. 19 Up & Down Wall Street item on Alex Herbage, founder of the International Newsletter Association.
> I read with interest your tale of woe about Caprimex and the IMAC Currency Hedge Fund. In addition to having computer problems, Alex Herbage also cannot do compound interest arithmetic. An investment that produces a profit of 257% in 6½ years (i.e., $100 grows to $357) has an [implicit] rate of return of _____ , not the 39.5% as quoted by Herbage. The 39.5% was evidently arrived at by dividing 257% by 6½ years. This calculation goes beyond the limits of reasonable puffery, certainly does not conform to U.S. financial advertising practice . . . and is totally without significance.
>
> Mark Hallinan
> Glastonbury, Conn.

14. What interest rate was used to determine the following settlement?

> The Treasury, after 775 years, has settled a debt for death and damage caused by Oxford people in 1209.
> The Government has been paying £3.08 a year compensation to Oxford University after people in the city hanged the students for helping a student to murder his mistress.
> Now the University has accepted a [once-and-for-all] payment of £33.08 in settlement.[6]

15. A developer is contemplating a four-year investment in a skateboard emporium in Cucamonga, California. Since she firmly believes that inflation will average 4 percent over the next five years, she says that 4 percent is the appropriate rate to use in discounting the projected cash flows. A financial adviser says that her required rate of return should be 10 percent since she can earn 10 percent by investing in government bonds. Explain why both are wrong.

16. United States per capita gross national product (GNP) was $205 in 1885 and $16,704 in 1985. Because 1985 prices were 14.17 times 1885 prices (that is, on average, something costing $1 in 1885 cost $14.17 in 1985), real per capita 1885 GNP, in terms of 1985 prices, is (14.17)($205) = $2905. What was the annual rate of growth of real per capital GNP during the period 1885–1985?

17. When a child loses a baby tooth, an old U.S. tradition is for the tooth to be put under the child's pillow, so that the tooth fairy will leave money for it. A survey by a Northwestern University professor indicates that the tooth fairy paid an average of 12 cents for a tooth in 1900 and $1 for a tooth in 1987.[7] The Consumer Price Index was 25 in 1900 and 340 in 1987. Did the real value of tooth-fairy payments rise or fall over this period? If tooth-fairy payments had kept up with inflation, how large should the 1987 payment have been?

18. The "annualized" return is calculated by ignoring compounding; for example, for a credit card company that charges 1.5 percent a month on unpaid balances the annualized rate is 12(1.5%) = 18%. What is the effective interest rate, taking monthly compounding into account?

19. An article in *The Wall Street Journal* claimed that a 9.25% annual interest rate, compounded daily, was more attractive than a 9.40% annual interest rate, compounded quarterly; a reader wrote in to say that his calculations showed just the opposite.[8] Which rate is more attractive?

20. A million-dollar state lottery pays $25,000 a year for forty years, beginning immediately.

At a 10 percent required return, what is the present value of this payoff?

21. In its 1985 annual report, Internorth estimated that the total future cash flow from its proven oil and gas reserves amount to $1.8 billion and that if these estimated flows were discounted at a 10 percent rate, their present value would be $0.6 billion. What is the present value at a 10 percent required return if the $1.8 billion is divided into thirty annual flows of $1.8/30 = $0.06 billion, beginning a year from today?

22. Professor Jones expects to earn royalties on his new statistics book of $50,000 a year for ten years, beginning a year from today. If he invests all of these royalties at 10 percent, how much will he have accumulated (call it W) after ten years? If he were to sell his rights to these royalties, what lump sum, L, received now and invested at 10 percent would grow to W after ten years?

23. The Brooklyn Botanical Gardens offered members this choice: annual dues of $10 *or* a one-time payment of $120 for a lifetime membership. For what values of the required return is the lifetime membership more financially advantageous if the member expects to live ten years? Fifty years? (Assume that the $10 dues begin immediately and will not increase over time.)

24. Explain why you either agree or disagree with this argument made by an anonymous economics major:

> Your great-grandfather has just died and left you $120,000, which you will invest in a small winery. Because this inheritance cost you nothing, your required rate of return is 0 percent.

25. In 1983, Colonel Parker bought a BMW 320i for $16,440 cash. He could have leased the car by making an initial payment of $540, then made five annual payments of $3790 each (beginning one year from the date of purchase),

and finally made a residual payment of $9270 at the end of the five years (at which time he would have become the legal owner of the car). Either way, he would have to pay insurance, repairs, maintenance, and other operating expenses out of his own pocket. Should he have leased instead?

26. A study of the effects of Proposition 13, which limited California property taxes,[9] found that in northern California each $1 decrease in property taxes tended on average to increase the market price of a house by $7.275. If we think of this $1 tax reduction as a perpetual constant annual saving, what value for the required return is consistent with this $7.725 estimate?

27. Following are some data from the Commerce Department's index of U.S. home prices (with the average cost of a home in 1925 equal to 100):

Year	Home Price Index
1885	60
1925	100
1935	60
1980	1000

Calculate the annual percentage increase from 1885 to 1980, from 1925 to 1980, and from 1935 to 1980. Why, in addition to their neglect of taxes and maintenance expenses, are these numbers an inadequate measure of the rate of return from buying a house?

28. Use Table 2–2 in this chapter to find the tax, average tax rate, and marginal tax rate for a single person with the following amounts of taxable income in 1988.
a. $30,000 **b.** $50,000 **c.** $100,000

29. A financial-education service gave this advice:

> Sometimes an investment makes sense even when it results in a loss because it keeps the investor from advancing to a higher tax bracket. The loss reduces income below the level on which a higher percentage of tax is demanded by the government.[10]

Consider a single person facing the 1988 income-tax brackets shown in Table 2–2 and assume that taxable income is $20,000. How much tax is owed, and how large is after-tax income? Now assume that this individual has, in addition, an investment that loses $2150, reducing taxable income to $17,850. How much tax is owed now, and how large is after-tax income? Does your answer confirm or contradict the argument made by this education service?

30. Before the 1986 Tax Reform Act, taxpayers were allowed to deduct state and local sales taxes in calculating their federal taxable income. For someone in a 50 percent tax bracket in 1985, what was the effective cost of paying a 6 percent state sales tax? Why did some states with large sales taxes urge rejection of this provision of the Tax Reform Act? The act continues to allow the deduction of state and local income and property taxes. How could a state use the distinction between sales and income taxes to reduce the tax burden on its citizens without reducing its overall tax revenue?

31. In 1987, the College Savings Bank introduced the CollegeSure CD, what its president called "the single most important financial product of the century and that's an understatement."[11] By paying $14,570 in 1987, the parent of a five-year-old buys one year of private-college education thirteen years later— when its estimated cost will be $28,580. If the cost does turn out to be $28,580, what is the implicit rate of return on such an investment? If the cost of a comparable year of college education was $11,500 in 1987, what annual rate of increase in college prices is assumed in the $28,500 estimated future cost?

32. It has been proposed that the government issue perpetuities paying a constant real amount (that is, if the price level increases by 5 percent, then the annual cash payment automatically rises by 5 percent). How much would an investor with a 0 percent real required return be willing to pay for such a bond?

33. In 1985, one-year Treasury bills yielded about a 7 percent return. What is the after-tax return for someone in the following tax brackets?
a. 0 percent
b. 30 percent
c. 50 percent

34. In 1979, Treasury bills yielded a 10.7 percent return, and the inflation rate was 13.3 percent. In 1982, Treasury bills yielded 14.9 percent, and the inflation rate was 3.9 percent. What were the real after-tax returns during these two years for someone in a 30 percent tax bracket?

35. A college is considering establishing a publishing house. It can borrow at 10 percent or use endowment funds currently invested in bonds earning an average return of 12 percent. One trustee says that the appropriate required return is 10 percent, while another says it is 12 percent. What do you say?

36. A bond selling for $100 promises to pay, after one year, $102 plus $102 times the percentage change in the Consumer Price Index. What are the nominal and real percentage returns if prices increase by 5 percent during this year?

37. You are in a 28 percent tax bracket. If the before-tax return from a certain investment is 10 percent and the inflation rate is 2 percent, what is your real after-tax return? What happens to your real after-tax return if inflation increases to 12 percent and your nominal rate of return increases to 20 percent? How much would the nominal rate of return have to increase to hold the real after-tax return constant?

38. It has been argued that nominal interest rates move up and down with inflation so that real interest rates hold constant at, say, 2 percent. If a 5 percent *fall* in prices is anticipated, what nominal rate of return will give a 2 percent real return? (Ignore the effect of taxes.) How much does a $100 investment have to pay a year from now to give this nominal return? Why won't people make such an investment?

39. The Social Security Administration estimated that someone twenty-eight years old earning $16,000 a year in 1985, who works steadily and retires at age sixty-five in 2022, would begin receiving annual benefits of about $27,500 in 2023.[12] This calculation assumes a 4 percent inflation between 1985 and 2023. If so, how much will this $27,500 buy in terms of 1985 dollars; that is, how much money in 1985 would buy as much as $27,500 will buy in 2023?

40. The Dow Jones Industrial Average of stock prices closed at 144.13 on December 31, 1935, and at 1546.67 on December 31, 1985. The Standard and Poor's 500 (S&P 500) index closed on these same dates at 10.60 and 211.28. What was the effective annual rate of increase in each index over these fifty years?

41. The S&P 500 closed at 92.15 on December 31, 1970, and at 211.28 on December 31, 1985; the corresponding values for the Dow were 838.92 and 1,546.67. The Consumer Price Index was 119.1 in December 1970 and 327.4 in December 1985. Did stock prices increase by more or less than consumer prices over this fifteen-year period? If stock prices had increased by just as much as consumer prices, what would the value of the Dow have been on December 31, 1985?

42. In 1984 a Harvard Business School professor observed that from 1926 to 1976 the average real rate of return on long-term Treasury bonds was 1.1 percent and reasoned that, "With long-term Treasury bonds yielding a nominal return of 11% [in 1984], this suggests that investors harbor long-term inflation expectations close to 10%."[13] What is the implicit assumption?

43. In September 1987 a market analyst published a graph comparing the path of Treasury-bond yields and raw-materials prices since 1980.[14] The graph was constructed so that the two series roughly coincided in mid-1984 (when the price index was at 290 and the bond yield at 12.5 percent) and in mid-1986 (when the price index was at 215 and the bond yield at 7.5 percent). A year later, the price index had risen to 290 and the bond yield to 10 percent, suggesting that "harmonic convergence" required a jump in bond yields to 12 percent— and that investors should dump bonds before it happens. What logical reason is there for commodity prices to affect interest rates? What is the fundamental error in this analyst's comparison? (Hint: what if the price level stays at 290 indefinitely?)

44. You are considering the renovation of an aging municipal sports arena, with the following projected expenses and rental income (both paid at the beginning of each year):

Year	Renovation Expenses (millions of dollars)	Rental Income (millions of dollars)
1	$1	$2
2	4	1
3	0	4
4	0	6
5	0	7

The city has offered two deals. Assuming you are a tax-exempt institution, use a 12 percent required return to determine if either of these deals is financially attractive, and identify the more attractive of the two. In each case, you must make the renovations and will be entitled to collect the rental income through Year 5. The deals are as follows:

Option A—You can lease the arena for five years at $3 million per year (payments due at the beginning of each year), with the $5 million in renovation expenses reimbursed at the end of Year 5.

Option B—You can buy the sports arena now for $20 million, but must sell it back at the end of Year 5 for $22 million.

45. The purchase price is but part of the cost of owning an automobile. In 1984, the U.S. Federal Highway Administration estimated the expected annual costs of operating a large-size

TABLE 2–B

Year	Miles Driven	Repairs and Maintenance	Replacement Tires	Accessories	Gasoline	Oil	Insurance	Garaging and Parking	Taxes and Fees	Total Costs
				Operating Costs (cents per mile)						
1	14,500	0.69	0.13	0.10	6.85	0.06	4.38	0.94	5.45	18.60
3	12,500	3.92	0.22	0.10	6.85	0.13	5.08	0.94	1.63	18.87
5	10,300	12.87	0.94	0.11	6.85	0.19	6.16	0.94	1.62	29.68
7	9,200	13.32	0.94	0.23	6.85	0.12	4.28	0.94	1.91	28.59
10	7,800	2.10	0.94	0.24	6.85	0.16	5.05	0.94	1.65	17.93
12	6,700	0.87	0.94	0.24	6.85	0.08	5.88	0.94	1.65	17.45

four-door sedan as shown in Table 2–B. It calculated the purchase price to be $11,554 and assumed that the car would last twelve years and be driven 120,000 miles. The figures given in the table are real (constant-dollar) cents per mile, with the number of miles driven for each stated year shown in the second column. Calculate the total cost in each of the six years shown (cents per mile times number of miles), and interpolate to estimate the total costs in the six omitted years. Then calculate the present value, using a 5 percent real required return, with the assumption that each annual expense is at the beginning of the year.

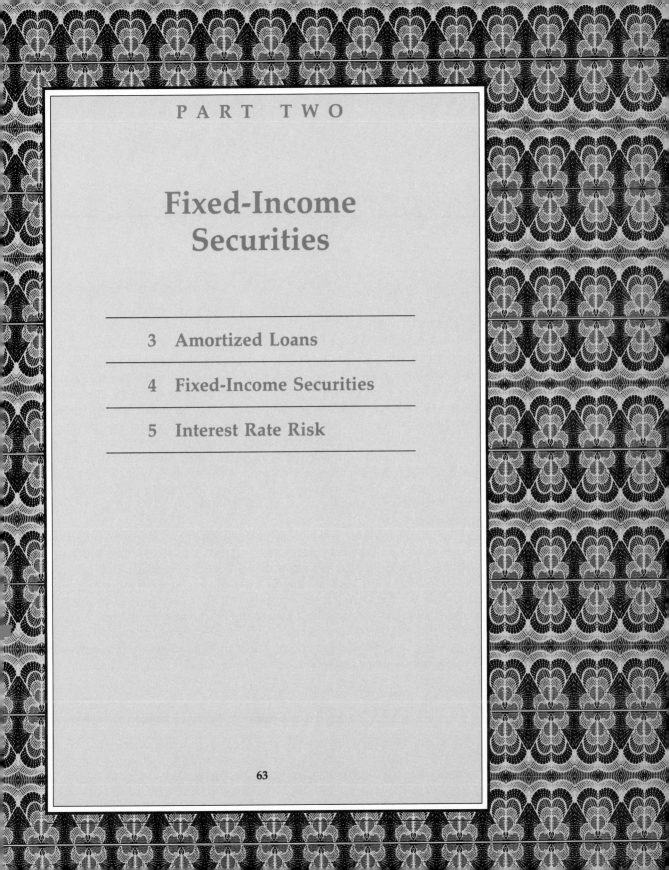

PART TWO

Fixed-Income Securities

CHAPTER 3

Amortized Loans

I'm going to do you a favor . . .
anonymous car dealer

Individuals not only invest money but also borrow money to finance the acquisition of a car, a home, household appliances, and other real assets. Some people also borrow money to buy stocks and bonds. Businesses borrow to finance expansion, either the construction of new plant and equipment or the takeover of existing businesses. Financial intermediaries borrow from some to lend to others. For each borrower, such loans are debts—obligations to repay the borrowed money plus interest. For each lender, loans are an investment comparable to the purchase of bonds, stocks, or real assets. In every case, there is an initial outlay and a cash flow with a present value that can be determined using an appropriate required return.

In this chapter, we will look at how loan payments are determined and see how each payment is part interest and part principal, which eventually reduces the unpaid balance to zero. You will learn why the common practice of comparing loans on the basis of the total payments is wrong and see the incorrect decisions caused by this error. Then we turn to a variety of complicating factors, including points and prepayment penalties, variable-rate loans, and an optional section on graduated-payment loans. We begin with a discussion of the general principle that the investment of borrowed money can magnify gains and losses.

THE POWER OF LEVERAGE

We have all seen news reports of people, perhaps even relatives or neighbors, who lost their home, farm, or business because they could not repay a loan. This is one reason why many people consider debt to be one of those four-letter words that decent people avoid: if you cannot pay cash,

TABLE 3–1 Potential Returns on a $10,000 Investment with
10-to-1 Leverage

Investment Rate of Return, R (percent)	Dollar Return on Total Investment	Interest Payable on $90,000 Loan	Dollar Return on Cash Investment of $10,000	Rate of Return on Cash Investment (percent)
0	$ 0	$9,000	− $ 9,000	− 90
10	10,000	9,000	1,000	10
20	20,000	9,000	11,000	110
30	30,000	9,000	21,000	210

then you cannot afford it. Yet, others swear by, not at, debt. Borrowing allows you to invest other people's money and many a fortune has been built with other people's money.

Debt has these two faces, like the proverbial two-edged sword, because it creates **leverage,** a situation in which a relatively small investment reaps the benefits or losses of a much larger investment. Suppose you have $10,000 of your own money and borrow another $90,000 of other people's money, giving you a total of $100,000 to invest. For simplicity, we will look a year into the future and assume that the $90,000 is a simple one-year loan at 10 percent. Thus, you must pay $99,000 at the end of the year. Your net financial gain depends on the rate of return, R, that you earn on your $100,000 investment. Table 3–1 shows some possibilities, ignoring tax complications.

Look first at $R = 10$ percent. A 10 percent return on $100,000 is $10,000, enough to pay the $9000 interest due on the $90,000 loan with $1000 left over—a 10 percent return on the $10,000 that is your own money. This return illustrates the general principle that if you borrow at 10 percent in order to invest at 10 percent, the borrowing is neither an advantage nor disadvantage.

leverage
Leverage occurs when a relatively small investment reaps the benefits or losses from a much larger investment.

If the rate of return on the total investment is equal to the rate of interest owed on other people's money, then this interest rate will also be the rate of return on your own money.

Now, what if the rate of return on the total investment turns out to be 20 percent? Twenty percent of $100,000 is $20,000, minus $9000 interest leaving an $11,000 gain on your $10,000—a rewarding 110 percent return. You more than double your wealth in a year by borrowing at 10 percent and investing at 20 percent!

In general, the exact magnitude of the gain can be figured by taking the degree of leverage into account. Because the total $100,000 investment is ten times the size of your own $10,000, you have ten-to-one leverage. The consequence is that every percentage point by which the investment return exceeds the loan rate is multiplied by 10 in order to determine the return on your own money. A total return of $R = 20$ percent is a 10 percent excess over the 10 percent loan rate, and multiplication by 10 pushes the excess return up by 100 percent. To formalize this logic, a few mathematical symbols are helpful.

> **If a fraction x of an investment is your own money, then your degree of leverage is $1/x$. If you pay a rate B on the borrowed money and earn a rate of return R on the total investment, then the rate of return on your own money is $B + (1/x)(R - B)$.**

Let's apply this rule to our specific example with $R = 30$ percent. If R were 10 percent, the borrowing would have no net effect, and you would have a 10 percent return on your own money. Because $R = 30$ percent is 20 percentage points above $R = 10$ percent and you have ten-to-one leverage, the return on your own money is $10\% + 10(20\%) = 210\%$. The step-by-step dollar calculations in Table 3–1 confirm that this rule is correct.

The two-edged sword comes into play because leverage works on the downside too, multiplying shortfalls. If your $100,000 investment just breaks even, with $R = 0$ percent, this result is ten percentage points less than the loan rate, and multiplication by the ten-to-one leverage gives you a return of $10\% + 10(-10\%) = -90\%$. You have $100,000 at the end of the year and, after paying your $99,000 debt, are left with $1000—a $9000 loss on a $10,000 investment. Notice that your total investment does not have to lose money for leverage to be a disaster; what hurts is that the investment's rate of return is less than the rate you are paying on the borrowed money. You will lose money borrowing at 10 percent to invest at less than 10 percent, and the more you borrow, the more you lose. Investment Example 3–1 recounts how highly leveraged real-estate investments have caused some to live and die by this two-edged sword.

CALCULATING LOAN PAYMENTS

When a bank loans you money, you sign an agreement promising to pay back the amount borrowed plus interest. No matter how the payments are structured, the general rule for all loans is very simple:

> **The present value of the loan payments, discounted at the quoted loan rate, is equal to the amount borrowed.**

balloon loan
On a balloon loan, the periodic payments include little or no repayment of the principal.

Before the Great Depression in the 1930s, most mortgages were three- to five-year **balloon loans** requiring the payment of interest until maturity, at which time a final, or balloon, payment equal to the size of the loan is

THE DOWNFALL OF THE NO-MONEY-DOWN GURUS

Many have made fortunes using borrowed money to invest in rapidly appreciating real estate; others have grown wealthy selling their "secrets" to people with dreams of getting rich quickly. Look at Table 3–1 again, but this time, label your investment as real estate, and dream along with the following sales pitch: If you borrow $90,000 at 10 percent and buy a $100,000 property that appreciates by 30 percent in a year's time, your $10,000 will increase by 210 percent, to $31,000. Now you sell this property, and use your $31,000 as a 10 percent down payment on a $310,000 property. If you again borrow the remaining 90 percent at a 10 percent interest rate and this property appreciates by 30 percent, then—presto!—your personal wealth increases to $96,100. After two more years of trading up—dare to believe it—you are virtually a millionaire with $923,521 in personal wealth. It sure beats waiting tables or pumping gas. You don't have the $10,000 to get started? No problem. You can begin with no money down—just attend a $495 seminar, listen to an inspirational pep talk, and buy a $19.95 book and $79.95 tape.

Two of the most well-known real estate enthusiasts, Albert J. Lowry (How You Can Become Financially Independent By Investing in Real Estate) and Robert Allen (Nothing Down), had books on the New York Times best-seller list in 1980. Inspired by their success, dozens of imitators bought television time, gave hotel seminars, and wrote books preaching the no-money-down gospel, using such alluring titles as Millionaire Maker, Million Dollar Secrets, Two Years to Financial Freedom, and How to Wake Up the Financial Genius Inside You. At its peak, it has been estimated that the promoters took in $150 million a year.* As it turned out, most of the eager buyers were not latent financial geniuses after all. It is not all that easy to buy property with no money down, and it became very difficult to make money borrowing at double-digit mortgage rates when the rate of growth of real-estate prices slowed to single-digits. By 1987, many of the gurus were bankrupt, and most had moved on to other schemes.

One of the ironies of the business is explained by a cassete supplier: "We laugh about it. They talk about buying stuff with no money down, but when we deal with them we demand our money up front. That's what you learn after you get burned enough times." Similarly, a cable-TV distributor observed, "In broadcasting, the preachers, the politicians, the car transmission shops and the get-rich-quick guys are all money up front." If you reflect on it, there is a fundamental reason for skepticism about any get-rich-quick advice. As the ex-president of one of Lowry's seminar companies said of the no-money down gurus,

I've known most of them and I don't know of one who made a fortune investing in real estate, at least prior to the time they amassed some wealth putting on seminars. If you know how to make a fortune in real estate, you would spend your time doing it, rather than conducting seminars.

*This estimate and the quotations in this example are from James Bates, "Promoters of Easy Street Seen on Bankrupt Lane," Los Angeles Times, April 6, 1987. See also Robert Guenther, "'Nothing-Down' Gurus Wane; Critics Say Concept Is Flawed," Wall Street Journal, January 14, 1987.

due. For instance, on a $10,000, four-year balloon loan with annual 10 percent interest payments, the homeowner pays $1000 a year for four years and then repays the $10,000 loan or, more likely, refinances it.

In the 1920s, balloon loans were routinely renewed at maturity. But the 1930s were not routine, and many banks and other lending institutions were unable or unwilling to renew loans. Homeowners who were out of work or earning reduced wages had trouble paying interest let alone a balloon, and, by 1935, more than 20 percent of the assets of savings and loan associations was real estate, mostly foreclosed properties.

amortized loans
On an amortized loan, the periodic payments include principal as well as interest.

Today, most mortgages and other loans are **amortized,** which means that the periodic payments include principal as well as interest so that the loan is paid off gradually rather than with a single balloon payment at the end. The most common amortized loan involves constant monthly payments over the life of the loan. These monthly payments are set so that their present value at the stated loan rate is equal to the amount borrowed. For the general formula, we will use the following notation:

P = amount borrowed

X = monthly payments

R = monthly loan rate (annual percentage rate/12)

n = number of monthly payments

The size of the monthly payment is the value of X that solves the present-value equation

$$P = \frac{X}{(1 + R)} + \frac{X}{(1 + R)^2} + \cdots + \frac{X}{(1 + R)^n} \tag{1}$$

The solution is given by Equation 6 from Chapter 2, renumbered here,

$$X = \frac{RP}{1 - \dfrac{1}{(1 + R)^n}} \tag{2}$$

For instance, if we borrow $4000 for a year at 12 percent, the values

$P = \$4000$

$R = 0.12/12 = 0.01$

$n = 12$

imply that

$$X = \frac{0.01(\$4000)}{1 - \dfrac{1}{(1.01)^{12}}}$$

$$= \$355.40.$$

Twelve monthly payments of $355.40, discounted at a 12 percent annual rate, have a present value equal to $4000.

The Unpaid Balance

The present-value logic can be confirmed by dividing each monthly payment into interest and principal. The example of a twelve-month $4000 loan at 12 percent can again be used. After one month the borrower owes one month's interest on $4000. At a 12 percent annual rate, the monthly interest rate is $12\%/12 = 1\%$ and the interest due is $0.01(\$4000) = \$40$. The $355.40 monthly payment covers this $40 in interest, and, in addition, the extra $355.50 - \$40.00 = \$315.40$ reduces the principal (or unpaid balance) to $\$4,000.00 - \$315.40 = \$3,684.60$.

For the second month, the amount borrowed is only $3,684.60, and the interest due at the end of the month is $0.01(\$3,684.60) = \$36.85$. The monthly $355.40 payment includes this interest and $\$355.40 - \$36.85 = \$318.55$ repayment of principal, reducing the unpaid balance to $\$3,684.60 - \$318.55 = \$3,366.05$.

Table 3–2 on p. 70 gives the month-by-month details. At the end of eleven months, the unpaid balance has been reduced to $351.88, and the final $355.40 monthly payment covers this unpaid balance plus interest: thus, as intended, the loan is fully repaid after twelve months.

Loan payments calculated such that their present value is equal to the amount borrowed will, period by period, pay the interest due on the unpaid balance and reduce the principal until, after the last payment, the unpaid balance is zero.

Notice in Table 3–2 on p. 70 that the total interest payments on this one-year loan only add up to $264.80, although 12 percent interest on a $4000 loan seemingly should come to almost twice this amount, or $0.12(\$4000) = \$480$. The answer to this apparent paradox is that $480 in interest would be due if one borrowed the $4000 for a full year, but the unpaid balance on an amortized loan shrinks month by month. In this case, $4000 is borrowed for the first month, then $3,684.60 for the second month, $3,366.05 for the third month, and so on until the last month, when only $351.88 is borrowed. The average amount borrowed is only about half

TABLE 3–2   Payments on a Twelve Month, $4000 Loan at 12 Percent

Payment Number	Total Payment	Interest Portion of Payment	Principal Portion of Payment	Unpaid Balance After Payment
1	$ 355.40	$ 40.00	$ 315.40	$3,684.60
2	355.40	36.85	318.55	3,366.05
3	355.40	33.66	321.74	3,044.31
4	355.40	30.44	324.96	2,719.35
5	355.40	27.19	328.21	2,391.14
6	355.40	23.91	331.49	2,059.65
7	355.40	20.60	334.80	1,724.85
8	355.40	17.25	338.15	1,386.70
9	355.40	13.87	341.53	1,045.17
10	355.40	10.45	344.95	700.22
11	355.40	7.00	348.40	351.82
12	355.40	3.52	351.88	−0.06
	$4,264.80	$264.74	$4,000.06	

the $4000, and, therefore, the interest is only about half of what would be due if $4000 were borrowed for the entire year.

Table 3–2 also shows that as time passes and the unpaid balance declines, the monthly payments are composed increasingly of less interest and more repayment of principal. This shift from interest to principal is particularly pronounced for a long-term loan, such as a thirty-year mortgage. Table 3–3 on p. 71 shows some highlights for a thirty-year loan of $100,000 at 12 percent.

The initial monthly payments in Table 3–3 are almost entirely allocated to paying interest, so that after the first year's payments of more than $12,000, the unpaid balance has declined by less than $400. After two years, the unpaid balance is only down to $99,228.22, and after five years it still amounts to $97,663.22. The loan is not half repaid until the twenty-fourth year, when the monthly payments finally become more repayment of principal than interest, and the unpaid balance then shrinks rapidly during the last five years of the loan.

People who buy a house and then move, paying off their mortgage after only a few years, are often surprised to find that all the money they have paid month after month has made barely a dent in the principal. They have not been cheated. Each month they paid the interest due on their loan, which was fairly calculated, and every dollar they paid beyond that did reduce the principal. What they do not realize is that an amortized loan does not reduce the principal equally each month (because more interest is due when the loan is large and less when it is small).

TABLE 3–3 Payments on a Thirty-Year, $100,000 Loan at 12 Percent

Payment Number	Total Payment	Interest Portion of Payment	Principal Portion of Payment	Unpaid Balance After Payment
1	$1,028.61	$ 1,000.00	$ 28.61	$99,971.39
2	1,028.61	999.71	28.90	99,942.49
3	1,028.61	999.42	29.19	99,913.30
⋮				
12	1,028.61	996.69	31.92	99,637.12
⋮				
24	1,028.61	992.64	35.97	99,228.22
⋮				
60	1,028.61	977.15	51.47	97,663.22
⋮				
120	1,028.61	935.11	93.50	93,418.00
⋮				
240	1,028.61	720.03	308.58	71,694.83
⋮				
293	1,028.61	505.74	522.88	50,050.82
⋮				
300	1,028.61	468.02	560.59	46,241.32
⋮				
358	1,028.61	30.25	998.36	2,026.77
359	1,028.61	20.27	1,008.34	1,018.43
360	1,028.61	10.18	1,018.43	0.00
	$370,299.60	**$270,299.60**	**$100,000.00**	

Effective Loan Rates

Another often overlooked fact is that just as monthly compounding increases the interest earned on a savings account, monthly compounding also increases the effective interest rate paid on a loan. Look again at the one-year $4000 loan at 12 percent summarized in Table 3–2. The present value of the twelve monthly payments is $4000, computed as follows:

Payment	Present Value	
1	$355.40/(1 + 0.12/12) =	$351.88
2	$355.40/(1 + 0.12/12)^2 =	348.40
.		
.		
.		
12	$355.40/(1 + 0.12/12)^{12} =	315.40
		$4000.00

We can think of these twelve payments as twelve separate loans: the first, $351.88 loaned for a month; the second, $348.40 loaned for two months; and so on. From the standpoint of the lender, these are twelve separate investments—$351.88 grows to $355.40 after one month; $348.40 grows to $355.40 after two months: and so on through the last payment. Each of these investments is earning a 12 percent annual rate of return compounded monthly, making the effective rate of return on the loan somewhat higher than 12 percent; thus,

$$(1 + 0.12/12)^{12} = 1.1268$$

implies an effective yield of 12.68 percent. If the lender earns an effective rate of 12.68 percent, this rate is also the effective rate that borrowers are paying.

When banks pay depositors or charge borrowers an annual percentage rate divided by 12 each month, this monthly compounding increases the effective interest rate. Bank reporting, however, is asymmetrical in that eye-catching advertisements inform us that the effective rates paid on deposits are higher than the annual percentage rates, but similar information about loan rates is nowhere to be found.

If you do not have a pocket calculator handy, just remember that you should not compare effective rates on deposits with the annual percentage rates on loans; nor should you compare the annual percentage rates on competing deposits (or loans) unless they are compounded equally often.

EVALUATING LOANS: TOTAL PAYMENTS VERSUS PRESENT VALUE

Truth-in-lending laws require lenders to reveal not only the annual percentage rate, but also the total amount (principal plus interest) that will be paid over the life of the loan. Unfortunately, the prominent diplay of this information encourages borrowers to make the mistake of judging loans by the total payments. (See Investment Example 3–2 on pp. 74–75.) This approach is a mistake because it does not take into account when the payments are made, and a dollar paid today is more burdensome than a dollar paid thirty years from now.

A simple-minded comparison of total payments suggests that a one-year loan at a 100 percent interest rate is better than a 150-year loan at a 1 percent interest rate, a conclusion that present-value logic rebukes as nonsense. A total-payments analysis also implies that, for any given loan rate, you are always better off borrowing less money and repaying the loan as soon as possible, because this reduces your total payments. The optimal strategy, according to a total-payments analysis, is to never borrow any money at all—no matter what the loan rate! A present-value analysis, in contrast, implies that if the loan rate is favorable (as with Pomona College's 0 percent computer loan), you want to borrow as much as you can for as long as you can. In general, a comparison of total payments is misleading because it ignores present value completely. (An even more complex present-value error is described in Investment Example 3–3 on pp. 76–77.)

CREATIVE FINANCING

The typical home buyer finances most of the purchase with a mortgage from a bank, savings and loan association (S&L), or other lending institution. If you buy a house for $100,000, you might put up $20,000 of your own money (the down payment) and borrow $80,000 from an S&L, to be repaid over thirty years. At the closing, when the deal is finalized, your $20,000 plus the S&L's $80,000 are given to the seller, some of which may be used to pay the remaining unpaid balance on the mortgage that financed the seller's original purchase years earlier. The seller is, thus, paid in full, as is the seller's mortgage institution, and you will now make monthly payments to the institution that holds your mortgage.

In the 1970s and early 1980s, the lethal combination of inflation and the Federal Reserve efforts to wring inflation out of the economy drove nominal interest rates upward. Meanwhile, banks, S&Ls, and other deposit intermediaries were restricted by Regulation Q on the rates they could pay depositors. They tried monthly, daily, and then continuous compounding. They gave away dishes, toasters, and even color television sets. But, still, they could not compete with market interest rates, and they lost depositors.

These credit crunches battered the housing market. In the midst of the 1980 crunch, Federal Reserve Chairman Paul Volcker was quoted as saying that he wouldn't be satisfied "until the last buzz saw is silenced."[1] When he was asked if the Fed's tight monetary policies would bring a recession, he responded, "Yes, and the sooner the better."[2] Lending institutions raised mortgage rates to unprecedented levels, and, even then, they rejected loan applications because they had no money to lend. The president of a major savings and loan made the typical comment that the mortgage rate is 16⅜ percent, but "we're not making any" loans and that he didn't know anyone who was.[3] Home buyers were dissuaded by high mortgage rates and rejected loan applications; sellers were discouraged by the lack of buyers.

In this environment, buyers and sellers turned to **creative financing,** novel ways of financing real-estate deals, usually involving a loan from the seller. Investment Example 3–4 on pp. 78–79 gives a detailed example. In 1980 and 1981, roughly half of all sales of existing homes involved some sort of creative financing. If possible, instead of paying off the seller's mortgage, the buyer assumed the mortgage by taking over the monthly payments. If the old mortgage is at, say 8 percent, then assumption is clearly better than borrowing money at 18 percent to pay off the old mort-

creative financing
Creative financing refers to novel ways of financing deals, usually involving a loan from the seller.

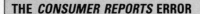

THE *CONSUMER REPORTS* ERROR

It is not only unwary borrowers who fall into the total-payments trap; so do otherwise sensible advisors. For example, in 1972, *Consumer Reports* compared two alternatives for purchasing a washing machine, clothes dryer, and automatic dishwasher for a new home:

a. Buy the appliances from a store for $675, financed by a two-year loan at 15 percent interest.
b. Buy the appliances from the home builder for $450, financed by a 27-year loan at 7.75 percent interest.

The application of Equation 2 gives the requisite monthly payments: $32.71 a month for twenty-four months to the store or $3.32 a month for 12(27) = 324 months to the builder. Which alternative is more attractive? *Consumer Reports* compared the total payments

Builder:	324(3.32)	= $1075
Store:	24(32.71)	= $ 785
		$290

and concluded that "the appliances would cost $290 more from the builder than from the store."

Our intuition hesitates to follow this advice. If the builder charges a third less for the appliances and half the interest rate, why is the store's offer the better deal? It generally isn't. *Consumer Reports* erred by comparing the total payments, ignoring the fact that the payments to the store must be made during the next two years, while the payments to the builder are spread over twenty-seven years. In the view of *Consumer Reports,* time isn't money; a dollar paid two years from now is the same as

*"Notes to Home Buyers on Financing Future Schlock," *Consumer Reports,* April 1972, pp. 258-9.

a dollar paid twenty-seven years in the future.

If we accept the argument that time is money, then we want to compare the present values, *P,* of the following two cash flows, with *S* for the store and *B* for the builder:

$$P_S = \frac{\$32.71}{(1+R)} + \frac{\$32.71}{(1+R)^2} + \cdots + \frac{\$32.71}{(1+R)^{24}}$$

$$P_B = \frac{\$3.32}{(1+R)} + \frac{\$3.32}{(1+R)^2} + \cdots + \frac{\$3.32}{(1+R)^{324}}$$

Consumer Reports implicitly uses $R = 0$ when it just adds up the undiscounted monthly payments. It makes more sense to use a required rate of return that reflects the reality that a dollar today is worth more than a dollar tomorrow. Assume that instead of buying from the store and paying $32.71 a month for twenty-four months, we buy from the builder, pay $3.32 a month, and deposit the difference, $32.71 − $3.32 = $29.39, in a bank earning a modest 5 percent return. If so, we should use 5 percent as our annual required return (and $R = 0.05/12$ as the corresponding monthly return) in the above present-value formulas. The answers (computed using Equation 5 in Chapter 2) then work out to be as follows:

$$P_S = \left[\frac{\$32.71}{.05/12}\right]\left[1 - \frac{1}{(1+.05/12)^{24}}\right] = \$745.59$$

$$P_B = \left[\frac{\$3.32}{.05/12}\right]\left[1 - \frac{1}{(1+.05/12)^{324}}\right] = \$589.66$$

Instead of costing $290, the builder actually saves, in present-value terms, $745.59 − $589.66 = $155.93.

We could also figure out the monthly details, showing the twenty-four $29.39 deposits, followed by the three hundred $3.32 withdrawals to pay off

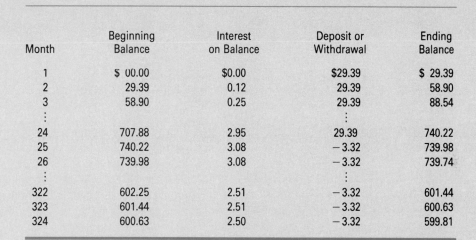

Month	Beginning Balance	Interest on Balance	Deposit or Withdrawal	Ending Balance
1	$ 00.00	$0.00	$29.39	$ 29.39
2	29.39	0.12	29.39	58.90
3	58.90	0.25	29.39	88.54
⋮			⋮	
24	707.88	2.95	29.39	740.22
25	740.22	3.08	−3.32	739.98
26	739.98	3.08	−3.32	739.74
⋮			⋮	
322	602.25	2.51	−3.32	601.44
323	601.44	2.51	−3.32	600.63
324	600.63	2.50	−3.32	599.81

the builder and the interest (at a monthly rate of 5/12 = 0.4166 percent) along the way. The accompanying table summarizes the results of such calculations. After 324 months, there is still $599.81 left in the account. This balance is, of course, a future value—the savings, including interest, after 324 months. To convert to a present value, we discount as follows:

$$P = \frac{\$599.81}{(1 + .05/12)^{324}}$$
$$= \$155.93$$

the very same answer obtained earlier. Thus, the initial present-value comparison did answer the question without the need for all the monthly step-by-step details.

Now, 5 percent is not the only possible value for the required return. For some values (such as 0 percent), the store is more attractive, while, for others (such as 5 percent) the builder looks better. In general, the higher is the interest rate, the more attractive is the builder's offer, because those distant payments are less and less burdensome in present-value terms. The accompanying figure compares the present values of the cash flows for a variety of interest rates. As it happens, for any required return above 2.7 percent, the builder's deal is the better option.

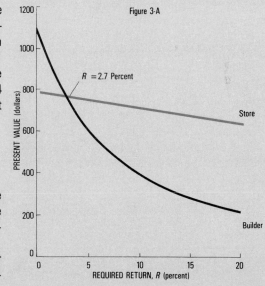

Figure 3-A

INVESTMENT
EXAMPLE
3–3

CAN YOU MAKE MONEY BORROWING AT 12 PERCENT TO INVEST AT 7 PERCENT?

Car buyers who try to pay cash are sometimes dissuaded by sales managers who claim that a car buyer can save hundreds of dollars by leaving, say, $12,000 in the bank earning 7 percent and borrowing through the dealer at 12 percent.* This is their persuasive, but fallacious, argument. If the $12,000 is kept in the bank for four years, the total interest, compounded monthly, comes to $3864. The monthly payments on the amortized car loan are $316, and the total interest comes to $3168, which is $696 less than the interest earned on the bank account.

How can 7 percent interest be more than 12 percent interest? The gimmick is that the loan is amortized, so that the amount borrowed is $12,000 only for the first month. Each month's $316 payment covers the interest due and also reduces the

*See S.J. Diamond, "Credit or Cash? The Difference Can Add Up," *Los Angeles Times,* September 23, 1985; S.J. Diamond, "Credit Doesn't Always Rate Better Than Cash," *Los Angeles Times,* September 30, 1985; and Gary Smith, "The Car Financing Fallacy," *Sylvia Porter's Personal Finance Magazine,* September 1986, pp. 75–76.

principal, so that each month the unpaid balance declines, until it reaches zero at the end of the last month. Instead of borrowing $12,000 for four years, the car buyer borrows $12,000 at the beginning and almost nothing at the end, and the average amount borrowed is about half the initial loan. This is the sales manager's trick: comparing 7 percent interest on $12,000 with 12 percent interest on roughly half of $12,000. It is also the basis for Sperling's Rule, named after a bank vice president who advised that borrowers come out ahead if the loan rate is less than twice the interest rate earned on the bank deposit.

This apples-and-oranges comparison is illogical and Sperling's Rule is wrong. If the sales manager's advice is followed, the car buyer will not earn interest on the entire $12,000 for four years. At the end of the first month, the bank deposit will have earned only $12,000(0.07/12) = $70 in interest, and the $316 car payment reduces the amount in the bank account by $316 − $70 = $246. Month after month, the bank-account balance declines in order to pay off the loan. The sales manager uses the fact that, on average, the buyer pays interest on roughly half of $12,000, but ignores the fact that, on average, the buyer only earns interest on half of $12,000 too. The buyer would break even earning 7 percent and

gage. Creative financing also typically involves some owner financing, with the buyer borrowing money from the seller at, say, 12 percent rather than borrowing from an S&L at 18 percent. The buyer appreciates the lower interest rate, and the seller is relieved to have sold the house. Many owner-financing deals have balloon payments due after three to five years, with

	Car Loan at 12 Percent				Bank Account Paying 7 Percent			
Month	Unpaid Balance	Monthly Payment	Interest Due	Principal Payoff	Bank Balance	Earned Interest	Car Payment	Net Payout
1	$12,000.00	$316.00	$120.00	$196.00	$12,000.00	$70.00	−$316.00	−$246.00
2	11,804.00	316.00	118.04	197.96	11,754.00	68.56	−316.00	−247.44
3	11,606.04	316.00	116.06	199.94	11,506.56	67.12	−316.00	−248.88
⋮								
43	1,831.40	316.00	18.32	297.68	330.66	1.92	−316.00	−314.08
44	1,533.72	316.00	15.34	300.66	16.58	.10	−316.00	−315.90
45	1,233.06	316.00	12.34	303.66	−299.32	−1.74	−316.00	−317.74
46	929.38	316.00	9.30	306.70	−617.06	−3.60	−316.00	−319.60
47	622.68	316.00	6.22	309.78	−936.66	−5.46	−316.00	−321.46
48	312.90	316.00	3.12	312.88	−1,258.12	−7.34	−316.00	−323.34
49	0.00				−1,581.46			
	$15,168.00	**$3,168.00**	**$12,000.00**			**$1,586.52**	**−$15,188.00**	**$13,581.48**

paying 7 percent, but must inexorably lose money earning 7 percent and paying 12 percent. In our example, the bank account runs dry midway through the fourth year, and to make the last five car payments, the buyer must use other funds. As the accompanying table shows, at the end of four years, the buyer is not $696 ahead, but $1581 behind.

What if the buyer leaves the $12,000 in the bank untouched and makes the car payments out of monthly income? The answer is the same, since each $316 monthly car payment could have been deposited to earn 7 percent interest. At the end of four years, the $12,000 will have grown to $15,865, but the buyer will have lost forty-eight deposits plus interest, a total of $17,446—on balance, a deficit again of $1581. It really doesn't matter whether each $316 monthly payment comes out of old savings or new. Either way, intuition is right. You cannot make money borrowing at 12 percent in order to invest at 7 percent.

borrowers hoping that loan rates will fall by then so they can refinance inexpensively through a conventional lending institution. Observers called the balloons launched in 1980 and 1981 "the ticking time bomb" in the residential real-estate market. Fortunately, mortage rates finally did drop in 1986, a bit late for some, but just in time for others.

78

BUYING A HOUSE WITH CREATIVE FINANCING

In order to analyze the mechanics of creative financing, consider an actual, fairly typical, real-estate transaction made in 1980 in Cape Cod, Massachusetts. At the time, Cape Cod mortgage institutions were charging a minimum of 18 percent and rejecting most loan applications. One home seller agreed to a price of $66,000, with the buyer putting $30,000 down and borrowing $36,000 from the seller at 10.5 percent "amortized over ten years, with a balloon after five." This agreement means that the buyer makes monthly payments as if paying off a ten-year amortized loan, but after five years makes a balloon payment to cover the unpaid balance.

The use of Equation 2 with these values

$$P = \$36,000$$
$$R = 0.105/12 = 0.00875$$
$$n = 120$$

shows the appropriate monthly payments to be $485.78. What is the size of the unpaid balance after five years? We can make month-by-month calculations as in Table 3–3, or apply the principle that the present value of all the payments must equal the amount borrowed, so that

$$\$36,000 = \frac{\$485.78}{1.00875} + \ldots + \frac{\$485.78}{1.00875^{60}} + \frac{B}{1.00875^{60}}$$

where B is the balloon payment. This equation can be solved to give

$$B = \$22,599.08.$$

Now we can determine the value of this below-market loan to the buyer. The seller's 10.5 percent rate is substantially below the 18 percent plus charged by lending institutions; but it is only a five-year loan. Is this deal worth hundreds or thousands of dollars? To answer this question, we calculate the present value of the payments, using an 18 percent interest rate, as follows:

$$(.18/12 = .015 \text{ monthly})$$
$$P = \frac{\$485.78}{1.015} + \ldots + \frac{\$485.78}{1.015^{60}} + \frac{\$22,599.08}{1.015^{60}}$$
$$= \$28,379.86$$

The present value of the payments is about $7600 less than the $36,000 borrowed; that is, the buyer is indifferent between this creative-financing deal and borrowing from the bank at 18 percent with the seller reducing the price by $7,600.

As it turned out, this seller's subsequent purchase of a new home was financed by a bank at a very high interest rate and, twenty-six months later, the seller was very eager to pay off some of this debt. The seller offered to cut $5000 off the remaining

unpaid balance on the first home if the buyer would repay the loan at that time. Now the buyer had to weigh the financial advantage of a $5000 drop in the unpaid balance against giving up a 10.5 percent loan that still had thirty-four months remaining.

The first step, as always, is to figure out the cash flow. After twenty-six monthly payments, the unpaid balance is that amount B such that the present value of all the payments is equal to the amount borrowed, or

$$\$36,000 = \frac{\$485.78}{1.00875} + \ldots + \frac{\$485.78}{1.00875^{26}} + \frac{B}{1.00875^{26}}$$

which implies that

$$B = \$31,038.29$$

with the seller willing to settle for $26,038.29. The buyer's choices, therefore, are to pay $26,038.29 now; or (as originally agreed) pay $485.78 a month for thirty-four months and then $22,599.08. As usual, a present-value comparison is in order. If the buyer needs to borrow the $26,038.29 to make the early payoff, then the interest rate on such a loan (still 18 percent plus at the time) would be appropriate; if, as it happens, the buyer can take the $26,038.29 out of another investment yielding 12 percent, then 12 percent is appropriate. But before settling on a specific interest rate, to three decimal places, notice that the early payoff has the lower present value for low required returns, and the original agreement wins for high required returns. There is a break-even required return where the two alternatives are equally attractive (they have the same present value). The equality

$$\$26,038.29 = \frac{\$485.78}{\left(1 + \dfrac{APR}{12}\right)} + \ldots +$$

$$\frac{\$485.78}{\left(1 + \dfrac{APR}{12}\right)^{34}} + \frac{\$22,599.08}{\left(1 + \dfrac{APR}{12}\right)^{34}}$$

can be solved by trial and error to give

$$APR = 0.1882 \ (18.82 \text{ percent}).$$

(A more accurate analysis—which takes into account the fact that interest payments, but not principal, are tax-deductible—gives a break-even after-tax required return of 15 percent for a 30 percent tax bracket and 12.75 percent for a 50 percent tax bracket.) Since the buyer was earning substantially less than this return, the loan was repaid early.

POINTS AND PENALTIES

During the 1960s and most of the 1970s, mortgage rates averaged some 1½ to 2 percentage points above the interest rates on long-term U.S. government bonds. However, government bond rates jumped to 10.8 percent in 1980 and then to 12.9 percent in 1981, while many lending institutions were prohibited by state usury laws from charging more than 10 percent on mortgage loans. Unable to charge mortgage rates comparable to the rates of return they could earn on bonds and other investments not subject to usury ceilings, some lending institutions stopped making mortgages. Others discovered that they could circumvent usury ceilings, which restrict stated rather than effective interest rates, by charging **points** (sometimes called an origination fee or buy down), a fee equal to a specified percentage of the loan that is paid at the time the loan is made. For example, if you borrow $100,000 through a conventional thirty-year mortgage at 12 percent plus 5 points, you only receive $95,000 ($100,000 less the 5 percent points charge), but pay 12 percent interest on the full $100,000 loan.

points
Points are loan fees, equal to a specified percentage of the loan, paid at the time the loan is made.

The Impact of Points on the Effective Loan Rate

Because you pay 12 percent interest on $100,000, the implicit interest rate on the $95,000 you actually receive is somewhat higher. How much higher depends on the length of the loan. If your loan is a one-year balloon with $112,000 due at the end of the year, then you receive $95,000 now and pay $112,000 a year from now, for an effective interest rate R of almost 18 percent; that is,

$$\$95,000(1 + R) = \$112,000$$

implies that

$$R = \$17,000/\$95,000$$
$$= 0.179 \text{ (that is, 17.9 percent).}$$

With a thirty-year amortized mortgage, the arithmetic is more complicated. First, we can use Equation 2 to determine the requisite monthly payments on a $100,000 loan at a 12 percent annual loan rate (a 1 percent monthly rate):

$$X = \frac{0.01(\$100,000)}{1 - \dfrac{1}{(1 + .01)^{360}}}$$
$$= \$1028.61.$$

Now the key question is, if you pay $1,028.61 a month but only receive $95,000, what is the implicit loan rate? That is, on a $95,000, thirty-year loan, what annual percentage rate implies monthly payments of $1,028.61? The answer can be determined from Equation 1, setting the present value of the monthly payments equal to the amount actually borrowed, as shown in the following:

$$\$95,000 = \frac{\$1,028.61}{(1 + R)} + \ldots + \frac{\$1,028.61}{(1 + R)^{360}}$$

Then, it is a matter of solving, by trial and error, for the implicit monthly interest rate. (Financial calculators can do the figuring very quickly). The solution turns out to be $R = 0.010583$, implying an annual percentage rate of $12(0.010583) = 0.1270$ (or 12.7 percent), so that a borrower has the same monthly payments at a 12 percent interest rate with 5 points and a 12.7 percent interest rate with no points. Thus, 5 points raises the implicit interest rate on this thirty-year mortgage by nearly a percentage point.

The average U.S. family moves every six years. What if a borrower changes jobs, marries, divorces, has children, or for some other good reason decides to pay off the mortgage before thirty years passes? This effectively shortens the loan and raises the implicit interest rate. Suppose that the loan is paid off after 10 years. The unpaid balance at this point is shown in Table 3–3 earlier in this chapter: $93,418. That is, at a 12 percent annual percentage rate (a 1 percent monthly rate), the present value of 120 monthly $1,028.61 payments and a $93,418 balloon is $100,000, the stated size of the loan. The calculations are as follows:

$$\$100,000 = \frac{\$1,028.61}{(1 + 0.01)} + \ldots + \frac{\$1,028.61}{(1 + 0.01)^{120}} + \frac{\$93,418}{(1 + 0.01)^{120}}$$

Of course, in reality, the borrower receives only $95,000 and the implicit interest rate is larger than 12 percent. If we solve

$$\$95,000 = \frac{\$1,028.61}{(1 + R)} + \ldots + \frac{\$1,028.61}{(1 + R)^{120}} + \frac{\$93,418}{(1 + R)^{120}}$$

by trial and error, the monthly interest rate works out to be $R = 0.0107583$. We can then calculate the annual percentage rate, $12(0.0107583) = 0.1291$ (or 12.91 percent), a rate somewhat higher than when the mortgage is kept until the very end. If the mortgage is paid off before ten years passes, the implicit interest rate rises very quickly, as shown in Table 3–4 on p. 82. A rule of thumb might be that five points adds about one percentage point to the effective interest rate for a thirty-year mortgage that is not paid off for at least ten years, and from one to five percentage points if it is paid off sooner.

TABLE 3–4   Implicit Interest Rates for Various Payoff Dates of a Thirty-Year Mortgage at 12 Percent Plus 5 Points

Prepayment Date (year)	Implicit Interest Rate (percent)
1	17.5
2	14.9
5	13.4
10	12.9
20	12.7
30	12.7

The Plight of S&Ls

Interest rates have fallen from their 1981 peaks, and most usury ceilings have been abolished; but points continue to be added on to mortgage loans. Many savings and loans now routinely resell mortgages to the Federal National Mortgage Association (Fannie Mae), Government National Mortgage Association (Ginnie Mae), Federal Home Loan Mortgage Corporation (Freddie Mac) and other nationwide mortgage pools. These pools raise money to purchase mortgages either by selling bonds or by selling shares to investors, who then receive the monthly payments that are forwarded from the original lender. The points charged the homebuyer provide an immediate, certain profit to the S&L.

The primary reason S&Ls now resell so many of their mortgages is in remembrance of past problems. In the 1960s and early 1970s, S&Ls paid their depositors interest rates ranging from 2 percent to 5 percent, and loaned the money out in mortgages at 4 percent to 8 percent—enough to pay depositors, cover expenses, and make a profit too. Mortgage rates topped 8 percent in 1971 and hit an unprecedented 10 percent in 1978. Most observers thought that interest rates would soon fall to more normal levels. They were wrong. Interest rates went higher still, to 18 percent plus in 1981, and those who borrowed at 8 percent to 10 percent were lucky to have what, in retrospect, were low-interest loans. The S&Ls they had borrowed from were not so lucky.

Having loaned virtually all their depositors' money in long-term mortgages, S&Ls literally could not afford substantial deposit withdrawals. While compelled to raise deposit rates to double-digit levels to hold onto depositors who otherwise would invest their money elsewhere, the S&Ls were receiving fixed, single-digit interest rates on mortgages written in the 1960s and 1970s. In 1982, the U.S. League of Savings Associations estimated that the average cost of funds (mainly deposit rates) for S&Ls was 11½ percent and that a mortgage would have to yield 13 to 13½ percent to cover the cost of funds and other expenses. Yet 87 percent of the outstanding mortgages at that time had rates below 13 percent, and 58 percent had rates below 10 percent.[4] As a result, the aggregate net worth of S&Ls fell from $23 billion at the end of 1977 to a frightening −$44 billion at the end of 1981,[5] and nearly a quarter of the S&Ls operating in the 1970s collapsed or merged in the 1980s.[6] Collecting single-digit rates on their mortgages while paying double-digit rates to depositors, S&Ls suffered alarming losses simply because interest rates had risen unexpectedly.

What if interest rates had instead fallen unexpectedly? S&Ls would have made enormous profits if they could have reduced to 1 percent the rates paid depositors while still collecting 4 percent to 8 percent on mortgages. But, in reality, they would not have been able to hold on to these high-interest mortgages, because borrowers would simply have refinanced at the new, low interest rates. S&Ls made a very asymmetrical bet in the 1950s, 1960s, and early 1970s. Depositors could refinance if rates fell, but S&Ls could not renegotiate if rates rose. Heads, depositors win; tails, S&Ls lose.

When S&Ls realized how expensive this asymmetrical bet could be, they changed the rules of the game by revising their standard mortgage contracts in two important ways. First, they inserted *due-on-sale clauses* to make mortgages nonassumable; now, if the borrower sells the house, the old, possibly low-interest mortgage, must be repaid and cannot be passed on to the buyer. Second, to discourage or at least penalize borrowers who refinance when interest rates go down, they inserted **prepayment penalties,** additional charges that the borrower must pay the lender if the loan is repaid early. Borrowers naturally dislike prepayment penalties, and fourteen state legislatures have outlawed their use. Points can, however, serve as a rough substitute, since five points on a new loan is about as discouraging as a 5 percent prepayment penalty on the old.

prepayment penalties
Prepayment penalties are fees the borrower must pay the lender if the loan is repaid early.

The Effect of Prepayment Penalties

A prepayment penalty increases the effective interest rates on a loan that is repaid early. Consider a thirty-year, $100,000 mortgage at 12 percent with a $5000 prepayment penalty (penalties can be specified as some dollar amount, as some percentage of the unpaid balance, or by other rules). How does this penalty change the effective interest rate? The analysis is very similar to the case of points, the main difference being that points are tacked on at the beginning and prepayment penalties at the end. For instance, you will recall that if the loan is paid off after ten years, the unpaid balance at the time is $93,418. A $5000 prepayment penalty compels the borrower to pay $98,418, and the implicit monthly interest rate is the value

TABLE 3–5   Implicit Interest Rates for Various Payoff Dates of a Thirty-Year Mortgage at 12 Percent with a $5000 Prepayment Penalty

Prepayment Date (year)	Implicit Interest Rate (percent)
1	16.6
2	14.2
5	12.7
10	12.3
20	12.1
30	12.0

of R that solves the following present-value equation:

$$\$100,000 = \frac{\$1,028.61}{(1 + R)} + \ldots + \frac{\$1,028.61}{(1 + R)^{120}} + \frac{\$98,418}{(1 + R)^{120}}$$

Trial and error gives $R = 0.0102167$, for an annual percentage rate of $12(0.0102167) = 0.123$—that is, 12.3 percent. As with points, the effect is larger the sooner the loan is repaid, as shown in Table 3–5. A $5000 pre-payment penalty does not raise the effective interest rate as much as $5000 in points, because the points are paid right away and the prepayment penalty is paid later (and can be avoided entirely by not prepaying the loan).

Does Refinancing Pay?

We can also answer a somewhat different question: how low do interest rates have to fall to make refinancing financially attractive, despite the prepayment penalty? To keep the analysis straightforward, we will assume that when a thirty-year mortgage is refinanced after n years, the new loan is for $30 - n$ years and the new amount borrowed is such that the monthly payments are unchanged. Refinancing is then profitable if the amount borrowed is enough to pay off the old loan plus the prepayment penalty (and any other fees), with something left over. If homeowners voluntarily choose to borrow a different amount for a different period of time, then presumably they are even better-off. (This analysis ignores two complications. First, the borrower may pay off the new loan at some future date and, if so, the unpaid balance is not the same as with the old loan. Second, even if refinancing is profitable today, it may be even better to wait for still lower interest rates.)

TABLE 3–6 Maximum Profitable Interest Rates for Refinancing a Thirty-
Year Mortgage at 12 Percent with a $5000 Prepayment
Penalty

Refinancing Date (year)	Maximum Profitable Interest Rate (percent)
1	11.4
2	11.3
5	11.3
10	11.2
20	10.4
25	7.6

We will continue to use the $100,000, thirty-year mortgage with a $5000 prepayment penalty as an example. If the loan is repaid after ten years, the homeownwer pays the bank $98,418. How low must the monthly interest rate R on the refinanced loan be so that the twenty years of $1,028.61 monthly payments will allow the homeowner to borrow $98,418? The value of R that solves the present-value equation is

$$\$98,418 = \frac{\$1,028.61}{(1 + R)} + \ldots + \frac{\$1,028.61}{(1 + R)^{240}}$$

and the solution is $R = 0.009325$, for an annual percentage rate of $12(0.009325) = 0.112$—that is, 11.2 percent. Similar calculations for other prepayment dates yield the values shown in Table 3–6.

Even with a seemingly stiff $5000 prepayment penalty, a 1 percent drop in interest rates makes refinancing attractive in the first ten years. As time passes and the number of years remaining at the original, high interest rate dwindle, it takes a bigger and bigger drop in interest rates to make refinancing profitable.

ADJUSTABLE-RATE LOANS

Imposing prepayment penalties and selling mortgages to mortgage pools were two S&L responses to the losses sustained in the early 1980s. Another response was shifting from fixed-rate mortgages to **adjustable-rate loans**— loans in which the loan rate rises and falls with market interest rates. If the problem is that the interest rates on old mortgages stay low while deposit rates rise, then the solution is either to fix deposit rates or to adjust mortgage rates. S&Ls use both alternatives—encouraging time deposits

adjustable-rate loan
Adjustable-rate loans have interest rates that rise and fall with market interest rates.

with rates that are fixed for two, five, or even ten years, and encouraging mortgages with interest rates that vary with market interest rates. Most bank loans to businesses today are also variable rate—for example, an interest rate equal to the current prime rate charged the most creditworthy businesses, plus 2 percent.

These flexible-rate loans are known by a variety of names: adjustable-rate loans, variable-rate loans, renegotiable-rate loans, rollover loans, and so on. In each case, the lender is allowed to adjust the interest rate to reflect current financial conditions. Often there is a formula that ties the loan rate to current market rates—approximating the rates paid depositors plus a few extra percentage points to cover expenses. Many S&Ls use the yield on one-year Treasury bills; other use explicit industry estimates of the average cost of funds. Many variable-rate mortgages have caps limiting the rate adjustment in specific ways—say, for example, 2 percent in any given year and 5 percent during the life of the mortgage. The widespread use of variable-rate mortgages was first permitted in April 1981, and during the years 1982–85 roughly half of all new mortgages were variable rate.

There are a number of ways to adjust the payment stream as the loan rate varies. The essential rule is that the present value of the payments equals the amount borrowed (using Equation 4 in Chapter 2), or, equivalently, the amount by which the monthly payment exceeds the interest due on the unpaid balance reduces the unpaid balance each month, until it reaches zero.

Variable Payments

A benchmark payment structure is provided by amortizing the loan at a certain interest rate to obtain a planned constant stream of payments; for instance, a thiry-year, $100,000 mortgage at 12 percent implies monthly payments of $1,028.61, some of which is interest on the unpaid balance and some of which is a reduction of that balance. Then, with a variable-payment loan, each month's payment can rise or fall with changes in the interest charged on the unpaid balance, the reduction of principal following the plan initially established by the benchmark. The borrower pays somewhat more than $1,028.61 if the interest rate rises above 12 percent and somewhat less if it falls below. Since the unpaid balance declines as scheduled, the loan is fully paid off after thirty years.

As an example, look again at Table 3–3. As shown, after the first month's payment, the unpaid balance declines to $99,971.39. If the interest rate stays at 12 percent, the planned $1,028.61 payment the second month will cover the $999.71 in interest due and reduce the unpaid balance by $28.90, to $99,942.49. What if, instead, the interest rate charged in the second month jumps to 12.2 percent? The interest due increases to

$$(0.122/12)\$99,971.39 = \$1,016.38.$$

The monthly payment must increase by $16.67 in order to reduce the unpaid balance by $28.90, as planned:

	Planned			*Actual*
Interest	$999.71		Interest	$1,016.38
Principal	28.90		Principal	28.90
Total payment	**$1,028.61**		**Total payment**	**$1,045.28**

Thus, the unpaid balance falls to $99,942.49, as planned, and adjustments of the monthly payments keep this unpaid balance falling on schedule until it reaches zero after thirty years.

Negative Amortization

Another possibility with variable-rate loans is for the lender to hold the monthly payments constant (at least temporarily) by varying the division of the monthly payment between interest and principal. Instead of increasing the monthly payment by $16.67 to cover the extra interest due, the repayment of principal can be reduced by $16.67:

	Planned			*Actual*
Interest	$999.71		Interest	$1,016.38
Principal	28.90		Principal	12.23
Total payment	**$1,028.61**		**Total payment**	**$1,028.61**

If the interest rate rises so much that the fixed $1,028.61 monthly payment is insufficient to cover the interest charge, there is **negative amortization**— the unpaid loan balance actually increases.

    If the monthly payments are held constant and the interest rate stays above 12 percent, then the unpaid balance will continue to decline more slowly than originally planned and will not reach zero after thirty years. A balloon payment can be made at that time, or the loan term can be lengthened. If, on the other hand, the interest rate averages less than the planned 12 percent, the loan will be paid off before the end of thirty years.

    A variation is a variable-rate loan with temporarily fixed payments. Here the borrower selects a period of time, usually one to five years, over which the monthly payments are constant even while the interest rate being charged varies. The unpaid balance declines less than planned if the interest rate rises and more than planned if the interest rate falls. After the specified period of fixed monthly payments is over, a new payments schedule is established to ensure that the unpaid balance declines to zero at the end of thirty years.

negative amortization
Negative amortization, an increase in a loan's unpaid balance, occurs when the loan payment is insufficient to cover the interest charge.

In many business and personal loans (for example, a line of credit from a bank, a loan from a stockbroker, or a credit-card balance), there is no set repayment schedule. Each month, interest is charged at a fixed or variable rate on the unpaid balance, and the borrower chooses how much to repay. The unpaid balance grows if the payment does not cover the interest charge, and declines if the payment does.

GRADUATED-PAYMENT LOANS (optional)

A conventional amortized loan sets a constant dollar payment for the length of the loan. During inflationary periods, the real value of these monthly payments declines steadily. For instance, if prices rise by 10 percent a year, the price level will nearly double every seven years

$$1.10^7 = 1.95$$

and, at the end of a thirty-year mortgage, be some 17½ times higher than when the loan began:

$$1.10^{30} = 17.45$$

Thus, the real value of the constant monthly payments at the beginning of the mortgage is some 17½ times the real value at the end, and so is the financial sacrifice needed to make these payments, particularly for a young household. Even at a 5 percent inflation rate, the price level doubles in fourteen years and at the end of thirty years is some 4.3 times the initial level.

It is more reasonable to have monthly payments that are constant in real rather than nominal terms. Imagine, for example, that you are just beginning a career and expect your salary to grow at the same rate as prices in general. If you have a mortgage with constant monthly payments, then the fraction of your income spent on housing is highest when you are young and then declines steadily. Is it not more sensible to have mortgage payments grow with your income, keeping the ratio of housing expenses to income roughly constant?

Unaffordable Housing

As a practical matter, constant mortgage payments may represent such a large fraction of income in the early years that a young household cannot qualify for a mortgage even though it will have plenty of income later. Fannie Mae requires a 20 percent down payment and advises that housing expenses (including mortgage payments, homeowner's insurance, and taxes) not exceed 28 percent of household income. (For many years, the rule at lending institutions was a more conservative 25 percent of income.) In 1982, with prices rising at double-digit rates, the average price of a new home was $94,600, and the average conventional mortgage was for $69,800 for 27.6 years at a 14.47 percent interest rate, plus three points. The average new buyer put $24,800 down (plus nearly $3000 in points) and signed a mortgage with monthly payments of $858, which, according to Fannie Mae's guidelines and ignoring insurance and taxes, required an annual income of about $37,000. Needless to say, few young households had $27,000 in cash and an annual income of $37,000.

Mortgage Payments That Increase With Income

To ease the financial burden on young households who expect nominal income to grow steadily (which is particularly likely during inflationary periods), there are **graduated-payment mortgages (GPM)**—loans in which the monthly payments are initially low and then grow with income. Consider a household who has a monthly income, now amounting to $2000, that is expected to grow by about 5 percent a year and who wants to borrow $100,000 for thirty years at the prevailing 10 percent mortgage rate. With a conventional loan, Equation 2 gives the requisite monthly payment as follows:

graduated payment mortgage (GPM)
In a graduated payment mortgage, the monthly payments are initially low and then increase over time, to ease the financial burden on young households who expect nominal income to grow steadily.

$$X = \frac{(0.10/12)\$100,000}{1 - \dfrac{1}{(1 + 0.10/12)^{360}}}$$
$$= \$877.57$$

This fixed monthly payment is 44 percent of the household's current income (which, no doubt, would cause the loan application to be rejected) but only 10 percent of the household's expected $8935 monthly income thirty years from now.

We can construct an alternative, graduated-payment plan with mortgage payments growing by 5 percent a year, subject only to the constraint that the present value of these payments is equal to the amount borrowed. (The exact formula is not important here, but will be developed in Chapter 7 to value a firm with constantly growing dividends.) The first monthly payment works out to be $537.79 and the last $2,402.69, each amounting to 27 percent of monthly income. A graduated-payment mortgage attempts to keep housing expenses at a relatively constant share of household income, making mortgages more accessible for people who expect their income to rise as time passes.

In practice, the typical GPM contract does not increase the monthly payment at the same rate every month. More often, the payment begins low, rises gradually for five to ten years, and then levels off. If the early payments are not enough to cover the interest due on the loan, then there is negative amortization for a while. This principle holds true in our example in that the first month's $537.79 payment does not cover the interest of $(0.10/12)\$100,000 = \$833.33$. The unpaid balance grows for several years until the rising monthly payments overtake the monthly interest.

Franco Modigliani, a Nobel Prize winning economist and enthusiastic advocate of GPMs, attributes their lukewarm acceptance by lenders and borrowers to an irrational distaste for negative amortization.[7] Even some otherwise informed observers are put off by this characteristic. In a 1983 article on mortgage alternatives, *Business Week* treats negative amortization as a drawback and goes on to state the following:

> In the long run it's more expensive than other mortgages. In fact, a $67,000 GPM at a fixed 15% rate would start out with monthly payments that are $120 cheaper than the conventional mortgage but would end up costing about $16,000 more over 30 years.[8]

Yes, it is the *Consumer Reports* error once again! You as the borrower pay more total interest with a GPM, because the unpaid balance grows at first instead of declining; and you pay more interest whenever you borrow more money for a longer period of time. In this instance, your monthly payments are lower at the beginning and higher at the end, and *Business Week* obtains its $16,000 difference by simply adding up the total payments, regardless of when they are made. Discounted at the mortgage rate, the present values of a GPM and a conventional mortgage are exactly the same, equal to the amount borrowed.

SUMMARY

Borrowed money is often used to finance the purchase of real and financial assets. This use of other people's money creates leverage in that the return on one's relatively small investment depends on the profitability of a much larger investment. If the total investment earns a rate of return larger than the interest rate paid on the borrowed money, this differential is multiplied by the degree of leverage. Leverage is a double-edged sword in that any shortfall between the investment's return and the loan rate is magnified too.

Loan payments are calculated so that the present value of the payments, discounted at the quoted loan rate, is equal to the amount borrowed. In a conventional amortized mortgage, the constant monthly payments cover the interest due and also reduce the principal—slowly at first, then rapidly at the end—so that the last payment reduces the unpaid balance to zero. In a balloon loan, the periodic payments do not reduce the principal sufficiently (often not at all), and a large payment must be made at maturity to cover the still substantial unpaid balance.

Loans are often evaluated and compared on the basis of the total (undiscounted) payments made during the life of the loan—a flawed procedure that favors borrowing as little as possible for as brief a period as possible. A total-payments analysis concludes that it is better to borrow for one year at 100 percent than for 150 years at 1 percent, and that it is better still to never borrow. Instead of a total-payments calculation you should use a present-value analysis—discounting your loan payments by your required rate of return, which depends on market interest rates.

Points, a percentage fee paid when a loan is made, raise the effective interest rate on the loan—especially if it is a short-term loan or a long-term loan that is repaid early. Prepayment penalties are fees charged when a loan is repaid early; these raise the effective loan rate more the sooner the loan is repaid. Nonetheless, despite the prepayment penalty, it is often profitable to refinance a long-term, fixed-rate loan at a low interest rate after only a few years, thereby avoiding many years of high interest payments.

On an adjustable-rate loan, the interest rate is periodically adjusted to reflect current market rates or the lender's cost of funds. These adjustments either alter the size of the payments or the amount of time it takes to repay the loan. When the loan rate increases and monthly payments do not increase, there can be negative amortization—the loan payments don't cover the interest due and the unpaid balance increases.

In a conventional constant-payment mortgage, the fraction of household income devoted to mortgage payments is high when the household is young and declines as its income grows over time. Graduated-payment mortgages were developed so that monthly payments would rise with income and, thus, represent a relatively constant fraction of household income. In either case, the present value of the payments, at the quoted loan rate, is equal to the amount borrowed.

EXERCISES

1. You want to invest $80,000 for one year but have only $20,000. You borrow an additional $60,000 at 10 percent and owe $66,000 one year from now. What is the percentage return on your $20,000 if the rate of return earned on the entire $80,000 is 10 percent? 50 percent? −10 percent?

2. You have inherited $50,000 and hope to multiply your new wealth by buying undeveloped land in a resort area. You are considering borrowing $50,000 and buying a $100,000 parcel, or else borrowing $450,000 and buying a $500,000 property. Assume that either way you will have to pay back your loan plus 12 percent interest after a year and that each property will appreciate equally. If, for instance, property in this area appreciates by 20 percent, you will either make $20,000 − $6,000 = $14,000 or $100,000 − $54,000 = $46,000, depending on which property you buy. Fill in the rest of Table 3–A on p. 92, showing the net gain on your $50,000 wealth. For what rate of property appreciation do these two strategies work equally well? How much leverage do you have with each strategy?

3. Banks make profits with other people's money, investing what they have borrowed from their depositors. For a typical bank, out of every $100 that it invests, $95 is borrowed and $5 is net worth. The rate of return that it pays its depositors is generally specified ahead of time, while the rate it earns on its investments depends on loan defaults and other economic conditions. What is the annual rate of return on its net worth if it borrows at 7 percent and invests at 7 percent? What if it borrows at 7 percent and invests at 9 percent? If it borrows at 7 percent, what rate of return on its investments will bankrupt the bank (a −100 percent on net worth)?

TABLE 3–A

Property Appreciation (percent)	Return on $50,000 Investment with $50,000 Loan		Return on $50,000 Investment with $450,000 Loan	
	Dollars	Percent	Dollars	Percent
−10				
0				
10				
20	$14,000	28	$46,000	92
30				
40				

4. You are going to borrow $10,000 for ten years at a 10 percent interest rate. What is the size of your payment if you make constant annual payments? What size is your payment if you make constant monthly payments? Why are the annual payments more than twelve times the monthly payments?

5. In 1980, Chrysler announced that interest rates (then about 20 percent on car loans) were 7 percent too high and that it was consequently giving a 7 percent rebate on new cars financed by car loans. Consider a new car costing $10,000 for which you will put $2000 down and pay the remainder over five years with a conventional amortized monthly car loan. Would you rather have the price reduced 7 percent to $9300, or have the loan rate reduced to 13 percent?

6. Before the 1969 Truth-in-Lending Act, a finance company using the add-on method could loan you $1000, charge you $100 interest (with $1100/12 = $91.67 due each month for twelve months), and say that the interest rate was only 10 percent. What is the true annual percentage rate on such a loan? If the annual percentage rate were really 10 percent, how big would the monthly payments be?

7. At age eighty-two, Fred Benson won a $50,000 state lottery, paying $100 a month for 500 months. He sold his claim to a local bank for $13,500 and threw the biggest party in the history of Block Island. What is the bank's implicit rate of return on its investment? (That is, if this were a $13,500 mortgage to be repaid in 500 monthly $100 installments, what would be the implicit mortgage rate?)

8. Rent-A-Center rents televisions and other appliances by the week without using a credit check, and allows its customers to apply the rental payments toward eventual purchase; for example, for a nineteen-inch portable TV that can be purchased from a discount store for $229, Rent-A-Center charges $9.95 a week for seventy-eight weeks.[9] If a customer does buy the set by paying $9.95 a week for seventy-eight weeks, what is the implicit annual interest rate on this $229 TV?

9. Colonel Parker sold his BMW 320i in 1985 and bought a BMW M635 C51. He could have paid $47,000 cash, but he decided to lease the car instead, agreeing to make an initial payment of $7000, forty-eight monthly payments of $750, and a final residual payment of $22,000 at the end of forty-eight months (at which time he would become the legal owner of the car). Either way, he is required to pay insurance, repairs, maintenance, and other operating expense out of his own pocket. Should the colonel have paid cash instead?

10. On August 28, 1986, General Motors announced "The Big One," a 2.9 percent interest rate on thirty-six-month loans for its 1986 models; Ford and Chrysler followed with similar deals. If at the time you were buying a $12,000 car and had $2000 for a down payment, would you rather have borrowed the difference at 2.9 percent, or have had the price reduced by $1000 and borrowed from a credit union at 10 percent instead?

11. A 1986 *Newsweek* article said the following about the 2.9 percent loan rate offered by GM and the 0 percent rate from American Motors:

> Don't think this is a never-again opportunity. The American auto market is going to be flooded with new cars in the years ahead . . . there seems no way to avoid a market where there will be too many cars chasing too few passengers. So what will come next—a pitch featuring negative interest rates?[10]

How would a negative interest rate work? In particular, what would be your monthly payment on a four-year amortized monthly loan of $10,000 at −5 percent? Is the total of the monthly payments more or less than $10,000?

12. If you save $2000 a year for forty years, starting a year from today, and earn a 3 percent after-tax rate of return each year, how much will you have after forty years? (Hint: find the present value of this cash flow, and then convert it to a future value.)

13. A consumer finance book advised, "A second method of reducing costs is to make the largest downpayment possible and repay in the shortest period of time."[11] How does this strategy reduce costs? Would you recommend this strategy, no matter what the loan rate?

14. The owner of a Washington, D.C., real-estate firm said that an equation basic to real estate is:[12]

Principal × Interest Rate per Period × Interest Periods (time) = Total Interest Paid

Explain why the total interest paid on a $100,000 conventional thirty-year mortgage at 10 percent is *not* $100,000 × 10 percent/year × 30 years = $300,000.

15. Mr. I. M. Gone moved to Houston in 1978 and had to sell his home in Philadelphia. He asked $100,000, but mortgage rates were 18 percent, and many banks were not approving any new mortgage loans. Mr. Gone finally agreed to owner-financing by which he would lend the buyer $80,000 for thirty years at 12 percent. The buyer paid the remaining $20,000 in cash. From the buyer's standpoint, how large a price cut was the owner-financing equivalent to?

16. Mr. Gone discovers that he has an assumable $60,000, thirty-year mortgage at 9 percent with twenty-five years remaining. He offers to owner-finance an additional $20,000 over twenty-five years at 20 percent. What is the buyer's effective interest rate?

17. Ms. Yup must sell her Houston home in order to take a job in California. She has two offers on her house. The first is $160,000 cash. The second is $180,000, of which $30,000 is cash and the remaining $150,000 an owner-financed, thirty-year mortgage at 8 percent. Which offer is the more financially attractive?

18. Pomona College has agreed to lend Professor Smith $85,000 at 7 percent and an additional $40,000 at 12 percent. Both of these loans will be conventional thirty-year mortgages with constant monthly payments. For simplicity, the Pomona College business office wants to combine these two loans into one thirty-year mortgage with a single interest rate. What is the appropriate interest rate?

19. You need $100,000 to start your new business. One lender requires sixty monthly payments of $2150, due at the end of each month (beginning a month from the signing of the loan papers). A second lender requires twenty quarterly payments of $6450, due at the beginning of each quarter (starting on the day the loan is signed.) Which lender charges the higher effective loan rate? How much higher is it?

20. In 1985, a Los Angeles mortgage company was charging 15 percent plus 10 points on second mortgages. What is their implicit annual percentage rate of interest on a twenty-year, $100,000 loan that is not repaid early?

21. Consider a thirty-year, $100,000 mortgage at 10 percent with constant monthly payments. If it costs five points to get this mortgage and there is a $5000 prepayment penalty, what is the annual percentage rate of return to the bank if the loan is paid off after five years?

22. On May 1, 1986, Imperial Savings in California offered conventional fifteen-year, fixed-rate mortgages for either 9.875 percent with 1 point or 9 percent with 4.5 points. How would you as the home buyer choose between these two alternatives?

23. In 1986, a former reporter for *The Wall Street Journal* told how he had been tempted to refinance his twenty-five-year, 13.25 percent, $55,000 mortgage at 9 to 10 percent, but he had become discouraged by the $3500 to $4000 he would have to pay in points and other closing costs. Critically evaluate his logic, as explained in the following statement:

> But with, say, a saving of $100 a month in principal and interest payments, I still would pocket $36,000 over 30 years, I thought at first. Not so. Since I have only 22½ years left on my existing contract and if I convert it to 25 or 30 years to keep the payments low, I discovered that I could end up paying more total dollars in the long run. And I can't afford the monthly payments for a shorter loan term of 15 or 20 years, which would make the deal work.[13]

24. In 1985, the *Los Angeles Times*[14] described the "sudden, almost explosive, acceptance of the 15-year fixed rate mortgage," in place of the traditional thirty-year mortgage. It cited a Mortgage Bankers Association estimate that, coming from "minimal acceptance" just a year ago, fifteen-year mortgages now account for one-seventh of all new mortgages. In explanation, the *Los Angeles Times* cited "common sense economics" as the basis for its popularity:

> At the end of 30 years, that $100,000 mortgage [at 13%, with $1,106.20 monthly payments] has cost the home buyer a grand total of $398,232—a mind boggling $298,232 in interest . . . . by cutting the same mortgage down to 15 from 30 years (and raising the monthly payments from $1,106.20 to $1,265.25), the total cost to the home buyer is $227,745 for a net saving in interest of $170,487.
>
> "While you certainly can't quarrel with the arithmetic of the 15-year mortgage—and the sudden popularity of it . . . there are limits on how far the trend can go," according to Fred E. Case of UCLA's Graduate School of Management. "Not everyone who sees the sense of the 15-year mortgage is in a position to qualify for one."

The *Los Angeles Times* also quoted an anonymous "cynical" midwestern lender:

> I'd like to think that home buyers have suddenly gotten smart—that they've looked at those figures and realized how much interest they're paying over 30 years. God knows they've been dumb about it long enough.

Why, by their reckoning, is a thirty-year mortgage so expensive? Is there any interest rate at which you would choose a thirty-year rather than fifteen-year mortgage at the same interest rate?

25. Find the error in the following financial analysis of three auto deals (Chrysler [no rebate], Ford [5 percent rebate], and General Motors (GM) [12.8 percent financing]):

> Assume, for instance, that you are going to buy a car with a $10,000 sticker price. It would normally be financed for 48 months at 16.5% interest . . . after a 20% or $2000 down

payment. If the manufacturer doesn't provide any assistance in the purchase of the car, the total cost at the end of the four-year financing period would be $12,979.04 according to Detroit Bank & Trust. Monthly payments would amount to $228.73. That is what a buyer would pay under Chrysler's incentive plan, which offers no help on the purchase price.

If you bought that same car from Ford, the purchase price plus financing interest would amount to $12,479.04, reflecting a 5% or $500 rebate paid to you by Ford and used as part of your $2000 down payment. Again monthly payments would be $228.73. You could lower the total cost and the monthly payments slightly if you used the rebate to increase the down payment to $2500.

The same $10,000 car purchased from a GM dealer under the 12.8% financing program, which expires May 31, would cost $12,263.68. Monthly payments would drop to $213.83. Thus, it appears that the GM financing plan saves the customer the most money in the direct purchase of the car, all other things being equal.[15]

26. Find the error in the following comparison of car leasing with buying:

> Consider a moderately equipped Pontiac Grand Am that would sell for $11,288. GM calculates that the standard lease on the car would be $229 a month for 48 months, or a total of $10,992. With a 5% tax on the monthly payments, the cost would total $11,542.
>
> If a person were to buy the car with the standard minimum down payment of 13%, or $1,481, and finance the rest at 11% for 48 months, the monthly payments would be $253, or a total of $12,144. Including the downpayment and lost interest earnings on that amount, as well as the 5% sales tax, the buyer's cost would be $14,840.
>
> But with the loan paid, the buyer would own a car with a value of at least $4,400, according to GM. If the buyer sold the car for that price, his net cost would be $10,440, compared with the lessee's $11,542.[16]

27. A real-estate broker argues that Mike, after buying a $100 raffle ticket, might walk away from the prize, a $150,000 house, because (a) he will have to pay the IRS $75,000 (in a 50 percent tax bracket); (b) "Mike does not have $75,000 in cash to pay the tax—he hardly had the $100 for the raffle ticket;" and (c) if he borrows $75,000 to cover the tax from a bank at 18 percent for twenty years, he will have to pay $1157 a month $\times$ 12 months/year $\times$ 20 years $=$ $333,120 total mortgage payments on the house.[17] Would you walk away from this prize?

28. In 1985, Lucy Cooper (a former librarian) was receiving $350 each month in Social Security benefits, while her husband Jack (a retired principal) had received $550 a month until his death that year. As a sixty-four-year-old widow, Lucy was entitled to part or all of her husband's benefits in place of her own, depending on whether she elected to begin receiving them immediately or to wait a year until her sixty-fifth birthday. Her alternatives were to (a) give up her own benefits immediately and receive 94 percent of Jack's benefits for the remainder of her life, or (b) continue to receive her benefits for another twelve months and then receive 100 percent of Jack's benefits for the remainder of her life. If we assume that Social Security benefits increase each month at the rate of inflation and that Lucy's real required return is 3 percent, which option should she choose?

29. *Consumer Reports* gave the following advice about auto loans:

> The nice thing about auto loans is that you can locate the lemons before you sign on the dotted line. Just keep your eye on the APR— the Annual Percentage Rate . . . . Obviously, the lower the APR, the better. Another point to keep in mind: the shorter the loan the better . . . . a one-year loan is much cheaper than a four-year loan. Say you borrow $4000 at 11%. For a one-year loan, the total interest would be $242. The total interest for a four-year loan would be $963—about four times as

much. Of course, the monthly payments for the longer loan would be smaller, but remember that you pay heavily for that convenience.[18]

a. Why is the $242 total interest on a one-year loan far less than 11 percent of $4000?

b. Why is the total interest on a four-year loan more than on a one-year loan?

c. Why are the monthly payments smaller on the four-year loan?

d. What is the present value of each stream of monthly payments, discounted at an 11 percent required return?

e. Assuming the same interest rate on each loan, are there any circumstances in which the adage "the shorter the loan, the better" is not true?

30. Joanna graduated from college today and will immediately begin working at a salary of $24,000 a year, payable monthly. She expects her salary to rise at the rate of inflation, keeping her real income constant. If so, what is the value of her human capital (that is, the present value of her lifetime wages) if she anticipates working for forty-five years and has a real required return of 2 percent.

31. Critically evaluate the following advice:

Want to build equity in your home fast, slash 60 percent off the total interest you pay on a mortgage held to maturity, retire the major debt of your lifetime—your home loan— before the kids' college bills come steamrolling in?

The 15-year-fixed- or adjustable-rate mortgage (ARM) can help you accomplish all that for a relatively low price. For $105 more per month, a 15-year, fixed rate mortgage saves you $115,000 in interest charges (compared to a 30-year fixed-rate mortgage) over the life of the mortgage. A 15-year ARM saves you $95,400 in interest charges (compared to a 30-year fixed-rate mortgage) in this example [$75,000 borrowed for thirty years at 12 percent or for fifteen years at 9.25 percent

the first year and 15 percent thereafter] provided by Carteret Savings and Loan Association of Morristown, New Jersey. Even though monthly ARM payments may increase each year (if interest rates rise), you come out ahead, thanks to a maximum 15 percent interest-rate ceiling built into this loan agreement . . . .

If you can afford modestly higher monthly payments and meet stricter borrowing requirements, there's no denying the advantages of a 15-year versus a 30-year mortgage.[19]

32. In 1981, the Federal Home Loan Bank Board approved the Reverse Annuity Mortgage (RAM) as a means of allowing homeowners, especially elderly ones with valuable houses but little cash income, to convert the equity in their homes into monthly income without having to sell their homes. Consider a sixty-six-year-old widow living in a $300,000 home with no outstanding mortgage. With a 10 percent RAM, she could receive $1000 a month for, say, ten years until she dies, at which time her estate would have to pay the lending institution the amount the widow had borrowed, including interest charged each month (at a 10 percent annual percentage rate) on the outstanding balance. How much would this future payment be? [Hint: you can convert this future value into a present value by using Equation 5 in Chapter 2, and then convert back to a future value.]

33. The owner of a Washington, D.C., real-estate firm warns that elderly homeowners can get "RAMed" by reverse annuity mortgages (RAMs):

An $80,000 RAM at 13% interest paid monthly to the homeowner over 15 years would give the homeowner monthly payments of approximately $145/month.

But wait a minute.

$145/month × 12 months/year ×

15 years = $26,100

Yes, the homeowner gets $26,100 (much less if inflation is figured in) and owes $80,000 in 15 years![20]

Explain why the homeowner pays $80,000 while getting only $26,100. Explain why inflation should not be figured in.

34. After studying the insurance industry, one analyst estimated that "Insurance companies tend to be leveraged at between 10 and 20 to 1 for life companies and 4 or 5 to 1 for casualty companies."[21] If you were assigned to estimate the leverage ratio for a company, which of these data would you use and how: sales, before-tax profits, after-tax profits, assets, liabilities, net worth, or stock price?

35. If you borrow $10,000 at a 15 percent annual interest rate and make annual payments of $2000, how many years will it take to pay off this loan?

36. Critically evaluate these excerpts from a newspaper column:

At first, Berkeley psychology professor Geoffrey Keppel rejected out of hand his Toyota dealer's offer of financing. He had saved up the price of a new Corolla and, like many people, didn't want a loan because "that's the way I'd been brought up." The dealer even told him he could earn more on the same $8300 in a 8% certificate of deposit than he'd pay out on a 14.2% car loan, "but you just don't believe it," he says . . . .

That night, however, Keppel awoke and went to his computer to "work it out for myself, month by month." Calculating different investment yields and weighing them against the total interest that he'd pay on the 14.2% loan, he saw that he'd break even with only a 7% investment, and if he could earn 10%, he'd make almost $1,500.[22]

37. In a biweekly mortgage, monthly payments are calculated as if the mortgage were a conventional thirty-year amortized monthly mortgage, but then half this calculated monthly amount is paid every other week. The result has been described as follows:

At 9.25% interest, a biweekly $100,000 mortgage pays off in slightly more than 21 years, instead of 30, and saves $63,819 in interest. On a $200,000 mortgage, the interest saved is $126,637.

"And," as G. Randall Kinst, director of secondary marketing for Mortgage Loans America, a large wholesale mortgage banking firm located in Campbell, Calif., says, "a 30-year conventional loan would need an unheard of 6.7% interest rate to achieve the same savings realized on a biweekly."[23]

How do biweekly payments reduce the interest paid and the length of the mortgage? Would you choose a 9.25 percent biweekly or a 6.7 percent monthly?

38. One California mortgage banker set up a "simulated" biweekly plan that works in the following way:

It simply sets itself up as a trust, collects biweekly mortgage payments from its clients and then turns around and pays their lender the regular monthly payment . . . . What it amounts to is simply one extra payment a year being made on the mortgage.[24]

Why would a mortgage banker do this for its clients?

39. In July 1986 an elderly couple received a letter from their savings bank that began as follows:

We are very pleased to offer you the opportunity to save a minimum of $1,370.91 in future interest on your mortgage loan. Yes, you can save $1,370.91 in future interest by increasing your monthly payment by only $25.00 per month beginning in August. This extra $25.00 per month will also pay off your mortgage 3 years and 7 months early.[25]

An enclosed analysis showed that this couple had an unpaid balance of $8,479.53 on a 7.25 percent loan, with eleven years and eleven months of $89.00 monthly payments remaining, and that

With your present monthly payment of $89.00, your future interest paid over the next 11 years 11 months will be	$4,185.04
By increasing your monthly payment by $25.00 per month, your future interest over the next 8 years 4 months will be	2,814.13
Interest savings (will also pay off your mortgage 3 years 7 months early)	$1,370.91

After reviewing the analysis, answer the following questions:
a. If we look at the total payments, principal plus interest, how much does the couple save?
b. Why does an extra $25 a month reduce the length of the mortgage?
c. Why do you think the bank offered this opportunity?

40. The owners of the Fifth Street Bar and Grill have used almost all of their available funds to establish their restaurant and are now considering a bank loan to raise more cash. One imaginative owner has suggested that Fifth Street issue a Gold Card for $3000 that would enable the purchaser to have their next $5000 in meals at Fifth Street for free. Does this Gold Card make good financial sense? If they do issue a Gold Card, which of the following deals is more financially advantageous to Fifth Street: a card that costs $3000 and can be used for $5000 in meals or a card that costs $6000 and can be used for $10,000 in meals? One owner has suggested a $500 monthly limit on the use of the Gold Card. Why might such a limit be financially advantageous to Fifth Street? Act as a financial advisor to Fifth Street. You will have to make some assumptions, including acceptance of the owners' presumptions that the food is so good that the Gold Card holder would have eaten at Fifth Street anyway and that the restaurant will not go out of business prematurely. State any additional assumptions, and set up any necessary calculations.

CHAPTER 4

Fixed-Income Securities

Good intelligence is nine-tenths of any battle . . .
Napoleon

The preceding chapter examined amortized loans—the debts most commonly used by household borrowers. In this chapter, the focus is on fixed-income securities, which are issued by governments and businesses and bought by individual and institutional investors. These securities, also called bonds or debt, are fixed-income in the sense that the cash flow is specified in advance. Their market prices are by no means fixed. Bond prices can and do vary, for reasons that will be explained in this chapter and the next.

We will look first at the general characteristics of bonds and at the present-value logic behind the calculation of their prospective return. You will see that bond prices and yields are inversely related and learn why some bonds sell for discounts from face value while other, very similar, bonds sell at a premium over face value. Then we will look two important characteristics that make some bonds very dissimilar from others: default risk and taxes.

TREASURY BILLS

Just as households borrow to buy cars and houses, and businesses borrow to buy buildings and equipment, so the government borrows to buy missiles and paper clips. When the federal government's expenditures exceed its tax revenues, the U.S. Treasury sells securities to raise cash. *Treasury bonds* are securities that have maturities of more than ten years: *Treasury notes* have maturities of one to ten years: and **Treasury bills,** the subject of this section, mature in less than 1 year.

Treasury bills
T-bills are federal government securities with maturities of less than one year.

The Trading of T-Bills

Treasury bills (often called T-bills) are auctioned off by the Treasury in minimum $10,000 denominations. Thirteen-week (91 days) and 26-week (182 days) T-bills are sold every Monday, while 52-week (364 days) T-bills are sold every fourth Thursday. After issuance, T-bills, like all government securities, are traded over the counter.

At each auction, some forty dealers submit bids to the Federal Reserve's New York trading desk, stating the quantity they want and the price they are willing to pay. The Federal Reserve fills these orders, starting with the highest price, until the supply of T-bills is exhausted. (Some dealers end up paying slightly more than others.) Individual investors can buy T-bills at the average price by mailing a certified check for $10,000 or else appearing before 1 PM eastern time at a Federal Reserve Bank or branch with $10,000 in cash or certified check: refunds are distributed once the price is determined. The Treasury Direct system, started in 1986, allows investors to reinvest the proceeds from maturing T-bills automatically with refunds deposited directly in a bank account or money market fund.

There are no periodic interest payments on T-bills. Instead, an investor earns interest by purchasing a T-bill at a discount from the $10,000 face value received when the security matures. For example, if you buy a one-year T-bill for $9400, you receive $10,000 after a year; the return on your investment is the $600 difference between the purchase price and the redemption value of the bill. The IRS considers this $600 return interest, not a capital gain, and taxes it as such, the same as interest on a bank account.

Why T-Bill Rates are Misleading

discount basis
Treasury-bill rates are calculated on a discount basis, relative to face value rather than purchase price.

Unlike virtually all other securities, the financial press traditionally calculates the returns for T-bills on a **discount basis,** calculating the profit as a percentage of the face value rather than the purchase price. If you buy a 52-week T-bill for $9400, the $600 interest is a 6 percent discount from the $10,000 face value, and the T-bill rate is reported conventionally as 6 percent. But from the standpoint of the investor, this is a $600 return on an investment of $9400, not $10,000, and the actual rate of return is $600/$9400 = 0.0638 (or 6.38 percent).

> **Because T-bill rates traditionally are calculated on a discount basis (relative to the maturation value rather than the purchase price), they understate the investor's actual rate of return.**

The federal government does not allow banks to calculate consumer-loan rates on a discount basis but uses this misleading arithmetic on its own borrowing—thereby understating the rate it pays investors. Perhaps the calculation of T-bill rates on a discount basis made sense long ago when computations were done by hand and it was easier to divide by $10,000 than by $9423.19. Today, however, we have computers to do our arithmetic for us, and this anachronism either misleads investors or forces them to do the computations themselves.

Another quaint practice, left over from the days of hand calculations, is to pretend that the year has 360 days. Consider, for instance, a T-bill with 30 days until maturity purchased in the over-the-counter market for $9934.38. The discount is

$$\$10,000 - \$9,934.38 = \$65.62,$$

which, relative to $10,000, is

$$\frac{\$65.62}{\$10,000} = 0.006562 \text{ (or 0.6562 percent)}.$$

Because 30 days is one twelfth of 360 days, the annual rate is reported as

$$12(0.6562 \text{ percent}) = 7.87 \text{ percent.}$$

More generally, if there are n days until maturity and P is the purchase price, the reported T-bill rate is calculated as

$$RT = \left(\frac{360}{n}\right) \frac{(\$10,000 - P)}{\$10,000}. \tag{1}$$

It makes more sense to calculate the return as

$$R = \left(\frac{365}{n}\right) \frac{(\$10,000 - P)}{P}. \tag{2}$$

In our example,

$$R = \left(\frac{365}{30}\right) \frac{(\$10,000 - \$9,934.38)}{\$9,934.38}$$
$$= 0.0804 \text{ (or 8.04 percent).}$$

Many newspapers report the bid and ask prices (at which dealers are willing to buy and sell T-bills) as rates of return calculated on a discount basis using Equation 1; and they also report a more logical yield calculated with the use of Equation 2. For instance, the May 17, 1986, *Los Angeles Times* reported the following data on a T-bill traded the previous day:

Maturity	Bid	Asked	Yield	Bid Ch.
Nov 13 86	6.27	6.25	6.54	+0.11

This T-bill matures on November 13, 1986, which is 180 days beyond May 17. The bid and ask numbers are percentage rates of return calculated on a discount basis, assuming a 360-day year. By manipulating Equation 1,

$$P = \$10,000 - RT(\$10,000)/(360/n)$$

we can determine the following prices:

$$\text{Bid } P = \$10,000 - 0.0627(\$10,000)/(360/180) = \$9,686.50$$
$$\text{Ask } P = \$10,000 - 0.0625(\$10,000)/(360/180) = \$9,687.50$$

(Notice how small the bid-ask spread is in the T-bill market.)

The 6.54 percent yield reported in this newspaper was calculated using Equation 2 with the ask price, which is what you would have to pay to buy this T-bill:

$$R = \left(\frac{365}{180}\right)\frac{(\$10,000 - \$9,687.50)}{\$9,687.50}$$
$$= 0.0654 \text{ (or 6.54 percent)}$$

The bid change shows the change in the bid discount rate, since bid prices apply if you want to sell your T-bill. Because interest rates generally change by only a fraction of a percent each day, financial-market participants use the term **basis points** to describe hundredths of a percentage point. Here, the T-bill rate was up eleven basis points, from 6.16 percent to 6.27 percent.

The yield data reported by some papers are logical and useful for investors who want to compare the returns from T-bills with bank deposits and other investments. Bid and ask *prices* would also be useful. However, it is confusing and potentially misleading to have the bid and ask returns calculated on a discount basis, as are the T-bill rates reported in the *Federal Reserve Bulletin. Economic Report of the President, Statistical Abstract*, and virtually all other sources of historical data. (Each of the Treasury-bill returns graphed in Figures 2–1, 2–2, and 2–3, for example, had to be converted from a discount basis.)

TREASURY AND CORPORATE BONDS

To finance the federal deficit, the U.S. Treasury sells not only short-term T-bills, but also longer-term Treasury notes and bonds. **Corporate bonds** are analogous fixed-income securities of various maturities that are issued by corporations to purchase new plant and equipment, pay current bills, and finance the takeover of other companies. Specific corporate bonds have a number of ever-changing labels, some of which were concocted for marketing purposes. Their different labels are less important than the general characteristics that will be discussed in this chapter.

Unlike T-bills, most bonds make periodic (usually semiannual) interest payments in addition to a final payment when the bond matures. The interest payments on bonds are called **coupons** because, traditionally, they were literally part of the bond certificate, to be clipped with scissors and redeemed through a local bank or security dealer. The final payment when the bond matures is called the *maturity value*, (also, *principal, par value*, and *face value*). Most corporate bonds have maturity values of $1000 or $5000; Treasury bonds have maturity values of $1000 and higher.

coupon
Coupons are the periodic (usually semiannual) interest payments on a bond.

Corporate bonds generally involve a trustee, usually a bank, that handles the payment of interest and principal, and that represents the bondholders as a group in any dispute with the firm, including bankruptcy. The trustee also ensures that the firm complies with any protective covenants that have been written into the indenture agreement to protect bondholders. For example, one covenant might prohibit the firm from selling its assets and distributing the proceeds as an extraordinary dividend to shareholders, leaving bondholders with worthless certificates. Another covenant might restrict the amount of debt that the firm can issue and stipulate that any additional debt must be subordinate (or junior) to the present issue—thus, prohibiting the firm from making payments of interest or principal if it has not satisfied the terms of more senior debt.

Bearer bonds are coupon bonds for which proof of ownership is demonstrated simply by possession of the security. With **registered bonds,** in contrast, the name of the owner is registered with the trustee and payments can be mailed directly to the owner without the physical presentation of the bond certificate. Registered bonds are safer from theft than bearer bonds and reduce the paper shuffling involved with clipping coupons. Since 1983, all Treasury securities have been in registered form.

bearer bonds
A bearer bond's proof of ownership is demonstrated by possession of the security.

registered bonds
Registered bonds are registered with the bond's trustee and the owner receives coupon payments without the physical presentation of the bond certificate.

Call Provisions

Some Treasury bonds and almost all corporate bonds have **call provisions** that allow the issuer to redeem the bond before maturity at a specified price. These provisions give the issuer the opportunity to refinance if interest rates fall, just as a homeowner can benefit by refinancing a home loan if mortgage rates decline. An issuer can choose to call all of the bonds issued or a randomly selected subset. Purchasers of callable bonds typically have some call protection, provisions specifying that the bond cannot be called in the first few years after issuance and that the issuer must pay a premium over face value (analogous to a mortgage's prepayment penalty) if the bond is called. Callable Treasury bonds can be redeemed at face value, typically during the last five to ten years before maturity; a Treasury

call provisions
Call provisions allow the issuer to redeem a bond before maturity at a specified price.

bond with a maturity stated as 2012–2017 matures in the year 2017 and is callable after 2012.

Investors understandably prefer noncallable bonds. If interest rates fall, those investors who have their bonds called will have to reinvest their money at low interest rates, while those with noncallable bonds have locked in higher interest rates. Because a callable bond is less attractive to investors, it must offer a somewhat higher interest rate than a comparable noncallable bond. The size of this rate premium depends on the degree of call protection the bond provides and on investor perceptions of the probability that it will be called.

Sinking Funds

sinking funds
Sinking funds are used to retire a firm's bonds.

Many corporate bonds have provisions for a **sinking fund,** an account into which the issuer is required to deposit a certain amount of money each year in order to redeem some of its bonds, thereby reducing its indebtedness. These bonds can be called by lottery at a specified premium over face value or repurchased in the secondary market if the market price is lower than the call price. Bond issues that are considered risky often use sinking funds to reassure investors that the firm will repay its debt in an orderly fashion and not have to scramble for funds at maturity. But investors should be unsettled by the possibility that their bonds will be called away if interest rates decline.

Bond Trading

Treasury bonds are initially sold, like Treasury bills, at public auctions and then traded over the counter. Corporate-bond issues that are sold to the public must be registered with the Securities and Exchange Commission and must include an indenture agreement, which specifies the various terms of the bond issue in precise legal detail that can fill hundreds of pages. Publicly issued corporate bonds are marketed by investment bankers and then traded either over the counter or, to a limited extent, on the stock exchanges. Bond transactions on the New York Stock Exchange (NYSE) are handled by designated specialists in a small room off the main trading floor.

private placement
Privately placed securities are sold by investment bankers to small groups at a negotiated price.

About half of all corporate debt is issued privately, either term loans from banks and insurance companies or **private placements**—bond sales arranged by investment bankers in which fewer than thirty-five investors (typically pension funds and life insurance companies) purchase all of a bond issue at a negotiated price. Bonds acquired through a private placement cannot be resold for at least two years. Private placements have relatively low underwriting and administrative expenses offerings, particularly for small issues. Private placements also tend to have stronger restrictive covenants; but, in cases of financial distress, it is easier to renegotiate a bond's terms with a few investors than with hundreds or thousands of bondholders. Overall, the interest rates on privately placed bonds average about a half percentage point above the rates on comparable public issues.[1]

YIELD CALCULATIONS

The rate of return on a Treasury bill held to maturity depends on a relatively straightforward comparison of the purchase price with the $10,000 received when the bill matures. Bonds are more complex because there are coupons in addition to the maturation value that must be considered in determining rate of return. To illustrate the logic, we'll use these May 17, 1986, data for four corporate bonds traded on the NYSE, as reported in the *Los Angeles Times:*

Bond		Current Yield	Close	Chg.
AT&T	3⅞s90	4.4	89	−¼
IBM	9⅜ 04	9.1	102½	−⅜
IBM	10¼ 95	9.3	110	−2
Navstr	9s04	11.0	81⅞	+⅞

Each of these bonds was issued by a large corporation: AT&T, IBM, and Navistar. The first number after the company's name gives the **coupon rate,** the annual stated coupon as a percentage of the bond's face value. For a $1000 AT&T bond, the annual coupon is 3⅞ percent of $1000 = $38.75, paid in two semiannual installments of $38.75/2 = $19.375. Similarly, the $1000 Navistar bond pays $45.00 every six months. The next number in the table is the year the bond matures, 1990 for AT&T, 2004 and 1995 for the two IBM bonds, and 2004 for the Navistar bond. You must consult a dealer or a bond fact book to find the exact payment dates for the coupons and maturation value. (The *s* that sometimes appears between the coupon rate and maturation date is inserted for stylistic purposes, to help separate two numbers or because the natural pronunciation of the coupon rate includes an *s*.)

Bond prices are quoted as a percentage of the bond's face value; for example, if a bond with a face value of $10,000 sells for $9,900, then its price is reported as 99, meaning 99 percent of its face value. The AT&T bond reported above had a closing price of 89, down ¼ from the day before; for a bond with $10,000 face value, this translates to a price equal to 89 percent of $10,000 = $8900, down from $8925. While corporate bond prices use fractions such as ½ and ⅞, Treasury bond prices are reported as decimals, with the numbers to the right of decimal point representing 32nds of a point; thus a reported price of 99.11 signifies a price equal to 99¹¹⁄₃₂ of face value. In addition to the quoted price, a bond buyer must also pay the seller a proportionate share of the next coupon payment; for example, if a bond is bought five months after the last coupon and one month before the next, the buyer must pay the seller an amount equal to five-sixths of the next coupon.

It is striking that the Navistar bond, which pays virtually the same coupons, and matures in the same year as the first IBM bond, sells for 20 percent less. Similarly, we might wonder why the AT&T bond is relatively inexpensive and why one IBM bond sells for less than the other. We will answer these questions in this chapter and the next.

The current yield shown in the table is the annual coupon, stated as a percentage of the current price. Thus, $3\frac{7}{8}$ is 4.4 percent of 89, or

$$\frac{3\frac{7}{8}}{89} = 0.044.$$

The 4.4 percent yield is not a very informative statistic. It is true that if you purchase a $100 AT&T bond for $890, the annual $38.75 coupon represents a 4 percent on your $890 investment. But this calculation ignores the face that you are going to make another $110 profit when the bond matures in 1990 and pays you $1000. A complete accounting of your return must take into consideration both coupons and maturation value.

Yield to Maturity

yield to maturity
A bond's yield to maturity is that discount rate such that the present value of the bond's coupons and maturation value is equal to its price.

Logically, the price investors are willing to pay for a bond is the present value of the cash flow—that is, the coupons and maturation value discounted by a required rate of return. Conversely, the **yield to maturity** on a bond is defined as that discount rate such that the present value of the coupons and the maturation value is equal to the price. We will use the following notation:

P = Bond price

C = Semiannual coupons

n = Number of years until maturity

M = Maturation, or face value

y = Annual yield to maturity

The yield to maturity y is given by

$$P = \frac{C}{\left(1 + \frac{y}{2}\right)} + \frac{C}{\left(1 + \frac{y}{2}\right)^2} + \ldots + \frac{C}{\left(1 + \frac{y}{2}\right)^{2n}} + \frac{M}{\left(1 + \frac{y}{2}\right)^{2n}} \qquad (3)$$

TABLE 4–1   Prices and Yields of Four Bonds on May 17, 1986

Bond	Current Yield	Closing Price	Yield to Maturity (percent)
AT&T 3⅞ 90	4.4	89	7.1
IBM 9⅜ 04	9.1	102½	9.1
IBM 10¼ 95	9.3	110	8.6
Navstr 9 04	11.0	81⅞	11.4

(Notice that because the coupons are paid semiannually, the annual discount rate y is divided by 2, and the number of periods is $2n$.) Since we know P, C, and M, we can solve Equation 3 for the yield to maturity y by using a financial calculator or computer program that, by trial and error, tries different tentative values of y until the right-hand side of Equation 3 is approximately equal to the price.

For the AT&T bond discussed above,

P = $890

C = $19.375

n = 4

M = $1000

and the appropriate present-value equation is

$$\$890 = \frac{\$19.375}{\left(1 + \frac{y}{2}\right)} + \ldots + \frac{\$19.375}{\left(1 + \frac{y}{2}\right)^8} + \frac{\$1000}{\left(1 + \frac{y}{2}\right)^8}$$

The solution is $y/2 = 0.0354$, or $y = 2(0.0354) = 0.0708$, rounded off to 7.1 percent. Table 4–1 shows the yields to maturity for all four of the bonds discussed earlier. The puzzles to be explained here and in the next chapter are why the Navistar bond is priced to have such a high yield to maturity and why there are variations among the other three bonds, two of which are issued by the same company.

Yield to Call

If the market price of a callable bond is above its call price, then it is unrealistic to count on holding the bond until maturity. In place of the yield to maturity, many investors instead calculate the more conservative **yield to call,** which assumes that the bond will be called at the first opportunity. To do so, Equation 3 is used, replacing the number of years until maturity n with the number of years until the first call date and replacing the maturation value M with the call price.

Consider, for example, a 20-year bond with a 12% coupon and a market price of 115, which is callable in 5 years at a call price of 105. The yield to maturity is given by solving Equation 3 with $P = 115$, $C = 12/2 = 6$, $n = 20$, and $M = 100$:

$$115 = \frac{6}{\left(1 + \frac{y}{2}\right)} + \frac{6}{\left(1 + \frac{y}{2}\right)^2} + \ldots + \frac{6}{\left(1 + \frac{y}{2}\right)^{40}} + \frac{100}{\left(1 + \frac{y}{2}\right)^{40}}$$

The yield to maturity works out to be 10.22 percent. Because of its generous 12% annual coupon, this bond sells for a premium above its face value. But investors will not receive this 12% coupon for 20 years if the bond is called before maturity. To compute the yield to call, we assume that the bond will, in fact, be called after 5 years at a price of 105. Thus we replace $n = 20$ with $n = 5$ and replace $M = 100$ with $M = 105$:

$$115 = \frac{6}{\left(1 + \frac{y}{2}\right)} + \frac{6}{\left(1 + \frac{y}{2}\right)^2} + \ldots + \frac{6}{\left(1 + \frac{y}{2}\right)^{10}} + \frac{105}{\left(1 + \frac{y}{2}\right)^{10}}$$

The yield to call turns out to be 9.02 percent, which is 1.20 percentage points lower than the yield to maturity.

Yield to Maturity Versus Price and Coupon Rate

When members of the financial press refer to *interest rates*, they usually mean yields to maturity, and we will use the same language. The yield to maturity is that discount rate for which the present value of the coupons and principal are equal to the price of the bond. Equation 3 shows mathematically the inherent inverse relationship between a bond's yield and price. Bonds have a fixed cash flow and the higher is the required return used to discount this cash flow, the lower is the present value. To put it somewhat differently, because the cash flow is fixed, the only way investors can get a higher return, if they require it, is if the price is lower.

> **Bond prices fall when interest rates (yields to maturity) increase and rise when interest rates decline.**

Thus, whenever the front page of the daily newspaper reports that interest rates have increased, the financial pages report a drop in bond prices.

People are sometimes puzzled by the fact that a drop in the price raises the yield. Don't investors lose money when the price falls? The answer lies in the distinction between *ex ante* (before) and *ex post* (after). The price falls so that, for those who buy at the new price, the future cash flow provides the requisite higher yield. Investors who bought before the price fell experience a capital loss—a loss that is no doubt unexpected, since they would have sold yesterday if they had known the price would be lower today.

Even experienced investors sometimes comfort themselves with the argument that such losses are not real, merely paper losses, as long as they do not sell their bonds. They rationalize that they can continue to collect their coupons and maturation value, the very same cash flow previously anticipated. Nevertheless, they have lost, in the same sense that any investor loses when the market value of an asset plummets. If they want to sell, they could have sold yesterday for more than they can get today. If they are content to hold, they should regret the fact that higher interest rates have reduced the price of the cash flow they purchased, just as someone who buys a television set regrets learning that is it now on sale.

The inverse relationship between a bond's price and its yield to maturity has an important corollary. Notice that the first IBM bond in Table 4–1 has a price (102½) that is close to its face value (100) and a yield to maturity (9.1 percent) that is close to its coupon rate (9⅜). The second IBM bond, on the other hand, has a price above its face value and a yield to maturity below its coupon rate, while the AT&T and Navistar bonds have prices below face value and yields to maturity above their coupon rates. This is no accident.

> **When the yield to maturity is equal to the coupon rate, the price of a bond is equal to its face value. A bond sells for a premium above its face value when the yield is below the coupon rate, and at a discount when the yield is above the coupon rate.**

For the economic logic, think of the first IBM bond with its coupon rate and yield to maturity of approximately 9 percent. If you put $1000 in the bank for eighteen years at 9 percent compounded semiannually, you could collect $45 in interest every six months and then withdraw your $1000 at the end of eighteen years. That is effectively what you are doing by purchasing this IBM bond with a yield equal to the coupon rate. And because the price is inversely related to the yield, it follows that a bond's price is above or below face value, depending on whether the yield to maturity is smaller or larger than the coupon rate.

When a bond is first issued, the coupon rate is usually set close to the prevailing yield to maturity on similar bonds, so that the bond will sell for close to face value. If interest rates then fall, the bond's price will rise above its face value. If interest rates instead rise, the bond will sell for a discount from face value: for example, the AT&T bond in Table 4–1 was issued back in 1956, when interest rates were about 4 percent, and sold for a discount in 1986 when it was priced to yield 7 percent.

TABLE 4–2   Effect of Semiannual Compounding on Bond Yields

Stated Yield, y (percent)	Effective Yield, R (percent)
6	6.09
8	8.16
10	10.25
12	12.36
14	14.49

Effective Yields

Equation 3 follows the conventional practice of dividing the annual yield by 2 to obtain the semiannual discount rate; but, as with any investment, semiannual compounding increases the effective annual yield. The effective yield to maturity on a bond with semiannual coupons is the value of R given by

$$(1 + R) = \left(1 + \frac{y}{2}\right)^2. \tag{4}$$

Some sample calculations are shown in Table 4–2. Investors should compare R, not y, to the effective yields offered on bank deposits.

Realized Return

It is tempting to interpret a bond's yield to maturity as the investor's rate of return if the bond is held until maturity. But the investor's overall return depends critically on the rate of interest that the investor is able to earn on the coupons received and reinvested before maturity. To illustrate this point, consider a two-year $1000 bond selling for par that pays 10 percent coupons *annually*. Since it sells for par, it has a yield to maturity equal to its coupon rate, 10 percent. The investor buys the bond for $1000 and receives one coupon of $100 after one year and a second coupon of $100 plus the $1000 maturation value after two years. If the investor is able to invest the first coupon at 10% for a year, then this will grow to $110 by the end of the second year and the total value of the investment will be:

Reinvested first-year coupon	$ 110
Second-year coupon	100
Maturation value	1000
Total future value of investment	$1210

The investor's overall return on this investment requires a comparison of this future value with the initial cost of the bond. In particular, the **realized rate of return** on an investment is the rate of return that, applied to the initial cost, gives a future value that is just equal to the actual future value of the investment including the proceeds from the reinvestment of the cash flow, if any. If P is the initial cost of the investment and F is the future value after n years, then the realized rate of return R is given by

$$P(1 + R)^n = F$$

Here, the initial \$1000 investment has grown to \$2210 after two years, and the realized rate of return R is determined by

$$\$1000(1 + R)^2 = \$2210$$

In this case, the realized return R is 10 percent, exactly equal to the bond's yield to maturity. But it immediately follows that if the reinvested coupon earns more (or less) than 10 percent, then the total future value will be more (or less) than \$1210 and the investor's realized rate of return will be larger (or smaller) than 10 percent. This illustrates the general point:

The realized rate of return on a bond held until maturity is larger or smaller than its calculated yield to maturity, depending on whether the coupons are reinvested to earn a rate of return that is larger or smaller than this yield to maturity.

For another example, consider a 20-year bond selling for par with 8 percent coupons, paid semi-annually. The realized rate of return on this bond will not be equal to its 8 percent yield to maturity unless the coupons can be reinvested to earn an 8 percent rate of return. The following table illustrates how the reinvestment rate pulls the investor's realized return above or below the calculated yield to maturity.

Interest Rate on Reinvested Coupons (percent)	Realized Rate of Return on Bond (percent)
12	10.11
10	9.01
8	8.00
6	7.07
4	6.24

realized rate of return
The realized rate of return compares the initial cost with the future value, including the proceeds from the reinvestment of the cash flow.

DEFAULT RISK

Why were investors content with a 9.1 percent yield from IBM in May 1986 when they could get 11.4 percent from Navistar? These 9.1 percent and 11.4 percent yields are the *promised* returns if the coupons and principal are paid as scheduled. If the company doesn't pay or delays the payments, the *actual* return may turn out to be far below what was promised. In 1986 investors were more confident of IBM's promises than they were of Navistar's.

Those who borrow money are not always able to pay back their loans plus interest. Individual borrowers may lose their jobs, firms may lose customers, and state and local governments may lose their tax base. Only the federal government is absolutely certain of always having enough money to repay its debt—because the Treasury and the Federal Reserve can literally print money.

default
A borrower defaults
when the terms of the
debt contract are
violated.

Borrowers **default** when they don't pay what was promised when it was promised. A default is not necessarily a complete loss for an investor; it may represent merely a temporary suspension of coupon payments or a prelude to a partial payment. In the first month after default, a bond typically trades at about 40 percent of its face value.[2]

Defaults are infrequent because likely defaulters are not able to issue bonds in the first place. Nevertheless, even among relatively safe bonds, some appear safer than others. In addition, unexpected financial difficulties several years down the road can turn an initially safe bond into a nightmare. Penn Central, Chrysler, Lockheed, New York City, and Texaco were all safe investments, until the unexpected happened.

Professional rating agencies such as Moody's and Standard & Poor's monitor the financial condition of bond issuers and assign the quality ratings summarized in Table 4–3 on p. 113. Finer gradations are made within the categories Aa (or AA) to B, with Moody's using the numbers 1, 2, and 3 and Standard & Poor's the symbols + and −.

Treasury securities are not rated, because the chances of default are negligible. Corporate bonds along with state- and local-government bonds are rated because, as many investors have learned painfully, they can and do default. Unfortunately, many municipalities do not provide enough information to gauge their financial condition accurately. In 1980, the SEC concluded that "the market for municipal securities provides investors with only limited protection compared with corporate, [federal] government or other issuers." A Harvard Business School professor wrote in 1985, "Within wide limits, government accounting rules permit accountants to play games that lead to whatever bottom line the mayor or governor wants," usually a small surplus so that voters will neither be upset by a deficit nor demand lower taxes.[3]

Standard & Poor's estimated that about half of the state and local governments issuing bonds in 1980 did not comply with generally accepted accounting principles. Most only reported current expenditures and rev-

TABLE 4–3   Bond Ratings of Two Professional Rating Agencies

Moody's		Standard & Poor's	
Aaa	Best quality	AAA	Highest rating
Aa	High quality	AA	Very strong
A	Upper medium grade	A	Strong
Baa	Medium grade	BBB	Adequate
Ba	Speculative elements	BB	Somewhat speculative
B	Lack characteristics of desirable investment	B	Speculative
Caa	Poor standing; may be in default	CCC–CC	Highly speculative
Ca	Speculative in a high degree; may be in default	C	Income bonds with no interest being paid
C	Lowest rated class; extremely poor prospects	D	In default

Source: Moody's Bond Record, October 1988; *Standard & Poor's Bond Guide,* October 1988.

TABLE 4–4   Selected Corporate Bond Ratings, 1989

Rating	Corporate Bond Issuers
AAA	Exxon, General Electric, IBM
AA	AT&T, Citicorp, Sears
A	Teledyne, Merrill Lynch, Xerox
BBB	Chrysler, Manufacturers Hanover, Texas Power & Light

Source: Standard & Poor's Bond Guide, April 1989.

enues and ignored anticipated revenue and spending commitments. Many habitually omit important information, and most do not submit to independent audits. Standard & Poor's has since gone so far as to threaten to stop rating the bonds of municipalities that ignore sound accounting practices.

Corporate borrowers provide better information and are rated more confidently by Standard & Poor's and Moody's. Those bonds placed in the first four rating categories are considered investment grade, and historically, about 90 percent of all rated corporate issues are placed initially in the first three categories. (This does not mean that 90 percent of all corporations are this financially sound, only that less secure companies do not issue many bonds.) Table 4–4 shows some examples of corporate ratings in 1989. Those bonds rated outside of the first four categories are somewhat speculative and considered imprudent investments by many institutional investors. Investment Example 4–1 on pp. 114–115 discusses the market for poor-quality bonds.

JUNK BONDS

Junk is the generic label for low-quality bonds—unrated bonds or low-rated bonds issued by companies that are either not well known or else known to be risky. Some of these bonds are new junk, sold to finance risky ventures; and some are fallen angels, bonds issued by companies that once were financially secure and now are not. In the past, most investors wouldn't touch junk; this was particularly true of mutual funds, pension funds, and other institutional investors who feared lawsuits if they breached their fiduciary duties with imprudent investments.

Then, according to popular legend, Mike Milken, a student at the University of Pennsylvania, decided that this aversion to junk bonds was excessive. Most companies whose bonds were low rated or unrated were not on the verge of default. Some were experiencing temporary financial difficulty; many were just unknown or did not have a lot of tangible assets. According to Milken's calculations, the occasional default was more than offset by the fact that the bonds' prices were very low and the promised returns were high. Milken joined a small securities firm, Drexel Burnham, and made his argument over and over to anyone who would listen, selling junk bonds to those he persuaded.

Once Milken found junk buyers, more sellers appeared. A takeover wave hit the United States in the 1980s, as corporate raiders acquired companies that appeared to have grown large and lazy and then resold them, often in parts, to those who thought they were better managers. Sometimes, a company's managers borrowed money to buy up the shareholder's stock—a leveraged buyout that converted the firm from a public corporation to a private business. These raiders, external or internal, need financing. Few investors have enough funds to buy billion-dollar companies. Instead, they can finance their takeovers by issuing junk bonds, implicitly using the assets of the target company as collateral.

With willing buyers and sellers, Milken thus created a junk-bond market, with Drexel Burnham acting as the middleman. Those businesses that want to issue junk can come to Drexel, which has established a long list of buyers; those investors who want high potential returns know that Drexel is a place to buy junk bonds. But there is more to it than that. Drexel does not just know the names of buyers and sellers; it has their confidence. With traditional investment-grade bonds, the ratings by Moody's and other services give a stamp of approval that facilitates trading: The seller of a triple-A bond knows that there are plenty of buyers; the buyers know from the independent ratings that they are buying quality securities. The same is not true for junk bonds. By definition, junk bonds have not been certified as safe investments by independent rating services. Junk buyers are relying on the knowledge and reputation of Drexel (or whoever the middleman might be) that this bond is a chance well worth taking. Issuers count on the middleman's reputation, too, to ensure that all their bonds will be sold quickly, at less than exorbitant interest rates.

Junk buyers are also interested in the possibility of reselling their bonds in the future, and, here again, a secondary market requires a middleman who knows the players and has their confidence. By 1988 there was some $160 billion worth of actively traded

Type of Security	Promised Yield (percent)	Actual Return (percent)
Government bonds	10.80	12.25
Low-rated junk	14.54	13.24

Source: Edward I. Altman, "The Anatomy of the High-Yield Bond Market," *Financial Analysts Journal,* July/August 1987, pp. 12–25.

junk bonds, with more than half of the trading through Drexel. Mike Milken was at the core of this market, with first-hand knowledge of most of the buyers and sellers, and has an ability to recite the terms of every single junk bond in the country. Under him were 150 traders who worked twelve to fifteen hours a day, beginning at 4:30 in the morning. Junk bonds turned Drexel into a major securities firm and now provides it with some $2 billion a year in revenue. Milkin's 1987 salary and bonus was reportedly $550 million, and he became a billionaire in 1988 at age 42. However, as you will see in Chapter 11, Drexel was accused of a variety of securities fraud charges in 1988 and agreed to plead guilty to six felonies, pay $650 million in penalties and accept Milkin's resignation. Milkin was separately indicted for 98 counts of racketeering, with the outcome still unknown.

Junk bonds are generally priced to yield 4 to 6 percentage points more than less speculative securities and so far, on average, some 2 percent of all junk bonds have defaulted each year. The accompanying table compares the average promised yields to maturity and actual realized returns (coupons plus capital gains) from junk bonds and long-term government securities during the years of 1978–86. However, these low default rates are

somewhat misleading. Because of the extremely rapid growth of the junk bond market, the overwhelming majority of junk bonds have been issued very recently and relatively few defaults occur during the first few years after issuance. Perhaps only 2 percent of the bonds defaulted this year because 98 percent were issued in the last six months. In 1988, a study by Paul Asquith, David Mullins, and Eric Wolf calculated cumulative default rates for junk bonds of various ages.[1] They found that 34 percent of the junk bonds issued in 1977 and 1978 and 23 percent of those issued between 1979 and 1983 had defaulted by 1988. In addition, the years 1982 to 1988 were recession free. Many observers worry that junk is being used to finance increasingly dubious ventures, gambles that will collapse when a recession does come. In October 1988, a senior partner of a prominent investment firm that had acquired several corporations without using junk wrote, "Surely, when the history books are written, the reason so many investors bought these bonds will be the financial riddle of our age."[2]

[1] Matthew Winkler, "Junk Bonds Are Taking Their Lumps," *Wall Street Journal,* April 14, 1989.
[2] Theodore J. Forstmann, "Violating Our Rules of Prudence," *Wall Street Journal,* October 25, 1988.

Financial Ratios and Bond Ratings

How do Moody's and Standard & Poor's decide the appropriate rating for a company's bonds? They conduct a quantitative evaluation of its current and past financial condition and make a subjective assessment of the firm's future. The key question in their analysis is: will this firm have enough profits (and, in particular, enough cash flow) to meet the mandated payments on its debts? Among the data examined are the four financial ratios shown in Table 4–5 on p. 117, the numbers showing average values for seven Standard & Poor's ratings categories.

The *pre-tax fixed charge coverage ratio* is the ratio of profits (before taxes and interest payments) to bond payments, lease payments, and other non-discretionary expenses. Pre-tax profits are used because interest payments are tax deductible; if a firm has $1 million of pre-tax profits and $1 million of interest to pay, it can pay this interest because it owes no taxes. If this pre-tax fixed-charge ratio is less than one, the firm is having trouble making ends meet. For the most highly rated firms, profits are many times more than enough to cover mandated expenses.

Of course, the profit calculations of sometimes creative accountants do not ensure that sufficient dollars really are on hand to meet expenses. Cash flow measures the money actually coming into the firm, and the *cash flow to debt ratio* (or, more relevantly, a comparison of this ratio with the interest rate on this debt) gauges the adequacy of the cash flow. The most highly rated firms have both high profits and a generous cash flow relative to interest expenses and other fixed charges.

The *pre-tax return on long-term capital ratio* is a measure of the firm's basic profitability: a firm that doesn't make money is not economically healthy.

The *long-term debt to capitalization ratio* is the ratio of the firm's long-term debt to the sum of its short-term debt, long-term debt, and stock—essentially the total value of the firm, because those who own its debt and stock receive all the money (interest and dividends) paid out by the firm. If the value of these debt and stock claims is approximately equal to the value of the firm's assets, then the liquidation of an AAA-rated firm with a 0.12 ratio would yield eight times the amount of money needed to retire its long-term debt.

Risk and Promised Return

Calculated yields to maturity use market prices of bonds and promised cash flow, promises that may or may not be kept. The larger is the probability that a firm will default, the lower is the market prices of its bonds, and the higher is the computed yield to maturity. Thus, bonds from IBM and Navistar with very similar coupons and maturation dates sold for very different prices in May 1986.

IBM bonds had Standard and Poor's highest rating (AAA) while Na-

TABLE 4–5 Four Financial Ratios Used to Judge Financial Condition

Rating Category	Pre-Tax Fixed-Charge Coverage	Cash Flow To Total Debt	Pre-Tax Return on Long-Term Capital (percent)	Long-Term Debt to Capitalization
AAA	6.05	0.48	23.8	0.12
AA	4.68	0.32	21.9	0.19
A	2.97	0.13	17.9	0.28
BBB	2.32	0.07	12.4	0.34
BB	1.74	−0.01	11.5	0.48
B	1.45	−0.06	10.6	0.57
CCC	0.12	−0.02	−2.2	0.73

Source: Standard & Poor's Corp., *CreditWeek*, September 5, 1988.

TABLE 4–6 Yield to Maturity by Rating Category, May 1986

Rating Category	Yield to Maturity (percent)
AAA	9.19
AA	9.51
A	9.75
BBB	10.32

Source: Standard & Poor's Guide, January 1987.

vistar bonds were rated a speculative B. Under its former name, International Harvester, Navistar lost staggering amounts of money for five straight years, from 1980 through 1985, and by the end of 1985 had a total long-term debt of $888 million as compared to a net worth of $42 million, calculated by subtracting its debts from its assets. Its long-term-debt-to-capitalization ratio was nearly 1.0, and one more bad year would push its net worth into the red.

Thus, nervous investors paid only 81⅞ for Navistar's bonds but were willing to spend 102½ for similar promises from IBM, giving Navistar a 11.4 percent calculated yield to maturity and IBM just 9.1 percent. These yields are consistent with the May 1986 average yields to maturity by rating category that are shown in Table 4–6.

When a bond's rating changes, so do its price and promised yield to maturity. For instance, as a company's financial difficulties mount and its chances of bankruptcy grow, Moody's and Standard & Poor's downgrade

TABLE 4–7 Corporate Defaults by Rating Category, 1900–1943

Initial Rating (composite of rating agencies)	Promised Yield to Maturity	Fraction Defaulted (percent of par value)	Actual Yield to Maturity
1 (highest)	4.5	5.9	5.1
2	4.6	6.0	5.0
3	4.9	13.4	5.0
4	5.4	19.1	5.7
5–9 (lowest)	9.5	42.4	8.6

Source: W. Braddock Hickman, *Corporate Bond Quality and Investor Experience* (New York: National Bureau of Economic Research, 1958).

the bond while its price slips in financial markets. There is some evidence that investors see changes in the financial condition of firms before the rating agencies do. One study found that bond prices reflect changing default conditions a full six to eighteen months before subsequent rating changes, and that the rating changes themselves (being so late) have no perceptible effect on bond prices.[4]

Realized Returns

W. B. Hickman made an exhaustive study of the corporate bonds issued between 1900 and 1943. Some of his findings are summarized in Table 4–7. First, notice that the promised yields to maturity (assuming coupon and maturation value will be paid as promised) are higher the lower is the bond's rating. Second, notice the striking correlation between a bond's initial quality rating and its chances of eventual default. The overall fractions of these bonds that actually defaulted were pretty high, because the Great Depression brought down so many firms in the 1930s. Since World War II, very few firms in the top three rating categories have defaulted.

The fourth column in Table 4–7 shows the actual yields, taking into account that defaulting companies did not pay all that they had promised. The realized yields are virtually identical for the first three rating categories and rise somewhat for the last two. One complication with these data is that the substantial drop in interest rates in the 1930s made it profitable for many firms to exercise the call provisions in their bonds, by paying bondholders a premium over the bond's face value (but a discount from the current market price). Hickman's data include these call payments, which push the actual yields above the promised yields for the first four rating categories. Two other authors redid Hickman's calculations for the first four rating categories—this time assuming that no bonds had not been called, so as to focus solely on how defaults affected yields. They found that the actual yields, taking into account defaults, were the same, 4.3

percent, in each category—the higher promised yields just offsetting the higher chances of default.[5]

Matters have turned out differently since World War II. There have been so few defaults that low-rated, high-yielding bonds have outperformed more highly rated bonds. This does not mean that, at present, AA bonds are a better investment than AAA and that junk bonds are better still; it only means that risky bonds are priced to take into account their susceptibility to default during bad times, and times, as it turns out, have been relatively good since World War II.

ZERO-COUPON BONDS

A zero-coupon bond (zero) differs from ordinary bonds because, as the name implies, it pays no coupons; as with T-bills; the buyer receives a single, lump-sum payment at maturity. J. C. Penney issued a corporate zero in 1981, and a year later a number of brokerage firms began marketing zeros created from coupon-paying Treasury bonds. Merrill Lynch introduced its version of zeros—Treasury Investment Growth Receipts (Tigers, for short)—in 1982 by purchasing a pool of $500 million in long-term Treasury bonds. Merrill Lynch then placed these Treasury bonds in a trust and created a series of zeros maturing at six-month intervals by "stripping" away the coupons. For example, a twenty-year bond paying $5000 semi-annual coupons and $100,000 at maturity can be separated into forty $5000 zeros, with maturities ranging from six months to twenty years, and one twenty-year $100,000 zero. These zeros can be split into smaller denominations or combined with pieces of other bonds to give larger zeros. Salomon Brothers sells similar zeros, labeled Certificates of Accrual on Treasury Securities (Cats), and other firms use other labels. Encouraged by their success, the U.S. Treasury now strips it own bonds and sells zeros too; their name is less colorful though accurate: Separate Trading of Registered Interest and Principal of Securities (STRIPS).

> **zero-coupon bonds**
> Zeros pay no coupons; as with T-bills, the buyer receives a single, lump-sum payment at maturity.

The implicit annual rate of return R on a zero costing P that pays an amount F in n years is given by the following compound-interest formula:

$$P(1 + R)^n = F$$

For instance, a $10,000 Tiger purchased in 1984 will pay $300,000 in 2014. These data

$$\$10,000(1 + R)^{30} = \$300,000$$
$$(1 + R)^{30} = 30$$

imply

$$R = 0.12 \text{ (or 12 percent)}.$$

PREPAID TUITION PLANS

In 1985, Duquesne University introduced a novel way to prepay college expenses, an idea that has since been imitated by dozens of other colleges and universities. By making a single $5700 payment in 1985, parents could buy four years of tuition payments for a child enrolling at Duquesne fourteen years later, in 1999.

Prepaid tuition is very similar to a zero-coupon bond; but the maturation value, Duquesne's tuition in 1999, is uncertain. In 1985, tuition was $5850 and Duquesne officials assumed that it would increase by 6 percent a year, to

$$\$5850(1.06^{14}) = \$13,226$$

in 1999. They then simply multiplied by 4 to obtain a four-year figure of $4(\$13,226) = \$52,905$.

How much should the university charge for this future value? Duquesne treated the $52,905 payoff as a zero-coupon bond with a 17.25 percent annual return and calculated the cost X from

$$X(1 + 0.1725)^{14} = \$52,905,$$

implying that

$$X = \$5700,$$

which is what the university charged parents for prepaid tuition.

In fact, Duquesne invested each $5700 payment that it received in 11 percent zero-coupon bonds maturing in 1999 with a payoff of

$$\$5850(1.11^{14}) = \$25,216.$$

Thus, Duquesne's future receipt was only about half their own estimated future cost of tuition. From the parents' standpoint, they were implicitly credited with a 17.25 percent annual return on their investment, when market returns were only 11 percent.

Many investors appreciate the simplicity of zero-coupon bonds and the fact that they don't have to worry about reinvesting future coupons at uncertain interest rates. But, as we will see in the next chapter, zero-coupon bonds are hardly worry free. Investment Example 4–2 discusses a recent variation on the zero-coupon concept.

Although zero-coupon bonds do not pay any interest until maturity, the investor must pay taxes each year as if interest had been paid. For tax purposes, the value of the investment is assumed to increase each year at the implicit rate of return R, and taxes are levied on this implicit income. In the first year, taxes are paid on the implicit interest RP, and the adjusted cost basis is increased from P to $P(1 + R)$. In the second year, taxes are paid on $RP(1 + R)$ and the basis is raised to $P(1 + R)^2$. This procedure continues until maturity. With this tax accounting, the implicit after-tax yield to maturity (the discount rate that equates the present value of the

Rate of Growth of Tuition (percent)	Total Four-Year Tuition in 1999	1985 Cost of Zero-Coupon Bond at 17.25 Percent
4	$40,521	$4,366
6	52,905	5,700
8	68,730	7,406
10	88,861	9,575

There were a number of uncertainties with this program. One uncertainty was the tax status, which is still not resolved. Another was the actual rate of growth of tuition, as illustrated in the accompanying table. The third important uncertainty was whether the child, then three years old, would be accepted and want to attend Duquesne fourteen years later. Under Duquesne's plan, if the child decided not to attend, the parents would get only their $5700 investment back, with no interest at all. The parents' alternatives were to invest $5700 at 11 percent on their own, which would give $25,216 in cash to spend as they wish, or to invest $5700 in Duquesne's prepayment plan—which would give $5700 if the child did not attend Duquesne or free tuition, worth some $40,000 to $90,000, if the child did attend the university for four years. The plan was initially marketed only to Duquesne alumni, and about 500 signed up.

During the subsequent three years, interest rates declined, and Duquesne also raised its estimated tuition growth rate to 8 percent. Together, these events boosted the parents' prepayment to $25,300 in 1988, prompting the school to suspend the plan until the cost could be improved significantly.

cash flow to the purchase price) is exactly equal to $(1 - t)R$, where t is the investor's marginal tax rate. For example, in a 28 percent tax bracket, the implicit after-tax yield is $(1 - 0.28)12$ percent $= 8.64$ percent.

TAX-EXEMPT BONDS

Interest on bonds issued by state and local governments is generally exempt from federal income taxes, while interest on U.S. Treasury securities is not subject to state and local taxes. Because federal income taxes are the more substantial of the two, state and local government bonds are usually called **tax-exempt bonds.** They are also known as *municipals,* and *munis.*

Most states that have income taxes do not tax interest on their own bonds, making these bonds double tax-exempt; for example, Californians

122

INVESTMENT
EXAMPLE
4–3

WHOOPS—A DISAPPOINTMENT FOR INVESTORS

Municipal-bond defaults have been infrequent, and usually involve the postponement of payments—particularly with revenue bonds, where the project financed by the bond may take longer than expected to earn sufficient revenue. For instance, some West Virginia Turnpike bonds issued in 1952 were in default for twenty years before enough toll revenue finally accumulated to pay off the bonds.*

In 1975, the municipal-bond market was rocked by New York City's financial troubles. With a weak economy and a shrinking tax base, the city declared a moratorium on some $2.4 billion in short-term notes. After the courts ruled this action unconstitutional, the city found ways to pay its bondholders, though the principal payments were delayed for up to two years and only 6 percent interest was credited during this delay.

In 1983, it was the Washington Public Power Supply System (WPPSS), widely known by the ironic

*Lynn Asinof, "Possible Effects of a WPSS Bond Failure are Visible in Past U.S. Municipal Bond Defaults," *Wall Street Journal*, July 13, 1983.

lable Whoops, that disappointed investors. A consortium of nearly 100 public utilities in the Pacific Northwest established WPPSS to sell $8.4 billion in municipal revenue bonds to finance the construction of five nuclear power plants, with the income from the plants used to pay off the bonds. These public power agencies backed the bonds by signing take-or-pay (also known as come-hell-or-high-water) contracts, agreeing to pay for specified amounts of electricity at set prices regardless of whether or not the power was actually delivered.

Construction costs turned out to be much higher than originally estimated and the region's demand for electricity much lower. Two of the plants (Projects 4 and 5) were terminated in January 1982 after spending almost all of the $2.25 billion raised by bond sales to finance their construction. Projects 1 and 3 were later suspended semipermanently, leaving only Project 2 producing any electricity. WPPSS stopped making payments on its Project 4 and Project 5 bonds in January 1983 and formally defaulted on them later that year, after the Washington State Supreme Court ruled that the public utilities had no authority to sign take-or-pay

who buy bonds issued by the state of California do not have to pay state or federal income taxes on the interest. New York City levies a city income tax, making its bonds triple tax-exempt for residents.

There are two primary kinds of state and local securities: general-obligation bonds and revenue bonds. *General-obligation bonds* are backed by the full faith and credit of the issuer and, more importantly, by its ability to levy taxes to pay the promised coupons and maturation value. *Revenue bonds*, in contrast, are issued to finance specific projects, such as a road, sports facility, or water project, and will be repaid by the income from the completed project. Usually, the agency issuing a revenue bond has no taxing authority and the bond is not an obligation of the state or local

contracts and, therefore, had no obligation to fulfill them. Coupons and principal continue to paid on the bonds for Projects 1, 2, and 3, which (unlike Projects 4 and 5) are backed by the Bonneville Power Administration, a federal agency that distributes electricity to public utilities in the Pacific Northwest.

WPPSS was the nation's largest issuer of municipal bonds, and the $2.25 billion default on its Project 4 and Project 5 bonds was, by far, the largest ever. Moody's gave these bonds an A1 rating until June 1981, and Standard and Poor's rated them A until January 1982. Investors were shocked and then enraged that these seemingly safe investments were made a shambles through a court-backed default. A collection of lawsuits alleging fraud by WPPSS, the Wall Street firms that marketed the bonds, and other convenient targets (ninety-one defendants in all) is now working its way through the courts.

Despite dire warnings in 1983 of shock waves from this precedent, the municipal-bond market recovered quickly, leading some people to call WPPSS a "no-fault default." To reassure nervous investors (and reduce their interest costs), many local governments and agencies now buy special insurance that guarantees the payment of principal and interest on their bonds. Standard & Poor's automatically gives an AAA rating to bonds that are backed by either of the two major insurers—

the Municipal Bond Insurance Association or the American Bond Assurance Corporation. Nonetheless, these insured bonds have been priced to yield up to a ½ percent more than noninsured AAAs, because the latter are rated AAA on the strength of the issuing municipality and there is apparently some fear that a wave of defaults would bankrupt the insurers.

As for WPPSS, in 1986 the bonds for Projects 1, 2, and 3 were all selling at premiums over par (due to their generous coupons), while the bonds for Projects 4 and 5 were priced at roughly 10 percent of their face value, evidently purchased by speculators hoping that the next surprise would be a pleasant one. If you check the prices in the latest issue of *Barron's*, you will see if their gamble has paid off.

government. Investment Example 4–3 describes the default of an important revenue bond.

About half of the state and local bonds issued in 1985 were private-purpose revenue bonds, for such things as hotels, stores, irrigation projects, and industrial parks.[6] Concerned about apparent abuses, Congress put restrictions in the Tax Reform Act of 1986 on the amount and type of munis used to finance essentially private projects. Bonds falling outside of these restrictions are not exempt from federal taxes, which has created a new class of bond—taxable munis. For instance, municipal bonds used to finance sports stadiums or convention facilities owned by private interests are no longer exempt from federal taxes. Congress did include a grandfather clause that allows an exemption for existing bonds and even for some private projects that had been planned, but not financed, before the Reform Act.

When first issued, state and local bonds are sold to syndicates of investment bankers on the basis of competitive bids. The bonds are then marketed to investors. Later, they can be bought and sold in the over-the-counter market, though not always inexpensively. One authority says

> *If you have $100,000, you can begin to think about trading, but it's only at a close to $500,000 that you can adequately trade municipals.*[7]

A trade involving less than $100,000 par value is considered an odd lot, subject to larger brokerage fees. Fees on round-lot trades generally range from 1 percent to 3 percent; those on odd lots can be 5 percent or even higher. Some 50,000 different authorities have issued over a million different tax-exempt securities; most are traded seldomly, or not at all,[8] and significant price concessions may be required to consummate a trade.

Municipal bonds were traditionally bearer bonds, with ownership proven simply by physical possession of the bond certificate and the presentation of clipped coupons at a local bank, which was then reimbursed by the issuing agency. Federal law now requires all state and local bonds (issued since July 1, 1983) to be registered bonds, with the issuing agency keeping a computerized list of owners and mailing them the semiannual coupon payments. The intent of the federal law is to assure reporting of any taxable income and to discover suspicious wealth that may have been acquired with unreported income and then tucked into tax-exempt bonds.

Because of the tax advantages, investors in high tax brackets buy state and local bonds even when the before-tax yields to maturity are substantially below those on equally safe, but taxable, corporate bonds. In recent years, as Figure 4–1 on p. 125 shows, the interest rates on highly rated state and local bonds generally have been some 1 percent to 2 percent below the rates on similarly rated corporate bonds. For instance, in January 1986 yields to maturity averaged around 10 percent on highly rated corporate bonds and about 8 percent on comparable state and local bonds. College endowments and other investors who do not pay taxes prefer the 10 percent corporates, while those in high tax brackets prefer 8 percent tax-exempts. What is the break-even tax rate that would make an investor indifferent between the two bonds? If t is the marginal tax rate, the after-tax yields are $(1 - t)10$ percent and 8 percent, and these yields are equal

$$(1 - t)10 \text{ percent} = 8 \text{ percent}$$

for

$$t = 0.20.$$

FIGURE 4–1 Yields on high-quality corporate and municipal bonds.
(*Source:* Federal Reserve *1987 Historical Chart Book.*)

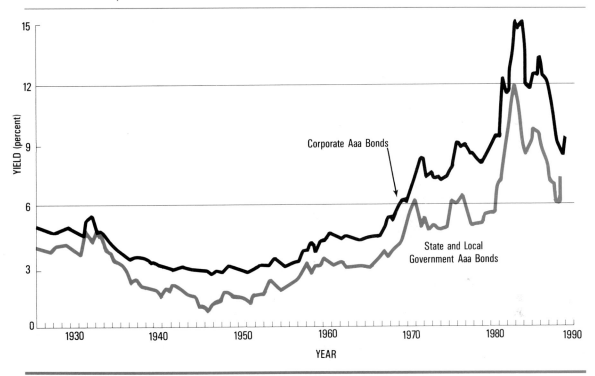

This example is one of many we will encounter in which tax considerations encourage investors in different tax brackets to choose different investments. Here, tax exempts appeal to those with marginal tax rates above 20 percent and don't make much sense for those in lower tax brackets.

CONVERTING ORDINARY INCOME INTO LIGHTLY TAXED INCOME (optional)

Some returns, such as interest on a bond or bank account, are considered ordinary income and taxed fully, at a tax rate that depends on one's tax bracket. Other investments (such as municipal bonds) are tax-advantaged, in that the returns are taxed lightly or not at all. Such differences in effective tax rates can make a big difference to one's wealth.

Suppose that a certain investment yields a 15 percent return, compounded annually, year after peaceful year. If you invest $10,000 now, how much will you have after ten years? After thirty years? It all depends on

TABLE 4–8   Effect of Tax Rates on Wealth

Type of Income	Tax Rate (percent)	After-Tax Return (percent)	Wealth After 10 Years	Wealth After 30 Years
Ordinary	28	10.8	$27,887	$216,867
Tax-free	0	15.0	40,456	662,117
Even better		19.2	57,911	1,942,172

how heavily this 15 percent return is taxed. If the return is ordinary income and you are in a 28 percent bracket, then your annual after-tax return shrinks to $(1 - 0.28)15$ percent = 10.8 percent. If the 15 percent return is tax-free, you keep the full 15 percent. In this way, the tax code determines whether your after-tax return is 10.8 percent or 15 percent and, hence, what happens to your $10,000, as seen in Table 4–8.

Can you do better than tax-free? Surprisingly, you can, by using other people's money to exploit the fact that different types of income are taxed at different rates. To illustrate the general principle as simply as possible, suppose that the 15 percent annual return referred to earlier is tax-free, and that you borrow another $10,000 at a 15 percent interest rate, giving you $20,000 in all to invest. Why is borrowing at 15 percent to invest at 15 percent profitable? Because the after-tax interest rates are not the same. The 15 percent income is untaxed, leaving a 15 percent after-tax return; while the 15 percent interest expense is deductible from ordinary income, reducing the after-tax cost to $(1 - 0.28)15$ percent = 10.8 percent.

Here are the first year's details. You invest $20,000 in all, obtaining an untaxed income of $0.15(\$20,000) = \$3000$. You pay $0.15(\$10,000) = \$1500$ in interest, but this interest can be deducted from ordinary income, saving you $0.28(\$1500) = \$420$ in taxes. Thus, the after-tax cost of the borrowed money is $\$1500 - \$420 = \$1080$ (that is, 10.8 percent), and your net return is $\$3000 - \$1080 = \$1920$ (that is, 19.2 percent), as shown in the following:

Income		*Expenses*	
Interest	$3000	Interest	$1500
Taxes	− 0	Tax saving	− 420
	$3000		$1080

This strategy boosts your net after-tax return to 19.2 percent, and it increases your wealth to $57,911 after ten years and to $1,942,172 after thirty years. Here you borrow at 10.8 percent after taxes to invest at 15 percent after taxes. This general lesson is that

Investing borrowed money is profitable as long as the after-tax cost is less than the after-tax return.

There is another useful way of understanding this strategy. The $10,000 you borrow the first year gives you $1500 in income that is taxed at a 0 percent rate and $1500 in interest expenses that can be used to offset ordinary income taxed at a 28 percent rate. Thus, instead of paying a 28 percent tax on $1500 of ordinary income, you pay a 0 percent tax on $1500 of tax-advantaged income. Borrowing effectively converts $1500 of heavily taxed ordinary income into $1500 of untaxed income, and this tax saving of 0.28($1500) = $420 provides the extra 4.2 percentage points that boost your return from 15 percent to 19.2 percent. This example illustrates a general tax-shelter principle:

Borrowing, with interest that can be deducted from ordinary income, in order to make tax-advantaged investments converts ordinary income into lightly taxed income.

Before the 1986 Tax Reform Act, the tax rate on capital gains was only 40 percent of that on ordinary income, and many tax shelters had been set up to convert ordinary income into capital gains by borrowing money to buy stock, land, buildings, gold, paintings, or other assets that, it was hoped, would appreciate in value. This conversion was profitable as long as the after-tax cost of borrowing was less than the after-tax investment return. One objective of the Tax Reform Act was to make these shelters less attractive.

The tax advantages of borrowing money to buy tax-free municipal bonds are so obvious that, in theory, the Internal Revenue Service will not allow you to deduct the interest on money borrowed to buy tax-free securities. But, in practice, if you are borrowing with one hand and investing in a seemingly unrelated fashion with the other, your deduction is likely to stand. For example, imagine that your are moving from Texas to Ohio and receive $100,000 from the sale of your home in Texas. You are about to buy a house in Ohio for $150,000 and have these choices: (a) put down $100,000 and borrow $50,000; or (b) invest $70,000 in municipal bonds, put down $30,000, and borrow $120,000. Clearly, the difference between (b) and (a) is that you borrow an additional $70,000 in order to invest $70,000 in municipal bonds. Yet the financing of a home purchase and the decision to invest in municipal bonds can be interpreted as separate decisions, and, indeed, in 1986 the IRS ruled explicitly that the interest is deductible, because the purchase of a home is of "such a personal nature" that it does not "taint" the acquisition of municipal bonds.[9] Another example is the following: You have $100,000 invested in municipal bonds yielding 10 percent and a $100,000 home mortgage at 10 percent. Should you sell your municipal bonds and pay off your mortgage? The answer is no; doing so converts untaxed income into taxable income—an expensive mistake.

TAX DEFERRAL (optional)

Another tax-shelter principle is to defer taxes. If you can postpone a $1000 tax liability for a year, that $1000 can be temporarily invested. If you earn 10 percent on this $1000, you will have $1100 after a year, pay the original $1000 tax liability plus (in a 28 percent tax bracket) $28 in taxes on the extra $100 that you earned, and still have $72 left over. By deferring $1000 in taxes for a year, the government implicitly loans you that $1000 at 2.8 percent, which is pretty hard to resist. More generally, tax deferral allows you to borrow money at an interest rate equal to your tax rate times the rate of return you earn on this money; in this case, 28 percent of 10 percent is 2.8 percent.

A very important example involves capital-gains taxes, which are deferred until the gain is realized by the sale of the asset. By not taxing unrealized gains, the government implicitly loans investors their tax liability at a very attractive interest rate. Another simple example is the rescheduling of income and expenses. Income received and expenses paid from January 1, 1990, to December 31, 1990, are reported on your 1990 tax return, which must be filed by April 15, 1991. If you receive taxable income on January 1, 1991, instead of December 31, 1990, then the taxes on this income are deferred for a full year. If you make a charitable contribution on December 31, 1990, instead of January 1, 1991, then you get the tax saving in 1990 instead of 1991, and again, some taxes are deferred for a year. The rule in general is:

Accelerate your deductions, and postpone your income.

Retirement Plans

Another important example of deferring taxes is seen in annuities, deferred-compensation plans, and (in some cases) Individual Retirement Accounts (IRAs)—tongue-twisting names for investment plans that offer the powerful though frequently misunderstood advantage of tax deferment.

The investor avoids current income taxes on each dollar put into a tax-deferral plan, but must pay taxes later on each dollar (plus interest) withdrawn from the plan.

Many knowledgeable bankers and investment advisors claim that the advantage of such tax deferral is that income is shifted to retirement years, when the investor will presumably be in a low tax bracket. Others worry that by putting so much money into tax deferral plans, they will actually be in the same, or an even higher, tax bracket when they do retire.

The truth is that the advantages of tax deferral do not hinge on lower future tax brackets. Even if an investor is in the same tax bracket throughout his or her entire life, tax deferral is still an extraordinarily powerful tax shelter. A simple rule summarizes the power of tax deferral:

If the tax rate is the same when money is placed in the plan and when it is withdrawn, then the implicit after-tax return is equal to the before-tax return earned while the money is in the plan.

The Power of Tax Deferral

To keep the arithmetic simple, consider an investor in a 50 percent tax bracket who puts $1000 of wage income into a tax-deferred plan for one year, earning a 10 percent (before-tax) rate of return. At the end of the year, she pays a 50 percent tax on the $1100 withdrawn from the plan, leaving $550. If, instead, the investor does not put $1000 into the tax-deferral plan, she must pay a $500 tax on this wage income immediately, leaving her only $500 to invest. For this $500 to grow to the $550 provided by the tax-deferral plan, she would have to earn a 10 percent *after-tax* rate of return. Thus, tax deferral allows the investor to earn an effective after-tax return equal to the before-tax return on these funds. Whether we use five, ten, or fifty years, the principle is the same. Nor does the value of the before-tax rate of return matter, nor the tax bracket, as long as it is the same at the beginning and end.

Consider now a second example, a 28 percent tax bracket and $1000 invested at 8 percent a year for thirty years. After thirty years of tax deferral, the initial $1000 will have grown to

$$\$1000(1.08)^{30} = \$10{,}062.66,$$

and a 28 percent tax leaves $7,245.11. If the investor does not defer taxes, then the initial 28 percent tax leaves only $720 to invest. What after-tax return is needed for this $720 to grow to the $7,245.11 provided by tax deferral? Not surprisingly, it is 8 percent

$$\$720(1.08)^{30} = \$7{,}245.11$$

Again, the effective after-tax yield from tax deferral is equal to the before-tax return, whatever this happens to be.

There are several implications. Any investor tempted to invest funds outside of tax-deferred plans should remember that one needs to earn an after-tax return outside the plan that is higher than the before-tax return on money inside the plan—no easy feat. A second implication is that tax-deferred plans should not invest in tax-advantaged investments that offer low before-tax returns. It is foolish to invest tax-deferred funds in municipal bonds. The natural candidates are instead heavily-taxed corporate and Treasury bonds, especially zero-coupon bonds (which give no cash flow, but are taxed anyway).

What if the investor has no current savings to put into a tax-deferral plan? If our investor in a 50 percent tax bracket puts $1000 in a tax-deferred plan, this will save $500 in taxes. She can borrow the remaining $500. As before, at a 10 percent interest rate she will have $550 after taxes at the end of a year. For what tax-deductible interest rate does such borrowing make sense? If she borrows $500 for a year at 20 percent, she will owe $500(1.20) = $600, of which $100 is tax deductible (saving her $50 in taxes), leaving a $550 out-of-pocket cost:

The investment of borrowed funds in a tax-deferred plan is profitable if the plan's before-tax return is at least equal to the after-tax interest rate on the loan.

The one serious fly in the tax-deferral ointment is that the money invested in such plans may be illiquid, in that it cannot be touched (or touched only with penalty) before retirement. An investor anticipating major preretirement expenses, such as a child's education or a vacation home, may want to keep funds near at hand, in more liquid investments. However, some tax-deferred plans (for example, some tax-sheltered annuities) can be liquidated before retirement, and others, even though involving penalties for early withdrawal, may still be attractive, so powerful is the tax-deferral arithmetic.

SUMMARY

Treasury bills mature within a year and pay a single lump sum at maturity. The interest rates on T-bills are often quoted on a discount basis, relative to face value rather than current price, and therefore understate the actual rate of return. The yield to maturity on a bond, coupon paying or not, is that interest rate for which the present value of the cash flow, coupons and principal, is equal to its current price.

Bond prices and interest rates (yields to maturity) are inversely related. When interest rates rise, bond prices fall; when interest rates decline, bond prices increase. A bond's yield to maturity is equal to its coupon rate (the ratio of its annual coupon to face value) if the bond's price is equal to its face value. Since the price and yield to maturity are inversely related, a bond sells at a discount from face value when

its yield is larger than its coupon rate and at a premium when the yield is below the coupon rate.

Bond issuers with assets, profits, and cash flow that are relatively small in comparison with their debts are given low quality ratings by Standard & Poor's, Moody's, and other professional rating agencies. Their bonds must have low prices and high (promised) yields to maturity in order to compensate investors for the risk of default. Low-rated and unrated issues are called junk bonds. Some junk bonds are issued by small, little-known companies; some are fallen angels, once-safe bonds issued by once-strong companies; and some are issued to finance takeovers.

Bonds issued by state and local governments are called municipal bonds, munis, or tax-exempts, because most are exempt from federal income taxes. If a corporate bond yields 10 percent and a comparably risky tax-exempt bond yields 8 percent, investors with marginal income-tax rates larger than 20 percent can earn a higher after-tax return from the tax-exempt bond; the reverse is true of those in lower tax brackets.

EXERCISES

1. One financial observer wrote that a government bond is "backed by the full faith and credit of the national government. To put it more directly, government paper is backed by the federal government's power to tax."[10] If a balanced-budget amendment or other law restricted the federal government's ability to increase taxes, would there be serious doubts about the government's ability to pay the interest due on its debt?

2. Consider a T-bill paying $10,000 at maturity that is priced to yield an annual return of 10 percent. (Ignore transactions costs and assume a 365-day year.) What is the price at the following times until maturity?
a. 364 days
b. 180 days
c. 90 days
d. 30 days
e. 1 day

3. The May 17, 1986, *Los Angeles Times* reported the following T-bill data for trading on May 16:

Maturity	Bid	Asked	Yield	Bid Ch.
Jun 12 86	5.84	5.80		+0.09

a. What price did buyers pay on May 16?
b. What price did sellers receive on May 16?
c. What is the yield value omitted above?
d. What was the bid price of this bill on May 15?

4. Must the reported yield on T-bills always be larger than the bid and ask returns, calculated on a discount basis?

5. Following are four bonds and their yields to maturity on November 8, 1988. Which bonds were selling for a premium over face value and which at a discount?
a. Texaco 13s 91, yield = 11.9 percent
b. Texaco 13⅝ 94, yield = 11.5 percent
c. Texaco 5¾ 97, yield = 10.0 percent
d. Texaco 7¾ 01, yield = 10.3 percent

6. Explain why the following two 1984 statements by the same author are either consistent or inconsistent:[11]

> Daily price fluctuations of government securities are minimal. [p. 44]
> Since the late seventies, interest rates have fluctuated widely and wildly, with significant changes occurring not only week to week, but even daily. [p. 45]

7. Does the following argument imply that bond transaction costs are small?

> Commissions on bonds are quite reasonable . . . In fact, in many bond transactions there is no commission charge. In this instance (especially in new issue transactions), the seller has a profit built into the selling price.[12]

8. Critically evaluate the following statement:

> Investors flee from bonds when interest rates rise—or when they think they're going to rise—because bond prices move in the opposite direction from interest rates. Thus

bonds—which are interest-bearing debt securities issued by governments and corporations to raise money—are a good investment during periods of low interest rates.[13]

9. Explain this observation by the author Andrew Tobias:

> Even without checking the ratings, you can tell the quality of a bond just by looking at how its yield compares with the yield of other bonds . . . . If anything, you should shy away from bonds that pay exceptional interest: there is a reason they pay so well.[14]

10. The text states that if a company defaults or delays the payments on its bonds, the *actual* return on these bonds may turn out to be far below what was promised. Why does a delayed payment reduce your actual return? For a simple example, consider a bond selling for $1000 that has only one payment left, a $50 coupon and the $1000 maturation value scheduled to be paid six months from now. What is your (annual) rate of return if the company
a. makes the payment on time?
b. delays the payment for six months?
c. delays the payment for four years?
11. The noted economist John Kenneth Galbraith wrote that "anyone who buys a junk bond known as a junk bond deserves on the whole to lose."[15] Why would any rational investor buy a junk bond when it is clearly labeled a junk bond?
12. Some relatives bought thirty-year corporate bonds at par ($1000 apiece) yielding 4.3 percent in 1963. Seven years later, in 1970, the yields to maturity had risen to 9.1 percent, and the prices had fallen to $541. They shrugged and said, "As long as we do not sell, we have not lost anything. We will still get our $1000 when these bonds mature in 1993." Explain why you agree or disagree with their logic.
13. A bond paying a 10 percent annual coupon

for ten years is selling for $1000. What is the annual yield to maturity?
14. Consider a thirty-year bond with a 10 percent coupon that is callable after five years at a price of 110 (10 percent over face value). What is your yield to call if you buy this bond at a price of 115 and it is called after five years? After ten years? Why would a corporation exercise its call right and pay 110, instead of waiting until maturity when it need pay only 100?
15. A firm that markets time-share condominiums offers prizes to those who endure a tour and sales talk. One prize is a $1000 savings account maturing in forty-five years, in return for a $55 fee for "handling, processing and insurance."[16] What is the implicit annual rate of return to someone who takes this prize?
16. A home seller was offered $290,000 for her property: $140,000 cash plus zero-coupon bonds paying $150,000 after twenty years.[17] If the annual interest rate on these bonds is 10 percent, what is the buyer's actual cost for the property?
17. In 1986, Duquesne University offered these prepaid tuition options:

Number of Years Until Enrollment	Cost if Prepaid Today	Estimated Cost at Enrollment
10	$13,061	$54,675
15	8,837	76,685

What are the implicit rates of return if we think of each of these plans as a zero-coupon bond paying the estimated enrollment cost, in a single lump sum at enrollment?
18. Explain why you either agree or disagree with the following reasoning:

> Another way of achieving security is to put up as little money as possible to purchase financial instruments that will almost certainly appreciate in future years. Inevitably, many bond issues are at a discount because they

were originally offered with lower coupon rates than are presently obtainable. Deep discount bonds may also be the result of interest rate fluctuations or a business's running into difficulties and not paying its bondholders. While the company struggles to revamp itself or undergoes reorganization under the court's protection, the bonds will fall sharply. Buyers of such deeply discounted bonds stand to make substantial capital gains and accrued interest if or when the company emerges from its troubles.[18]

19. For each choice offered below, other things being equal, decide which security you would expect to have the higher yield to maturity.
a. Corporate or Treasury bonds
b. Corporate or municipal bonds
c. AA or A corporate bonds
d. Public issue or a privately placed bond that cannot be resold for two years
20. A wealthy Californian with $100,000 of taxable income had to pay a 28 percent federal income tax and a 9.3 percent California state income tax in 1988. Individuals could, however, deduct their state income taxes from their federal taxable income; that is, every $1 of state taxes reduces by $1 the income on which they have to pay federal taxes. What is the effective after-tax return for each of the following securities?
a. A Treasury bond yielding 10 percent
b. A corporate bond yielding 10 percent
c. A Massachusetts bond yielding 8 percent
d. A California bond yielding 8 percent
21. Critically evaluate the statement, "Even in periods of towering interest rates, when debt instruments generally are not wise investments, municipal bonds are desirable because they are tax exempt."[19]
22. The following is a 1987 analysis of municipal-bond prices:

Demand for the bonds of states, cities and public authorities, which offer tax-exempt interest payments, has been tremendous. So many have rushed to buy what bond houses advertise as the last tax shelter of the middle class that customary price differentials between tax-exempt and taxable bonds have narrowed. Crowd psychology rather than economics is at work.[20]

Consider equally risky tax-exempt and taxable bonds with equal coupons. Which will have the higher price? If the demand for tax-exempts surges, will the price differential narrow?
23. Consider the following three alternative investment strategies over a five-year horizon. Assuming no default and no state or local income tax, which strategy has the higher after-tax return if you are a tax-exempt pension fund? An individual in a 15 percent tax bracket? An individual in a 28 percent tax bracket?

Strategy 1: At the beginning of each year, buy one-year T-bills paying an effective yield of 8 percent a year.

Strategy 2: Spend $9750 on a five-year, zero-coupon corporate bond with a maturation value of $15,000.

Strategy 3: Buy a thirty-year, zero-coupon municipal bond with a maturation value of $1000 and a yield to maturity of 7 percent. Hold this bond for five years, and then sell it. Assume that the yield to maturity stays at 7 percent.

24. A company is considering the purchase of a new machine that costs $500,000 and will generate an after-tax cash flow of $10,000 a month for ten years, at which time it will have a salvage value of $50,000. If the company requires a 10 percent after-tax return on its investments, is this machine an attractive acquisition? (Assume that the $10,000 cash flow begins one month after the purchase of the machine.)
25. Consider two ten-year bonds, both priced at $100. Bond A has a $10 annual coupon and $100 maturation value; Bond B has a $5 annual

coupon and $170 maturation value. The yields to maturity are 10 percent for Bond A and 9.5 percent for Bond B. For the following required returns, which bond has the higher present value?

a. 5 percent

b. 10 percent

c. 15 percent

26. Historically, the yields on tax-free municipal bonds have averaged about 70 percent of the yields on comparable taxable corporate bonds; for instance, municipals might yield 7 percent when corporates yield 10 percent. If so, investors in which tax brackets receive a higher after-tax return from municipals?

27. An article in *The Wall Street Journal* began, "Pay $1200 or more for a municipal bond that will return only $1000 [at] maturity? That strikes most investors as a stupid idea."[21] Would it ever be a good idea?

28. Explain this observation regarding the municipal-bond market:

> General-obligation bonds . . . generally carry lower interest rates than various kinds of . . . revenue bonds sold by hospitals, housing authorities, and electrical power authorities.[22]

29. The 1986 Tax Reform Act imposed restrictions on municipal bonds that are used to finance private projects. Why did private projects financed by municipal bonds have what some people considered an unfair advantage over projects financed by corporate bonds?

30. Historically, banks have been major purchasers of municipal bonds; but the Tax Reform Act of 1986 changed the tax code so that when banks and other financial institutions calculate their taxable income, they can no longer deduct the interest paid for deposits and other money that is borrowed to finance the purchase of munis. Can you think of any reason for this change? How do you think it affected bank demand for municipal bonds?

31. The fine print in an advertisement for a municipal bond fund says that it is "not suitable for retirement plans." Why not?

32. A financial writer made this observation regarding the Tax Reform Act of 1986: "The new rules crack down on a tax maneuver that often served as a primary impetus for incorporating. Professional and certain other closely held businesses would generally be required to use the calendar year as their fiscal year."[23] Before, a doctor might form a corporation with a fiscal year that ends on January 31, while paying his personal income taxes on a calendar year that ends on December 31. Then in January 15, 1985, he could pay himself $50,000 and record this payment as an expense for the corporation and income to himself. What is the advantage of this if the corporate and individual tax rates are approximately the same?

33. In the spring of 1986, Congress debated legislation that would reduce the tax rates for high-income taxpayers from 50 percent to 27 percent, and Prudential-Bache economist Edward Yardeni asked:

> Do you want to know how you can get an absolutely tax-free, and nearly risk-free, return of 23%? All you have to do is defer as much of your 1986 income into 1987 as possible . . . . What if you can't defer income . . . ? Accelerate 1987 deductions into this year. Prepay next year's mortgage interest . . . Be more charitable this year than next year.[24]

Explain his logic.

34. Investors do not have to pay capital-gains taxes until they sell an asset; and when a person dies, any capital gains on assets in the estate are not taxed. (When a beneficiary sells an inherited asset, the taxable capital gain is the difference between the sale price and the price on the date of the deceased's death.) Intending to convert ordinary income into untaxed capital gains, an elderly widow borrows $100,000 at

TABLE 4–A

Interest expense (15 percent of $100,000)	− $15,000
Tax saving (for a 50 percent tax rate)	+ 7,500
Property taxes (1 percent of $100,000)	− 1,000
Property-tax deduction (50 percent tax rate)	+ 500
Insurance and maintenance (1 percent of $100,000)	− 1,000
Rental saving and capital gains (15 percent of $100,000)	+ 15,000
	$6,000

10 percent interest to buy undeveloped land, which she will hold until her death. If she is in a 28 percent tax bracket and is able to deduct the $10,000 interest expense from her taxable income each year, what is the minimum annual percentage capital gain necessary for her heirs to benefit from this strategy?

35. Financial consultants advise that you should wait until April 15 to file your return if you owe the government money, but file early if you are due a refund. Why is this strategy financially advantageous?

36. A company issued thirty-year 12 percent bonds ten years ago. Now it can exercise the call provisions and retire these bonds by paying 110 percent of par value. The firm can issue new twenty-year bonds at 9 percent, but it will have to pay its investment banker a fee equal to 2 percent of the par value of the new issue. Is it profitable for the company to call these bonds and issue new ones?

37. Some returns are taxed at very low rates; the most important example for a majority of people is the purchase of a house in which to live, an investment that yields untaxed capital gains and rent savings. There are also expenses such as mortgage interest and property taxes (which are tax deductible) as well as insurance and maintenance (which are not deductible). Assume that property taxes are 1 percent of the house's value and that insurance and maintenance together are another 1 percent. Table 4–A shows the bottom line when you are in a 50 percent tax bracket and borrow $100,000 at

15 percent to buy a $100,000 house yielding 15 percent in rental saving and capital gains. (The numbers would be the same if you borrow, say, $80,000 and put up $20,000 that could instead earn a 15 percent return.)

This strategy is profitable as long as the rent plus capital gain is greater than 9 percent. Fill in the table below, showing the minimum percentage home-rental savings plus capital gains needed to profit from purchasing a home in order to convert ordinary income into untaxed rent and capital gains. How did the 1986 Tax Reform Act's reduction of the top tax rate from 50 percent to 28 percent affect the appeal of housing?

	Minimum Rent Saving Plus Capital Gains (percent)	
Mortgage Rate (percent)	*In 50 Percent Tax Bracket*	*In 28 Percent Tax Bracket*
10		
15	9	

38. Check and evaluate the calculation in the following statement:

You're 25 years old, but you wait until age 26 to start your IRA. If we assume the interest rate you earn on your funds is 10% annually, and you deposit the maximum $2000 IRA contribution into your account each year, by the time you reach age 65, that one year delay would cost you over $90,000![25]

39. In January 1986, *Money* magazine gave the following advice:

> In 1986, as always, you'll likely make fullest use of your IRA's tax advantages by stocking it with such income-producing investments as CDs, corporate and government bonds, and income mutual funds.[26]

Why did this publication encourage investors to stock their retirement plans with assets that have lots of fully-taxable income, as opposed to precious metals, real estate, and other assets that produce capital gains, which at the time were lightly taxed?

40. It has been reported that "roughly half of all zero-coupon bonds are bought with IRA money."[27] Why are zeros attractive for IRAs?

CHAPTER 5

Interest-Rate Risk

The adviser's strategy was long and wrong . . .
Wall Street trader

Investors who bought long-term bonds yielding 4 percent in the 1960s lost money when long-term rates went to 9 percent in 1970. Business that sold thirty-year bonds in 1982 at 15 percent were dismayed when rates fell below 10 percent in 1986. People who bought Treasury bills yielding 8 percent in 1985 were frustrated when they reinvested their money at 6 percent in 1986. Many savings and loans that borrowed short and lent long in the 1960s and 1970s went bankrupt in the 1980s.

These are all examples of interest-rate risk, gambles on the future course of interest rates. The cases cited are all gambles lost; there are an equal number of gambles won. The objective of this chapter is to understand the wagers being made and the stakes at risk.

First, we will look at why securities of different maturities usually have different interest rates. Then, we will compare the risks borne by those who buy long-term bonds with the risks inherent in buying short-term securities. Finally, we will look at some tools that have been developed to measure risk and, if possible, to reduce it.

THE TERM STRUCTURE OF INTEREST RATES

In May 1985, short-term Treasury bills were priced to yield less than 8 percent while long-term Treasury bonds yielded more than 11 percent. Neither security had any default risk, yet some investors willingly settled for an 8 percent yield on one Treasury security when another offered 11 percent. Was the long-term bond an overlooked bargain, or is there some other rational explanation?

FIGURE 5–1 Term structure of interest rates for zero-coupon bonds, May 16, 1985

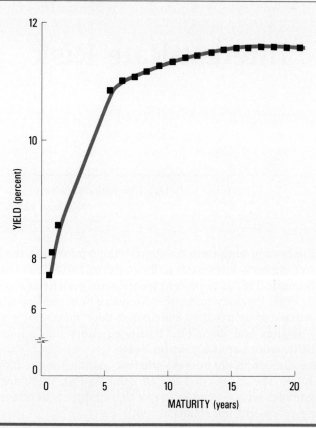

Figure 5–1 shows the yields on several zero-coupon Treasury bonds in May 1985, with maturities ranging from one to twenty years. There is a whole spectrum of interest rates, beginning with relatively low yields on the shortest maturities rising to higher yields for bonds with longer maturities. This figure provides an example of the **term structure of interest rates,** describing the yields to maturity on zero-coupon bonds that have different maturities, but are otherwise identical. It is crucial to restrict our attention to bonds of similar risk. If we compare the yields on a short-term Treasury bond and a long-term BB corporate bond, we do not know if the difference in yields reflects the term structure or the default risk.

Notice also that the term structure compares the yields on zero-coupon bonds, which, for reasons that will be explained shortly, are not necessarily

term structure of interest rates
The term structure describes the yields to maturity on zero-coupon bonds that have different maturities, but are otherwise identical.

equal to the yields on coupon-paying bonds. A **yield curve** describes the yields to maturity on coupon-paying bonds with different maturities. In understanding the effect of maturity on interest rates, it is easiest to work with zero-coupon bonds because then we can associate a single future payment with a single interest rate.

yield curve
The yield curve is similar to the term structure, but compares the yields to maturity on coupon-paying bonds with different maturities.

THE EXPECTATIONS HYPOTHESIS

Figure 5–1 shows that the term structure in May 1985 was upward sloping, with longer-term bonds yielding more than those with shorter maturities. Sometimes the term structure is flat, with short-term and long-term bonds having the same yields, and sometimes the term structure is inverted, with short-term bonds having the highest yields.

The most important explanation for these variations in the term structure is interest-rate expectations. Consider two default-free, zero-coupon securities—the first security to mature in a year and the second in two years. Each costs $1; the first pays F_1 after 1 year, with an implicit rate of return R_1, or

$$\$1(1 + R_1) = F_1,$$

and the second pays F_2 after two years with an implicit annual rate of return R_2,

$$\$1(1 + R_2)^2 = F_2.$$

To compare these investments, we need to focus on equal horizons, either one year or two. Consider a two-year horizon first. A prospective purchaser of the two-year security should consider the alternative of "rolling over" one-year securities by purchasing a one-year bond and then, when it matures, purchasing a new one-year bond. We denote the yield on one-year bonds a year from now as R_1^{+1}. Every dollar now invested in two-year securities will grow to $(1 + R_2)^2$, while every dollar invested in a sequence of one-year bonds grows to $(1 + R_1)(1 + R_1^{+1})$. The **Expectations Hypothesis** states that securities must be priced so that both strategies do equally well, as shown in the following formula:

$$(1+R_2)^2 = (1+ R_1)(1 + R_1^{+1}) \tag{1}$$

Otherwise, investors will shun the inferior bond, causing its price to decline and its return to rise until it is competitive.

What if investors have a one-year horizon? The alternative to the one-year security is to buy the two-year bond and sell it after a year, when it

Expectations Hypothesis
The Expectations Hypothesis explains the term structure by interest rate expectations.

will be priced at P to give the same return as new one-year bonds, $P(1 + R_1^{+1}) = F_2$. Since $F_2 = (1 + R_2)^2$,

$$P = \frac{(1 + R_2)^2}{(1 + R_1^{+1})}.$$

Thus, \$1 invested in a one-year bond grows to $1 + R_1$, while \$1 invested for a year in a two-year bond grows to P. Their equality confirms Equation 1.

Similar logic applied to longer-term securities gives the following extrapolation of Equation 1:

$$(1 + R_n)^n = (1 + R_1)(1 + R_1^{+1})(1 + R_1^{+2}) \ldots (1 + R_1^{+n-1}) \qquad (2)$$

where R_n is the annual yield on an n-year, zero-coupon security and the returns on the right-hand side are the one-year rates over the next n years. Equation 2, sometimes called the **Hicks Equation** in recognition of John Hicks' pioneering work, is the fundamental equation of the Expectations Hypothesis.

Hicks Equation
The Hicks Equation states that long-term interest rates are the product of the current and anticipated future short-term rates.

According to the Expectations Hypothesis, the relationship between short-term and long-term interest rates reflects the anticipated future course of interest rates.

If the one-year rate is 10 percent now and will be 10 percent next year, then two-year securities must yield 10 percent also in order to be competitive, as the following shows:

$$(1 + R_2)^2 = (1 + R_1)(1 + R_1^{+1})$$
$$= (1 + 0.10)(1 + 0.10)$$
$$= (1.21)$$

and $\qquad 1 + R_2 = \sqrt{1.21}$
$$= 1.10$$

If, on the other hand, the one-year rate is currently 10 percent and will be 12 percent next year, then comparable two-year assets must yield approximately 11 percent a year, as shown in the following:

$$(1 + R_2)^2 = (1 + R_1)(1 + R_1^{+1})$$
$$= (1 + 0.10)(1 + 0.12)$$
$$= 1.232$$

and $\qquad 1 + R_2 = \sqrt{1.232}$
$$= 1.10995$$

FIGURE 5–2   Three term structures

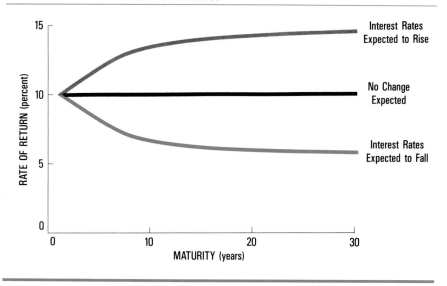

If, instead, the one-year rate is expected to decline from 10 percent this year to 8 percent next year, then two-year assets must yield about 9 percent a year:

$$(1 + R_2)^2 = (1 + R_1)(1 + R_1^{+1})$$
$$= (1 + 0.10)(1 + 0.08)$$
$$= 1.188$$

and

$$1 + R_2 = \sqrt{1.188}$$
$$= 1.08995$$

The general rule is short and easy: the two-year rate will be either above or below the one-year rate depending upon whether the one-year rate is expected to rise or fall. Extending the lesson to longer-term assets:

> **When no change in one-year rates is anticipated, comparable assets of differing maturities will all be priced to have the same yield. Longer-term rates will be above the current one-year rate if rates are expected to rise in the future and below the current one-year rate if rates are expected to decline.**

Three simple term structures are shown in Figure 5–2. More complex interest-rate expectations (for example, rates expected to rise for a few years and then decline) imply more complicated term structures.

Is the Term Structure Always/Ever Right?

The Expectations Hypothesis is a straightforward yet elegant theory. Because rolling over short-term assets (shorts) is an alternative to holding long-term assets (longs), and because holding a long-term asset for a short while is an alternative to buying a short-term asset, the yields on short- and long-term assets are linked by interest-rate expectations. Anticipated movements in short-term rates determine whether long-term rates will be above or below short-term rates. Conversely, we can use the observed relationship between short- and long-term rates to infer the interest-rate expectations of financial experts. For instance, long-term rates are above short-term rates in the May 1985 term structure shown in Figure 5–1; the expectations-hypothesis interpretation is that at the time investors expected interest rates to increase.

Figure 5–3 shows that interest rates fell by several percentage points during the twelve months after May 1985, causing investors to regret, in retrospect, that they had not bought long-term securities and locked in high rates of return. Those investors who passed up long-term bonds yielding more than 11 percent in the spring of 1985 and bought one-year Treasury bills yielding less than 8 percent, counting on a rise in interest rates, found that in the spring of 1986 they had to roll over their money at lower interest rates.

This episode was not the first time the term structure mispredicted interest rates. Interest rates are notoriously difficult to forecast, and investors have made many costly errors. In 1982 and 1983, as in 1985, long-term Treasury bond rates were some two percentage points above the yields on short-term Treasury bonds, indicating that interest rates were expected to increase sharply; yet, interest rates tumbled. In 1979 and 1980, long-term rates were below short-term rates, and interest rates rose.

Figure 5–4 on p. 144 shows that in the 1930s and 1940s short-term rates on corporate bonds dropped below 1 percent while the yields on long-term corporate bonds held at around 2 to 3 percent. Evidently, long-term rates stayed above shorts because investors expected interest rates to return to the 5 percent levels typical of the 1920s and before. This persistent belief went unrewarded. Short-term rates stayed well below long-term rates until the 1950s, and investors who patiently rolled over shorts, waiting for interest rates to rise, were repeatedly disappointed.

Some recent detailed studies[1] have found evidence that the term structure mispredicts the direction of interest rates as often as not. The safest conclusion is that the term structure may well reflect investors' best guesses about the future course of interest rates, but these guesses are far from guarantees.

Of course, investors are not unanimous in their opinions about the future direction of interest rates. In December 1986, *The Wall Street Journal* asked thirty-five top forecasters to predict the interest rates on three-month Treasury bills and thirty-year Treasury bonds that would prevail six months later, in June 1987. Then, in June 1987, they asked for predictions for De-

FIGURE 5–3   A drop in the term structure

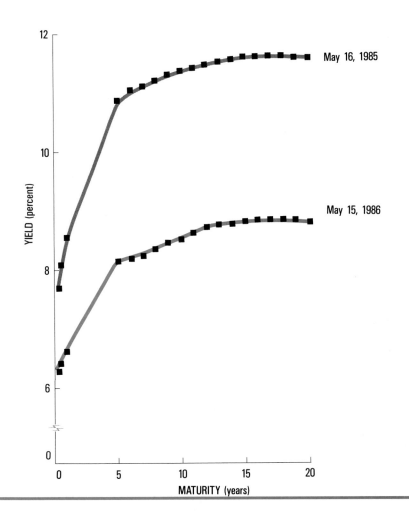

cember 1987. The results are shown in Table 5–1 on p. 145. In December 1986, average prediction for the T-bill rate in June 1987 was 4.98 percent— with the individual forecasts ranging from as low as 4.1 percent to as high as 6 percent, a span of nearly two percentage points. The actual value turned out to be 5.73 percent, seventy-five basis points above the average prediction. The June 1987 thirty-year bond rate was 8.5 percent, a full 1.5 percent above the average prediction and, indeed, outside the range spanned by the predictions. Not one of these thirty-five experts was within fifty basis points of the actual value. There was even more disagreement in the predictions for December 1987, with the average T-bill forecast turning out to be slightly too high and the long-term bond forecast much too low.

FIGURE 5–4 Long- and short-term interest rates. *Note:* data for AAA corporate bonds are not available after 1983. (*Source:* Federal Reserve *1987 Historical Chart Book.*)

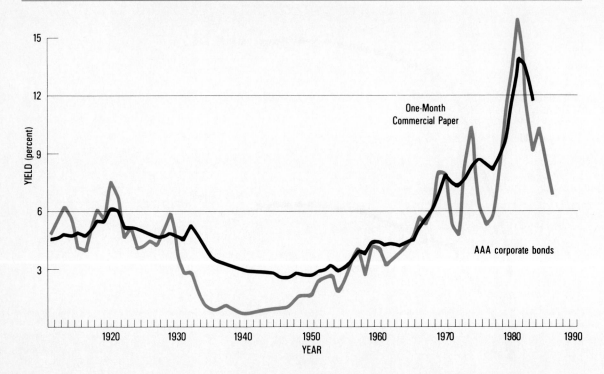

Nine of these forecasters had been surveyed by *The Wall Street Journal* over all ten of the preceding six-month periods (from December 1981 through June 1986). On six of these ten occasions, the actual Treasury bill rate was outside the range of the nine forecasts made six months earlier. Of the ninety individual forecasts of the T-bill rate, there were thirty-eight correct and fifty-two incorrect predictions of the direction of change of the T-bill rate. The average error was 1.6 percentage points.[2]

The problem in making accurate predictions is not that forecasters are uninformed, but that interest rates are of necessity difficult to forecast. There are large capital gains and losses made in financial markets, and each gain or loss is largely unexpected. No one voluntarily buys securities expecting a large capital loss, and any professional who is really confident of capital gains would buy virtually unlimited amounts of an underpriced security and make unheard-of fortunes. Instead, there are continual uncertainties, disagreements, and surprises in the securities market.

TABLE 5–1   Interest-Rate Forecasts Versus Actual Outcomes

	December 1986 Predictions of June 1987 Interest Rates		June 1987 Predictions of December 1987 Interest Rates	
	For Three-Month Bill (percent)	For Thirty-Year Bond (percent)	For Three-Month Bill (percent)	For Thirty-Year Bond (percent)
Average prediction	4.98	7.05	5.91	6.19
Range of predictions	4.10-6.00	6.10-8.00	4.25-6.63	5.88-9.40
Actual outcome	5.73	8.50	5.77	9.12

Source: Tom Herman and Mathew Winkler, "Economic Expansion Will Keep Going for at Least Another Year and Interest Rates Won't Change Much, Say Analysts in Survey," *Wall Street Journal*, July 6, 1987.

The Expectations Hypothesis was derived by assuming that future interest rates are known with certainty. A sure knowledge of future interest rates compels levels of short- and long-term rates such that all strategies do equally well. Investors will not hold long-term bonds if they know they can do better rolling over shorts, and they will not hold shorts if they are certain that longs are more profitable. When the future is certain and short- and long-term rates reflect this certainty, there is no basis for choosing a particular strategy over another. Shorts and longs are guaranteed to do equally well.

In reality, the future course of interest rates is unknown, and investors gamble, whichever strategy they follow. If they roll over shorts, they can be hurt by an unexpected drop in interest rates; if they buy longs, an unexpected increase in interest rates is their downfall.

Betting Against the Term Structure

For any given term structure, we can infer the future interest-rate values for which the strategies of buying longs and rolling over shorts do equally well. If we disagree with the projections, we have a reason for choosing between shorts and longs. Suppose that one-year bonds are priced to yield 8 percent and two-year bonds to yield 9 percent a year; that is, $R_1 = 0.08$ and $R_2 = 0.09$. The Hicks Equation (either Equation 1 or 2 shown earlier) implies that shorts and longs, in retrospect, will do equally well if the one-year rate a year from now turns out to be the value of R_1^{+1} such that

$$(1 + R_2)^2 = (1 + R_1)(1 + R_1^{+1})$$
$$(1 + 0.09)^2 = (1 + 0.08)(1 + R_1^{+1}),$$

which implies

$$1 + R_1^{+1} = \frac{(1 + 0.09)^2}{(1 + 0.08)}$$
$$= 1.1000925$$

and

$$R_1^{+1} = 0.1000925, \text{ about 10 percent.}$$

The two-year bond pays 9 percent a year. To do as well buying a one-year bond at 8 percent, the investor has to be able to reinvest the second year at 10 percent. For ease of comparison, we can say that the two-year bond at 9 percent implicitly pays 8 percent the first year, like the one-year bond, and then 10 percent the second year. The implicit future rates of return imbedded in the term structure are called **forward rates.** The question then is whether the investor expects the one-year rate next year to be above or below the 10 percent forward rate implicit in the term structure.

forward rates
Forward rates are the implicit future interest rate values for which the strategies of buying longs and rolling over shorts do equally well.

If you personally predict a 10 percent rate next year (or have no basis for making an informed prediction), then you have no reason for believing that shorts will do better or worse than longs. If, however, you disagree with the term structure's implicit 10 percent forward rate, you have cause for betting against the term structure. You choose the two-year bond if you do not think the one-year rate will rise to 10 percent; you favor the one-year bond if you believe that the one-year rate will be above 10 percent next year.

Notice that a belief in rising interest rates is not sufficient reason for buying short-term bonds. If you think interest rates will rise from 8 to 9 percent, a two-year bond at 9 percent still does better. You must believe that interest rates will rise above the 10 percent forward rate that is already imbedded in the term structure.

Investors can bet that future interest rates will be lower than the forward rates implied by the term structure by buying long-term bonds or bet that they will be higher by rolling over shorts.

Whether or not your decision is an informed bet, you are gambling, whichever strategy you choose. If you buy a two-year bond yielding 9 percent when one-year bonds yield 8 percent, you are betting implicitly that next year's rate will be below 10 percent. If it is, you earn more than you would have rolling over shorts. If it is not, you are long and wrong, as with advisor mentioned in the chapter's opening quotation.

Either way you go, buying shorts or longs, there is the possibility of disappointment—with longs, if interest rates rise unexpectedly; with

TABLE 5–2   Three Strategies for Investing in Zero-Coupon
Treasury Bonds

Type of Bond Purchased (1)	Current Price (2)	Price of Bond Next Year	
		If Rates Stay at 10 Percent (3)	If Rates Rise to 20 Percent (4)
One-Year	$10,000 = $\dfrac{\$11,000}{1.10}$	$11,000	$11,000
Two-Year	$10,000 = $\dfrac{\$12,100}{1.10^2}$	$11,000 = $\dfrac{\$12,100}{1.10}$	$10,083 = $\dfrac{\$12,100}{1.20}$
Thirty-Year	$10,000 = $\dfrac{\$174,494}{1.10^{30}}$	$11,000 = $\dfrac{\$174,494}{1.10^{29}}$	$882 = $\dfrac{\$174,494}{1.20^{29}}$

shorts, if rates drop unexpectedly. The first danger is called capital risk;
and the second is income risk.

CAPITAL RISK

The short-term purchase of a long-term asset creates **capital risk,** the possibility that an asset's price will be affected by unexpected changes in
interest rates. To illustrate, consider an investor with $10,000 at a time
when interest rates on default-free Treasury bills are 10 percent and are
widely expected to stay at 10 percent for the foreseeable future. In accord
with the Expectations Hypothesis, one-year, two-year, and thirty-year zero-
coupon Treasury bonds all are priced to yield 10 percent a year, as shown
in column (2) of Table 5–2. The future values of these three assets are such
that the present value of each at a 10 percent required return is $10,000.
Column (3) in the table shows that if interest rates stay at 10 percent as
anticipated, the present value of each asset a year from now will be
$11,000—providing the requisite 10 percent return.

What if interest rates rise unexpectedly to 20 percent? The one-year
asset will still be worth $11,000 in a year because it matures then. The
present value of the two-year asset, in contrast, is $900 less than expected.
In one year's time, this asset will have one year left until maturity; and
investors will not pay $11,000 then to get $12,100 a year later, a mere 10
percent return, when interest rates on other one-year assets have risen to
20 percent. They will only pay an amount such that $12,100 provides the
requisite 20 percent return, and that amount is $12,100/1.20 = $10,083, as
shown in column (4) of the table. As we have come to expect, an increase

capital risk
Capital risk exists
because unexpected
interest rate changes
affect asset prices.

in the required return reduces the present value of a given future cash flow. This price variability is capital risk.

Capital risk refers to the fact that the present value of an asset (and hence the price others are willing to pay for it) fluctuates with interest rates and required returns.

Capital risk is, of course, two-sided; just as an unexpected rise in interest rates reduces the present value, so an unexpected drop in interest rates raises the present value.

The drop in the value of the two-year asset in our example is disappointing, but it is not nearly as crushing as the collapse of the value of the thirty-year asset when interest rates rise to 20 percent. One year after purchase, there are still twenty-nine years until maturity and the present value of this bond at a 20 percent required return is $882, some 92 percent less than the $11,000 that had been anticipated.

The startling magnitude of this collapse in the value of the thirty-year asset is the converse of the power of compound interest. Small differences in returns can make a big difference to future values many years from now; conversely, for a *given* future value, small differences in required returns can have a large effect on the present value. The 92 percent capital loss is a dramatic example of a general principle that we will explore in more depth later in this chapter: the longer the term of the asset, the more sensitive its price is to interest-rate fluctuations and the larger is the capital risk.

INCOME RISK

Should nervous investors forgo long-term assets to avoid the terrors of capital risk? Not necessarily, because rolling over short-term assets is risky too. If you invest in a perfectly safe one-year Treasury bill, then you are guaranteed $10,000 when the bill matures a year from now (and the price won't stray far from $10,000 in the meantime). But what rate of return will you earn when you reinvest your $10,000 a year from now, and the year after that? This uncertainty about the rates of return available when money is reinvested is called **income risk** (or reinvestment risk).

income risk
There is income risk because the future value of the proceeds from an investment depends on the rates of return prevailing when the cash flow is reinvested.

Income risk refers to the fact that the future value of an investment depends on the rates of return prevailing when the cash flow is reinvested.

Consider again the three assets in Table 5–2. If the thirty-year Treasury zero is purchased, the investor is assured of $174,494 thirty years from now, representing a 10 percent annual rate of return. If, instead of locking in this 10 percent return, the investor rolls over one-year assets, year after year, $11,000 is assured at the end of the first year, but there are no guarantees beyond that. If, as is currently anticipated, interest rates stay at 10 percent, then the investor's wealth will grow to

$$\$10,000(1.10^{30}) = \$174,494$$

the same as with the thirty-year asset. But if interest rates drop unexpectedly to 5 percent after a year, and stay there, the future value will be only

$$\$10,000(1.10)(1.05^{29}) = \$45,277$$

some 75 percent less than with the thirty-year asset.

The purchase of a thirty-year zero guarantees a payment in thirty years, when the asset matures, but it does not guarantee its present value in the intervening years. Rolling over one-year assets guarantees a payment next year, but not beyond that. With capital risk, you may experience a sudden large loss; with income risk, you may suffer slowly.

The purchase of long-term assets is profitable if interest rates fall unexpectedly; rolling over short-term assets does well if interest rates rise unexpectedly.

INFLATION RISK

There is another, more subtle point. The thirty-year asset in our example locks in a fixed dollar amount, but still there is **inflation risk**—uncertainty regarding the future purchasing power of the investment's cash flow.

If the price level today is at $1 and there is no inflation for the next thirty years (just pretend, OK?), the price level will still be $1 and $174,494 will buy as much then as it does now. If there is instead 5 percent inflation each year, the price level will more than quadruple, to

inflation risk
Inflation risk is created by uncertainty about future prices and, hence, the purchasing power of the proceeds from an investment.

$$\$1(1.05^{30}) = 4.322,$$

and $174,494 will only buy then what $40,374 buys now, as shown by the following:

$$\frac{\$174,494}{4.322} = \$40,374$$

For a third possibility, a 10 percent inflation, year after year, just offsets the 10 percent nominal return, giving a 0 percent real return. Wealth goes up by a factor of 17, but so do prices, so that the real value of the investment stays at $10,000. For a final scare, if prices rise by 20 percent a year, the investor with $10,000 who locks in a guaranteed 10 percent nominal return a year winds up with only enough money to buy what $735 buys today.

> **An unexpected increase in the rate of inflation erodes, while an un-expected decrease swells, the purchasing power of fixed nominal cash flows.**

A long-term asset with a guaranteed nominal payoff does not protect investors from unanticipated inflation. We saw in Chapter 2 that inflation and interest rates do not move in locked step. Still, a strategy of rolling over short-term assets at least offers the likelihood that nominal interest rates will increase if inflation does.

DURATION

So far, we have focused on zero-coupon securities, which pay a lump sum at maturity. However, most investments provide a regular cash flow—for example, the monthly payments from an amortized loan, the semiannual coupons from a bond, and the quarterly dividends from corporate stock. A thirty-year, zero-coupon bond has much more capital risk than a two-year zero. But does a ten-year bond with large coupons have more capital risk than a five-year bond with no coupons? You have to wait longer to receive the maturation value of the ten-year bond, but you also receive some coupons before the five-year bond matures. The overall sensitivity of an asset's present value to changes in its required return, taking into account all of the cash flow, is gauged by an asset's **duration,** which is a measure of the average wait until the cash flow is received. We will look first at how duration is measured and then how it can be used to gauge capital risk.

duration
An asset's duration, the present-value weighted average number of years until the cash flow is received, gauges the sensitivity of its present value to changes in its required return.

The Duration Formula

The present value, P, of an n-year investment with cash flow X_t in year t and a constant required return R is calculated as follows:

$$P = \frac{X_1}{(1 + R)} + \frac{X_2}{(1 + R)^2} + \dots + \frac{X_n}{(1 + R)^n} \qquad (3)$$

The value of an asset's duration is given by the following:

$$D = (1)\frac{X_1/(1 + R)}{P} + (2)\frac{X_2/(1 + R)^2}{P} + \dots + (n)\frac{X_n/(1 + R)^n}{P} \qquad (4)$$

An understanding of this formula may be aided by an analogy to a course grade that depends on the scores on two midterms and a final examination, with 50 percent of the grade determined by the final exam score and 25 percent by each midterm. A student who gets scores of 82 on the first midterm, 75 on the second midterm, and 93 on the final has a course score of

$$X = 84(0.25) + 78(0.25) + 93(0.50) = 87.$$

The course score is a weighted average in that the individual scores are multiplied by weights of 0.25, 0.25, and 0.50 to reflect the relative importance of each score.

Duration is also a weighted average. Those items in Equation 4 in parentheses—1, 2, . . . , and n—are the number of years the investor must wait to receive the cash flow; X_1 is received after one year, X_2 after two years, and so on. An asset's duration is a weighted average of these years, based on weights that reflect the fraction of the total present value received at that time—for example,

$$\left(\frac{X_2/(1 + R)^2}{P} \right)$$

is the fraction of the present value received in the second year.

Let us now consider a two-year asset paying $100 one year from today and $100 the year after. At a 10 percent required return, the present value is

$$
\begin{aligned}
P &= \frac{X_1}{(1 + R)} + \frac{X_2}{(1 + R)^2} \\
&= \frac{\$100}{(1 + 0.10)} + \frac{\$100}{(1.10)^2} \\
&= \$90.91 + \$82.64 \\
&= \$173.55.
\end{aligned}
$$

The second $100 payment has a lower present value than the first because it occurs a year later. Of the total $173.55 present value, the first $100 payment represents $90.91/$173.55 = 0.524, slightly more than 52 percent, and the second $82.64/$173.55 = 0.476, the remaining 48 percent. The duration is

$$
\begin{aligned}
D &= (1)(0.524) + (2)(0.476) \\
&= 1.476,
\end{aligned}
$$

a bit less than one and one-half years.

Using Duration to Gauge Capital Risk

So far, we have seen that an asset's duration is the average wait until the investor receives its cash flow. Duration is also of interest for another reason—because it gauges the sensitivity of present value to a change in the required return. In particular, the use of calculus to differentiate Equation 3 shows that the percentage change in an asset's present value, written as %P, resulting from a small change dR in the percentage required return is given by

$$\%P = -D \, dR/(1 + R) \tag{5}$$

or, approximately

$$\%P = -D \, dR. \tag{6}$$

In the preceding example, the two-year asset has a duration D of about 1.5 years, and Equation 6 shows that a one-percentage-point change in the required return ($dR = 1$) will therefore reduce the present value by about 1.5 percent. Let's see if the formula works. If R rises by one percentage point, to 11 percent,

$$
\begin{aligned}
P &= \frac{X_1}{(1 + R)} + \frac{X_2}{(1 + R)^2} \\
&= \frac{\$100}{(1 + 0.11)} + \frac{\$100}{(1.11)^2} \\
&= \$90.91 + \$82.64 \\
&= \$171.25,
\end{aligned}
$$

about a 1½ percent decline: ($171.25 − $173.55)/$173.55 = −0.013. This confirms that

An asset's duration, the present-value weighted average number of years until the cash flow is received, is approximately equal to the percentage change in the asset's present value resulting from a one-percentage-point change in the required return.

For a zero-coupon bond, all of the present value is received in year n and, therefore, asset duration is simply equal to n, the number of years until maturity. Long-term zero-coupon bonds have a great deal of capital risk. The duration of a thirty-year zero is thirty years, implying that a one-percentage-point rise in interest rates *reduces* its present value by roughly 30 percent. The other side of the coin is that a one-percentage-point drop in interest rates *raises* the present value by about 30 percent.

Empirical confirmation of the usefulness of duration for gauging risk is provided by the data in Table 5–3, which shows the annual standard

TABLE 5–3 Annual Standard Deviations of Treasury Zero-Coupon
Bonds, 1984–1987

Maturity (years)	Standard Deviation (percent)
5	10.8
10	20.7
15	28.8
20	38.1

Source: Gary Smith, "Coping with the Term Structure," in *Essays in Honor of James Tobin,* William C.
Brainard, ed. (Cambridge, Mass.: MIT Press, 1990).

deviations of the prices of zero-coupon Treasury bonds in the years 1984–
87. Since the duration of a zero is equal to its maturity, we might expect
ten-year, fifteen-year, and twenty-year zeros to have, respectively, about
two, three, and four times as much capital risk as a five-year zero. During
this period, judging by the relative standard deviations, this was indeed
the case.[3]

The duration of a coupon bond is less than its maturity and is shorter
the larger are the coupons. For instance, a twenty-year bond selling at par
with a 10 percent coupon and 10 percent yield to maturity has a duration
of 9.01 years, less than half that of a twenty-year zero-coupon bond. A
corollary of this principle is that the price of a long-term bond with high
coupons may be less affected by interest rates than is the price of a shorter-
term bond with low coupons. Therefore maturity is an inaccurate measure
of capital risk. For instance, the twenty-year bond with 10 percent coupons
has a lower duration than does a ten-year, zero-coupon bond.

LIQUIDITY PREMIUMS

The Expectations Hypothesis predicts that short-term and long-term securities will all be priced to have the same anticipated return, taking into
account investor expectations of future interest rates. But because interest
rates are uncertain, there is income and capital risk; and risk-averse investors may prefer shorts to longs, or vice versa, even if the expected returns
are equal. If so, the inferior asset will have to offer a higher expected
return—a *risk premium*—to attract investors.

If income risk is the predominant concern, then short-term rates will
be high and long-term rates low relative to the levels implied by the Expectations Hypothesis. The **liquidity-premium hypothesis** holds that
investors are more concerned with capital risk than income risk and there-

**liquidity premium
hypothesis**
The liquidity premium
hypothesis says that
investors have a natural
preference for short-
term assets and require
relatively high returns
on long-term bonds.

fore have a natural preference for short-term assets and require relatively high returns on long-term bonds—higher than predicted by the simple Expectations Hypothesis. According to this theory, the term structure is normally upward sloping.

The **market-segmentation hypothesis,** in contrast, is a theory holding that investors have diverse preferences and specialize in different maturities. Some investors, such as life-insurance companies and pension funds, have long horizons. To the extent such institutions have promised to pay out relatively fixed nominal amounts many years from now, based on assumed nominal rates of return, there is considerable danger for them in a strategy of rolling over short-term investments. Insurance and pension funds are, in fact, the largest holders of long-term bonds. Other investors, particularly those most concerned with real rates of return, consider long-term bonds very risky and prefer to roll over short-term investments.

If the market is sharply segmented, then the interest rates on different maturities might depend solely on demand and supply within that segment of the market—resulting in very different interest rates for bonds with only slightly different maturities. While some investors do have preferred habitats, the evidence is that there are no discontinuities in the term structure; maturities are linked by the willingness of many investors to seek out the highest returns.

On balance, capital risk seems to be the predominant concern of investors in that, over the long run, rigorous studies confirm what Figure 5–4 in this chapter and Table 1–2 in Chapter 1 suggest—that long-term rates have, on average, been somewhat higher than short-term rates, evidence that investors need some extra return to persuade them to hold long-term bonds.[4] Similarly, comparisons of the term structure with actual surveys of rate expectations indicate that longer-term securities carry a risk premium.[5]

YIELD CURVES

The pure term structure of interest rates reflected in the Hicks Equation applies to zero-coupon bonds, but most bonds pay semiannual coupons. A yield curve showing the yields to maturity for coupon-paying bonds of differing maturities is not identical to the term structure of returns on zero-coupon bonds, except in the special case of a flat term structure. To demonstrate this point, we will assume annual coupons for simplicity. The present value P of an n-year bond, with annual coupons C and maturation value M, is obtained by summing the present values of the payments, using the appropriate required returns,

$$P = \frac{C}{(1 + R_1)} + \frac{C}{(1 + R_2)^2} + \cdots + \frac{C}{(1 + R_n)^n} + \frac{M}{(1 + R_n)^n}$$

The yield to maturity y is the *constant* required return that solves the present-value equation

$$P = \frac{C}{(1 + y)} + \frac{C}{(1 + y)^2} + \ldots + \frac{C}{(1 + y)^n} + \frac{M}{(1 + y)^n}$$

If the term structure is flat ($R_1 = R_2 = \ldots = R_n$), then the calculated yield to maturity equals R_n, and the yield curve and term structure coincide. If, on the other hand, the term structure is upward sloping, then the yield to maturity is an average of the R_t and will be somewhat less than R_n, depending on the size of the coupons. If $C = 0$, then y obviously equals R_n; panel (a) of Figure 5–5 shows that as C increases, the calculated yield to maturity falls below the return on a zero-coupon bond. Similarly, panel (b) of the figure shows that when the term structure is downward sloping, the yield to maturity is above R_n.

The most important implication is that the term structure provides a logical explanation for why bonds from the very same issuer with the same maturity have different yields to maturity. If you look in the newspaper now, you might find two ten-year U.S. Treasury bonds, one with, say, an 8 percent yield to maturity and the other an 8.5 percent yield to maturity. The latter is not necessarily an overlooked bargain. Perhaps the second bond has low coupons and the term structure is upward sloping.

A SAFE HORIZON

Because a coupon-paying bond or similar investment has both income and capital risk, an increase in interest rates is both good and bad news. Higher required returns reduce the present value of the bond (the bad news), but higher interest rates also increase the amount earned when the coupons are reinvested (the good news). The same is true of any cash flow. When interest rates go up, the market value of the asset declines but, paradoxically, the future value (including reinvestment of the cash flow) increases.

Consider, for instance, an eighteen-year Treasury bond with a maturation value of $1000, paying annual coupons of $100, and selling for par with a 10 percent yield to maturity. The duration is 9.02 years. Table 5–4 on p. 157 shows the future value of the coupons if these are reinvested at 10 percent and the market value of the bond if the yield to maturity stays at 10 percent. At the end of one year, the bond pays one $100 coupon and has seventeen years yet to run. With the yield to maturity still equal to the coupon rate (10 percent), the bond continues to sell for par, $1000. Thus, the value of the investment has grown to $1100, representing a 10 percent realized rate of return. After another year, a second $100 coupon is paid and the reinvestment of the first coupon has earned one year's interest at a 10 percent annual rate, giving a future value for the coupons of $210.

FIGURE 5–5 Yields to maturity on coupon-paying bonds

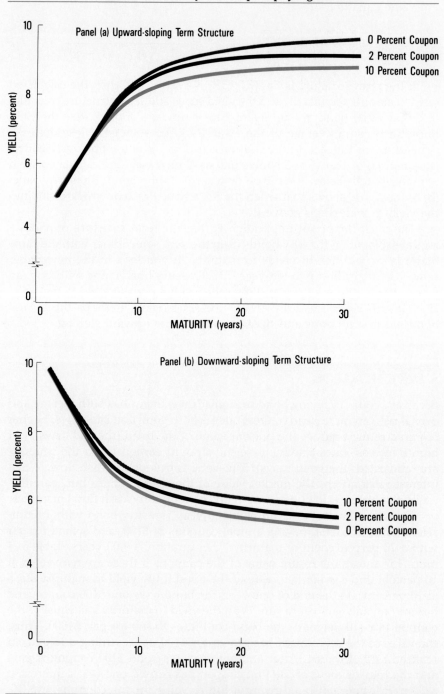

TABLE 5–4   Bond Results When Interest Rates Stay at 10 Percent

Year	Future Value of Coupons	Bond Price	Total Future Value	Realized Rate of Return (percent)
1	$ 100.00	$1,000.00	$1,100.00	10
2	210.00	1,000.00	1,210.00	10
3	331.00	1,000.00	1,331.00	10
4	464.10	1,000.00	1,464.10	10
5	610.51	1,000.00	1,610.51	10
6	771.56	1,000.00	1,771.56	10
7	948.72	1,000.00	1,948.72	10
8	1,143.59	1,000.00	2,143.59	10
9	1,357.95	1,000.00	2,357.95	10
10	1,593.74	1,000.00	2,593.74	10
11	1,853.12	1,000.00	2,853.12	10
12	2,138.43	1,000.00	3,138.43	10
13	2,452.27	1,000.00	3,452.27	10
14	2,797.50	1,000.00	3,797.50	10
15	3,177.25	1,000.00	4,177.25	10
16	3,594.97	1,000.00	4,594.97	10
17	4,054.47	1,000.00	5,054.47	10
18	4,559.92	1,000.00	5,559.92	10

With the yield to maturity still 10 percent, the price of the bond stays at $1000, and the total $1210 future value (coupons plus bond) represents a 10 percent realized rate of return, compounded annually. So it goes, period after period, the bond continuing to sell for par while the reinvested coupons accumulate, providing a realized annual rate of return of 10 percent.

Now what if interest rates do not stay at 10 percent? Table 5–5 on p. 158 shows the effects of a general decline in interest rates to 9 percent. The price of the bond initially rises by about 9 percent (as predicted by the nine-year duration), and, together with the $100 coupon, the total invest-ment has a realized return of 18.54 percent. As time passes and interest rates stay at 9 percent, the price of the bond falls inexorably toward its $1000 maturation value while the reinvested coupons earn 9 percent a year. Comparing Tables 5–4 and 5–5, one can see that the price of the bond is higher with a 9 percent interest rate in every period until maturity (the good news), but the value of the reinvested coupons is lower in every single period (the bad news). Overall, a 9 percent interest rate increases the total future value (bond price plus reinvested coupons) in the early years, but decreases it in the later years, when the reinvested coupons

TABLE 5–5   Bond Results When Interest Rates Fall to 9 Percent

Year	Future Value of Coupons	Bond Price	Total Future Value	Realized Rate of Return (percent)
1	$ 100.00	$1,085.44	$1,185.44	18.54
2	209.00	1,083.13	1,292.13	13.67
3	327.81	1,080.61	1,408.42	12.09
4	457.31	1,077.86	1,535.17	11.31
5	598.47	1,074.87	1,673.34	10.85
6	752.33	1,071.61	1,823.94	10.54
7	920.04	1,068.05	1,988.10	10.31
8	1,102.85	1,064.18	2,167.02	10.15
9	1,302.10	1,059.95	2,362.06	10.02
10	1,519.29	1,055.35	2,574.64	9.92
11	1,756.03	1,050.33	2,806.36	9.83
12	2,014.07	1,044.86	3,058.93	9.77
13	2,295.34	1,038.90	3,334.23	9.71
14	2,601.92	1,032.40	3,634.32	9.66
15	2,936.09	1,025.31	3,961.40	9.61
16	3,300.34	1,017.59	4,317.93	9.57
17	3,697.37	1,009.17	4,706.54	9.54
18	4,130.13	1,000.00	5,130.13	9.51

become more important. As we saw in the previous chapter,

> **At maturity, the realized rate of return on a bond, including the reinvested coupons, is higher or lower than the quoted yield to maturity, depending on whether the rate of return earned on the reinvested coupons is larger or smaller than the yield to maturity.**

Here, the reinvestment of the coupons at 9 percent rather than 10 percent reduces the final future value from $5,559.92 to $5,130.13, representing a 9.51 percent rather than a 10 percent realized rate of return.

Table 5–5 also shows that, whether the interest rate is 10 percent or 9 percent, the future value is approximately the same after nine years, which, not so coincidentally, is the duration of the bond.

> **For an horizon equal to the duration, the future value of a bond and its reinvested coupons is unaffected by (small) changes in the required return.**

TABLE 5–6 Bond Results When Interest Rates Rise to 11 Percent

Year	Future Value of Coupons	Bond Price	Total Future Value	Realized Rate of Return (percent)
1	$ 100.00	$ 924.51	$1,024.51	2.45
2	211.00	926.21	1,137.21	6.64
3	334.21	928.09	1,262.30	8.07
4	470.97	930.18	1,401.15	8.80
5	622.78	932.50	1,555.28	9.23
6	791.29	935.08	1,726.36	9.53
7	978.33	937.93	1,916.26	9.74
8	1,185.94	941.11	2,127.05	9.89
9	1,416.40	944.63	2,361.03	10.02
10	1,672.20	948.54	2,620.74	10.11
11	1,956.14	952.88	2,909.02	10.19
12	2,271.32	957.69	3,229.01	10.26
13	2,621.16	963.04	3,584.20	10.32
14	3,009.49	968.98	3,978.47	10.37
15	3,440.54	975.56	4,416.10	10.41
16	3,918.99	982.87	4,901.87	10.45
17	4,450.08	990.99	5,441.08	10.48
18	5,039.59	1,000.00	6,039.59	10.51

To confirm these lessons, Table 5–6 shows the case of a rise in interest rates to 11 percent, which reduces the bond's price during every period prior to maturation and simultaneously increases the value of the reinvested coupons. The total value of the bond at maturation (and the realized rate of return) is pulled up by the 11 percent rate of return on the reinvested coupons. The date at which the reduced value of the bond is just offset by the increased value of the coupons is again the bond's duration, nine years. Figure 5–6 on p. 160 shows this relationship graphically.

This constancy of the future value nine years hence only holds for small changes in interest rates, because the future value is nonlinear and the duration depends (inversely) on interest rates. As the interest rate rises, the duration shrinks and so does the horizon for which the total future value is constant. Consider, for instance, a jump in interest rates from 10 percent, where this bond has a duration of 9.02 years, to 17 percent, where the bond's duration works out to be 6.93 years. Table 5–7 on p. 161 shows that the horizon with constant future value is roughly eight years, about halfway between these two durations.

FIGURE 5–6   Realized return from a bond

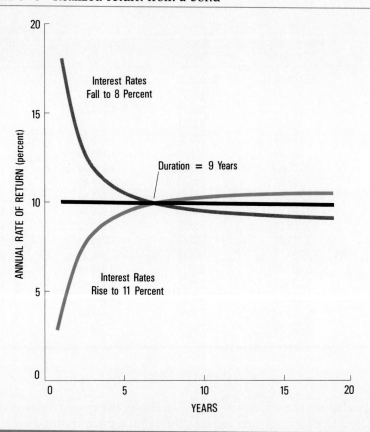

IMMUNIZATION

immunized
An investment's future value is immunized from interest rate changes if the holding period is equal to its duration.

If the holding period of an asset is equal to its duration, the investment is said to be **immunized**—protected in the sense that its realized rate of return is equal to its required return, regardless of whether interest rates rise or fall. Thus, an investor with a definite horizon can minimize interest-rate risk by holding assets with a duration equal to that horizon. A young couple needing $30,000 for a down payment on a house five years hence can buy bonds with a duration of five years. A family needing $50,000 for their children's college education fifteen years from now can buy bonds with a fifteen-year duration. A life-insurance company expecting to pay $500,000 thirty years from now can hold bonds with a thirty-year duration.

Because duration is inversely related to interest rates, these investors may want to adjust their bond holdings as interest rates change. An in-

TABLE 5–7 Bond Results When Interest Rates Rise to 17 Percent

Year	Future Value of Coupons	Bond Price	Total Future Value	Realized Rate of Return (percent)
1	$ 100.00	$ 616.78	$ 716.78	−28.32
2	217.00	621.63	838.63	−8.42
3	353.89	627.31	981.20	−0.63
4	514.05	633.95	1,148.00	3.51
5	741.04	641.72	1,343.16	6.08
6	920.68	650.81	1,571.50	7.82
7	1,177.20	661.45	1,838.65	9.09
8	1,477.33	673.90	2,151.22	10.05
9	1,828.47	688.46	2,516.93	10.80
10	2,239.31	705.50	2,944.81	11.41
11	2,719.99	725.43	3,445.43	11.90
12	3,282.39	748.76	4,031.15	12.32
13	3,940.40	776.05	4,716.45	12.67
14	4,710.27	807.97	5,518.24	12.98
15	5,611.01	845.33	6,456.34	13.24
16	6,664.88	889.03	7,553.92	13.47
17	7,897.92	940.17	8,838.09	13.68
18	9,340.56	1,000.00	10,340.56	13.86

crease in interest rates, for example, reduces the bonds' duration, encouraging them to sell some of their shorter-term bonds and buy longer-term ones to maintain their target duration. Even if interest rates are unchanged, portfolio rebalancing may be desirable because (except for zero coupon bonds) the passage of a year's time does not reduce an asset's duration by a year. Consider again the eighteen-year bond in Table 5–4 with a 10 percent yield to maturity and a duration of 9.02 years, which is appropriate for a horizon of nine years. After a year passes, the investor has a horizon of eight years and would like a bond portfolio with a similar duration. But if the yield to maturity is still 10 percent, the duration of this now seventeen-year bond is 8.82 years. Clearly, investors have to balance their desire for an attractive duration against frequent transaction costs.

Asset and Liability Durations

Individuals and businesses have both assets and liabilities, each with associated future cash flows. Individuals take out mortgages and buy bonds; businesses sell bonds and buy plant and equipment. Each side of their balance sheets has some interest-rate risk, and, to the extent the durations of their assets and liabilities are not matched, they are making an implicit

BORROWING SHORT AND LENDING LONG

In the 1970s, the balance sheet of a small, traditional savings and loan association might appear as follows, with all entries stated in millions of dollars:

Assets		Liabilities	
Cash reserves	5	Deposits	96
Loans	95	Net worth	4
Total assets	**100**	**Total liabilities**	**100**

We will assume that the interest rates paid on its deposits change daily, giving deposits a duration of virtually zero, and that its loans are conventional thirty-year mortgages. At a 10 percent interest rate, the duration of a thirty-year mortgage works out to be 8.5 years, implying that a one-percentage-point change in interest rates reduces the present value of a thirty-year mortgage by about 8.5 percent. In practice, not all of any S&L's mortgages are made today; so, we will assume that in our example the mortgages are fairly evenly scattered—some with ten years to go, some with twenty, and so on—and that the average duration of the loan portfolio is roughly four years. If so, an unanticipated one-percentage-point increase in interest rates will reduce the present value of this portfolio by 4 percent (about $4 million), enough to wipe out the S&L's net worth:

Assets		Liabilities	
Cash reserves	5	Deposits	96
Loans	91	Net worth	0
Total assets	**96**	**Total liabilities**	**96**

(The present values of the deposits and reserves do not change, since they have a duration of zero.)

Duration provides a dramatic way of seeing how the traditional S&L strategy of borrowing short and lending long is a very dangerous bet on the future course of interest rates. In this stylized example, an unexpected one-percentage-point reduction in interest rates doubles net worth, but a one-percentage-point interest-rate increase leaves the S&L technically bankrupt.

As interest rates rose during 1979–82 (and, to make matters worse, there were significant defaults on farm, oil, and foreign loans), financial institutions with balance sheets comparable to those shown in this example were in a lot of trouble. Indeed, one influential analyst, Edward Yardeni of Prudential-Bache, based his 1984 and 1985 predictions of lower interest rates largely on his belief that the Federal Reserve would have to lower interest rates to bail out financial intermediaries that had borrowed short and lent long.

Duration also helps us understand how financial intermediaries have adjusted their portfolios to stabilize their net worth. A move to shorter-term loans (increasing the number of short-term consumer loans and fifteen-year mortgages in place of thirty-year mortgages) obviously reduces asset duration. Even more effective are adjustable-rate mortgages, which can have a duration of one year or less, depending on the adjustment provisions of the contract. On the liability side, longer-term deposits "with substantial penalties for premature withdrawal" can push duration upward. If these actions roughly match the duration of the loans to the duration of the deposits, then net worth is insulated from unanticipated interest-rate fluctuations. If the duration of loans exceeds deposit duration, then implicitly the institution is betting that interest rates will fall. A deposit duration in excess of loan duration is a wager that interest rates will rise.

wager on the future course of interest rates. In fact, it was investor anxiety over such wagers during the interest-rate turbulence in the late 1970s and early 1980s that led to the creation of financial-futures contracts and other hedging instruments that we will discuss in later chapters.

Banks, savings and loan associations (S&Ls), and other financial intermediaries provide an especially interesting example in that by borrowing from some to lend to others, there is a clear and controllable link between their financial assets and liabilities. In Britain, the actuaries who certify the financial soundness of an insurance company or a pension fund are required to compare the maturities of assets and liabilities. There is no such requirement in the United States, and, as Investment Example 5–1 explains, the interest-rate gambles that savings and loan associations have won and lost have not only shaken the S&Ls, but scared depositors and policymakers, too.

SUMMARY

The term structure of interest rates describes the relationship between the interest rates on comparable zero-coupon bonds with differing maturities. The Expectations Hypothesis states that the shape of the term structure depends on interest-rate expectations, with long-term rates above, equal to, or below short-term rates depending on whether interest rates are expected to rise, stay the same, or decline. Thus, we can infer from the shape of the term structure the direction in which investors expect interest rates to move.

Interest rates are very difficult to predict. Those investors who buy long-term zeros, locking in a certain rate of return, are betting that future interest rates will be lower than the forward rates implied by the term structure. Those investors who roll over short-term bonds implicitly wager that future interest rates will be higher than the term structure's forward rates. Short-term bonds have income risk since the interest rates at which the funds can be reinvested are uncertain. Long-term bonds have capital risk in that changes in interest rates affect their market value. Fixed-income securities, especially long-term ones, also have inflation risk, because the purchasing power of the cash flow depends on uncertain rates of inflation.

The liquidity-premium hypothesis holds that investors fearful of capital risk prefer short-term securities if the expected return on long-term bonds is no higher than the expected return on shorts. Therefore, long-term securities must have relatively high expected returns to compensate for their capital risk. The market-segmentation hypothesis says that some investors have short horizons and prefer short-term securities, but others, such as pension funds and life-insurance companies, have long horizons and a natural preference for long-term bonds.

An asset's duration is the present-value-weighted average length of time until its cash flow is received. Duration is of interest to investors because the percentage change in an asset's present value resulting from a one-percentage-point change in the required return is approximately equal to the asset's duration. Increases in interest rates reduce the present value (and the market price) of an asset's future cash flow, but they also increase the returns that can be earned on the reinvested cash flow. Therefore, an increase in interest rates is bad news in the short run, but good news in the long run. An asset's duration determines the horizon over which the change in an asset's market price is just offset by the change in the value of the reinvested cash flow, leaving the total future value unaffected.

A complete examination of exposure to interest-rate risk must consider assets and liabilities. A savings and loan association, for example, that borrows short and lends long has an asset duration that significantly exceeds the duration of its liabilities. Its net worth will be increased by an unexpected decline in interest rates, and it will be reduced by an unanticipated rise in interest rates.

EXERCISES

1. The rate of return on one-year T-bills is now 7 percent. This rate is expected to be 10 percent a year from now and 12 percent two years hence. According to the Expectations Hypothesis, what should be the current annual yield on a three-year, zero-coupon Treasury bond?

2. The annual rates of return on one-year and two-year bonds are 7 percent and 10 percent, respectively. According to the Expectations Hypothesis, what is the expected return on one-year bonds issued a year from now? (Assume that these are all zero-coupon bonds.)

3. The rate of return on one-year zero-coupon bonds is now 10 percent, and it is expected to be 15 percent next year and for at least two years after that. According to the Expectations Hypothesis, what should be the current annual yields on two-year, three-year, and four-year zero-coupon bonds?

4. The annual rates of return on one-year, two-year, and three-year zero-coupon bonds are 7 percent, 10 percent, 12 percent, respectively. According to the Expectations Hypothesis, what is the expected return on a one-year zero issued a year from now? two years from now?

5. Here is some advice offered in *Woman's Day* to bond investors:

Many conservative investors are attracted to "income funds"—mutual funds invested mostly in [long-term] bonds—but they are not always as safe as they sound. Bond funds do well when long-term interest rates fall . . . But bond funds do poorly when long-term interest rates rise . . . Michael Lipper of Lipper Analytical Services, which specializes in mutual-fund analysis, urges investors to think of bond funds as *speculative* securities: investments to buy and sell according to market conditions, rather than to hold for the long term . . . if rates rise again, he says, it will pay to sell income funds and switch to the greater security of short-term money market mutual funds.[6]

a. Why do bond funds do well when long-term rates fall and poorly when they rise?

b. What does the Expectations Hypothesis imply about the profitability of shifting to short-term securities after interest rates rise?

c. In what sense do short-term money-market funds offer greater security than do long-term income funds?

6. Will Rogers once said, "I am not so much concerned with the return on my money as with the return of my money." Would you say that he was more concerned with income risk or with capital risk?

7. Assume that the coupons on the following bonds are paid semiannually, beginning six months from today, and that each bond pays $1000 at maturity.

Bond	Maturity (years)	Semiannual Coupon Amount
A	5	$ 50
B	5	100
C	30	100

For each bond, use a computer program to calculate the present value and the duration if the yield to maturity is 10 percent. Also calculate the percentage change in the present value if the yield to maturity rises to 11 percent. What relationship, if any, is there between these percentage changes and duration?

8. Explain this observation: "A bond's duration will always be shorter than its maturity— much shorter for higher coupon bonds."[7]

9. In November 1988, two-year Treasury notes had 8½ percent yields to maturity while thirty-year Treasury bonds had 9 percent yields. An article in *The Wall Street Journal* began:

> Why would anyone buy 30-year Treasury bonds right now when they can earn nearly the same returns on short-term issues that aren't as susceptible to price decline?
>
> Investors are confronting that dilemma because of an unusual development in the bond market—a "flat yield curve."[8]

a. Why are long-term bonds more susceptible to a price decline?

b. Why is a flat yield curve unusual? What is the usual shape of a yield curve?

c. Why would anyone buy thirty-year bonds (and someone must) when the yield curve is flat?

10. In a May 1985 *New York Times* interview, John T. Haggerty, National Director of Personal Financial Planning for Prudential Bache Securities, advised

> I wouldn't buy any bond, except maybe a Treasury, that was 30 years in maturity. I don't know if the world is going to be around 30 years from now . . . If I had to buy, or if I wanted to buy, I'd probably be looking at discount bonds. There you have the maturities working in your favor. You know the bond's going to be going up in price, because it's getting closer to maturity with the passage of time.[9]

a. Why is the existence of the world thirty years from now of little relevance to an investor's choice between short-term and long-term bonds?

b. Evaluate Haggerty's apparent claim that the returns from bonds selling at a discount are inherently more certain than the returns from bonds selling at par or for a premium.

c. Interest rates dropped substantially in 1985. Why, in retrospect, would Haggerty have made especially large profits from the purchase of thirty-year bonds early in 1985?

11. Explain why you might hesitate to follow this financial advice: since short-term rates are currently lower than long-term rates, it is better to borrow short-term.

12. A vice president at E. F. Hutton says of zero-coupon bonds, backed by U.S. Treasury notes, "The beauty of it is that the investor knows exactly how many dollars go in, and how many dollars will come out." A Merrill Lynch vice president says, "This suits the little old lady in tennis shoes who's watching her nickels, and it's ideal for your kids."[10] Can you think of any reason why little old ladies and kids might be nervous about zeros? Is there any risk in such an investment?

13. In 1985, Ed Yardeni, Prudential Bache's chief economist, forecast "lower-than-expected interest rates."[11] Why was he careful not to say simply "lower interest rates"? For each of the following options, which choice would you have made at the time if you agreed with Yardeni?

a. Buy Treasury bills or long-term bonds.

b. Borrow at a fixed interest rate or at a variable interest rate.

c. Sell fifteen-year bonds or thirty-year bonds.

14. Critically evaluate the following advertising statement:

> Why spend your valuable time worrying and fretting about falling interest rates? Forget it! And while you're at it, forget about making frequent, difficult financial decisions. Invest

in one of the Pomona First Federal's longer term (18–29 month) high-yield money market certificates.[12]

15. A textbook states that "bond investors will prefer to buy short-term bonds whenever they expect interest rates to rise."[13] What is the logic behind this assertion? Why is the statement incorrect?

16. Following is an excerpt from a syndicated newspaper column:

> For all their importance, interest rates remain a subject of immense confusion and mystery. The striking aspect of the current decline is that long-term interest rates have dipped far more than short-term rates. Since January 1985, for example, rates on long-term Treasury bonds have fallen more than 3 percentage points while those on short-term Treasury bills have declined roughly 1 percentage point . . .
>
> The implication is that the Federal Reserve has so far played a secondary role in lowering rates. Its direct influence is concentrated on short-term rates.[14]

If the Expectation Hypothesis is correct, how can long-term rates fall more than short-term rates? How can the Fed affect long-term interest rates, even if it only buys and sells short-term Treasury bills?

17. The following are excerpts from an article in *The Wall Street Journal:*

> With inflation abated and interest rates down sharply on money-market funds and bank accounts, consumers are turning to bond products for higher yields. Many investors have shifted dollars out of money funds paying around 7% and into "long-term" Treasury securities paying more than 10% . . .
>
> A California real estate attorney admits that he was "dumbfounded" to find that $192,000 in Treasury zeros he bought in January 1984 were valued at $156,000 when he went to sell them four months later . . .

> Nelson Chase, a West Blomfield, Mich., attorney is representing a group of zero-coupon bond investors that is suing New York-based Merrill Lynch & Co. "All the literature talks about how safe these investments are," he says. "Unless you can be absolutely sure you will hold to maturity, these aren't safe investments."[15]

Answer these three questions:

a. What circumstances, if any, would dissuade you from shifting out of a bank paying 7 percent into Treasury securities paying 10 percent?

b. How could Treasury zeros lose nearly 20 percent of their value in four months?

c. Why may zeros held to maturity not be safe?

18. In February 1987, a Los Angeles investment banker explained why he would not finance his house with an adjustable-rate mortgage: "I don't want to throw the dice and get burned."[16] In what sense is a fixed-rate mortgage also a throw of the dice? What is a losing roll?

19. A conventional, amortized, 30-year mortgage for $100,000 at 10 percent has a duration of 8.5 years. Without doing any calculations, do you think this mortgage's duration is longer or shorter than

a. a thirty-year zero-coupon bond?

b. a thirty-year bond with a 10 percent yield to maturity selling for par?

c. a conventional, amortized, thirty-year mortgage for $200,000 at 10 percent?

20. Many lending institutions have been touting the fifteen-year mortgage in place of the traditional thirty-year mortgage. Why do they prefer the fifteen-year mortgage?

21. In the 1960s, the U.S. government wanted to reduce long-term interest rates to stimulate corporate investment while raising short-term interest rates to improve the balance of payments. The Fed tried Operation Twist, a strategy of trading in short- and long-term government securities to twist the term structure. Should they have bought shorts and sold longs or vice-versa? What are the implications, if any,

TABLE 5–A

Bond	Maturity (years)	Annual Coupon	Current Price	Yield to Maturity (percent)
A	5	$100	$1,000.00	10
B	7	150	1,243.42	10
C	10	50	692.77	10

of the Expectations Hypothesis for Operation Twist?

22. In the spring of 1986, David Marks, Senior Vice President of Cigna Investments, explained how he used duration to implement his fixed-income strategy:

> To look at maturity alone, you are generally not taking into account interest income and reinvestment income . . . If you're bullish, expecting interest rates to go down and prices up, then your duration should be slightly longer than the [Shearson Lehman bond] index. If you're bearish, your duration should be slightly shorter or the same.[17]

Explain the advantages of a long-duration portfolio when you are bullish, and a short-duration portfolio when you are not. Are there any circumstances in which you, confident that interest rates will fall, would choose a short-duration portfolio?

23. Consider the three bonds, each with a $1000 maturation value, described in Table 5–A. You want to lock in a 10 percent return over the next five years. What is the future value of each of these bonds, including reinvested coupons, five years from now if, immediately after purchasing the bond, interest rates drop to 9 percent? rise to 11 percent? Which bond does a better job of guaranteeing a 10 percent return?

24. Write a brief critique of the following advice:

> With a growing sense of gloom hanging over the bond market, many investment analysts

said they're urging clients to switch away from long-term securities into the shortest possible maturities. "You can get almost as good yields at the short ends without the worry," says Data Resources' Mr. Eckstein.[18]

25. In 1980, U. S. Steel pioneered the issuance of thirty-year, floating-rate bonds. The yield on these bonds is adjusted weekly, based on the current yields on Treasury securities. In gauging capital risk, would you consider such floating-rate securities to be short-term or long-term?

26. Evaluate the following argument by a prominent economics professor:

> We should curb the political influence that the banking community has achieved through its formal alliance with the Fed. It is not surprising, of course, that creditors are more interested in relatively tight money and high interest rates than debtors and consumers.[19]

27. Critically evaluate this discussion of unit bond trusts, which are mutual funds that purchase long-term bonds:

> Unlike conventional mutual funds, which can buy and sell securities as economic or market conditions change, unit trusts normally hold their original bonds until they mature . . . the terms of the trust forbid it to sell one bond in order to buy another, even one that is less likely to decline in price.
>
>   An investor who is content to hold his units until the last bond matures—perhaps

well into the 21st century—can cheerfully ignore temporary declines in the value of the bonds in the trust. Indeed, the longest term trusts often appear to be the most attractive. In today's market, bonds maturing in 25 to 30 years pay up to a full percentage point more than five-to-ten-year bonds from the same company or municipality. But many people will have to sell their units before maturity, and here a trust can turn out to be an expensive mistake.[20]

28. Long-term rates are generally more stable than short-term rates: for example, when the one-year rate jumps from 10 percent to 13 percent, the twenty-year rate might only rise from 10 percent to 12 percent. How would the Expectations Hypothesis explain the relative stability of long-term rates?

29. A commonplace bank procedure to control for interest-rate risk is gap management, where gap = (rate-sensitive assets − rate-sensitive liabilities)/total assets. The following explains this concept:

> Interest-sensitive assets are those that mature, or are repriced, within a designated time-frame. For example, a loan may have a stated maturity of one year, but can be subject to rate changes tied to the prime rate and is, therefore, immediately sensitive to interest rate changes. Similarly, rates paid on money market accounts generally can change daily and, are therefore, immediately sensitive to interest rate movements.
> . . . When the gap is zero, net interest income is fully insulated from interest rate risk because the maturity of rate-sensitive assets and liabilities should cause them to offset each other and to leave the net interest margin unchanged.[21]

For example, if 10 percent of assets and 12 percent of liabilities have their rates change with market rates, then the gap is −2 percent.

a. If a bank has a negative gap, will its net interest income rise or fall if interest rates increase?

b. If a bank wants to bet that interest rates are headed downward, should it have a positive or negative gap?

c. Explain how a bank with a gap of zero can find itself bankrupted (with its market value driven to zero) by an unexpected decline in interest rates.

30. In 1986, *The Wall Street Journal* reported the following:

> Falling interest rates prompt corporations to refinance short-term, high-cost debt with bonds with lower rates and longer maturities, reducing costs and making them less vulnerable to interest-rate moves . . . Still, many corporations delay refinancing, expecting interest rates to drop further.[22]

Why might long-term debt have lower interest rates than short-term debt? In what way are those who borrow long-term still vulnerable to interest-rate moves?

31. Explain the reasoning that underlies this advice:

> A portfolio duration of eight years is about as long as one can obtain on conventional coupon-paying bonds, given double-digit interest rates, but investment horizons of 40 years are not uncommon for pension funds or life insurance companies . . . such portfolios will surely suffer when interest rates decline, even though the associated temporary increase in market value . . . may create the illusion of investment success.[23]

32. Explain why you either agree or disagree with this reasoning: "Long-term bonds tend to have the highest current yields; this reflects the greater uncertainty of future events. That uncertainty is compensated for, as it were, by higher interest rates."[24]

33. Here are some excerpts from a 1986 *New York Times* article:

> "In my view, making long-term fixed-rate mortgages is simply not a viable strategy any

longer," said Dennis Jacobe, director of research at the United States League of Savings Associations.

The widespread issuance of fixed-rate mortgages in the 1970s led to the collapse or merger of nearly a quarter of the nation's 4,000 savings associations then existing . . . Of those that survived, some remain in extremely poor shape . . .

Adjustable-rate mortgages reached their height of popularity in late 1984, when 70 percent of the mortgages issued by savings and loan associations were adjustable-rate, according to the savings league.

. . . Fixed-rate loans, [however], were the only type Washington Federal [a Seattle S&L] was making . . .

"You can't be reckless, but right now we're in a deflationary cycle . . . ," Mr. Knutson [the company's president and chief executive] said. Referring to 1981, he added that "you can't operate based on one devastating period; otherwise you leave too much profitability on the table."[25]

a. What economic event caused trouble for S&Ls with fixed-rate mortgages? How do adjustable-rate mortgages provide protection?
b. Some S&Ls have moved to shorter-term mortgages and longer-term deposits. If the duration of their liabilities is greater than the duration of their assets, are they protected from interest-rate fluctuations?
c. Why do you suppose the management at many S&Ls now wish they had issued fixed-rate mortgages during 1981–84?

34. The Student Loan Marketing Association (Sallie Mae) is a private corporation that uses borrowed money to buy government-guaranteed student loans from banks. The interest rates on all of its assets and liabilities adjust up or down with changes in T-bill rates. What is the duration of its assets? of its liabilities? How is its net worth affected by interest rates?

35. Explain the logic behind the following assertion, and then explain why it is misleading:

The essential difference between fixed- and adjustable-rate mortgages is the party at risk. In fixed mortgages, the lender takes all the risk, profiting or suffering from changes in the interest rate . . . . With an ARM, the borrower, not the lender, is at the mercy of fluctuating interest rates.[26]

36. An April 1987 article titled "Interest Rates Likely to Head Higher" explained its prediction this way:

Bond purchasers don't enjoy months like March; the brokerage firm of Salomon Brothers reported that price declines in the domestic bond market last month produced negative total returns for the first time since May 1986. That sort of situation leads to higher interest rates."[27]

a. Can we infer that monthly bond prices had not declined from May 1986 until March 1987?
b. Do lower bond prices raise or lower bond yields to maturity? Are bonds then more or less attractive?
c. What pattern in bond-price behavior is implicit in the prediction that bond-price declines will cause interest rates to rise soon?
37. Explain why you agree or disagree with the advice, "In an inflationary era, when depreciation of the currency is the order of the day, a fixed, long-term obligation is not the thing to own."[28]
38. Explain why you either agree or disagree with this reasoning by the director of research for the American Association of Individual Investors: "Certificates of Deposit, unless they are the large-denomination, negotiable type, have no market interest-rate risk because they are not traded and have no market price."[29]
39. A March 1989 *U.S. News & World Report* story contained this advice:

With interest rates up and expected to head higher this year, the case is strong for short-term investments that let you ride the upward spiral without risk. Yields on one-year T-bills, recently 9.32 percent, are at the highest levels in four years . . . Meanwhile, the 30-year and six-month issues both yield about 9 percent . . . The wisest course may be to pick short maturities, but be ready to shift to longer terms when rates have clearly peaked.[30]

a. Is there any risk in buying short-term Treasury bills?

b. How would the Expectations Hypothesis explain the shape of yield curve?

c. Explain the flaw in the advice to "shift to longer terms when rates have clearly peaked."

40. A *U.S. News & World Report* writer reported that, "Of the $10,000 an investor paid for a one-year bill in mid-February [1989], $868.50 was returned immediately. But it will not count as income until maturity in 1990 and thus escapes taxation until April 15, 1991."[31] What is the before-tax rate of return on this T-bill? Explain why there either is or is not a tax advantage as compared to a one-year bank certificate of deposit that pays the same before-tax return as the T-bill.

Common Stock

CHAPTER 6

The Stock Market

*If you don't know who you are, the stock market is an
expensive place to find out . . .*

George Goodman

The preceding two chapters dealt with bonds and other fixed-income securities, legally binding agreements by issuers to pay specified amounts
of money to investors holding the securities. Corporate stock is very different because it represents equity, ownership of a company, and the return
is not at all fixed. The profits from owning stock, dividends plus capital
gains, depend ultimately on the profitability of a company, because current
profits allow the firm to pay dividends and because anticipated future
profits influence the price others are willing to pay for the company's
shares. In this chapter, we will examine the nature of corporate stock and
the markets in which it is traded. The next three chapters will be concerned
with valuation models—how investors value stock and, hence, the prices
they are willing to pay.

First, we will consider some of the reasons that a company chooses to
incorporate and some of the consequences. Then we will explore how
secondary-market trades are handled on the stock exchanges and in the
over-the-counter market. Next is a discussion of the types of orders that
investors can place with their brokers and the inherent conflict between
the interests of investors and brokers. Finally, we will look at the Dow
Jones Industrial Average and other indexes that monitor stock prices.

CORPORATE STOCK

common stock
The holders of a
corporation's common
stock are the legal
owners of the firm.

There are two general types of shares. The legal owners of a corporation,
hold **common stock**—the name indicating that the shareholders own the
firm in common. Although the stockholders do not personally make production, pricing, and personnel decisions, they do elect (normally with

one vote per share) a board of directors, which hires the top executives and supervises their management of the firm. Some firms have two or more classes of common stock. For example, Ford Motor Company has a Class B common stock, owned by the Ford family and related trusts, which is not publicly traded and has 40 percent of the total stockholder vote even though it is only 15 percent of the total outstanding shares. Similarly, New York Times Class B common, held mostly by an Ochs family trust, has voting control even though it is only 6 percent of the company's outstanding common stock.

Preferred stock is a second type of stock similar to a bond in that there are often no voting privileges, the shares have a stated liquidation value, and the dividend payments are specified when the stock is first issued—usually a constant dollar amount, but sometimes (for adjustable-rate preferred) an amount linked to the current level of interest rates. Unlike bondholders, the owners of preferred stock cannot force the company into bankruptcy if dividend payments are missed. If the preferred dividends are cumulative, the unpaid dividends accumulate (without interest), and a firm is generally prohibited from paying dividends on its common stock until it has paid all of the current and cumulative dividends due on its preferred stock. If the firm is liquidated, preferred stockholders must be paid a specified value before common stockholders receive anything.

preferred stock
Preferred stock is similar to a bond in that there are often no voting privileges, the shares have a stated liquidation value, and the dividend payments are specified when the stock is first issued.

The dividends common stockholders receive are not contractually fixed; rather they are decided periodically by a firm's board of directors. Unlike interest, dividends are not a tax-deductible expense for the corporation. The stockholders, as owners of the firm, are entitled to the profits that the firm makes after wages, materials, rent, interest, and other expenses. The firm's directors, acting on behalf of the shareholders, decide how much of these profits to distribute as dividends and how much to retain for buying more plant and equipment to expand the firm.

Debt and Equity

The loans, bonds, and other fixed-income securities issued by a corporation are legal *debts*, while common stock is *equity*—a claim to the residual value of the firm after its debts have been paid. An extremely condensed balance sheet of a hypothetical firm is shown in Table 6–1. This firm has $100 million in assets, mostly plant, equipment, and other real assets. Because it has $40 million in debts outstanding, *shareholders' equity*—what would be left if the firm were liquidated and its debts repaid—comes to $60 million. If there are 5 million shares outstanding, this works out to $12 a share. This estimate of the firm's value per share is called the **book value** of the firm's stock, since it is derived from the firm's books—that is, the accountants' balance sheets.

book value
A company's book value is the net worth (assets minus liabilities) shown on its balance sheets.

The market price of the stock may be above or below the book value, because investors do not value a firm in the same way as accountants.

TABLE 6–1   Balance Sheet of a Hypothetical Firm

Assets (millions of dollars)		Liabilities (millions of dollars)	
Financial assets	$10	Debt	$40
Real assets	90	Shareholders' equity	60
Total assets	**100**	**Total liabilities**	**100**

The market price of the stock may be above or below the book value, because investors do not value a firm in the same way as accountants. Assets are generally carried on the books at original cost and, in the case of buildings and equipment, depreciated over time to indicate wear and tear. When a business buys a building that will be productive for fifty years, accountants say it is misleading to record all of the cost in the first year, giving a huge loss that year. Instead, they spread the cost over the life of the building and, to balance the books, show these costs as *depreciation*— a decline in the value of the building.

However, if land prices and construction costs increase, the replacement cost of a firm's real assets may be far larger than their original cost, let alone their depreciated cost. If so, the firm's stock may be worth far more than its book value. Yet, a firm may have very expensive assets that are not profitable, and shareholders will not pay $12 a share for a company that does not make money and cannot afford to pay dividends.

Bondholders have legally binding promissory notes and have first claim on the firm's revenue and assets. If there is not enough money to pay a company's debts in full, then the firm may be forced into bankruptcy, with its assets sold and the proceeds paid to the bondholders and other creditors. The stockholders get nothing but their worthless stock certificates and, we are told, an expensive lesson. On the other hand, if the firm grows and prospers, the bondholders receive only the fixed income they have been promised, nothing more, while the stockholders, as owners of the firm, share the growing profits.

Bondholders have a relatively secure investment because their returns are part of a binding contract, and, if the firm does experience financial difficulty, they are paid first. The stockholders' investment is far less certain, because their return hinges on the firm's success and the dividends that are declared by the firm's directors. The stockholders may lose every penny of their investment, or they may share in an unending succession of larger and larger profits.

Limited Liability

The legal concept of corporate shareholders began in England in the early stages of the Industrial Revolution. Large companies are too big to be owned by any single individual or handful of partners. The most extreme example today is IBM with a total market value of approximately $70 billion in 1989. No one individual has enough money to own IBM or other large, modern businesses. In addition, most persons are reluctant to have all of their wealth concentrated in a single company. Instead, the affluent, like the not-so-rich, invest in many different companies, and IBM has millions of different stockholders. Most investors today are *outside shareholders*— people who invest money but have nothing to do with the day-to-day operations of the company, which they leave to the firm's management.

The legal concept of a corporation was devised not only to divide ownership among many investors, but also to protect investors if the firm is mismanaged. While stockholders are the legal owners of a corporation, they are not personally responsible for its debts. Shareholders have **limited liability** in that their potential loss is limited to the amount of money they have invested in the firm's stock. Limited liability is the reason many British and Canadian firm's have the word *Limited* or the abbreviation *Ltd.* as part of the company's name. Similarly, a *limited partnership* is a special arrangement that allows investors to share in the profits of a firm, but limits their liability to the size of their investment.

> **limited liability**
> Stockholders have limited liability in that they are not personally responsible for the firm's debts.

If a corporation cannot pay its debts, then its bankruptcy leaves the shareholders with worthless stock certificates—a disappointing outcome, but, still, far better than having to turn over additional money to satisfy the firm's creditors. Presumably, limited liability encourages people to invest in stock, enabling them to become part owners of large businesses.

There are disadvantages to being a public corporation, perhaps the most important being the double taxation of earnings. Suppose that a company earns $10 a share and wants to distribute the earnings to the owners. If the company is not a corporation, the owners receive $10 and pay perhaps a 28 percent personal income tax, which allows them to keep $7.20. If the business is a corporation, however, it must pay a 34 percent corporate income tax, leaving $6.60 to be distributed as dividends, on which shareholders then pay a 28 percent tax and keep only $0.72(\$6.60) = \$4.75$. The double taxation, thus, amounts to an effective 52.5 percent tax rate!

Corporations also must keep investment bankers and stockholders happy and comply with the various disclosure requirements and other regulations enforced by the Securities and Exchange Commission, chores that some consider intrusive and expensive. As the director of investment banking at Prudential Bache put it, "You can't have the trappings of many private companies—Mercedes, jets, maids on the company payroll. You have to clean up your act, and some people don't like that."[1]

THE PROCESS OF INCORPORATION

Businesses typically begin as small, privately held companies. Imagine that you have an idea for the proverbial better mousetrap, and you want to produce and market this wonder. After exhausting your own savings, you may be able to borrow some additional funds at, say, a 10 percent interest rate from relatives, a bank, or sympathetic investors. The enthusiasm of these potential investors, however, may be dampened by your inexperience and lack of tangible assets. If sales turn out to be disappointing, as is usually the case with new businesses, you will not be able to repay your debts and the investors' hoped-for 10 percent interest will turn into a 100 percent loss.

If you cannot find lenders willing to accept these odds you may have to settle for *partners*, investors willing to bankroll your expansion in return for a share of the profits. While these investors accept the possibility of 100 percent loss, they also have the chance of large profits. You can form a partnership or, instead, a corporation to obtain limited liability. Businesses can incorporate without selling shares to the public: individuals can form sole-owner corporations, and small groups (thirty-five or fewer investors) can form a privately held corporation. If your small business eventually proves successful, there may come a point at which your ambitious plans for expansion require a great deal of money and you decide to sell shares to the public at large.

A public offering has to meet the disclosure requirements of the SEC. An investment banker (such as Morgan Stanley, Salomon Brothers, or Goldman Sachs) prepares a *prospectus* for potential investors—a document that reveals relevant data regarding the company's past performance, lays out the company's plans, and gives boldface warnings to investors, like **"These shares are very risky."** An advertisement may appear in one or more publications, such as *The Wall Street Journal*, that announces the planned incorporation and states, "This announcement is neither an offer to sell nor a solicitation to buy any of these securities. The offering is made only by the Prospectus." Listed in this ad are several underwriters, including your investment banker and others that have agreed to distribute the shares. This syndicate of investment bankers has regular customers—including insurance companies, pension funds, and individual investors—who can be persuaded to buy shares. The underwriters may also agree to buy for their own accounts any shares that they cannot sell to the public.

You and your investment banker agree on a price at which the shares are to be offered. Experienced financial analysts scrutinize your books and come up with an estimate of what the company is worth—that is, how much you could sell it for. Suppose the estimate is $20 million. (If this is a dream, we may as well make it a good one.) Now, you do not intend to sell your company and walk away. You just want funds to expand and, in return, are willing to share your company with others. If you are to raise, say, another $20 million, then you will have $40 million in assets—your company, which is worth $20 million by itself, plus $20 million in cash. In addition, this cash will not sit idle, but rather be used to enlarge your business. With this new money and your patented mousetrap, you can make enough profits so that the company will be worth perhaps $50 million.

So, armed with these conservative estimates, you issue ten million shares of stock, priced at $5 a share. You keep six million shares for yourself and your original partners, and your investment banker pledges to sell four million shares at $5 a share to raise the desired $20 million. The buyers are getting, with each share, one ten-millionth of a $50 million company. You and your initial partners get shares worth $30 million—$20 million for the company as it is today, plus $10 million for the profits you can make with this new money. If things work out as planned, everyone will be happy.

Notice that incorporation apparently creates instant millionaires. You were plugging along, building mousetrap after mousetrap, working long hours and plowing every penny back into the firm. You lived a frugal, workaholic lifestyle and didn't look at all like the rich and famous seen on television. Then along came incorporation, and, all of a sudden, you (and your initial partners, if any) had stock worth $30 million. George Goodman called these instant riches *supermoney* and wrote a book with this word as its title. What should not be overlooked is that, as owner of a profitable firm, you were really a millionaire all along. Your mousetrap business was worth millions, and incorporation disclosed this fact by transforming your illiquid human capital into liquid securities.

THE STOCK EXCHANGES

Once issued, shares of stock trade in the secondary market, either over the counter or on an organized exchange. The most important exchange is the New York Stock Exchange (NYSE), followed by the American Stock Exchange (AMEX), and various regional exchanges (such as Boston, Philadelphia, and the Pacific). Some securities that aren't listed on organized exchanges are said to be traded **over the counter (OTC).** The prices of many, but by no means all, OTC securities are reported on the National Association of Securities Dealers Automated Quotation System (NASDAQ).

The exchanges are closed on weekends and some holidays. On a typical trading day on the NYSE, about 110 million shares are traded with an aggregate market value of around $4 billion. Although individual investors own about 60 percent of the outstanding shares, 80 percent of the daily trading is by institutions. Many households are content to buy and hold stock, while some institutions buy and sell feverishly, looking for short-term profits.

Table 6–2 on p. 178 compares the NYSE, AMEX, and NASDAQ at the end of 1985. (The regional exchanges, added together, are roughly comparable to the AMEX.) While the number of companies listed on the NYSE was only twice that on the AMEX and less than half that on the NASDAQ system, the aggregate value of NYSE listed companies was far larger than

over the counter
Securities that aren't listed on organized exchanges are said to be traded over the counter (OTC).

TABLE 6–2 Stock Trading, 1985

	New York Stock Exchange, NYSE	American Stock Exchange, AMEX	National Association of Securities Dealers Automated Quotation System, NASDAQ
Companies listed	1540	783	4136
Shares of listed companies (billions)	52	6	30
Volume of shares traded (billions)	28	2	21
Value of shares listed (billions of dollars)	$1950	$87	$287
Value of shares traded (billions of dollars)	$970	$27	$233

Source: National Association of Securities Dealers, *1986 Fact Book.*

the others. The average NYSE company had a market value of $1.3 billion, eleven times the size of the average AMEX firm and eighteen times the average NASDAQ company. The NYSE is called the big board, not only because of the number of listed companies and the volume of trading, but also because the NYSE companies are mostly the biggest and the best (the best companies, not necessarily the best stocks to invest in).

To be listed on the NYSE, a corporation must have $18 million in tangible assets, $2.5 million in before-tax profits, 1.1 million or more publicly held shares with an aggregate market value of at least $18 million, and 2000 or more stockholders each owning at least 100 shares. Some large companies have chosen not to be listed: for example, Apple Computer, and (to avoid the NYSE's disclosure requirements) many financial institutions. Most companies, however, believe that listing on the NYSE makes their stock more attractive to investors, and, indeed, about half of all investors own only NYSE stocks.

How Trading Activity is Reported

Daily newspapers record summaries of stock trading on the previous business day. Here is an example of the trading in one stock on May 13, 1986, as reported in *The Wall Street Journal* on May 14:

52 weeks				Yld	P-E	Sales				Net
High	*Low*	*Stock*	*Div.*	*%*	*Ratio*	*100s*	*High*	*Low*	*Close*	*Chg.*
72⅞	29¼	Polarid	1	1.6	29	1575	63	61⅜	62⅜	+¾

Most company names are abbreviated to save space. Here, for example, "Polarid" is an abbreviation of Polaroid. The translation of more difficult abbreviations sometimes takes a bit of detective work. After finding the company, investors invariably look first at the last two columns on the right, showing the closing price and the change in price from the day before. For Polaroid on May 13, 1986, the last trade of the day was at a price of $62\frac{3}{8}$ a share, up $0.75 from the closing price the day before. Moving leftward, we see the high and low prices for the day and the volume of trading (in 100s). On this particular day, 157,500 shares of Polaroid were traded at various prices ranging from $61\frac{3}{8}$ per share to $63 per share.

Right after the company's name is the latest declared annual dividend, for Polaroid $1 a share. The "Yld %" is the dividend yield, calculated by dividing the annual dividend by the closing price of the stock ($1/$62\frac{3}{8}$ = 0.016, or 1.6 percent). A 1.6 percent dividend yield may seem like a modest return on an investment. Shareholders were undoubtedly expecting dividends to increase from year to year and to earn capital gains, too. In the next chapter, we will look at the relationship between dividend growth and capital gains.

The reported *P/E (price-earnings) ratio* is the ratio of a firm's closing price to its latest annual earnings. (We will examine the importance of the P/E ratio to investors in Chapter 8.) On the far left, *The Wall Street Journal* provides some historical perspective by showing the highest and lowest prices during the past fifty-two weeks.

U.S. stock exchanges quote prices in fractions of a dollar—½, ¼, ⅛, ¹⁄₁₆, and even ¹⁄₃₂—apparently an anachronistic remnant of earlier days when arithmetic was done by hand. Calculations are done by computers now, and most foreign exchanges quote prices in decimals, a logical practice that is still resisted by U.S. exchanges.

Exchange Membership

The NYSE and other organized exchanges are physical locations, trading floors, where securities are bought and sold by exchange members, who are said to have seats on the exchange (dating back to when members had armchairs to rest in). There are 1366 seats on the New York Stock Exchange, which are bought, sold, or leased at negotiated prices reflecting supply and demand. The price of a seat began at $1000 in 1850; reached $625,000 in 1929, before the stock-market crash; and has fluctuated considerably since—trading for $250,000 in 1965, $40,000 in 1976, and $1 million in 1987.

Exchange memberships can be divided into four categories, as described in the following sections.

Specialists Each stock traded on the NYSE is assigned to a **specialist,** a person who acts as both a broker (an agent trading for others) and a dealer (an individual trading for himself or herself). As a broker, the specialist

specialist
Stock exchange specialists collect and execute orders, trading, as needed, for their own accounts.

TABLE 6–3 Brown and Company Commission Schedule, 1987

Stock Price	Commission for the First 1000 Shares	Commission for Each Additional Share
0-10	$25 + $0.04 per share	$0.035
10⅛-20	$25 + $0.05 per share	$0.045
20⅛-25	$25 + $0.06 per share	$0.055
25⅛-30	$25 + $0.07 per share	$0.065
30⅛ or more	$25 + $0.08 per share	$0.075

collects orders from other members of the exchange and executes a transaction when someone is willing to buy at a price at which another member is willing to sell. Specialists have an obligation to maintain a fair and orderly market; in this capacity, they act as dealers by buying or selling, as needed, for their own accounts. At any moment, specialists will quote bid prices at which they will sell and ask prices at which they will buy. The bid price is, of course, somewhat lower than the ask price.

At present, there are nearly 400 specialists on the NYSE, working for 90 specialist firms. Some specialists handle only one or two stocks, while others work with thirty or more. A committee of specialists decides who can be a specialist and which stocks they are assigned.

Commission Brokers Another 400 NYSE seats are owned by representatives of brokerage firms such as Merrill Lynch, E. F. Hutton, and Salomon Brothers. When an investor places an order with a brokerage firm, that firm contacts a *commission broker*—a broker who forwards the customer's order to the appropriate specialist for execution. When the trade is completed, the brokerage firm charges the customer a commission and the customer then generally has five working days to settle the trade by paying for purchased securities or by delivering securities that were sold.

Discount brokerage firms do little more than answer the phone, give the current bid-ask prices of securities, and record trades for customers. *Full-service brokers*, in contrast, give investment advice in person, over the phone, and in periodic newsletters. They compile vast quantities of data, prepare in-depth analyses, make buy/sell recommendations, and provide reassurance to timid investors. They are also more expensive, since investors must pay the substantial salaries of investment analysts and advisors. Table 6–3 shows the rate schedule used by a leading discount broker, and Table 6–4 compares this broker's costs for several representative trades with the average cost of a full-service broker.

Floor Brokers *Floor brokers* are freelance brokers who do not work for any particular brokerage firm, but who instead handle orders from any com-

TABLE 6–4 Discount Versus Full-Service Broker Commissions for Specific Trades

Number of Shares	Cost per Share	Total Cost of Shares	Brown & Company		Full-Service Broker	
			Commission	Commission as Percentage of Total Cost of Shares	Commission	Commission as Percentage of Total Cost of Shares
200	$20	$ 4,000	$35.00	0.9	$99.50	2.5
300	15	4,500	40.00	0.9	114.68	2.5
100	50	5,000	33.00	0.7	96.10	1.9
500	20	10,000	50.00	0.5	203.60	2.0
800	25	20,000	73.00	0.4	357.42	1.8
1000	30	30,000	95.00	0.3	461.27	1.5
1000	60	60,000	105.00	0.2	630.86	1.1

mission broker who happens to have an excess of orders to process. It would be inefficient for each brokerage firm to employ enough commission brokers to handle all of its orders during the busiest times; instead, they employ only enough to handle a normal load and then share the services of floor brokers. Floor brokers are sometimes called two-dollar brokers because at one time their standard commission was $2 per order.

Floor Traders *Floor traders* are members of the exchange who trade for their own accounts. They pay no commissions but still must pay state and federal transfer taxes. Most are speculators who hope that being present on the floor will give them an intuitive sense, or "feel," of the market, enabling them to buy at an opportune time and sell for a small profit a short while later. Floor traders may act as quasi-specialists by stepping in when there is a temporary imbalance between buy and sell orders. They also can act as floor brokers during hectic times, though exchange rules prohibit traders from trading for their own accounts and acting as brokers on the same day, because of the potential conflict of interest.

A Fair and Orderly Market?

The specialist keeps track of buy and sell orders (until recently, in a notebook, now on a computer), to which only the specialist has access. When a specialist quotes a price of "25 bid, 25¼ asked," specialists may be holding orders in the book to buy and sell at these prices, or the specialist may be willing to buy or sell for his or her own account. The specialist is supposed to offset temporary imbalances between demand and supply by buying when there is an excess of sellers and selling when the reverse is true. The specialist is, thus, a buffer who maintains a fair and orderly market, assuring that investors can always make a trade at a price not very different from the prices of other recent trades.

The work of a specialist is very lucrative. If you are buying at 25 and selling at 25¼ a few moments later, you make a 1 percent profit in very little time. Repeated over and over, day after day, your transactions can be a lot more profitable than money in the bank at 5 percent a year. The specialist does have the expense of maintaining a stock inventory and does bear the risk of buying heavily before prices collapse or selling large amounts before prices soar. But these risks are manageable, since the specialist is the only one with access to the accumulated order book.

Imagine that you are a specialist and are holding orders to buy thousands of shares at 24½ to 24⅞ with relatively few orders to sell. You can safely quote "25 bid, 25¼ asked" and make trades for your own account at these prices. If demand picks up and sellers are still scarce, you can raise the price, sell the stock you acquired at 25, and make a substantial profit. If, on the other hand, there is a flood of sellers, you can join the crowd and sell to those orders you are holding between 24½ and 24⅞, taking a small loss.

Knowledge of the accumulated orders is valuable and specialists, on average, make large profits. An SEC study found that the average annual rate of return per dollar invested was 80 percent for high-activity specialists and 190 percent for those with low activity.[2] Not only are these returns far above those of other professional investors, but it is disconcerting that the largest profits are made by specialists who are less active (perhaps because they set wide bid-ask spreads and do not actively maintain a fair and orderly market).

When there is a severe demand-supply imbalance, specialists naturally tend to be more concerned with their own pocketbooks than with orderly markets. Instead of buying when there is an avalanche of sell orders, they are tempted to step aside and let the price collapse to a level where outside buyers can be found. Instead of an orderly market, there is an air pocket. For example, when President John F. Kennedy was assassinated at 1:40 P.M. (eastern time) on Friday, November 22, 1963, some specialists dropped prices sharply and bought for their own accounts from panicked investors. The exchanges closed at 2:07 P.M. that day with prices, on average, down about 3 percent and reopened on Tuesday, November 26, with prices close to their levels before the assassination. Investors had calmed down while specialists had cleaned up. The *New York Times* editorialized as follows:

> *An investigation of their activities by the Securities and Exchange Commission shows that some specialists contributed to the extremely disorderly conditions that took place in the 30 minutes that the Exchange remained open following the news of the shooting in Dallas. Its findings reveal that specialists dumped shares on the market ahead of the public, which led to a nosedive in prices and was hardly consistent with the claim by the New York Stock Exchange that specialists play a vital role in maintaining stability.*[3]

Similarly, during the October 19, 1987 stock market crash (which is discussed in detail in Chapter 12), specialists should have bought stock to stabilize prices; but 30 percent of the specialists were net sellers that day. On the following day, Terrible Tuesday, 82 percent of the specialists were net sellers. A presidential task force concluded that the actions of some specialists was "poor by any standard."

A National Market System

All the organized exchanges restrict members from trading listed stocks outside the exchanges. Since most major brokerage firms are exchange members, these restrictions hamper the trading of listed stocks off the exchanges. Critics have long accused the exchanges of operating monopolies that enrich specialists. Prodded by perceived abuses, Congress passed the Securities Acts Amendments of 1975, instructing the SEC to develop a national market system that would be more competitive and efficient than the exchanges. Many economists envision a national auction market, linked by computers, with the specialist nowhere to be seen. But, by and large, the NYSE has resisted this vision successfully.

One opening in the exchanges' virtual stranglehold on listed stocks is SEC Rule 19c–3, which eliminated off-board restrictions for stocks listed (or delisted) after April 26, 1979. When AT&T split into eight holding companies, the seven spinoffs were newly listed and fell under Rule 19c–3, so that they are traded over the counter as well as on the exchanges. About 10 percent of the trades in these seven spinoffs have been made off-exchange and, more importantly, the opportunity to trade off the exchanges has limited the discretionary power held by specialists (though not their privileged access to their books of limit orders).

The specialist system was designed to handle the intermittent arrival of small orders at a central location. It is less appropriate for active trading among large institutional investors who can be linked by a nationwide, indeed worldwide, computer network. In 1965, only 3 percent of the volume of trading on the NYSE involved large *blocks* of more than 10,000 shares traded by mutual funds, pension funds, and other institutional investors; now more than half the volume of NYSE trading involves such blocks. Block trades are generally negotiated in the *upstairs market*, an informal market that uses telephones and linked computers to arrange private deals among brokerage firms and institutional clients, before being executed on the exchange floor. Except for Rule 19c–3 stocks, block deals negotiated by member firms must be brought to a specialist where they are subject to the exchange's commission.

Because of these restrictions, it is helpful to distinguish four types of secondary markets. The trading of listed stocks on an exchange is called the first market, while the trading of nonlisted stocks over the counter

(OTC) is the second market. The third market encompasses the trading of exchange-listed stocks off the exchanges using brokers—either by using brokers that are not exchange members or by making trades that involve Rule 19c–3 stocks. The fourth market refers to the off-the-exchange trades in listed stocks that are directly negotiated between investors without using brokers.

TRADING OVER THE COUNTER

Off the exchanges, trades are handled quite differently from the specialist system. Dealers voluntarily maintain a market in a security by quoting bid and ask prices at which they are willing to buy or sell shares. Market makers must register with the Securities and Exchange Commission, but there is no limit to their number or their geographic location. At present, the average OTC stock has about eight active market makers. All of the market makers' bid and ask prices are public knowledge, both to each other and to interested investors.

When you place an order to buy an OTC stock, your broker determines who the market makers are and then uses a computer to find their latest price quotations. Some 500 market makers, representing more than 4000 stocks, belong to the *National Association of Securities Dealers Automated Quotation System* (NASDAQ), a computerized system for giving and receiving price quotations. Level I subscribers, mostly individual investors and brokers, can obtain median bid and ask prices on any NASDAQ-listed security as well as data on the latest transaction price, daily high and low prices, and trading volume. Level II subscribers can see all bid-ask prices, while Level III subscribers can enter their own bid-ask prices. The market makers and prices of inactively traded OTC stocks are published in the National Quotation Bureau's daily "pink sheets."

NASDAQ, itself, does not hold inventories of securities or make trades. It is an information service that helps buyers and sellers find each other. If your brokerage firm has a level II subscription, it can survey current bid-ask prices, find the most advantageous offer, and then make a transaction with that market maker, by either using the computer or making a phone call. The transaction is then reported to NASDAQ's data bank. Members like to call NASDAQ the national market system, and they think of it as the stock market of the future. It may well be, if the London Stock Exchange does not earn the title first. (See Investment Example 6–1.)

TYPES OF TRANSACTIONS

Investors can place a variety of orders through their brokers. We will discuss three important types of orders first. Then we will look at buying stock with borrowed money and selling borrowed shares.

INVESTMENT EXAMPLE 6–1

LONDON'S BIG BANG

On October 1, 1986, London's financial markets were transformed by extensive deregulation, changes so significant that they were labeled the "big bang." Before, the London Stock Exchange was much like a private club, where well-bred gentlemen in bowler hats showed up at 10:00 A.M. and went home at 4:00 P.M., with a leisurely two-hour lunch in between. In this relaxed, noncompetitive atmosphere, the brokers made a fixed 1.65 percent commission on each trade, and all trades passed through jobbers on the floor who, like the New York Stock Exchange's specialists, quoted bid and ask prices and made their profits on the spread.

Foreign banks and securities firms were allowed to join the London Stock Exchange in 1986, and within a year one-third of the members were foreign. Fixed commissions were abolished, as was the distinction between brokers and jobbers. In its place, authorized members act as market makers, quoting prices at which they are willing to buy or sell

securities. To keep track of the competing prices, the exchange spent millions on a massive computer system, and once computerized prices defined the market, there was no real need for the floor of the exchange at all.

Today, transactions are made from securities houses, by traders watching computer screens. The gentlemen in bowler hats have been replaced by American-style whiz kids driving Porsches, who show up at 7:00 A.M. and work until the New York Stock Exchange closes, at 10:00 P.M. London time. Their wide-ranging trades for worldwide clients make London the model international stock exchange, the center of trading in currencies, Eurobonds (dollar-denominated bonds issued by non-U.S. institutions), and some commodities such as gold, tin, and rubber. In addition, hundreds of U.S. stocks are traded on the London Exchange, as are the stocks of a dozen other countries. In 1987, some 15 percent of the trading in French stocks took place on the London Exchange; for some Dutch companies, the figure was closer to 40 percent.

Market Orders

The most common order is a **market order**—a directive to buy or sell at the best price currently obtainable, the market price. The transaction is executed very quickly, sometimes while the customer is still on the telephone with the broker. For a listed stock, the trade may be at the specialist's bid or ask price. Over the counter, the broker identifies the market maker with the best price and makes the transaction. A market order ensures a timely transaction, and the customer relies on the market to provide a reasonable price.

market order
A market order is an order to buy or sell a security at the best price currently obtainable.

Limit Orders

In a **limit order,** the customer puts a limit on the price—a maximum in the case of a buy order, a minimum for a sell order. This type of order ensures an acceptable price if a trade is made, but does not guarantee that a trade will occur.

Suppose that a certain listed stock is quoted currently at "25 bid, 25¼ asked," so that, if you want, you can immediately buy the stock for $25¼ a share or sell for $25. If you want to buy, but at a lower price, you can place a limit order offering to buy, say, 200 shares at $24 a share. The specialist records this order on a computer and executes it if the price falls to $24 a share. (Specifically, the specialist is not allowed to buy for himself or herself at a price of $24 a share or less, without executing your order first.) Similarly, if you want to sell, but for more than $25¼, you can place a limit order to sell for, say, $27, which is executed if the price reaches $27.

A limit order that is not immediately executed is either a day order, which expires at the end of the day, or good-till-cancelled, which lasts until withdrawn by the investor.

Stop Orders

Investors can also place **stop orders**—directives to sell if the price falls to a specified level or to buy if the market price rises to a specified level. The most common are stop orders to sell, also called **stop-loss orders**. Suppose that you buy a certain speculative stock for $25 a share and do not want to lose more than $5 a share. You can place a stop-loss order for $20, which will be converted into a market sell order (not a limit order) if the price drops to $20 or below. Unfortunately, if the price does collapse, there is no guarantee that you will be able to sell at $20. The specialist may drop the price from $21 to $15, executing your sell order at $15. If there are more stop-loss sell orders than the specialist wants to absorb, he can even ask the exchange to suspend trading in the stock until buyers are found, perhaps at a price even lower than $15 a share.

Round- and Odd-Lot Transactions

A **round lot** is a trade involving some multiple of a standard-size trade. For most stocks, 100 shares is the standard size, and any multiple of 100 shares is a round lot. For a few high-priced or lightly traded stocks, however, ten shares is the standard size. For most bonds, the standard size is $1000 of par value. Trades of a nonstandard size are **odd lots.** The sale of 5 shares of AT&T is an odd lot; the purchase of 505 shares involves 5 round lots and one 5-share odd lot. Odd-lot trades may be handled by the specialist, as are round lots, or the customer's brokerage firm may simply buy or sell the stock itself. In either case, the customer pays an added cost, called the *odd-lot differential*, generally one-eighth of a point ($0.125 a share) for stocks selling for less than $40 and one fourth of a point ($0.25 a share) for more expensive stocks.

Margin

You can buy stock with other people's money, in particular, money borrowed from your brokerage firm. Buying stock with borrowed money is called **buying on margin,** where the margin is the amount of money put up by the stockholder. If you buy 200 shares of ZYX stock for $50 a share (a total cost of $10,000), a brokerage firm with a 60 percent margin requirement will require you to put up at least $6,000 (and lend you the remainder). Since 1934, the Federal Reserve Board has been empowered to set the *margin requirement*, the minimum margin that brokerage firms must require of their customers. The margin requirement has been as low as 40 percent and as high as 100 percent; it has been 50 percent since 1974.

buying on margin
Buying on margin is the purchase of stock with borrowed money.

> **When stock buyers buy on margin with an x percent margin requirement, they must pay at least x percent of the cost of the stock and borrow the rest from their brokerage firm.**

To protect itself when it buys stock for you on margin, the brokerage firm registers the stock purchased in its **street name,** the name under which the brokerage firm does business, rather than your name. Your margin agreement also allows the firm to use your stock as collateral for its borrowing and to lend your stock to short sellers (more on this subject later). When a dividend is paid, it is credited to your account, reducing the outstanding loan balance. Annual reports and other correspondence are forwarded to you.

street name
Street name securities are registered in the name of the brokerage firm, rather than the customer.

The brokerage firm charges you interest on this loan, but, as with any levered investment, you come out ahead if the rate of return on your stock exceeds the interest rate on your loan. Suppose that you put up $5,000 of the $10,000 cost of your ZYX purchase and borrow the rest from your broker. Neglecting the commission, the value of your brokerage account is calculated as shown in part (a) of Table 6–5, with your equity equal to the current market value of the stock minus the loan balance.

The rate charged on your loan fluctuates with the broker's **call rate,** the cost of borrowing from banks the money that the broker lends to investors. Active shareholders who borrow large amounts pay the call rate plus (or, in rare cases, minus) a fraction of a percent, while less active borrowers pay the call rate plus 2 percent or even more. For simplicity, we will use a fixed 12 percent annual interest rate and assume that a month has passed since your purchase.

call rate
The call rate is a brokerage firm's cost of borrowing money from banks to lend investors.

If the stock does not pay a dividend this month but its price rises 1 percent, to $50.50, the 1 percent return on the stock and the 1 percent loan rate cancel each other, leaving a 1 percent profit on your $6000 cash investment, as shown in part (b) of Table 6–5. If the stock's price goes up by more than 1 percent this month, the power of leverage is unleashed. Part (c) of Table 6–5 shows that if the price goes up by 10 percent, to $55, your equity increases by $950—a 19 percent return on your initial $5000

TABLE 6–5 Buying Stock with a 50 Percent Margin at 12 Percent Annual Interest

(a) Initial purchase

Market value of stocks (200 shares @ $50)	$10,000
Loan balance	−5,000
Equity	5,000

(b) Price rises 1 percent in a month

Market value of stocks (200 shares @ $50.50)	$10,100
Loan balance	−5,050
Equity (1 percent gain)	5,050

(c) Price rises 10 percent in a month

Market value of stocks (200 shares @ $55)	$11,000
Loan balance	−5,050
Equity (19 percent gain)	5,950

(d) Price falls 10 percent in a month

Market value of stocks (200 shares @ $45)	$9,000
Loan balance	−5,050
Equity (21 percent loss)	3,950

(e) A margin call

Market value of stocks (200 shares @ $35.75)	$7,150
Loan balance	−5,050
Equity (only 30 percent of market value)	2,100

investment. (As explained in Chapter 3, you get your 1 percent, and, in addition, with two-for-one leverage the 9 percent profit on other people's money is doubled to 18 percent.) Part (d) of Table 6–5 shows that if the stock drops 10 percent, your losses are magnified (as with any levered position), because not only do you lose 10 percent on the $5000 of your own money, but there is also an 11 percent shortfall on the borrowed money that is doubled by two-for-one leverage.

If your *equity*—the market value of your stock minus your current loan balance—falls below a specified *maintenance margin*, you will get a margin call from your broker requesting additional funds to reduce you indebtedness (or the deposit of more securities to build up your equity). The stock exchanges require a 25 percent maintenance margin, but most brokers use a more conservative 30 percent of market value. Part (e) of Table 6–5 shows that you will get a margin call if the price falls to $35.75, since $2100/ $7150 = 0.294 <0.30.

If you fail to meet a margin call, your broker unilaterally sells your stock and pays off your loan for you. In 1929, when 10 percent margin buying was the norm and leveraged speculation the rage, every significant drop in stock-market prices set off an avalanche of margin calls and forced sales, adding to the downward pressure on prices.

Short Sales

If you think a stock's price is heading downward, you can sell your shares; if you are very confident of an impending price drop, you even can sell shares you do not own—by borrowing through your broker. Selling stock this way is referred to as a **short sale**—the sale of borrowed stock, which must later be covered by a purchase. With a short sale, you try to follow the age-old advice to buy low and sell high, but you sell first and buy later.

short sale
A short sale is the sale of borrowed securities, which must later be covered by a purchase.

Suppose that you want to sell 100 shares of Stock XYZ short at $25 a share. Your broker will find someone who owns 100 shares of XYZ, borrow these shares temporarily, and sell them for you at $25 or thereabouts. Your hope is that later the price will drop to, say, $20, allowing you to purchase 100 shares to replace those you borrowed and keep a $500 profit, less expenses.

Notice that the most you can make on this short sale is $2500 (if the price goes to $0), while your potential losses are unlimited. If you are forced to cover at $100 a share, you will be out $7500; if you must cover at $1000, you lose $97,500. As the Wall Street adage goes, "He who sells what isn't his'n, has to buy back or go to prison." The potential for enormous loss is the reason the short seller is stereotyped as a nervous pessimist who sleeps little at night and spends the day checking the latest stock prices.

Why are anonymous donors willing to lend their stock to you, a short seller? Typically, they have margin accounts, and one of the conditions of the margin agreement is that their stock is held by the broker in that broker's street name and can be lent to short sellers. In practice, the investors never know their stock is gone, since they continue to receive dividends (paid by you) and can sell their stock whenever they want (the broker just finds someone else to lend you shares).

The rules of the game are: You do not receive the $2500 proceeds from your short sale; the brokerage firm retains it and uses it to earn some interest for itself (you might persuade the broker to share this interest if you are a valued trader who pays frequent commissions). Also, your broker requires that you put up margin equal to some fraction of $2500, perhaps 50 percent, and then charges you interest on the remaining fraction. It is no wonder that brokerage firms do not discourage short sales. With each such transaction, they get a commission on the short sale and a commission when you cover your position. They invest the proceeds of the sale plus your margin requirement, and then they charge you interest on the remainder. In the example described earlier, for example, the brokerage firm earns interest on $5000 that is not even its own money.

As for you, the courageous short seller, you must pay an in-and-out commission, lose the interest you could be earning on your margin deposit, pay interest on the rest, and pay dividends on the underlying stock—seemingly expensive penalties for being a pessimist. Investment Example 6–2 tells of the effort some short sellers make to spread their pessimism.

Short sales on the New York Stock Exchange and the American Stock Exchange are also governed by what is known as an uptick rule. In the bad old days, market manipulators (bear raiders) reportedly used short-sale orders to drive stock prices down and thereby panic honest investors, activate stop-loss orders, and force those investors who could not meet margin calls to liquidate their positions—in all, unleashing a flood of sale orders that caused prices to collapse and allowed the manipulators to cover their positions at profitably low prices. To thwart such manipulation, the SEC established the *uptick rule*, a regulation that allows a short sale to be executed only at a price that is higher than the price in the preceding trade (or at an unchanged price if the most recent price change was upward). The intent is to keep short sales from adding to the momentum of a falling market.[4]

Short sales are sometimes used to defer a profit until the next tax year. If you are sitting on a big capital gain and are fearful that it will evaporate, but do not want to realize it immediately, you can sell *short against the box* (an allusion to the presumption that you have your shares in a safe-deposit box)—a tax-deferment strategy in which you sell borrowed shares and later cover your short sale by turning over shares that you have owned all along. You have locked in your profit (the difference between the price of the short sale and your earlier purchase price) but have postponed its realization for tax purposes until the short sale is covered. The costs of this strategy are the brokerage fee and the interest expense of the short sale. Clearly, the most attractive time to take this action is late in the year, when a few weeks of interest can postpone a capital-gains tax for a year.

CHURNING IS DANGEROUS TO YOUR WEALTH

Beginning brokers generally try to build a client base by making "cold calls" to a list of people who have been identified as potential customers, often as a result of newspaper or magazine advertisements offering a free, no-obligation financial report.[5] Those people who respond to such an ad receive follow-up phone calls from brokers hoping to find investors who will buy securities and pay commissions. These cold calls are known as "dialing for dollars," because the only way a broker can make money is by having clients who make trades.

THE DARK SIDE OF SHORT SELLING

Some prominent investors are habitual short sellers, searching out companies with as yet undetected difficulties and then shorting their overvalued shares. Just as those investors who own a stock extol its virtues, hoping that other buyers will push the price higher, so short sellers publicize a company's difficulties, hoping that additional sellers will drive the price lower. A three-month investigation of such short sellers by *The Wall Street Journal* in 1985 concluded:

Lying, espionage, impersonations, and threats have become increasingly common, among both short sellers and some of their equally combative targets . . . [A] relatively small, though also growing, group of speculators . . . specialize in sinking vulnerable stocks with barrages of bad-mouthing. They use facts when available, but some of them aren't above innuendo, fabrications and deceit to batter down a stock.[1]

There are laws against stock manipulation, but hard evidence is sometimes difficult and application often murky. Among the incidents recounted by *The Wall Street Journal,* one involves a company that shorted Coleco, the maker of Cabbage Patch dolls, in late 1984 and early 1985 as its price fluctuated about $15 a share. After orally criticizing Coleco for months, the shorting company issued a report saying that it may be "only a question of time" until banks call in Coleco's loans, "forcing the company to liquidate." Then Dan Dorfman, a syndicated stock-market columnist, was persuaded to mention the report and quoted the short seller as predicting that "Coleco will go bankrupt some time before year-end [1985]." Copies of the negative report were mailed to other newspeople and to Coleco's creditors. In March 1985, an employee of the short seller telephoned Toys "R" Us and pretended to be a reporter from *The Wall Street Journal* working on a story dealing with declining Cabbage Patch sales, apparently intending to spook Toys "R" Us into reducing its Cabbage Patch orders.

As it turned out, this short-seller's pessimism, though premature, was eventually born out. Coleco had long been a toy maker on the brink of disaster, what *The Wall Street Journal* called "the high-wire act of the toy industry."[2] Coleco lost $10 million in 1983, lost $75 million in 1984 and then, riding the Cabbage Patch craze, made $80 million in 1985. But the company had a hard time finding a sequel and made some ill-timed acquisitions, including the purchase of the maker of Trivial Pursuit in 1986, right after its sales had peaked.

Coleco's stock reached a high of $20.50 in March 1986. But the company lost more than $100 million in 1986 and 1987, defaulted on its bonds in April 1988, and filed for bankruptcy-law protection in July 1988. In May 1989, Coleco stock continued to trade at about $1 a share, purchased by those who hoped that a restructured Coleco could emerge from bankruptcy court as a smaller, but profitable firm.

[1] Dean Rotbart, "Aggressive Methods of Some Short Sellers Stir Critics to Cry Foul," *Wall Street Journal,* September 5, 1985.

[2] Joseph Pereira, "Coleco Is Looking for Lettuce as Cabbage Patch Wilts," *Wall Street Journal,* March 18, 1988.

Once a broker has clients, there is a persuasive economic incentive to recommend active portfolio management (*"account upgrading"* is the euphemism, "churning" is the goal)—selling General Motors (GM) to buy Ford; then selling Ford to buy Chrysler; then selling Chrysler to buy GM; and on and on. One cynical observer put it this way, "Movement is [the broker's] breath of life. Like the shark, he will drown if he lies still."[6] Investment Example 6–3 tells some horror stories about broker sharks.

Transaction Costs

Active portfolio management costs investors money in two ways, in commissions and in capital-gains taxes. For small trades, commissions can be staggering; for example, Brown and Company has a $25 minimum commission, even if you just buy one share of a $5 stock. Brokerage fees decline for larger trades, but these savings may be offset by the effect of the transaction on the market price. Although a stock may have just traded at $25 a share, there is no guarantee that the next order will be executed at this price. The specialist's bid-ask spread increases for lightly traded securities and for large orders.

If the order is large relative to the normal volume of transactions in a particular security, it may take a significant price increase to find a seller and a substantial decrease to find a buyer. The story is told of an investor who placed an order to buy 1000 shares of Fly by Night, which was then selling for $4 a share. The order was executed at $4.50 and the investor, excited by the price increase, bought another 1000 shares, this time at $5. Once again encouraged by the price increase, the investor bought another 1000 shares, and so on until the price reached $10. He then decided to take his profits and instructed his broker to sell all of his holdings. "Fine," the broker replied, "to whom?"

Knowledgeable observers estimate that transaction costs generally run from 2 percent to 3 percent of the dollar value of a transaction, with these expenses mostly brokerage fees for modest trades and mostly bid-ask spreads and price concessions for larger trades. A careful empirical study found that bid-ask spreads for small trades average about 0.5 percent for companies with a total market value above $1.5 billion and 6.6 percent for those companies with less than $10 million in market value. The total costs, commission plus price spread, range from 1 percent to 8 percent for large companies (depending on the size of the trade) and from 17 percent to 44 percent for small companies.[7] Of course, if you sell one asset to buy another, you have to pay two transaction costs. At, say, 5 percent a round trip, active trading becomes pretty expensive. Trading once a year, the stock you buy has to have a 5 percent higher annual return than the stock you sell to cover the cost of the trade; that is, if the stock you sell has a 10 percent annual return, the stock you buy has to give 15 percent. The required differential rises to 20 percent if you trade every three months.

JAWS: STOCKBROKER HORROR STORIES

Most brokers are hard working, conscientious professionals who, while realizing that they make money from customer transactions, also recognize that excessive expenses and dismal performance will alienate their customers. As with any profession, though, there are some unscrupulous brokers who, like vicious sharks, churn their clients' accounts mercilessly and then move on to feed elsewhere.

The front page of the June 19, 1985, *Los Angeles Times* carried a story subtitled "Beware, Unwary" that detailed some stockbroker abuses.[1] In one case, a broker who had earned only $4,782 in commissions in five months and had filed for personal bankruptcy found a divorcee with $400,000 in corporate bonds. In ten months time, he had churned $143,754 in commissions while losing all of her $400,000, and then some—just like the Woody Allen joke, "A broker is someone who invests other people's money until it is all gone." A federal jury awarded the divorcee $175,000 in compensatory losses and $3 million in punitive damages (later reduced to $1.5 million), to be paid by the broker and the firm that employed him. In another case, a seventy-year-old, retired radio actress saw her $550,000 nest egg shrink to $67,000, while thousands of pointless trades generated $310,000 in commissions. When she asked her broker about the blizzard of trade confirmation slips mailed to her, she says he told her to just "throw them away."

A freshman at Princeton turned his trust account of 20,000 shares of Natomas Corporation over to a stock broker who, during two years in which the market rose 40 percent and the price of Natomas rose 60 percent, allegedly charged $92,000 in commissions while losing $300,000. Other cases cited by the *Los Angeles Times* involved a seventy-three-year-old blind woman and a man who lost a leg in a car crash and most of his legal settlement in stock churning.

In 1986, an even more astounding story came to light. During two years at two brokerage firms, a twenty-three-year-old aspiring actor turned stockbroker generated a staggering $5 million in commissions, which, it later turned out, came almost entirely from churning the account of a millionaire great-uncle whose $16 million account was allegedly whittled down to $8 million.[2] (This is eerily like the old joke: How do you make a small fortune in the stock market? You start with a large fortune.)

According to the *Los Angeles Times* article, brokers at Merrill Lynch, the nation's largest brokerage firm, are paid roughly half of their customer's commissions, and those who do not generate $250,000 a year in commissions after three years are asked to leave Merrill Lynch. Despite these strong economic incentives to churn accounts, most broker-client relationships are not like the horror stories described earlier. Nevertheless, these tales do warn that the broker's and customer's objectives are not identical, and that investors should understand their transactions and be vigilant that their brokers are carrying out their instructions. In explaining why the compensatory damages to the divorcee discussed above were less than her actual losses, the jury said that her "inattention to her own affairs, as well as her incredible gullibility, contributed to her losses." Or as the *Los Angeles Times* put it, "Beware, Unwary."

[1]Michael A. Hiltzik, "Churning: Trading in Stock Abuse," *Los Angeles Times,* June 19, 1985.

[2]Roger Lowenstein, "How a 23-Year-Old Broker Went From Riches to Scandal and Jail," *The Wall Street Journal,* February 27, 1986.

TABLE 6–6 Buy and Hold Versus Portfolio Turnover

	After 10 Years		After 20 Years		After 30 Years	
	After-Tax Profit	Brokerage Fees	After-Tax Profit	Brokerage Fees	After-Tax Profit	Brokerage Fees
Buy and Hold	$9,963	$720	$33,173	$1,483	$85,787	$3,214
Turnover once a year	4,995	4,903	12,484	12,254	23,714	23,276
Turnover four times a year	−3,536	12,753	−6,006	21,017	−7,532	26,124

Capital-Gains Taxes

The second, more subtle, argument against active trading is that taxes are postponed on unrealized gains, allowing you to continue making profits on money owed to the Internal Revenue Service (IRS). Suppose that you bought an asset for $10,000 that is now worth $20,000. If you are in a 28 percent tax bracket and sell, you must pay the government 28 percent of $10,000 = $2800, leaving that much less to reinvest. If you realize your gain and pay a $2800 tax, you only have $17,200 to put back in the market; if you do not sell, you can continue earning dividends and capital gains on the full $20,000. In essence, the IRS has loaned you the $2800 tax liability, with the stipulation that you share some of the profits with the IRS; in particular you will have to pay a 28 percent tax on the extra dividends and capital gains. No bank will loan you $2800 at such favorable terms.

Of course, if you are convinced that the price of your $20,000 asset is going to collapse, then by all means sell. If, however, you have no good reason for believing that other investments will do better than this one, then the avoidance of brokerage fees and the postponement of taxes are persuasive reasons for doing nothing at all.

To quantify these considerations, a computer program was used to simulate the results when $10,000 is invested in three different ways—buy and hold, turn over the portfolio once a year, and turn over the portfolio four times a year. Table 6–6 shows the results for a brokerage fee of 2 percent, a 28 percent marginal tax rate, a 5 percent annual dividend, and a 5 percent annual price appreciation.

Turnover deflates performance dramatically, illustrating the old saying, "The broker made money, the IRS made money, and two out of three ain't bad!"[8] To do as well as buy and hold, a strategy of turning over the portfolio once a year would have to earn an average before-tax return of roughly 15 percent a year, as compared to the buy-and-hold strategy's 10 percent a year before taxes. Turning over the portfolio four times a year has to earn an unrealistic 30 a year before taxes and commissions to match the buy-and-hold strategy.

TABLE 6–7   After-Tax Stock-Trading Profits for Two Different Strategies with No Commissions

Number of Trading Years	After-Tax Profits	
	Buy-and-Hold Strategy	Yearly-Turnover Strategy
10	$10,732	$10,042
20	35,223	30,169
30	91,106	70,509

In the short run, the major advantage of a buy-and-hold strategy is the avoidance of brokerage fees; in the long run, the postponement of capital-gains taxes becomes more important. One way to see this distinction is to redo the simulation with no brokerage fees at all; the after-tax profits are shown in Table 6–7. The difference—$700 for ten years and $20,000 for thirty years—gauges the value of postponing capital-gains taxes. A convenient way of expressing this advantage is to calculate the effective capital-gains tax rate—that is, the tax rate levied on unrealized gains that would give the same after-tax profits as the postponement of the current tax. In these simulations, postponing the tax for ten years reduces the effective tax rate on capital gains from 28 percent to 20 percent and a thirty-year postponement reduces it to 11 percent. An investor can reduce the tax all the way to 0 percent by holding the stock until death, since the heirs do not pay taxes on capital gains that occur before they receive their inheritance.

Should You Take Profits or Cut Losses?

An old Wall Street adage advises investors to overcome greed and cash in their profits while they still can, cautioning, "Nobody ever went broke taking a profit." Others have pointed out that if you sell your winners and hold on to your losers, you will soon have a portfolio full of losers; instead, you should sell your disappointments and let your winners run. Thus, one seasoned observer argued that losses "must be cut quickly before they become of any financial consequence . . . Cutting losses is the one and only rule of the market that can be taught with the assurance that it is always the correct thing to do."[9]

The problem with each such rule is that it is backward looking, a rearview mirror when you need a crystal ball. Selling winners and keeping losers is advantageous if stocks that have done poorly in the past are likely to outperform stocks that have done well in the past. Keeping winners and shucking losers is profitable if the reverse is true. However, since past performance is an unreliable guide to future performance (we will look at the reasons and evidence in future chapters), neither of these rules is a guarantee of success.

Yet, even if the stocks that have gone down and those that have gone up are equally likely to do well in the future, there are sound tax reasons for treating the winners and losers differently. We have already seen that the postponement of capital-gains taxes is a good reason for not selling stocks that have gone up in price. Conversely, the realization of losses provides a tax refund from the IRS, giving you more money to invest. A simple rule (assuming you have no good reason for thinking some stocks will do better than others) is: hold on to stocks that have gone up in price, and sell those stocks that have gone down in price far enough so that the tax rebate is significantly larger than the transaction costs.

STOCK-MARKET INDEXES

stock market indexes
Stock market indexes are statistical averages that are intended to summarize changes in stock prices.

More than 100 million shares of more than 1500 different stocks are traded daily on the New York Stock Exchange alone, creating a virtual mountain of statistical data, more than anyone could absorb or appreciate. **Stock-market indexes** are statistical averages that are intended to summarize changes in stock prices as time passes. We will look first at the most well known index, the Dow Jones Industrial Average, and then at some other indexes.

The Dow Jones Industrial Average

Dow Jones Industrial Average
The Dow Jones Industrial Average is a simple average of the stock prices of thirty prominent blue-chip companies.

In 1880, Charles Dow and Edward Jones started a financial news service that they called Dow-Jones. Today, the most visible results are *The Wall Street Journal,* the most widely read newspaper in the United States, and the **Dow Jones Industrial Average**, an average of thirty stock prices that is the most widely reported stock-market index.

The Dow Jones Average began as a barometer of economic activity. Dow was convinced that stock prices reflect informed opinion about future business conditions and, thus, that stock prices provide advance information about the economy. Two indexes were constructed; one, the industrial average, reflected production while the other, the railroad average, monitored commerce. The rail average has always been the less prominent of the two indexes, an imbalance exacerbated by the decline of railroads in the United States. In 1969, eight of the twenty railroad stocks in the index were replaced by six airlines and two trucking firms, and the rail average was renamed the transportation average; but, still, the industrial average gets the headlines.

How the Average is Calculated The Dow Jones Industrial Average began with twelve stocks in 1896 and grew to its present size, thirty stocks, by 1928. These select stocks represent the nation's most prominent companies, the so-called blue chips (a term derived from poker, in which blue chips are the most valuable). It is a measure of economic evolution in the United States that only one company, General Electric, has been in the Dow Industrial Average from the beginning (and even this firm was dropped for a while). The current other twenty-nine stocks have been added over time as other, once powerful companies faded. The Great Depression was, of course, the blow that killed many of the mightiest firms. Twenty-five of the thirty blue chips in the Dow Industrial Average were dropped in the 1930s and replaced with healthier companies.

Another company substitution was made in 1956; four more in 1959; and MMM was added in 1976 after the Anaconda Copper Company was taken over by Atlantic Richfield. In 1979 an ailing Chrysler and an unglamorous Esmark (formerly Swift, a meat-packing firm) were replaced by Merck, a leading producer of health-care products, and by IBM, the company with the largest market value of any company ($43 billion at the time and soon more than double that). In 1982 American Express replaced the troubled Manville, and in 1985 Philip Morris (manufacturer of such products as Marlboro and Benson & Hedges cigarettes, Miller beer, and 7-Up) acquired General Foods and took its place in the Dow, while McDonald's was substituted for American Brands (manufacturer of Pall Mall and Tareyton cigarettes as well as Sunshine biscuits) to avoid overweighting the Dow with tobacco and packaged foods. In 1987 Boeing and Coca Cola replaced Owens-Illinois (which disappeared in a leveraged buyout) and Inco (a producer of nickel and other metals). A list of the 30 firms currently included in the Dow is shown in Table 6–8.

The Dow Industrial Average is computed by adding the per-share prices of thirty prominent companies and dividing by the current value of the divisor *k:*

$$DJ = \frac{P_1 + P_2 + \ldots + P_{30}}{k}$$

Originally, the Dow Average was computed simply by adding the prices of the twelve stocks and dividing by 12. This computation had to be modified as other companies were added or substitutions were made; otherwise, the Dow would have jumped or plummeted for no real reason. Suppose, for instance, that all twelve of the original stocks were selling for $50 a share, giving an average of 50, and a thirteenth stock was added, which happened to be selling for $10 a share. If we add the thirteen prices

TABLE 6–8   The Dow Jones Industrial Average, 1989

Stock	Price per Share (on May 1, 1989)	Number of Shares (millions)	Total Market Value (billions of dollars)
Allied Signal	33½	148.7	5.0
Alcoa	62¾	88.3	5.5
American Express	32½	417.1	13.6
AT&T	34½	1073.7	37.0
Bethlehem Steel	22½	74.5	1.7
Boeing	77⅛	153.2	11.8
Chevron	53⅝	342.1	18.3
Coca Cola	54¾	359.0	19.7
DuPont	109¼	239.4	26.2
Eastman Kodak	47⅛	324.2	15.3
Exxon	42⅞	1289.0	55.3
General Electric	48¾	900.5	43.9
General Motor	41¼	612.9	25.3
Goodyear	52¼	57.3	3.0
IBM	113⅜	591.4	67.0
International Paper	49⅛	111.1	5.5
McDonald's	55⅜	188.0	10.4
Merck	67⅜	396.5	26.7
MMM	71½	226.8	16.2
Navistar	5⅜	252.8	1.4
Philip Morris	126⅜	231.0	29.2
Primerica	21⅛	96.0	2.0
Procter & Gamble	97⅝	169.4	16.5
Sears Roebuck	45¾	380.0	17.4
Texaco	54¼	244.3	13.3
Union Carbide	31⅝	135.6	4.3
United Technologies	51⅜	130.7	6.7
USX	34½	260.8	9.0
Westinghouse	57½	144.0	8.3
Woolworth	52¼	63.9	3.4

and divide by 13, we get an average of

$$DJ = \frac{50 + 50 + \ldots + 50 + 10}{13} = \frac{610}{13} = 46.92,$$

indicating that the average stock price dropped by more than 7 percent when, in fact, all that happened was that the index was broadened from twelve to thirteen stocks. A similar false signal would be given if one stock was substituted for another that happened to be selling for a different price.

A like difficulty arises whenever a stock splits. In a two-for-one split, each original share is replaced with 2 new shares, so that every owner of 100 old shares now has 200 new shares. For the company as a whole, the number of shares outstanding is doubled, and the value of each share is halved. For instance, a shareholder with 100 out of 1 million old shares owns 0.01 percent of the company and receives 0.01 percent of the total dividends distributed to shareholders. After a two-for-one split, this shareholder has 200 out of 2 million shares, still 0.01 percent of the company and its dividends. The market value of the 200 new shares should be the same as the value of 100 old shares, implying a halving of the price per share.

The Dow Jones Average allows for such cosmetic changes by adjustments to its divisor. In our first example, if we do not want the inclusion of a thirteenth stock to change the average, we can divide by some number k that keeps the average at 50. Thus,

$$DJ = \frac{50 + 50 + \ldots + 50 + 10}{k} = \frac{610}{k} = 50$$

implies a divisor of $k = \frac{610}{50} = 12.2$, rather than 13. The Dow is then calculated as follows:

$$DJ = \frac{50 + 50 + \ldots + 50 + 10}{12.2} = \frac{610}{12.2} = 50$$

By the same logic, the divisor is adjusted every time a substitution is made or a stock splits. The cumulative effects of these adjustments was to reduce the Dow industrial divisor to 0.682 by May 1989. (The current divisor is published in *The Wall Street Journal* every day.)

Thus, the Dow Industrial Average is an average of thirty prices, using a divisor that changes from time to time to maintain a logically consistent daily index of stock prices running all the way back to 1896.

Criticism of the Dow There are two primary objections to the Dow Industrial Average. One is that the index includes only thirty stocks. Admittedly, the thirty are among the biggest and the best, but, still, all other stocks are ignored completely. At present, these thirty companies represent one-fourth of the total market value of the 1500 stocks traded on the New York Stock Exchange and about a tenth of the exchange's daily volume. It is impressive that these 2 percent of the total number of companies have 25 percent of the market value, but it may be misleading to ignore the other 75 percent—particularly since the excluded companies are quite different from those included.

The thirty stocks in the Dow Industrial Average are not a random sample. The Dow seems top-heavy with representatives of smokestack America, industrial giants of the past, while U.S. growth now seems to be with high-technology and service companies. In addition, stocks are chosen for the Dow because they are large, well-established companies, the bluest of the blue chips, and, as such, their performance may not be representative of other, smaller and less prominent, companies. The excluded companies may grow faster and be riskier than the giants, and there may well be systematic differences in the behavior of their prices. Indeed, some security analysts compare movements in the Dow Industrial Average with broader averages (such as the NYSE composite index) in order to gauge the mood of the market. If the broader averages are soaring while the Dow is slumbering, this result is interpreted as a signal that the speculators are loose again, gambling on risky stocks.

In the long run, it can make all the difference in the world which particular thirty stocks are annointed the biggest and the best. IBM was originally added to the Dow in 1932, replacing National Cash Register, but then was dropped mysteriously in 1939 in favor of AT&T. If IBM had not been excluded for forty years, from 1939 to 1979, the Dow would have grown much faster and the stock market would have seemed much healthier. By 1979, the Dow would have been twice as high, at 1700 rather than at 850.

Similarly, one analyst calculated that the Dow increased by fifty points in September and October of 1985 solely because of large increases (fueled by takeover speculation) in the prices of just two stocks, General Foods and Union Carbide. Without these two stocks, the Dow would have fallen, "which is what it should have done, since we have seen a falling market."[10]

A second criticism is that the Dow Average reflects per-share prices instead of market values. We have seen how per-share prices are dramatically affected by stock splits. The more general lesson is that the per-share price depends on how many shares the company happens to have issued. If one of two otherwise equivalent companies has issued twice as many shares as the other, it will also have a per-share price half the size of the other. This fact is unimportant for the company and its shareholders, but it makes a big difference to the Dow Average in that a company's influence on the Dow depends on how many shares it happens to have issued.

Look at Table 6–8 again. In May 1988, Merck was the highest-priced stock among the Dow industrials, selling for $150 a share. But on May 26, 1988, Merck split three-for-one and its price dropped to $50 a share, reducing its importance to the Dow. At that time, the Dow divisor was about 0.754, so that, before the split, a 10 percent drop in the price of Merck (from 150 to 135) would have reduced the numerator of the Dow average by 15, causing the Dow to drop by $\frac{15}{0.754} = 20$ points. After the split, however, Merck lost its premier position; a 10 percent drop in the price of Merck would reduce the Dow by only 7 points.

In May 1989, Philip Morris at 126⅜ had the highest price and Navistar at 5⅜ the lowest, so that a 4 percent drop in the price of Philip Morris would force the Dow down 8 points, the same as if the price of Navistar fell by 100 percent.

The Dow Average treats a $1 change in any of the thirty included stock prices the same, regardless of whether the stock affected is selling for $10, $50, or $200 a share.

The Dow Average also pays no attention to how many shareholders are affected by the price changes. In May 1989, General Electric (GE) and Goodyear were both selling for about $50 a share, so that a $5 increase in either price meant a $\dfrac{5}{0.682}$ = 7.3-point increase in the Dow and a 10 percent gain for shareholders. GE had sixteen times as many shares outstanding as Goodyear, however—so a $5-per-share increase represented only $28 million in capital gains to Goodyear shareholders but $4.5 billion in capital gains to GE shareholders. The Dow treats such events as identical when they are, in fact, quite different—both as a barometer of the economy and in their implications for consumer wealth.

Market-Value Indexes

For just three reasons, most analysts prefer an index of stock prices based on market values, such as the following:

Market value index = (number of shares)(price per share).

For an example, consider an index based on just two stocks—GE and Goodyear:

$$(48¾)(900.5) + (52¼)(57.3) = 46,893$$

(The index, of course, could be scaled to equal 100 in a chosen base period.) In a market-value index, a 10 percent change in the value of the index represents a 10 percent change in the aggregate market value of the companies included in the index.

Most stock indexes, unlike the Dow, show changes in the market value of stocks. The Standard & Poor's 500 (S&P 500) contains 500 NYSE stocks, representing about three-fourths of the market value of all NYSE stocks, and the NYSE composite index includes all NYSE stocks. (Both have sub-indexes covering industrials, utilities, financial firms, and transportation companies.) The AMEX index covers the American Stock Exchange; the NASDAQ index tracks over-the-counter stocks; and the Wilshire 5000 includes 5000 stocks from all of these sources.

Each of these indexes is weighted by the number of outstanding shares, as illustrated by the two-stock index of GE and Goodyear so that it reflects the aggregate market value of the stocks in the index. Market-value indexes are a more accurate gauge of what really is happening to investor portfolios than is the Dow Average. But the Dow has its long tradition and an entrenched spot in the newspaper headlines. When the Dow is up fifty points, people can interpret that statistic readily as very good news about the stock market, simply because they remember that the Dow seldom goes up as much as fifty points in a single day. If they were to read that the NYSE composite index was up four points, they would not know what to make of that statistic, even though it is describing the same events and probably describing them more accurately. Undoubtedly typical of many market watchers, one securities analyst said of the Dow:

> *Statistically it isn't very good, but I follow it avidly. It's a kind of love-hate relationship. When you get down to it, it's the most convenient shorthand for the market.*[11]

SUMMARY

Common stock is equity, representing ownership of the company, and the dividends received depend on the company's profitability. Because dividends are not a tax-deductible expense for the corporation, they are taxed twice, once as corporate profits and again as shareholder income. On the other hand, shareholders have limited liability in that, even though they are owners of the firm, they are not personally responsible for its debts.

Stock is initially offered through investment bankers and then traded on a stock exchange or over the counter. The largest and most prominent companies are generally listed on the New York Stock Exchange. On stock exchanges, representatives of brokerage firms bring investor orders to a specialist who accumulates orders and executes trades when possible. The specialist also buys or sells for his or her own account, if such activity is necessary to fulfill an obligation to maintain a fair

and orderly market. Off the exchanges, trades are made by consulting the bid and ask prices quoted by competing market makers. Many trades today are large blocks of stock sold between institutions, which either bypass the exchanges or are privately negotiated before being recorded by a specialist.

Stock can be bought on margin, by borrowing money from a brokerage firm. This borrowing creates leverage that multiplies the gains or losses when the return on the stock is not equal to the interest rate on the loan. Stock can be sold short by borrowing shares from another investor (through a broker), selling these shares, and then purchasing shares later (at a lower price, it is hoped) to replace the shares that were borrowed.

Stockbrokers make money when investors make trades, giving them an economic incentive to encourage trading. A buy-and-hold strategy minimizes transaction costs and postpones the payment of capital-gains taxes. It may be profitable to realize losses if the tax credit is significantly larger than the transaction cost.

The Dow Jones Industrial Average is calculated by adding up the per-share prices of thirty blue-chip companies and dividing by the current value of the divisor k, which is adjusted periodically for stock splits and the inclusion of new securities. The thirty Dow stocks are large, established firms—not a random sample of all stocks. In addition, the Dow Average only considers the per-share prices, not the number of shares outstanding. The S&P 500, NYSE composite, and most other stock indexes are market-value indexes, in which each stock's price is multiplied by the number of shares outstanding, thereby reflecting what is happening to the market value of investor portfolios.

EXERCISES

1. Before the 1986 Tax Reform Act, the corporate tax rate was 46 percent, and the top individual tax rate was 50 percent. Taking into account the double taxation of dividends, what was the effective tax rate on a dollar of corporate profits paid out as dividends to someone in a 50 percent tax bracket?

2. Critically evaluate the following analysis of a new corporation:

> The founder of the Widget Works decides to sell 100,000 shares at $10 out of a total issued capitalization of 250,000, thus leaving him with three-fifths, or 60%, of the company. He retains majority control while the corporation receives the proceeds of the sale—$1,000,000 less expenses . . . the investors' shares are immediately devalued, since the $1 million reflects the worth, not of the 100,000 shares that were purchased, but of the total issued capitalization of 250,000. And these 250,000 shares are now worth $4 apiece.[12]

3. *The Wall Street Journal* awarded its tongue-in-cheek 1986 Charity Begins at Home Award with the following comments:

> To Merrill Lynch Capital Markets, for its underwriting of Home Shopping Network. Merrill priced the stock at $18 a share. The day it began trading, the stock more than doubled to $42.625 . . . By June the stock had more than doubled again to $100.[13]

Why is the price, $42.625, given to three decimal places? The creators of Home Shopping Network sold two million shares to the public and kept ten million shares for themselves. What was the total market value of the company at a price of $18? At $42.625? At $100? At $5, the price one year later? Did it really make any difference to anyone whether the two million shares were initially sold at $18 or $42 a share?

4. The investment banking firm of Morgan Stanley went public on March 21, 1986, by selling 4,500,000 shares at 56½. In the secondary market, the stock closed at 71¼ that day on the NYSE. Who gained and lost from this mispricing?

5. Look in the most recent Friday newspaper to see what happened to IBM on the NYSE the previous day, and answer the following questions:

a. What is IBM's current annual dividend?

b. How many shares were traded on Thursday?

c. What was the price of the last trade on Thursday?

d. What was the closing price on Wednesday?

6. Look in the most recent Friday newspaper to see what happened to Apple in the OTC market the previous day, and answer the following questions:

a. What is Apple's current dividend?

b. How many shares were traded on Thursday?

c. What was the price of the last trade on Thursday?

d. What was the closing price on Wednesday?

7. Check Moody's, Standard & Poor's, Value Line, or some other stock reference manual to find the number of shares outstanding for IBM and Apple. Then look in the most recent Friday newspaper to find the per-share price of these two stocks and the number of shares traded.

a. What fraction of the total outstanding shares of each of these stocks was traded the day before?

b. What is the total market value (price per share times number of shares) of each of these stocks?

8. In April 1987, the bid and ask prices for a seat on the NYSE were $750,000 and $1.5 million. Which price was the bid, and which was the ask? Do you think this market is very efficient? In what sense?

9. Explain how stop-loss orders could do the damage described in the following statement:

> A friend of mine who was out in the Far East in 1963 had stop-loss orders on all his stocks. When President Kennedy was assassinated . . . the market took a fierce immediate plunge . . . The market then recovered its nerves, turned around almost immediately and went right up past its previous level. But by the time the news reached my unfortunate friend, all he could do was get back in with 80 shares where he had formerly had 100.[14]

10. An astute market observer wrote, "Margin is how brokerage firms make it easy for you to overextend yourself with leverage."[15] Another says, "If you and your broker are nonetheless determined to give margin a try, be prepared for an intense and perilous relationship that may well last till debt do you part."[16] Explain how margin gives you leverage and why it might be a perilous strategy.

11. If you buy 400 shares of stock at $25 a share, what is your percentage gain (neglecting taxes and commissions) if the price immediately jumps to $30? Now assume that instead of buying 300 shares, you had used 50 percent margin to buy 800 shares. Show your debt and equity and calculate the percentage return on your investment if the price jumps to $30. If instead the price immediately drops to $20.

12. In 1929, many speculators bought stocks with a 10 percent margin. Assuming a very short period of time, so that dividends and interest costs are negligible, how much do stock prices have to increase to double the speculator's equity? How much do stock prices have to fall to wipe out the speculator?

13. During the 1920s, some investors would pyramid their position by borrowing more money as stock prices went up. For instance, an investor might use $2000 of his money and $8000 in borrowed money to buy 1000 shares at $10. If the price goes up to $16, the total market value is $16,000—of which $8000 is debt and $8000 equity. The investor now can borrow an additional $24,000 and buy 1500 more shares, giving $32,000 debt and $8000 equity—still a 20 percent margin. Fill in Table 6–A showing the debt, equity, and total market value when the following events then happen in succession: the price rises to $20; the investor buys another 2000 shares with borrowed money; the price rises to $25; the investor buys an additional 3600 shares with borrowed money; the price falls back to $20.

14. Bonds can be bought on margin—30 percent for corporate bonds and as little as 5 percent for Treasury bonds. Why would anyone want to buy Treasury bonds on margin, since the loan rate charged by the broker is presumably higher than the interest rate on Treasury bonds?

15. If you donate stock instead of cash to a charity, you can deduct the market value of the stock from your taxable income. Why might it be advantageous to donate stock instead of selling the stock and donating the cash received from the sale?

16. Explain the following description of bear

TABLE 6–A

Price per Share	Number of Shares	Debt	Equity	Total Value
$10	1000	$ 8,000	$2,000	$10,000
16	1000	8,000	8,000	16,000
16	2500	32,000	8,000	40,000
20	2500	32,000		
20	4500			
25	4500			
25	8100			
20	8100			

raiding to someone who does not understand stop-loss orders or margin calls:

> One is the effort to depress a certain stock a few points in the hope of "touching off" some stop-loss orders . . . . A more extensive operation, looking for a larger profit, is to help depress stocks to the point where margin calls will be sent out.[17]

17. In the spring of 1920, there was a struggle between investors who sold shares of Stutz Motor Company stock short and Allan Ryan, the president of Stutz, who personally bought up virtually all of the company's stock. The stock's price surged from 100 in early 1920 to 391 on March 31, at which point Ryan announced that he was willing to sell stock to the short sellers at $750 a share. The New York Stock Exchange responded by announcing an indefinite suspension of trading in Stutz stock and declaring the short sellers' contracts void. It explained that "there is not a word of truth in the statement that the action...was dictated by a desire to benefit the short interests."[18] Why would short sellers buy stock from Ryan at $750 a share? Why would short sellers benefit from a voiding of their contracts?

18. Explain the following recommendation in PaineWebber's analysis of the 1986 Tax Reform Act:

> Investors who have current short-term [capital] gains should try to defer them,

whenever possible, into 1987 when they will be taxed at a maximum rate of 38.5%, much lower than the current 50%. One possible strategy is to "short against the box"[19]

19. Look in the most recent Monday *Wall Street Journal* for the large box labeled "The Dow Jones Averages" that appears next to the New York Stock Exchange price quotations. Are the 30 stocks in the Industrial Average the same as in Table 6–8 in the text? If not, what substitutions have been made?

20. Look in *The Wall Street Journal* and find the current value of the divisor for the Dow Jones Industrial Average. What would be the effect on the Dow Industrial Average if the price of IBM went up by $10? If the price of Primerica went up by $10?

21. Look in the "Stock Market Data Bank" printed in the most recent Monday *Wall Street Journal* (near the NYSE price quotations). Did the Dow Jones Industrial Average or the NASDAQ composite change by a larger percentage on the preceding Friday? Over the past 12 months?

22. Look in the "Stock Market Data Bank" in the most recent Monday *Wall Street Journal*. Which stock had the largest percentage increase and which had the largest percentage decrease in trading the preceding Friday on the NYSE? Among stocks listed in the NASDAQ system?

23. On May 25, 1988, Merck closed at 150 and the Dow Jones Industrial Average closed at 1961.37 (with a divisor of 0.754). Merck then split three-for-one before the market opened on May 26. What new value of the divisor was needed to keep the Dow Industrial Average at 1961.37 as Merck split?

24. One observer said the following of the Dow Jones Average:

> It's taken as gospel. The state of the economy, the fate of politicians, often are read in the twists and turns of Wall Street's most recognizable indicator, the Dow Jones Industrial Average.[20]

In 1979, Chrysler and Esmark, which had fallen by 44 percent and risen by 42 percent respectively during the preceding twenty years, were replaced by IBM and Merck, which had each increased by nearly 400 percent. If the substitution had been made twenty years earlier, would the Dow have told a happier or sadder tale during the 1960s and 1970s?

25. In July 1979, IBM (at $70 a share) and Merck (at $68) replaced Chrysler and Esmark (at $9 and $26, respectively) in the Dow Industrial Average. To keep the Dow index at 850, did the divisor of 1.443 have to be adjusted up or down? What was the new value of the divisor?

26. One observer said the following of the substitution described in the previous exercise:

> It points to greater volatility in the Dow Average, since two higher-priced stocks are replacing two lower-priced ones. The higher a stock's price, the more the likelihood of substantial dollar fluctuations in a day's trading.[21]

(That is, a 10 percent change in a $70 stock is $7, while a 10 percent change in a $20 stock is only $2.) Does this argument that the Dow will be more volatile apply to changes in all of the Dow's thirty stocks or just to changes in IBM and Merck? Taking into account the changed divisor discussed in the preceding exercise,

how would you summarize the effect of this substitution on the volatility of the Dow Jones Average?

27. The same observer cited in the preceding exercise went on to say the following about the Dow's inclusion of Chrysler and Esmark in 1979: "The two additions are stocks in growth areas that seem likely to be candidates for split in the future . . . . and thus increase the volatility of the average." How can a stock split increase the volatility of the average? Again, you may want to distinguish between these stocks and the other twenty-eight in the Dow Average.

28. In a market-value stock index, how must the divisor be adjusted for stock splits? Use the index given in the text for General Electric (GE) and Goodyear, and assume that GE splits two-for-one, doubling the number of shares and halving its price.

29. Use the data in Table 6–8 to answer the following questions regarding the effects of a $3 decrease in the price of AT&T and a $3 decrease in the price of Allied Signal, roughly 9 percent in each case.
a. Using a Dow divisor of 0.682, how much does each of the price decreases affect the Dow Industrial Average?
b. How much does each of these price decreases affect shareholder wealth?

30. Union Carbide split three-for-one on March 14, 1986, tripling the number of outstanding shares. In comparison with the numbers in Table 6–8, assume that without this split there would have been 45.2 million shares outstanding, each selling for $94⅞. Using a Dow divisor of 0.682, compare the effects of a 10 percent price increase with the split and without the split on the following:
a. The Dow Industrial Average.
b. Shareholder wealth.

31. Following are the closing prices on Friday, October 16, 1987, and on Monday, October 19, 1987. Do these data indicate that stock prices fell more on this Black Monday for large, established companies or for smaller, more speculative firms?

	Closing Prices	
Index	*Friday, October 16, 1987*	*Monday, October 19, 1987*
Dow Industrial Average	2246.74	1738.74
NYSE composite	159.13	128.62
AMEX composite	323.55	282.50
NASDAQ	406.33	360.21

32. The Dow Jones Industrial Average closed at 144.13 on December 13, 1935, and at 1546.67 on December 31, 1985. The Standard & Poors' 500 closed on these same dates at 10.60 and 211.28. Which index increased more in percentage terms? Tell in words the story represented by these numbers.

33. In late 1985, Congress changed the tax laws so that all realized capital gains, beginning in 1986, would be taxed at the same rate as wages, dividends, and other income. Before that, realized long-term gains (on assets held more than six months) were taxed at only 40 percent of the tax rate on other income. Some observers predicted that the elimination of the distinction between short-term and long-term gains would lead stock-market investors to make use of more frequent trading and shorter-holding periods. Can you think of any reason why this tax change might persuade investors to use longer holding periods?

34. In the first eight months of 1986, Japanese stock prices rose 44 percent, putting prices at fifty times earnings. Comparing this run-up with the 1929 surge in stock prices in the United States, two *Financial Times* correspondents wrote that "a major difference is that most of it is now being done with real money, not on margin, so that there is no monetary reason why it cannot go on."[22] What difference do you think it makes to a speculative boom whether the buying is done on margin or not?

35. A staff reporter from *The Wall Street Journal* described as follows the shorting of what was referred to as "ghost stock":

> Even riskier is shorting stock without borrowing it first, a practice limited almost exclusively to brokerage firms that sell short for their own accounts. Shorting "ghost stock" might seem impossible because no delivery takes place to settle the trade. But greed can make some brokers less than vigorous in pursuing settlement.
>
> When an invester unwittingly buys ghost stock, he writes a check to his brokerage firm and his account is credited with the stock. The funds aren't released to the short seller's broker until the stock is actually delivered.[23]

Why do you suppose the buyer's broker is less than vigorous in demanding delivery of the stock?

36. In 1980, *The Wall Street Journal* reported the following:

> Earlier this year, fast-growing Loral Corp needed a lot of money and found a cheap place to get it—the stock market.
>
> By issuing one million new shares, Loral took in $55 million. If that money had been borrowed—at a time when banks' basic lending rate was nearly 20%—[Loral] would have burdened itself with paying $11 million a year in interest . . . "We made one very good decision," Mr. Schwartz [Loral's chairman] says.[24]

Overall, corporations raised $83 billion in 1980 by borrowing and only $13 billion by selling stock. Why do you think most companies chose to borrow (and pay interest) rather than sell stock (and pay dividends)?

37. Suppose that at the age of twenty-five you invest $10,000 in a stock for your retirement forty years later. After twenty years, the value of your stock may quadruple to $40,000—a not unreasonable 7.2 percent a year. If you sell at that time and pay a 33 percent tax on your $30,000 capital gain, you will have $30,000 left to invest. Suppose that, whether you sell or not, your investment will quadruple again over the next twenty years. How much will you have after taxes if you sell once, at age sixty-five? If you sell twice, at age forty-five and again at the age of sixty-five?

38. A full-page newspaper advertisement in February 1988 boasted that D. H. Blair and Company had managed "the top performing initial public offering and 4 of the top 5 performers."[25] A table showed that the price of Management Technologies stock had increased by 370.83 percent between its initial sale and December 31, 1987, more than any other new stock. Three other Blair-managed offerings increased by 135.42 percent, 130 percent, and 127.50 percent between the initial sale and December 31, 1987. Investors who "believe in investing in exciting super growth stocks early" were urged to contact D. H. Blair about its investment programs. Why are such comparisons potentially misleading? Which readers of this advertisement were not happy to see the price of Management Technologies stock quadruple?

39. A 1981 *New York Times* article recommended bond-swapping—selling a bond that had gone down in price and buying a similar bond:

> Some 30-year A-rated bonds of Municipal Electric Utilities, for example, were marketed four or five years ago with a 7% coupon. Currently, many of these bonds are worth only sixty cents on the dollar . . . . The process of turning lemons into lemonade, so to speak, involves bond-swapping.[26]

Why do you suppose these bonds were only worth sixty percent of their face value? What possible advantage could there be to bond-swapping if bonds are fairly priced?

40. This exercise is intended to compare active and passive trading strategies. You have been given a portfolio of $10,000 worth of stocks to manage for five years. If you simply hold onto these stocks, they will appreciate by 10 percent per year. (Assume throughout that the stocks pay no dividends, so that all returns are in the form of capital gains.) How much will you have, before taxes, at the end of five years? How much will you have after taxes, if you are in a 28 percent tax bracket? What is the implicit annual after-tax return? Alternatively, you can sell all your stocks each month in order to buy stocks more likely to appreciate during the next month. Assume that the stocks selected by this active portfolio management appreciate by 5 percent per month. (What is the annual price appreciation for stocks that increase by 5 percent a month?) Assume also that you pay a 2 percent commission on every transaction, buying or selling, and that you pay a 28 percent capital-gains tax at the end of the year. How much will you have after paying transaction costs and taxes at the end of one year? What is the implicit annual after-tax return? How much money will you have after five years?

C H A P T E R   7

Fundamental Analysis:
Dividend-Discount Models

Investors should buy stocks as if they were groceries
instead of perfume . . .
Benjamin Graham

When we buy groceries, clothing, or a television set, we ask not merely whether the food is good, the clothing attractive, or the television well built, but also how much it costs. Is it really worth the price? When we buy stock, we should ask the same question—not whether it is issued by a good company, but whether the price is right. Is it worth the cost? Everyone knows that IBM is a better company than Sears. The relevant question is whether IBM stock, at $120 a share, is a better buy than Sears stock, at $45.

This simple insight is the basis for John Burr Williams's 1938 book *The Theory of Investment Value*, in which he intended to set forth "a new subscience . . . that shall comprise a coherent body of principles like the theory of Money and The Theory of International Trade."[1] A classmate of Paul Samuelson, Williams wrote this book as his Harvard doctorate thesis; but his dissertation committee would not approve it until it became a bestseller. The book did succeed, and so did Williams, who not only got his degree but became a Harvard professor.

While Williams was writing for academicians, Benjamin Graham and David Dodd wrote *Security Analysis*,[2] popularly referred to as the "Bible of Wall Street"—an enduring work that is still studied by investment analysts today, more than fifty years after its initial publication. After World War II, Graham published a condensed version for laymen, called *The Intelligent Investor*. Graham, like Williams, was an academic—a Phi Beta Kappa from Columbia who was fluent in Greek and Latin. Graham was offered teaching jobs in English, math, and philosophy at Columbia but, instead he worked on Wall Street and taught finance part-time for twenty-five years at Columbia—David Dodd was one of his students—and then for fifteen years at UCLA. Through the many editions of his two classic books, Graham urged investors to resist glamorous images and romantic dreams, the emotions that sway perfume choices, and instead, as with groceries, consider the quality of the ingredients and compare brands and prices. The best groceries are quality products at bargain prices—and the same is true of stocks.

In this chapter and the next, we will look at the approach developd by Williams and Graham that is now called fundamental analysis. You will see how the value of a stock depends on its dividends, earnings, and assets as well as on interest rates. Several examples will be given to show how professionals use fundamental analysis and how you can too. We begin by distinguishing between investment and speculation.

INTRINSIC VALUE AND SPECULATION

intrinsic value
The intrinsic value of a stock is the present value of its prospective cash flow, discounted by the investor's required return.

What is the value of 100 shares of IBM? We do not buy stock certificates to eat, wear, or watch at night. We buy stock for its cash flow—for its dividends and then the price received when we sell it to someone else. The **intrinsic value** of a stock is the present value of its prospective cash flow, discounted by our required return, taking into account the returns available on alternative investments, the stock's risk, and other salient considerations. The intrinsic value is not necessarily equal to the market price. The very first sentence of Williams's book is, "Separate and distinct things not to be confused, as every thoughtful investor knows, are real worth and market price." A stock is worth buying if its intrinsic value is higher than its price and not otherwise. As elaborated by Dodd and Graham and countless others, Williams's insight is the basis for what is now called **fundamental analysis,** efforts to compare the price of a security to the present value of the anticipated cash flow.

fundamental analysis
Investors using fundamental analysis compare the price of a security to the present value of the anticipated cash flow.

John Burr Williams considered stocks a long-run investment with a cash flow consisting of an endless stream of dividends. In his view, an investor should not buy a stock unless he or she is willing to hold it forever, happily cashing the dividend checks. A stock that will never pay dividends is of no value, just as a used postage stamp has no intrinsic value. True investors avoid assets with no cash flow. Williams, the Harvard economics professor temporarily turned poet, wrote:

A cow for her milk
A hen for her eggs
and a stock, by heck
For her dividends.

An orchard for fruit
Bees, for their honey
and stock, besides
For their dividends.[3]

In contrast to investors who are willing to hold an asset for keeps **speculators** buy not for the long-run cash flow, but to sell a short while later for a profit. To speculators, a stock (or a used postage stamp) is worth what someone else will pay for it, and the challenge is to guess what others will pay tomorrow for what you buy today. Keynes put it this way:

> *It is not sensible to pay 25 for an investment of which you believe the prospective [cash flow] to justify a value of 30, if you also believe that the market will value it at 20 three months hence.*[4]

speculators
Speculators buy not for the long-run cash flow, but to sell the asset a short while later for a profit.

This sort of guessing game is dangerously close to the Greater Fool Theory: you buy shares at an inflated price, hoping to find an even bigger fool who will buy these shares from you at a still higher price. The retort of speculators is that everyone hopes to sell for a large profit; those who hold for keeps do so reluctantly, still waiting for the capital-gains dream that has never come true.

Fundamental analysts readily admit that many who buy and sell stock are speculators, hoping for fast and easy profits, and that speculative binges can cause prices to depart from intrinsic values. Speculators are like the wind that blows a boat about its anchor, present value. The task is to determine intrinsic value, since this knowledge can help identify a speculative bubble and also can help discover opportunities after the bubble pops.

Benjamin Graham was a very conservative practitioner of fundamental analysis. He favored blue-chip companies with a well-established history of earning profits and paying dividends, with substantial, tangible assets and few liabilities. Because the future cash flow is uncertain for even the best of companies, he insisted on an adequate safety margin, so that the stock would still be attractive even if projections proved somewhat optimistic. He was not much interested in growth stocks, whose anticipated rosy future might prove to be just a dream. He never bought a single share of IBM, the best growth stock; but for every IBM he missed, there were hundreds of failed dreams he passed up too.

THE PRESENT VALUE OF DIVIDENDS

We will begin our examination of the details of fundamental analysis with an investor who intends to hold a stock forever. If D_t is the dividend t periods from now and R is the shareholder's required return, then the present value of this cash flow is as follows:

$$PV = \frac{D_1}{(1 + R)} + \frac{D_2}{(1 + R)^2} + \frac{D_3}{(1 + R)^3} + \cdots \tag{1}$$

(Companies usually pay dividends quarterly and, hence, a quarterly required return is in order; but, for simplicity, we use annual dividends and annual required rates of return.)

Suppose that a large, mature firm will pay a $5 annual dividend forever. This payout is equivalent to that of a consol bond and, as seen in Chapter 2, the present-value equation simplifies to

$$PV = \frac{D_1}{R}.$$

If the required return is 10 percent ($R = 0.10$), the present value of this perpetual $5 annual dividend is $PV = \$5/0.10 = \$50$. It follows that if the dividend grows over time, the present value must be somewhat larger than $50; if the dividend declines, the present value is less than $50.

THE CONSTANT-GROWTH MODEL

constant-dividend-growth model
The constant-dividend-growth model assumes that dividends grow at a constant rate.

A special case is the **constant-dividend-growth model,** in which the dividend grows at a steady rate g each period:

$$D_2 = (1 + g)D_1$$
$$D_3 = (1 + g)^2 D_1$$

$$\cdot$$
$$\cdot$$
$$\cdot$$

Substituting into Equation 1, we find the following:

$$PV = \frac{D_1}{(1 + R)} + \frac{D_1(1 + g)}{(1 + R)^2} + \frac{D_1(1 + g)^2}{(1 + R)^3} + \cdots$$

If $g<R$, then, as shown in the appendix to this chapter, the present value simplifies to the following, the central equation of fundamental analysis:

$$PV = \frac{D_1}{R - g} \tag{2}$$

This equation is the present value of a dividend, D_1, growing at a rate g.

TABLE 7–1   Present Value of a $5 Dividend with a Required Return of
10 Percent

Growth Rate, *g* (percent)	Present Value, *PV*
0	$ 50.00
2	62.50
4	83.33
6	125.00
8	250.00

Of course, dividends never grow at a completely constant rate. The appeal of Equation 2 is that it is a reasonable initial approximation that has some very logical implications.

The Value of Growth

Notice, particularly, how important the growth rate is to the value of a stock. At a 10 percent required return, a stock paying a $5 dividend is worth $50 if no growth is expected, and it is worth twice as much if the dividend is expected to grow by 5 percent a year: $PV = \$5/(0.10 - 0.05) = \$100$. The present values for other growth rates are shown in Table 7–1.

Growth makes a big difference because of the power of compounding. The difference between 0 percent and 5 percent growth may not seem like much (and it really isn't for the first few years); but fifty years down the road, the first company still will be paying a $5 dividend while the second pays $5(1.05^{50}) = \$57.34$. A present-value calculation whittles down the difference somewhat, but, still, when all is said and done, taking into account the small difference in near dividends and the big difference in distant dividends, the second company is worth twice as much as the first.

This logic explains the lure of **growth stocks,** shares in companies with relatively high anticipated growth rates. Why, in August 1986, were investors willing to pay $74 a share for Lilly, a pharmaceutical company paying a $1.80 dividend, and only $59 a share for Kansas Power and Light, which was paying a $3.16 dividend? The explanation provided by fundamental analysis is that while both were very strong, financially secure companies, Lilly's dividend was expected to grow faster than Kansas P&L's. Value Line, a widely read investment-advisory service, gave both companies A+ ratings for financial strength, but estimated Lilly's growth rate at 12.5 percent and Kansas P&L's at only 6 percent.[5] Since long-term Treasury securities yielded about 8 percent at the time, shareholder required returns for these two stocks were probably at double-digit levels. Kansas P&L's price was about right for an 11.5 percent required return and, even with

growth stock
A growth stock has a higher present value than otherwise similar firms with lower growth rates.

a 15 percent required return, Lilly's higher price was justified fully by its faster growth rate, as shown by the following:

$$\text{Kansas P\&L } PV = \frac{\$3.16}{(0.115 - 0.06)} = \$57.45$$

$$\text{Lilly } PV = \frac{\$1.80}{(0.15 - 0.125)} = \$72.00$$

The conclusion that growth is valuable works in reverse, too. Sometimes, a company with bright prospects will announce an increase in its earnings and the price of its stock free-falls downward. This price decline occurs because the announced increase in earnings (and, hence, future dividends) is not as large as had been previously anticipated, and small differences in growth rates can make a big difference to the value of a company's stock; for example, in Table 7–1, a scaling down of growth prospects from 8 percent to 6 percent cuts the present value in half.

As Table 7–1 indicates, the effects of revised growth projections are largest for a growth stock because what you are buying with such a stock is large future dividends, which do not materialize if the growth rate slows. A particularly dramatic example is Disney, a favored growth stock whose price fell from a high of $121½ in 1973 to a low of $16⅝ in 1974, even while its earnings were increasing. Its 1973 earnings of $1.64 a share were a full 16 percent above 1972's $1.41 earnings, but they were far below most analysts' optimistic $1.80 to $2.00 predictions. Even the revised prediction of $1.95 for 1974 proved to be optimistic, as earnings only increased slightly, to $1.66. Recession, inflation, and the energy crisis took their toll, but worst of all was the fear that Disney had changed from a glamorous growth stock to something a bit more mature and much less exciting.[6]

An unsettling corollary is that the present value of a growth stock is a slippery calculation, since it is so sensitive to the assumed growth rate. A good example is Professor J. Peter Williamson's calculation in 1968 of the present value of IBM, then priced at $320 a share.[7] He assumed a growth rate for IBM during the next ten years of 16 percent, slightly under the growth rate of the preceding ten years, which would be followed by a 2 percent growth rate thereafter. A 7 percent required return gave Williamson's calculation a present value of $173, about half the current price at the time. He then assumed 16 percent growth for twenty years, followed by 2 percent growth, and thus obtained a present value of $433, almost 50 percent above the 1968 price. While the value of growth cannot be doubted, the difficulties in valuing rapidly growing companies is what kept Benjamin Graham away from IBM and other, more temporary, high fliers.

To condemn the dividend-discount model because the future is difficult to predict is to shoot the messenger for delivering unpleasant news. The dividend-discount model demonstrates very forcefully that whether a stock is attractive or unattractive depends not on its past history, but on its uncertain future. The purchaser of stock is buying the future, not the past;

and the perceived value of a stock, as with all present-value calculations, hinges on assumptions about an unknowable future. Yet, this uncertainty does not require us to pick stocks blindly, hoping for a Greater Fool. While we may know little about the manufacture of television sets or automobiles, rational choice still requires an informed judgment, based on what we do know and what we are willing to assume. The same is true with the purchasing of stocks.

Fundamental analysis helps us ask the right questions. The safest answers use a variety of assumptions to gauge the sensitivity of our conclusions—Graham's margin of safety. If the buy/sell decision hinges on a debatable assumption, you then know the relevant question that must be asked.

The Growth-Stock Paradox

If the growth rate, g, is not smaller than the required return, R, then Equation 2 does not hold (for mathematical reasons detailed in the appendix to this chapter). Otherwise, Equation 2 would give the nonsensical conclusion that stocks with very high growth rates have a negative present value! To determine the correct present value for rapidly growing stocks, think first of one whose growth rate is just equal to R, say 10 percent. The $5 dividend to be paid a year from now is worth $5/1.10 = 4.55. The year after that the dividend will be $5(1.10) = 5.50, with a present value of $5.50/1.10^2 = 4.55, again. The dividend three years from now will be $5(1.10)^2 = 6.05, and its present value is $6.05/1.10^3 = 4.55 once again. At a 10 percent required return, a 10 percent growth rate for the dividend keeps the present value of each dividend at $4.55. The total present value of this unending stream of dividends is infinite:

$$PV = \$4.55 + \$4.55 + \$4.55 + \ldots \rightarrow \infty$$

Obviously, the present value is also infinite if the growth rate is larger than R. This infinite present value for $g \geq R$ is called the **growth-stock paradox.**

The answer to the apparent paradox is that investors should indeed be willing to pay an unlimited amount for a stock with a long-run growth rate that exceeds shareholders' required return, but that such a permanently high, long-run growth rate is not really plausible. Firms can grow very rapidly in their early years, when they are starting from a small base with new products in undeveloped markets. However, such rapid growth cannot be maintained forever, because markets become saturated, competitors arise, and the very size of the company imposes resource constraints. Inevitably, companies mature and either wither or grow at the rate of ordinary companies. Investment Example 7–1 uses IBM to illustrate this argument.

growth-stock paradox
The growth-stock paradox is that a stock with $g > R$ has an infinite present value.

THE INEVITABLE SLOWING OF IBM

IBM is the premier growth stock of all time. In 1968, its revenues had been growing (in real terms) by about 16 percent a year; if this growth continued and the overall U.S. economy continued to grow at its long-run 3 percent rate, IBM would comprise 2.6 percent of the total gross national product in ten years and 8.5 percent in twenty—an impressive achievement but not beyond the realm of possibility. What if IBM's 16 percent growth rate were projected indefinitely? After thirty-five years, half of the GNP would be IBM products and, after forty-one years, everything would be made by IBM! At this stage in our fanciful exercise, since IBM cannot be bigger than the economy, something would have to give—

either IBM's growth rate would have to drop to 3 percent, or the economy's growth rate would have to rise to 16 percent. The latter scenario—sustained 16 percent growth for the entire economy—is plainly implausible, because aggregate output is constrained by the rates of growth of the labor force, capital stock, and productivity. Mathematically, rapid rates of growth for individual companies cannot persist indefinitely, without unprecedented and almost unimaginable changes in the entire economy.

In IBM's case, the company's 16 percent growth rate did not persist. By 1986, IBM revenues were 1.2 percent of GNP, an average real growth rate of 5.5 percent over the preceding eighteen years, with similar growth projected over the next five years.

Sources of Growth

The cash that firms pay out in dividends comes from profits earned on their assets. A slight elaboration of the constant-growth model brings out the important relationship between assets, profits, and dividends. First, we will link dividends D to after-tax earnings E:

$$D = dE$$

payout ratio
A firm's payout ratio is the fraction of its earnings paid out as dividends.

The parameter $d = D/E$ is the **payout ratio,** the fraction of earnings that a firm's board of directors elects to pay out as dividends; the remainder $1 - d$ is the **retention ratio,** the fraction of earnings plowed back into a firm to finance expansion.

Earnings, E, depend on the profitability of assets, A,

retention ratio
A firm's retention ratio is the fraction of earnings retained by the firm.

$$E = ROE \, A$$

The parameter $ROE = E/A$ is a firm's *profit rate,* the rate of return earned on its assets (or return on equity).

For now, we assume that a firm's expansion in financed solely by retained earnings (internal financing); Chapter 8 considers borrowed money and the sale of additional stock (external financing). With internal financing, the increase in a firm's assets is equal to its retained earnings, or

$$\Delta A = (1 - d)E.$$

The substitution of the equation for earnings gives

$$\Delta A = (1 - d) \, ROE \, A,$$

and

$$\frac{\Delta A}{A} = (1 - d) \, ROE,$$

so that the rate of growth of assets is equal to $(1 - d) \, ROE$, the retention ratio times the profit rate. Because profits are proportional to assets and dividends proportional to profits, these too grow at this same rate, $(1 - d) \, ROE$. Thus, the rate of growth of dividends, profits, and assets in the constant-growth model is equal to the retention ratio times the rate of return a firm earns on its assets, or

$$g = (1 - d) \, ROE. \tag{3}$$

Equation 2 can now be modified to

$$PV = \frac{d \, ROE \, A}{R - (1 - d) \, ROE} \tag{4}$$

to show that the present value of a stock depends on four fundamental factors,

$$PV = PV[\overset{+}{A}, \overset{+}{ROE}, \overset{-}{R}, \overset{?}{d}] \tag{5}$$

with the signs indicating whether the effects on present value are positive, negative or ambiguous. For a given profit rate and other factors, a stock is worth more, the more assets, A, are owned by a firm. The next two influences, ROE and R, must be distinguished carefully. The *profit rate, ROE*, is the rate of return a firm earns on its assets, depending on the strength of the economy, the appeal of its products, and the efficiency of its production methods. The *required rate of return, R*, in contrast, is decided by shareholders, taking into account the returns available on alternative investments and the riskiness of the company's stock. These two rates of return have very different effects on present value. A high profit rate for the firm increases the cash flow to shareholders, making the stock more valuable, while a high shareholder required rate of return discounts the cash flow more heavily, reducing its present value.

The fourth influence, *d,* is the firm's payout/retention policy. A high value of *d* means that the firm pays more of its earnings out as dividends and retains less for expansion; a low value of *d* means that the firm spends potential dividends on expansion. A change in *d* has conflicting effects on a stock's value in that when *d* is reduced, current dividends are diminished, but, because more funds are retained for expansion, future dividends are enhanced. Whether such a sacrifice of current dividends for future dividends benefits shareholders depends on whether the rate of return the firm earns on its investments is larger or smaller than the shareholders' required return. If the firm earns a higher rate of return on its investments than shareholders require on their stock, expansion benefits shareholders. If, on the other hand, the firm's investments yield less than the shareholders' required return, then the shareholders prefer that earnings be distributed as dividends and not be reinvested.

The plowing back of retained earnings is the trading of current dividends for future dividends—of a bird in the hand for two in the bush. The firm's return on its investments is clearly crucial to this exchange. Some companies like IBM and Lilly have earned high returns (around 20 percent for many years), while others like Kansas Power & Lighting earn less than 10 percent, and still others like Bethlehem Steel and People Express have earned nothing at all. Not surprisingly, IBM and Lilly retain about 60 percent of their earnings, and Kansas P&L retains only 30 percent.

USING INTRINSIC VALUE FOR BUY/SELL DECISIONS

Unlike fixed-income securities, a share of common stock has no contractual payments and no maturity date. Because dividends depend on the success of the company and the dividend policy of its directors, the estimated cash flow from owning a share of stock must be a subjective guess, based on the investor's knowledge of the company, the industry, and the overall economy. Some analysts formalize these guesses by building computer models that predict the path of earnings under different hypothetical scenarios.

Intrinsic Value Versus Market Price

Once the cash flow has been estimated, practitioners of fundamental analysis use Equation 1 or the simplified Equation 2 to gauge whether stocks are undervalued or overpriced. These equations give the present value of the anticipated dividend stream, using the investor's required return (which takes into account the returns available on alternative investments).

If the market price is less than this present value, then the stock is undervalued by the market; others are willing to sell for a price that is less than you are willing to pay, and you should take advantage of this bargain price. If, on the other hand, the market price is higher than your present value, the stock should be avoided because it is not worth its cost.

Such analyses can be done for individual stocks or for the market as a whole. In the first case, the analyst tries to identify specific stocks that are attractively priced (these are put on a buy list) and those that are too expensive (these go on a sell list). In the second case, the analyst tries to determine whether stocks in general are cheap or dear. If stocks appear cheap, the recommendation is to buy more; if stocks seem expensive, then the best strategy is to liquidate stocks and invest elsewhere. Investment Example 7–2 gives an example of such reasoning.

Of course, not everyone agrees on whether stocks are cheap or expensive. That is why there is a stock market. While you believe that a certain stock is very attractively priced, other investors, with more pessimistic growth projections or higher required returns, consider the price too high. They sell what you are buying.

Implicit Versus Required Return

Equation 2 gives the present value as

$$PV = \frac{D}{R - g}.$$

If we replace PV with the market price P, then we can solve for the implicit rate of return such that the discounted value of the cash flow is just equal to the market price, as follows:

$$P = \frac{D}{\text{return} - g}$$

Rearranging this equation, the implicit rate of return is

$$\text{return} = \frac{D}{P} + g. \tag{6}$$

If this implicit return is larger than the shareholder's required return, then the present value, calculated using this required return, must be larger than the market price. Thus, a comparison of the implicit return and required return is equivalent to a comparison of intrinsic value with market price. Investment Example 7–3 shows how one investment company, Goldman, Sachs, applies this principle to the overall stock market.

A slightly more complicated model was constructed by assuming that, each year, investors expect dividends for the S&P 500 index to return gradually to a long-run trend path estimated from dividend data for the preceding ten years.[8] The implicit shareholder required return can be

220

INVESTMENT EXAMPLE
7–2

AN INTRINSIC-VALUE CALCULATION IN 1983

In November 1983, the firm of L. F. Rothschild, Unterberg, Towbin prepared a stock-market outlook for "year-end 1985."* At the time, the S&P 400 industrials index was at 183.94, up 16.7 percent since the beginning of the year (largely due to the ending of the 1981–82 recession). The 1983–84 economic recovery was consistent with previous business-cycle expansions in the percentage increases in output, employment, sales, productivity, and so on. The company consequently forecast a continued brisk expansion of profits and dividends, as shown in the accompanying table.

After admitting that interest rates are notoriously difficult to forecast and discussing a variety of considerations—including an approaching presidential election, a predicted drop in inflation, growing federal deficits, and the strength of the dollar—the firm ventured a guess that the yields on thirty-year Treasury bonds would drop by about a percentage point, from 11.75 percent to 10.8 percent. To this calculation was added a 1 percent risk premium to obtain a required return on stocks: $R = 10.8\% + 1\% = 11.8\%$. To develop a long-run growth rate for dividends, a 5.5 percent inflation forecast was added to the economy's 1.25 percent average real growth rate over the preceding thirty years: $g = 1.25$ percent $+ 5.5$ percent $= 6.75$ percent. Thus,

$$PV = \frac{D}{R - g}$$
$$= \frac{10.25}{(0.1180 - 0.0675)}$$
$$= 202.97$$

*Alexander Bing III and Michael F. Wilcox, "Market Commentary," L. F. Rothschild, Unterberg, and Towbin, November 4, 1983.

Year	S&P 400 Earnings	S&P 400 Dividends
1982	$13.18	$ 7.38
1983*	15.70	7.50
1984*	19.50	9.00
1985*	22.60	10.25

*Figures were estimated at time outlook was prepared, November 1983.

Compared to the prevailing level of 183.94, this figure represented a modest 10 percent capital gain in two year's time, less than 5 percent a year. Adding a 4 to 5 percent annual dividend yield gave a projected total return of less than 10 percent a year at a time when Treasury bonds were yielding nearly 12 percent. Since the company considered its earnings and dividend forecasts relatively optimistic, they concluded that for the stock market to do better than had been anticipated, interest rates would have to fall farther than had been assumed, a drop that would benefit bonds as well as stocks: "any major advance in equity prices must be accompanied by a major advance in bond prices."

As it turned out, 1985 earnings were $15.36 (far below the company's predicted $22.60), dividends were $7.93 (rather than the projected $10.25), and thirty-year Treasury bond yields were 9.5 percent (instead of the 10.8 percent). The S&P 400 index ended 1985 at a robust 234.56, up 27.5 percent in two years, giving an annual rate of return, including dividends, of about 17 percent. As the company anticipated, this advance was due to a sharp drop in long-term interest rates, which provided an annual return in coupons and capital gains on thirty-year Treasury bonds of about 21 percent.

INVESTMENT
EXAMPLE
7–3

IMPLICIT-RETURN CALCULATIONS AT GOLDMAN, SACHS

The highly respected investment banking firm of Goldman, Sachs uses a dividend-discount model to indicate whether stocks are underpriced or overvalued. For dividends D, the firm multiplies current trend earnings (earnings adjusted for the business cycle) for the S&P 500 stocks times the average payout ratio over the preceding five years. Division by the current level P of the S&P 500 index gives the dividend yield, D/P. The growth rate g is estimated by multiplying the five-year average return on equity by the five-year average retention rate—all in accord with intrinsic value principles. Thus,

$$\text{return} = \frac{D}{P} + g$$

$$= \frac{D}{P} + (1 - d)\, ROE$$

For the required return R, Goldman, Sachs uses the yield on five-year government bonds plus a 2.5 percent risk premium. The difference between the implicit and required returns is the risk-adjusted excess return,

$$e = \text{return} - R,$$

with a positive excess return giving a signal that stocks are attractively priced.

In one test of the model, Goldman, Sachs used monthly data for the years 1961–67, and found that e averaged 0.8 percent with a standard deviation of 5.6 percent.[1] Then, for the years 1968–82, the firm varied its relative holdings of bonds and stocks according to a mechanical rule that called for 50 percent bonds and 50 percent stocks when e is 0.8 percent (the historical mean), 0 percent stocks and 100 percent bonds when e is −4.8 percent or lower (one standard deviation below the historical mean), 100 percent stocks and 0 percent bonds when e is 6.4 percent or more (one standard deviation above the mean), and proportionate holdings at intermediate values of e. At the market peaks in November 1968, December 1972, and November 1980, the recommended stock holdings were 12 percent, 0 percent, and 10 percent, respectively. At the market bottoms in June 1970, September 1974, March 1978, and August 1982, the respective recommended allocations were 100 percent, 100 percent, 100 percent, and 60 percent in stock holdings.

Shortly before the October 1987 crash (which was mentioned in Chapter 1 and is discussed in detail in Chapter 12), their model indicated an excess return of −2.5 percent or, equivalently, that the intrinsic value of stocks was about 30 percent below the market price. Goldman, Sachs consequently shifted the composition of their equity portfolio from 85 percent stocks and 15 percent cash to 65 percent stocks and 35 percent cash.[2]

[1] Steven G. Einhorn and Patricia Shangquan, "Using the Dividend Discount Model for Asset Allocation," *Financial Analysts Journal*, May-June 1984, pp. 30–32.

[2] Goldman, Sachs, "Portfolio Strategy," October 22, 1987, p. 1.

calculated by equating the present value of these forecast dividends to the current market price of the S&P 500.

The results are shown in Figure 7–1, which compares these calculated implicit stock yields with the yields on long-term Treasury bonds. In the

FIGURE 7–1   Implicit yield on stocks

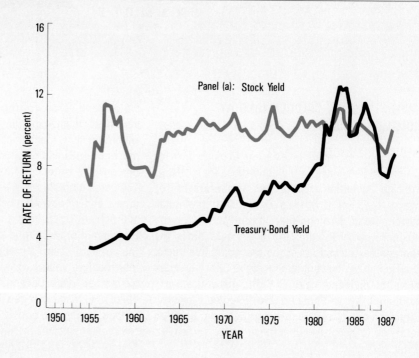

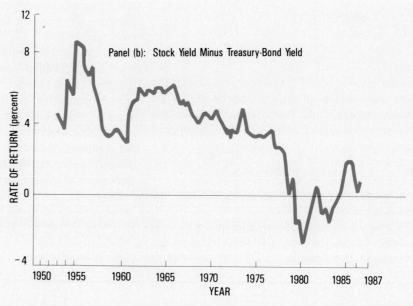

1950s, Treasury-bond yields were below 4 percent while dividend yields were above 4 percent, and anticipated dividend growth pushed the implicit return on stocks substantially above long-term interest rates, indicating that stocks were relatively cheap. Benjamin Graham, in fact, did make this argument in the 1950s; but, even as late as 1958, most investors allowed the strong dividend and earnings data to be overwhelmed by their lingering fears of a return to the economic depression that preceded World War II.

Between 1959 and 1979, bond and stock yields generally moved up and down together, with stocks priced to yield some 3 percent to 5 percent more than long-term Treasury bonds, presumably because stocks were perceived to be the riskier investment. The exceptions to this 3 percent to 5 percent risk-premium rule are interesting. The first exception occurred in 1961, when the prices of growth stocks and new issues jumped upward and reduced the stock-bond yield below 3 percentage points, suggesting that stocks were no longer inexpensive. This run-up in stock prices was a speculative house of cards that tumbled down in 1962, in what the *New York Times* called "something like an earthquake."[9]

In late 1966, in contrast, the stock yield was a full 6½ percentage points above the bond yield, suggesting that stocks were relatively cheap. In retrospect, stocks would have been a superior investment, as stock prices rose sharply in 1967 and 1968, eliminating the abnormally large yield spread. The spread narrowed again in 1973, and this imbalance was corrected by a drop in stock prices in 1973–74. The correction was excessive in that the yield differential topped 5 percent in the fourth quarter of 1974, now suggesting that stocks were relatively cheap. In retrospect, they *were* cheap, as the stunning market advance in late 1974 and early 1975 rewarded past investors while it lowered the yields for future investors. Stock yields were again brought back to within 3 percent to 5 percent of bonds.

A very important change in the relationship between bond and stock yields occurred shortly after October 1979, when the Federal Reserve Board decided to abandon thirty years of interest-rate stabilization and, instead, try a now-discredited experiment in monetarism. Without the Fed's stabilizing hand, interest rates went through some truly breathtaking gyrations. In 1980, the federal funds rate jumped from below 13 percent in mid-February to above 19 percent in early April, then fell to below 10 percent in May. As interest rates swung wildly, investors decided that bonds had become as risky as stocks. The president of the brokerage firm, E. F. Hutton, said, "This market has made traders queasy, uneasy, and at times shaken. The greatest problem of all is the volatility. Even in government securities, prices have sometimes changed in a single day more than they did in an entire year in the past."[10] The risk premium between stocks and bonds disappeared when the Federal Reserve stopped stabilizing interest rates.

In 1981, the yield differential hit an unprecedented −2.5 percent, with Treasury bond yields at 13.6 percent and the yield on stocks only 11.1

percent. Stock prices fell by 15 percent over the next twelve months, giving stocks a slight yield advantage. The yield spread fluctuated over the next five years, but never returned to the 3 percent to 5 percent range typical of the years before 1979. In comparison with earlier decades, through most of the 1980s, stocks did not appear cheap relative to bonds. Stock prices did increase sharply between 1982 and 1987, giving shareholders large capital gains. As Investment Example 7–3 relates (and the data in Table 1–3 in Chapter 1 confirm), the cause of the stock-price increases was a sharp drop in interest rates, which provided long-term bondholders with capital gains that matched the gains of stockholders.

Using the Required Growth Rate

For a long-term investor who values assets for their cash flow, the question of whether stocks are cheap or expensive can be rephrased as a question of whether the investor's projected dividend growth rate is high enough to justify the current price. For instance, stock prices increased by about 80 percent between October 1985 and October 1987. Was this run-up justified by the underlying fundamentals? The disappearance of the yield spread shown in Figure 7–1 suggests a negative answer.

Another way to answer this question is to rearrange Equation 2 to find the dividend growth rate consistent with a given required return and the current dividend yield, as shown in the following:

$$g = R - \frac{D_1}{P} \tag{7}$$

On October 2, 1987, the S&P 500 Stock Index closed at $P = 328.07$, and S&P 500 dividends were $D_1 = 9.03$, for a dividend yield of $D_1/P = 9.03/328.07 = 0.0275$—that is, 2.75 percent. Thus,

$$g = R - 0.0275.$$

The required return on stocks is influenced by the yield on alternative investments, and on October 2, 1987, the average yield on long-term Treasury bonds was 9.75 percent. For an investor satisfied with a 9.75 percent required return on stocks (the same as Treasury bonds), a 7 percent annual dividend growth rate is necessary for stocks to have a present value equal to market price, as the following shows:

$$g = 0.0975 - 0.0275$$
$$= 0.07$$

With a 12.25 percent required return (3 percent higher than bonds), the requisite growth rate is 10 percent. Either number, 7 percent or 10 percent, in October 1987 was above the economy's predicted long-run growth rate.

Those who bought stocks early that October were either very optimistic about dividend growth or else short-term speculators hoping to profit from higher prices rather than dividends.

Multistage Dividend Models

The constant-growth model is most appropriate for large, mature companies (and for the stock market as a whole, where the vagaries of individual companies offset one another and average out). One way to evaluate younger, more erratic companies is to use the constant-growth model to estimate what their value will be at some distant date, when they have matured, and to use other means to project dividends and earnings in the interim. Young companies can be assigned short-term, unsustainable growth rates, which are then eroded as the company matures, new competitors enter the industry, or their markets become saturated. For a cyclical company, short-term earnings can be tied to anticipated booms or recessions.

Typically, a security analyst provides annual earnings and dividend forecasts for the next five years, a growth rate for a subsequent specified period of time until the firm matures, and then a growth rate during maturity.[11] Such three-stage models are used at many major brokerage firms, including Salomon Brothers, Merrill Lynch, Drexel Burnham, and Kidder, Peabody.

AN INTRINSIC-VALUE EXPLANATION
OF STOCK PRICES

Economic theorists use fundamental analysis not to make buy/sell decisions, but to explain stock prices. They assume that the prevailing market price is equal to the present value calculated according to Equation 1, using the market's required rate of return. This fundamental-analysis model is appealing because it is logical and internally consistent.

Consider an investor who buys a stock just after a dividend has been paid, planning to hold the stock until the next dividend and then immediately sell the stock. According to Equation 1, the current price is

$$P = \frac{D_1}{(1 + R)} + \frac{D_2}{(1 + R)^2} + \frac{D_3}{(1 + R)^3} + \cdots$$

Analogously, in the next period, when this investor sells the stock, the price will be

$$P_1 = \frac{D_2}{(1 + R)} + \frac{D_3}{(1 + R)^2} + \cdots$$

Comparing the two prices, we find that

$$P_1 = (1 + R)P - D_1.$$

One reflection of the internal consistency of this model is the solution for P:

$$P = \frac{D_1 + P_1}{1 + R}$$

That is, the current price is equal to the present value of the cash flow to the investor who holds the stock for one period, receiving one dividend and then selling the stock.

We can also solve for R as follows:

$$R = \frac{D_1}{P} + \frac{P_1 - P}{P}$$
$$= \text{dividend} + \text{capital gain}$$

The left-hand side of the equation is the required return R, while the right-hand side is the actual return, dividend plus capital gain, calculated as a percentage of the purchase price. Again, the model's implications are very sensible. The stock is priced so that the investor's total return, dividend plus capital gain, is just equal to the investor's required return.

The present-value model is internally consistent in that for a given required return and anticipated dividend stream, the present value of the cash flow is equal to the current price, no matter whether the investor holds for a single period or forever (or somewhere in between).

The same internal consistency also applies to the special case of constant growth. The current market price is given by Equation 2,

$$P = \frac{D_1}{R - g}$$

Next year, the price will be

$$P_1 = \frac{D_2}{R - g}$$

Now, because $D_2 = (1 + g)D_1$, we have

$$P_1 = \frac{(1 + g)D_1}{R - g}$$
$$= (1 + g)P.$$

That is, if dividends grow at a constant rate g, then so will the stock's price, allowing us to make a simple interpretation of the following rearrangement of Equation 2:

$$R = \frac{D_1}{P} + g \tag{8}$$

The first term on the right-hand side of Equation 8 is the dividend yield; the second term is the capital gain.

In the constant-growth model, the stock's price grows at the same rate as dividends, keeping the dividend yield (dividend/price) constant. The investor's return (the dividend yield plus capital gain) is equal to the required return. If a stock selling for $100 a share pays a dividend of $5 that will grow by 10 percent a year, then it yields a 15 percent annual return.

Consider this conclusion carefully, because it is very important and yet not always fully appreciated. If you were to borrow $100 from a bank at a 15 percent rate and pay this loan off on a graduated-payment plan, your payments could be $5.00 this year and 10 percent higher every year thereafter: $5.00 this year, $5.50 the second year, and so on. The initial $5.00 plus 10 percent growth provides the bank a 15 percent return on its $100 loan. By the same logic, if you invest $100 and receive $5.00 plus 10 percent growth each year, then you are receiving a 15 percent return on your investment.

The Stock Market and the Economy

The National Bureau of Economic Research has long considered an index of stock prices to be one of the best leading indicators of changes in economic activity. Stock prices usually decline shortly (on average, four and a half months) before a recession begins and rise shortly before a recession ends. Figure 7–2 compares the nation's employment rate and the S&P 500 index of stock prices with the shaded time periods marking economic sions. Each of the eight recessions since 1948 was, in fact, preceded by a noticeable decline in stock prices. However, stock prices also fell sharply in 1962, 1966, 1977, 1984, and 1987 without a recession. To paraphrase Paul Samuelson, the market has predicted thirteen of the last eight recessions.

Nonetheless, there does seem to be a striking correlation between the stock market and the economy. There are three possible explanations, all consistent with fundamental analysis: The stock market may influence the economy, the economy may influence the stock market, or some third factor may influence both. Most likely, all three explanations are correct. As is so often true in economics, everything really does depend on everything else, though in varying degrees.

FIGURE 7–2 Stock prices and the economy. (Periods of economic recession are indicated by shaded bars.)

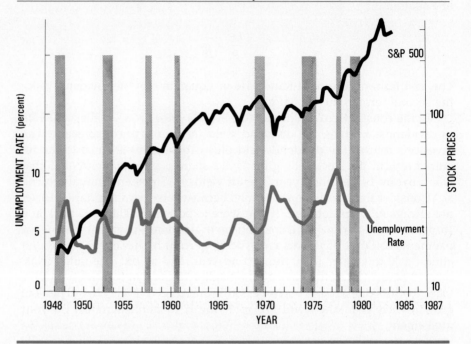

Let us look first at how the stock market influences the economy. When stock prices are high, those investors who own stock feel richer (with good reason—they are richer). They tend to spend more and live in a manner befitting their new wealth. When stock prices decline, households are likely to retrench, increasing their saving and trying to rebuild their lost wealth. One of the Federal Reserve Board's economic models estimates that each dollar change in the market value of stocks tends to change consumer spending by about 5 cents. With the substantial fluctuations in stock prices in recent years, those nickels add up. In 1973–74, the aggregate market value of stocks dropped by about $500 billion, implying a $25 billion depressant for consumer spending that helps explain the 1974–75 recession. The 1985–86 bull market increased stock values by nearly a trillion dollars, and the implied $50 billion spending stimulus helps explain why household spending as a fraction of income reached record levels. The $500 billion crash on October 19, 1987 made many, including the Federal Reserve, fearful of recession. The Fed immediately responded by increasing the nation's money supply to support financial markets and the economy.

The economy, in turn, undoubtedly affects the stock market. Stock prices are influenced by anticipated dividends, and when the economy is strong, profits surge and dividends follow close behind. When recession hits, profits slump, and dividends grow slowly—or even drop. Why does the market go up or down four and a half months *before* the economy does likewise? Perhaps stock analysts can see booms and recessions coming, in advance of their actual arrival (at least, in thirteen out of eight cases).

Another explanation for the observed correlation between the stock market and the economy is that some third factor influences both. The possibilities are endless, ranging from skirt lengths to the heights of the Great Lakes. A more plausible factor is interest rates. As Andrew Tobias put it, "The key to everything financial, and to nearly everything economic, is interest rates."[12]

Interest Rates and the Stock Market

When investors' required rate of return increases, asset prices must fall in order for a given cash flow to provide this higher rate of return. Earlier chapters have discussed this inverse price-yield relationship for bonds; the very same logic applies to stocks. For a given dividend stream, a high rate of return requires a low price while a low required rate of return necessitates a high price.

Duration, Once Again The sensitivity of stock prices to changes in the required return, as with bond prices, can be gauged by the asset's duration, the present-value-weighted average number of years until receiving the cash flow. For the constant-growth model, a stock's duration is shown in this chapter's appendix to be

$$\text{duration} = \frac{1 + R}{R - g}. \tag{9}$$

This simple formula confirms our common-sense expectation that growth stocks, with so much of the cash flow in the distant future, are, like very long-term bonds, extremely susceptible to capital risk. A twenty-year bond with a 10 percent coupon selling for par has a duration of nine years; a stock with a 12 percent required return and a 5 percent anticipated growth rate has an even longer duration of $(1 + R)/(R - g) = 1.12/(0.12 - 0.05) = 16$ years.

Consider again the example of a stock with a forthcoming $5 dividend and a variety of possible growth rates, this time comparing 11 percent with 10 percent required returns, as in Table 7–2. Notice, first, that stock prices are very sensitive to required returns and, second, that the faster is the growth rate, the larger is the price decline required to raise the yield from 10 percent to 11 percent. Because a large part of the present value consists of distant dividends, stocks (especially growth stocks) are long-term assets with substantial capital risk.

It is often thought, wrongly, that the only reason high interest rates depress the stock market is that they may mean increased costs for busi-

TABLE 7–2 The Effect of Required Return on a Stock's Present Value

Growth Rate, g (percent)	Present Value, PV		Change in Present Value (percent)
	When Required Return, R, Is 10 Percent	When Required Return, R, Is 11 Percent	
0	$ 50.00	$ 45.45	− 9.1
2	62.50	55.55	−11.1
4	83.33	71.43	−14.3
6	125.00	100.00	−20.0
8	250.00	166.67	−33.3

nesses or a weaker economy and depressed sales. Even if costs are constant and the economy stable, higher interest rates depress stock prices for the same reason they depress bond prices. Assets are, to varying degrees, substitutes in investors' eyes, and the required rates of return that investors use to discount the cash flow from assets depend on the yields available on alternative investments. When the returns available on Treasury securities rise, so do the required returns on corporate bonds and stocks, pushing these asset prices downward. Otherwise, investors would foresake corporate stocks and bonds for the higher yields available on Treasury securities.

Because financial markets are competitive and efficient, these interest rate ripples are felt almost immediately. Stock-market analysts pay close attention to other financial markets and to news of government financial policies. Stock prices jump immediately after (and sometimes before) the Fed announces a cut in the discount rate or Chase Manhattan announces a drop in its prime loan rate. Daily reports on the stock market commonly refer to interest-rate developments and to perceived changes in financial policies. For instance, one *New York Times* story began, "Stock prices tumbled yesterday, with the Dow Jones Industrial Average dropping more than 11 points, following apparent confirmation that the Federal Reserve was permitting short-term interest rates to move higher."[13] More dramatically, the 1973–74 stock-market crash ended just when interest rates peaked, and the 1985–86 surge in stock prices coincided with a three-percentage-point drop in long-term bond rates. The October 1987 crash began after interest rates rose, and the market recovered when the Federal Reserve acted to reduce interest rates.

The Relationship Between Bond and Stock Prices The fact that low interest rates push both bond and stock prices upward (and higher interest rates push both downward) does not mean that bond and stock prices always move in the same direction. To the extent that bonds and stocks are substitutes, their yields move up and down together, true enough. Bonds have a fixed cash flow (except in defaults), while stocks have a variable cash flow, with dividends that go up and down with the economy. Because the economy and interest rates can move in the same or opposite directions, sometimes bond and stock prices move together, and at other times they diverge.

If the economic outlook is unchanged while interest rates fluctuate, stock and bond prices will move together. If the economic outlook changes, then the relative movements of bond and stock prices depend on whether the economy and interest rates move in the same or the opposite direction. When interest rates rise, bad economic news reinforces the drop in stock prices, while good economic news cushions the drop, perhaps even propelling stock prices upward at the same time that bond prices are falling. When interest rates decline, good economic news reinforces rising stock prices, while a weak economy restrains stock prices.

THE TAXATION OF DIVIDENDS AND CAPITAL GAINS (optional)

Before the 1986 Tax Reform Act, only 40 percent of a realized capital gain was taxable for individual investors, making the tax rate on capital gains 40 percent of the tax rate on ordinary income. This preferential treatment of capital gains encouraged investors to buy stocks, particularly growth stocks. The 1986 change, taxing capital gains at the same rate as ordinary income, has had a significant negative effect on stock values.

Consider the standard constant-growth model, taking taxes into account. A stock is priced to give an after-tax return of

$$r = (1 - t)\left(\frac{D}{P}\right) + (1 - c)g, \tag{10}$$

where D is the current dividend, P the price, g the growth rate, t the tax rate on ordinary income, and c the tax rate on capital gains. If we set $r = (1 - t)R$, then R is the before-tax rate of return that fully taxed investments of comparable risk must offer to be competitive with stocks. Letting $a = (1 - c)/(1 - t)$, we can solve for R and also for the stock's price as follows:

$$R = \frac{D}{P} + ag \tag{11}$$

$$P = \frac{D}{R - ag} \tag{12}$$

Since 1987, dividends and capital gains have been taxed at the same rate ($a = 1$), giving the familiar equations that ignore taxes altogether: $R = D/P + g$ and $P = D/(R - g)$.

TABLE 7–3   The Effect of Capital-Gains Taxes on Stock Values

	Tax Bracket	Value of a^*	Present Value of Stock			
			At Growth Rate of 0 Percent	At Growth Rate of 4 Percent	At Growth Rate of 5 Percent	At Growth Rate of 6 Percent
After 1986 tax reform	all brackets	1.0	$16.67	$25.00	$25.87	$33.33
Before 1986 tax reform	0.0	1.0	$16.67	$25.00	$25.87	$33.33
	0.1	1.1	16.67	25.86	30.00	35.71
	0.2	1.2	16.67	27.03	32.00	39.22
	0.3	1.3	16.67	28.69	35.00	44.87
	0.4	1.4	16.67	31.25	40.00	55.56
	0.5	1.6	16.67	35.71	50.00	83.33

$^* a = (1-c)/(1-t)$ where c is the tax rate on capital gains and t is the tax rate on ordinary income.

The end to the preferential treatment of capital gains reduced the value of a, thereby reducing both the interest rates needed to make bonds more attractive than stocks and the prices investors are willing to pay for stock. For some ballpark estimates of the effect of this change, Table 7–3 considers a company paying a $2 annual dividend, with a required before-tax return of 12 percent. (If, for instance, long-term Treasury securities yield 8 percent before taxes, investors requiring a 50 percent higher after-tax return on risky stocks require $R = 12$ percent, no matter what their tax bracket.)

With dividends and capital gains taxed at the same rate, P is the same for all tax brackets. Before the 1986 tax change, investors in high tax brackets were attracted to growth stocks with their lightly taxed capital gains. For $g = 5$ percent, for instance, the 1986 tax reform reduces the stock's value for an investor in a 30 percent tax bracket by 18 percent, from $35.00 to $28.57. For those investors in a 50 percent tax bracket, the stock's value falls by 43 percent, from $50.00 to $28.57. With the 1986 tax reform's reduction of the top tax bracket to around 30 percent, the total loss in stock value can be separated into two parts: In a 50 percent tax bracket, the stock is worth $50.00. A drop in the overall tax rate to 30 percent, but maintaining the preferential tax treatment of capital gains, reduces the value of this stock to $35.00. The taxation of capital gains at the same rate as dividends reduces the value still further, to $28.57. The effects are larger for stocks with brighter growth prospects, and they are smaller for those stocks whose return is mostly in the form of current dividend yield.

There are two cautions to add to this analysis. First, the effective capital-gains tax rate can still be reduced somewhat by postponing the realization of gains. Second, many shareholders, such as pension funds and nonprofit institutions, do not pay taxes and, so, do not care whether dividends and capital gains are taxed equally.

SUMMARY

Fundamental analysis advises investors to compare a stock's market price with its intrinsic value, the present value of the prospective dividends or other cash flows. Investors should not buy a stock unless they will be satisfied holding it and receiving the projected dividends. Speculators, in contrast, buy a stock not for cash flow, but with the hope of selling it a short while later for a profit.

The present value of a stock paying constant dividends is D/R; if the dividends grow at a constant rate g, the present value is $D/(R - g)$, which may be considerably larger than the value of a no-growth stock. If the growth rate permanently exceeds shareholders' required return, the present value is infinite; in practice, companies cannot sustain such rapid growth forever, and their intrinsic value must be estimated using multistage dividend models.

Dividends come from the profits generated by assets. Other things being equal, the value of a company's stock is enhanced by an increase in its assets, an increase in the rate of return it earns on its assets, or a drop in shareholders' required return, perhaps because of a decline in interest rates. If a firm retains more of its earnings, paying less dividends now in order to acquire assets that will yield additional dividends later, this action increases the value of its stock if the profit rate on these assets exceeds the shareholders' required return on their stock, but not otherwise.

Fundamental analysis bases buy/sell decisions on a comparison of a stock's market price with its intrinsic value, the projected cash flow discounted by the shareholder's required return. Equivalently, we can find the implicit discount rate that equates the present value to the current market price and compare this rate with the required return. The shareholder's required return depends on the returns available on other investments and on the relative riskiness of these investments. Although stocks are generally riskier than bonds, the riskiness of bonds varies with Federal Reserve policy.

The intrinsic-value model can also be used to explain why stock prices are buoyed by a strong economy and low interest rates. Stock prices tend to change direction a few months before a change occurs in the economy, suggesting either that investors anticipate economic developments before these developments are reflected in unemployment and GNP data or that changes in the stock market influence the economy. Because stocks are long-duration assets with substantial capital risk, stock prices, like the prices of long-term bonds, are very sensitive to interest rates. Stock and bond required returns move together because these assets are substitutes for each other, but their prices need not move in lockstep. For example, if the economy is strong while interest rates are increasing, stock prices can rise even though bond prices are falling.

Historically, one advantage that stocks enjoyed over Treasury and corporate bonds was that much of the return occurred in the form of lightly taxed capital gains, earned as share prices increased along with corporate assets, profits, and dividends. The 1986 tax reform eliminated this preferential treatment of capital gains, reducing the appeal of stocks to individual investors.

APPENDIX

Present Value With Constant Growth

If the dividend t periods from now is D_t and the required rate of return is R, the present value of this cash flow is

$$PV = \frac{D_1}{(1 + R)} + \frac{D_2}{(1 + R)^2} + \frac{D_3}{(1 + R)^3} + \ldots$$

as given by Equation 1 in Chapter 7. If dividends grow at a constant rate g, so that $D_t = D_1 (1 + g)^t$, then

$$PV = \frac{D_1}{(1 + R)} + \frac{D_1 (1 + g)}{(1 + R)^2} + \frac{D_1 (1 + g)^2}{(1 + R)^3} + \ldots + \frac{D_1(1 + g)^{n - 1}}{(1 + R)^n}$$

This rearrangement,

$$PV = \frac{D_1}{(1 + R)} (1 + b + b^2 + \ldots b^{n - 1}),$$

where $b = (1 + g)/(1 + R)$, allows the substitution used in the appendix to Chapter 2.

$$PV = \frac{D_1}{(1 + R)} \frac{(1 - b^n)}{(1 - b)}$$

If $g < R$ and n is infinite, then $b < 1$ and b^n is small enough to be neglected, so that

$$PV = \frac{D_1}{(1 + R)} \frac{1}{(1 - b)}$$

$$= \frac{D_1}{(1 + R)} \cdot \frac{1}{1 - (1 + g)/(1 + R)}$$

$$= \frac{D_1}{(1 + R) - (1 + g)}$$

$$= \frac{D_1}{R - g}$$

as given by Equation 2 in the text. (If $g > R$, then b^n approaches infinity rather than zero as n increases, and the present value is infinite.)

For the duration, the derivative of the above equation with respect to $1 + R$ gives

$$\frac{\Delta PV}{\Delta(1 + R)} = \frac{-D_1}{(R - g)^2}.$$

Converting to percentages,

$$\frac{-\%(PV)}{\%(1 + R)} = \frac{(1 + R)}{PV} \cdot \frac{D_1}{(R - g)^2}$$

$$= \frac{1 + R}{R - g}$$

as shown in Equation 9 in the text.

EXERCISES

1. In 1981, a New York retailer paid $24,000 for the first case of wine (using 1979 grapes) produced in a joint venture by Robert Mondavi and Baron Philippe de Rothschild from Cabernet Sauvignon and Cabernet Franc grapes. A reporter wrote

> With such a beginning, one wonders if any bottles of the 1979 will ever be enjoyed at a meal. Would you drink up part of your investment portfolio?[14]

Would John Burr Williams classify the purchaser of this wine as an investor or a speculator?

2. A Wall Street saying, "A bargain that stays a bargain isn't a bargain," suggests that an investment in a stock that seems undervalued is not a good investment if the price does not increase afterwards. Does fundamental analysis agree?

3. Bruce Meyer, the president of Geary's, a Beverly Hills, California, gift store, stated that something is most likely to be a good investment if it has "some intrinsic value." He explained,

> If you buy a silver piece for $100, and melt it down, you can still get $30 for the silver. With a porcelain tea set, the sand it's made from is worth zero.[15]

Why do people buy tea sets made from worthless sand? How does Meyer's definition of intrinsic value differ from John Burr Williams's definition? Indicate whether Meyer and Williams agree or disagree that the following have substantial intrinsic value: a 200-year-old pos-

TABLE 7–A

Year	Profits	Dividends
1925	$ 2,753,697	$ 1,329,610
1935	7,090,531	4,300,987
1945	10,893,707	6,861,000
1955	55,872,633	16,386,489
1965	476,902,000	210,767,482
1975	1,989,877,000	968,988,000
1985	6,555,000,000	2,703,000,000

tage stamp, a Picasso painting, and a U.S. Treasury bill.

4. You have decided to endow an economics chair at your college named, coincidentally, in your honor. Assuming that salaries are paid once a year, at the end of each year, and that the college can earn 10 percent per year on your gift, how much must you donate in order to provide $100,000 a year forever? $100,000 a year for fifty years? A trustee points out that salaries may rise each year. If so, how large an endowment is needed to provide $100,000 at the end of the first year and 5 percent more each succeeding year, forever? 10 percent more each succeeding year, forever?

5. A certain company is expected to pay an end-of-year dividend of $10 a share. What is the stock's present value under each of the following circumstances?

a. The dividend is not expected to increase, and the shareholders' required return is 10 percent.

b. The dividend is expected to grow by 5 percent per year, and the shareholders' required return is 10 percent.

c. The dividend is expected to grow by 10 percent per year, and the shareholders' required return is 15 percent.

6. In 1924, Computing-Tabulating-Recording Company became International Business Machines (IBM). Table A shows some data on its net after-tax profits and dividends. Calculate IBM's annual rate of growth of profits and dividends for each ten-year period 1925–35, 1935–45, and so on up until 1985, and also for the following periods:

a. 1925–75

b. 1925–85

7. Your human capital is the present value of your lifetime wages. Assume that you begin work at $30,000 a year (paid annually, beginning a year from today) and will work for forty years. Using the appropriate formula in the appendix, determine the value of your human capital if your required return is

a. 8 percent and your wages grow by 5 percent a year.

b. 10 percent and your wages grow by 10 percent a year.

8. This exercise illustrates how you might calculate the monetary value of an MBA degree. Assume that you are twenty-five years old and will retire at age sixty-five. Also, assume that if you begin work immediately your salary will be $30,000 to start and will grow by 5 percent a year (paid at the end of each year). If instead you go to business school full-time, you lose two years of wages and pay $12,000 annual tuition (at the end of each year); but when you begin working two years from now, you will start at $40,000, and your salary will grow by 7 percent a year (again paid at year end). Use the appropriate appendix formula to determine which career path is the more financially rewarding, assuming each of the following conditions:

a. An 8 percent required return.

b. A 10 percent required return.

9. In December 1986, the Texas Comptroller released the Texas Stock Index, based on the prices of seventy-seven companies headquartered in Texas.[16] From 1980 to 1986, the Texas Stock Index increased from 100 to 126, while the S&P 500 rose from 114 to 242. Assuming that shareholder required returns for Texas stocks are comparable to those for the nation as a whole, what does this difference in stock performance say about the past, present, and future performance of the Texas economy?

10. A famous stock advisor once remarked that a conspiracy between stock specialists and bankers is suggested by the fact that "when you're having a decline in stock prices, you can always anticipate an increase in interest rates."[17] What he apparently meant was that when specialists lower stock prices so that the insiders can accumulate stocks cheaply, banks raise interest rates so that the public cannot borrow money to purchase stocks at these bargain prices. Is there any nonconspiratorial explanation for the observation that a drop in stock prices is often accompanied by an increase in interest rates?

11. Explain why you either agree or disagree with this reasoning by a panelist on the television show "Wall Street Week": "It's true that interest rates are rising, but that shouldn't affect growth stocks since they don't yield much anyway."[18]

12. On July 19, 1984, Chrysler sold all of the stocks in its pension fund and bought bonds with the proceeds. In January 1987, rumors that Chrysler was going back into stocks inspired the following report:

> [The rumors] prompted some guffaws on Wall Street because, on the surface, it might appear that Chrysler has missed an enormous stock rally and now wants to get back in at the top.

> But is isn't quite that simple, because the bond market did nearly as well as the stock market in the 2½ years between July 1984 and December 1986.
>
> In that period . . . the S&P 500 stock index returned 25% annually, counting dividends . . . [while] the Shearson Lehman aggregate bond index returned 22.4% annually . . . In fact, the bonds held by Chrysler equaled the stock market's performance because they were slightly longer in maturity than the Shearson index.[19]

What economic event would explain simultaneous bond- and stock-market rallies? What does maturity have to do with performance?

13. Between March 1985 and March 1986, long-term Treasury-bond yields dropped from 11.8 percent to 8 percent, while stock prices rose by some 33 percent to 45 percent depending on the price index used. Assuming that required returns on stocks dropped by an amount comparable to the decline in long-term bond rates—with dividend and earnings forecasts unchanged—what duration of stocks is consistent with these data?

14. Merrill Lynch routinely tracks the characteristics of the stocks in the S&P 500 and has found that stocks with relatively high dividend yields consistently have low projected earnings growth. For instance, in April 1986, for the 100 stocks with the lowest dividend yield (an average of 0.6 percent), the earnings per share were expected to grow by 35 percent in 1986. For the 100 stocks with the highest dividend yield (an average of 6.4 percent), earnings per share were projected to increase by only 6 percent in 1986.[20] How do you explain this empirical finding?

15. In May 1987, David A. Wyss, chief financial economist with Data Resources, estimated that "every percentage point on the bond yield gives you something like 200 points on the Dow."[21] At the time, long-term Treasury bonds yielded 9 percent, and the Dow was at 2240. If every percentage point of bond yield raises shareholders' required return by one percentage point, what is the implied duration for the Dow?

16. Write a rebuttal to the following August 1987 argument for buying stocks:

> The power of any market move is limited because at some price, something else becomes more attractive. The exception is when the returns on other investments are considered to be so poor by comparison as to be irrelevant.
>
> Consider the alternatives. Look at the stock market so far this year. The industrial indexes such as the Dow and the S&P 400 are up roughly 40 . . . Most conventional investment alternatives such as money-market funds or bonds, or even most real asset investments, aren't anywhere close to that eight-month return.[22]

17. Each week *Barron's* reports a "Stock/Bond Yield Gap," showing the spread between the dividend yield for stocks listed in the Dow Jones Industrial Average and the yield to maturity on the best grade corporate bonds. In August 1986, for instance, this spread was −5.19 percent. How might investors use such data to gauge whether stocks are underpriced or overvalued?

18. National Polyester currently pays a dividend of $10 a share, but the company expects its dividend to decline steadily by 5 percent a year. If shareholders require a 10 percent return on their investment, what price will they pay now for this stock? What will happen to the stock's intrinsic value as time passes? (Be specific.) Why would anyone ever invest in a negative-growth stock? Would you?

19. Give an economic explanation of the following empirical observation:

> If we look back over the long history of markets, not just the postwar ear, we find a whole string of economic indicators that seem to turn with remarkable regularity either shortly before or coincidentally with stock market bottoms . . . The most significant of these is interest rates.[23]

Do you think interest rates tend to turn up or down at stock-market bottoms? Why?

20. An article in the *ABA Banking Journal* discussed the estimation of commercial damages when one company's violation of a contract forces another company to go out of business. Instead of trying to estimate the firm's liquidation value, the author argues that a company with current net earnings of $50,000 growing at 5 percent a year would have, at a 25 percent discount rate, a "capitalization rate" of 5, giving it a value of 5($50,000) = $250,000. Where does the value 5 for the capitalization rate come from? The author went on to argue that "it is common for appraisers in lawsuits to use a capitalization rate that is based on broad industry norms . . . This method should be used with caution."[24] Why?

21. Century-Minus-One Village is a complex of condominiums, which legally reverts back to the developer after 99 years. Assume that each unit yields its owner a constant real yearly income of $2000 (after repairs and maintenance fees) and is priced in the real-estate market to yield a 5 percent real annual return (in rental income plus price appreciation). What will be the market price of a unit at the end of 99 years, just before it reverts to the developer? after 98 years? after 97 years? What will be the initial price? Roughly sketch a graph showing the market price over the first 200 years.

22. In 1986, Michael Sherman, who heads Shearson Lehman's investment-policy committee, recommended a portfolio of 70 percent stocks, 30 percent long-term bonds, and no short-term bonds. He advised, "If you have cash [short-term bonds] in your account, it means you don't trust what you're doing . . . More stocks than bonds generally indicate a positive outlook both in Treasury rates and the economy."[25] (The opposite occurred in early 1982, when more bonds than stocks in portfolios indicated that investors liked interest rates but not the economy.) Explain why forecasts of interest rates and the economy should influence your portfolio allocation between stocks and bonds. Are there any circumstances in which you would recommend holding a substantial amount of "cash"?

23. Stock and bond prices generally moved in opposite directions during most of the 1960s, but in the same direction in the 1970s.[26] How would fundamental analysis explain this change?

24. The following are excerpts from a 1986 newspaper article:

> The underlying U.S. economy today is not strong enough to support the market's enthusiasm, and it is not gaining. The force driving stock prices up is declining interest rates (and oil prices). Well, interest rates decline when lenders have lots of money but borrowers don't have lots of need for it, that is, when business is slow. Like now.
>
> Every new statistic—retail sales off a bit, unemployment up a bit—indicates that the economy is only so-so. Which wouldn't be so bad if the outlook for the economy were better. But it's not.
>
> Despite lower interest rates, business doesn't seem in a hurry to invest in new plant and equipment . . .
>
> What does it all mean? Only that the economy will putter along—no disaster but no great glory either—and the stock market will probably take a sharp decline.[27]

Is there any rational explanation for why the stock market might be strong, even while the economy is not?

25. If a stock's price declines shortly after they purchase it, many investors conclude that they made a bad investment and sell the stock, looking for something better. Yet one portfolio manager said "I never sell anything that goes down. I buy more."[28] Which reaction is more consis-

tent with intrinsic value principles? Explain your reasoning.

26. In 1985, a stock analyst argued

> Generally, you are close to a top when the Dow price-to-dividend ratio is 30 to 1. That would be 1800 on the Dow [using $60 in dividends during the past 12 months], where, historically, we'd say, "This is a market where speculation and greed have taken over; that is clearly overvalued." . . . Something like 22.7 times dividends is the 50-year norm. That would give you a Dow about 1404, so the market right now is pretty reasonably valued and at 1800 it would be overvalued.[29]

Is there any logical reason why the price-to-dividend ratio should provide information about the attractiveness of stocks? Is there any logical reason why stocks could be attractive even if their price-to-dividend ratio is well above the fifty-year norm of 22.7?

27. Provide a logical explanation for the claim that "low interest rates are far more friendly to stocks than to cash or bonds."[30]

28. In October 1987, a commentator argued that the investors were overly worried about rising interest rates: "We are creatures of habit in this business. We have grown accustomed to interest rates that go down and stocks that go up. But through most of history, *rising* interest rates have gone hand in hand with a rising stock market."[31] He then presented a table of annual data between 1950 and 1986 that is summarized here:

	Years Stock Market Was Up	Years Stock Market Was Down
Years interest rates were up	17	5
Years interest rates were down	9	6

(In twenty of these thirty-seven years, the change in interest rates was less than one percentage point.) What logical explanation is there for the observation that interest rates do not appear to have a consistently positive or negative association with stock prices? Why did this commentator soon regret his advice?

29. Explain this reasoning regarding the use of cash or a mortgage to buy property:

> A mortgage can increase the investment return when the rate of appreciation on a property is greater than the difference between the mortgage interest rate and the initial yield at purchase [the rent less expenses, divided by the price]. Here's an example: A $100,000 property that is increasing in value at 5% a year has an 8% yield; mortgage money is available at 11%. In such a case, debt makes sense . . . [It] makes more sense to pay all cash if the rate of appreciation on the property drops to 2%.[32]

30. An investment analyst wrote the following about Avon stock in the early 1970s:

> You had to pay $60 or more to get a $1 slice of Avon's profit pie, so excited were investors by Avon's ability to earn 25 to 30% on that $1 . . . What investors failed to note was that, while 25% was a boffo return on that one reinvested dollar, $1—no matter how well it was reinvested—was a pretty lousy return on a $60 investment. Subsequently, Avon stock fell about 75% even though profits kept growing admirably.[33]

Use the constant-growth model to estimate the shareholders' rate of return if a stock sells for $60 a share and the company earns $1 a share, earns a 25 percent return on its assets, and pays out 50 percent of its earnings as dividends.

31. In summer 1987, a group bought thirteen acres with 1100 feet of beachfront on Martha's Vineyard, a Massachusetts island. This group sold shares for $25,000 each that enabled the purchaser to use this beach forever. This investment is unique, but still its value can be gauged by the dividend-discount model. If we let X be the annual fee that a person would

pay to use the beach and assume that X increases by 5 percent a year, for what value of X does a price of $25,000 imply a 15 percent required return?

32. In 1986, real-estate experts estimated that a reduction in the top marginal tax rate from 50 percent to 30 percent would reduce the prices of expensive homes by some 20 percent. A columnist commented in *The Wall Street Journal* that:

> What's interesting is that all the tax breaks for owner-occupied housing—principally the mortgage interest and property tax deductions—are retained in both current versions of tax reform. It's lower tax rates themselves that arguably will lower house prices.[34]

Use the intrinsic-value model of stock prices to recreate the argument of these real-estate analysts and to obtain a rough estimate of the damage to housing values from the lower tax rates. Assume that the house is held forever and remember that the shelter provided by a house is tax free.

33. In 1986, the managing director of the Bond Portfolio Analysis Group at Salomon Brothers argued that the duration of a portfolio of bonds and stocks may be much greater than the duration of the bonds alone.[35] How is this possible?

34. Mrs. Cooper has been renting a house for $600 a month, and her landlord has offered to sell her the house for $90,000. She has considered putting $20,000 down and borrowing $70,000 with a conventional thirty-year mortgage at 10 percent, giving her monthly payments of $641.30. Since this amount exceeds her monthly rent, she has decided to continue renting. Explain why her approach, comparing the monthly mortgage payments with the rent, is flawed, in that it can advise her to buy when she should rent, and vice versa. Suggest a better rule of thumb for choosing between buying and renting.

35. Respond to the following argument, explaining why simultaneously higher rents and lower property prices are or are not logically possible:

> As for rental housing, the National Apartment Association has announced, with comic precision, that the loss of tax breaks under the Finance Committee bill "will force rents to increase approximately 39.3% or property values to decline by 28.3%." Since the value of a rental property is the capitalization of future rents, it's hard to understand these alternatives. If rents go up, so should property values; if values go down, so should rents.[36]

36. Two virtually identical firms, ABC and XYZ, have 1 million shares outstanding and $10 million in assets. Both consistently earn 20 percent returns on their asets. The only differences between these two companies is that ABC pays out all of its earnings as dividends and its stock sells for $10 a share, while XYZ pays out 50 percent of its earnings and its stock sells for $12.50 a share. Using the constant-growth model, what are the shareholders' before-tax rates of return, taking both dividends and capital gains into account? If the year is 1986 and the tax rate on capital gains is 40 percent of the tax rate on dividends (for example, an investor paying a 50 percent tax on dividends pays a 20 percent tax on capital gains), for which tax brackets will investors earn a higher after-tax rate of return on XYZ stock? If the tax code is suddenly changed so that dividends and capital gains are taxed at the same rate, investors in which tax brackets will prefer XYZ stock? What do you predict will happen to the price of XYZ stock? (Throughout, assume that capital gains are realized and taxed each year.)

37. In 1986, Trammell Crow was considering the construction of an office building (the McKee Building) adjacent to a prestigious Denver golf course. One option was to buy five acres at $3.00 per foot and construct one 30,114 square-foot building. A second possibility was to purchase 8.75 acres at $2.75 per foot and build two 30,114 square-foot buildings—a choice described as follows:

> The latter option would cost less per square foot of building area to develop and would eventually yield double the rental income of the first option. However, due to the softness of the office leasing market in Denver, it would be necessary to offer 18 months free rent in order to lease the second building. (The first building would be entirely pre-leased.)[37]

Detailed cash-flow projections gave the relationship between net present value and required return shown in Figure 7–A. In fifty words or less, summarize the implications of this figure.

FIGURE 7–A

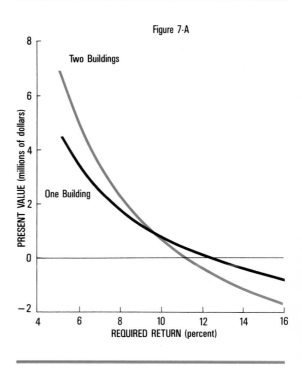

Figure 7-A

38. Imagine that you are John Burr Williams, and write a brief critique of the following reasoning:

> If bonds yielded 3%, then equity should return 5% or 6%. Today, all that has been turned on its head. [The dividend-price ratio] on the Dow Jones Industrial Average in 1983 was 4.59%, while the yield on ten Dow Jones industrial bonds was 10.78%—a stock-bond yield gap of −6.19%. The role of dividends in a period of high interest rates has markedly changed. Furthermore, a variety of growth companies declare no dividends, but reinvest all their earnings back into the company. The future stream of dividends theory of ascertaining present value is logical, but impractical and out of date.[38]

39. In this exercise, you will explore the effects on shareholders of the merger of two companies when there is no change in their economic operations. Assume that market price is determined by fundamental value and that the shareholders' required returns are the same. If we let $D1$ and $D2$ be total dividends, $n1$ and $n2$ be the number of shares outstanding, and $p1$ and $p2$ be the per-share prices, then the total market values of these two firms before the merger are:

$$n1\,p1 = \frac{D1_1}{(1 + R)} + \frac{D1_2}{(1 + R)^2} + \cdots$$

$$n2\,p2 = \frac{D2_1}{(1 + R)} + \frac{D2_2}{(1 + R)^2} + \cdots$$

In the merger, the shareholders of the first company retain their shares while the shareholders of the second company exchange each share of their stock for $p2/p1$, newly issued shares of Company 1 stock. The total market value of the merged company is

$$\frac{(D1_1 + D2_1)}{(1 + R)} + \frac{(D1_2 + D2_2)}{(1 + R)^2} + \cdots$$

Compare the per-share price of the stock of the merged company with the premerger price $p1$. Which stockholders gain from the merger?

40. In this exercise, you will analyze the shareholder implications of a firm selling stock in order to increase dividends, when taxes are taken into account. Assume the market value of the firm is the present value of the after-tax dividend stream,

$$mp1 = (1 - t)D_0 + \frac{(1 - t)D_1}{(1 + R)}$$
$$+ \frac{(1 - t)D_2}{(1 + R)^2} + \cdots$$

where t is the tax rate, m the number of shares outstanding, and $p1$ the per-share price. (Notice that there is a current dividend, D_0, whose payment is imminent.)

The firm now sells n new shares at a per-share price $p1$, with the proceeds distributed as current dividends. The new aggregate market value is

$$(m + n)p2 = (1 - t)(D_0 + n\,p1)$$
$$+ \frac{(1 - t)D_1}{(1 + R)} + \frac{(1 - t)D_2}{(1 + R)^2} + \cdots$$

Is the new per-share price $p2$ larger or smaller than $p1$? What if $t = 0$? Explain your answer.

CHAPTER 8

Fundamental Analysis: Earnings and Assets

*My favorite definition of a growth stock is a stock that
somebody is trying to sell you . . .*
Burton Crane

In theory, the value of a stock should be gauged by the present value of
its dividends. In practice, most investors look beyond dividends to a company's earnings and assets—earnings because they give firms the means
to pay dividends, assets because they are the source of earnings (and, cash
if the firm is liquidated).

In this chapter, we will examine the logical basis for considering earnings and assets, and identify some of the errors that investors make when
doing so. You will see why the ratios of dividends to price and earnings
to price are useful, but not decisive, in valuing securities. You will also
learn that, in theory, growth is valuable, but, in practice, the pursuit of
growth stocks often is an expensive mistake. We will explore why the
market value of a firm need not equal either the book value or the replacement cost of its assets. Finally, we will use an important conservation-of-
value principle to understand the implications of several financial events,
including mergers and stock splits. We begin with two rules of thumb that
are helpful, but not sufficient, for valuing securities.

DIVIDENDS, PROFITS, AND RETAINED EARNINGS

The financial press commonly reports a stock's dividend-price and earnings-price ratios, and many investors use one or the other ratio as an
estimate of a stock's rate of return which they then compare with bond

FIGURE 8–1 Dividend and earnings yields, 1925-1987

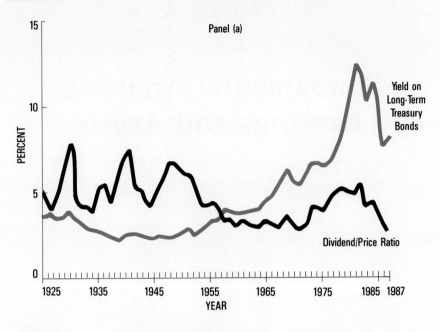

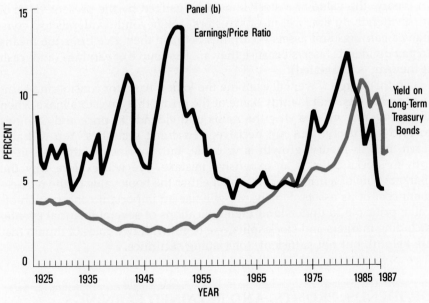

yields. Figure 8–1 shows some historical values of the dividend-price ratio, the earnings-price ratio, and the yield on long-term Treasury bonds. There appears to be little relationship between either ratio and the Treasury yield. It is interesting, though, that the dividend-price ratio was generally above the bond rate before 1958 and consistently below afterwards, and that the earnings-price ratio fell below Treasury yields from 1981 through 1987.

There are persuasive reasons why neither ratio is a completely satisfactory measure of a stock's return and, as a consequence, why neither is closely correlated with interest rates. We will analyze the earnings-price ratio first and the dividend-price ratio second.

The Earnings-Price Ratio

A stock's **earnings-price ratio *(E/P)*,** or **earnings yield,** is the ratio of the firm's annual earnings per share to the stock's price per share, which, for many investors, is a rough estimate of the stock's rate of return. If a stock sells for $100 a share and the company earns $10 a share in after-tax profits, these investors reason that the shareholders, as legal owners of the company, have earned $10, which is a 10 percent return on their investment. The problem with this logic is that, unless it is paid out as dividends, the shareholders have not received $10—and getting $10 is a whole lot better than reading about $10 in earnings in the annual report.

earnings yield
A stock's earnings yield is the ratio of the firm's earnings per share to the stock's price per share.

If the company only pays out, say, a dividend of $5 per share, then shareholders should consider the fate of the remaining $5. If these retained earnings are squandered on worthless projects, the $5 might just as well not have been earned in the first place. If the $5 is invested in projects that barely break even, the shareholders may eventually get $5, but $5 eventually is not the same as $5 now. At a 10 percent required return, the present value of $5 received five years from now is only $5/1.10^5 = $3.10. Therefore, the present value to shareholders of $10 in profits, $5 of which is paid out now and $5 paid out five years from now, is $5.00 + $3.10 = $8.10.

What if, instead, the firm makes a 10 percent annual after-tax profit on its retained earnings? After five years, the initial $5 of retained earnings grows to

$$\$5(1.10^5) = \$8.05.$$

The present value of this $8.05, if it is paid out as dividends after five years, is

$$\frac{\$8.05}{1.10^5} = \$5.00.$$

In this special case, $5 of retained earnings is worth $5 to shareholders.

This specific example illustrates a very important point. For a dollar of retained earnings to be worth a dollar to shareholders, the firm must earn an after-tax rate of return on these retentions that is equal to the shareholders' required rate of return on their stock. If the firm earns less than this required rate of return, then a dollar of retained earnings is worth less than a dollar in current dividends to shareholders. If the firm earns more than the shareholders' required return, a dollar in retained earnings is worth more than a dollar to shareholders. This principle explains why a firm that is interested in the well-being of its shareholders should use an estimate of the shareholders' required return as the minimum profit rate that is required of its investment projects.

A more general point is that the earnings-price ratio, E/P, is not a satisfactory measure of the rate of return to stockholders. Earnings are very important, since earnings are the source of dividends. However, earnings are the means to an end, not the end itself. Dividends are the cash flow to shareholders, and retained earnings are only of value to the extent that they yield future dividends.

The Dividend-Price Ratio

dividend yield
A stock's dividend yield is the ratio of its dividends per share to its price.

Some investors, accepting this argument use the **dividend yield,** the ratio of dividends per share to price, D/P, as a measure of shareholder return. In our example, these investors see the stock's $5 dividend and its $100 price, and they estimate the stock's yield to be $D/P = \$5/\$100 = 0.05$, or 5 percent. Yet, such a calculation is only logical if the dividend is expected to remain at $5 indefinitely. A $5 receipt, year after year, on a $100 investment is, indeed, a 5 percent return. However, if a firm retains $5 per share for expansion, dividends can be expected to grow as time passes, and, if so, the shareholders' return logically must be larger than 5 percent. How much larger depends on how fast dividends are expected to grow, which, in turn, depends on how much the firm is investing and on the profitability of these investments.

A Better Alternative

Neither of these two simple yield measures, E/P or D/P, is persuasive. The earnings-price ratio looks at profits rather than dividends. The dividend-price ratio ignores the future growth of dividends. A better rule of thumb would be to add to the dividend-price ratio an estimated growth rate for dividends, $R = D/P + g$. Equation 3 in Chapter 7 shows how g can be estimated from the firm's retention rate $(1 - d)$ and return on equity $ROE: g = (1 - d)ROE$.

FIGURE 8–2   Price-earnings ratios for the S&P 500, 1925-1987

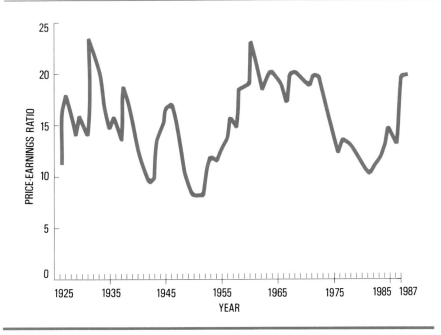

THE PRICE-EARNINGS RATIO

A stock's **price-earnings ratio,** P/E, is obtained by dividing the price per share by the annual earnings per share. The earnings might be for the most recent year, four times the earnings for the most recent quarter, or estimated earnings for the coming year. The price-earning ratio, P/E, is the inverse of the earnings-price ratio, E/P, and its mechanical use to gauge whether stocks are cheap or expensive can lead to misjudgments similar to those discussed in the preceding section.

Many investors have long considered a P/E ratio of 10–1 as normal and the purchase of a stock at or below a 10–1 P/E ratio as a sound investment. For example, Burton Crane, a *New York Times* financial writer from 1937 to 1963, observed that "most of us over the age of forty, unless we are completely without market knowledge, subconsciously think of [dividend] yields of 6 per cent and price-earnings ratios of 10 as about right."[1] Figure 8–2 shows that the price-earnings ratio for the S&P 500 has varied considerably, falling close to 5 in some years and topping 20 in others. For individual securities, some observers believe that P/E ratios are determined primarily by risk differences with the appropriate P/E ratios

price-earnings ratio
A stock's price-earnings ratio is its annual earnings divided by its price.

above 10 for safe stocks and below 5 for risky ones. However, such aggregate and individual rules of thumb are unreliable.

A Low *P/E* is Not Necessarily a Bargain

Crane correctly cautions that "no market is cheap because the price-earnings ratio is low and no market is dear because the ratio is high."[2] The mechanical *P/E* rules of thumb that so many use, if only subconsciously, ignore some very logical explanations of why individual stocks or the market as a whole may be cheap even if the *P/E* ratio is high and expensive even though the *P/E* is low.

Look again at the constant-growth model discussed in Chapter 7:

$$P = \frac{D}{R - g}$$
$$= \frac{dE}{R - g}$$

Division by *E* gives the following *P/E* ratio:

$$\frac{P}{E} = \frac{d}{R - g} \tag{1}$$

For the market as a whole, *d* may be relatively constant at around 50 percent, but *R* and *g* may vary considerably from year to year, and so should the *P/E* ratio.

> ***P/E* ratios tend to be high when projected growth rates are high and when shareholder required returns are low.**

For individual companies, required rates of return depend on risk perceptions, with high-risk stocks having high required returns and relatively low *P/E*s. In addition, Equation 1 tells us that high-growth stocks should have higher *P/E* ratios than slow-growth stocks and that, for any given growth rate, a firm with high dividends is worth more than one whose growth is at the expense of current dividends.

Growth rates, especially, vary substantially from one stock to the next, and the evidence is clear that investors are willing to pay more for fast-growing firms. Table 8–1 illustrates this point, using the five-year earnings growth rates predicted by professional security analysts for roughly 900 companies. Bauman and Dowen calculated the 1983 average predicted growth rate for each company, divided the companies into five groups ranging from those having the highest growth forecasts to those having the lowest, and calculated the average *P/E* for the stocks in each group. This exercise was repeated in 1984 and 1985, and Table 8–2 averages their

TABLE 8–1   Predicted Growth and Price-Earnings Ratios, 1983–1985

Stock Group	Average Predicted Growth Rate (percent)	Average Price-Earnings (P/E) Ratio
1	27.3	15.7
2	21.0	12.4
3	18.1	11.4
4	15.5	10.1
5	9.3	7.7

Source: W. Scott Bauman and Richard Dowen, "Growth Projections and Common Stock Returns,"
Financial Analysts Journal, July/August 1988, pp. 79–80.

results, showing, as expected, that the higher is the predicted growth rate, the higher is the *P/E*.

The constant-growth model neglects two additional important influences on *P/E* ratios: first, short-run fluctuations in earnings and, second, creative accounting. If earnings are depressed temporarily by an economic recession or a corporate misfortune, the stock's price stays relatively firm as current earnings sag, driving the *P/E* ratio skyward. In these circumstances, the *P/E* ratio is unusually high because current earnings are abnormally low. In the reverse situation, there may be a temporary bulge in earnings due to some extraordinary good luck. Recognizing that earnings will usually be much lower, the price does not rise much, and the *P/E* ratio slumps. Similarly, if investors believe that the firm has used dubious accounting procedures to boost reported earnings, the *P/E* ratio is deceptively small because earnings are fictitiously large.

THE GROWTH TRAP

Years ago, many investors focused almost solely on a stock's dividend yield to gauge its attractiveness. Indeed, as Figure 8–1 shows, for many years the average dividend yield exceeded the interest rate on Treasury bonds, indicating that investors attached little importance to dividend growth. As late as 1950, the average dividend yield was over 6.6 percent, while the yield on Treasury bonds was 2.3 percent. Fundamental analysis shows that dividend growth, too, is important. If a stock selling for $100 a share pays a $7 dividend that will grow by 10 percent a year, the shareholders' annual rate of return is 17 percent, not 7 percent. Similarly, of two stocks paying $7 dividends, the stock with a dividend growing at 10 percent annually is

THE NIFTY FIFTY

In the early 1970s, the attention of institutional investors was focused on the "nifty fifty"—a small group of so-called one-decision stocks, stocks so appealing that they should always be bought and never sold. Among these select few were IBM, Xerox, Disney, McDonald's, Avon, Polaroid, and Schlumberger. In each case, earnings had grown by at least 10 percent a year over the past five to ten years, and no reason for a slowdown was in sight. Each company was a leader in its field, with a strong balance sheet, able to earn close to 20 percent on its investments.

David Dreman recounted the following tales of missed opportunities that danced in the heads of feverish money managers:

> Had someone put $10,000 in Haloid-Xerox in 1960, the year the first plain copier, the 914, was introduced, the investment would have been worth $16.5 million a decade later. McDonald's earnings increased several thousand times in the 1961–66 period, and then, more demurely, quadrupled again by 1971, the year of its eight billionth hamburger. Anyone astute enough to buy McDonald's stock in 1965, when it went public, would have made fortyfold his money in the next seven years. An investor who plunked $2,750 into Thomas J. Waston's Computing and Tabulating Company in 1914 would have had over $20 million in IBM stock by the beginning of the 1970s.[1]

Think of it—to invest at the beginning of the next Xerox, McDonald's, or IBM! Or, as a second best strategy, think of investing in these great companies now. It is better late than never. Perhaps more importantly, if you do invest in such stocks today, how can you be faulted for investing in the very best?

The unfortunate consequence of this fixation on the nifty fifty was the belief that there is never a bad time to buy a growth stock, nor is there too high a price to pay: "The time to buy a growth stock is now. The whole purpose in such an investment is to participate in future larger earnings, so *ipso facto* any delay in making the commitment is defeating."[2] This advice is suspiciously similar to the Greater Fool Theory, and it contradicts the main tenet of fundamental analysis—that stocks, like groceries, should not be selected without regard for price. IBM is a fine company, but is its stock worth $100 a share? $1000? Any price, no matter how high?

The subsequent performance of many of the nifty fifty was disappointing; yet, even today, some money managers still believe that you cannot go wrong with a good growth stock, no matter what price you must pay. In 1986, Michael Lipper, President of Lipper Analytical Services, was very blunt: "[Suppose] an investor's timing was exquisitely wrong and he bought a growth stock at its peak. If he held that stock until the top of the next market cycle, such an investor would be better off with a growth stock than a value play."[3]

Not necessarily. Avon was a hot growth stock in 1973 when it sold for $140 a share, 60 times earnings. In 1974, the price collapsed to $18⅝; twelve years later, in 1986, it was still selling as low as $25 a share. Polaroid sold for $149½ in 1972 (an astounding 115 times earnings), $14⅛ in 1974 and $42¼ in 1986. Xerox hit $171⅞ in 1972 (60 times earnings), $49 in 1974, $27⅛ in 1982 and $48⅝ in 1986. An investor with exquisitely wrong timing would have been better off putting money under the mattress, not to mention buying value.

[1] David Dreman, *The New Contrarian Investment Strategy* (New York: Random House, 1982) p. 48.

[2] J.F. Bohmfalk, Jr., "The Growth Stock Philosophy," *Financial Analysts Journal,* November/December 1960, p. 122.

[3] Quoted in Beatrice E. Garcia, " 'Nifty 50' Tactic Tied to Growth Is Resurrected," *Wall Street Journal,* March 24, 1986.

worth far more than the stock whose dividend grows at only 5 percent or not at all.

As the value of growth was increasingly recognized in the 1950s and 1960s, investors were willing to buy stock at prices for which dividend yields were below bond yields. By the early 1970s, the pendulum had swung to an extreme, with institutional investors appearing to be interested exclusively with growth and, consequently, only in the premier growth stocks—labeled the "nifty fifty." Investment Example 8–1 tells how the myopia of these investors led them to pay what, in retrospect, were ridiculous prices for growth stocks.

There are two reasons why growth stocks are sometimes disappointing. Investors appraising a stock with their hearts instead of their heads see short-term profit increases and think they have found permanently rapid growth. However, statistically, unusually high profits are unlikely to be sustained. In addition, knowing that investors are looking for growth, some firms create an appearance of growth to boost the price of their stock. We will examine each of these pitfalls in turn.

The Dangers of Incautious Extrapolation

Graham and Dodd were consistently wary of growth stocks, since rosy growth projections were often based on little more than simple-minded extrapolations of past successes. They wrote, "It must be remembered that the automatic or normal economic forces militate against the indefinite continuance of a given trend. Competition, regulation, the law of diminishing returns, etc. are powerful foes to unlimited expansion."[3]

The value of a growth stock lies in the distant future, and it is risky to extrapolate a few years of past data several decades into the future. Many ludicrous examples have been concocted to dramatize the error of incautious extrapolation. In 1940, there was an average of 2.2 people in each car on the highways in the United States. By 1950, this average had dropped to 1.4. At this rate, by 1960 every third car on the road should have been empty! One observer, with tongue firmly in cheek, extrapolated the following observation that automobile deaths declined after the maximum speed limit in the United States was reduced to 55 miles per hour:

> *Prof. Thirdclass of the U. of Pillsbury stated that to reach zero death rate on the highways, which was certainly a legitimate goal, we need only set a speed limit of zero mph. His data showed that death rates increased linearly with highway speed limits, and the line passing through the data points, if extended backwards, passed through zero at zero mph. In fact, if he extrapolated even further to negative auto speeds, he got negative auto deaths, and could only conclude, from his data, that if automobiles went backwards rather than forwards, lives would be created, not lost.[4]*

More than a hundred years ago, Mark Twain came up with this example:

In the space of one hundred and seventy-six years the Lower Mississippi has shortened itself two hundred and forty-two miles. This is an average of a trifle over one mile and a third per year. Therefore, any calm person, who is not blind or idiotic, can see that in the Old Oolitic Silurian Period, just a million years ago next November, The Lower Mississippi River was upward of one million three hundred thousand miles long, and stuck out over the Gulf of Mexico like a fishing rod. And by the same token any person can see that seven hundred and forty-two years from now the Lower Mississippi will be only a mile and three-quarters long, and Cairo and New Orleans will have joined their streets together . . . There is something fascinating about science. One gets such wholesale returns of conjecture out of such a trifling investment of fact.[5]

Regression Toward the Mean

regression towards the mean
Regression towards the mean is the statistical tendency of extreme observations to be followed by more average values.

Another reason that profit extrapolations often prove to be wildly optimistic is a phenomenon that statisticians call **regression toward the mean,** a tendency of extreme observations to be followed by more average values.

Will All of Our Grandchildren Be 5'8"? Regression toward the mean was first noticed by Sir Francis Galton in a study of the relationship between the heights of fathers and their sons. Galton found that unusually tall fathers tend to have sons shorter than themselves, while very short fathers usually have somewhat taller sons, which suggests (erroneously) that the world is "regressing towards mediocrity." Such data do not mean that soon everyone will be the same height; instead, they reflect the statistical consequences of two chance factors.

The first is genetic. A person's height depends on the heights of both parents, and very tall men generally marry women who are not as exceptionally tall as themselves—not because they prefer short women, but because height is not the only factor they consider in choosing a mate. Because most very tall men marry women who are not as exceptionally tall as themselves, they have sons whose heights are not as extreme either.

The second chance factor is that because diet, exercise, and other environmental factors influence how tall a person is, observed height is not a perfect reflection of one's genes and, hence, not a perfect predictor of the genetically expected height of one's children. A 6'4" man might have had a genetically predicted height of 6'2" and positive environmental influences, or a genetically predicted height of 6'6" with negative environmental factors. The former is more likely, simply because there are many more men with 6'2" genetically predicted heights than with 6'6" predicted heights. Thus, the observed height of a very tall father is usually an overstatement of his genetic height and, thus, the expected height of his child.

These explanations do not imply that we will soon all be the same height. Indeed, we could just as well turn the argument upside down by noting that most very tall people had somewhat shorter parents, while most very short people had somewhat taller parents. Does this imply that heights are diverging? No, heights are neither converging nor diverging. There will always be unusually tall and unusually short people. The regression-toward-the mean fallacy is to conclude that some important trend is at work, when it is really just the complex implications of chance.

Test Scores and Corporate Profits Professors observe that those students who score highest on the midterm exam usually do not do quite as well on the final exam, while those who receive the lowest scores at midterm improve somewhat by the time of their final test. Does this imply that students converge to a depressing mediocrity, with the weak students learning and the strong forgetting? Or, turning the argument on its head, does the fact that the highest scorers on a final exam did not get the highest scores on the midterm show that scores are diverging from the mean? The answer is no—twice! The most plausible explanation is that high scores on any exam involve a bit of good luck, and low scores reflect some misfortune. Those students with the highest scores on any particular test are mostly above-average students who did exceptionally well because the questions asked happened to be ones that they were well prepared to answer. It is more probable that they are good students who did unusually well rather than great students who had an off day. The highest scorers on any given test most likely did not do as well on their last exam and will not do as well on their next exam.

We also see the regression towards the mean in IQ scores:

> *4 year olds with IQs of 120 typically have adult scores around 110. Similarly, 4 years olds with scores of 70 have an average adult score of 85 . . . . This does not mean that there will be fewer adults than children with very high or very low IQs. While those who start out high or low will usually regress toward the mean, their places will be taken by others who started closer to the mean.*[6]

An economic example is provided by a book published some time ago with the provocative title *The Triumph of Mediocrity in Business*. The author discovered that businesses with exceptional profits in any given year tended to have smaller profits the following year, while most firms with very low profits did somewhat better the next year. From this evidence, he concluded that strong companies were getting weaker, and the weak stronger, so that soon all will be mediocre. The author's fallacy is now obvious. A famous statistician explained it as follows:

While [businesses] at the margins . . . often go toward the center, those in the center of the group also go towards the margins. Some go up and some down; the average of the originally center group may, therefore, display little change . . . while for an extreme group, the only possible motion is toward the center.[7]

The natural tendency in the stock market, where all investors hope to find the next IBM, is to see a year or two of rapidly increasing earnings and conclude that this is the beginning of many years of never-ending growth. The regression-toward-the-mean phenomenon teaches us that a company with earnings up by 20 percent this year (or over the past few years) is more likely to have experienced good luck than bad that year and most likely, will regress towards the mean next year, disappointing overly optimistic investors.

Creating an Illusion of Growth

Fundamental analysis shows that rapidly growing firms should command high *P/E* ratios. However, a few caveats sometimes get overlooked by growth enthusiasts. An increased plowback of earnings always raises the firm's growth rate (as long as its *ROE* is positive) but does not raise the value of the stock unless *ROE* is larger than the shareholders' required return. The stockholders' return includes *both* the current dividend yield and the growth rate, and the trading of current dividends for future growth does not benefit shareholders unless *ROE* is larger than *R*.

Another pitfall for investors who focus myopically on earnings growth is that conglomerates can manufacture such growth merely by acquiring companies with low *P/E* ratios. For a simple example, consider two firms, each with $100 million in assets and one million shares outstanding. The first company (Smith) earns a 10 percent profit rate on its assets, and shareholders require a 10 percent return on their stock. The second company (Cooper) earns a 20 percent return on its assets, and shareholders require a 20 percent return. Both companies pay out all their earnings as dividends. Both are no-growth companies, and each has a total market value of $100 million, or $100 a share.

Now assume that Smith takes over Cooper, issuing a million new shares of stock which are exchanged one-for-one for shares of Cooper stock. The two companies continue to operate exactly the same as before, with the only difference that their balance sheets are combined. The results are in Table 8–2. Since there are no changes in their operations or in the current and future cash flow to investors, the market value of the combined companies should be the sum of the market values of the two separate firms, $100 million + $100 million = $200 million, and the per-share price should stay at $100. Another way to see this is to recognize that the merger has not increased the opportunities available to investors. Before, an investor

TABLE 8–2 The Balance Sheets of Smith and Cooper, Before and After Merger

Category	Smith	Cooper	Smith and Cooper
Total shares	1 million	1 million	2 million
Total assets	$100 million	$100 million	$200 million
Assets per share	$100	$100	$100
Total earnings	$10 million	$20 million	$30 million
Earnings per share	$10	$20	$15
Total dividends	$10 million	$20 million	$30 million
Dividends per share	$10	$20	$15
Price per share	$100	$100	$100(?)
Price-earnings ratio	10	5	6.67(?)

could pay a total of $200 for one share of each firm and receive $30 in dividends. Why would this investor pay more for two shares of the merged company?

Yet, from the standpoint of Smith, earnings per share have jumped 50 percent, from $10 to $15. Conversely, from the standpoint of Cooper, earnings per share have slumped from $20 to $15. If the merged company is named Smith, investors might compare last year's $10 per-share earnings with this year's $15, decide Smith is now a growth company, and apply a price-earnings ratio of 10+, thus pushing the price above $150. If they do so, Smith will be even better positioned to manufacture more earnings growth next year by taking over another low-*P/E* company. If, on the other hand, the new company is named Cooper, investors may compare last year's $20 earnings with this year's $15 and flee a disaster in the making. The lesson is that investors should look at the reasons for earnings growth (or decline), before mechanically applying *P/E* ratios.

BOOK VALUE

Many analysts look beyond earnings to assets, since assets are the source of earnings. In addition, firms sometimes raise cash by selling some or all of their assets. In the extreme, but not uncommon, case where one firm is taken over by another, the price shareholders receive may depend on the perceived liquidation value of the target firm's assets.

The *book value* of a firm is the net worth shown on the accountants' books. It is commonly calculated on a per-share basis: total assets minus liabilities (including preferred stock at redemption value), divided by the number of shares of common stock outstanding. Tangible book value is calculated by deducting such intangibles as good will, patents, and copyrights. Neither of these measures of a firm's assets necessarily equals the market value assigned by shareholders.

Book Value Versus Market Value

In their classic *Security Analysis*, Graham and Dodd downplay book value as an explanation of market value, observing that stock prices appear to depend on earnings and dividends and that there is little correlation between earnings and book value, with the possible exception of regulated utilities whose authorized customer rates are influenced by book value. Nonetheless, they endorse book value as one factor in identifying undervalued or overvalued stocks. Stocks priced at many times book value should be viewed cautiously, while those selling at a "small fraction" of book value may have "speculative possibilities—especially so if there is no substantial debt."[8]

Others put more emphasis on book value. Whitman and Shubik (the first a practitioner, the second an academician) argue that book value is at least as significant as earnings: "In choosing a starting point within financial statements for an analysis, book value seems to us to be the better starting point most of the time than accounting earnings."[9] To the extent book value is a good approximation of the replacement cost of a firm, it serves as a benchmark of the firm's *liquidation value*—the price another firm might pay for a liquidating firm's assets as an alternative to building such assets from scratch. In addition, Whitman and Shubik point out that there may be substantial tax benefits from acquiring the assets of a profitable company at a steep discount from book value, since the difference can often be treated as a capital loss for the acquired company and offset against past profits in order to obtain a tax refund from the IRS. Whitman and Shubik give several historical examples of asset sales that involved tax-loss carrybacks.[10]

A substantial problem with book-value data, which Whitman and Shubik freely acknowledge, is that such data are calculated according to accounting conventions that allow considerable divergence from replacement cost or liquidation value. Some assets carried at cost or, even worse, depreciated cost, actually may have appreciated in value considerably. The replacement cost of soundly constructed buildings, scarce real estate, and valuable mineral rights may be several times their book value. Some assets, such as management expertise, do not show up on balance sheets, and other assets, such as patents and brand-name recognition, are exceedingly difficult to value. On the other side of the balance sheet, the firm may have liabilities that are not fully reflected in book value—pension-fund obligations or federal requirements that plants be made safer or pollute less, for example.

In addition, if the firm is not going to be liquidated, its value to shareholders is the cash flow the assets generate, no matter what their original or replacement cost. A firm that loses money year after year is of little value to shareholders even if it would cost billions to construct its money-losing plant and equipment. Conversely, a high-technology company operating out of a garage can be worth millions even though its garage is only worth thousands. In the first case, the firm will sell for a substantial discount from book value or replacement cost; in the second case, the company will sell for a large premium. Whether a particular company's stock sells for a premium or a discount depends on the profitability of its assets, in particular whether its rate of return on equity is larger than shareholders' required rate of return.

Tobin's *q*

Early in this chapter, we saw that the retention of earnings to finance expansion raises a stock's price if the return on these investments, *ROE*, is larger than shareholders' required return on their stock, *R*. In particular, an investment that costs $5 a share is worth more than $5 a share to stockholders if $ROE > R$. This principle suggests that whether a firm's stock sells for a premium or a discount from the cost of its assets also depends on *ROE* in relation to *R* and, further, that a firm's investment decisions ought to hinge on a comparison of *ROE* with *R*.

Shareholders' required return is determined and revealed in financial markets: taking into account the yields offered on other assets, shareholders price stock to yield a competitive return. This comparison is one of the primary ways in which financial markets affect real economic activity. When interest rates fall, required stock returns decline, making it more likely that the profits from prospective investments are sufficient to make these investments attractive.

How do firms (or economic forecasters) calculate shareholders' required returns? The stock market is the place to look, but the financial pages do not report the anticipated rates of returns on stock. An ingenious alternative, suggested by James Tobin, is to look at stock prices. Specifically, Tobin argues that we should look at how financial markets value a firm relative to the replacement cost of the firm's assets:

$$q = \frac{\text{market value of firm}}{\text{replacement cost of firm}} = \frac{P}{A}$$

where *P* and *A* are, respectively, the firm's aggregate market value and replacement cost or, equivalently, its price per share and assets per share. (If a firm has bonds outstanding, then these should either be added to the market value, *P*, or substracted from the firm's assets, *A*.)

Tobin's *q*, the ratio of market value to replacement cost, can be calculated in a fairly straightforward manner. The market value uses the stock-market prices printed in daily newspapers. The replacement cost of a firm's assets can be estimated by listing these assets and then adjusting for wear and tear and current construction costs. The book value reported by firms

Tobin's *q*
Tobin's *q* is the ratio of market value of a firm to the replacement cost of its assets.

is a rough approximation, a starting point, that takes into account depreciation, but not current costs.

Implications for Investment Decisions A connection between business investment spending and market value relative to cost was pointed out many years ago by John Maynard Keynes:

> *The daily revaluations of the Stock Exchange, though they are primarily made to facilitate transfers of old investments between one individual and another, inevitably exert a decisive influence on the rate of current investment. For there is no sense in building up a new enterprise at a cost greater than that at which a similar existing enterprise can be purchased; whilst there is an inducement to spend on a new project what may seem an extravagant sum, if it can be floated on the stock exchange at an immediate profit. Thus, certain classes of investment are governed by the average expectation of those who deal on the Stock Exchange as revealed in the price of shares.*[11]

Similarly, Tobin argues that a firm should expand (by investing in new plant and equipment) if the stock market will value the project at more than its cost (that is, if its $q > 1$). Put more plainly, the appropriate question a firm should ask is whether, if it were to sell shares in its new venture, it could raise enough money to cover the project's cost.

The persuasive logic can be illustrated by a home builder's choice of location and housing plans: home construction is attractive only if the potential market value exceeds the construction cost. The same reasoning applies to all corporate investment. A firm should compare the cost of new capital with the value that financial markets will place on that capital. If the market value is larger than the cost ($q > 1$), shareholders prefer that the firm build this plant and equipment rather than distribute its cost as dividends, gladly giving up a dollar of dividends in exchange for a two-dollar increase in the value of their stock.

Similarly, the firm should compare the price it can get for selling its existing capital with the value that financial markets place on that capital. If the financial market value is less than the selling price ($q < 1$), the firm is worth more dead than alive, and it should sell off its assets and distribute the proceeds as dividends. Shareholders prefer two dollars of dividends to one dollar of market value.

In recent years, many prominent firms have benefited their shareholders by selling assets. For example, in 1980 Seagram sold $2.3 billion in energy properties, and the market value of its stock promptly doubled. Similarly, Esmark more than doubled the value of its stock in 1980 by selling 42 percent of its assets and using the proceeds to buy up 55 percent of its shares. A low market value relative to replacement cost also frequently motivates takeover bids. An outside group may be able to profit by purchasing enough stock to gain control of a company and then liquidating its assets. Indeed, it was a Mobil Oil offer to buy Esmark stock that helped persuade Esmark executives to unload low-value assets.

What Determines q? How can assets be valued in financial markets at other than their replacement cost? Assets are of value to shareholders only to the extent they yield profits which, sooner or later, finance dividends. It matters not at all that a plant cost $700 million to build if it does not produce a dime of profits. For a plant to be worth what it costs shareholders, it must earn the shareholder's required rate of return.

For a simple example, consider a hamburger chain that pays out all its earnings as dividends. Assume also that a new restaurant costs $1 million to build and is expected to earn a constant 20 percent profit ($ROE = 0.20$), $200,000 a year forever. The value that financial markets place on the $200,000 annual dividend depends on how highly hamburger earnings are valued. If Treasury bonds yield 5 percent, then perhaps stock in risky hamburger restaurants is priced to yield 10 percent ($R = 0.10$). Because the anticipated dividends are a constant $200,000, we can use the consol formula, $P = D/R$ from Chapter 7, to show that the market value of the restaurant is

$$P = \frac{\$200,000}{0.10} = \$2,000,000.$$

Valued at $2 million, the $200,000 annual dividend provides stockholders their requisite 10 percent return.

In this case, the market value of the restaurant is twice its cost of construction: $q = 2$. Stockholders endorse this kind of investment, since the use of $1 million in potential dividends to build the restaurant provides $2 million in market value. The underlying reason is that the restaurant's 20 percent profit rate is larger than the stockholders' 10 percent required rate of return.

If, on the other hand, shareholders' required rate of return is 25 percent, then

$$P = \frac{\$200,000}{0.25} = \$800,000.$$

Now $q = 0.8$, and shareholders oppose construction of the restaurant. Shareholders require a 25 percent return on their stock, and because the restaurant earns only 20 percent on its cost, the stock must be valued at less than asset cost to provide shareholders their requisite return.

The observation that q is larger or smaller than 1 depending on whether the firm's return on equity is larger or smaller than shareholders' required return is not a peculiar accident in this example. Look again at the formula

TABLE 8-3   The Twenty Largest Firms in the Computer and Office Equipment Industry, 1989

Company	Market Value (millions of dollars)	Book Value (millions of dollars)	Tobin's q	Return on Equity (percent)
IBM	94,644	66,299	1.43	14.7
Xerox	20,122	18,787	1.07	11.2
Hewlett-Packard	14,865	6,335	2.35	18.0
Digital Equipment	14,853	10,553	1.41	17.4
Unisys	11,394	12,203	0.93	9.0
Apple	6,692	1,764	3.79	39.9
Pitney-Bowes	6,016	3,925	1.53	18.7
Tandy	5,521	3,211	1.72	19.7
NCR	5,412	3,204	1.69	19.6
Automatic Data Processing	3,687	1,868	1.97	17.3
Compaq	3,453	1,248	2.77	30.5
Wang Laboratories	3,410	3,769	0.90	5.8
Control Data	2,633	2,872	0.93	3.5
Amdahl	2,397	1,388	1.73	21.2
Prime Computer	2,293	1,892	1.21	10.2
Tandem Computers	2,256	1,466	1.54	11.7
Sun	1,907	912	2.09	18.0
Cray Research	1,756	906	1.94	23.1
Intergraph	1,133	925	1.22	12.5
Seagate Technology	1,053	798	1.32	17.7

Source: Value Line Investment Survey, May 5, 1989, pp. 1076-1118.

for the fundamental value of a constant-growth firm, Equation 4 in Chapter 7:

$$P = \frac{d(ROE)A}{R - (1 - d)ROE}$$

This can be rearranged as

$$q = \frac{P}{A} = \frac{d(ROE)}{R - ROE + d(ROE)}$$

$$= \frac{1}{1 + \left(\dfrac{R - ROE}{dROE}\right)}$$

to demonstrate that Tobin's q is larger than one if the firm's rate of return on equity is larger than shareholders' required rate of return, and less than one in the reverse case.

FIGURE 8–3 The twenty largest firms in the computer and office equipment industry, 1989

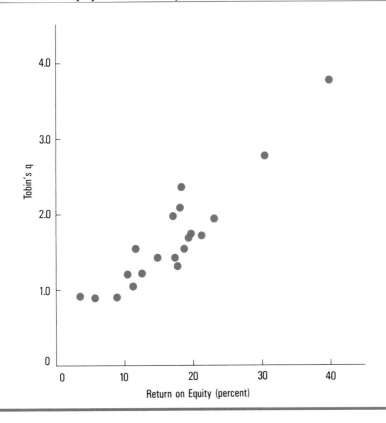

Table 8–3 shows the market value, book value, and return on equity for the twenty largest U.S. firms in the office-equipment and computer industry in 1989. The return on equity reflects only a single year's profits, and the ratio of market value to book value is a crude estimate of Tobin's q—crude because book value uses historical cost and assets purchased years ago may be expensive to replace today. Nonetheless, those firms with high profit rates tend to have high q values (market values that are far above book values), while firms with low profit rates have low qs. The scatter diagram of q and *ROE* shown in Figure 8–3 confirms this tendency.

The data in Figure 8–3 represent a cross section of twenty firms in one particular year, 1989. Figure 8–4 shows some time series data for the firms in the S&P 400 industrials index, using Goldman, Sachs's estimates of the replacement value of the companies' assets. In the 1960s, profit rates were much higher than Treasury-bond rates, and market values were substantially above replacement cost. After 1973, profits fell below interest

FIGURE 8–4 Interest rates, profit rates, and *q*. (*Source*: Goldman, Sachs, "Portfolio Strategy," September 1988, p. 11.)

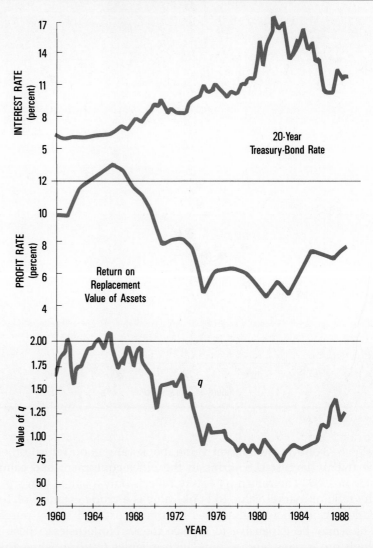

rates, and *q* slumped, touching bottom in 1982 with the unemployment rate at 10 percent and the market value of these corporations less than half the replacement cost of their assets. In the economic recovery that followed, interest rates came down, profits went up, and *q* rose to a value of about 1.

GRAHAM'S APPROACH TO SECURITY ANALYSIS

Benjamin Graham, together with David Dodd, wrote the investment classic *Security Analysis* that underlies much of modern fundamental analysis. The first edition was published in 1934 and the fifth edition (updated by three associates) in 1988, with 750,000 copies sold in-between. Adam Smith said in *Supermoney*, "There is only one Dean of our profession, if security analysis can be said to be a profession. The reason that Benjamin Graham is undisputed Dean is that before him, there was no profession and after him they began to call it that."[12] We will look briefly at Graham's views on earnings and assets.

Investment Opportunities

Despite the homage paid to his ideas, Graham felt that investors inevitably price some stocks too high and others too low because, as he observed wryly, his books were not only the most widely read, but also the most commonly disregarded. He was especially critical of highly paid institutional money managers who had "degenerated from the standpoint of sound investment to this rat race of trying to get the highest possible return in the shortest period of time."[13] The inevitable outcome of their short horizons is that, according to Graham, "nine out of ten so-called investors— and this includes the big institutions—are really speculators. This is fortunate because it means the tenth can make a decent profit."[14] To be successful investors, Graham believes that "people don't need extraordinary insight or intelligence. What they need most is the character to adopt simple rules and stick to them. They have to avoid greediness and overenthusiasm—that's a silly thing to say, because I know they won't do it; it's not human nature."[15]

Earnings and Assets

Graham and Dodd advised focusing on not more than 100 companies that "are large, prosperous, soundly capitalized and well known to investors," with the 20 to 30 most favorable ones included in the portfolio.[16] Investors should value a company's stock by considering how much they would pay for the company itself. This perspective encourages the view that you are buying "for keeps" and discourages speculation about which way the stock price will move tomorrow.

Businesses report two interrelated sets of financial data that are of interest to serious investors: (1) a *statement of operations*, that shows a firm's current income and expenses, and (2) a *statement of financial condition*, that discloses a firm's assets and liabilities. Profits and assets are interrelated in that a company with few assets has a hard time making profits, and a firm with little profits has trouble maintaining its assets, let alone expanding.

Graham recommended examination of a firm's earnings and dividends over a substantial period, say, ten years, covering both booms and recessions, supplemented by a careful scrutiny of the firm's assets, debts, lines of credit, expansion plans, pension reserves, management capabilities, and other factors that might impair the firm's ability to maintain earnings and dividends. He advised tracking many of the financial ratios used to rate the quality of a firm's bonds, such as:

1. Return on equity (after-tax profits divided by net worth)
2. Pretax return on sales (before-tax profits divided by sales)
3. Current ratio (current assets, omitting plant and equipment that is illiquid and difficult to value, divided by current liabilities)
4. Long-term debt to capitalization (long-term debt divided by total debt and stock)

If a firm cannot pay its debts, it cannot pay dividends either. Financial strength, the ability to generate a substantial cash flow in good times and bad, allows a firm to pay interest and dividends with ease.

Graham argued that investors should treat retained earnings with caution, because the profit rate on such retentions is likely to be disappointing. Earnings paid out as dividends are usually worth more to investors than earnings retained for expansion: "Of two companies with the same earning power and in the same general position in an industry, the one paying the larger dividend will almost always sell at a higher price."[17] The exceptions are, as fundamental analysis teaches, situations in which a company's return on its investments is unusually large:

> The higher the [P/E ratio], the greater the proportion of issues which presumably should retain all or nearly all of their profits . . . For—presumably again—the rate of return on reinvestment will substantially exceed, in a typical case, what the stockholder could earn on the same money received in dividends.[18]

The approach advocated by Graham is conservative, emphasizing the ability to maintain current dividends and earnings. The famed analyst had little interest in concept stocks, or stocks with a "story," such as these: "Curtiss-Wright owns the North American patent on Wankel rotary engines, which will revolutionize the automobile industry." "Upjohn has developed a cure for baldness that is going to be bigger than contact lenses." "Home Shopping Network has this new concept, peddling discount merchandise in a game show format, that is absolutely sensational." In *Security Analysis,* Graham and Dodd admitted, "We are haunted as it were by the spectre of growth stocks—by the question of how best to deal with them in the context of our own basic principles."[19] In practice, they avoided them.

Some Guidelines

If the dividends and earnings are sound, then Graham used the price-earnings ratio to judge whether the company's stock is overpriced or underpriced, using for comparison the returns available on long-term bonds. In his later years, Graham seemed to focus increasingly on the balance sheet, assets and liabilities, rather than current income. He advised careful scrutiny of financial statements to identify asset-rich companies with real estate, natural resources, or inventories that are valued on the books at less than the replacement cost. An interviewer, in 1974, reported Graham's views at the age of eighty: "If there is a factor that Mr. Graham considers crucial—one that could even be used as a single buy indicator—it's the net asset value. He can't conceive of a better bargain than a stock of a well-known prosperous company that is selling below its book value."[20] Again, this is a very conservative approach, inquiring not about a firm's potential growth, but asking simply, "What are the company's assets worth?" Such asset seekers make little or no attempt to predict which direction an industry, the economy, or the stock market is going.

In 1976, shortly before he died, Graham was reported to have pared his criteria to two alternatives: (1) stocks selling at low *P/E* ratios (below 7 in 1976, for an earnings yield of 14 percent at a time when long-term Treasury bond yields were about 7 percent), with current assets (cash on hand, inventories, and accounts receivable) that exceed current liabilities plus long-term debt; and (2) stocks with a per-share price less than asset value per share, counting as assets only current assets less current liabilities, long-term debt and preferred stock.[21] To follow Graham's approach, an investor needs only a pencil, paper, and Standard and Poor's monthly stock guide.

THE CONSERVATION OF VALUE

One of the main principles of finance is the **conservation of value**: in its most general form, it holds that the present value of A + B is equal to the present value of A plus the present value of B. This principle means that nothing is gained or lost by combining two cash flows or by splitting a cash flow in two. There are several implications for the valuation of corporate stock.

Mergers

The most obvious application of the conservation-of-value principle is to mergers. If two companies combine without changing their operations (so that the cash flow of the merged company equals the sum of the separate cash flows), then the market value of the postmerger company should equal the sum of the premerger values. For example, if BIG is worth $100 million and SMALL $30 million, the two companies together should be worth $130 million. We used this principle earlier in the example of Smith and Cooper, and a formal proof using the dividend-discount model was given as an exercise in Chapter 7.

What if BIG pays $30 million to acquire SMALL? BIG has gained something worth $30 million (SMALL's assets) and given up something worth $30 million (cash to SMALL's former shareholders). The market value of BIG should stay at $100 million.

According to the conservation-of-value principle, mergers only create value if the cash flow of the whole is greater than the sum of the separate cash flows. Perhaps one of the firms involved in a merger was mismanaged, and the merger brings in new people and policies to increase the company's cash flow. Possibly there are economies of scale that allow two merged firms to live, if not as cheaply as one, at least less expensively than two separate companies. For instance, if each company has its own separate accounting department, some parts may become redundant with the merger. Maybe each company has large facilities that are underutilized: together, they can share one facility and sell the other. These are good reasons for mergers; without such reasons, mergers do not create value.

Most mergers, in practice, seem to have little or no economic rationale.[22] Some seem motivated by the chief executive officer's personal desire to rule a larger company. Other mergers, particularly those that occurred during the conglomerate boom in the 1960s, seem mainly intended to manufacture earnings growth through the acquisition of companies with low *P/E* ratios. In the 1970s came the realization that a hodge-podge of essentially unrelated companies did not create automatic economies of scale or better management. If anything, large companies run by distant bureaucracies who do not know the business are poorly managed. In the 1980s, almost all of the conglomerates were broken up, with the pieces spun off as smaller, separate entities, or sold to other firms who know the business or have genuine economies of scale.

Some of this restructuring was involuntary, forced by outside corporate *raiders*. One of the most prominent, Carl Icahn, relates how he took over a company operating in the Midwest that had a headquarters staff of 173 in New York:

> *I couldn't understand what they were doing [at headquarters] . . . . So I went to the guys in the Midwest and said, "Look, you have to tell me, how many of these guys in New York do you need to support you?" And they looked at me and said, "We don't need any of them. We'd be better off without them— we could save 20 percent of our staff who are around just to report numbers to them every week."*[23]

Icahn hired an outside consulting firm that assigned five people with M.B.A. degrees from Harvard to determine what the New York staffers were doing. The consultants could not figure out why the headquarters staff was needed, and so Icahn fired all 173 of them.

In contrast, a financial analyst said the following about Hanson Trust, a successful British conglomerate:

> *Hanson Trust may be the last conglomerate, but it appears to be the first to make [the concept] work. The conglomerates of the 60s failed because they bought anything if the [low P/E] arithmetic worked, kept everything they bought, didn't worry about managing or improving operations, had to keep making more and bigger acquistions to maintain the growth rate, and inevitably were swallowed up by the problems they bought or created. How does Hanson do it? Hanson has carefully bought strong basic operations with potential for improvement, has recovered a large part of its acquisition costs by astute pruning of the companies it has bought, and has demonstrated its capabilities in profit improvement largely through decentralized management that gives full authority and responsibility and ample incentives to divisional management.*[24]

Stock Splits and Stock Dividends

Another example of the conservation-of-value principle is a **stock split,** which increases the number of shares outstanding and reduces the value of each share proportionately. Consider a company with one million shares valued at $60 apiece, an aggregate market value of $60 million. If the company declares a two-for-one split, each stockholder's shares are doubled, and the total number of shares increases to two million. With no change in the company's actual operations, its aggregate market value should stay at $60 million, implying a $30-per-share market value:

stock split
A stock split increases each stockholder's shares proportionately.

> **If the number of shares is doubled, the conservation-of-value principle implies that the value of each share is halved.**

The individual shareholder with, say, 100 shares before the split held 0.01 percent of the outstanding shares and received 0.01 percent of the dividends, a privilege that the market valued at $60(100) = $6,000. After the split, this shareholder has 200 out of two million shares—still 0.01 percent of the company and 0.01 percent of the dividends, a claim that should still be worth $6000 and will be if the market price of a share falls to $30.

Why Split Stock? If stock splits are nonevents, why do firms bother? One explanation is that if a growing company allows its price to rise to $200,

$500, or $1000 a share, some investors will not be able to afford purchases, particularly in the 100-share round lots that both investors and brokers favor. Periodic splits that maintain a price per share of under $100 keep both happy.

Nevertheless, in a market dominated by large institutions and wealthy individuals, the affordability argument is a bit strained and sometimes preposterous. American Telnet, a television production firm, went public in March 1979 at 50 cents a share. By August 1980, the firm had yet to sell a TV production, and the price had sagged to 43¾ cents a share. At this point, the firm split its stock five for one so that, according to its president, it would be "more affordable."[25] Given the structure of commissions, however, it does not make sense to buy only one share of an 8-cent stock. On the other hand, if you can afford to invest hundreds or thousands of dollars, it does not make much difference whether you buy 1000 shares at 40 cents each or 5000 shares at 8 cents each.

A somewhat more satisfactory argument for stock splits is that, traditionally, blue-chip stocks have traded in the $20-to-$100 range, and by manipulating the number of shares to keep the per-share price in that range, firms acquire some of the luster of blue chips. An important implication of this argument is that if a stock's price runs up to $80 and the firm declares a two-for-one split, reducing the price back to $40, this stock split communicates to investors that the board of directors is confident the run-up was justified—not just mindless speculation that, when it has run its course, will result in the price collapsing to below $20, where lesser stocks trade. A stock that falls below $20 can do a reverse split; for example, a one-for-two split would halve the number of shares and double the price. However, resort to this tactic would appear to be a damaging admission by the company's board that prospects for the firm are not bright enough to increase the price soon.

For American Telnet, the most logical explanation for its five-for-one split is that penny stocks have a reputation for being very risky, and a company that splits its stock down to the penny range may attract speculators who habitually restrict their attention to penny stocks. In sharp contrast, Berkshire Hathaway (B-H) run by Warren Buffett, has never split its stock, allowing its price to top $7000 a share in 1989. In a Christmas card to a friend, Buffett wrote "May you live until B-H splits."

stock dividend
A stock dividend is the distribution of additional shares of stock rather than cash.

Is a Stock Dividend a Real Dividend? A **stock dividend** is a stock split, only smaller; for instance, with a 5 percent stock dividend, a stockholder with 100 shares receives 5 additional shares. The conservation-of-value principle implies that the value of each share promptly drops by 5 percent, leaving shareholders no better or worse off than before. Nonetheless, *Barron's Finance and Investment Handbook* says:

From the corporate point of view, stock dividends conserve cash needed to operate the business. From the stockholder point of view, the advantage is that additional stock is not taxed until sold, unlike a cash dividend.[26]

This argument is misdirected and misleading. Companies and their shareholders may well want to retain earnings to finance profitable expansion. However, there is no need to declare a stock dividend to do so. Given that the company is going to retain earnings and expand as planned, it really does not matter whether the company leaves the number of shares unchanged, declares a 2-for-1 split, or declares a 21-for-20 split (a 5 percent stock dividend).

Andrew Tobias, a keen observer of the stock market, offers a very different and disturbing explanation of why companies declare stock dividends:

> *The only difference between a stock dividend and a stock split is that, being a very small split, it is hoped that no prospective buyers will notice that it has taken place.*
>
> *Stock dividends are under no circumstances to be confused with real dividends. Their (dubious) value is entirely psychological—it is hard to believe that it merits the cost of issuing all those extra little stock certificates and answering the questions of confused stockholders.*
>
> *Prior to the dividend, 100% of the company was divided among the shareholders. Then, in an attempt to keep those shareholders happy without having to pay them anything, each one is given 5% more shares. Now they have exactly what they had before—100% of the company. It is just divided into smaller pieces.*
>
> *You pay no tax on a stock dividend, because is adds no value to your holdings. What you hope, however, is that Wall Street will not notice that your company has made this quiet little "split" and, accordingly, will keep paying what it used to pay for each now-slightly-less-valuable share.*
>
> *Sometimes it actually works.[27]*

By this logic, stock dividends are like candy-bar inflation: the company shrinks the bar, hoping that consumers will continue to pay full price.

Ex-Dividend

Dividends are paid to those who own the company's shares on a specified day known as the *record date*. For instance, the board of directors might meet on February 1 and declare a $2 dividend to be paid on March 1 to those who own stock on the record date of February 15. To allow for the processing of transactions, the NYSE and most other exchanges stocks use an **ex-dividend** (excluding dividend) date four business days before the record date. In our example, those who buy the stock ex-dividend do not

ex-dividend
Those who buy a stock ex-dividend (excluding dividend) do not receive the dividend.

FIGURE 8–5 The sawtooth pattern created by periodic stock dividends

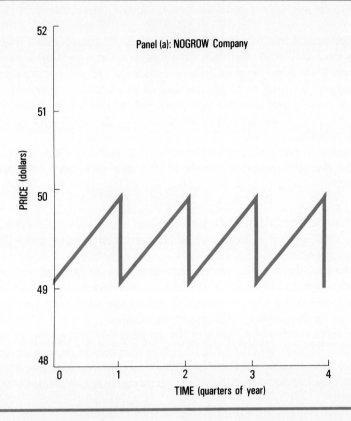

receive the March 1 dividend. Newspapers use an *x* to indicate that a stock is trading ex-dividend.

After a firm pays a dividend, its market value should fall by the size of the dividend, since its assets have declined by this amount. Consider, for instance, a company with one million shares valued at $50. If the company pays a $1 dividend, the price of each share should drop by $1 to $49. The aggregate market value of the company falls too, from $50 million to $49 million, because the $1 million paid in dividends has reduced the firm's assets by this amount. (If the price falls by less than $1, profits can be made by buying just before it goes ex-dividend and selling just after the ex-dividend date; if the price falls by more than $1, stockholders can profitably sell before the ex-dividend date and buy afterwards.)

Figure 8–5 displays the sawtooth price pattern that accompanies the regular payment of dividends. In order to focus on the ex-dividend behavior, this figure assumes (unrealistically) that there are no fluctuations in profits or required rates of return. NOGROW is a fictitious company

FIGURE 8–5, *cont'd* The sawtooth pattern created by periodic stock dividends

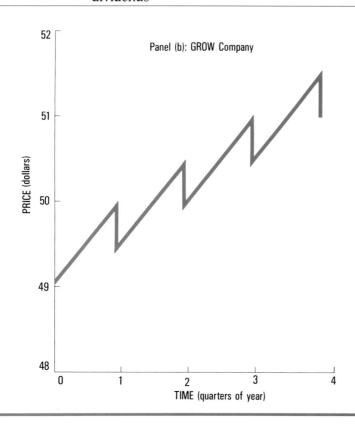

that earns a $1 million after-tax quarterly profit and distributes it all as dividends. A shareholder who buys at $49 waits a full quarter to get the $1 dividend. As time passes, the wait shortens, and the price increases so as to keep the effective rate of return constant. The price reaches $50 just before the stock goes ex-dividend, giving stockholders the option of selling for $50 or taking the $1 dividend and holding the stock as its price drops back to $49. The second company in Figure 8-5, GROW, retains some of its profits and expands over time, but, still, each time a dividend is paid the price falls back by the amount of the dividend.

Stock Sales and Repurchases (optional)

Corporations can raise money by selling additional shares of stock or distribute money by repurchasing shares from their stockholders. To understand the consequences, it is helpful to separate the firm's financial and real decisions. We know already that expansion—investment in new plant

TABLE 8–4 Equivalence of Stock Repurchase to a Dividend

Category	Company's Initial Position	Company's Position After Paying $2 Dividend (ex-dividend)	Company's Position After Repurchasing 1 Million Shares
Number of shares	10 million	10 million	9 million
Price per share	$20	$18	$20
Total value	$200 million	$180 million	$180 million

and equipment—makes sense if a company's profit rate is larger than the shareholders' required rate of return. So we will hold constant the firm's investment plans, which allows us to invoke the conservation-of-value principle and focus on financing choices.

Consider a firm with ten million shares outstanding that are each valued at $20 (an aggregate market value of $200 million), which has $20 million in cash that it would like to distribute to its shareholders. One alternative is to pay a $2 dividend per share; another is to purchase one million of its shares at $20 apiece. Table 8–4 shows the consequences of each of these actions. If the company pays a $2 dividend, there is a $2 drop in the price per share, and shareholder wealth is unchanged. If the company repurchases shares, the number of shares declines by one million and its assets decrease by $20 million, leaving the price at $20 and again making shareholders no better or worse off. As long as the company is neither wasting the money nor investing it profitably, shareholders do not care if the company holds the cash for them or distributes it, either as dividends or through share repurchases. It is true that a dividend puts cash in their pockets, but they can always get money by selling some of their shares.

Remember that we are comparing purely financial transactions in our example, to show that share repurchases are equivalent to dividend payments. Repurchases no doubt increase the price of a firm's stock if the cash is raised by abandoning an unprofitable venture. But it is the abandonment of the money-loser that raises the price of the stock, not the decision to distribute the proceeds through repurchases. Shareholders would benefit equally well if the company abandons the project and distributes the proceeds as dividends.

Table 8–5 also shows that the issuance of new shares is equivalent to reducing dividends. The company's stock in this example is selling for $22 and will fall to $20 after it pays a $2 dividend. If the company eliminates the dividend, the stock's price stays at $22 and the stock's aggregate market value increases by the $20 million that the company keeps. Instead of cutting its dividend, the firm can raise $20 million by selling one million

TABLE 8–5   Equivalence of Stock Sale to a Dividend Reduction

Category	Company's Initial Position (ex-dividend)	Company's Position After Eliminating Dividend	Company's Position After Issuing 1 Million New Shares
Number of shares	10 million	10 million	11 million
Price per share	$20	$22	$20
Total value	$200 million	$220 million	$220 million

new shares, either at $22 including a dividend or at $20 ex-dividend. Either way, its assets increase to $220 million, and the number of shares expands to eleven million, leaving shareholders with a $2 dividend and a $20 stock— a total of $22, the same result as when the dividend is cut. This outcome is not surprising, since a firm can neither help nor hurt its stockholders by selling securities for what they are worth.

Taxes create a slight complication that makes share repurchases somewhat better than paying dividends, and cutting dividends better than stock sales. Shareholders have to pay taxes on dividends, but they do not have pay capital-gains taxes until they realize their gains by selling. A dividend gives shareholders no alternative but to take the cash and pay taxes. In the absence of a dividend, shareholders have a choice. Either they can sell some shares and pay taxes, or they can let their investment ride. This distinction was even more important before the 1986 Tax Reform act, when the tax rate on capital gains was only 40 percent of the tax rate on dividends. Then, stock repurchases were much better than paying dividends, and stock sales were much worse than reducing dividends.

Taking into account the complication of taxes, our conclusion regarding stock repurchases and sales is:

> **Except for the possible deferral of capital-gains taxes, a stock repurchase is equivalent to paying dividends, and a stock sale is equivalent to reducing dividends.**

Debt Versus Equity (optional)

A third option for raising money is to borrow, either by getting a loan from a bank or by selling bonds. Either way, when a firm borrows, it creates leverage. Consider a firm with the balance sheet shown in Table 8–6. This firm has $200 million in debt outstanding and 10 million shares valued at $20 each. The firm's total value is $400 million, in that those investors who own all of its debt and stock receive all the cash flow from its assets.

Because its assets are twice the size of shareholders' equity, the firm

TABLE 8–6 Balance Sheet of a Hypothetical Levered Firm

Assets (millions of dollars)		Liabilities (millions of dollars)	
Plant and equipment	$400	Debt	$200
		Equity	200
Total assets	**$400**	**Total liabilities**	**$400**

has two-for-one leverage. To the extent the firm earns a rate of return on its assets that is larger or smaller than the interest rate on its debt, this difference is doubled for shareholders. For example, if the firm earns 15 percent and pays 10 percent interest on its debt, the profit rate for shareholders is $10 + 2(15 - 10) = 20$ percent. (Checking, we find that a 15 percent profit on the firm's assets is 0.15($400) = $60, and 10 percent interest on its debt is 0.10($200) = $20—leaving $40 for shareholders, and $40/$200 = 0.20, or 20 percent.) Is this leverage good or bad for shareholders? It clearly makes the stock riskier, but it also raises the anticipated return because presumably the firm does not borrow unless management believes there will be money to pay the interest, and then some. On balance, is it a benefit or a detriment for a firm to have debt?

The Modigliani-Miller Theorem The surprising answer given by the **Modigliani-Miller theorem**—one of the most famous theorems in finance, is that a firm's leverage does not affect shareholders at all. To understand this theorem's logic, consider Table 8–7, which shows what a company's balance sheet might look like if it had no debt.

Modigliani-Miller theorem
The Modigliani-Miller theorem holds that shareholders are not affected by changes in a firm's debt-equity ratio.

The first insight of the Modigliani-Miller hypothesis is that shareholders can unlever the levered stock by purchasing some of the firm's debt. Consider a stockholder who buys 1 percent of an unlevered firm's stock, thereby receiving 1 percent of the company's cash flow. Alternatively, if the firm is levered, this investor can buy 1 percent of its bonds and 1 percent of its stock, again receiving 1 percent of the cash flow, no matter how it is divided between bondholders and stockholders. There is no disadvantage to leverage because shareholders can undo the leverage. If shareholders value the cash flow from the unlevered company at $400 million, they should value the debt plus equity of the levered firm (which gives the very same cash flow) at $400 million too.

The second Modigliani-Miller insight is that shareholders can use "homemade" leverage to lever unlevered stock. An investor who buys 1 percent of a levered stock can get the same two-for-one leverage with an unlevered company by buying 1 percent of its stock and borrowing half

TABLE 8–7 Balance Sheet of a Hypothetical Unlevered Firm

Assets (millions of dollars)		Liabilities (millions of dollars)	
Plant and equipment	$400	Equity	$400
Total assets	**$400**	**Total liabilities**	**$400**

the cost. There is no advantage to corporate leverage because it simply does what shareholders can do on their own.

> **The Modigliani-Miller theorem states that because there is no advantage or disadvantage to corporate leverage, the total market value of a company depends on the profitability of its assets, not on its debt/equity ratio.**

There are three assumptions implicit in this argument. The first is that firms and shareholders borrow at the same interest rate; if not, corporate leverage is advantageous to investors who otherwise would have to borrow at higher interest rates. The second assumption is that bankruptcy is not a possibility. In fact, corporate leverage is better than the homemade kind for investors because, as shareholders they are not personally responsible for the company's debts. An individual investor who borrows money to buy stock must repay the loan even if the stock does poorly. Limited liability does not make unlimited leverage optimal: a firm that borrows too much and is forced into bankruptcy will find its assets squandered on expensive lawyers and accountants. Although these arguments are correct, for most major corporations the chances of bankruptcy are slight and can be safely neglected.

Debt as a Tax Shield The third assumption underlying the Modigliani-Miller theorem gives a clear advantage to debt. The assumption is that money distributed to bond and stock holders is treated equally by corporate tax laws. In fact, corporations can deduct interest payments but not dividends; thus, money disbursed to bondholders is taxed just once, when they receive it, while money paid to stockholders actually is taxed twice.

Consider the example shown in Table 8–8 on p. 277). The unlevered company pays a 34 percent corporate income tax on its $100 million in earnings, leaving $66 million for dividends. The individual investors who receive these dividends then pay up to a 33 percent personal income tax on them. If the firm is instead levered with $20 million in interest payments,

LEVERAGED BUYOUTS

Takeovers are based on a belief that the potential value of a company is substantially larger than its current market value. One reason might be that the current management is incompetent. Another is that the company would have more after-tax cash flow if the target firm had more debt to use as a tax shield. The tax advantage of debt is a primary motivation for the leveraged buyout (LBO) where, using the target firm's assets as collateral, the takeover group uses borrowed money to purchase the target firm's stock. Once the takeover group has control of the firm, there is less equity, more debt, and a bigger tax shield. Realizing that this debt-equity restructuring is the ultimate objective of many takeovers, some target firms have, for self protection, borrowed heavily, using the proceeds to repurchase stock or pay a special dividend (sometimes equal to more than half the value of the stock). Once they have created a sufficient tax shield, there is little to be gained by a takeover.

Overall, the Federal Reserve Board estimated that between 1984 and 1988, U.S. nonfinancial corporations issued $440 billion in corporate bonds and repurchased $425 billion in corporate stock, thereby swapping roughly a half trillion dollars of debt for equity. This increased leverage also makes firms more vulnerable to default. The median rating of industrial bonds was A in 1981 and fell to BB in 1988, leading the managing director for industrial and utility ratings at Standard & Poor's to comment that "Most companies are junk today."*

One group that doesn't benefit from this debt/equity substitution consists of those investors who held the firm's bonds before the restructuring and, now that the firm is more highly levered and more vulnerable to bankruptcy, find their bonds downgraded. For example, after the 1988 $17.7 billion, debt-financed buyout of RJR Nabisco, existing RJR bonds lost 20% of their value as they were downgraded from single-A to junk. In response, some big institutional investors began pushing for "takeover-proof" bonds that can be redeemed at par if the firm merges with another company or borrows money to repurchase its stock or to pay a large dividend. Other investors migrated to Treasury bonds, which presumably aren't susceptible to a leveraged buyout.

*Bill Sing, "Mega-Mergers Leave Bondholders Counting Their Losses," *Los Angeles Times*, November 9, 1988.

tax shield
Because corporate interest payments are deducted from corporate taxable income, this income is shielded from corporate taxes.

then this interest is a **tax shield**—a tax deduction that reduces taxable corporate income, thus enabling more of the company's cash flow to reach investors. Instead of $66 million, investors receive a total of $20 million + $52.8 million = $72.8 million, the extra $6.8 million being the taxes that were not paid on the money distributed as interest: 0.34($20) = $6.8.

If the company is unlevered, an investor who owns 1 percent of the stock receives $660,000. If the company is levered, this investor can get an unlevered position by buying 1 percent of the bonds and 1 percent of the

TABLE 8–8   The Effect of Leverage on Cash Flow

Unlevered Company (millions of dollars)		Levered Company (millions of dollars)	
Gross income	$100	Gross income	$100.0
Interest	0	Interest	20.0
Taxable income	$100	Taxable income	$ 80.0
Taxes at rate of 0.34	34	Taxes at rate of 0.34	27.2
Dividends	$ 66	Dividends	$ 52.8
Cash flow (dividends + interest)	$ 66	Cash flow (dividends + interest)	$ 72.8

stock, and receive $728,000. Because the cash flow is higher, the company has a higher total market value (debt plus equity) if it is levered. (There are limits, of course; interest payments in excess of income do not reduce taxes and may cause bankruptcy.) Investment Example 8-2 tells how leveraged buyouts are often motivated by the tax advantages of debt.

There are several lessons for investors in this discussion. Despite the ingrained aversion that many investors have to debt, corporate borrowing can benefit shareholders by increasing the after-tax cash flow. High debt/equity ratios do create leverage, making a firm's profits more volatile, but shareholders made queasy by this volatility can undo the leverage by buying debt as well as equity. On the other hand, shareholders interested in volatility need not restrict their attention to companies with lots of debt; they can create homemade leverage by borrowing money to buy stock in companies with little debt.

SUMMARY

Many investors use the dividend-price or earnings-price ratio to estimate a stock's rate of return. The dividend-price ratio ignores the fact that retaining earnings will increase future dividends; the earnings-price ratio implicitly assumes that the profit rate on retained earnings is equal to the shareholders' required rate of return. The price-earnings ratio is the inverse of the earnings-price ratio, and it, too, is used to gauge whether stocks are cheap or expensive. In theory, the P/E is positively related to growth and negatively related to shareholders' required return, two good reasons why a stock with a low P/E is not necessarily a bargain and one with a high P/E is not necessarily overpriced. In addition, the P/E ratio compares the stock's price to current reported earnings, while the price itself depends on anticipated future dividends and earnings. It is not irrational for a company with unreliable accounting or a temporary earnings surge to have a relatively low *P/E*.

For a given level of current dividends and shareholders' required return, the faster a company's dividends grow, the more valuable is its stock. Yet, the pursuit of growth stocks is often unrewarding. Growth *per se* is not valuable. A company that reduces current dividends in order to increase future dividends always increases its growth rate, but only benefits shareholders if the return on its retained earnings exceeds shareholders' required return. A company that absorbs a firm with a lower *P/E* ratio creates earnings growth but does not benefit shareholders unless the acquisition is worth more than its cost, perhaps because of economies of scale or other savings. Too often, hopeful investors extrapolate observed short-term earnings growth into predictions of permanently rapid growth. The regression toward the mean teaches us that exceptional performance usually deteriorates to merely above average.

If a firm earns a rate of return on its investments just equal to the rate of return required by shareholders (*ROE* = *R*), it is immaterial whether its earnings are reinvested or paid out as dividends, the earnings-price ratio gives a quick calculation of shareholders' return *R*, and the market value of the company is equal to the replacement cost of its assets. If, on the other hand, the firm earns a higher rate of return on its investments than is required by shareholders, then the earnings-price ratio understates the shareholders' anticipated return, the firm's *q* exceeds 1, and a reinvested dollar is more valuable to shareholders than dividends. The opposite is true when the firm's profit rate is less than the shareholders' required return.

The conservation-of-value principle says that the value of the whole is equal to the value of its parts. Mergers, breakups, stock splits, and stock dividends that do not affect the aggregate cash flow do not help or hurt shareholders. Except for tax consequences, shareholders do not gain or lose wealth from the disbursement of cash through a dividend or stock repurchase, or from the raising of funds by cutting dividends or selling additional shares.

Corporate borrowing creates leverage, but conservation of value (in the form of the Modigliani-Miller theorem) implies that the value of the firm does not depend on how the cash flow is split between debt and equity. The most important exception is that debt is a tax shield that increases the firm's after-tax cash flow.

EXERCISES

1. A company has a 20 percent return on equity, a 50 percent plow-back rate, and now earns \$4 a share. Use the present-value equation, $P = D/(R - g)$, where $g = (ROE)$(plow-back rate), to calculate the dividend-price ratio, the earnings-price ratio, and the price-earnings ratio when the shareholders' required return is each of the following:

a. 20 percent.

b. 14 percent.

Now redo parts (a) and (b), assuming that the company increases its plow-back rate to 60 per-cent. Explain why this increase in the plow-back rate does or does not affect the price-earnings ratio.

2. IBI stock is selling for \$70 a share. The company has \$35 in assets per share and consistently earns a 20 percent return on its assets. This coming year, it is expected to earn an after-tax profit of \$7 a share and to pay a dividend of \$3.50 per share. Analyst 1 calculates the stockholders' return as \$3.50/\$70 = 0.05 (or 5 percent). Analyst 2 calculates the stockholders' return as \$7/\$70 = 0.10 (or 10 percent). Analyst

TABLE 8–A

Year	Year-End Price	Dividend	Earnings	P/E Ratio
1977	$ 831.17	$45.84	$ 89.10	9.3
1978	805.01	48.52	112.79	7.1
1979	838.74	50.98	124.46	6.7
1980	963.99	54.36	121.86	7.9
1981	875.00	56.22	113.71	7.7
1982	1046.54	54.14	9.15	114.4

3 argues that the stockholders' return must equal the firm's profit rate of 20 percent. Explain and evaluate the logic behind each analyst's calculation. If you had to make a rough estimate of the shareholders' return using the data, what would your estimate be?

3. What is the value of q for the firm in Exercise 2? If IBI were to reduce its dividend by ten cents a share and use these additional retained earnings to expand its operations, would you predict that this action will raise or lower the price of its stock? Explain your reasoning.

4. Why do the stocks of financially shaky companies tend to sell at relatively low P/E ratios? Shouldn't these stocks command a risk premium?

5. Use logic, not numbers, to provide a rational explanation for this 1988 observation by a newspaper columnist:

> [E]ven though IBM sells far more computers in a year than Apple—far more than all its small competitors combined—the stock market gives Apple shares a price that, proportionate to the profits of the company, is twice as high as IBM's stock price. And it gives Microsoft, the software leader, a price three times as high.[28]

6. Some argue that, because shareholders own the firm, the value of their stock should equal the present value of the firm's current and future profits. Explain why this would be double counting, which exaggerates the value of shareholder stock. (You may find an example helpful.)

7. Some annual data on the Dow Jones 30 Industrials are shown in Table 8–A. Is there any conceivable explanation for the 1982 jump in the P/E ratio from 7.7 to 114.4, other than mindless speculation?

8. A September 1986 article entitled "This Time, the Great Crash is More likely to Happen in Japan Than Here," included the observation, "Price-earnings ratios are breathtaking at 50 or better."[29] Why are P/E ratios of 50 breathtaking? At the time, long-term bond rates in Japan were 5 percent; add a 5 percent risk premium to get a 10 percent required return. For a P/E ratio of 50, what are the necessary values of the rate of return on equity and the growth rate in the constant-growth model if the payout ratio is 50 percent? if it is 25 percent?

9. Benjamin Graham made the following observation:

> Long experience has taught investors to be somewhat mistrustful of the benefits claimed to accrue to them from retained and reinvested earnings. In very many cases, a large accumulated surplus failed not only to produce a comparable increase in the earnings and dividends, but even to assure the continuance of the previously established rate of disbursement.[30]

Under what circumstances are retained earnings of benefit to shareholders?

10. To gauge the percentage of stocks that are "overpriced," the American Association of Individual Investors sees how many have P/E ratios larger than $1/$(long-term risk-free interest rate $+ 5$ percent). For instance, on April 29, 1983, the long-term interest rate was 10.39 percent and $1/(0.1039 + 0.05) = 6.5$, and the association found that "93% of stocks have P/Es of more than 6.5 and are thus overpriced."[31] Explain the logic of this criterion and any possible pitfalls.

11. Explain the logic underlying these empirical observations by William H. Pike, a portfolio manager with Fidelity Management Research of Boston:

> Companies with a high return on equity generally have higher *P-Es* [price-earnings ratios] than companies with a low return on equity . . . Regarding interest rates, *P-Es* of most stocks tend to be low when interest rates are high . . . When interest rates are low, *P-Es* tend to be relatively high . . . While these observations are generally true, they are not always so.[32]

12. Explain and evaluate this September 1986 analysis (the S&P 500 closed the previous day at 234.93):

> Long-term Treasury bond rates now are running about 8% . . . let's assume that long Treasuries will be at 8% to 8.5% by mid-1987.
>
> The stock market has to compete with alternatives in the bond market. Thus, it's not surprising that there's a close connection between bond yields and P/E ratios on stocks.
>
> The P/E ratio implied by our interest rate guess, (12 to 12.5 times earnings), when combined with an earnings estimate [for the S&P 500] of $17.50 for next year, suggests that present stock prices are fairly fully priced.[33]

13. Of those major-league baseball teams that win more than 100 out of 162 games in a season, 90 percent win fewer games the following season.[34] How would you explain this statistical pattern?

14. In 1972 Xerox's market value was $10.5 billion greater than its book value; ten years later, its market value was $0.5 billion less than book value. In which period do you think its return on equity was larger than the shareholder's required return, and in which period less?

15. A 1985 article on John Neff, a highly respected managing partner of Wellington Management Company, gave the following example of market irrationality:

> Neff cites the example of two companies, one expected to grow at 8% and the other expected to grow at 15%. Both have the same total return—because an 8 percent grower typically pays a [dividend] yield of 7% while the 15 percent grower pays little or no yield. Yet the fast grower usually sells at a much higher [price-earnings] multiple. "Now does that make sense?" asks Neff with exasperation. "The market gives away yield. It's just damn stupid."[35]

To investigate the rationality of such data, consider the three companies described in Table 8–B. For each firm, use the constant-growth model to determine the plow-back rate, the growth rate, the price (assuming a 15 percent required return), the dividend yield, and the price-earnings ratio. Why are the price-earnings ratios higher for the low-yield, high-growth stock than for the high-yield, low-growth stock? What are the shareholder rates of return on these three companies? In 1985, capital gains were taxed at 40 percent of the tax rate on dividends; would this differential tax treatment make the first or second company more attractive to individual investors?

16. A prominent investment advisor recommends that investors gauge a stock's attractiveness by calculating the "value ratio": the

TABLE 8–B

Firm	Earnings per Share	Dividends per Share	Return on Equity (percent)
1	$10	$6	20
2	10	3	20
3	10	6	35

company's projected growth rate divided by the current price-earnings ratio. For example, a company with a 20 percent growth rate that is selling for ten times earnings would have a value ratio of 2, "a very attractive ratio that would make the company an immediate buy."[36] Explain the general logic of comparing the growth rate to the price-earning ratio. Then, use the constant-growth model to show a specific hypothetical example of a company with a value ratio of 2 that is not an "immediate buy."

17. As of 1989, there had been twenty-four Superbowls in professional football, and only four of the winning teams were able to repeat their feat the following year. In baseball as of 1989, only four World Series champions repeated since 1964. The 1988 Los Angeles Lakers were the first professional basketball team to repeat as NBA champion since the Boston Celtics won in 1968 and in 1969. Write a one-paragraph sports column, using regression toward the mean to explain these data.

18. Between March 1985 and March 1986, bond rates dropped by about three percentage points, while the economy muddled along, with essentially unchanged profit expectations. Do you think Tobin's q went up or down during this period? Does this change in q foretell an increase or decrease in business investment spending? Why might businesses change their investment plans even if profit expectations are unchanged?

19. Supply a logical explanation for the following observation:

Our studies of stock prices indicate that when common stock are selling at low price-earnings ratios relative to average historic earnings, the same common stocks are also selling at large discounts from book value . . .

[For example, on May 28, 1976, among the thirty Dow industrials stocks] six of the seven common stocks selling at the highest premiums above book value—Eastman Kodak, Procter and Gamble, General Electric, International Paper, DuPont, and Sears Roebuck—were also selling at the highest price-earnings ratios. Furthermore, six of the seven common stocks selling at the biggest discounts from book value—American Can, Woolworth, Westinghouse Electric, International Harvester, Chrysler and Anaconda—were selling at the lowest price-earnings ratios.[37]

20. Table 8–C on p. 282 shows annual data for 1982–87 on the number of home runs hit by Wade Boggs of the Boston Red Sox and the earnings per share for Digital Equipment, a computer maker.[38] Make rough predictions of the respective values for 1992. Explain why you did or did not use the same procedure for both predictions.

21. In 1986, a columnist bemoaned the tax breaks that make real estate more attractive than other investments:

In general, generous tax breaks for rental and owner-occupied housing have not served to make housing more affordable or to increase

TABLE 8–C

	1982	1983	1984	1985	1986	1987
Home runs hit by Wade Boggs	5	5	6	8	8	24
Earnings per share, Digital Equipment	$3.77	$2.50	$2.87	$3.18	$4.81	$8.53

the supply. Most of the value of these breaks has simply been capitalized into higher prices for land and existing structures.[39]

Is there any logical reason for high market prices to influence housing construction?

22. A 1980 article in *The Wall Street Journal* observed:

> In February, Allied sold four million shares for $216 million. It thereby saved $35 million in annual interest payments, by paying off $137 million in short-term borrowing . . . Based on Allied's annual dividend rate of $2.20 a share, the four million additional shares will cost the company $8.8 million in payouts.[40]

In 1980 corporations as a whole raised $83 billion by borrowing and only $13 billion by selling stock. Why didn't all companies reduce their interest expense by selling stock?

23. Explain the error in this reasoning:

> A company that buys any of its stock increases its earnings on the remaining shares outstanding. Over the past two years, for example, Wisconsin Electric has repurchased 1 million of its 34 million shares. Partly as a result, the stock has gone up nearly 75%.[41]

24. An investment textbook stated that, "Multistage dividend-discount models assume that, ultimately, economic forces will force the convergence of the profitability and growth rates of different firms."[42] To support this assumption, the author identified the 20 percent of firms with the highest profit rates in 1966 and the 20 percent with the lowest profit rates that same year. Fourteen years later, in 1980, the profit rates of both were more nearly average, the author commenting that "convergence . . . is apparent . . . the phenomenon is undoubtedly real." Why might the explanation be statistical rather than economic?

25. On April 30, 1985, Atlantic Richfield (Arco), the nation's sixth largest oil company, unveiled a massive restructuring plan "designed to confront what it sees as weakening oil markets:"[43] The company announced that it would repurchase $4 billion of its stock; increase its dividend by a third; sell all of its refining and marketing operations east of the Mississippi; and reduce its investment spending to about $2.8 billion annually, down from a previously budgeted $3.6 billion. The day this program was announced, Arco was the most actively traded stock on the New York Stock Exchange, and its price jumped $5.25, from $53.00 to $58.25. How could the stock price rise so much, when Arco seemed to be in so much trouble?

26. Explain why you either agree or disagree with the following reasoning:

> The price-earnings ratio has the simple virtue of indicating whether the company's shares are overpriced or underpriced . . . If the Dow Jones Industrial Average is selling with a price-earnings ratio of 12, the company with a price-earnings ratio of 8 may well be

underpriced compared to the market. But if that industry rarely sells at a price-earnings above 5, the company is probably overpriced, and it's drastically overpriced if over the last five years the average price-earnings high was 6 and the low, 3.[44]

27. A Harvard Business School professor wrote, "High growth may look good on paper—but it could destroy your stock market value."[45] How is this theoretically possible? Is it not true that a high growth stock always should be worth more than a low-growth one?
28. An investments text states, "Book and market values will probably be equal when the stock is issued, but after that, it appears that only coincidence will keep them equal at any given moment."[46] If a firm's book value is approximately equal to the replacement cost of its assets, can you think of any logical, non-coincidental reason why market value should be above, below, or equal to book value?
29. A *Washington Times* writer made the following observation:

> The money center banks are highly profitable indeed. Bankers Trust's $371.2 million 1985 profit set a record, and for the seventh year in a row the bank was able to raise its cash dividend, then send its shareholders one share of stock for each one they owned.[47]

Why does the bank's profitability have little to do with its ability to send shareholders one share of stock for each one they owned? How much are these extra shares worth to stockholders?
30. Explain why you either agree or disagree with this logic:

> Many companies use stock repurchase to increase earnings per share. For example, suppose that a company is in the following position:
>
> | net profit | $ 10 million |
> | number of shares | 1 million |

earnings per share	$ 10
price-earnings ratio	20
share price	$200

The company now repurchases 200,000 shares at $200 a share. The number of shares declines to 800,000 shares and the earnings per share increase to $12.50. Assuming the price-earnings ratio stays at 20, the share price must rise to $250.[48]

31. A 1987 article in *Harper's Magazine*, drawing parallels to 1929, argued that unproductive takeovers had helped drive stock prices "out of touch with economic reality . . . corporate investment was dead flat in January 1987, and had been for many months. Why invest in making a better widget, when funding the takeover of a widget company can make you money so much faster and easier?"[49] Why is this argument logically inconsistent?
32. A 1987 *Business Week* article was entitled "How to Double Your Shares Without Spending a Dime."[50] The secret is to buy a stock that splits two for one. What is the catch?
33. In its *Get Rich Investment Guide, Consumers Digest* discussed the fact that an investor who buys a stock ex-dividend does not receive the latest dividend:

> Obviously, one strategy is to know when the stock will go ex-dividend and buy a day or two before the cutoff. Then you can receive the dividends, and you can sell the shares as soon as you have [received the dividend].[51]

What is the flaw in this strategy?
34. Explain why you agree or disagree with the following comment:

> A fast-growing company that can generate the bulk of the funds it needs internally is of course far more desirable than one that must rely heavily on outside borrowing or on the sale of stock, which would dilute the present shareholders' equity.[52]

35. Explain the flaw in this argument:

> Here's a sneaky one: A number of major
> corporations in recent years have announced
> programs for buying their own stocks,
> especially at times when the prices of those
> stocks were depressed . . . Now, on the
> surface, an investor might think that this is a
> splendid confirmation of his own fine
> judgment; after all, if the corporation itself is
> buying its stock, it must augur great things to
> come, right? Well, maybe, but don't count on
> it. It could be a device to increase earnings
> per share. When those shares come into the
> company's treasury, there are that many
> fewer shares outstanding—so the same
> amount of earnings will produce higher
> earnings per share.[53]

36. In January 1984, Pennzoil thought it had a
deal to acquire three sevenths of Getty Oil for
$112.50 a share, but the entire company was
sold instead to Texaco for $128 a share.[54] Penn-
zoil sued Texaco and was awarded $7.5 billion
plus punitive damages. The $7.5 billion figure
was arrived at by estimating that it costs Pennzoil about $10.90 a barrel to find oil and that
three sevenths of Getty's oil reserves represented 1 billion barrels. At $10.90 a barrel, it
would have cost Pennzoil $10.9 billion to find
this oil on its own; at $112.50 a share, it would
have cost Pennzoil only $3.4 billion to acquire
three sevenths of Getty. The difference is
$10.9 − $3.4 = $7.5 billion. Imagine that you
are an economist hired by Texaco to defend
against this suit. How might you attack their
argument? (Hint: what if it costs Pennzoil $100
a barrel to find oil?)

37. Explain the error in the following explanation of stock repurchases from a best-selling
corporate-finance textbook:

> [ADC] earned $4.4 million in 1984, and 50%
> of that amount, or $2.2 million, had been
> allocated for distribution to common
> shareholders. There were 1.1 million shares

outstanding, and the market price was $20 a
share. ADC felt that it could use the $2.2
million to repurchase 100,000 of its shares
through a tender offer or could pay a cash
dividend of $2 a share.

The effect of the repurchase on the
[earnings per share (EPS)] and the market
price per share of the remaining stock can be
determined in the following way:

1. Current EPS $= \dfrac{\text{total earnings}}{\text{number of shares}} =$
   $\dfrac{\$4.4 \text{ million}}{1.1 \text{ million}} = \$4$ per share
2. P/E ratio $= \$20/\$4 = 5$
3. EPS after repurchase $= \dfrac{\$4.4 \text{ million}}{1 \text{ million}} =$
   $4.40 per share
4. Market price after repurchase $=$
   $(P/E)(EPS) = \$22$ per share

It should be noticed from this example that
investors would receive benefits of $2 per
share in any case, either in the form of a $2
cash dividend or a $2 increase in the stock
price.[55]

38. Many companies have dividend-reinvest-
ment plans that allow their shareholders to
specify that their dividends be automatically
used to purchase additional shares of stock,
either newly issued or purchased for them by
the company. The shareholders avoid brokerage fees, and the company raises some money
without paying fees to an underwriter. The
shareholders must still pay taxes on their dividends though. Carefully explain why shareholders who take advantage of a dividend-rein-
vestment plan would prefer instead that the
firm eliminate its dividend altogether and use
the money to repurchase its shares.

39. When a stock is about to declare a dividend, investors can buy the stock with the dividend or wait and buy the stock at a lower price
ex-dividend. One study divided stocks into
groups, based on the dividend yield (dividend/
price).[56] At the time of this study, the tax rate

on capital gains was 50 percent of the rate on dividends. For the lowest-dividend stocks, the dividend yield was about 1 percent, and the price ex-dividend declined by two thirds of the size of the dividend—that is, the price of a stock selling for $100 that paid a $1 dividend dropped to $99⅓ ex-dividend. For stocks paying a 5.5 percent dividend, the ex-dividend price decline was about equal to the size of the dividend. In each case, for which tax bracket would an investor be indifferent between buying the stock with dividend or ex-dividend? Would an investor in a 30 percent bracket want to buy low-dividend stocks with dividend or ex-dividend? Would the same investor want to buy high-dividend stocks with dividend or ex-dividend?

40. On March 9, 1987, Martin T. Sosnoff offered $28 a share for Caesars World. In response, the company's management proposed borrowing $1 billion in order to pay shareholders a special cash dividend of $25 a share and, in addition, giving top management 1.5 million shares of stock before the dividend and another 1.5 million shares at a later date. How would each of these three actions affect the price of Caesars World stock? Be as specific as possible.

41. William G. Campbell, president of the Hartwell and Campbell Fund, advised:

> If you took the ten best companies you could find in every industry—or not even industry, just take ten companies that you thought met your four- or five-point criteria, whatever criteria you had—and you bought them blind twenty years ago or ten years ago or five years ago or today, without any consideration of price, I will bet you my last dollar you will make more money than the man who is trying to decide when to buy and when to sell.[57]

Pretend that you are Benjamin Graham, and write a paragraph criticizing Campbell's advice.

42. Critically evaluate the following statement:

> [W]hat about stock dividends, which are theoretically used as a way of sharing profits while conserving cash? . . . As I see it, the trouble with this approach is that shares outstanding increase as a compound rate. It's a 5% stock dividend this year, but next year it's 5% of 105%, and so forth. This pattern holds down growth in earnings per share.[58]

CHAPTER 9

Measuring Profits and Managing Assets

Things are seldom what they seem
Skim milk masquerades as cream . . .
W. S. Gilbert

The preceding chapter explained the importance of earnings and assets for shareholders who are trying to determine the intrinsic value of a firm. Unfortunately, the earnings and assets reported by accountants do not always answer investor questions. Instead, accountants sometimes resemble Humpty Dumpty in Lewis Carroll's *Alice in Wonderland*, who proclaimed "When I use a word it means just what I choose it to mean—neither more nor less." Even worse, a few firms use creative accounting to mislead shareholders, by exaggerating earnings and assets.

In accounting and other matters some companies apparently consider stockholders an unwelcome nuisance. Instead of trying to maximize the value of shareholders' stock, these managers appear to be self-centered, ego-driven creatures, out to enrich themselves.

In this chapter, we will look at some subjective accounting practices, particularly during inflationary periods, and see whether stocks have been an effective hedge against inflation. We also will discuss creative accounting, asset mismanagement, and other alleged managerial misdeeds—not because such practices are typical, but because investors should be aware of the dangers.

CREATIVE ACCOUNTING

The Securities and Exchange Commission (SEC) requires that financial statements conform to **generally accepted accounting principles (GAAP)**, guidelines adopted by the *Financial Accounting Standards Board* (FASB) to encourage a general standard for reporting procedures among companies.

The FASB is an independent group, financially supported by the accounting industry, which, from time to time, publishes its opinions on accounting practices that it considers acceptable. FASB recognizes that no two situations are identical and its general guidelines allow a wide range of permissible practices.

Profit calculations might seem to be simple, mechanical drudgery—a matter of merely adding up the dollars coming in and subtracting the dollars going out. However, such myopic arithmetic ignores changes that are just around the corner and might, as a consequence, paint a misleading picture of the financial viability of a company. A very important example involves the distinction between operating and capital expenses.

Many goods are consumed very quickly—raspberries, gasoline, and cheap sandals. Others—such as a farm, automobile, or shoe factory—have long economic lives, yielding a stream of products or services for many years. For a household, the former are labeled *consumption goods,* and the latter are called *investment goods.* For businesses, accountants call quickly consumed items *operating expenses* and long-lived goods *capital expenses.* The distinction is important because operating expenses are here and gone, while capital expenses give the firm valuable assets. In recognition of this distinction, accountants record operating expenses as a current expenditure and spread capital expenses over the useful economic life of an asset.

Consider, for instance, the purchase of a $10,000 snack machine to be installed at your school. This machine will last ten years, during which time its annual revenue will be $5000 and its annual expenses (for snack foods, servicing, and so on) will be $3000. If the purchase of the machine is recorded as a $10,000 expense in the first year, the books will show an $8000 loss that year, followed by nine years of $2000 profits. Accountants reason that reporting an initial $8000 loss is misleading, because it reflects the purchase of a machine that will yield revenues over ten years, rather than just one year. So the $10,000 purchase price is spread over ten years, with the imputed annual cost of the asset called *depreciation,* a term suggesting the gradual wearing out of the machine as it is used to produce revenue. The simplest assumption made by accountants is straight-line depreciation—dividing the $10,000 cost by ten years, giving a constant annual $1000 depreciation. By this method of calculation, the annual cost is $4000 ($3000 operating expenses plus $1000 depreciation), and annual profits are a rock-steady $5000 − $4000 = $1000.

One obvious problem with the accountants' reasoning is its neglect of present value: to the accountant there is no difference between spending $10,000 on a machine that lasts ten years and spending $1000 a year for ten years. The second problem with accountants moving away from cash flow to present a "fair" picture of the firm's profitability is that fairness requires subjective judgments, which can be influenced by an all-too-human desire to please the firm that is paying the accountant's bills.

Instead of a mechanical reporting of income and expenses, there is

Generally Accepted Accounting Principles (GAAP)
Generally Accepted Accounting Principles are adopted by the independent Financial Accounting Standards Board.

latitude for creative accounting—adjusting the numbers to get the desired results. Sometimes, the adjustments are fradulent and the perpetrators are censored, fined, or sent to prison. More often, the many judgments made by accountants are well within the wide boundaries allowed by flexible, generally acceptable accounting principles. One of the most respected critics of creative accounting is Abraham Briloff, a professor of accountancy and author of numerous articles in Barron's and three books.[1]

Reporting Anticipated Revenue

Business expenditures for labor, materials, and other production expenses generally precede the sale of a product and the receipt of revenue. In some cases, such as a long-term construction project, the delay between expense and revenue may stretch over many years. Accountants reason that it is misleading to book the initial expenses and ignore the eventual revenue because this cash flow accounting would show a string of losses on what might eventually be a very lucrative project.

Instead, accountants use accrual accounting to show that the firm is engaged in profitable work, even if it has not been paid for it yet. Suppose that a firm has just completed the first year of a five-year project that is expected to cost $40 million and for which it will be reimbursed $50 million when done. The accountants can use the percentage-of-completion method, recording a $2 million profit in the first year, because they estimate that the firm has completed one-fifth of a project that is expected to produce a $10 million profit. Alternatively, they can use the cost-to-cost method, figuring that since the overall profit is 25 percent of expenses, they can prorate profits to be 25 percent of whatever costs have been incurred so far; for example, if the firm spends $20 million the first year, they show $5 million in profits. (The perverse consequence of cost-to-cost accounting is that the higher the expenses, the larger the reported profits.)

One deficiency with reporting anticipated revenue is that a dollar five years from now is not the same as a dollar today. Another problem is that anticipations may be influenced by hopes and dreams, which do not always come true.

Sterling Homex, a builder of modular housing, was a very popular company in 1971 when it reported "with pleasure and pride" a $3.3 million profit, up 60 percent from the year before. However, this profit resulted from Sterling Homex's practice of reporting revenue whenever a unit was manufactured and assigned to a specific contract, even though the company would not be paid until the housing was in place and occupancy permits issued.[2] Much of the company's anticipated revenue did not materialize; and in 1972 Sterling Homex reported a $26 million loss, defaulted on $38 million in bank loans, and petitioned for bankruptcy. Investigators subsequently found 10,000 housing modules, worth $65 million, stored in fields—only 900 of which had been paid for. A front-page article in *The Wall Street Journal* explained:

As early as 1970, it thus appears, the company's accounting policies may have overstated sales and earnings. Testimony at bankrutpcy hearings has suggested that many of the contracts Homex relied on to justify its financial reports were less than ironclad. In some cases, federal financing for module purchases couldn't be had. Or building permits were harder to get than project developers thought. Or letters of commitment to buy modules weren't made firm. Or Homex exaggerated the size of a contract. Its 1970 annual report, for example, said that the Akron (Ohio) Metropolitan Housing Authority had "purchased" 1,500 townhouse apartments. In fact, an authority spokesman says, it had bought only 1,000.[3]

Another example of the problem of reporting anticipated revenue involves a company known as Talley (later merged with General Time). In calculating its annual profits, Talley added projected sales and costs for the coming year to its current figures, and it calculated a profit margin for the total amount that was applied then to current sales. Abraham Briloff related the following example of this logic. Current revenue is $20 million, and costs are $45 million, apparently a $25 million loss. If the company projects $100 million in sales for the next year and only $27 million in costs, then total revenue for *both* years will be $120 million—with total costs for the two-year period being $72 million. The $48 million difference represents a 40 percent profit ($48/$120 = 0.40). Applying this 40 percent profit for two years to actual sales of $20 million in the current year gives a profit of 0.40($20) = $8 million. However, for there to be an $8 million profit on $20 million of revenue, costs must be $12 million: so, presto, $12 million is what is reported this year rather than the actual $45 million in costs. The $33 million discrepancy is tucked into inventories and the books magically balance, showing a $8 million profit rather than a $25 million loss. In Talley's case, an SEC complaint alleged that the profits reported twelve months before the merger with General Time were predicated on an unsupported forecast of $100 million in revenue for that year, and that the interim profits reported three months before the merger continued to use this $100 million forecast, even though only $18 million in sales had materialized during the first nine months of the year.

Deferring Costs

Another way accountants handle the timing problem of expenses preceding revenues is to defer some costs until the firm receives the revenue. Depreciation, amortization, or depletion of such long-term assets as buildings, patents, and oil wells all are intended to spread costs over a useful economic life. One complication that makes the reporting of depreciation confusing is that the tax laws allow firms to use various accelerated depreciation methods in calculating taxable income, depreciating assets faster than they really wear out. Because time is money, accelerated depreciation is profitable for firms and encourages them to invest in plant and equipment.

Businesses, consequently, keep two sets of books. One, the financial statement shown to shareholders, generally uses straight-line depreciation, which reduces reported costs and increases reported profits. The other set of books, prepared for tax purposes, uses the most rapid depreciation allowed by the IRS—thereby increasing reported costs and minimizing taxable profits.

The depreciation expenses reported to shareholders depend on accounting judgments regarding the useful economic life of assets. There is plenty of room for well-intentioned accountants to differ—and room for controversial depreciation schedules too. What, for example, is the useful economic life of a computer whose components will not wear out for decades but which might be technologically obsolete in a few years? Leasco, a company which buys computers and leases them to other businesses, depreciated its IBM SYSTEM/360 computers (the bulk of which were purchased from 1968 to 1970) over ten years (straight-line) even in the face of IBM's 1972 introduction of system/370 machines.[5]

Occidental Petroleum and some other oil companies defer the cost of unsuccessful exploration. Until prohibited by the SEC in 1974, McDonald's (and others) deferred interest expenses incurred during construction. Another commonplace example of deferred expenses is research and development (R&D) costs that are intended to yield future revenue. There is obviously considerable judgment involved in estimating when hoped-for revenues will occur and, indeed, if they will occur at all. One dramatic example is Lockheed's deferral of $418 million in R&D costs that it incurred before 1973 on the TriStar jet, whose future sales were very questionable. When the Financial Accounting Standards Board prodded Lockheed to revise its accounting policy in 1974, shareholder net worth was revised downward from $283 million to $3 million.[6]

Making Miscellaneous Adjustments

Among the other problems accountants wrestle with are long-term leases that represent committed future expenses for a company, the provision of adequate reserves for accounts receivable that may never be received, and the size of pension reserves whose adequacy depends on many unknowables—including retirement ages and the rates of return on bonds, stocks, and other investments. Slightly different assumptions here and there can easily turn a 20 percent drop in profits into a 20 percent gain.

A more general problem with accountants' books is that they generally value assets at their depreciated cost. Only when a gain is realized by the sale of an asset do accountants admit that the asset is worth more than what the firm originally paid for it. This approach may be safer than making subjective estimates of current market value, but it means the books do not reflect unrealized gains on land, buildings, precious metals, bonds, and debt. This omission makes it difficult for shareholders to value a company's stock, and it also allows management to manipulate reported profits by choosing if and when to realize gains by selling some of the company's appreciated assets. In the third quarter of 1986, Bank of America reduced its losses from $146 million to $23 million by realizing $123 million in capital gains on asset sales, including a $58 million profit on some Tokyo property acquired in 1946 for $50,000. The property had long been worth millions and was worth $58 million in 1986, whether or not Bank of America decided to sell. To the accountants, however, it wasn't worth more than $50,000 until the bank actually sold it.

A less innocent variation used by many conglomerates is to acquire a company with unrealized gains and then realize those gains in order to boost reported profits. For example, between 1961 and 1968, ITT used $1.3 billion in stock and other securities to acquire thirty companies and, using perfectly legal pooling-of-interest accounting, entered the cost on its books as $535 million—the reported book value of the acquired companies— leaving some $700 million in suppressed costs to be reported as future profits as ITT realized these unreported gains. Similarly, in 1970 ITT acquired Hartford Fire Insurance Company for $1.08 billion in securities, but it entered the cost at $485 million—Hartford's book value. A large part of the $600 million difference was due to the fact that Hartford owned stocks that were worth $716 million but were carried on its books at their $434 million cost. The realization of these unreported gains was enough to boost ITT's reported profits by $50 million a year for the next five years.[7]

A fradulent variation is for a company to set up dummy corporations, or *shells*, to buy its assets at inflated prices. Perhaps the company even lends the shells money to buy the assets. Similarly, associated firms may arrange to trade assets back and forth among themselves at ever inflated prices, reporting an unending string of paper profits.

As businesses have become more international, an issue of increasing importance is the valuation of foreign currency and other assets when exchange rates fluctuate. These profits (or losses) are invariably unexpected, evaporate if exchange rates move in the other direction, and distort the books if lumped in with normal operating profits. Further, the foreign currency, raw materials, and equipment that represent necessary components of a firm's foreign operations must be replaced at current prices rather than original cost. For an example of the importance of how such assets are valued, in the first half of 1974 Marathon Oil reported a doubling of profits, from $1.40 to $2.79 a share. Of this $1.36 increase, however, 47 cents was foreign–currency gains, 30 cents was inventory profits, and 49 cents was the result of a lower tax rate. Only 10 cents was operating profits.[8]

In the Shareholders' Best Interests?

All firms recognize that there is considerable flexibility in generally accepted accounting principles, and many companies believe that creative account-

292

INVESTMENT
EXAMPLE
9–1

NATIONAL STUDENT MARKETING

Cortes Wesley Randell, a personable 29-year-old, founded National Student Marketing Corporation (NSMC) in 1965, a private company that was to use a network of college students to distribute product samples, conduct market research, and sell posters, records, and similar products. By 1968 NSMC had 600 campus representatives and a million dollars in sales and was ready to sell stock to the public. The stock was initially offered at $6 a share on April 24, 1968, traded at $14 that same day and at $30 six weeks later. Soon after, the company's lawyers (Covington and Burling) and its accountants (Arthur Anderson and Company) both resigned mysteriously; but the stock's price kept rising, hitting a 1968 high of $82 a share, nearly fourteen times the initial offering price.

With a price-earnings (P/E) ratio of 100-to-1, NSMC was able to create an illusion of earnings growth by acquiring a succession of 22 relatively low P/E companies in two years. Randell also cultivated the appearance of financial success by buying a castle, a jet, and a 55-foot yacht for entertaining security analysts. An expensive set of golf clubs was prominently positioned outside Randell's office, but apparently used only by the custodial staff to hit wadded up paper. Analyst enthusiasm was also encouraged by gifts of stock. Nine days after Kidder Peabody published a positive report on NSMC, it received 4,000 shares, worth half a million dollars, ostensibly a finder's fee for suggesting that NSMC acquire a company that made college rings.

Randell boasted that earnings would triple in 1969 and triple again in 1970, but had to use increasingly dubious accounting methods to meet these projections. In 1969 NSMC showed a $3 million profit by deferring a half million dollars in expenses and anticipating $7 million in income, of which half was from target companies that hadn't yet been acquired. The stock's price hit $144 per share in December 1969. At the February 1970 *Institutional Investor* conference of 2000 top money managers, National Student Marketing was selected as the favorite stock for the coming year. A few days later, Randell abruptly resigned as president and, a week after that, NSMC reported a first-quarter loss of $1.5 million. The stock plunged to $50 a share and in July to $3½. Four people eventually went to prison including Randell, who served eight months for stock fraud, and a partner of NSMC's accounting firm, who was sentenced to sixty days for submitting misleading financial statements to the SEC.

This example is based on John Brooks, *The Go-Go Years,* New York: Ballantine, 1973; and Rush Loving, Jr., "How Cortes Randell Drained the Fountain of Youth," *Fortune,* April 1970, pp. 94-97.

ing can be used to bolster stock prices, at least temporarily. Some corporations even argue that such deception is really in the best interests of shareholders, whose short-sighted perspective causes an overreaction to bad news. Thus some firms with extraordinary profits in good years purposely delay their reporting, setting aside a reserve that can be used to offset losses in bad years. Other companies adjust the timing of year-end expenses and income to smooth out profits and reassure nervous investors, as illustrated by this example:

> *Orders came down from above to generate as many expenses as possible before the fiscal year-end. The year had been a good one but bad times were on the horizon. The obedient manager immediately purchased more than $10 million in postage metering—charged off as an expense when purchased even though it wouldn't be consumed for years, if not decades.*[9]

It is hard to see how this company benefited from stockpiling postage metering, an investment guaranteed to earn a 0 percent return, and it is even harder to see how investors benefit from misinformation. When the truth comes out, the surprise is usually expensive:

> *In the go-go market of 1967–68, two computer leasing firms, Data Processing & Financial General and Levin-Townsend, both traded at 40 times earnings, almost triple the average ratio of the S&P 500, thanks to their rapidly growing earnings produced solely by clever accounting. When more conservative reporting policies were adopted, their earnings disappeared entirely, and both dropped 90 percent from their highs. And University Computing, a Dallas-based computer service company of the era, topped even this, trading as high as 118 times accounting-manufactured earnings before plummeting 98 percent.*[10]

Investment Example 9-1 tells of another expensive surprise.

STOCK PRICES AND ACCOUNTING PRACTICES DURING INFLATION

Inflation is a persistent, continuing increase in the prices of goods and services. Logically, an investor ought to find protection from such inflation by stocking up on goods and services that are rising in price. But it is impossible to stockpile some things, such as medical services, and it is expensive to store others, such as automobiles. Some assets are beyond the budgets of most individual investors—Iowa farmland, Arizona shopping centers, and Chicago skyscrapers.

inflation
Inflation is a persistent, continuing increase in the prices of goods and services, often measured by the change in the Consumer Price Index (CPI).

Stock Investment as a Hedge Against Inflation

One way to invest in real assets that are presumably appreciating with inflation is to buy stock in companies that own land, buildings, and other tangible assets. To analyze the effect of inflation on stock prices, consider the dividend discount model:

$$P = \frac{D}{R - g}$$

TABLE 9–1 Inflation and Stock Prices, 1900–1987

Index Name	1900 Index	1987 Index	1987 Price Index Divided by 1900 Price Index	Average Annual Price Increase, 1900–1987 (percent)
S&P 500 Stock Price Index	6	320	53.3	4.7
Consumer Price Index	25	340	13.6	3.0

First, assume that with no inflation $D = \$1$, $R = 0.10$, and $g = 0.05$, so that

$$P = \frac{\$1}{(0.10 - 0.05)}$$
$$= \$20.$$

The 10 percent annual return is half current dividend and half capital gain, as the following shows:

$$R = \frac{D}{P} + g$$
$$= 0.05 + 0.05$$
$$= 0.10$$

If a 5 percent inflation raises both the shareholders' required return and the rate of growth of dividends and earnings by 5 percent, $R - g$ is constant and so is the current value of the stock.

$$P = \frac{\$1}{(0.15 - 0.10)}$$
$$= \$20$$

As for the future value, because stock prices grow at the same rate as dividends, the rate of growth of stock prices increases by 5 percent to 10 percent annually too, increasing the shareholders' annual nominal return by 5 percent and thereby keeping the real return at 10 percent.

Shareholders are fully protected from an x percent inflation that increases both the nominal required return and dividend growth rate by x percent.

In practice, required returns and dividend growth do not change in lockstep with inflation, and neither do stock prices. In the long run, stock prices have increased faster than the prices of consumer goods. From 1900 to 1987, the Consumer Price Index increased by a factor of 13.6 while the S&P 500 stock index increased by a factor of 52.3, as shown in Table 9–1.

FIGURE 9–1 Nominal and real S&P 500 stock price indexes, 1950–1987

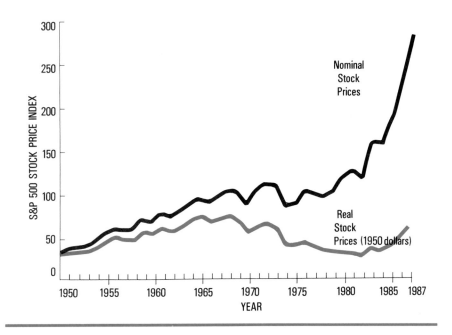

If we add in dividends, investors have averaged well over a 5 percent real return from stocks in the long run.

In the short run, however, increases in the rate of inflation have not increased stock prices reliably. For instance, compare the high-inflation 1970s with the low-inflation 1960s. In each decade, real output increased by more than 30 percent. Between 1960 and 1969, consumer prices rose by 25 percent, and stock prices nearly doubled. Between 1969 and 1979, in contrast, consumer prices doubled, and stock prices were virtually unchanged, causing the real value of stocks to fall by 50 percent! Figure 9–1 shows the nominal value of the S&P 500 and the real value, adjusted for inflation. You can see the large drop in real prices in the 1970s. Despite the impressive increase in stock prices in the 1980s, the real value of the S&P 500 in 1987 still had not reached the level of the late 1960s.

Many investors who suffered through the inflationary 1970s drew the understandable conclusion that inflation must be bad for the stock market. However, the data do not support this simple belief any better than the opposite, equally simple, belief that inflation is always good for the market. Figure 9–2 is a scatter diagram of the rate of inflation and the return on stocks (dividend plus capital gain) each year from 1926 to 1987. As the figure shows, there is no relationship at all between the annual inflation

FIGURE 9–2 Stock returns and inflation, 1926–1987. (*Source:* Gary Smith, *Statistical Reasoning*, ed 2. Copyright © 1988 by Allyn and Bacon. Reprinted with permission.)

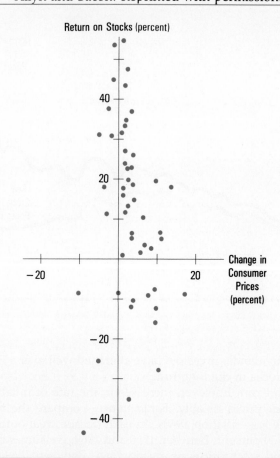

rate and stock returns. Whether it is a year of deflation or double-digit inflation does not seem to affect the stock market's chances of collapse or boom.

Although the prices of real assets increase during inflations, the prices of common stock, which represent ownership of tangible corporate assets, don't increase consistently with inflation. One explanation is that stockholders are not buying assets but rather the profits that flow from these assets, and corporate after-tax profits do not always keep up with prices during inflations.

Accounting for Inflation

After-tax corporate profits often suffer during inflations because corporate taxes are levied on profits calculated according to more or less standard accounting principles, and some of these principles do not make much sense during inflations. For instance, the cost of a machine that can be used for ten years is spread over ten years, with an annual depreciation expense that is intended to show the cost of the capital being used to produce output. In theory, depreciation expenses reflect current costs—what it costs to replace machines as they wear out. In practice, however, firms calculate their capital expenses each year of the basis of the original cost of plant and equipment, which is like figuring labor costs on the basis of wage rates ten or twenty years ago. The result is that inflation causes capital costs to be understated and profits to be overstated, so that businesses, particularly those with lots of old capital pay relatively more taxes.

Inventory accounting methods can also overstate profits during inflations. Businesses keep inventories of raw materials, intermediate products, and final goods that are finished but not yet sold. Though identical, these goods were purchased or produced at different times and at different costs. Which cost should be used in figuring profits? Before the inflationary 1970s, virtually every U.S. company used *FIFO (first in, first out) accounting*, calculating inventory costs as the cost of the good purchased or produced earliest and still in inventory—an accounting convention that, during inflations, understates current production costs and overstates profits. In the 1970s, many firms switched to *LIFO (Last In, First Out) accounting*, a sensible alternative that uses the cost of the item most recently purchased or produced to establish inventory costs. The difference between costs calculated by the LIFO and the FIFO approaches is inventory profit.

Suppose that at the beginning of the year a firm purchases enough raw material to sustain the coming year's production and that the cost of these materials was $1 million. By the end of the year, a 20 percent inflation has increased the cost of these materials to $1.2 million. With FIFO accounting, the cost of materials is calculated to be $1 million, which is what the firm actually paid; with LIFO, the reported cost is $1.2 million. The $200,000 difference is an inventory profit, reflecting the fact that the firm bought materials for $1 million that would now be worth $1.2 million. The problem is that the firm has used the materials in production and now must replace them for $1.2 million. Even worse, firms that use FIFO accounting pay taxes on their inventory profits (those that use LIFO accounting do not). The U.S. government estimates that reported corporate profits would have been $50 billion lower in 1979 (a year of 11.3 percent inflation) if all firms had been using LIFO.

The failure to adjust profit calculations for inflation raises the effective tax rate on inflation-adjusted profits (with inventory profits omitted and depreciation expenses calculated on the basis of replacement rather than original cost). Corporate taxes averaged between 40 percent and 50 percent of profits in the early 1960s, when there was little inflation, but in 1979 corporate taxes were about 40 percent of reported profits and 60 percent of inflation-adjusted profits.

On the other hand, conventionally measured profits are misleadingly *low* during inflations to the extent that they ignore capital gains on some corporate assets and liabilities. Just as households who buy a house and borrow long term at fixed interest rates profit from an inflation, so do corporations that borrow to acquire plant and equipment. Yet, such gains are not included in reported profits unless these gains are realized by the firm's sale of its real-estate holdings or retirement of its debt.

The effects of accounting practices on profits and taxes vary, of course, from firm to firm. Two Stanford professors, John Shoven and Jeremy Bulow, estimated that, with a full inflation adjustment for depreciation, inventories, and debt, General Motors' taxable income in 1974 (a year of 11 percent inflation) would have been only $410 million, rather than the $950 million reported, because the company had little debt. For American Telephone and Telegraph (AT&T) which had lots of debt, taxable income would have increased from $3.2 billion to $8.2 billion. Inflation with imperfectly calculated profits and taxes hurt General Motors' shareholders, but it benefited AT&T stockholders.

Did the Stock Market Make a Mistake?

The Council of Economic Advisors has adjusted aggregate corporate-profit data for depreciation, inventory profits, and capital gains on debt and found, in the aggregate, no systematic deterioration during inflation.[11] Inflation-adjusted profits did decline during the recessions in 1969–70 and 1974–75, but they were higher in 1979, for instance, than in the low-inflation late 1950s and early 1960s. Similarly, Martin Feldstein and Lawrence Summers, two Harvard professors, found that it was recession, not inflation, that depressed profits in the 1970s.[12] In addition, despite the fact that financial institutions, publishing houses, and service companies have relatively little capital to distort their earnings during inflationary times, their stocks also fared poorly in the 1970s—suggesting that the relatively weak stock market cannot be explained solely by inflation-distorted earnings.[13]

A study by Franco Modigliani and Richard Cohn of M.I.T. also concluded that corporate profits adjusted for depreciation, inventory profits, and capital gains on debt kept up with inflation during the 1980s.[14] In the spring of 1979 they made the provocative argument that "had equity values been rationally appraised, they would have been not far from twice as high as they then were."[15] They argued that this incredible undervaluation was due to two distinct errors by investors. The first error was neglect of the capital gains on corporate debt as interest rates rose: the second error was that investors compared price-earnings (P/E) ratios calculated with real, inflation-adjusted earnings to nominal rather than to real interest rates.

We have already discussed the first error. The second can be explained with the constant-growth model,

$$P = \frac{D}{R - g}$$

using nominal values for D, R, and g. Earlier in this chapter, we saw that an x percent inflation that raises both the shareholders' nominal required return, R, and the nominal growth rate, g, by x percent does not affect the current value of stock, but it does increase the rate of growth of stock prices by x percent. Because current prices and earnings are unchanged, so is their P/E ratio; and because prices and earnings both grow by x percent, future P/E ratios are unchanged, too, even while nominal (but not real) interest rates are rising.

Modigliani and Cohn argued that investors apparently believe that the earnings-price ratio is an estimate of the stockholders' nominal rate of return and so should move with nominal interest rates. Instead, the earnings-price ratio should be interpreted as a real return, which should not be affected by an increase in inflation that leaves real interest rates (and real growth rates) roughly constant.

A telling example of this error is provided by Benjamin Graham, who recommended a maximum P/E ratio of 15 in the early 1960s when the nominal interest rates on long-term, high-grade corporate bonds were around 4½ percent, but who halved his maximum P/E ratio to 8 in 1974 when nominal corporate bond rates moved above 9 percent.[16] Similarly, Modigliani and Cohn reported that estimates of five-year earnings growth rates from Value Line and E. F. Hutton security analysts showed "only a modest decline in the anticipated real growth rate of earnings . . . In particular, there was essentially no change from the end of 1973 to the end of 1978, a period during which the average price-earnings ratio for the firms in our sample declined 36 percent."[17] Figures 8–1 and 8–2 in Chapter 8 confirm that price-earnings ratios fell as earnings-price ratios rose with nominal interst rates in the 1970s.

A contrary argument, offered by Richard Kopcke, of the Federal Reserve Bank of Boston, is that the profit data discussed so far neglect the fact that inflation may inflict losses on corporate pension plans. Retirement pay is commonly based on an employee's salary during the five years before retirement, and a firm prepares for this future expense by setting aside funds that are invested in stocks and bonds. To the extent a firm's pension reserves are invested in fixed-income assets, an unexpected inflation forces the firm to set aside more money, money that ultimately comes out of stockholder dividends. Kopcke argues that, since aggregate pension re-

FIGURE 9–3   Real dividends for the S&P 500, 1950–1987

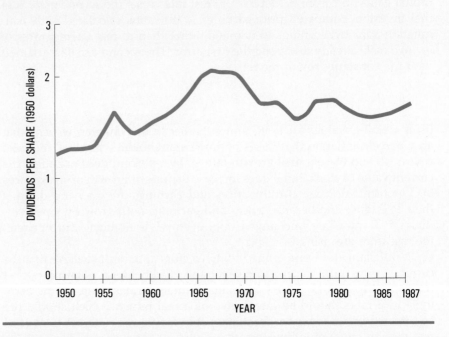

serves are about the same magnitude as aggregate corporate debt, the capital losses on the first roughly offset the capital gains on the second, leaving no net advantage to corporations.[18]

The establishment of adequate pension reserves is a very difficult challenge, and the calculation of inflation-adjusted profits, in general, is full of ambiguities. A more straightforward approach for valuing stock during inflation is to recognize that what investors are buying is not some accountant's reckoning of profits, but the actual cash flow, the dividends, that stocks provide. Figure 9–3 shows real dividends per share for the S&P 500 from 1950 to 1987. After growing at a 3.4 percent annual rate from 1950 to 1966, real dividends peaked in 1966 and declined sharply in the early 1970s. In 1987, real dividends were still below their level of twenty-one years earlier. The real rate of growth of dividends not only slowed, but turned negative.

Also, stock prices anticipate the future, and during inflations investors may well expect the Federal Reserve to tighten its monetary policy—driving interest rates up and the economy down—in order to wring inflation out of the economy. When investors act on such fears, the stock market is a casualty, too, with depressed stock prices during inflations a reflection of the possible high-interest recession just around the corner. While the 1960s were virtually recession-free, the United States has had four recessions since 1969, including the two worst since the Great Depression in the 1930s. A variation of this argument is that investors in the 1970s, while not certain that inflation is the prelude to recession, were unaccustomed to double-digit inflation and had an all-too-human fear of the unknown. Consequently, inflation made stocks riskier and, therefore, less attractive to nervous investors.

In general, investors try to peer into the distant future to anticipate not only inflation, but also interest rates and output. One year, investors might anticipate low inflation with an improving economy and low interest rates. Another year, they might foresee low inflation with a sluggish economy and high interest rates. As a consequence, there is no dependable, simple relationship between stock prices and inflation.

THE MANAGEMENT OF CORPORATE ASSETS

Incorporation allows the ownership of enormous businesses to be shared by millions of relatively small investors. However, if shareholders are a diffuse, diverse group with power so diluted that it is meaningless, corporate executives may be able to slight shareholder interests. When shareholders are scattered with no convenient way of communicating with each other and with little knowledge (other than through management announcements) of a company's actions, let alone foregone opportunities, it is not surprising if they exercise little control over management.

The Separation of Management and Ownership

An early study found that by 1929 nearly half of the 200 largest U.S. nonfinancial corporations were management controlled, with no identifiable group of shareholders owning more than 20 percent of the stock or otherwise exhibiting discernible outside control over management.[19] A later study raised this figure to 85 percent by 1963.[20] One of the authors of the initial study made the cynical, but no doubt correct, observation that "an overwhelming majority of [stockholders] are 'little people' . . . who know little or nothing about corporate activities, whose advice is not sought in running the corporation and probably would be worth little if it were given."[21]

John Kenneth Galbraith has done much to popularize the view that shareholders have little influence over the managers of large corporations.[22] In theory, at the annual meetings shareholders can reject management decisions and impose their own will. But, in practice, the vast majority of shareholders simply cash their dividend checks and acquiesce to all but the most blatant lootings of their company. At annual meetings, shareholders are permitted to ratify the company's auditors and board of directors and to approve a few general management decisions; most stockholders give management their proxy to vote as it sees fit. A handful of proposals from dissident shareholders may be considered, but are almost always overwhelmingly rejected—10 percent support is considered a moral victory. Only when a well-financed shareholder acquires a significant block of stock, say 10 percent of the outstanding shares, does management become alarmed by the prospect of shareholder votes at annual meetings.

Some people argue that since a firm raises little, if any, funds through the sale of new shares, it need not concern itself with the price of the company's stock. As long as the price does not sag enough to unite lethargic shareholders in mutiny, management is free to do as it wishes. Corporate executives who are insulated from shareholder accountability can live like royalty, receiving astounding salaries and benefits, no matter how poorly the company does. Many such executives are driven by personal objectives of power and associated prestige, priorities that lead them to sacrifice profits for the sake of growth.[23] Empire builders use expensive advertising campaigns and low prices to boost sales; construct new facilities by rote; and acquire other companies feverishly, spending whatever funds are available while showing scant regard for profit margins and the effects on share prices.

One study that supports these allegations found that owner-controlled firms have profit rates nearly double those of management-controlled companies.[24] Similarly, a survey of fifty years of research on mergers found that "no one who has undertaken a major empirical study of mergers has concluded that mergers are profitable . . . A host of researchers working at different points in time and utilizing different analytic techniques and data, have but one major difference: whether mergers have a neutral or negative impact on profitability."[25]

These criticisms of insulated management have some merit, but their conclusions are exaggerated. There are compelling reasons why stock prices should influence management decisions, and there is persuasive evidence that they do. Many top executives have part of their wealth invested in company stock, and much of their compensation is in the form of stock options and other incentive plans whose value hinges on the price of the company's stock. Also, a high stock price makes it easier to take over other firms, and, conversely, a low stock price encourages other firms to buy up enough shares to take control of the company and replace its management. These are good reasons why even the most selfish executive is likely to keep any eye on stock prices.

Indeed, some seemingly illogical actions by management, such as the use of FIFO rather than LIFO accounting, appear motivated by a zealous concern for stock prices. Whitman and Shubik observe:

> *It is well known that privately held corporations . . . usually attempt to report earnings in a manner that minimizes income taxes—an important consideration to these businessmen in realizing wealth-creation goals. Publicly held*

corporations, on the other hand, frequently attempt to report the best earnings possible . . . because the ability to report favorable current earnings may have the most favorable impact on stock prices and in this instance provides the greatest potential for wealth creation.[26]

The Role of the Board of Directors

A corporation's board of directors is supposed to provide some oversight on behalf of shareholders; but because most directors are handpicked by a company's chief executive officer (with passive approval by shareholders), they often, as *Business Week* put it, "operate in the traditional mode: as a rubber stamp for management."[27] A former SEC commissioner, A. A. Sommer, estimated that "in 95 percent to 99 percent of all cases, management is basically self-perpetuating. Even when the chief executive is retiring, he generally picks his own successor, not the board. The board will go along with the CEO unless he's really off the wall."[28] Peter Drucker joked that the only way to get rid of an incompetent chief executive "is a heart attack. But it usually strikes the wrong person. It's not reliable."[29]

The Question of Independence Roughly half of the directors of firms nationwide are *insiders*, members of senior management. Of the other half, *Business Week* remarked that "there are a lot of so-called outside directors who are not all that independent: They are close friends of the chief executive, or perhaps the company's banker, lawyer, or management consultant."[30] The president of the National Association of Corporate Executives acknowledged in 1986 that many directors are "put on boards for the wrong reason—name recognition. Gerald Ford's not a businessman."[31] Yet, the former President sat on at least eleven boards in 1986.

Even those outside directors who are reasonably independent and well-informed are not eager to make enemies by being troublemakers. Victor H. Palmieri puts it more graphically, "No one likes to be the skunk at the garden party. One does not make friends and influence people in the boardroom or elsewhere by raising hard questions that create embarrassment or discomfort for management."[32] Carl Icahn, a troublemaking corporate raider, related his impression of one company's board meetings:

> I was on the board of one company and really it's a frightening thing . . . . They used to have board meetings at 8 in the morning out in Cleveland. Here's what goes on. Literally, half the board is dozing off. The other half is reading The Wall Street Journal. And then they put slides up a lot and nobody can understand the slides and when it gets dark they all doze off.
>
> The CEO at that time was a very intimidating sort of guy. A big, tall guy, strong personality, and he was in control of that board. I mean nobody would say anything.[33]

Shareholder Recourse One line of defense for shareholders is the Securities and Exchange Commission (SEC), which can institute civil and criminal proceedings against insiders who mislead shareholders or loot the company. Individual shareholders can also use class action lawsuits to recover damages. In practice, the hundreds of shareholder suits filed each year are mostly just a nuisance to companies, because the broad "business judgment" rule protects the board of directors from personal liability unless there is blatant negligence. John C. Coffee, a Columbia Law School professor, commented, "The chances of being held personally liable are about as high as the chances of getting hit by lightning when you walk across the street."[34] On the other hand, the fact that shareholders win relatively few lawsuits may be because the threat of suit effectively deters serious wrongdoing, leaving only frivolous lawsuits.

Management Strategies to Repel Takeovers

Carl Icahn has often said that "the only way you get these top executives off the golf course is when . . . a 13D [is filed]," notifying the SEC that one has acquired more than 5 percent of a company's stock. Icahn adds the punchline, "Then I sometimes think they're better off on the golf course than in the office."[35] What brings the top executives off the golf course is fear that the company will be taken over and new management brought in. The most public examples of management disregard for shareholder interests are the bitter, expensive campaigns fought by entrenched executives to repel takeover attempts and protect their jobs.

Takeover Bids Most takeovers begin with one company making a "friendly" offer to acquire another company. After some negotiation, the target company's board of directors may approve the offer and submit it to shareholders with its recommendation that it be approved. If instead the board does not approve the offer, the bidder may go to the shareholders anyway and make an "unfriendly" tender offer to buy enough of their shares to gain effective control.

When a company's stock is selling for $30 a share and an outside group offers shareholders $40 a share to gain control of the company, it is hard to see how shareholders benefit by takeover defenses that cost the company millions of dollars and keep the price at $30 or below as assets are squandered. Yet that is exactly what many managements have done.[36]

Why would an outside group pay $40 a share for stock that is selling for $30? First, the organized exchanges can easily accommodate the trading of individual shareholders, the volume of purchases needed to gain control of a company might create a demand-supply imbalance that would drive the price well above $40. Takeover attempts often begin with modest purchases on the exchanges, made surreptitiously until the 5 percent reporting threshold is reached (because news of a possible takeover would cause the price to jump upward in anticipation of higher prices yet to come). Invariably, however, these attempts at takeover end with tender offers, inviting shareholders to sell their shares to the takeover group directly, off the exchanges.

This is why the acquiring firm has to pay $40; the second question is why it is willing to do so. Takeover battles are struggles over the control of a company's assets. Under current management, the cash flow produced by these assets is valued by the stock market at $30 a share; however, the bidder believes that a new management can do better. Either the company as a whole can be run better, increasing its earnings and dividends, or parts can be spun off to other owners and uses because this corporation is worth more dead than alive. As *Barron's* said of the department-store chain Marshall Field, "the dismal management . . . makes the company far more valuable as commercial real estate (or possibly a parking lot) than a going concern."[37] Yet Marshall Field's management fiercely resisted repeated takeover attempts, including an offer of $42 a share in 1978, when its stock was selling below $20; finally, in 1982, to avoid Carl Icahn, it agreed to a merger for $30 a share.

Shark Repellents On average, takeovers give the shareholders' target companies a 30 percent gain.[38] Yet the managements of target companies often resist mightily, and the takeover defenses, called **shark repellents.** They employ in their no-holds-barred maneuvering have come to be labeled by a variety of colorful names.

Greenmail occurs when a company pays a raider to go away; for example, Goodyear paid Sir James Goldsmith nearly $100 million to drop his takeover attempt. A greenmail of sorts occurred in December 1986, when General Motors (GM) made headlines, not for designing a better car, but for ousting H. Ross Perot from its board of directors. When GM acquired Perot's Electronic Data Systems, it gave him 11.4 million shares of GM Class E stock and a seat on its board. A long-time maverick, Perot took the job seriously and began suggesting changes at GM. For instance, when he learned that GM executives get new, specially serviced cars every three months, he pointed out that they might get a more accurate impression of GM's product if they spent some time in the same cars the public was supposed to buy. Seeing GM's falling sales and plant closings, he suggested that management did not deserve large bonuses. The chairman of a pension-fund group called Perot "the best thing that happened to General Motors since Frigidaire."[39] But GM decided to get rid of Perot by paying him $100 million plus $56.50 a share for his stock, then trading at 31⅜. In return for this $400 million premium, Perot resigned from GM's board of directors and agreed to stop criticizing its management (or pay fines up to $7.5 million).

Scorched earth is another shark repellent, in which a company sells its prized assets to make the company less attractive. For instance, Pabst

shark repellents
Shark repellents are aggressive defenses used by target companies to ward off unfriendly takeovers.

greenmail
Greenmail occurs when a company pays a raider to drop a takeover attempt.

scorched earth
A scorched-earth strategy occurs whe firm resists an unf takeover by sellir prized assets.

Brewing Company used the defense when it was a company in trouble, in 1981. Its market share was shrinking, and its earnings had dropped by two-thirds over the previous five years. Its chief executive officer (CEO) described the situation as follows:

> *There was extravagance everywhere, lack of control in the sales area, people didn't have the direction they should, marketing money was being spent on brands that shouldn't have been . . . there was overcapacity at the plant level and there was a tremendous morale problem.*[40]

After a year-long fight against a variety of takeover attempts, Pabst finally drove away its suitors by selling its three best plants to another brewery. The CEO explained: "We realized we had to do something really drastic to get the thing over with. So, we sold off the crown jewels." Pabst emerged as a beaten company, close to bankruptcy. From a broader perspective, the takeover pressure did succeed in reallocating the company's assets to a more successful brewer.

In another scorched-earth example, Whittaker Corporation attempted to acquire Brunswick in 1982, primarily for its very profitable medical-products subsidiary. Brunswick sold the subsidiary to someone else, Whittaker went away, and Brunswick stock dropped from $25 to $14. Interestingly, the failed takeover traumatized Brunswick into promoting a new chief executive officer who quickly laid off redundant executives, tied management pay to performance, sold two of the three company planes, and rented out two-thirds of what he called the "big corporate palace we were in."[41] Within two years, the price of Brunswick stock was up to $70.

poison pills
Poison pills provide for exorbitant cash payments in the event of an unfriendly takeover.

Poison pills are corporate rules that provide for excessive cash payments if the firm is ever taken over. For instance, a company might specify that if any group acquires more than 20 percent of the company's stock, it will sell new shares to others at bargain prices, in effect giving away assets. **Golden parachutes** are similar in that they provide lavish severance pay to displaced executives. For example, when Allied took over Bendix, it had to pay a total of $18 million to twenty-two top executives. Herman Miller, an office-furniture company, created "silver parachutes" specifying that any employee with two years' service who is let go after a takeover will receive a full year's severance pay.

golden parachutes
Golden parachutes provide lavish severance pay to displaced executives.

Takeovers can be a wrenching experience, not only for a company's executives, but for its rank-and-file workers and the communities in which they live. Unfortunately, such dislocations sometimes are necessary economically, and takeovers in these instances are merely the catalyst that overpowers management resistance to change. The empirical evidence is that, overall, takeovers have a positive effect on corporate performance.[42]

Admittedly, some managers have devoted their lives to their companies, and many firms have long, admirable, even noble traditions that are worth preserving. There is something to be said for continuity and for the plight of managers whose shares are buffeted by economic events or stock-market speculation over which they have no control. Some dislodged managements may not deserve their fate, but some do. Shark repellents protect not only the unlucky, but also the incompetent.

There is a very persuasive alternative to shark repellents for any company that really believes that its unreasonably low market price invites an unwarranted takeover. The firm can always boost the price of its stock by repurchasing shares. Shareholders are then given the opportunity to sell at a higher price, and if the market price really is too low, the purchases will turn out to be a great investment for the company.

Dilution of Shareholder Power The limited power of diffuse, diverse shareholders may be changing as institutions come to dominate the stock market. A few institutions can band together easily and monitor management more closely, with sufficient votes in hand to enforce their opinion. So far, such monitoring has largely been restricted to institutional support for the takeover offers of corporate raiders. Institutions could exert a more positive, and less drastic, influence on companies by insisting on aggressive, neutral directors and by leading the fight against antishareholder actions by management.

Unfortunately, the takeover binge in the 1980s (and a growing management fear of institutional shareholders) prompted many managements to reduce shareholder power. Former SEC Commissioner Bevis Longstreth observed cynically, "As long as shareholder democracy is a myth, the business community seems to tolerate it. But as soon as it's got the bite of reality, the business community tries to eliminate it."[43]

Among the management-sponsored changes that shareholders approved in the 1980s are rules that stagger the terms of directors so that a majority cannot be replaced in any year, that require 75 percent or even 80 percent votes to approve mergers and other important changes, and that prohibit shareholders from calling a special meeting. In 1986 (with no takeover attempt in sight), Chase Manahattan's shareholders approved (in some cases, barely) a series of rules giving the board of directors sole authority to accept or reject a takeover bid and making it virtually impossible to remove a member of the board. Further, these rules cannot be changed or a decision of the board overruled without a 75 percent majority vote by shareholders. J. M. Smucker and American Family Corporation now give long-term shareholders ten votes per share and short-term shareholders (who have owned stock less than four years) only one vote. MCI has reduced the voting power of those investors who acquire more than 10 percent of its outstanding stock with a rule that gives every share beyond 10 percent only one one-hundredth of a vote. (Thus, for a company with 100 million shares outstanding, someone who acquires 20 million shares would have only 10 million + 10 million/100 = 10.1 million votes.) In 1987, the Supreme Court upheld an Indiana state law that keeps stockholders who hold more than 20 percent of a company's shares from voting at all, unless specifically approved by a majority of the remaining shareholders.

Figgie International used a variety of rules to entrench the conglomerate's founder, Henry E. Figgie, Jr. First, two classes of stock were created, and existing shareholders were offered a dividend of 8 cents per share to choose the second class, which has only one twentieth of a vote per share. Second, the company's retirement fund bought up much of the full-vote stock. Third, any shareholder owning more than 10 percent of the stock of either class was allowed only a one hundredth of a vote for each of the additional shares. Fourth, Henry Figgie was exempted from these restrictions, which effectively gave him 80 percent of the votes even though he owned only 10 percent of the outstanding stock.[44]

Such measures were not invented in the 1980s—since 1956, the Ford family has retained control over Ford Motor Company through its ownership of nontrading Class B shares. Nevertheless, the 1980s brought an unsettling explosion of takeover defenses in which shareholders voluntarily relinquished even the appearance of control over management. An SEC study found that the adoption of antitakeover rules, even when no takeover is in sight, reduces stock prices by an average of 3 to 5 percent.

How do such measures pass? Apparently because many shareholders, even supposedly alert and sophisticated institutional investors, are apathetic or easily persuaded by management. James E. Heard, of the Investors Responsibility Research Center, was blunt: "Institutional investors are voting for these proposals either on a completely uninformed basis or to preserve their commercial relationships with clients."[45] It is easy to see why a bank, investment banker, insurance company, or pension-fund manager might be reluctant to mount an aggressive challenge that could antagonize a potential business customer. The College Retirement Equities Fund (CREF) for college professors is one of the few institutions in the country that consistently votes against takeover-defense rules.

SUMMARY

Generally accepted accounting principles allow considerable flexibility in reporting assets and earnings. Instead of estimating the market value of a firm's assets, accountants generally report the depreciated cost. Instead of recording a firm's cash flow, accountants anticipate revenue, defer costs, and make a variety of adjustments that are intended to give a more accurate picture of a firm's profitability. These practices allow for judgment, and some firms have abused this flexibility in order to exaggerate their earnings and assets and to boost the market price of their stock.

Conventional accounting practices are particularly ill suited for inflationary periods when the historic costs of plant, equipment, and inventories substantially understate current costs. Because reported profits are overstated during such periods, firms pay more taxes than they would with inflation-adjusted accounting.

If a 5 percent inflation increased shareholder required returns and the rate of growth of corporate dividends by 5 percent, stock prices would increase with inflation. In the long run, stocks have been a superior investment, with a return that has substantially outpaced inflation. In the short run, however, stocks have not been a hedge against inflation because, when inflation increases stock prices are as likely to fall as they are to rise. One reason that stock prices do not reliably increase during inflations is that conventional accounting increases corporate taxes faster than prices. Another reason is that the Federal Reserve often uses a tight monetary policy to cause a recession that will wring inflation out of the economy. A very different argument, by Modigliani and Cohn, is that investors undervalued corporate stock in the inflationary 1970s because they neglected to consider capital gains on corporate debt and because they priced stock to give an earnings-price ratio that was comparable to nominal rather than to real interest rates.

In most large corporations the owners and managers are different people, with interests that do not always coincide. Shareholders want to maximize the value of their stock, while a firm's executives may want to maximize their compensation or the size of the firm. Yet, even self-interested managers will pay attention to stock prices if their compensation includes incentives tied to stock prices and if low prices encourage takeovers and management dislodgment. Shark repellents installed to discourage takeovers seem an especially clear case of management putting its own interests above those of shareholders. An easy alternative for discouraging takeovers, which benefits stockholders, is for a firm to repurchase its stock when the managers believe that the price is too low.

EXERCISES

1. A firm is considering spending $1 million on a machine that lasts 20 years and produces $100,000 in revenue (net wages, materials, and other expenses) at the end of each year for 20 years. Ignoring taxes, determine whether or not this machine is financially attractive according to each of the following investment criteria:

a. Dollars in, dollars out. Compare the total amount spent on the machine with the total revenue over the machine's life.

b. Accounting profits. Calculate total profits (revenue minus depreciation) over the machine's life, using straight-line depreciation over 20 years.

c. Net present value. The present value of the machine's cash flow is calculated using a 15 percent required return.

2. For tax purposes, the company in Exercise 1 can either depreciate the machine staight line over 20 years or over 10 years. How much difference does this make to the net present value if the firm's tax rate is 34 percent and it's after-tax required rate of return is 10 percent?

3. A New York University professor analyzed the major-league baseball teams' 1984 financial statements to determine if they were making or losing money.[46] After adjusting for several questionable accounting practices, he estimated that they lost $27 million, about $1 million per team. A typical adjustment involved a player earning $500,000 a year, of which $400,000 was paid each year and $100,000 was to be deferred to the year 2000. The clubs generally recorded this as an annual $500,000 expense. Do you think that the professor adjusted this expense up or down? Why?

4. Does a company whose accounting exaggerates its profits tend to have a high or a low *P/E* ratio? Explain your answer.

5. In 1970 Chrysler's profits were increased by $40 million by a switch from LIFO to FIFO accounting. What are LIFO and FIFO? How can such an accounting change increase a firm's profits? Why might a firm nonetheless prefer LIFO accounting?

6. Brazilian accountants developed NIFO (Next In, First Out) accounting, in which the reported cost of an inventory good used in any given year is equal to an estimate of the cost of its replacement. Why might firms find this accounting system advantageous? Is it closer to LIFO or FIFO accounting?

7. A 1982 survey of companies still using FIFO accounting found that 16 percent were experiencing declining prices for the goods they held in inventory.[47] Why do firms with declining inventory prices benefit from FIFO accounting?

8. A 1986 promotional letter from Forbes magazine stated:

> America's companies are its real wealth . . . Shares in these companies are practically the only things that have undergone *deflation*. In 1965 dollars, a Dow Jones at 1,000 today would have to be at 2,637 to be the equivalent of a 1965 Dow of 1,000. This imbalance must reverse itself, and the Dow will surge dramatically to even higher levels.[48]

Can you think of any rational reason why the real value of American stock could decline?

9. Look up the values of the Consumer Price Index (CPI) and the Dow Jones Industrial Average in December 1969 and in December 1989. Did consumer prices or stock prices increase more over this twenty-year period? Did the real value of stocks increase or decline?

10. Two professors calculated real stock prices, adjusted for changes in the Consumer Price Index, back to 1857 and concluded that

> inflation-adjusted stock prices were approximately equal to nominal stock prices in 1864-1865, were greater than nominal prices through 1918, tracked them rather closely . . .

following World War I and were nearly equal to them throughout the World War II period. Since the end of World War II, however, the nominal and real stock price series have begun to diverge, with the real price moving further below the nominal price.[49]

What does this conclusion, by itself, tell us about stock prices and consumer prices during these years?

11. The authors of the study cited in the preceding exercise go on to consider what would have to happen for nominal stock prices to again equal real stock prices. What is the answer?

12. David Dreman, a well-known author and portfolio manager, said "Throughout the past ten years of accelerating inflation, earnings of S&P's 500 have increased at an almost 11 percent annual rate, considerably faster than the climb in prices. In a word, our major corporations have fared far better against inflation than is generally realized."[50] Explain why stock prices depend not only on whether the level of nominal profits and dividends keep up with consumer prices, but also on their ability to increase faster than consumer prices. In particular, explain why stock prices might drop while nominal profits and dividends grow at exactly the same rate as consumer prices.

13. A 1986 *Business Week* report explained the 1985–86 bull market in the following way:

> Stunted and disfigured by more than a decade of rising inflation, the stock market has been restored to vigor by the balm of disinflation. Falling inflation makes lower interest rates possible. And as interest rates fall, stock prices rise. That's because anticipated growth in corporate earnings becomes more valuable to investors. Such are the elemental but potent economics of this bull market to date.[51]

Critically evaluate this analysis, being very careful to distinguish between nominal and real.

14. In 1983, an investor interested in the relationship between the earnings yield and the risk-free rate of return developed the following equation, using annual data for the preceding sixteen years:[52]

$$(E/P) = 1.22 + 0.85(I + 3)$$

where (E/P) is the earnings-price ratio for the Dow Jones Industrials, I is the inflation rate, and the real interest rate is assumed to be a constant 3 percent. Interpret his results.

15. A 1984 Harris poll of 602 senior corporate executives found that 70 percent believe that takeovers are bad for the economy, but 80 percent think that takeovers are good for shareholders.[53] How would you interpret this apparent contradiction in their opinions?

16. Some people argue that golden parachutes encourage takeovers by making the top management of a target company less fearful of losing their jobs and salaries. Why might golden parachutes discourage takeovers?

17. In 1987, a financial writer argued as follows for more laws governing takeovers:

> Raiders shouldn't be permitted to invest first and disclose later. Investment banking firms shouldn't be permitted to set up the financing for a takeover without disclosing their intention first. And no one should be permitted to buy a publicly owned company without having to pay for it. Margin requirements were invented to halt just such abuses.[54]

How would such laws affect takeover activity? Explain your reasoning.

18. U.S. managers have been criticized for being more interested in the size of a firm than its profitability. Two financial analysts argue that this misguided aim is reinforced by shareholders who focus on the rate of growth of earnings and dividends.[55] They give the following example: Suppose you invest $10,000 in a money-market fund that buys Treasury bills earning a 10 percent rate of interest. If the fund distributes all the interest to shareholders, its rate of growth is 0 percent. If the fund distributes half the interest and reinvests the other half, its earnings and dividends will grow by 5 percent a year. If the fund distributes 20 percent and reinvests 80 percent, it will grow by 8 percent a year. How were these growth rates calculated? What is the shareholder's rate of return in each case? Why, despite the differing growth rates, does reinvestment not benefit shareholders? What criterion do you suppose these financial analysts recommend for judging whether growth benefits shareholders?

19. A certain closed-end mutual fund began by issuing 1 million shares at a price of $10 each, using the $10 million raised to purchase securities, with dividends and realized capital gains distributed to shareholders. Unlike an open-end fund, closed-end funds do not issue or redeem their shares at net asset value. An investor who wants to buy in must buy shares from a current shareholder; a shareholder who wants out must find a buyer. The shares of closed-end funds are traded on the stock exchanges, and they may trade at a premium or a discount from their net asset value. For example, the value of the securities owned by the closed-end fund in our example has risen to $15 million, giving a net asset value of $15 per share, while the fund's shares trade on the New York Stock Exchange at only $12 a share. What is the value of this mutual fund's q (market value/replacement cost)? Should the fund expand or contract if it wants to benefit its shareholders? How?

20. In November 1985, the *Los Angeles Times* reported:

> Hospital Corp. of America, bolstered by its strong financial position, was authorized by its board of directors Friday to spend up to $350 million to repurchase shares of its common stock, the company's chairman said.
> "In view of HCA's strong financial position

and the recent market prices of our stock, we believe that repurchase of our own shares represents an attractive investment opportunity, which will benefit both the company and our shareholders," Thomas F. Frist, Jr., Chairman and Chief Executive, said in a written statement . . . .

"HCA clearly thinks their stock is a better investment than buying more hospitals," said Randall S. Huyser, a health-care analyst with San Francisco-based Montgomery Securities.

"They (HCA) may also be worried about a takeover . . ."[56]

In February 1986, *The Wall Street Journal* reported that Honeywell had adopted a new antitakeover measure, giving shareholders the right to buy Honeywell stock at a discount in the event of a takeover attempt.

> Separately, [Honeywell] said it plans to repurchase as many as five million common shares [out of 45.5 million outstanding]. A company spokeswoman said there isn't any connection between the stock repurchase plan and the antitakeover measures. The company made a similar repurchase last year.[57]

Under what circumstances does the company's repurchase of its own shares, in lieu of more hospitals or other investments, benefit shareholders?

21. Explain the error in management's reasoning: "We are considering the construction of a shopping center. Since we will finance this project by borrowing money from Security Pacific at 12 percent, this is the rate we should use to discount the projected cash flow."

22. A professor has noted that businesses are advised to gauge projects by discounting the dollar cash flow by nominal interest rates or, equivalently, by discounting the real cash flow by real interest rates. He argues that the latter course simplifies matters because real cash flows are easier to forecast than nominal flows (which depend on unknown rates of inflation), and real interest rates are approximately equal to zero. As evidence, he cites the fact that during the years 1948–78, the average value of the long-term AAA corporate-bond rate was approximately equal to the average value of the annual rate of inflation. Why, as your business's chief financial officer, might you hesitate to follow the professor's advice?

23. The Financial Accounting Standards Board (FASB) and the SEC both require companies with proven oil and gas reserves to estimate the future cash flows from these reserves using current year-end prices and costs (unless other prices are established by existing contractual arrangements) and to take into account the timing of these flows by applying a 10 percent discount rate. The FASB has noted that 70 percent of 102 petroleum-evaluation engineers it surveyed believe that the present value of proven reserves should be reported and that 58 percent support a standard 10 percent discount rate. Yet, the FASB has remarked, "The Board is concerned, at the same time, that users of financial statements understand that [the required calculation is] neither fair market value nor the present value of future cash flows. It is a rough surrogate for such measures."[58] Why has the FASB made this qualification?

24. Consider a firm that makes craft items selling for $10 each. The raw materials needed to make one item cost $1. Labor costs $10 an hour, and each worker can make two items an hour. What is this firm's total cost (materials plus labor) per item and profit per item? If all prices and wages double, with productivity unchanged, what happens to the firm's profit? In real terms, does its profit increase or decline? What if all wages and prices double and productivity increases to 2.5 items an hour? If the cost of materials and the price of the product both double, while productivity increases by 25 percent to 2.5 items an hour, how much can this firm afford to raise real wages without reducing its real profit per item?

25. Explain why you agree or disagree with the following argument:

Since 1938 a not implausible argument could be presented to show that accounting is not even an art, but just a state of mind. In that year occurred those two fantastic accounting cases—McKesson and Robbins, and Interstate Hosiery Mills. For some time both corporations had flourished like the green bay trees, chiefly on assets that simply weren't there, but which everyone thought were there. Everyone, that is, save one man in each case, who had created the assets all by himself, using only a pen, some ink, and a lot of skillful dishonesty. Presumably these corporations' securities would never have taken those two dives if only the nonexistent assets had not been destroyed by having their nonexistence discovered.[59]

26. Put yourself in the shoes of a pension-fund manager, and answer this criticism of your willingness to accept tender offers from corporate raiders:

At present, institutional money managers operate under what they call a fiduciary duty to sell when the price of a stock is driven up by a takeover attempt. There is some suspicion that "duty" is a convenient excuse to cover a somewhat less noble reason—the competition to out-perform other money managers over the short term.[60]

27. The federal government's budget is calculated on a cash-flow basis. In 1987, several private borrowers from the Federal Export-Import Bank prepaid their loans, reducing the bank's deficit for that year by $1.5 billion. Why do you think these borrowers voluntarily repaid their loans early? Explain how a loan prepayment reduces the bank's deficit. Do you think that the loan prepayments in the example

strengthened or weakened the financial condition of the Export-Import Bank?

28. The federal government has loaned billions of dollars to students, farmers, homeowners, and others. Some people have proposed that the federal government sell some of these loans to private investors, who will then receive the loan payments from the borrowers.[61] Since the federal government's budget is calculated on a cash-flow basis, how do you think the federal deficit has been affected by the initial issuance of these loans? How do you think the deficit would be affected by the sale of federal loans to private investors? Why does cash-flow accounting give a misleading financial picture in this situation?

29. In September 1988, the portfolio strategy group at Goldman, Sachs advised clients that "We do not believe that bond yields are 'too high' relative to inflation."[62] To support this argument, they compared the 4 percent inflation rate then prevailing with an estimate of the implicit inflation rate imbedded in bond yields, which was calculated by using a 9 percent Treasury bond yield, an 18 percent marginal tax rate for Treasury bond purchasers, and a 3.5 percent assumed real after-tax bond yield. What was their estimate of the inflation rate implicit in bond yields?

30. A few pages after making the argument described in Exercise 29, this portfolio strategy group went on to argue that the real interest rate on Treasury bonds is above its historical average and that if the inflation rate is used in place of interest rates in the dividend discount model of stock prices, the S&P 500 appears to be fairly valued rather than 15 percent overvalued.[63] Logically, is the inflation rate or the Treasury bond yield more appropriate as a required return for stocks? Defend your choice.

CHAPTER 10

Technical Analysis

If you torture the data long enough, Nature will confess . . .

Coase

Fundamental analysis applies present-value principles to the valuation of corporate stock, using dividends, earnings, assets, and interest rates to judge whether a stock is really worth its current price. **Technical analysis,** in contrast, tries to gauge the mood of the market by studying changes in market prices, the volume of trading, and investor attitudes. Technicians are not concerned with a firm's dividends or profit projections: indeed, they need not even know the name of the company or its line of business. It is enough to know whether investors are buying or selling.

Academicians are overwhelmingly skeptical of technical analysis, often likening it to astrology or palm reading. Yet virtually every investment firm employs technical analysts. In this chapter we will look at some popular technical indicators and the reasons for skepticism. We begin with the nature of technical analysis and its early roots.

technical analysis
Technical analysis tries to gauge the mood of the market by studying changes in market prices, the volume of trading, and other barometers of investor attitudes.

THE NATURE OF TECHNICAL ANALYSIS

Technical analysis generally starts with a scrutiny of stock prices, trying to discern from past price movements which way prices are headed. John Magee, one of the most influential technical analysts, explains that

The market price reflects . . . the hopes and fears and guesses and moods, rational and irrational, of hundreds of potential buyers and sellers, as well as their needs and resources—in total, factors which defy analysis and

FIGURE 10–1   A vertical-line stock price chart

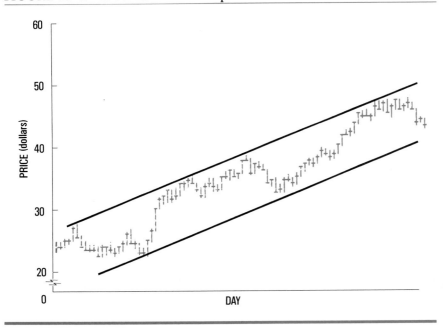

for which no standards are obtainable, but which are nevertheless all
synthesized, weighed, and finely expressed in one precise figure [the
price].[1]

A technical analyst can be compared to a person watching a computer
program draw lines on a screen. Not having access to the software, the
analyst looks for a pattern that will reliably predict the lines to be drawn
next. The lines themselves are all-important, and it would be distracting
to think about daily news events or speculate on the author of the computer
program. In the same way, the mood of the stock market can be gauged
by watching stock prices: additional news about the economy or the fortunes of specific companies is merely distracting. Magee reportedly
boarded up the windows of his office so that his readings of the hopes
and fears of the stock market would not be influenced by the sight of birds
singing or snow falling.

   The technician's primary tool is a chart of stock prices, whose visual
inspection yields exploitable patterns. The most popular are vertical-line
charts, normally using daily data for short-run forecasting and weekly
or monthly data to give a long-run perspective. As illustrated in Figure
10–1, each vertical line spans the high and low prices, with the horizontal
slash showing the closing price. A technician studies the chart and draws

in lines, like the channel in Figure 10–1, to show a trend or other interesting pattern.

There are virtually as many technical theories as there are technical analysts (evidently no single theory does well enough to win over other analysts). However, because most present day-chart reading is derived in one way or another from the Dow Theory, the flavor of technical analysis can be learned from a study of this approach.

THE DOW THEORY

Charles Dow and Edward Jones founded the Dow-Jones Company in 1880 as a financial-news service, and this venture evolved into *The Wall Street Journal* in 1889, for which Dow wrote a series of influential editorials on the direction of the stock market until his death in 1902. After Dow's death, a reporter on the newspaper, Samuel Nelson, reprinted several of these editorials in a small book and for the first time referred to "Dow's Theory." William Hamilton, a disciple of Dow, became editor of *The Wall Street Journal* in 1908 and, in his editorials, popularized his interpretation of Dow's theories until his death in 1929.

Ironically, Dow, the founder of technical analysis, was convinced that stock prices depend on dividends and profits—the essential ingredients of fundamental analysis. In fact, the Dow-Jones price indexes were constructed because of Dow's belief that stock prices are based on informed opinion about future business conditions and, therefore, are a barometer of economic activity. The Dow Jones Industrial Average reflects production and the transportation average monitors commerce, with increases in both indexes revealing the collective opinion of knowledgable analysts that economic activity is expanding.

Predictable Cycles

Both Dow and Hamilton believed that there are regular cycles in the economy and elsewhere. Indeed, the opening sentence of Hamilton's book, *Stock Market Barometer*, cites William Stanley Jevons's sun-spot theory of economic cycles. If the economy does go through regular cycles and stock prices mirror the economy, then it seems plausible that stock prices go through predictable cycles, too, and it is to the investor's advantage to know which direction the cycle is going.

Dow was interested in the oceans, and all chart reading traces back to Dow's idea that financial markets are like the sea, with tides, waves, and ripples. All these movements are of irregular length and magnitude, but can be characterized roughly as follows:

Primary trends are market movements similar to the tide in that they reflect the direction in which the market is inevitably moving. There are

FIGURE 10–2 A bull market

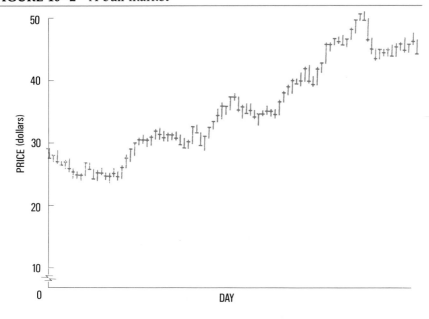

setbacks and reversals along the way, but in a *bull market* (see Figure 10–2), each intermediate high or low point is higher than the one before; in a *bear market* (see Figure 10–3 on p. 320), each intermediate high or low is lower than the one before. (The origin of the labels *bull* and *bear* are obscure; one explanation is that a bull walks with its head up and a bear with its head down.) Major trends last at least a year and may last four years or even longer.

Intermediate reactions are market movements similar to the waves crashing on the shore and then retreating. As shown in Figure 10–2, each advance in a bull market brings a countermove or reaction (a technical correction), which lasts from a few weeks to a few months and retraces from one-third to two-thirds of the preceding movement—two steps forward, and one step back. Similarly, in the bear market shown in Figure 10–3, each retreat is followed by a partly offsetting advance.

Minor fluctuations are market movements like the ripples on top of the ocean, meaningless fluctuations, lasting from a few hours to several weeks, that the analyst must try to ignore.

For both Dow and Hamilton, the analyst's primary objective is to determine whether the primary trend is bullish or bearish. Every bull market eventually turns into a bear market, which then inevitably turns bullish once again. The two competing forces that make analysis difficult are momentum and reaction, and, unfortunately, no one knows when an inter-

FIGURE 10–3 A bear market

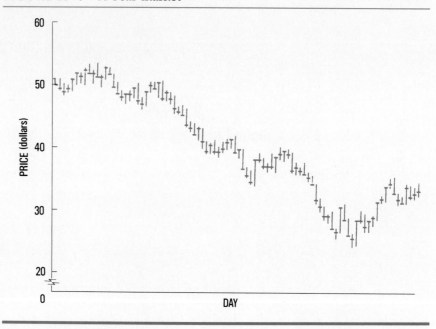

mediate reaction will begin, end, or turn into a reversal of the major trend. No one rings a bell when it is time to sell. Or as Dow put it,

> *There is no way of telling when the top of an advance or the bottom of a decline has been reached until some time after such top or bottom has been made. Sometimes people are able to guess when prices are at the top or at the bottom, but . . . it is a proverb of Wall Street that only a foolish speculator hopes to buy stocks at the lowest and sell them at the highest.*[2]

Both Dow and Hamilton considered the understanding of stock-market cycles a defensive tool for conservative investors, not a key to easy riches for speculators. Instead of trying to guess which way prices will zig or zag next, they hoped merely to identify the direction of the long-run primary trend, freely acknowledging that they could not detect a change in the direction of the primary trend until some time after the fact.

Hamilton's most spectacular prediction was his editorial "A Turn of the Tide," appearing on October 25, 1929 (after two sharp breaks in the market on October 23 and 24), which correctly predicted that the six-year bull market had ended. (Dow enthusiasts pay less attention to the fact that Hamilton made the same prediction three years earlier, after which the Dow Industrial Average nearly tripled.) The 1929 prediction was published some time after the market peaked (on September 3), but it still appeared

TABLE 10–1 The 1929—1932 Bear Market

Date	Dow Index	
	Industrial Stocks	Rail Stocks
September 3, 1929	381	189
October 23, 1929	301	167
July 8, 1932	41	13

in plenty of time to save investors from the ravages of the prolonged bear market that did not touch bottom until July 8, 1932. (See Table 10–1.)

A Belief in Momentum

Both Dow and Hamilton emphasized the momentum in major trends, that a rising market will continue rising and a bear market will continue slumping (admittedly with temporary setbacks and reversals). Their explanation for this momentum was that the economy goes through regular boom-and-bust cycles and that the market, a barometer of the economy, does too.

An alternative explanation for momentum in stock prices is that investors use the past to gauge the profitability of the future. When stock prices increase substantially, many investors envy the profits their neighbors have made and rush to buy stocks so that they, too, can make money. This eager buying has the effect, for a while at least, of a self-fulfilling prophecy, keeping the bull market going. In bear markets, on the other hand, investors observe past price declines, decide that stocks are not a profitable investment, and withdraw—again fulfilling their prophecy.

A third explanation for momentum is that information about stocks spreads through the investment community like the ripples from a large stone tossed into a pond. When something good happens to a company or to the economy, a few insiders learn of this news first, and their buying pushes stock prices somewhat higher. As the news spreads to wider and wider circles, the buying of increasingly larger groups keeps pushing stock prices higher still. (Yet, it really does not seem plausible that a bull market lasts for years, because it takes years for information to be disseminated.)

Support and Resistance Levels

The primary objective of the Dow Theory is a timely identification of a change in the primary trend. To again use the analogy of the sea, you can determine the direction of the tide by watching the large waves and seeing whether succeeding waves end higher or lower on the shore. In the same way, each high point of an intermediate stock-price movement should be

FIGURE 10–4 A support level at $38

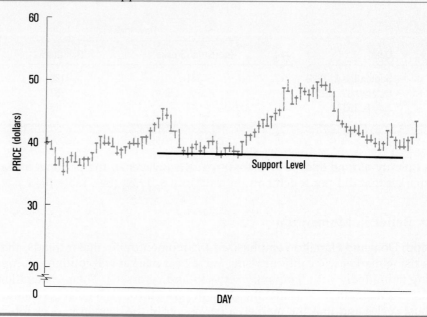

higher than the preceeding high if it is a bull market (with the tide coming in) and not as high if it is a bear market (when the tide is going out). The preceding intermediate high price is a **resistance level;** Dow chartists watch closely as prices approach a resistance level to see whether prices will now go even higher (a bullish signal) or will fall short (a bearish signal). Similarly, the preceding intermediate low price is a **support level;** as prices fall, technicians watch anxiously to see whether the support level will be pierced.

A logical explanation of support and resistance levels is suggested by the observation that, while prices have no memory, investors do. Look at Figure 10–4, where this stock traded at around $38 a share for several days before gradually moving up to near $50 and then back down again. Those investors who bought at $38 and still own the stock missed a chance to sell for a substantial profit and will only break even if they sell now for $38; a natural human inclination is to wait and see if the price goes back up again. All those who bought during the rise to $50 and after are even more reluctant to sell at $38; they remember that they paid more than $38 and are well aware that they will take a loss if they sell now. Those who bought at more distant times may also resist selling, noticing that $38 is the lowest price in a long time; they want to buy low and sell high, not the other way around.

Potential buyers, on the other hand, may think that now is the time

resistance level
A resistance level is an intermediate high price for a stock, which presumably poses a psychological barrier to further advances.

support level
A support level is an intermediate low price for a stock, which is said to provide a psychological cushion against a price decline.

FIGURE 10–5 A strongly established support level at $20

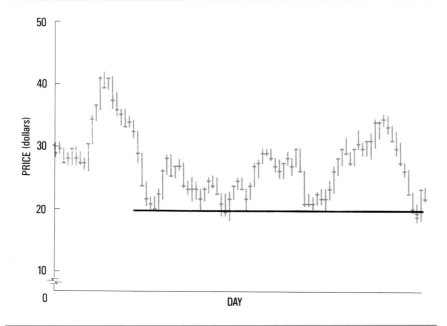

to buy low. Perhaps, they were thinking of buying the last time the stock was at $38, but did not. After the stock went up to $50, came the inevitable second-guessing: "I knew I should have bought at $38." When opportunity knocks twice as the price falls back to $38, they may take advantage of their second chance. These are plausible psychological reasons why, as the price drops to $38, there may be few sellers and many buyers. The $38 price is then a support level, as the psychological tilt toward buying provides support for the stock's price at $38. It is a bearish signal if the stock's price falls through the $38 support level (a breakout), since only very bad news about the company could overcome these psychological propensities.

Figure 10–5 shows a support level at $20 that has been confirmed time and again. To chartists, the more strongly a support level has been established, the more significant is its violation. Sometimes the bouncing off of a support level resembles the outline of a head and shoulders, with the support level being the neckline. Since stock patterns are in practice asymmetrical and ill-behaved, technicians use such labels as *multiple, deformed,* and *aborted head and shoulders* to describe the deviations from a perfect chart pattern.

Figure 10–6 shows a resistance level at around $45 a share. All those investors who bought below $45 will consider taking their profit at $45, the highest price in recent memory, while those considering buying may be reluctant to pay the highest price in some time. Similarly, those who

FIGURE 10–6 A resistance level at $45

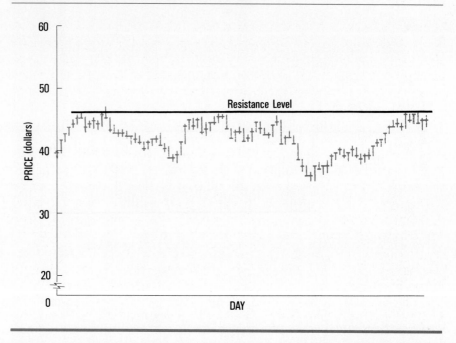

had bought earlier at $45 and watched with disappointment as the price fell may now be happy to break even. If so, the psychological reluctance to buy and eagerness to sell make it difficult for the price to rise above $45. If the company news is good enough to overcome this psychological barrier and the price pierces the $45 resistance level, this is a bullish signal. In the chart shown in Figure 10–6, the $45 resistance level has been confirmed time and again, and, indeed, it may be an inverted, deformed head-and-shoulders formation in the making.

These memories and psychological inclinations apply more plausibly to the individual stocks that people buy and sell than to the averages as a whole. Yet, investors trying to buy low and sell high may well watch the averages and let their memories of recent highs and lows influence their desicions. Psychologists are familiar with similar behavior in other contexts, using the term *anchoring* to describe how people simplify their interpretation of events by comparison to some benchmark. One simple example is an experiment in which subjects who were asked to estimate the height of a post tended to underestimate the heights of tall posts and overestimate the heights of short posts, apparently using the height of a standard fence post as a benchmark.[3] In the same way, investor perceptions of whether stocks are cheap or expensive may be influenced by past prices.

OTHER TECHNICAL INDICATORS

Technicians today watch a variety of indicators, looking for a reliable signal of the direction of the market. Not all, though, hold to Dow's objective of identifying the long-run primary trend—the direction of the tide; many instead try to profit from intermediate moves—the waves. Different technicians watching the same technical indicator may interpret its signal very differently—suggesting that indicators must not be very reliable; otherwise, analysts would surely agree on which are the useful ones and how to interpret them.

One helpful way of characterizing technicians is to remember the central tension in Dow's Theory between the forces of momentum and reaction: the *momentum* of the market is the tide, the bullish or bearish direction; *reaction* is the intermediate countermove. Technicians, too, divide into the momentum or reaction camp. When market prices surge upward, some analysts, the believers in momentum, recommend buying—"A body in motion tends to remain in motion." Others, trying to profit from intermediate reactions, see the very same data and advise selling—"What goes up must come down."

A good example of technical analysis by the momentum camp is the combining of data on price and trading volume—interpreting an upward move on heavy volume as more bullish than an upward move on light volume. Momentum enthusiasts also monitor relative performance, recommending those stocks that have been doing better than average. A technial indicator used by some analysts in the reaction school is the number of short sales on the Amex. When short sales in these relatively speculative securities reach an unusually high level, a sign that investors are very bearish, reaction believers interpret this as a buy signal.

Wall Street Week's Ten Technical Indicators

"Wall Street Week" is a popular Public Broadcasting System television show, hosted by Louis Ruckeyser. One segment of the show reports the latest readings of ten technical indicators developed by Robert J. Nurock, a broker, investment consultant, and regular panelist on the show. Nurock's ten selected indicators first appeared in 1972 and have been revised at least five times since; the ten indicators tracked in 1986 are shown in Table 10–2 on p. 326.[4] The exact parameters for each indicator are updated annually.

Wall Street Week's interpretation of these indicators is generally in the reaction camp: when the market seems strong, they advise selling. The specific indicators are interesting because, they are representative of the many varied barometers technicians watch. Their evolution since 1972 is also instructive, because it shows that technical analysis is not infallible. For these reasons, we will examine several in depth.

TABLE 10–2   "Wall Street Week" Technical Indicators

Indicator	Buy Signal
Dow Jone momentum ratio	The current value of the Dow Jones Industrial Average is significantly below the average value over the preceding thirty days.
NYSE hi-lo index	The number of stocks making new highs during the preceding ten days rises from less than ten to more than the number of new lows.
Market-breadth index	The number of stocks advancing over the preceding ten days minus the number declining has increased and then declined substantially.
Arms (trading) index	The average volume of trading in declining stocks over the preceding ten days substantially exceeds the volume for advancing stocks.
Prices of NYSE stocks versus their moving averages	The current prices of most NYSE stocks are below their average prices over the preceding ten and thirty weeks.
Premium ratio on options	The average premium on puts is large relative to that on calls.
Advisory-service sentiment	Leading advisory services are bearish.
Low-price activity ratio	Trading in speculative stocks is low relative to trading in more seasoned issues.
Insider-activity ratio	Most corporate officers and directors and those who own more than 10 percent of a company's stock are buying rather than selling.
Fed policy	The federal funds rate on interbank loans is low relative to the discount rate charged on bank loans from the Federal Reserve, signaling that money is plentiful and business borrowing is encouraged.

advance-decline index

An advance-decline index compares the number of stocks advancing with the number declining.

Advance-Decline Index   Many analysts construct an **advance-decline index** to monitor the number of stocks advancing relative to the number of stocks declining. Unlike the Dow Jones Industrial Average and other market price indexes, advance-decline indexes pay no attention to the value of a stock or to the size of an advance or decline—a 25-cent change in Fly-By-Night Marketing counts the same as a $5 change in IBM. Instead, the index simply counts whether most stocks went up or down. "Wall Street Week" initially used an advance-decline index that was a five-week average of the daily ratio of the number of stocks advancing plus 50 percent of those unchanged to the total number of stocks traded. A value of 0.50 shows that the market is mixed, with the number of stocks increasing equal to the number declining. Consistent with the reaction school, "Wall Street Week" interpreted a large value for this index (when most stocks are rising) as evidence that you should sell and a low index value (when most stocks are falling) as a signal to buy. The specific cutoff values depend on whether

TABLE 10–3 "Wall Street Week" Advance-Decline Index, 1972

	Buy Signal (percent)	Neutral (percent)	Sell Signal (percent)
in a bull market:	43 to 45	45 to 57	57 to 60
in a bear market:	38 to 40	40 to 50	50 to 54

a bull or bear market prevails, as shown Table 10–3. The bull/bear distinction is discomforting, since we have no objective way to gauge which type of market exists at a specific time. A few years after its original advance-decline index was introduced, "Wall Street Week" revised the 38–40 percent bear-market buy signal to 36-40 percent and, in a later second revision, the television show dropped the index entirely.

The ambiguities in interpreting technical indicators are demonstrated very vividly by the fact that Louis Rukeyser's explanation of the advance-decline index used on his show is contrary to Nurock's. Here is Ruckeyser's interpretation:

> *Practically every technician uses some variant of this [approach], which tots up how many stocks went up versus how many stocks went down. The result is a measure of the market's "breadth" —and bad breadth stinks. If the averages are rising but breadth is declining, technicians will assume that the market is already beginning to deteriorate.*[5]

Some technicians do draw this conclusion but, contrary to Ruckeyser, "Wall Street Week" did not. When most stocks were falling, "Wall Street Week" gave a buy signal.

A second advance-decline index was added in the first revision of Nurock's ten indicators, replacing a comparison of the volume of trading on the American Stock Exchange and New York Stock Exchange. This new indicator was a ten-day average of the number of stocks advancing minus the number of stocks declining. A value below -1000 (showing that most stocks have been falling) was considered bullish, and a value above $+1000$ was seen as bearish. This indicator survived the second revision, but its interpretation was made considerably more complicated. The bullish signal became "an expansion of this index from below $+1000$ to the point where it peaks out and declines 1000 points from this peak."

Low-Price Activity Ratio Another interesting "Wall Street Week" indicator, similar to those followed by many technicians, is the **low-price activity ratio,** dividing the weekly ratio of the volume of trading in the stocks in *Barron's* Lo-Price Stock Index by the volume of trading in the stocks in the Dow Jones Industrial Average. If low-priced stocks are more speculative

low-price activity ratio
The low-price activity ratio tracks the volume of trading in low-price (and presumably speculative) stocks relative to the total volume of trading.

than the blue chips included in the Dow Jones Average, then a relative increase in their trading indicates increased speculative activity. In the reaction spirit, a low value of this indicator is interpreted as a signal to buy, and a high value is a signal to sell. The particular values used initially by "Wall Street Week" were:

Buy signal	Neutral	Sell signal
5 to 8 percent	8 to 10 percent	10 to 15 percent

In the first revision, these values were changed to

Buy signal	Neutral	Sell signal
5 to 7 percent	7 to 12 percent	over 12 percent

In the second revision, these were changed once again, to

Buy signal	Neutral	Sell signal
below 12 percent	12 to 18 percent	over 18 percent

Now they are

Buy signal	Neutral	Sell signal
below 4 percent	4 to 8 percent	over 8 percent

short interest
Short-interest data show the total number of uncovered short sales.

Short Interest Many technicians watch data on **short interest,** the total number of uncovered short sales. One interpretation in the momentum camp, is that a large number of short sales reflects a growing pessimism, a bearish signal. Some analysts draw the opposite conclusion—that when people are pessimistic, stocks become cheap. Yet another interpretation is that because shorts must eventually cover their positions, the strength of their eventual demand is a bullish signal.

For many technicians, the most interesting short-sale data involve *odd lots,* trades involving fewer than 100 shares, presumably made by those who cannot afford to trade in round lots. If the odd-lotters are not only poor but uninformed (cause and effect?), then odd-lot short-sale data gauge the pessimism of amateur investors. When uninformed amateurs become extremely pessimistic, borrowing money to sell stock they do not own, it is time for the smart money to start buying.

One explanation of odd-lot behavior fits into the reaction school—when the market has fallen greatly and gloom abounds, small investors increase their short selling; thus, their short selling is a signal of a depressed market that is ripe for the reaction in the other direction. Another interpretation is that amateurs are wrong more often than right; the next best thing to following the advice of an expert is to do the opposite of an amateur. At first, "Wall Street Week" used a ten-day average of odd-lot short sales divided by total odd-lot sales, with a value above 1.5 percent a signal to buy and a value below 0.5 percent a signal to sell. The buy signal was later revised to a value above 2 percent. Nowadays, most technicians have given up on the odd-lot short-sale indicator, and so has "Wall Street Week."[6]

Institutional-Block Ratio "Wall Street Week" also used to follow an **institutional-block ratio** indicator, a ten-day average of the number of trades of 10,000 shares or more at higher prices than the preceding trade, relative to the number of large trades at lower prices. A low value of this indicator (between 0.25 and 0.35), showing that big institutions are more interested in selling than buying, is bullish; a high value (0.65 to 0.75) indicates that institutions are more eager to buy, a signal that you should sell. Again, there are two interpretations. The first is that of the reaction school, as explained by Nurock: "At tops buying tends to be most urgent . . . At bottoms there is an urgency to sell." The second explanation is that professionally managed institutions are, like the hapless odd-lotters, wrong more often than right.

> **institutional block ratio**
> The institutional block ratio compares the number of trades of 10,000 shares or more at prices higher than the preceding trade with the number at lower prices.

"Wall Street Week" later revised the reading completely: The buy signal became "0.20 upside reversal from below 0.35" and the sell signal "0.20 downside reversal from above 0.60." They changed from the reaction to momentum camp! When institutional buying picks up after a slumber, join them. When institutional buying cools, you should sell too. Nurock's revised explanation reflects this about-face: "After market bottoms buying tends to pick up and the ratio improves . . . Around market tops selling becomes more urgent and the ratio declines." Urgent institutional selling was first a signal of a market bottom and, after the first revision, as a signal of a market top. In the second revision, the institutional-block ratio disappeared entirely. Apparently, it did not work either as a reaction or momentum indicator.

Advisory-Service Sentiment The first revision of the "Wall Street Week" technical indicators introduced another indicator of some interest: advisory-service sentiment. There are a wide variety of investment services that, for a fee, provide periodic recommendations to investors. Just as for every buyer of stock there is a seller, so there is always a division of opinion among the self-proclaimed experts who sell advice. On average, they tend to be bullish, though the fraction that is bullish varies with the market. One advisory service, *Investor's Intelligence,* subscribes to other leading services and provides its subscribers with a weekly tabulation of the fraction that are bearish. Interestingly, its interpretation (and that of "Wall Street Week") is that the more bearish are the advisory services, the more likely it is that the market will rise.

Nurock provides a reaction explanation: "When advisory service sentiment becomes overly onesided, it is viewed as a contrary indicator as services tend to follow trends rather than anticipate changes in them." Another explanation is that, like the much maligned odd-lotter, investment advisors are amateurs who are wrong more often than right. If they're so smart, why don't they make money by using their own advice rather than selling it? "Wall Street Week" initially signaled sell if the percent of investment advisors that are bearish is less than 15 percent and buy if the percent bearish is over 30 percent in a bull market or over 60 percent in a bear market. These signals were later changed substantially: sell if the percent bearish falls below 25 percent and buy if above 42 percent. Now the cutoffs are the misleadingly precise numbers, 35.7 percent and 52.4 percent.

Long-Term Treasury-Bond Prices The last "Wall Street Week" indicator we will examine is based on an index of the prices of long-term Treasury bonds. At first, the television show gave a signal to buy if bond prices improved for one to two months by at least two points and to sell if bond prices fell for one to two months by two points. This recommendation is, of course, consistent with fundamental analysis, because rising bond prices reflect falling interest rates and low required returns are good for the stock market. However, presumably any past rise or fall in interest rates has already affected stock prices. Nurock adds a momentum interpretation, explaining that this indicator provides a "guide to the direction of the bond market." Apparently, he believes that when bond prices are rising and interest rates are falling, they will continue to do so. It is interesting that he assumes reaction in the stock market, but momentum in the bond market.

In the first revision of this "Wall Street Week" indicator, the magnitude of the signaling movement in the prices was changed from 2 points to 4½. In the second revision, matters became considerably more complex and subjective:

> *A price rise of 4¼ points from a low results in a positive reading. The reading turns neutral on 2-point reversal from the subsequent rally high. A price decline of 4¼ points from a prior peak results in a negative reading. The reading turns neutral on a 2-point reversal from the subsequent trough.*

In the next revision, this indicator was dropped.

Robert Nurock is an intelligent, well-informed technical analyst who does the best he can and apparently has been reasonably successful. The indicators he follows are representative of those followed by technicians everywhere, and the many twists and turns his rules have taken over the years aptly demonstrate that technical indicators are imperfect.

Technical Gurus

The Wall Street adage, "There is nothing wrong with the charts, only the chartists," confirms the difficulty in finding unambiguous, successful signals. Nonetheless, technical analysts are employed by all major brokerage firms, and many operate their own successful advisory services. Periodically, a technical analyst is elevated to the status of financial guru when reports of astoundingly accurate predictions are recounted in the media. Thereafter, devoted followers avidly seek the advice of these celebrities.

The Elliot wave theory is one example. A thirteenth-century Italian, Leonardo Fibonacci, investigated the progression of numbers 1, 1, 2, 3, 5, 8, 13, 21, 34, 55, 89, . . . now called a Fibonacci series, where each number is equal to the sum of the two preceding numbers. The number of branches on a tree grows according to a Fibonacci series, as does the family tree of a male bee and the diameter of spirals on a seashell. Musical scales also conform to a Fibonacci series, and the Egyptians used Fibonacci series in designing the Great Pyramid at Giza.

The *Elliot wave theory* is R. N. Elliot's application of the Fibonacci series to stock prices, an application with, at best, mixed success. One writer observed that, "Although the theory is fairly widely followed, Elliot's students often disagree about the proper interpretation of a given swing, sometimes for years after the fact."[7] In March 1986, *USA Today* called one wave watcher, Robert Prechter, the "hottest guru on Wall Street," after a bullish forecast made in September 1985 came true.[8] The same article advised readers of his forecast of a Dow at 3600–3700 by 1988. In October 1987, he said "The worst case [is] a drop to 2295." just days before the Dow collapsed to 1739.[9]

The stock market is very perplexing, and when people do not understand something, it is only human to seek the advice of professed experts— financial gurus—who will replace confusion and ambiguity with clarity and decisiveness. This search for unambiguous advice and in response, the emergence, of confident seers escalates during troubled times. As Nicolas Biddle observed more than 150 years ago, "When the condition of the patient is truly alarming, and the physician's skill is baffled by the disease, quacks gain confidence by their boldness and boasting."[10] Investment Example 10–1 on pp. 332–333 tells of one modern financial guru.

THE DATA-MINING TRAP

To many investors, the value of technical analysis is self-evident. Any reasonably alert person can plainly see the patterns evident in Figures 10–1 through 10–6 and in other charts of stock prices. The difficulty with such a conclusion is that it looks backward rather than forward. The analyst

JOSEPH GRANVILLE

Joseph Granville is one of the most flamboyant of financial advisors, sometimes doing vaudeville skits at his public lectures with a chimpanzee or ventriloquist's dummy and at other times preaching in a prophet's robes:

"The market is a jealous God," he shrieks, "it rewards winners and chastises losers. The Holy Bible is a record of winners and losers. The market follows every precept in that Book—if the market does not follow man's ways, what does it follow? God's ways . . ." Spellbound crowds of *"Granville Groupies," as veteran analyst Robert LeFevre calls them, roar their approval.*[1]

His forecasts were so inaccurate in the early 1970s (due, he says to an addiction to golf) that he abandoned the stock market completely. But then "golfers anonymous" turned his life around, and he wrote the book *How to Win At Bingo,* which sold 500,000 copies. Buoyed by this success and four

years of good stock-market predictions in the late 1970s, he boasted of having "cracked the secret of markets," promised to never make a serious mistake again, and nominated himself for the Nobel Prize in economics.[2] In his spare time, he predicted that Los Angeles would be destroyed by an earthquake in May 1981.

Granville issued a buy recommendation in April 1980, and the Dow jumped thirty points the next day. In September, he continued to predict a runaway stock market. "Short sellers are about to get the heat, and if you think hell is hot, watch."[3] On January 6, 1981, he abruptly turned bearish and his postmidnight calls to his biggest subscribers telling them to sell all their stocks (even while his normal market letter was advising smaller subscribers to buy), provoked the "Granville crash," a twenty-four-point drop in the Dow on January 7.[4] In his March 7, 1981, newsletter, he declared that the "March Massacre" had begun and that he could not possibly be wrong in his prediction that the Dow would fall at least 100 points and possibly 200 points by May 1.[5] In fact, the Dow rose from 965 to 996. Yet, his

needs a crystal ball, and stock charts only provide a rear-view mirror. In any set of data, even randomly generated data, it is possible to find some pattern if one looks long enough. Unfortunately, patterns identified in retrospect may be of little value in anticipating the future.

Theory Testing

To illustrate this pitfall, imagine that you are a statistician and that someone comes into your office claiming to have a psychic ability to predict the outcomes of coin flips. He does not claim to be perfect, only to get more

recycled sell recommendation in September 1981 sent tremors through financial markets.

In late September 1981, he appeared on British television, advising investors to sell everything in sight. He predicted that British interest rates would jump from 14 percent to above 17 percent and that their industrial-stock index would sink like a stone, from 480 to 150.[6] In fact, British interest rates peaked in the next month and headed downward, to 12 percent in 1982 and 10 percent in 1983. Stock prices bottomed at 474 in October 1981, too, and headed upward, to 580 a year later, 700 the year after and then to 900 in 1984, 1000 in 1985, and 1300 in 1986.

Meanwhile, back in the United States, Granville remained bearish throughout 1982–85, missing one of the greatest bull markets. In 1982 and 1983, he advised his subscribers to sell short; those who did lost 29.7 percent in 1982 and then another 25.2 percent in 1983 as the market rose sharply. For 1984 he cited "333 exact parallels with 1929" and forecast a comparable crash, driving the Dow below 700 by the spring of 1985. The Dow topped 1300 in the spring of 1985, and Granville stubbornly continued predicting a second Great Crash. His five-year record, from July 30, 1980, to June 28, 1985, was ranked dead last (down 45.3 percent while the S&P 500 was up 114.6 percent) out of forty-four investment letters monitored by Mark Hulbert.[7] His advice lost 79 percent for all of 1985, 61 percent in 1986, and another 61 percent in 1987.

[1]David Dreman, *The New Contrarian Investment Strategy* (New York: Random House, 1982), p. 22.

[2]Dreman, p. 22. See also Michael Sivy, "Joe Granville: Messiah or Menace?," *Financial World*, June 15, 1980.

[3]Joseph Granville's weekly market letter, quoted in *The Economist*, September 27, 1980, pp. 105–6.

[4]Dreman, p. 22.

[5]James R. Pierobon, "Preparing for the 'March Massacre'," *Houston Chronicle*, March 18, 1981.

[6]"They say that misery is jus a guy called Joe," *The Economist*, September 26, 1981, p. 83.

[7]Peter Brimelow, "Rating the Advisers," *Barron's*, July 15, 1985, pp. 6–7.

[8]John R. Dorfman, "Obscure Investment Letter Tops Performance Survey," *The Wall Street Journal*, June 7, 1988.

than 50 percent right. His system is that coin flips follow a momentum pattern: four heads, followed by four tails, and so on,

$$\mathrm{H\,H\,H\,H\,T\,T\,T\,T\,H\,H\,H\,H} \ldots$$

You pull out a pencil and paper, and prepare to test this theory by flipping a coin twenty times.

You recognize that, by sheer luck, a guesser might get eleven, twelve or even more correct. How many does this alleged psychic have to get right to convince you that he is not just a hapless guesser? Ten correct is unimpressive, while twenty out of twenty is astonishing. Where do we draw the line? Probability calculations show that a guesser has about a 5 percent chance of getting fourteen or more right, and this is the cutoff used in standard statistical tests. Because there is only a 5 percent chance of getting fourteen or more correct by guessing, he must do this well to persuade you that he is not just guessing. This logic is the very same as that used every day by statisticians to test whether Vitamin C helps ward off colds, whether one automobile gets better mileage than another, and hundreds of other interesting, if sometimes esoteric, theories.

In this case, the coin flips turn out as follows:

$$\text{H T T H H T T H H T T H H T H H T H H T}$$

Since the self-proclaimed psychic's system only gives nine correct predictions, you throw him out of your office and go back to work.

But as he goes out the door, another alleged psychic walks in with her theory that coin flips follow a reaction pattern: H T H T . . . A quick check of your data determines that she has eleven correct predictions. Better, but still not good enough. Out she goes and in comes another, with yet another theory: H H H T T H H T T T . . . Another check of your data and another fraud exposed.

Somewhere along the line, one of these frauds is going to get lucky and get fourteen or more right. If you set the cutoff so that a guesser has only a 5 percent chance of passing, about one out of twenty worthless theories will be confirmed by the data. Even if you never test anything but fraudulent theories, you are sure to give your statistical seal of approval to some, if only you test enough of them.

data mining
A data mining expedition is the testing of many theories, searching for a statistically significant result.

This testing of many theories is known as **data mining:** an eager researcher takes a body of data, tests countless theories, and reports the one that best fits the data. The end result—a statistically significant result—shows little more than the energetic efforts of the researcher. We know beforehand that, even if only worthless theories are examined, a researcher will eventually stumble on one that seems confirmed by the data, due to simple luck. Thus, we cannot tell whether the end product of a data-mining expedition shows the veracity of a useful theory or the perseverence of a determined researcher.

Sherlock Holmes Inference

Statistical tests assume that a theory is specified before data are collected. In practice, researchers often have the data in hand before they concoct the theories to be tested. An experienced observer can study the data and see quickly which theories are promising and which are not going to work. For example, a scrutiny of the twenty coin flips given earlier reveals that the following rule explains an incredible nineteen of the twenty observa-

HOW NOT TO WIN AT CRAPS

A book was written on how to win at the dice game craps after the author had recorded the outcomes of 50,000 dice rolls at a Las Vegas casino and carefully studied the sequence in which the numbers appeared. The sequence 4-4-11 can be expected about twenty times in 50,000 rolls, but it actually occurred thirty-one times. The book consequently advises betting on 11 whenever 4 comes up twice in a row. The author also found that on ten of thirty-eight occasions when the sequence 7–12–7 occurred, the next number was either a 2, 3, or 12. A $100 bet on each of these thirty-eight occasions would have won $4,200. This evidence is just like finding a pattern in twenty coin flips and should be overruled by common sense.

tions: coins follow a four-flip sequence, H T T H; except, if the pattern is broken, the sequence reverses to T H H T. Do you think this rule will predict nineteen out of twenty flips in the future? Of course not, because you known how we came up with this theory and the method is not convincing. This is pure and simple data mining. When you see how it is done and you see it applied to something like coin flips, where your intuition resists such theories, the results are not persuasive. Investment Example 10–2 gives a similar example. However, data mining is often applied to situations where we do not have much intuition and you do not see the data mining in action, only the final results.

If someone said that, as a professional economist, she had been studying the stock market and had come up with a theory that works, you might pay attention. If she then told you that in nineteen of the last twenty years, this theory had correctly predicted whether the stock market will go up by more than 5 percent, you might get very interested. And yet, she may have found her stock-market system the same way that we found a system for predicting coin flips. If H stands for a year when the market is up more than 5 percent and T stands for a year when it is not, then the twenty coin flips recorded earlier are, in fact, a history of the stock market over the twenty-year period 1968–87. A study of this history of ups and downs reveals a pattern that explains nineteen of the twenty years—which is pretty impressive, unless you know how we did it.

In the same way, Figures 10–1 through 10–6 all appear to show unmistakable patterns in stock prices. Yet each is, in fact, a graph of artificial data constructed by computerized coin flips, with heads giving an increase in price and tails a decrease. These figures illustrate the point that, after the fact, a little study reveals apparent patterns in past data, patterns that are of no use whatsoever in predicting the results of future coin flips.

Statistical tests assume that the researcher starts with a theory, and then gathers data to test the theory. However, many analysts work in the other direction, studying the data until they find a theory that fits. Sherlock Holmes used this method of reasoning: examine the data to discover theories that are consistent with the data. It can be a very useful method of operation. Many important scientific theories, including Mendel's genetic theory, were discovered by finding theories that explain data. However, Sherlock Holmes research has been the source of thousands of quack theories as well.

Antidotes to Data Mining

How do we tell the difference? How can we separate the genius from the quack? There are two good antidotes to unrestrained data mining: common sense and fresh data. The first question to ask when confronted with statistical evidence in support of some theory is, "Does it make sense?" If it is a ridiculous theory, then you should not be persuaded by anything less than mountains of evidence. One of the reasons you doubted the coin-flip system is that common sense tells you that coin flips are unpredictable. Even if someone claims to have predicted 99 out of 100 flips correctly, you still would be unconvinced. Instead of accepting that person's coin-calling prowess, you would suspect trickery. As Thomas Paine once wrote, "Is it more probable that nature should go out of her course, or that a man should tell a lie?" Most situations are not as clear-cut as coin predictions, but, nonetheless, you still should use common sense in evaluating statistical evidence.

The second antidote is fresh data. It is not a fair test of a theory to use the very data that were used to choose the theory. For an impartial test, we must state the theory before we see the data that will be used to test it. If some data have been used to concoct a theory, then the theory should be tested with fresh data that have not been contaminated by data mining. Consider the coin-flipping example again. When someone announces that a system is right nineteen out of twenty times, your likely response is, "I will flip a coin and see how well you do." The results will be fresh data, and most likely will expose a fraudulent system. You should do the same with any theory discovered by data mining.

In chemistry, physics, and the other natural sciences, such an approach is considered standard procedure. Whenever someone announces an important new theory, a dozen people rush to their laboratories to see if they can replicate the results. Unfortunately, investors do not have experimental laboratories. Instead, they may have to wait years or even decades to accumulate enough fresh data to test their theories.

When stock analysts test their theories with fresh data, the results usually are disappointing in that the theory does not explain fresh data nearly as well as it did the original data. The analysts' usual explanation is that there have been structural changes in the economy which necessitate modifications of their original models. They then mine the fresh data for a new theory. In this way, a provocative initial theory turns into a career.

PATTERNS IN THE STOCK MARKET

Because so very much money could be made in the stock market if only a reliable system could be found, millions of investors have spent billions of hours trying to discover some formula for success. It is not surprising that some have stumbled on rules that explain the past remarkably well but are disappointing in predicting the future.

Many such systems would be laughable, except for the fact that some people really believe in them. Burton Crane, a *New York Times* columnist for many years, told of two:

> There was once a man who ran a fairly successful investment advisory service based on his "readings" of the comic strips in The New York Sun . . . .
>
> I have been assured in utter seriousness that the dots between prices on the ticker tape are a code used by the Big Boys to signal each other for market coups. I have even been shown what purported to be a decoding of the dots. (The dots, in fact, are used in slow markets to move the last price out from under the typewheel so that it can be read.)[11]

Male stock analysts have been watching women's hemlines for a long time, believing that short skirts are bullish and long ones bearish; long heels on women's shoes are also supposed to be bullish and short heels bearish. For male fashions, thin ties are thought to be bullish and wide ties bearish, "There seems to be some confusion on this point, however, because some analysts put it the other way around while those who shop at Brooks Brothers aren't aware that tie widths can change."[12]

Other analysts have monitored sunspots, the water levels of the Great Lakes, and sales of aspirin and yellow paint. Some believe that the market does especially well in years ending in five—1975, 1985, and so on—while others argue that years ending in eight are best. In 1976, *Money* magazine reported that a Minneapolis stock broker had wonderful success over a five-month period, selecting stocks by spreading *The Wall Street Journal* on the floor and buying the stock touched by the first nail on the right paw of his golden retriever.[13]

Joseph Granville monitors what he calls the Confusion Index, keeping track of the number of times the word *confusion* appears in *The Wall Street Journal*. Tongue in cheek, Lawrence Ritter and William Silber found an astounding correlation from 1960 to 1966 between the Dow Jones Industrial

338

THE SUPER BOWL SYSTEM

On Super Bowl Sunday in January 1983, both the business and sports sections of the *Los Angeles Times* carried articles on the "Super Bowl Stock-Market Predictor."[1] The theory is that the stock market goes up if the National Football Conference—or a former National Football League (NFL) team now in the American Football Conference (AFC)—wins the Super Bowl. The market goes down if the AFC wins. In 1983, this theory had proven correct for fifteen out of sixteen Super Bowls—the one exception was 1970, when Kansas City beat Minnesota and the market went up 0.1 percent. Thus, the *Times* quoted a broker for Dean Witter Reynolds as saying, "Market observers will be glued to their TV screens . . . today it will be hard to ignore an S&P [market index] indicator with an accuracy quotient that's greater than 94%." An NFC team, the Washington Redskins, won that year, and the market went up. Next year, 1984, the Super Bowl system was back in the newspapers, stronger than ever—however, the AFC's L.A. Raiders won, and the market went up anyway. From its discovery through 1988, the Super Bowl system has been right five out of six times.

The accuracy of the Super Bowl system is obviously just an amusing coincidence, since the stock market has nothing to do with the outcome of a football game. Over these 22 years, the stock market has generally gone up and the NFC has usually won the Super Bowl. The correlation is made more startling by the gimmick of including the Pittsburgh Steelers, an AFC team, in with the NFC. The excuse is that Pittsburgh once was in the NFL; the real reason is that Pittsburgh won the Super Bowl four times in years when the market went up.

Inspired by the success of the Super Bowl indicator, a *Los Angeles Times* staff writer did a little data mining in 1989 and discovered several comparable coincidences.[2] The "Yo, Adrian Theory" holds that if a Rocky or Rambo movie is released, the stock market will go up that year. On average, the Dow increased by 173 points in the four years when a Rocky movie appeared and 245 points in the years when a Rambo movie was released. The Geraldo Rivera indicator notes that the Dow has fallen an average of 13 points on the day after seven major Geraldo Rivera specials. The George Steinbrenner indicator monitors his firing of Yankee managers. On the five occasions that he fired Billy Martin, the Dow rose an average of 5 points the following day; the eight times Steinbrenner fired someone else, the Dow fell an average of 3 points the next day.

[1] Sue Avery, "Market Investors Will Be High on Redskins Today;" and "Morning Briefing: Wall Street 'Skinish on Big Game," *Los Angeles Times,* January 30, 1983.

[2] James Bates, "Reality Wears Loser's Jersey in Super Bowl Stock Theory," *Los Angeles Times,* January 22, 1989.

Average and the number of strikeouts by the Washington Senators baseball team; unfortunately, the Washington Senators are no more.[14] Investment Example 10–3 tells of a similar sports system that is still making headlines.

The Dow Theory's Track Record

The logic of the Dow theory seems plausible, and William Hamilton's advocacy was influential; but the disappointing truth is that the theory has not been very successful in predicting the stock market. In one of the first careful studies of the value of investment advice, Alfred Cowles reread *The Wall Street Journal* editorials and found that Hamilton had made ninety forecasts of stock market changes. As it turned out, forty-five, exactly half of his recommendations, were profitable, and half were not. Perhaps the errors were small and the correct forecasts were very profitable? Following Hamilton's advice (and ignoring taxes and commissions), an investor would have averaged a return of 12 percent a year; the investor who ignored Hamilton and stayed fully invested averaged 15.5 percent a year.[15]

The Dow theory's limited success is indicated also by the subjective and often ambiguous signals it gives. On one memorable day, two leading Dow theorists looked at the charts and published diametrically opposed recommendations. One concluded that "high markets carry potentially large risks . . . the spring rise is probably in its culminating phase," while the other wrote that "the stock market is headed for much higher levels . . . is ripe for one of the greatest long-term advances in history."[16] If the theory really works, the users ought to agree at least on the signals.

"Wall Street Week" Data Mining

The complexity and fragility of Wall Street Week's technical indicators suggest data mining. For instance, its advance-decline index was initially a five-week average of the daily ratio of the number of stocks advancing plus 50 percent of those unchanged to the total number traded. There are a virtually unlimited number of other possibilities, many of which may have been tried by Robert Nurock before he settled on this particular one. Why is a five-week average used? Why not use four, eight, or some other number? Why is this indicator a *ratio* rather than a *difference* between advances and declines? If a ratio, why not advances divided by declines? The report that one particular variant explains earlier data fairly well is undermined by the sobering observation that there will always be some variant of even worthless theories that, by coincidence, happens to explain earlier data fairly well.

The introduction of powerful computers into technical analysis allows a technician to try hundreds, if not thousands, of ways of explaining past data, of finding patterns and rules that, as in Investment Example 10–4 on p. 340, would have been profitable if only the analyst had known the system beforehand. The fact that these rules must be revised or discarded after their application to fresh data is a discomforting reminder that the same is true of worthless, coincidental relationships.

COMPUTERS DON'T MAKE MISTAKES, PEOPLE DO

In 1982, *Fortune* magazine told of a company selling a computer program for forecasting the stock market eighty days ahead.* The company selling this program claimed to have found a complex pattern in stock prices that would have enabled a user to make a 72.1 percent profit over the preceding three years, while the stock market as a whole went down 6.1 percent. Just like the twenty coin flips and the 50,000 dice rolls, it should be easy to find such

*Daniel Seligman, "A Technical Error," *Fortune,* December 27, 1982, pp. 31-32.

apparent patterns even if the stock market, like coin flips and dice rolls, is completely random.

A *Fortune* editor ordered one of these programs and used it for eighty days, from August 13 through December 6, 1982. The August 13 forecast was that the market would drop 7.5 percent over the next eighty days. Indeed, every single day during this eighty-day period, the computer program advised selling stocks. However, the Dow Jones Industrial Average went up 11 points on August 13 and 300 more points over the next few weeks. This advance was one of the strongest in stock-market history, and the computer program missed it completely. Back to the charts.

SUMMARY

Technical analysis tries to gauge the mood of the market by studying charts of stock prices and data on various aspects of investor attitudes. Some analysts believe in momentum and buy when they see strength. Others emphasize reaction and sell when they think the market is overly strong. Many chart watchers try to identify support and resistance levels, reasoning that investor memories influence buying and selling at such critical points.

Most technical indicators can be given a plausible interpretation, but the data mining used to derive them is unsettling. The testing of many theories ensures that the determined researcher will find at least one theory that is consistent with the data, at least one pattern in the stock market that would have been profitable had it been known ahead of time. Since data mining inevitably leads to theories consistent with the data, we cannot tell whether the results of such exploration reflect the discovery of a useful theory or just perseverence. The only way to tell is with common sense and fresh data. Technical analysis, unfortunately, is much better at describing what happened yesterday than in predicting what will happen tomorrow.

EXERCISES

1. The Wall Street expression, "Don't fight the tape," means don't buy stock if prices are falling and don't sell if prices are rising. Would you characterize this as a momentum or reaction theory?

2. Burton Crane, stock-market columnist for the *New York Times* from 1937 to 1963, advised, "Buy stocks when they are making new highs and attracting attention, not when they are down at the bottom and nobody loves them."[17] Is this advice more consistent with the momentum or reaction school?

3. In 1987, the director of economic analysis for the National Association of Realtors said:

> If the rates for fixed-rate loans were to rise to the threshold level of 12% or above, as was the case in 1985, you'd see an extreme shift in behavior. The market buyer psychology would be altered and ARMs [adjustable rate mortgages] would storm back in alarming numbers.[18]

Would you interpret such home buyer behavior as a momentum or reaction approach to predicting bond prices?

4. Fidelity offers a variety of sector mutual funds, each investing in stocks in only one industry. An independent investment advisory service specializes in selecting the most attractive of these Fidelity sector funds:

> Our switch rules are simple. Invest in that fund that has been the strongest over the last 39 weeks. Stay with that strongest fund until it falls a full dollar below its 39-week weighted moving average, or more than two funds outrank it by a dollar or more. Then switch to the new strongest fund.[19]

Would you say that this advisory service is in the momentum or reaction school of technical analysis?

5. One of the ten technical indicators used on "Wall Street Week" gives a buy signal when the current prices of most NYSE stocks are below their average prices over the preceding ten and thirty weeks. Indicate whether this is a momentum or reaction interpretation of such data, and explain why.

6. "The main reason charts work is that investors have a nasty habit of remembering what they paid . . . The rest of the technique of chart reading is founded on the 'if you only had' idea."[20] Explain why such memories might establish a support level for a stock.

7. Technicians sometimes place a buy stop order to buy a stock now trading for, say, $26.50 if the price rises above $30. Why would they want to buy later at $30 when they could buy now at $26.50?

8. Some analysts monitor data on the fraction of mutual-fund assets invested in cash (Treasury bills and other short-term bonds). A buy signal might be given when the cash ratio exceeds 10 percent and a sell signal when mutual-fund cash drops below 5 percent. Give a logical explanation.

9. Louis Rukeyser once began his newspaper column with "Wonderful news: the experts are getting pessimistic about the stock market."[21] Why would anyone think that this is wonderful news?

10. The Boston Snow (B.S.) indicator uses the presence or absence of snow in Boston on Christmas Eve to predict the direction the stock market will go the following year: "the average gain following snow on the ground was about 80 percent greater than for years in which there was no snow."[22] How would you explain the apparent success of the B.S. index?

11. In 1987, a year with three Friday-the-13ths, the chief economist at a Philadelphia bank reported that in the past forty years there had been six other years with three Friday-the-13ths, and a recession started in three of those years.[23] Explain why you do or do not find this evidence persuasive.

12. Explain the following observation:

> There have always been a considerable number of pathetic people who busy themselves examining the last thousand numbers which have appeared on a roulette wheel, in search of some repeating pattern. Sadly enough, they have usually found it.[24]

13. Filter systems monitor price movements, looking for stocks that have changed direction.[25] Users adopt a mechanical rule of buying whenever a stock has risen x percent from a previous low and selling whenever a stock has fallen x percent from a previous high.

a. How can stop-loss orders be used to implement a filter-system strategy?

b. What is the implicit assumption underlying a filter-system strategy?

c. If this assumption is correct, what is the disadvantage of using a large value of x?

d. What is the disadvantage of using a small value of x?

14. Some technical analysts watch the number of short sales by stock-exchange specialists, believing that an increase in their short sales signals a bear market. Give two logical explanations of this indicator.

15. Explain why the following evidence does or does not persuade you that Dragon years are especially good years to buy stocks:

> Trying to discern any sort of seasonality in stock market movements may be a futile exercise. Perhaps the most ingenious "analysis" was done by the Rothschild firm, which noted that February begins the Year of the Dragon in the Chinese calendar.
> . . . during the 20th century . . . there were twice as many up Dragon years [4] as down Dragon years [2].[26]

16. Believing that changes in the money supply have an effect on the stock market, Beryl Sprinkel considered this strategy:[27]

> a. Keep track of the average monthly rate of growth of the seasonally adjusted money supply over the preceding six months.
> b. Buy stocks two months after a trough in this moving average.
> c. Sell stocks fifteen months after a peak in this moving average.

Neglecting brokerage fees, such a strategy would have given an average capital gain of 6 percent a year between 1918 and 1964, while simply buying and holding would have yielded 5.5 percent a year. Why might someone be skeptical of this evidence?

17. Explain the success of the following stock-market theory, advanced by a Tijuana brokerage firm, based on the clothes worn by television personality Vanna White: "If she sports a white, strapless dress, a 'buy' program appears to follows. 'Sell' programs are initiated if she wears neck-high garments."[28]

18. A computer program was advertised that had picked fourteen NYSE stocks, thirteen of which went up for a thirty percent return in four months. The promotional material stated:

> Each disk is valid for only four months. You pay only $199 for the program . . . and purchasing the disk entitles you to renew the disk every four months thereafter for the same $199 per disk . . . .
> Our guarantee of satisfaction is very compelling. If, after the four months, you are not satisfied with the program or have not seen it pay for itself many times over, please return it and get a full refund of your $199 investment. You can't lose.[29]

Is it true that this money-back guarantee insures that you cannot lose? Why do you suppose that the disk must be renewed every four months? Can you think of a way that an unscrupulous company could write a very simple computer program guaranteeing that half its subscribers will be satisfied during each four-month period?

19. While playing bridge recently, Ira Rate picked up his thirteen-card hand and found that it contained no spades (and very few honors, either). He promptly threw his cards down and declared that the deal had not been random. He read in a book on probability and statistics that (a) the probability of being dealt a hand with no spades is less than 5 percent and (b) this low a probability is sufficient evidence to reject the hypothesis that the deal was fair. Point out a fault or two in his reasoning.

20. A researcher wants to show that there is a statistically significant ability to predict the outcomes of coin flips. This researcher has decided that if a subject does not make enough correct predictions to pass the first test, then these results will be discarded and a second ten-coin test will be given. What is the probability that a guesser will eventually pass a test? Why are the results unconvincing evidence of psychic abilities?

21. Write a paragraph criticizing the *Telephone Switch Newsletter*'s investment philosophy:

For purposes of illustration, let us assume that the stock market can be divided into ten different segments . . . For example, included in these ten segments could be: blue chip stocks, energy-related stocks, stocks which concentrate in gold mining companies, bonds, utilities, and a cash position . . . Reviewing the past shows that no matter what the economic or political situation has been during the past 100 years, there has always been at least one of the segments of the stock market where you could make money . . . .

So what does our individual investment counselor actually do? He determines which segments of the market at present are in an uptrend and invests his money into mutual funds that specialize in these segments.

During the alloted one hour per week he gives to monitoring his plan, he sees whether the segment he is using is still in an uptrend. As long as the uptrend is still in place, he stays with the investment. When the trend is broken, funds are taken out of that segment and moved to a segment that is currently in an uptrend. If none of the segments being monitored are in an uptrend, he then goes to cash . . . The first benefit we experience is a feeling of contentment, along with peace of mind, because we are now in control. Once we realize that we are in control no matter what economic situation develops here or abroad, we know that there will always be some investment that will offer growth for our capital. The important word here is always.[30]

22. The following letter to the editor appeared in *Sports Illustrated:*

In regard to the observation made by *Sports Illustrated* correspondent Ted O'Leary concerning this year's bowl games (Scorecard, January 16), I believe I can offer an even greater constant. On Jan. 2 the team that won in all five games started the game going right-to-left on the television screen. I should know, I lost a total of 10 bets to my parents because I had left-to-right in our family wagers this year.

Gary M Wiesel
Interlochen, Mich.[31]

If right-to-left makes no difference, the chances of losing all five bets is 0.0312. Are you convinced, then, that right-to-left does matter? What other explanation can you provide?

23. "As January goes, so goes the year" is an old stock-market adage, meaning that if the market goes up from January 1 to January 31, then it will go up for the entire year, January 1 to December 31. If the market drops in January, then it will be a bad year. In its February 4, 1974, issue *Newsweek* reported that "this rule of thumb has proved correct in twenty of the

TABLE 10–A

Year	Return (percent)	Year	Return (percent)
1961	26.89	1971	14.31
1962	−8.73	1972	18.98
1963	22.80	1973	−14.66
1964	16.48	1974	−26.47
1965	12.45	1975	37.20
1966	−10.06	1976	23.84
1967	23.98	1977	−7.18
1968	11.06	1978	6.56
1969	−8.50	1979	18.44
1970	4.01	1980	32.42

past 24 years." Explain why you are skeptical about this evidence.

24. To test the theory given in Exercise 23, collect data on the Dow Jones Industrial Average for the years 1974 to the present and compare the profitability of the following two strategies (ignore brokerage fees, dividends, and interest):

a. Invest $10,000 on January 1, 1974, and hold the investment until December 31, 1989.

b. Each year invest all your money in the stock market on January 31 if the market has risen in January. Sell each December 31 and wait for the January signal.

25. Annual stock returns over the twenty-year period 1961–80 are shown in Table 10–A. Assume that you have initial wealth of $100,000, that there are no taxes, and that there is a 2 percent brokerage fee on each stock transaction. Assume a 5 percent return when funds are not invested in stocks. For each of the following strategies, calculate your wealth when the portfolio is sold at the end of 1980:

a. Buy and hold—buy stocks at the beginning of 1961 and hold until the end of 1980.

b. Momentum—buy stocks at the beginning of each year if the market return was positive the preceding year and sell stocks after the market has a negative annual return.

c. Reaction—buy stocks at the beginning of each year if the market had a negative return the preceding year, and sell stocks after the market has a positive annual return.

CHAPTER 11

The Efficient-Market Hypothesis

Is this a game of chance? Not the way I play it . . .
W.C. Fields

The preceding chapter suggested that technical indicators do not predict changes in stock prices. In this chapter, we will evaluate an even stronger assertion, that because financial markets are efficient, there are no profitable ways to forecast changes in security prices. As you might suspect, this theory is very important and provocative. The efficient-market idea can be applied to any asset; here we focus on the stock market. We will examine first the logic of an efficient market—what it implies and what it does not imply—and then some research supporting and contradicting this hypothesis.

You will see that the evidence is strongest in its rejection of technical analysis and also suggests that a great deal of fundamental analysis is of little value. On the other hand, the numerous insider-trading scandals that were exposed in the 1980s revealed that some people did know in advance which way certain stock prices were heading. You will learn how these people acquired their advance information and why the profits they made were illegal. We will conclude the chapter by looking at some investors who apparently have beaten the market legally.

THE IDEA OF AN EFFICIENT MARKET

Earlier chapters introduced the idea of an **efficient market** in which there are no obviously mispriced securities and, therefore, no transactions that can be counted on to make abnormally large profits. An efficient market

efficient market
In an efficient market there are no obviously mispriced securities and, therefore, no transactions that can be counted on to make abnormally large profits.

does not require zero profits. Stockholders receive dividends and, as time passes, expect stock prices to increase along with corporate assets, profits, and dividends. Since safe bank accounts and Treasury securities pay a positive return, stocks are priced to have positive anticipated returns, too—indeed, relatively high returns to the extent stocks are risky. The efficient-market hypothesis says that, compared to other investments—taking into account the risk and other characteristics thought to be relevant by investors—stocks are not priced to give a return that is clearly inadequate or excessive.

The stock market would be inefficient if some investors could take advantage of others' ignorance—for example, if some investors knew that a company had discovered an extremely profitable cure for baldness and they could buy stock at an unreasonably low price from other investors who were unaware of this discovery. If, on the other hand, information is disseminated quickly so that all investors have the same information, then market prices are efficient in that there is no advantage to *trading on information*—that is, buying or selling on the basis of information about a company or the market as a whole. An efficient market is a fair game in the sense that no investor can beat the market (except by luck), because no investor has an information advantage over other investors.

Required Disclosures

Investors are able to learn a great deal about U.S. corporations because of our free press, aggressive investment industry, and laws requiring corporate disclosures. It was not always this way. Early corporations in the United States told their shareholders remarkably little. Testifying before a congressional committee in 1899, the head of the American Sugar Refining Company defended the practice of not reporting earnings:

> *Let the buyer beware: that covers the whole business. You cannot wet-nurse people from the time they are born until the day they die. They have got to wade in and get stuck and that is the way men are educated and cultivated.*[1]

Today, the Securities and Exchange Commission (SEC) compels publicly traded corporations to disclose important financial information. Detailed prospectuses accompany the public sale of securities. Most companies must file an annual financial report (Form 10–K) and a quarterly version (Form 10–Q). Any extraordinary events of significance must also be reported to the SEC within fifteen days (Form 8–K). Mergers, liquidation, and other major asset transfers require detailed statements. Prospectuses, annual reports, and other disclosures can be obtained from most stockbrokers, the company itself, and the SEC.

Those investors who acquire more than 5 percent of a company's out-

INVESTMENT EXAMPLE
11–1

EQUITY FUNDING

Equity Funding was established in 1960 to sell a life insurance/mutual fund package.* Individuals were to invest in mutual funds and then borrow against this investment to buy life insurance. If the mutual funds did well, then the customer could, as the aggressive salesmen emphasized, pay back the loan plus interest and still have more than they invested—free life insurance plus some profits!

Equity Funding stock was an investor favorite when it reported that its profits were growing at 25 percent a year, and the company issued additional high-priced shares to finance a variety of acquisitions, including insurance companies, a savings and loan association, and even a cattle-breeding business. The stock price reached a high of $80 a share in 1969. Yet in 1973 (with its annual report at the printers, showing shareholders' equity of $143 million and 1972 profits of $22.6 million), the company went bankrupt when the public learned that at least $100 million of its assets were based on phony loans and phony insurance for nonexistent customers. Since the total reported profits during its thirteen-year history came to $75 million, Equity Funding had, in fact, lost money year after year. The president of Equity Funding was sentenced to eight years in federal prison for conspiracy and fraud; a partner in Equity Funding's accounting firm also served three months in prison.

*For more details on this episode, see Wyndham Robertson, "Those Daring Young Con Men of Equity Funding," *Fortune*, August 1973, pp. 81–85, 120–32.

standing shares must disclose these holdings (and each additional 2 percent) on Schedule 13D. Also required in certain circumstances is the filing of an **insider report**—a report required by the SEC from a corporation's directors and executives and those investors who own more than 10 percent of its shares whenever they buy or sell the firm's stock. These insiders are also prohibited from selling the firm's stock short and must turn over any profit made on stock held for less than six months.

insider report
A corporation's insiders must report purchases or sales of the firm's stock to the SEC.

Section 10(b)5 of the Securities Exchange Act of 1934 states that it is unlawful "to make any untrue statement of a material fact or to omit to state a material fact." Inadequate disclosure also invites class-action lawsuits by disgruntled shareholders. The professional bankers, accountants, and lawyers who prepare the requisite disclosure documents are, as a rule, cautious and truthful—unwilling to jeopardize their careers by making fraudulent statements that benefit them only indirectly if at all. The isolated cases of fraud, as in Investment Example 11–1, are newsworthy because they are unusual.

Anticipated Events and Surprises

Investors not only try to learn about events soon after their occurrence, but also to anticipate what will happen in the future. The efficient-market hypothesis implies an important distinction between events that have been anticipated in advance and those that have not. For instance, if a toy store's sales increase before Christmas, will the price of its stock rise too? When the stock trades in June, the price that buyers are willing to pay and sellers are willing to accept reflects the common knowledge that toy sales increase during the holiday season. Based on the information available in June, buyers and sellers estimate these sales and value the stock accordingly. If the actual increase in sales turns out to be equal to these forecasts, then there is no cause for a revision in the value of the stock. The price does change, however, if sales are unexpectedly brisk or disappointing.

Future events that are anticipated by investors are already imbedded in today's stock prices. Unexpected returns are caused by the occurrence of unexpected events.

As another example, consider the Dow theory, explained in the previous chapter, which states that regular cycles in the economy cause predictable cycles in stock prices. In an efficient market, any anticipated cycle in the economy should already be reflected in current stock prices. Investors seeing a recession coming will not buy stock unless today's price is low enough to give them their requisite return. Investors seeing an economic boom on the horizon will not sell their stock if the price is so low that holding on to the stock will give them more than their required return. Even if the economy goes through regular cycles, this cyclical pattern in the economy is not a good reason for buying or selling stock in anticipation of a similar pattern in stock prices. If the economic cycle is widely anticipated, stock prices at any point in the cycle give investors their required return. Excessive or inadequate returns are caused by random surprises, not anticipated events.

As Investment Example 11–2 illustrates, it is not enough to know that IBM will make more profits next year than Sears, that ice-cream sales increase in the summer, or that auto sales increase when the economy gets stronger. The question you have to ask yourself in order to establish a benchmark with which to gauge your investment ideas is not, "How will tomorrow differ from today?" but, "How does my perception of tomorrow differ from what others believe?" Do you really know something that the experts do not know? If you do, then you may be guilty of using inside information that is illegal for reasons discussed later in this chapter. If you do not, then your information is already imbedded in market prices.

THE COVER-PAGE JINX

Many sports fans believe that *Sports Illustrated* has a cover-page jinx, in that the athletes featured on the front cover of this weekly sports magazine often have disappointing performances afterward. Perhaps fame makes these athletes overconfident, or the history of the jinx makes them nervous. Regression toward the mean is another possibility, in that those athletes who have been spectacular successes recently cannot be expected to continue doing exceptionally well. On the other hand, it may be just a coincidence noted by disappointed fans.

Interestingly, the same sort of cover-page jinx has been observed for economic stories in the national media. For instance, the August 13, 1979, cover of *Business Week* dramatically proclaimed "The Death of Equities." During the next four years, the stock market rose by more than 50 percent, and in May 1983, *Business Week* was compelled to run a cover story proclaiming the "Rebirth of Equities." The market then fell 10 percent during the next twelve months. The May 21, 1984, cover of *Business Week* asked, "Are Utilities Obsolete?" emphasizing the troubles with nuclear power; nevertheless, utilities stocks strongly outperformed the market over the next two years. The May 28, 1984, cover story, "Government Bonds: A Market in Trouble," appeared the very week that bond prices bottomed; interest rates peaked at 14 percent that week and tumbled to 7 percent over the next two years.

News magazines are not incompetent, but most of what they report is old news. When their readers are informed that utility companies are in trouble, the prices of utility stocks already are very low. If bonds are reported to be unattractive, their prices are already depressed. If such bad news already is reflected in prices, it is not a reason to sell. As the old saying goes, "What everybody knows isn't worth knowing."

Uncertainty and Disagreement

The efficient-market hypothesis does not assume that the future is known with certainty or that everyone agrees on what a security is worth. The uncertainty of economic events is illustrated by these candid remarks made in October 1986 by one of the nation's top economic forecasters, Edward Yardeni of Prudential Bache:

> In our last forecast table dated July 29, we expected real GNP to fall by 2.4% during the third quarter of this year. Instead, real GNP rose by 2.4%. We had the magnitude right; we just got the sign wrong. So now we have to choose: Do we go back to our Muddling Through scenario? Do we turn into reaccelerationists? Or should we just push out our slump scenario?
> We pick Door #3.[2]

Four months later, Yardeni wrote

We're moving back into the muddling camp. We've been slumpers for the past few months. A slump is still possible, but now we feel more comfortable with a muddling scenario. Until recently, we assigned the slump scenario a subjective probability of 50%, with muddling at 30% and a boom given a 20% chance. Now, muddling gets 50%; bust gets 30%; and boom stays at 20% . . . . In the current economic environment . . . . quite honestly, anything is possible.[3]

Honest economic forecasters admit that they are practicing an imperfect art, not a precise science—or as one analyst quipped, "Economic forecasting is the occupation that makes astrology respectable."[4]

The twists and turns of individual companies and the aggregate economy (including output, interest rates, inflation and the like) depend in unknowable ways on a myriad of unpredictable developments, including the weather, new discoveries, and the moods of consumers, businesses, and policymakers. The best we can do is identify likely scenarios and use probabilities to describe their relative likelihood.

The efficient-market hypothesis does not assume that investors agree on these probabilities. Market opinion of IBM in the spring of 1987 provides a particularly dramatic example. IBM is probably the most widely followed company; the best analysts spend countless hours studying the company and its stock. In 1982, Value Line, one of the top stock-research firms, gave IBM stock an above-average rating and projected its 1985–87 price to be between 180 and 225. Five years later, in the spring of 1987, with IBM at 130, Value Line gave IBM stock its lowest rating, placing it among the bottom 10 percent in predicted performance over the next twelve months.[5] At the same time, Kidder, Peabody's widely respected research department gave IBM its highest rating and included it in its recommended model portfolio of twenty stocks, saying, "We consider IBM to be the most attractive low-risk stock in our universe of mainframe-computer companies."[6]

The stock market is dominated by institutions relying on intelligent and knowledgeable analysts. As with any stock, at IBM's current price there are as many buyers as sellers—as many people who think that the stock is overpriced as think it is a bargain. The efficient-market argument is that the price is not clearly too high or too low—for if it was, there would not be a balance between buyers and sellers. Assume you buy a stock for $30. If there is any obvious reason why the stock is worth much more than this price, other investors would not be willing to sell at $30 or to stand on the sidelines and let you get this bargain.

It does not follow that the price of IBM or any other stock is "correct," according to some external, objective criterion. A market price reflects only what investors are willing to pay for a stock. As long as the future is uncertain, there can be reasonable disagreement about the value of a stock.

Some observers believe that information about stocks spreads through the investment community like ripples in a pond, providing a momentum to stock prices as more and more people learn of the news. As reasonable as it may seem, this story does not explain why the first investors to learn good news, knowing that a stock is more valuable, do not buy heavily themselves—forcing the price to a level that will be justified once everyone knows the news. According to the efficient-market hypothesis, either everyone learns the news at the same time, or else there are a sufficient number of well-informed and well-financed investors to eliminate any bargains quickly.

ALTERNATIVE VERSIONS OF THE EFFICIENT-MARKET HYPOTHESIS

Investment decisions are influenced by many different bits and pieces of information, such as recent price movements, measures of investor sentiment, unemployment forecasts, perceptions of Federal Reserve policy, and takeover rumors. It is useful to group such disparate information into three general categories: past prices, other public data, and private information. The corresponding forms of the efficient-market hypothesis are referred to as weak, semi-strong, and strong; and we will discuss in turn each of these forms in the following sections.

The Weak Form

The **weak form** of the efficient-market hypothesis holds that past data on stock prices are of no use in predicting future price changes. Past price data are widely available, and there is no logical reason for investors to revise their opinions of a stock based on old data. The immediate implication is that most technical analysis is worthless. The weak form of the efficient-market theory often is called the **random-walk hypothesis** in that it states that each change in a stock's price is unrelated to previous changes, much as each flip of a coin is unrelated to previous tosses, and each step by a drunkard is unrelated to previous steps.

Tests of Filter Systems A number of get-rich books, including Ira Cobleigh's *Happiness is a Stock that Doubles in a Year* and Nicholas Darvas's *How I Made Two Million Dollars in the Stock Market*, advocate a **filter system:** Set some target price change, x percent, and then buy after the stock moves up x percent from a previous low or sell after it falls x percent from a previous high. This system implicitly assumes a momentum in stock prices. Fama and Blume applied this theory to a portfolio consisting of the thirty Dow Jones industrial stocks over a five-year period, during which a buy-and-hold strategy would have yielded about 10 percent a year. The results shown in Table 11–1 for different filter rules suggest some momentum in

weak form
The weak form of the efficient market hypothesis holds that past data on stock prices are of no use in predicting future price changes.

random walk hypothesis
The random walk hypothesis says that each change in a stock's price is unrelated to previous changes.

filter system
A filter system is a technical strategy of buying or selling after a specified percentage change in stock prices.

TABLE 11–1   Average Rate of Return from Filter System, 1957–1962

Value of x (percent)	Return before Commissions (percent)	Number of Transactions	Return after Commissions (percent)
0.5	11.5	12,514	− 103.6
1.0	5.5	8,660	− 74.9
2.0	0.2	4,784	− 45.2
4.0	0.1	2,013	− 19.5
6.0	1.3	1,071	− 9.4
8.0	1.7	653	− 5.0
10.0	3.0	435	− 1.4
12.0	5.3	289	2.3
14.0	3.9	224	1.4
16.0	4.2	172	2.3
18.0	3.6	139	2.0
20.0	4.3	110	3.0
30.0	− 0.5	51	− 1.4
40.0	− 2.7	21	− 3.5
50.0	− 21.4	4	− 23.0

Source: Data from Eugene F. Fama and Marshall E. Blume, "Filter Rules and Stock Market Trading," *Journal of Business*, January 1966, pp. 226–41.

small movements and some reaction in large moves, but that, once transaction costs are taken into account, only the brokers profit from filter systems—illustrating the truth of an old cartoon where a visitor says to a stockbroker at the boat club, "But where are the customers' yachts?"

Tests of Statistical Runs   Researchers have searched for evidence of momentum or reaction by counting the number of runs in stock prices also. To conduct such a test, we first divide the data into regular intervals (such as days or weeks) and determine whether the price change in each interval is larger or smaller than the median change. For instance, if we look at a ten-day period in the past, during which the median price change was zero, we can label the days when the market was up with a + and the down days with a −. The results might look like one of the following three patterns:

statistical runs

A statistical run is a sequence of uninterrupted above-average or uninterrupted below-average data.

+ + + + + − − − − −	2 runs (momentum)
+ − + − + − + − + −	10 runs (reaction)
+ − − + − + + + − −	6 runs (random)

A **statistical run** is a sequence of uninterrupted pluses or uninterrupted minuses. As indicated in the three patterns, stock prices will exhibit few

TABLE 11–2 Statistical Runs in Allied Chemical Stock

Frequency	Expected Number of Runs	Actual Number of Runs
Daily	713	683
4 days	162	160
9 days	71	71
16 days	39	39

Source: Eugene F. Fama, "The Behavior of Stock Market Prices," *Journal of Business*, January 1965, pp. 34–105.

runs if momentum is present and many runs if reaction is important. If the sequence of price changes is random, so that whether the market goes up or down today is unaffected by what happened on other days, then it can be shown that the number of runs should be close to $1 + n/2$, where n is the number of observations.

For instance, you might flip a coin ten times now, record the results, and count the number of runs. The outcome of each coin flip is independent of other flips, and we can expect about $1 + 10/2 = 6$ runs. More concretely, about 80 percent of the time, the number of runs will turn out to be between four and eight.

One study examined the prices of the thirty stocks in the Dow Jones Industrial Average over a five-year period, considering not only daily prices but also price changes over intervals of four, nine, and sixteen days. Table 11–2 shows the results for Allied Chemical, which are typical. There are somewhat fewer runs than expected in the daily data and virtually no difference between the actual and expected numbers over longer horizons. As was true of the filter tests, these results show evidence of momentum in short-term price changes, but this tendency is surely too slight to be profitable.

Other Tests Tests of filters and runs focus on momentum and reaction, the basic concepts underlying technical analysis. Since most technicians are looking for complex patterns, these rules, too, have been scrutinized by academic researchers. One programmed a computer to look for support and resistance levels, finding, after brokerage costs, this strategy to be inferior to a buy-and-hold approach.[7] Another study used a computer to identify patterns, such as head-and-shoulders formations, that are popular with chartists and found "no evidence of profitable forecasting ability."[8]

Technicians naturally defend their livelihood, arguing that technical analysis is an art rather than a science and that computers cannot be programmed to depict fairly what are inevitably subjective decisions. Even if this is so, it is at least an admission that markets are efficient to the extent that simple, get-rich-quick rules based on price patterns do not work. University researchers overwhelmingly believe that technical analysis as a whole does not work and that whatever patterns are discovered are simply the predictable result of data mining—chance relationships in the past that cannot be counted on to persist in the future.

The Semi-Strong Form

semi-strong form
The semi-strong form of the efficient market hypothesis says that abnormal returns cannot be consistently earned using publicly available information.

The **semi-strong form** of the efficient market hypothesis holds that abnormal returns cannot be consistently earned using publicly available information, not only past prices but also such data as interest rates, inflation, and corporate earnings. There are two different ways investors might use such information: in **market timing**—deciding when to hold stocks and when to hold bonds and other assets—and in the selection of individual stocks. We will consider these applications in turn and then look at the performance of those who practice both.

market timing
Market timers attempt to buy stocks at low prices and sell at higher prices, based on technical or fundamental analysis, or on both.

Market Timing Many investors, particularly institutions with large diversified portfolios, are concerned primarily with the overall direction of the stock market. If the economy suddenly turns sour or interest rates soar, most stock prices drop and so does the value of their portfolios: the only real protection is to be out of the market and in "cash" (T-bills and the like). During great bull markets, almost any portfolio of stocks will make satisfactory profits. The trick is to be on the sidelines when prices falter and fully invested when prices surge. Even better would be a nimble jumping in and out of the market to catch every rise and miss every fall. A longtime financial writer for the *New York Times* offered this attractive goal:

> *Since we know stocks are going to fall as well as rise, we might as well get a little traffic out of them. A man who buys a stock at 10 and sells it at 20 makes 100 per cent. But a man who buys it at 10, sells it at 14½, buys it back at 12 and sells it at 18, buys it back at 15 and sells it at 20, makes 188 per cent.*[9]

Such market timing can be based on either technical or fundamental analysis, or on both. Those who try to guess the direction of the market watch their favorite indicators of economic activity, charts of stock prices, and a variety of gauges of market sentiment.

Experienced professionals have long been skeptical of those who claim to be astute enough to jump in and out of the market at the appropriate times. Chapter 10 cited Charles Dow's observation that "only a foolish speculator hopes to buy stocks at the lowest and sell them at the highest."[10] More concise is the Wall Street adage that states, "Bulls and bears make money, hogs never." It certainly would be profitable to buy stocks before prices go up and to sell before prices go down, but how are we to know a stock's direction in advance? When the legendary J. P. Morgan was asked what would happen to stock prices next, he responded simply, "They will fluctuate."

If it were easy to see that stock prices are headed up, there would be no sellers at current prices. For there to be a balance between buyers and sellers, there must be considerable uncertainty about the direction of prices. The semi-strong form of the efficient-market hypothesis assumes that the disagreement between buyers and sellers is not due to one side's ignorance of publicly available information. Both buyers and sellers know the latest data on the economy, corporate profits, and interest rates. Their uncertainty is over future events that cannot be anticipated easily.

It is natural to try to buy low and sell high, but every trade involves a brokerage fee, and every realized capital gain forces a tax payment. In addition, stocks on average do better than Treasury-bills—so that if you switch between stocks and T-bills and are right only half the time, you will average a lower return than with stocks alone. It has been estimated that someone who jumps in and out, trying to guess which way the market will go, must be right three times out of four to do as well as buy and hold.[11] A study by Merrill Lynch concluded that "the great majority of funds lose money as a result of their timing efforts, and when the effects of commission costs are included, virtually everyone loses money."[12]

Stock Selection Stock selection involves picking stocks that will do relatively well, whether the overall market goes up or down. The logic of the efficient-market hypothesis suggests that it will be difficult to do so using publicly available information. For instance, most of the data printed in a company's annual report may be known months in advance by analysts who follow the company and are certainly known by investors in general once the report appears. It is hard to see how could consistently beat the market by trading on the basis of the information in annual reports, and, no surprise, academic studies indicate that such information is already imbedded in market prices in the sense that it is of little use in predicting prices *after* the report appears.[13]

One way of testing the efficient-market hypothesis is to identify an event, such as the publication of a company's annual report, and then to see if there is any evidence of a later effect on prices. Another approach is to look at significant price changes themselves. For instance, every day *The Wall Street Journal* lists those stocks that experienced the largest percentage price change on the preceding trading day. Two researchers randomly selected thirty-six days in 1977 and examined the behavior of the five stocks that experienced the largest percentage price increases on each of these days.[14] The researchers' intent was to see if these price increases, apparently the consequence of a change in the companies' fortunes, either were preceded or followed by similar price increases. If so, this would indicate that information spreads gradually through financial markets. If

FIGURE 11–1   Daily price changes before and after a large stock-price increase. (*Source:* Avner Arbel and Bikki Jaggi, "Market Information Assimilation Related to Extreme Daily Price Jumps," *Financial Analysts Journal,* November/December 1982, p. 62.)

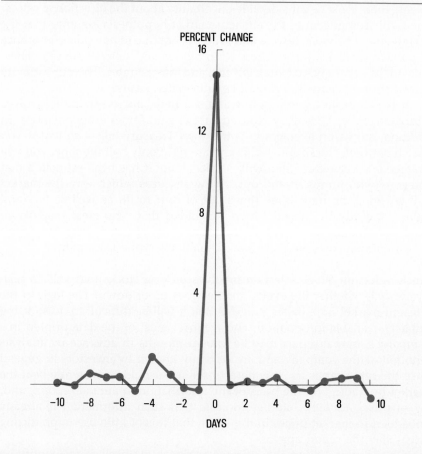

not, then whatever event triggered the price increase was apparently a surprise, whose full price effect was felt on a single trading day. Figure 11–1 summarizes their results. The price changes were small and seemingly random both before and after each large price increase, indicating that without warning some event caused a sudden jump in prices, followed by random fluctuations.

The Performance of Professionals   Another way of testing the semi-strong form of the efficient-market hypothesis is to review the records of professional investors, who presumably base their decisions, both in market-timing and in stock selection, on publicly available information. If these investors consistently beat the market, then public information is apparently of some value.

The record of professional investors as a group has been mediocre at best. In his persuasive book *The New Contrarian Investment Strategy*, David Dreman reports a compilation of fifty-two surveys of the stocks or stock portfolios recommended by professional investors during the years 1929–80. Of these, 77 percent underperformed the market.[15] Similarly, a tracking of forty-four prominent investment-advisory services from 1980 to 1985 found that only fourteen outperformed the S&P 500 while thirty underperformed.[16]

In addition, there is little or no consistency in which particular investors do relatively well and which do poorly. For instance, there is no correlation between a mutual fund's performance one year and its performance the next year; those funds in the top 10 percent this year and those in the bottom 10 percent are both equally likely to be in the bottom 10 percent next year.[17] A study of 200 institutional-stock portfolios found that of those institutions ranked in the top 25 percent in the period 1972–77, during 1977–82 26 percent ranked in the top 25 percent, 48 percent ranked in the middle 50 percent, and 26 percent were in the bottom 25 percent.[18] A similar scrutiny of thirty-two bond managers found no correlation at all between the performance rankings for 1972–76 and 1976–81.[19]

Many institutions have themselves been persuaded by such evidence and switched at least part of their portfolio to **indexing**—trying to replicate the market, rather than to outperform it—reasoning that matching a stock-market index will beat most of their competitors. The three largest stock managers—Wells Fargo Investment Advisors, Bankers Trust, and the College Retirement Equities Fund—are all index enthusiasts.

How Can We Distinguish Skill From Luck? Of course, some professionals do compile outstanding records (and publicize their successes). However, consider the following coin-calling experiment with a class of thirty-two students: Half the students predict heads for the first flip, and half the students predict tails. The coin is flipped and lands heads, making the first half right. The sixteen students who were right then predict a second flip, with half the students saying heads and the other half tails. It comes up tails, and the eight students who have been right twice in a row now try for a third time. Half the students predict heads and half tails, and the coin flip comes up tails again. The four students who were right divide again on whether the next flip will be heads or tails. This result is tails, and now we are down to two students. One student calls heads, and the other calls tails. The coin flip is heads, and we have our winner—the student who correctly predicted five in a row. The probability of correctly calling five coin flips in a row is $1/32 = 3$ percent, a seemingly convincing record. Are you confident, however, that the winner of this contest will call the next five flips correctly?

Even monkeys throwing darts and analysts flipping coins sometimes get lucky, an observation that cautions us that past successes are no guarantee of future performance. Even if it is true that some analysts are somewhat better than the vast majority, the limited information we have will be of little help in separating the skilled from the merely lucky. Imagine that there are 10,000 analysts, of whom 10 percent have a 0.6 probability of predicting correctly whether the stock market will do unusually well or poorly in the coming year. The remaining 90 percent, like monkeys throwing darts, have only a 0.5 probability of making a correct prediction.

We will call those analysts in the first group skilled and those in the second group lucky. If we examine their records over a ten-year period, probability theory tells us we can expect 6 of the 1000 skilled analysts to make correct predictions in all ten years. Among the merely lucky, 9 out of 9000 can be expected to make ten correct predictions. This expectation means that if we choose one of the 15 analysts who has been right for ten years in a row, there is only a 40 percent chance that we will choose a skilled analyst. This is considerably better than the 10 percent chance we have of picking a skilled analyst if we ignore their records; but still, and this is the point, past performance is far from a guarantee of future success. Less spectacular records are less helpful. Of those who have been right eight out of ten years, 25 percent are skilled. For seven of ten years, it is only 20 percent.

In practice, there is even more uncertainty, because we often do not have a complete, accurate record over a ten-year period. Some analysts are too young. Others distort their records, perhaps by selective reporting: if they manage five funds, they will only tell you about the one that did best; if they have been investing for ten years, they tell you about their five best years. Also, skills are not constant. By the time an analyst has acquired useful experience and compiled an impressive track record, some of the early energy and insight may be fading.

There are some money managers with outstanding records, who are much in demand and very expensive. The records of the rest are brief, mixed, or exaggerated, and there is no sure way to separate the talented from the lucky and the liars. The market is not all luck, but it is more luck than nervous investors want to hear or successful investors want to admit.

The Strong Form

In 1815, a series of special couriers and carrier pigeons gave Nathan Rothschild the first news in London that the British had defeated Napoleon at Waterloo. Rothschild had his agents sell British government bonds prominently, leading to rumors that he must have heard that the English had been crushed at Waterloo. In the subsequent rush to sell government bonds, prices collapsed. Rothschild's agents then discreetly purchased massive amounts of bonds at bargain prices shortly before government couriers reached London with the truth—the British had won.

Investors often buy a stock on the basis of what they believe to be a hot tip, some secret information that, while not as spectacular as the English victory at Waterloo, will soon be made public and cause a buying stampede. Usually they are disappointed, either because the hot tip turns out to be a false rumor or because the information, while correct, was known to many and already reflected in the price of the stock.

The **strong form** of the efficient market hypothesis holds that there is no information, public or private, that allows some investors to beat the market consistently. This hypothesis is contradicted by evidence that a few do profit by using information not available to other investors—often in violation of federal laws. Historically, these market beaters have typically been corporate insiders who bought or sold stock in the company they work for based on advance knowledge of new products, sales data, and so on. More recently, the feverish takeover activity in the 1980s provided valuable privileged information to accountants, lawyers, and investment bankers—a few of whom profited by purchasing stock in advance of the public announcement of the takeover bid.

strong form
The strong form of the efficient market hypothesis holds that there is no information, public or private, that allows some investors to beat the market consistently.

Insider Reports and Other Indirect Evidence The Securities Exchange Act of 1934 requires that a company's insiders, defined as its directors and executive officers and any stockholder who owns more than 10 percent of the outstanding shares, report any purchases or sales of the company's stock by the tenth day of the month following the transaction. The SEC reports these transactions to the general public in its monthly *Official Summary of Security Transactions and Holdings*.

A company's insiders are presumably well informed about the company and, while we cannot know what they know, we can do what they do—that is, buy if insiders buy and sell if they sell. A number of studies done in the 1960s and 1970s found that such imitative strategies would, in fact, have beaten the market by some 7 to 30 percentage points a year, even if the purchases were made a full two months after the insider transaction, by which time the trade had been reported to the SEC and published in its monthly *Summary*.[20] Here, apparently, was useful public information, a contradiction of not only the strong form, but also the semi-strong form of the efficient-market hypothesis.

These academic studies spawned a half dozen market newsletters devoted to reports of insider trading. These specialized advisory services sift through the SEC *Summary* or the actual insider filings, which are available in a public reference room at the SEC's Washington office, and select stocks that insiders are predominantly buying or selling. Value Line and many other advisory services also now regularly report insider trading activity. Since this information is now so widely reported, it may be of little value.

Other indirect evidence of the value of inside information is provided by the behavior of market prices shortly before important announcements, such as a takeover offer. According to an SEC study released in February 1987, trading volume usually increases noticeably ten days before a take- over announcement. On average, trading volume is three times normal three days before the announcement, five times normal the following day, and twenty times normal on the day of the announcement. The stock's price increases, on average, by 38.5 percent before the takeover attempt is formally announced. Much of this trading is an educated guess based on public information (both fact and rumor) that is widely reported in news- papers and on the Dow Jones ticker service; for instance, the filing of Form 13–D with the SEC when a raider has accumulated 5 percent of a company's stock. Other investors are lured into purchases by the scent of a rising price and surging volume. Some purchases are less innocent.

The Law and the SEC Section 10(b)5 of the 1934 Securities and Exchange Act makes it

> *unlawful for any person to employ any device, scheme or artifice to defraud or to engage in any act, practice or course of business which operates as a fraud or deceit upon any person.*

This law was a response to a variety of fraudulent activities in the 1920s that manipulated stock prices and misled naive investors. For instance, an investment pool would bid up the price of a selected stock, often by trading the stock back and forth among members of the pool, then sell to investors lured by the stock's upward momentum. The spreading of false rumors was another popular tactic during the 1920s.

Such activities have not disappeared completely. Some unscrupulous investors still plant false stories of scientific breakthroughs or of takeover attempts, hoping to boost a stock's price. In 1987, an investor was sentenced to 2½ years in federal prison after he pleaded guilty to conspiracy and fraud in manipulating the prices of two small stocks by buying and selling shares through fifty-three accounts at eighteen brokerage firms. The SEC charged that he tried to "create an illusion of widespread ownership and interest" in these two stocks, thereby inflating their prices.

The SEC also uses Section 10(b)5 for a very different purpose—to prosecute perceived insider trading abuses. Insider information is not even mentioned, let alone defined in the law, but over the years, through a series of cases, the SEC has successfully carved out a niche. In the past, many cases were settled by the accused not admitting guilt but agreeing to give back the disputed profits. Since August 1984, the SEC has been empowered to seek not only a return of profits, but also a penalty equal to three times profits. The SEC has also become more aggressive in seeking prison terms, not only for securities violations, but also for such related crimes as mail or wire fraud, obstructing justice, and income-tax evasion.

The SEC interprets illegal insider trading as that based on material information not yet made public if the information was obtained wrongfully (such as by theft or bribery) or if the person has a fiduciary responsibility to keep the information confidential. Further, investors are not allowed to trade on the basis of information that they know or have reason to know was obtained wrongfully. For example, the SEC charged that W. Paul Thayer violated Section 10(b)5 when, as chairman of LTV, he tipped his stockbroker about two takeover bids. Both were eventually convicted of obstructing justice and sentenced to four years in prison. The SEC is unlikely to press charges if it is convinced that a leak of confidential information was inadvertent—for example, a conversation overheard on an airplane. Many stock purchases and sales are, of course, made on the basis of tips and rumors, from unknown sources and of questionable accuracy. The boundaries of insider trading still represent a gray area that the courts are in the process of shaping.

The courts have consistently ruled that the officers and directors of a company cannot profit from buying or selling stock in their own firm prior to the public announcement of important corporate news. The SEC has also won a variety of cases against relatives and friends of corporate insiders, establishing the principle that a person tipped by an insider is an insider too. In the 1968 Texas Gulf Sulphur case, involving the purchase of stock by some company executives and outsiders who had been tipped before the public announcement of an enormous ore discovery, a federal appeals court ruled that "anyone—corporate insider or not—who regularly receives material non-public information may not use that information to trade in securities without incurring an affirmative duty to disclose."

The SEC has frequently taken the position that any trading in securities while in possession of material non-public information is illegal. By this definition, the SEC is trying to maintain a level playing field on which all traders have access to the same information—the economists' definition of an efficient market. The SEC worries that insider trading, playing with marked cards, will undermine the integrity of financial markets and drive away honest players.

The Theft of Information The SEC has also frequently won cases based on a different principle—that insider trading is robbery, the theft of information. In 1980, the SEC charged that Vincent Chiarella, an employee of a printing house, had defrauded investors when he decoded documents (with missing company names) that he was printing relating to mergers and takeovers and then bought shares in the target companies. The Supreme Court overturned his conviction, ruling that Section 10(b)5 "is premised upon a duty to disclose arising from a relationship of trust and confidence between parties to a transaction" and that Chiarella did not have such a duty to the shareholders of the target companies. At the same time, the Court refused to speculate on an argument that the government used in the appeal but not in the original trial—that Chiarella's misappropriation of information had defrauded the printing house that employed him, injuring its reputation, and had defrauded his employer's clients, who were forced to pay more for their target shares. (In a related civil case, Chiarella agreed to forfeit the $29,000 in profits that he had made.)

The Supreme Court again rejected the SEC's claim that the possession of superior information is, by itself, fraud in the 1983 case of Raymond Dirks, a stockbroker, who had been tipped by a former executive of Equity Funding that the company's reported profits were based on fraudulent insurance policies. Dirks confirmed the tip by interviewing some of the company's employees and then advised his clients to sell Equity Funding stock before he publicly disclosed the fraud. The Supreme Court ruled that the company's executives were not guilty of insider trading because they did not personally benefit from their disclosures to Dirks; thus, Dirks was not made an insider by their tips.

In 1984, a Federal Court of Appeals relied on the misappropriation argument in upholding the conviction of Anthony Materia, another printer, ruling that he violated a duty to his employer and its clients when he "stole information to which he was privy in his work . . . . Materia's theft of information was indeed as fraudulent as if he had converted corporate funds for his personal benefit." A landmark case involving an employee of *The Wall Street Journal* is recounted in Investment Example 11–3.

arbitrage

Pure arbitrage is a virtually riskless exploitation of price discrepancies.

Takeovers and Insider Trading Pure **arbitrage** is a virtually riskless exploitation of price discrepancies. If, for example, a stock sells for $20 a share on one exchange and $30 on another, arbitragers (arbs) can buy on the first exchange and sell on the second until the price discrepancy disappears. In takeovers, a corporate raider (such as T. Boone Pickens, Carl Icahn, and Irwin Jacobs) may offer $40 for a stock that had been selling for $30, driving the price immediately up to, say, $38—not all the way to $40 because there is a chance that the takeover attempt will fail. Arbitragers may buy the target stock at $38, betting that the takeover will succeed and, perhaps, that the raider will ultimately have to offer more than $40 a share. Because this type of arbitrage is not riskless, it is called *risk arbitrage*.

Even more money can be made in our example if the arbitrager can identify a likely takeover candidate ahead of time and buy shares at $30 before the $40 offer is announced—a strategy likely to be successful if the arbitrager has an inside tip from the corporate raider or the raider's investment banker. Investment Example 11–4 tells how Ivan Boesky profited from such information.

The scope of the Boesky scandal was stunning, both in the number of people involved and in the size of the illegal profits, and it unquestionably shook the public's confidence in the integrity and fairness of financial markets. It also tarnished takeovers because of an unfortunate confusion

HEARD ON THE STREET

The Wall Street Journal runs a regular column called "Heard on the Street," which reports financial rumors and gossip—a column sometimes derisively called "Herd on the Street" because of the imitative behavior of financial analysts. In 1983, R. Foster Winans was $18,000 in debt and earning $28,000 a year writing this column when Peter Brant, a leading broker at Kidder, Peabody, convinced him that they could make lots of money if Winans gave him the columns a day in advance of their publication.* Winans seemed to believe that his columns uncovered good reasons to buy or sell a particular stock; the broker thought that readers could be persuaded to buy or sell on the basis of a favorable or unfavorable story. Some of the trades worked and some did not; the SEC claims that, on balance, the profits came to $690,000, of which Winans received $31,000.

Computers at the SEC and the stock exchanges monitor trading continuously, looking for unusually heavy volume and sudden price changes (announcing any unusual patterns with a computer-generated voice or whistle). Investigators then ask the company about impending announcements and review brokerage records for suspicious connections. Even if there is no computer alert, after important news is released about a company employees of the SEC and the exchanges both go back and reinspect the numbers for suspicious prior trading activity. Considerable detective work may be needed to penetrate covers created by trades through friends, dummy corporations, and foreign banks. This search is aided by a computerized data bank that lists the personal and professional associations of a half million corporate executives and members of the securities industry.

In the Winans case, the stock exchanges were alerted almost immediately by an unusually heavy volume of trading and noticed that the stocks were subsequently mentioned in the column, "Heard on the Street." Soon the SEC learned that the broker, Brant, was the common denominator in the trades and established his ties to Winans, who admitted his actions. Winans was immediately fired by *The Wall Street Journal* and eventually fined and sentenced to federal prison for eighteen months. The broker pleaded guilty to two counts of fraud and testified against Winans.

The Winans case involved some tricky legal questions and was appealed all the way to the Supreme Court. Winans' lawyers claimed that he had no inside information and was merely passing along gossip. His information was literally heard on the street. Interestingly, the Securities Industry Association, which represents stockbrokers, was worried that stockbrokers might be prosecuted for doing the same thing, and filed a brief in support of Winans' appeal. The SEC claimed that Winans violated a fiduciary duty, not to the companies he wrote about, but to his employer, *The Wall Street Journal,* by misappropriating confidential information about the content and timing of columns that the newspaper planned to publish. The Supreme Court upheld Winans's conviction.

*For a first-person account, see R. Foster Winans, "The Crash of a Wall Street Reporter," *Esquire,* September 1986, pp. 233–41.

THE KING OF THE ARBITRAGERS

Ivan Boesky was a high-profile trader who bet millions of dollars on takeover candidates, usually in advance of any public offer, often winning big and occasionally losing big. (In 1984, he lost an estimated $70 million when T. Boone Pickens abandoned an attempted takeover of Phillips Petroleum.) In 1985, he had a very hot hand, consistently buying target stocks shortly before a takeover was publicly announced. He boasted of his success and attributed it to superior judgment and sleeping only three hours a night, adding:

We get up earlier and tend to go to bed later at night. Like all disciplines, when you apply a great deal of energy and work effort and careful judgment, then you have a greater chance of success.[1]

Another time, he claimed,

"What I am is the best odds-maker in the world. . . . I calculate risk better than anybody else, and that is why our firm has had the success it has. I take pride in that."[2]

As it turned out, there was little or no risk because Boesky was cheating—playing poker with marked cards.

In May 1985, the New York office of Merrill Lynch received an unsigned letter from its Caracas office alleging that two brokers there were buying in advance of takeover announcements. Merrill Lynch found that the brokers in Caracas were being tipped by a New York stock broker who was executing orders received from the Bahamian branch of a Swiss bank for an account in the name of Mr. Diamond. Merrill Lynch passed this information on to the SEC, who pressured the Swiss bank to reveal that Mr. Diamond was really Dennis Levine, the thirty-three-year-old co-director of Drexel Burnham's mergers-and-acquisitions department. Levine soon revealed sources for his tips and even agreed to tape-record conversations.

The SEC accused Levine of trading on the basis of inside information as far back as 1980, while holding jobs at a variety of firms, and, later, of supplying Ivan Boesky with advance notice of mergers and takeovers. In return, Boesky agreed to pay Levine 5 percent of his profits if he did not own the stock already and 1 percent if he already owned some shares. Boesky was to pay Levine $2.4 million shortly before Levine's arrest.

Levine agreed to pay the SEC $11.6 million in civil penalties and pleaded guilty to four felony charges,

of takeovers with insider trading. Takeovers make insider trading very profitable, but the reverse is not true. Insider trading is not the reason raiders want to acquire a company.

If anything, insider trading hurts corporate raiders, because the runup in the target stock's price prior to the takeover attempt forces them to offer an even higher price to persuade stockholders to tender their shares. This

for which he was fined $362,000 and sentenced to two years in prison. He also revealed a network of investment bankers and lawyers who supplied him with inside information. More than a dozen men, almost all under the age of forty, pleaded guilty to felony charges and, perhaps worse, had their reputations and careers ruined.

The SEC accused Boesky of making at least $50 million in illegal profits, based on inside information obtained from Levine, on seven major takeovers from April 1985 to April 1986. Boesky agreed to pay an astonishing $100 million—$50 million in illegal profits, to reimburse investors who sold their shares to Boesky, plus a $50 million fine paid (to the U.S. Treasury. (Shortly before his arrest, *Fortune* estimated Boesky's wealth at about $200 million.) Boesky also pleaded guilty to a felony (for which he was sentenced to three years in prison), agreed to withdraw permanently from the U.S. securities industry (except as an individual investor), and cooperated with the authorities (for example, by allowing the secret recording of all of his conversations for more than a month, until this eavesdropping was discovered).

Boesky's revelations eventually led to the indictment of Michael Milkin, Drexel Burnham's junk-bond star, for a variety of offenses, including insider trading, stock manipulation, parking of securities with associates to avoid ownership disclosure, the maintenance of false and misleading records, and false disclosures to the SEC. Drexel Burnham, Milkin's employer, settled an SEC civil suit alleging securities fraud by agreeing to $350 million in a fund to repay injured clients, sever ties with Milkin, transfer stock trading operations from Beverly Hills to New York, and appoint senior managers who are acceptable to the SEC, including the hiring of John Shad, a former SEC chairman, as chairman of Drexel. In a separate criminal case, Drexel pleaded guilty to six felony charges of securities fraud and paid $650 million in penalties. Milkin vowed to fight the charges against him in court.

Boesky was permitted to liquidate his $1.3 billion portfolio before the public announcement of his crimes, an apparent contradiction of the SEC's position that it is illegal to trade securities while in possession of material nonpublic information. One journalist reported that his "neighbors, not mincing their words, call [these sales] the greatest insider-trading scam in history."[3] The SEC defended its actions by arguing that forced sales by Boesky after the public announcement might have caused a "precipitous and uncontrollable liquidation of securities."

[1] Quoted in Michael A. Hiltzik, "Ivan Boesky: Prominence Led to Scrutiny, Charges," *Los Angeles Times,* November 16, 1986.

[2] Quoted in James Srodes, "We Have All Been Robbed by Deceit of 3 'Geniuses,'" *Los Angeles Times,* March 1, 1987.

[3] L.J. Davis, "The Next Panic," *Harper's Magazine,* May 1987, p. 44.

is why raiders try to keep their intentions secret, why they prefer investment bankers who keep valuable information confidential, and why they sue anyone who leaks their plans. The bankers, in turn, try to maintain a "Chinese wall" between investment banking and securities trading; if fearful of a breach, they put the stock on a restricted list, notifying traders that they cannot buy or sell the stock for the firm's own accounts. Morgan

Stanley's Manhattan offices are monitored by closed-circuit cameras, segregated by computerized access cards, and operated with a fortress mentality; their general counsel said, "The preservation of insider information is the backbone of our business."[21] Curbing takeovers to prevent insider trading makes about as much sense as outlawing oil drilling, medical research, or computer-software development to prevent the leak of inside information.

CAN THE MARKET BE BEATEN LEGALLY?

The efficient-market hypothesis does not require that all stocks be priced rationally, only that, because investors have access to the same information, there are no obvious bargains. Changes in stock prices can be unpredictable because of the market's rational absorption of new information, or they can result from unpredictable, irrational revisions in investor expectations and valuations.

It is tempting to think that, as in any profession, good training, hard work, and a skilled mind will yield superior results. It is especially tempting to think that you possess these very characteristics. By definition, however, half of all investors are below average. Someone will be successful in any game of chance, and, conversely, any one's superior skill can be undone by bad luck after an otherwise smart purchase. You may buy a stock at $30 and find that the market prices it inexplicably at $20 a few weeks afterward—as Keynes put it, "There is nothing so disastrous as a rational investment policy in an irrational world."

Researchers have uncovered a variety of apparent anomalies, or contradictions, of the efficient-market hypothesis. Some of the anomalies may reflect superior skill. Others seem inexplicable.

Blue Mondays

Mondays have a reputation on Wall Street for being wild and often downright nasty—a reputation that has been confirmed by a number of researchers. A study of the period 1952–65 found that the Dow rose on 64.6 percent of the Fridays, but on only 43 percent of the Mondays; on Tuesdays, Wednesdays, and Thursdays, the respective numbers were 54.0 percent, 56.3 percent, and 56.5 percent.[22] A calculation of daily percentage stock returns from 1963–78 obtained the results shown in Table 11–3. The overall average daily return was 0.0152 percent. Only Mondays had a negative average, and it works out to be a staggering −33.5 percent on an annual basis. The researchers who made these calculations tried to find a reasonable explanation and came up empty, concluding that it is "an obvious anomaly."

TABLE 11–3 The Day-of-the-Week Effect

	Stock Return by Day of the Week (percent)				
	Monday	Tuesday	Wednesday	Thursday	Friday
Average return	−0.134	0.002	0.096	0.028	0.084
Standard deviation	0.818	0.742	0.802	0.695	0.692

Sources: Mark Gibbons and Patrick Hess, "Day of the Week Effects and Asset Returns," *Journal of Business,* October 1981, pp. 579–95; a study of the period 1963–83 obtained similar results: Michael Smirlock and Laura Starks, "Day-of-the-Week Effects in Stock Returns," *Journal of Financial Economics,* September 1986, pp. 197–210.

One possibility, which the researchers did not consider, is that corporations and the government delay the release of bad news until after financial markets close on Friday, leaving Monday to bear the brunt of the resultant price decline. This explanation, even if correct, is of little help to analysts since they cannot predict which Fridays and which companies will have bad news. Even if the historical difference between the average return on Mondays and on other days persists, it is but a fraction of a percent on a daily basis—too slight to make it profitable to sell short on Fridays and buy on Tuesdays.

The Turn-of-the-Year Anomaly

Stocks, especially low-priced stocks, have consistently done very well in the last few days of December and the first five days of January.[23] One explanation is that institutional investors window-dress their portfolios in December by selling low-priced, risky securities that they are embarrassed to include in their year-end reports and then repurchase small risky securities early in January. Another possible explanation points to asymmetrical investor responses to capital gains and losses and to the relatively large bid-ask spreads on low-priced stocks.[24] As the end of the year approaches, investors are in no hurry to realize capital gains on stocks that have appreciated, but they are eager to realize capital losses for tax purposes by selling stocks that have declined. With an imbalance between sellers and buyers, much of the selling is to specialists at the bid price. Once the year has ended (or even slightly before), the balance between buyers and sellers is reestablished, and a trade is as likely to be at the specialist's ask price as at the lower bid price. For low-priced stock, the bid-ask spread can be several percentage points (for example, $1 bid and $1¼ asked is a spread of 25 percent), creating a misleading increase in the reported trading price. This increase is misleading because the bid-ask spread plus commissions will exhaust any profits that an investor hopes to obtain by buying in late December and selling in early January.

Warren Buffett and Other Contrarians

George Goodman, alias Adam Smith, best-selling author of *Money Game* and *Supermoney*, called Warren Buffett "easily the outstanding money manager of the generation." A student of Benjamin Graham, Buffett quietly scrutinized balance sheets in his hometown of Omaha, Nebraska.[25] Beginning in 1956 with a $100,000 partnership, he earned a 31 percent compound annual return over the next fourteen years. In 1969 believing stocks to be overpriced, Buffett left the stock market and dissolved the partnership. The "wizard of Omaha" returned to the stock market in the 1970s, making investments through Berkshire Hathaway, formerly a cloth-milling company. Continuing to earn nearly 25 percent a year, his net worth topped $1 billion in 1987. Before the market crash in 1987, he observed that stock prices had "become gloriously uncoupled from the plodding performances of the businesses themselves."

Institutional Myopia Like his mentor, Benjamin Graham, Warren Buffett has been critical of the hyperkinetic activity of institutional investors, who speculate fruitlessly on short-term price fluctuations instead of focusing on long-term investment values. In Berkshire's 1987 annual report, Buffett wrote, "The term 'institutional investor' is becoming one of those self-contradictions called an oxymoron, comparable to 'jumpo shrimp,' 'lady mud wrestler' and 'inexpensive lawyer.'"

Speculation not only incurs needless transaction costs and diverts attention from fundamental value, but also, in the effort to buy what others will buy, leads institutions to buy the same stocks. Ironically, caution can also lead institutions to imitative behavior. The Employee Retirement Investment Security Act of 1974 (ERISA) requires pension-fund managers to be "prudent," a traditional criterion for judging the competence of a money manager. Just as no purchasing agent ever got fired for ordering IBM equipment, so no money manager has ever been thought imprudent for buying IBM stock, nor any other glamour stock. To be out of step is to be incautious, bordering on the imprudent. One institutional investor explained his disdain for out-of-favor stocks, asking, "How can any prudent man look at companies like these with such unthinkably poor visability?"[26]

The "nifty fifty" in the late 1960s and early 1970s were, without question, successful companies—IBM, Xerox, McDonald's, Polaroid, Avon, Disney—the same companies identified by Peters and Waterman as America's best.[27] Nevertheless, a focus on a company's success overlooks the price of its stock, and an institutional willingness to buy no matter what the price virtually guarantees that a stock will be overpriced.

Andrew Tobias related a lunch discussion with an executive for a bank managing billions of dollars, more than half of which was invested in just fourteen stocks, only one having a price-earnings ratio below 20:

[He] told me that it was his bank's policy to invest only in companies whose earnings they expected to grow at an above-average rate. What about companies they expected to grow at only an average or subaverage rate? No, he said, they did not buy stock in such companies. Regardless of price? Regardless of price. Was there any *price at which the bank would buy stock in an average-growth company?*

This question made the money manager uncomfortable. He clearly wanted to answer no, because he clearly would be damned before he would buy stock in such a company. But he couldn't come right out and say that, because he knew that, theoretically, there must be some *price at which he should choose the stock of the mediocre company over the stocks of his nifty fifty.*[28]

A Contrarian Strategy If the herd-like instincts of institutional investors push the prices of glamour stocks to unjustifiable levels, then perhaps the road to investment success is to do the opposite—or, as J. Paul Getty (with a net worth estimated at $4 billion) advised in his autobiography, to "buy when everyone else is selling and hold until everyone else is buying." A deliberate attempt to do the opposite of what others are doing is called a **contrarian strategy,** and can be applied to individual stocks (buying the least popular ones) and to the market as a whole (buying when others are bearish).

contrarian strategy
A contrarian strategy is a deliberate attempt to do the opposite of what others are doing.

The experts have been notoriously wrong at dramatic market turning points: they were very bullish before the 1973–74 slump, overwhelmingly pessimistic in the summer of 1974 (just as the market touched bottom and surged upwards), and very optimistic just before the market crash on October 19, 1987. With individual stocks, the favorites often have done poorly. A representative example is *Financial World's* 1980 scrutiny of the recommendations of twenty "superstar" analysts selected in a pool of institutional investors. Of the 132 stocks they recommended, two thirds did worse than the S&P 500. The average gain for the 132 stocks picked by the most respected and highly paid security analysts was 9.3 percent, as compared to 14.1 percent for the S&P 500. A large institutional buyer of research concluded glumly, "It's uncanny, when they say one thing, start doing the opposite. Usually you are right."[29]

Low Price-Earnings Ratios Several researchers have found that stocks with low price-earnings (*P/E*) ratios—out of favor—outperform high *P/E* stocks. For instance, Benjamin Graham divided the Dow Jones thirty industrials into those having the ten highest, ten middle, and ten lowest *P/E* ratios.[30] For every five-year holding period between 1937 and 1969, the low *P/E* stocks outperformed the middle *P/E* stocks, which outperformed the high *P/E* stocks. If $10,000 had been invested and reinvested every five years in the ten stocks with the lowest *P/E* ratios at that time, this would have grown to more than $100,000 by 1969, more than twice the amount accumulated by investing and reinvesting in the ten highest *P/E*

TABLE 11–4 Annualized Compound Rates of Return by *P/E* Ratio

Group of Stocks with Similar *P/E* Ratios	Annualized Compound Rates of Return by Months Held until Portfolio Adjustment (percent)				
	3	6	12	36	108
1 (highest)	− 2.64	− 1.06	− 1.13	− 1.43	0.33
2	0.92	1.62	0.56	− 0.28	1.27
3	0.51	0.62	1.63	0.85	3.30
4	3.06	3.42	3.31	4.87	5.36
5	2.19	4.46	2.93	5.02	3.72
6	4.84	5.33	6.70	4.82	4.52
7	7.90	6.07	6.85	5.89	6.08
8	8.83	8.24	8.56	7.78	6.35
9	11.85	8.40	6.08	7.73	6.40
10 (lowest)	14.00	11.68	10.26	10.89	7.89

Source: The New Contrarian Investment Strategy, by David Dreman. Copyright © 1980–82 by David Dreman. Reprinted by permission, Random House, Inc.

stocks. (Other studies have confirmed the success of other Graham criteria, such as strong dividends, low debt, and high liquidation value.[31])

A study by David Dreman covering the period August 1968 through August 1977 divided 1250 stocks into ten groups of 125, according to *P/E* ratios.[32] As shown in Table 11–4, no matter how often the portfolio was readjusted, low *P/E* stocks outperformed those with high *P/Es*. A variety of starting and stopping dates for the study did not undo the remarkably consistent success of a low *P/E* strategy: "It did not matter whether the investor started near a market top or a market bottom; superior returns were provided in any phase of the market cycle." Nor could the results be explained away by the riskiness of low *P/E* stocks: "If anything, the low *P/E* stocks as a group were slightly less volatile." A comparable study by Sanjoy Basu came to a similar conclusion: low *P/E* stocks have been no riskier than high *P/E* stocks but outperform them consistently.[33]

Part of the explanation for the success of a low *P/E* strategy may involve the regression-toward-the-mean phenomenon discussed in Chapter 8. Investors tend to think that companies doing very well and those doing poorly will both continue to do so, overlooking the statistical fact that the former have undoubtedly had more than their share of good luck and the latter more than their share of bad. The future performance of very successful companies will, on average, disappoint those who do not realize that this success was, most likely, atypical.

TABLE 11–5   Rates of Return by Company Size

Group of Stocks of Similar Size Companies	Median Value of Companies (millions of dollars)	Median Share Price	Average Annual Return (percent)
1 (small)	$ 5	$ 5.24	32.8
2	11	9.52	23.5
3	19	12.89	23.0
4	31	16.19	20.2
5	47	19.22	19.1
6	74	22.59	18.3
7	119	26.44	15.6
8	209	30.83	14.2
9	435	34.43	13.0
10 (large)	1103	44.94	9.5

Source: Marc Reinganum, "Misspecification of Capital Asset Pricing: Empirical Anomalies Based on Earnings' Yields and Market Values," *Journal of Financial Economics,* March 1981, pp. 19–46.

Small-Capitalization Stocks Another explanation of the success of low *P/E* strategies is the herd-like behavior of investors, particularly large institutions. Some analysts who favor this explanation argue that a better measure of institutional interest or neglect is the size of a company. It is not profitable to do expensive research on small companies, because any attempt to buy a substantial number of shares will drive the price upward and a later sale will force the price down. Studies by Rolf Banz and by Marc Reinganum indicate that firms with a small total market value, called **small-capitalization (or small-cap) firms,** significantly outperformed larger companies.[34] Reinganum considered the performance of ten portfolios revised annually by dividing 2000 firms whose shares were traded on the New York Stock Exchange or the American Stock Exchange into ten groups based on their total market value at the time. The subsequent annual rates of return, neglecting transaction costs, are shown in Table 11–5 and indicate that portfolios containing smaller companies consistently outperformed portfolios of large companies.

small capitalization
Small-capitalization companies have a small total market value (debt plus equity).

Both Reinganum and Banz argue that small capitalization is a better criteria than low *P/E*—that while small firms tend to have low *P/Es,* it is their smallness that better explains their above-average returns. The low *P/E* enthusiasts predictably argue the opposite, that many small firms have been made small by a series of bad years, and that it is the unreasonably low *P/E* ratios attached to their unfortunate performance that explains the future success of their stock.[35]

Neglected Firms   Other researchers argue that investor neglect can be measured directly by counting the number of analysts who regularly follow a firm's stock and, further, that neglected stocks need not be small. Arbel and Strebel divided the S&P 500 into three categories based on analyst interest: highly followed, moderately followed, and neglected.[36] The groupings were revised at the beginning of each year because "analysts shift their attention quite frequently." Over the period 1970–79, an annually revised portfolio of highly followed stocks earned 9.4 percent a year, while the moderate-interest portfolio earned 12.7 percent, and the portfolio of neglected stocks earned 16.4 percent. When the portfolios were further divided into small, medium, and large companies, the researchers found that, for any size category, neglected stocks did better than the moderately followed, and the moderately followed did better than the highly followed. The reverse was not true, in that, for each category of analyst interest, there was no relationship between the size of the firm and the return on the stock.

Perhaps the safest conclusion is that the stock market is dominated by institutional investors who find some stocks attractive and neglect others. The unattractive firms tend to be small, with unimpressive earnings growth, and to have low price-earnings ratios. Not all unattractive firms have these characteristics; and not all their stocks have subsequently done well, although many have. Encouraged by this research, investors and advisory services have begun devoting more attention to small-cap, low *P/E*, and otherwise neglected companies, perhaps undermining this strategy's potential.

SUMMARY

The efficient-market hypothesis states that there are no clearly mispriced securities, whose purchase or sale would yield an abnormally large return, because all investors have the same information, or at least there are a sufficient number of well-financed investors to eliminate any obvious mispricings. One implication of the hypothesis is that to the extent anticipated future events are already imbedded in today's stock prices, most price revisions (and the accompanying capital gains or losses) are surprises, caused by the occurrence of unexpected events.

The efficient-market hypothesis does not assume that a stock's price is equal to some objective measure of its intrinsic value, or even that all investors agree on that value—only that investors cannot consistently make unusually large profits trading on information. The weak, semi-strong, and strong forms of the efficient-market hypothesis reveal, respectively, that abnormal profits cannot be made using information about past stock prices, all public information, and all information.

The evidence is strongest for the weak form—which denies the usefulness of technical analysis. There is also considerable evidence in support of the semi-strong form— denying the value of fundamental analysis. Nevertheless, there are anomalies, such as Blue Mondays and the turn-of-the-year effect, and some investors, such as Warren Buffett, who have compiled superior records. Of course, anomalies may self-destruct, and the existence of apparently superior investors is not a persuasive reason for assuming that you are one of them.

The strong form of the efficient-market hypothesis is contradicted by the excessive profits made by insiders, who used nonpublic information that was obtained wrongfully or who violated a fiduciary responsibility to keep the information confidential. Many spectacular cases in the 1980s involved the purchase of stock in advance of a public announcement of a takeover offer or other corporate restructuring.

EXERCISES

1. Explain why the following advice is not very helpful:

> Since we know stocks are going to fall as well as rise, we might as well get a little traffic out of them. A man who buys a stock at 10 and sells it at 20 makes 100 per cent. But a man who buys it at 10, sells it at 14½, buys it back at 12 and sells it at 18, buys it back at 15 and sells it at 20, makes 188 per cent.[37]

2. A study of corporate annual earnings reports found that these reports had little or no effect on stock prices. How can we reconcile this conclusion with economic theory, which says that stock prices depend crucially on a corporation's economic health—in particular, its dividends and earnings?

3. An old Wall Street adage states, "Buy on the rumor, sell on the news." Why would stock prices go up after a rumor and not go up when the anticipated event actually occurs?

4. A financial guru gives inspirational lectures on how to make a fortune in real estate by buying bargain properties; For example, "if you buy a $100,000 house for $80,000, you've got a $20,000 profit right off the bat." If so, is the real-estate market efficient? If the real-estate market is reasonably efficient, what is the flaw in his advice?

5. Briefly explain why each of the following allegations, if true, either would or would not provide evidence against the efficient-market hypothesis:

a. A well-known investment strategy consistently earns a return greater than zero.

b. Over the past twenty years, Mutual Fund A has had a significantly higher average return than Mutual Fund B.

c. When the stock market goes down in January, it usually goes down during the next eleven months.

d. The stock market almost always goes up at least 20 percent in the nine months preceding presidential elections and goes down 20 percent during the twelve months following elections.

e. Corporate bonds consistently give higher returns than municipal bonds.

6. Briefly explain why each of the following events is or is not a persuasive reason to buy stock:

a. Firm A has not missed a dividend payment in 119 years.

b. Firm A has a higher value of Tobin's q than does Firm B.

c. Yesterday, the Fed reported a $2.5 billion increase in the money supply last week.

d. The term structure is downward sloping, indicating that financial experts expect interest rates to fall.

7. Explain why the following advice is logical, but not very helpful:

> It is obviously good sense to buy bonds when the Federal Reserve Banks start lowering interest rates. It is just as obviously bad sense

to buy them at any time when, two or three or four months hence, the Fed is certain to start raising money rates and lowering the prices of outstanding bonds.[38]

8. A full-page 1982 advertisement was headlined, "If your stock portfolio didn't go up at least 41%, you should talk to one of our Financial Consultants."[39] Shown were pictures of three of the firm's consultants, one of which was quoted as saying, "In just 15 months our 'Aggressive Growth Portfolio' went up 41%." Another was shown as saying, "If you're interested in capital gains and are a reasonably venturesome investor, take a look at our 'Emerging Growth Stocks' portfolio. In the past 34 months these investments in companies that are in selected growth markets went up 110%." The third portfolio the ad was up 82 percent over the past five years. The ad went on to explain that this firm has "a wide variety of stock portfolios for a wide variety of investors." Why are you not persuaded that these certainly are superior investments?

9. An investment author made the following recommendation for buying stock in United Match Box, the maker of Rubik's Magic Puzzle:

> I'm not, however, recommending United Match Box just because of the Rubik phenomenon, which certainly isn't a secret. It has other attractions. A unique company, Match Box is based in Hong Kong and incorporated in Bermuda—and, as a result pays only 20 percent taxes. Most exciting, Match Box has a wedge into the People's Republic of China market, where it now has a joint venture with the Chinese government-owned toy company.[40]

Do you think any of these attractions are good reasons for trading on information? If a company has normal profits and pays low taxes, must its stock be a great investment?

10. Explain margin buying, and explain why you would be cautious about following this ad-

vice: "Margin buying is an excellent way to buy shares, when you are sure a stock has reached its bottom, or nearly its bottom."[41]

11. *The Palm Beach Post* invited twelve stockbrokers to pick five stocks that they thought would do especially well in 1983; they repeated the contest in 1984. As it turned out, the broker who did best in 1983 did the worst in 1984! Further, a portfolio picked by tossing a dart five times at the financial page beat all twelve brokers in 1983 and beat eleven of the twelve in 1984. How are these results possible?

12. Explain why you will not get rich following this advice in Consumer Digest's *Get Rich Investment Guide*:

> The ability to track interest rates as they pertain to bonds is made easier by following the path of the Prime Rate (the rate of interest charged by banks to their top clients). If the consensus shown in top business journals indicates that rates are going up, this means that bonds will go down in price. Therefore, when it seems that rates are moving up, an investor should wait until some "peaking" of rates is foreseen.[42]

13. An advertisement for a penny-stock report was headlined "5500% profit" and explained:

> EXAMPLE: On Sept. 1983 if you had purchased 25,000 shares of MAX AXAM at .25 a share ($6250), you could have sold on Feb. 1986 at $14.00 per share and pocketed $350,000. Imagine a gain of 5500%![43]

Why is this example unpersuasive?

14. During the 1988 presidential election campaign, it was widely believed that the stock market would benefit more from a George Bush presidency than from a Michael Dukakis presidency. Yet on Friday, January 20, 1989, the day of George Bush's inauguration as president, stock prices fell slightly, with the Dow down 3.75 points to 2235.36. How would the efficient-market hypothesis explain this apparent contradiction?

15. A *Wall Street Journal* article advised:

The long-term investor can make his
decisions based on information easily
available in his morning newspaper. Indeed,
Thom Brown, managing director of the
Philadelphia investment firm of Rutherford,
Brown & Catherwood, advises investors to
simply read a daily newspaper.
   "Look for anything that suggests the
direction of the economy," he says. "Auto
sales, for example, give you an idea about
how willing consumers are to part with their
money." An expanding economy usually
means rising stock prices.[44]

Write a letter to the editor of *The Wall Street
Journal* refuting this advice.

16. A graduate student once appealed to the
random-walk hypothesis in arguing that population growth follows a random walk. What
economic forces that imply a random walk of
stock prices might not apply to birth rates?

17. In November 1985, Edward Yardeni, of
Prudential Bache, said, "We still like stocks not
so much because we foresee better-than-
expected profits, but because we foresee lower-
than-expected interest rates."[45] Why are high
profits and low interest rates good for stock
prices? Explain why Yardeni said "better-than-
expected profits" and "lower-than-expected interest rates" instead of "high profits" and "low
interest rates."

18. A Harvard Business School professor
wrote, "The vast scientific evidence on the theory of efficient markets indicates that, in the
absence of inside information, a security's market price represents the best available estimate
of its true value."[46] In what sense does the market price represent true value?

19. Answer the question posed at the end of
the following quotation:

There are many who regard the stock market
as wholly perverse . . . How else, they
demand, can one explain a situation in which

a company announces increased earnings—
and sees its stock decline? What is the
justification for a day on which all the news is
bad—and the market rises?[47]

20. Several years ago, you bought 100 shares
of Takeoff at $30 a share and it is now selling
for $100 a share. You are considering (a) selling
this stock, taking your gains while you still can,
and buying Newimage with the proceeds, or
(b) holding on to Takeoff. Either way, you will
close out your position a year from now to help
pay for graduate school. What rate of return
on Newimage is needed for strategy (a) to beat
(b) if the rate of return on Takeoff is 10 percent
this year? If it is 0 percent? Assume that you
are in a 33 percent tax bracket, and ignore brokerage commissions.

21. Redo the calculations in Exercise 20, this
time assuming that you bought the stock at
$100 a share and it is selling now for $30. Explain any differences in your conclusions.

22. Explain why the following argument, even
if correct, does not refute the efficient-market
hypothesis:

I suspect that even if the random walkers
announced a perfect mathematical proof of
randomness I would go on believing that in
the long run future earnings influence present
value, and that in the short run the dominant
factor is the elusive . . . temper of the
crowd.[48]

23. Explain this observation by a *Forbes* columnist: "As a kid, I learned from my father
what moves stocks: it's the difference between
what a company is and what the world thinks
it is."[49]

24. An editorial in *The Wall Street Journal* related how Unocal sued Goldman, Sachs and
others for $2.5 billion in 1987, claiming that

[Goldman] gave "tainted and biased" advice
that caused the company in 1985 to pay more

than it needed when it bought back its own shares. Goldman bankers concocted the plan whereby Unocal bought back its shares, except those held by Mr. Pickens. Unocal took on a lot of debt, but the managers kept their jobs . . . .

The biggest problem with this lawsuit stems from confusion over determining who is harmed by "insider trading." To wit: Where's the victim?[50]

Can you think of any logical basis for *The Wall Street Journal*'s position that no one is harmed when a company pays too much to repurchase its shares?

25. In 1985, Anheuser-Busch sued W. Paul Thayer, a former director, alleging that he encouraged four associates to purchase Campbell-Taggert shares before the public announcement of a tender offer from Anheuser. According to the suit, these insider purchases pushed the market price of Campbell-Taggert shares upward, forcing Anheuser to raise its tender price and pay a total of $80 million more than it had planned. If true, who gained and who lost from these insider purchases?

26. In 1987, a brokerage firm observed that "since 1965, the Dow Jones Industrial Average declined 16 out of 21 times during the month of May. As of this writing, it appears as if another down May is in the offing. We offer no rational explanation for this 'May phenomenon.' We only observe that it often sets up attractive trading opportunities."[51] Does this evidence persuade you to buy stock on margin next April? Why or why not?

27. In 1987, a portfolio manager wrote the following:

I've long been fascinated by how much the market value of a company can change (in either direction) in only months (or even days) while the corporation itself is holding a steady course of growing revenues and solid profits. Consider IBM, which traded above $161 per share in February, and under $118 a share in October, a drop of 27.7%. Did IBM,

as a growing concern, lose $26 billion (610 million shares time $43) in *fundamental value* this year? Because per-share earnings in the September quarter were 27% lower than the year-ago level, is IBM really worth that much less as a corporation?

Of course not! . . . The stock market is rarely efficient in representing the fundamental worth of a corporation in the short run.[52]

Explain why the fundamental value of company might change drastically even while revenues and profits are rock-steady. Use some hypothetical numbers to illustrate your argument. Then explain why this portfolio manager's lament does not refute the efficient-markets hypothesis.

28. In 1983, the SEC enforcement chief said that "anyone who engages in insider trading is clearly a thief."[53] Explain what each of the following insiders are stealing and from whom they are stealing:

a. A chemist discovers a cure for baldness and buys stock in the company he works for before revealing his discovery.

b. A company's chief executive officer sells half of his stock in the company before releasing a disappointing earnings report.

c. A merger-and-acquisitions lawyer working for a corporate raider buys stock in a target company before a tender offer is announced.

29. On October 5, 1981, Kuwait National Petroleum Corporation announced its intention to acquire Santa Fe International for $51 a share. The SEC subsequently accused twenty-two people of illegal insider trading and recovered $10 million in profits, with the accused neither admitting nor denying guilt. Some people were also convicted of criminal charges, including contempt of court and obstruction of justice. Among the SEC's allegations were the following:

a. Using a false name on a Swiss bank account, one member of Santa Fe's board of directors bought 10,000 shares of Santa Fe stock at $23⅛ on September 22, 1981, the day of a special board meeting prior to the final agreement.

b. This director tipped a Jordanian business associate who bought stock options through secret foreign bank accounts.

c. Another director asked his accountant the tax implications of realizing large capital gains and, deducing that a takeover was imminent, the accountant bought Santa Fe stock options.

d. A lobbyist hired to defuse political opposition to the pending merger told a friend, who told his stockbroker, who told nine other brokers who bought Santa Fe options.

In each case, explain how the alleged action violated a fiduciary trust or duty for the sake of personal profit.

30. R. Foster Winans, who leaked stories that were published in *The Wall Street Journal*, wrote that "the only reason to invest in the market is because you think you know something others don't."[54] Is there any other reason to buy stock? If everyone has exactly the same information, would anyone buy stock?

31. Shortly before Dennis Levine's arrest, Ivan Boesky had agreed to pay him $2.4 million, based on the following profit-sharing formula: 5 percent of the profits on all purchases inspired by Levine, and 1 percent of the profits on positions that Boesky had established already and was persuaded by Levine to maintain. Based on the $2.4 million figure, what was the maximum profit that Boesky realized on these positions? The minimum profit? If Boesky's profits came to $50 million, did Levine's information generally persuade Boesky to maintain positions he already had or to take new positions?

32. In the aftermath of the Boesky scandal, one business writer said:

> The notion that the New York Stock Exchange is a "level playing field," where billionaire investors and grandmothers with 10 shares have equal access to information, is as untenable as suggesting that the rich man

and the poor man are equal because both have the same freedom to sleep under the bridge at night.[55]

Does the efficient-markets hypothesis require that every investor have the same information?

33. Put yourself in the shoes of a corporate raider, and refute this argument:

> The business community argues that much of the stock of major corporations is now held by big institutional traders—especially pension funds—looking for quick gains in the market. Companies are forced to keep profits growing rapidly just so these investors won't dump their stock. Add to that the activities of corporate raiders, looking around for undervalued stocks, and company executives find themselves under intense pressure to sacrifice future gains for what can be pumped into current earnings."[56]

In particular, what differences does this argument assume in the behavior of individual and institutional investors? What simple investment can a company make if its stock is undervalued?

34. Explain the logic of the following editorial excerpt from *The Wall Street Journal*:

> Ivan Boesky has done something wrong, but not exactly what the Securities and Exchange Commission thinks . . . . One result of this confusion is that the SEC is about to give the $100 million settlement to the wrong people [those who sold stock to Boesky] . . . . The truly injured parties were the companies that expected the investment bank to keep their takeover plans confidential only to have Mr. Levine sell those plans to Mr. Boesky.[57]

35. In thirty-one years, between 1956 and 1987, Warren Buffett's net worth grew from $100,000 to $1 billion. What was his annual compounded rate of return?

36. In May 1932, with stock prices at their lowest level in this century, Dean Witter sent a

TABLE 11–A

Year	Stock Return (percent)	Year	Stock Return (percent)
1961	26.89	1971	14.31
1962	−8.73	1972	18.98
1963	22.80	1973	−14.66
1964	16.48	1974	−26.47
1965	12.45	1975	37.20
1966	−10.06	1976	23.84
1967	23.98	1977	−7.18
1968	11.06	1978	6.56
1969	−8.50	1979	18.44
1970	4.01	1980	32.42

memo to his company's brokers and management, saying as follows:

> All of our customers with money must some day put it to work—into some revenue-producing investment. Why not invest it now, when securities are cheap?
>
> Some people say they want to wait for a clearer view of the future. But when the future is again clear, the present bargains will have vanished. In fact, does anyone think that today's prices will prevail once full confidence has been restored?[58]

Explain why you either agree or disagree with his logic.

37. Dennis Levine told one of his sources that he would buy small amounts of stock weeks before the public announcement of a takeover attempt.[59] Why would he want to follow such a course? Won't small trades made weeks in advance keep profits from being spectacular?

38. John Kenneth Galbraith observed that "all of the takeovers and all of the efforts to avoid takeovers have involved a substitution of debt for equity."[60] How can a company substitute debt for equity? Is there any rational reason why such a substitution would make the company more valuable? What problems are cre-ated by the substitution of debt for equity?

39. Explain, from the insider's point of view, the advantages and disadvantages of "keeping what they know under wraps:"

> When others see insiders trade, that often tells them nearly as much as an outright disclosure, and tends to push the stock's price closer to its real worth, that is, to where it would be if the insider's information had been disclosed outright . . . . Although insider trading is beneficial in this information-producing way, insider traders are not at all happy about the contributions they make to society. They would rather keep what they know under wraps. That's what would maximize their profits.[61]

40. Table 11–A gives annual data on stock returns over the twenty-year period 1961–80. We can apply a runs test to these data, determining first whether the return each year is unusually high (+) or low (−), then counting the number of sequences of uninterrupted pluses or uninterrupted minuses. If the annual returns are independent, as are twenty coin flips, the expected number of runs is eleven and there is a 0.95 probability that the number of runs will turn out to be between seven and fifteen. Does a small number of runs indicate momentum and a large number reaction, or is it the other way around? In this instance, the median return is 13.38 percent (halfway between the two middle values, 12.45 percent and 14.31 percent). For each of these twenty years, label the year "+" or "−" depending on whether the return that year is above or below the median value 13.38 percent. Count the number of runs and see whether these data convincingly demonstrate momentum or reaction in annual stock returns.

CHAPTER 12

The Human Factor in Investment

> *When beggars and shoeshine boys, barbers and beauticians can tell you how to get rich, it is time to remind yourself that there is no more dangerous illusion than the belief that one can get something for nothing . . .*
>
> Bernard Baruch

Investment decisions are based on more than arithmetic calculations and mechanical rules. Our information is usually incomplete and often contradictory, and there is always considerable uncertainty about the future. Inevitably, we make subjective decisions that are influenced by our all-too-human emotions. It is natural to hope that a clever investment will yield quick and easy wealth. This hope sometimes turns into greed, blurring our vision and dulling our common sense. In this chapter we will look at some of the swindlers who prey on get-rich-quick dreams and at the speculative bubbles that are fed by contagious hopes.

First, we will examine some purported investments that use financial flim-flam to offer returns that are literally too good to be true. Then we will look at the willingness of people to invest with strangers and in unknown companies. Finally, we will examine some examples of the madness of crowds, instances where investors as a group pushed asset prices to levels that, in retrospect, were far from intrinsic values.

PYRAMIDS AND PONZI SCHEMES

Almost everyone has received a chain letter, asking the recipient to send money to the person at the top of a list of names, to remove the top name and place his or her own name at the bottom, and to send the revised list on to several other people. The letter promises that, if all goes well, soon the mailbox will be overflowing with money. Chain letters are an illegal fraud as are Ponzi schemes, pyramids, and related get-rich-quick schemes based on the plausible, but fallacious, chain-letter argument.

Charles Ponzi's Sleight of Hand

The chain-letter principle can be illustrated by the infamous Charles Ponzi.[1] In 1920, Ponzi promised to pay Massachusetts investors 50 percent interest every forty-five days—compounded eight times a year, $1 would grow to $1.50^8 = 25.63, an effective annual rate of return of 2463 percent! His stated plan was to arbitrage the difference between the official and open-market price of Spanish pesos: he would buy Spanish pesos cheap in the open market, use these pesos to buy International Postage Union coupons, and then trade the coupons for U.S. postage stamps at the higher official exchange rate. If everything worked as planned, he could buy 10 cents worth of U.S. postage stamps for a penny. (But it was not at all clear how he would convert these stamps back into cash.) In practice, he received $15 million from investors and appears to have bought only $61 in stamps.

If he did not invest the money he received, how could he possibly afford to pay a 50 percent return every forty-five days? He couldn't. But he could create a temporary illusion of doing so. Suppose that one person invests $100, and Ponzi puts the investment in a safe place. If Ponzi now finds another two people to invest $100 apiece, then he can pay the first person $150, keep $50 for himself, and leave the original $100 untouched. Now, he has forty-five days to find four more people willing to invest $100, so that he can pay each of the last two investors $150 and keep $100 for himself. These four investors then can be paid off with the money from eight new ones, and these eight from sixteen more.

The Fallacy

In a **Ponzi scheme**, money from new investors is used to pay off earlier ones, and it works as long as there are enough new investors. The problem is that the pool of fish is exhausted surprisingly soon. The twenty-first round requires a million new people, and the thirtieth round requires a billion more. At some point, the scheme runs out of new people, and those in the last round (the majority of investors) are left with nothing. A Ponzi scheme merely transfers wealth from late entrants to early entrants.

Ponzi's 1920 scam collapsed after eight months when a Boston news-

Ponzi scheme
A Ponzi scheme uses the money of new investors to pay off earlier ones.

paper discovered that during the time that he supposedly bought $15 million in postage coupons, the total amount sold worldwide came to only $1 million. Despite his protestations that he could pay off his investors by incorporating and selling shares of stock to other investors, the state of Massachusetts froze his accounts and sent Ponzi to jail for ten years.

The same principles apply to chain letters. For example, one letter lists five names, asking you to send $10 to the top name and to mail copies of the revised list (with your name at the bottom) to ten new people. If the chain continues unbroken, you become a millionaire the easy way. However, for the chain to be unbroken, each of the ten people must send letters to ten more. The fifth round involves letters to $10^5 = 100,000$ people. If they each send you $10, you will indeed be a millionaire. But what about them? Each is hoping to reach another 100,000 people, so that their fifth round will involve 100,000(100,000) = 10,000,000,000 people, double the earth's population. They will never get what they hope for; and maybe you are actually one of them, a member of the fifth round, and bound to be disappointed. What can be stated with certainty is that a chain letter is a zero-sum game in which nobody makes money unless someone else loses it. If we figure in the cost of stationery and postage, the group as a whole has to lose money.

pyramid deal
A pyramid deal is a Ponzi scheme, a zero-sum game that transfers wealth from late entrants to early ones (and to the scheme's promoters).

A Ponzi scheme is also called a **pyramid deal**, since its workings can be visualized by imagining a pyramid with the initial investors at the top and the latest round on the bottom; the pyramid collapses when the next round does not materialize. At illegal pyramid parties, people pay a fee to go to one location and pass chain letters among themselves. Even though it is patently obvious that no one goes home richer unless others go home poorer, greed blinds the participants to the likelihood that they will lose money.

Investments That Were Too Good To Be True

Ponzi schemes typically lure investors by promising to channel their money to a unique investment or to a fabulous money manager. The best protection is sober reflection and common sense. If it looks too good to be true, it probably is. Of course, greed is a powerful emotion, and it often tramples common sense. Here are some notorious cases.

A scheme that began in the 1960s was supposed to import low-grade "industrial wine" from Europe for salad dressing, earning a minimum 30 percent return every nine months. There is no such thing as industrial wine, but this Ponzi scheme lasted ten years and took in $26 million before it collapsed.[2] A Florida investment advisor raised $61 million over a fourteen-year period beginning in the 1970s by paying investors tax-free returns of up to 15 percent. As it turned out, the income investors received was not tax-free and, according to a court-appointed receiver, came almost entirely from the cash deposited by new investors—a Ponzi scheme.[3]

Home-Stake managed a series of tax-advantaged oil- and gas-drilling projects from the early 1960s until 1972. Someone in a 70 percent tax bracket (the highest during this period) who invested $100,000 could deduct this entire amount from taxable income that year, saving $70,000 in taxes. If $75,000 of that $100,000 was borrowed, then a $25,000 outlay saved $70,000 in taxes. (The ultimate profitability depends on whether the cash flow from the drilling venture covers the loan plus interest.) In all, Home-Stake raised $130 million from 3000 wealthy, prominent, and supposedly sophisticated investors. In 1973, the Securities and Exchange Commission (SEC) discovered that Home-Stake was paying some investors more than others (apparently to mollify them), a clear indication of fraud. A subsequent investigation turned up a giant Ponzi scheme in which only $21 million was ever spent on drilling. Five officers or associates eventually pleaded guilty or no contest to a variety of charges.[4]

E.S.M. Government Securities was a Fort Lauderdale securities firm that promised investors above-average returns on perfectly safe government securities. Many, mostly small municipalities and thrift institutions, took the bait. The catch was that the investors had to leave their securities with E.S.M. As it turned out, E.S.M. bought only a few securities, which were pledged to multiple owners. Most of the money received was used in a Ponzi scheme to pay above-market interest and to buy yachts, jets, and other finery for E.S.M.'s officers. When the SEC closed E.S.M. for fraud in 1985, its customers were out $320 million—prompting a run on Ohio thrift institutions. Six E.S.M. officers pleaded guilty to a variety of charges and four others were convicted of felonies; two committed suicide. A 39-year-old managing partner of E.S.M.'s accounting firm was derailed from his fast track and sentenced to twelve years in prison for his role in covering up E.S.M.'s deception.

J. David Dominelli, a previously obscure stockbroker, founded J. David & Co. in 1979. Reports of 40 percent annual returns trading foreign currencies lured investors and millions of dollars, allowing Dominelli to build a financial empire that included six homes, three planes, and dozens of cars. Investor efforts to retrieve their money eventually exposed J. David's operation as a Ponzi scheme with an $80 million deficit and forced the company into bankruptcy in January 1984. In 1985, Dominelli admitted that he had lied about virtually every aspect of his operation, pleaded guilty to fraud and tax evasion, and was sentenced to twenty years in federal prison.

Multilevel Distribution Plans

Millions of dollars have also changed hands in Ponzi schemes disguised as business franchises. The avowed aim of these illegal schemes is to sell some product, such as cosmetics or a diet supplement, but virtually all of the activity involves selling franchises to people hoping to sell franchises to others. The pyramid collapses when it runs out of new people or when it is shut down as an illegal pyramid or lottery. The company founder then retires or moves on and starts another pyramid.

In a typical multilevel distribution plan, people sign up to become distributors by paying a fee and/or buying some of the product for resale. If they recruit other distributors, they get a percentage of the recruits' initial fees and a percentage of their sales. It usually costs less than $100 to start and offers a chance at financial independence—a dream that is exploited fully at motivational meetings ("sizzle sessions"). A few multilevel plans are legitimate, with distributors working hard to sell a product—Mary Kay sells cosmetics, A.L. Williams sells life insurance, and Shaklee sells diet supplements this way. Amway is perhaps the most well known, and in 1979 the Federal Trade Commission ruled that it is not an illegal pyramid for two reasons: (a) Amway distributors are paid for selling products, not for recruiting more distributors, and (b) the company buys unsold products back from its distributors.

In an illegal pyramid scheme, there are few or no ultimate consumers—just distributors passing money (and perhaps products) among themselves. Usually the product is virtually worthless—an inexpensive food additive or a few mimeographed pages explaining how to participate in a multilevel plan. One of the most famous illegal plans is described in Investment Example 12–1.

BLIND FAITH AND HIGH HOPES

The opening quotation for this chapter gives Bernard Baruch's advice to be wary of the get-rich-quick plans offered by barbers and beauticians. Unfortunately, people who are trusting (and a bit greedy) often invest in dubious plans recommended by virtual strangers. One cautionary rule is to be wary of any advisor who is eager for you to invest. If the plan is so good, why does the advisor need your money? A second rule is that if you do not understand it, don't invest in it.

Aggressive Salespeople

boiler room
Boiler room operations involve aggressive telephone marketing of very speculative or fraudulent securities.

Boiler-room operations involve aggressive salespeople dialing phone number after phone number, trying to persuade gullible people to buy desert land, take overpriced vacations, or invest in worthless or highly speculative securities. Investment Example 12–2 on p. 386 describes penny-stock boiler rooms.

One of the biggest boiler-room operations ever was exposed in 1988. Based in Switzerland, it took in an estimated $250 million from thousands of investors in forty countries, with individual losses ranging from $1000 to $750,000. The scam began with newspaper advertisements offering free

INVESTMENT
EXAMPLE
12–1

DARE TO BE RICH

Glenn Turner was the son of a South Carolina sharecropper.* After an up-and-down career as a door-to-door sewing-machine salesman, he was swindled out of $2500 by a dump-truck driver who offered him a chance to sell cosmetics distributorships. Angered and inspired by this loss, he borrowed $5000 at the age of thirty-three and founded Koscot Interplanetary Incorporated: the *Koscot* was a combination of *cosmetics* with *EPCOT,* the nearby Disney city of tomorrow, and *Interplanetary* reflected his grandiose reach. The cosmetics were to be made of mink oil, and people could sign up at the following levels for the prices indicated:

$10   Door-to-door salesperson, eligible to keep 45 percent of the sales proceeds

$125   Coordinator, eligible to hire salespeople and keep 10 percent of what they sell

$2000   Supervisor, eligible to earn a commission on every supervisor recruited

$4500   Distributor, eligible to earn a commission on every distributor recruited

Within twenty-four months, he had recruited 100,000 people and parlayed his $5000 into $100,000,000 (and was reportedly offered $50 million for a 49 percent share). In 1975, the Federal Trade Commission ruled that Koscot engaged in unfair and deceptive practices, and the pyramid collapsed as state after state prohibited its operation.

Turner turned to multilevel motivation schools, called "Dare to be Great!" This venture was less regulated because he was not selling a tangible product; it also was closer to what he was really selling, hope and confidence. Turner proclaimed, "If I can become rich and famous, anyone can!" But the SEC stopped these, too, labeling them unregistered securities.

*John Frasca, *Glenn W. Turner, Con Man or Saint?.*

samples of an investment newsletter. Those who responded were soon called by a persuasive British or American salesman. According to one attorney, "They all had James Bond-type names—James Church or Charles Snow, or Fleming Windsor. They were very smooth and they all knew how to close a deal."[5] The salesmen would promote obscure companies that were trading, or had once traded, in the U.S. over-the-counter market. After a purchase, investors received worthless stock certificates and meaningless computer printouts confirming the transaction. Every few months, the boiler room would move to a new Swiss city, to keep ahead of Swiss authorities who might have been alerted by suspicious investors.

THE TELEMARKETING OF PENNY STOCKS

Traditionally, penny stocks (those that sell for less than a dollar a share) have appealed to speculators. For instance, Chapter 1 told of the letter that began "IMAGINE turning $1000 into $34,500 in less than one year!" and then cited a stock that went from 2 cents a share to 69 cents. Some who are attracted to this sort of pitch reason that the price of a penny stock only has to rise a few cents to give a satisfactory profit and the reward will be enormous if the price ever reaches the $40-plus range typical of blue chips. Overlooked is the observation that the price only has to fall by a few cents to give a large percentage loss: Imagine turning $1000 into $500 or $0 in less than a year!

Most penny stocks are legitimate, though young and unproven, companies. But some are the fraudulent concoctions of boiler rooms operating out of Denver, Salt Lake City, Boca Raton, Florida, and Southern California. The operators begin by incorporating a shell company that has an exciting name, but no real assets or intentions of producing anything. To satisfy SEC regulations, they use a so-called "blank check offering," stating that they are raising money to acquire an as-yet-undetermined business. The initial offering of millions of shares at pennies apiece is sold to associates, who can then trade the shares among themselves at higher prices to create the illusion that the stock is popular.

Smooth-talking salespeople call prospective investors, generally using a sequence of three calls. The initial contact is a baiting call, stating that the salesperson has made a lot of money for other investors and will keep his eye out for interesting investments. Next comes a hook call claiming that a great investment is on the horizon, in a company that has made a high-technology breakthrough, discovered a cure for AIDS, or has some other fanciful potential. Then comes the closing call to persuade the gullible investor to send in hundreds or even thousands of dollars for shares. The stock is not listed on any organized exchange, and the boiler room is the only market maker. The promoters may quote ever higher prices, but investors will never see price quotations in the newspaper or be able to buy or sell the stock though legitimate dealers. Any attempts to sell the stock back to the boiler-room operators are rebuffed. The salespersons are instructed never to send money to a customer. The only way that a stock can be sold is if the proceeds are immediately reinvested in another of the boiler room's stocks. If the investor refuses this alternative, then the sales people grow increasingly evasive, stalling until the operation eventually moves to a new location and repeats its fraudulent cycle.

A variation is a *bucket shop*, where salespeople take orders to buy and sell legitimate securities but do not actually make the trades, because they assume that most of their customers will lose money. Instead of buying at $40 and then selling later for $30, the bucket shop holds on to the $40, returns $30 after the sale, and pockets the difference (plus the commissions charged for the nonexistent transactions). If the customers somehow make money, then the bucket shop packs up and moves on before the police arrive.

False Prophets

In 1940, an astute observer wrote about

> the romantic Wall Streeter—and they are all romantics, whether they be villains or philanthropists. Else they would never have chosen this business which is a business of dreams. They continue to dream of conquests, coups, and power, for themselves or for the people they advise.[6]

These dreams draw people to the get-rich-quick gurus discussed in earlier chapters. Faced with great uncertainty and the chance to make millions, people turn to seminars, newsletters, and books that combine the comfort of expert opinion with the excitement produced by unleashed greed. A wonderful example is *How I Made Two Million Dollars in the Stock Market*[7] (written by a gypsy dancer and, judging from the book itself, the answer to the title question is, "With a lot of luck").

Some gurus are doom-and-gloom prophets who exploit investor fears and insecurities by predicting the collapse of financial markets, the economy, and, indeed, civilization. The most extreme advise storing water, food, and ammunition and selecting a secure cave for survival in the barbaric times ahead. These professional pessimists are unfazed by the continued inaccuracy of their vision. If the prediction of runaway inflation does not work out, they change the forecast to uncontrolled deflation and sell some more books. There is always a market for fear.

Long Shots

The unfounded hopes and wild dreams of investors are also reflected in the ability of small, untested firms to market their securities to people looking for the next IBM, Xerox, or Avon. Carried to the extreme, the search is for a concept, a story, a hint of growth that will lead other investors to jump on the bandwagon—a few steps after your boarding. As one underwriter put it, "We're basically selling hope, and hope's been real good to us."[8]

This new-issue activity is especially feverish when the stock market is booming. In 1965, Western Oil Shale went public at $5 a share with no revenue, losses in the preceding two years, and three employees as its only assets. Its prospectus stated that "no commercially feasible method of extracting petroleum from oil shale has been developed to date," and it gave no evidence that one would be found soon. It also noted that "many companies are more financially able to fund research projects of studying various methods of extraction of petroleum from oil shale and to finance the development of such methods." Yet, the stock jumped to $14½, giving a market value of $50 million, before dropping back to $3.[9]

In 1967, investor hopes were rekindled, and the price of Western Oil Shale stock again surged from $3 in February to $30 in May, compelling the president of the company to issue a statement saying that

> *Any rumors or recent publicity regarding the present or future value of the company's shares aren't founded in any way upon any fundamentals known to the company's officers. . . . It must be emphasized that there is no commercial production of oil, gas hydrocarbons, or other valuable minerals from shale either in Utah or elsewhere in the U.S. at this time. . . . Such technology may never be accomplished.*[10]

Nonetheless, the company was able to sell another 150,000 shares to the public in October 1968 at $14.25 a share. The company had only a half-dozen employees and no significant income other than interest on the cash it had accumulated from its stock sales. The firm's only other assets were some unproductive Utah leases. Year after year, the firm lost money or barely broke even. In 1980, after fifteen years of never paying a dividend, the company was finally consolidated with three other energy-related companies. The price of its stock at the time was $5¾.

Apple Computer went public with a price-earnings (P/E) ratio of 100, and a total market value of $2 billion. Genentech, with the exciting idea of applying DNA technology, went public with a P/E ratio of 800 and a market value of $750 million. These companies survived, but many others have not. The president of a venture-capital company estimated the chance of success at one in a thousand.[11] A formal SEC study of five hundred randomly selected new issues from the 1950s and early 1960s found that 43 percent were confirmed bankrupt, 25 percent were losing money but still afloat, and 12 percent had disappeared without a trace. Of the remaining 20 percent, only twelve companies seemed solid successes—a mere 2 percent of the companies surveyed. A New York Stock Exchange study of 300 new issues underwritten by its member firms in 1962 found that the median price had declined by 97 percent.[12]

SPECULATIVE BUBBLES

speculative bubble
Speculative bubbles occur when people hope to profit not from the asset's cash flow, but from selling the asset at ever-higher prices.

From time to time, investors are gripped by what, in retrospect, seems to have been mass hysteria. The price of some commodity or security climbs higher and higher, beyond all reason, a **speculative bubble**, in that nothing justifies the rise in price except the hope that it will go higher still. Then, suddenly, the bubble pops and the price collapses. With hindsight, it is hard to understand why people were so foolish and bought at such crazy prices. Yet, paradoxically, at the time of the bubble it seems foolish to sit on the sidelines while others become rich.

Imitative Behavior

When humans are in an unfamiliar environment—confronted by events they do not fully understand, with consequences they cannot predict— they tend to imitate each other's behavior. In one interesting psychology experiment, subjects were told that they were testing an experimental vitamin supplement and then injected with epinephrine, a hormone that causes temporary rapid heart beats and hand tremors. Put in a room with actors who supposedly had been given the vitamin supplement too, the subjects typically imitated the actors' behavior, whether it was light-hearted or depressed.[13]

The same sort of imitative behavior is observed less formally every day, in our desire to purchase the latest in fashionable clothing, entertainment, and automobiles. In financial markets, we have a natural tendency to believe that something is a good investment if others think so too, which leads us to act collectively as an unthinking herd. After a Washington, D.C., investment club purchased a stock at $18 a share, it reported; "Club sold all holdings at 12½ due to decline in price; intends to reinvest when price moves up."[14] Clearly, these club members were being led by the market.

Professionals follow the same group-think, herd mentality, as illustrated by the story of National Student Marketing in Investment Example 9–1 in Chapter 9. Although National Student Marketing was selling for 100 times exaggerated earnings in February 1970, the most prominent money managers chose it as their favorite stock for the coming year. This consensus was not the result of independent evaluation; instead, all were swayed by the recent success of the stock and the enthusiasm of other money managers.

The Building of a Bubble

Speculative bubbles generally begin with important events of real economic significance, such as the building of a railroad, the discovery of gold, or an outbreak of war.[15] Seeing the profits made by some investors, others rush to get a piece of the action, pushing prices higher. Soon, greed displaces common sense, and swindlers emerge to part fools from their money. The upward rush of prices becomes a speculative bubble in the sense that most of the participants are buying not for the income that their investment might produce but in anticipation that prices will keep rising—a selfful-filling prophecy as long as there are more buyers than sellers. When everyone is convinced that the investment is a good one, there is no one left who will buy and push the price higher still. The bubble bursts when

TABLE 12–1   Two Hypothetical Speculative Bubbles

Year	Annual Dividend	Investment Having a Constant Required Return		Investment Having a Rising Required Return	
		Required Return (percent)	Price	Required Return (percent)	Price
0	$1.00	10	$20.00	12	$20.00
1	1.00	10	21.00	14	21.40
2	1.00	10	22.10	16	23.40
3	1.00	10	23.31	18	26.14
4	1.00	10	24.64	20	29.85
5	1.00		26.10		34.82

buyers no longer outnumber sellers. There is a selling stampede, and prices collapse. In the frantic rush for the exit, very few make it through the door.

A Hypothetical Example

Table 12–1 gives two specific numerical examples of hypothetical speculative bubbles. In these examples, there is a constant, perpetual annual dividend (or other cash flow) of $1. At a 10 percent required return, the investment's cash flow is worth $1.00/0.10 = $10 to an investor willing to hold the asset for keeps. What if the market price is $20? A $1 dividend on a $20 investment is inadequate, and investors should shun it. But what if the price of the asset is $20 now and is expected to be $21 a year from now? A $1 dividend plus a $1 capital gain will provide the requisite 10 percent return, thus justifying a price of $20. Why will people pay $21 a year from now for a $1 dividend? They will if they are confident that the price will keep rising, to $22.10 a year later. (A $1 dividend plus a $1.10 capital gain is a 10 percent return on a $21 investment.) By the same logic, $22.10 is justified by a price of $23.31 the year after that. No price is too high, as long as the price can be counted to go higher still. Does this seem like the Greater Fool Theory? It is, indeed. Investment Example 12–3 tells of experiments in which people behaved in just this way.

A speculative bubble is a runup of prices that is not justified by the underlying economic fundamentals (the present value of an asset's cash flow), but instead is sustained by a belief that prices will keep rising. The bubble bursts when participants are no longer willing to believe in ever higher prices. In Table 12–1, consider what happens in the fifth year if people begin to doubt that the price will continue rising. Even if they think

INVESTMENT EXAMPLE 12–3

EXPERIMENTAL BUBBLES

Several economists, including Vernon Smith at the University of Arizona, have set up experimental stock markets for volunteers (usually economics students, in some cases business executives) and have repeatedly observed speculative booms and crashes.[1] In Smith's experiments, the participants are given some shares of stock and money and are allowed to trade with each other using a computer for fifteen "days". Each trading day lasts less than 5 minutes and ends with the stock paying a dividend. All of the traders know that the dividend is determined randomly, with an average value of 24 cents, so that the intrinsic value of a share of stock is initially 15($0.24) = $3.60 and declines to $0.24 on the last trading day. Nonetheless, the market price typically rises to near $6.00 a share before crashing. Smith concludes that inexperienced traders never trade consistently near fundamental value, and most commonly generate a boom followed by a crash in stock prices.[2] After a few booms and crashes, traders learn to keep market prices closer to fundamental values. This learning from sad experience offers little hope for the real world, however, because markets are continually absorbing an influx of new traders who have not yet experienced bubbles and crashes.

[1]Vernon L. Smith, Gerry L. Suchanek, and Arlington W. Williams, "Bubbles, Crashes, and Endogenous Expectations in Asset Market Experiments," mimeo, 1986.

[2]Quoted in Jerry E. Bishop, "Stock Market Experiment Suggests Inevitability of Booms and Busts," *The Wall Street Journal*, November 17, 1987.

that the asset's price will hold at $26.10, a $1 dividend is only a $1/$26.10 = 3.83 percent return, far from the requisite 10 percent. If many rush to sell, putting downward pressure on the price, others may become convinced of an impending capital loss, creating panic selling with no buyers to be found.

The buildup of a speculative bubble is rational in the sense that higher prices today can be rationalized by even higher prices tomorrow. The participants may even be convinced that market prices have strayed far above economic fundamentals but be equally confident that they can get out before the bubble bursts. The inherent uncertainty of speculative bubbles may make them nervous, but that anxiety, too, can be overcome by sufficiently high anticipated prices. The last two columns in Table 12–1 show the case of a steadily rising required return, to compensate for increasing anxiety about when the bubble will pop. Sufficiently bullish price predictions can always satisfy those willing to believe—a point illustrated in Investment Example 12–4 on p. 392.

TULIPMANIA

Tulips were virtually unknown in western Europe until 1554, when an ambassador from Vienna brought bulbs back from Turkey. The offspring spread across Europe, catching the fancy of gardeners, especially wealthy ones in the Netherlands who were willing to pay handsomely for bulbs that would produce unusual flowers. (It is now understood that the most exotic flowers were produced from bulbs infected by a mosaic virus carried by aphids.) In 1634, rising prices and rumors that tulips were becoming fashionable in France lured nongardeners into the Dutch tulip market in force, looking for easy money and creating Tulipmania.*

With tulip prices rising briskly, it seemed a simple matter to buy a few bulbs and sell them a short while later for a substantial profit. In addition, each growing season a bulb can be split into two or three. Could there be an easier way to get rich? What seems to have escaped notice is that this same potential for multiplying the supply will cause prices to fall when the number of bulbs eventually exceeds demand.

Tulip bulbs must be in the ground from September until June; so trades made during these months are for future delivery, with the buyer agreeing to pay a specified price after the bulb is taken from the ground and the seller agreeing to deliver the bulb at that time. Trades among serious gardeners involved written contracts witnessed by notaries. By 1636, however, the tulip market was dominated by trading in taverns among nonprofessionals with little cash or bulbs. As there were no margin requirements, buyers could agree to pay a price beyond their means, anticipating that

they would resell the bulb for a profit before summer delivery. Others traded livestock and mortgaged their houses to participate. Swindlers soon entered, since it is impossible to identify the variety of a flower by inspection of the bulb.

By November 1636, speculation had spread to even the common tulip varieties, and during January 1637, the prices jumped by a factor of ten or twenty. For instance, a bulb that might have fetched $20 (in today's dollars) in the summer of 1636 traded for $160 in January and for $2000 a few weeks later. The prices of exotic bulbs topped $50,000, and one nobleman was reported to have paid $800,000 for an especially rare bulb. The prices agreed to in the taverns were even higher. Then, in February 1637, the market crashed virtually overnight. As people rushed to sell, prices collapsed, and buyers vanished, since no one wanted to buy tulips if the prices will be lower tomorrow.

Existing agreements were in limbo until April 1637, when Holland formally suspended all tulip contracts, allowing gardeners to sell the bulbs they would dig up that summer at fresh prices. Many cities later decreed that buyers could withdraw from earlier contracts for a 3.5 percent payment, but some buyers simply refused to honor earlier agreements. For trades among serious gardeners, the summer prices were down some 90 percent to 95 percent from February. A century later, tulip prices were less than one one-thousandth of the prices at the peak of Tulipmania.

*The most complete description of this historical episode is in Peter M. Garber, "The Tulipmania Legend," mimeo, Brown University, 1986.

STOCK-MARKET BUBBLES

There have been several dramatic historical episodes when the stock market was seized by a collective euphoria, as investors seemed to put aside common sense and, instead, were willing to believe whatever was necessary to justify ever higher stock prices. The subsequent, terrifying collapse of prices not only caused fortunes to evaporate, but persuaded many investors that they would never buy stock again. We will look first at an English bubble in the eighteenth century, then the stock market crash that accompanied the Great Depression, and, finally, at a more recent one-day crash of unprecedented magnitude.

The South Sea Bubble

In 1720, the South Sea Company took over the British government's debt in exchange for exclusive trading privileges with Spain's American colonies. Encouraged by the company's inventive bookkeeping, English citizens rushed to invest in this exotic venture. As the price of the South Sea Company's stock soared from 120£ on January 28 to 400£ on May 19, 800£ on June 4, and 1000£ on June 22, the investors became rich, and thousands of other people rushed to join their ranks. Soon entrepreneurs were offering stock in ever more grandiose schemes and were deluged by frantic inventors not wanting to be left out. It scarcely mattered what the scheme was. One promised to build a wheel for perpetual motion. Another was formed "for carrying on an undertaking of great advantage, but nobody is to know what it is." The shares for this mysterious offering were priced at 100£ each, with a promised annual return of 100£; after selling all the stock within five hours, the promoter immediately left England and never returned. Yet another stock offer was for the *nitvender*, or selling of nothing.[16] When the bubble burst, most of the stock for these myriad ventures became worthless, and fortunes and dreams were lost.

As with all speculative bubbles, there were many believers in the Greater Fool Theory. While some suspected that prices were unreasonable, the market was dominated by people believing that prices would continue to rise, at least until they could sell to the next fool in line. In the spring of 1720, Sir Isaac Newton said, "I can calculate the motions of the heavenly bodies, but not the madness of people," and sold his South Sea shares for a 7000£ profit. However, later that year, he bought shares again, just before the bubble burst, and lost 20,000£. Similarly, when a banker invested 500£ in the third offer of South Sea stock (in August 1720), he explained that "when the rest of the world are mad, we must imitate them in some measure."[17] After James Milner, a member of the British Parliament, was bankrupted by the South Sea bubble, he explained that "I said indeed that ruin must some come upon us but I owe it came two months earlier than I expected."[18]

The Great Crash

The 1920s were an exciting and turbulent decade—for the economy, for social mores, and for the stock market.[19] In 1924, the Dow Jones Industrial Average reached 100. In December 1927, it roared past 200, to 250 in October 1928 and 300 in December. Nine months later, in September 1929, it attained a peak of 386. It seemed as if investors could make money effortlessly by buying stock in rock-solid companies. Between March 1928 and September 1929, American Can went from 77 to 181⅞, American Telephone from 179½ to 335⅝, General Electric from 128¾ to 396¼, and U.S. Steel from 138⅛ to 279⅛.

Predicting the future is always treacherous, and history is full of well-informed people making what, with hindsight, are foolish statements. At breakfast before Waterloo, Napoleon remarked, "Wellington is a bad general, the English are bad soldiers; we will settle the matter by lunchtime." In 1899, the Director of the U.S. Patent Office said, "Everything that can be invented has been invented." Thomas Edison believed that "the phonograph is not of any commercial value," and President Hayes said of the telephone, "That's an amazing invention, but who would ever want to use one?" Lord Kelvin, a scientist and president of Britain's Royal Society proclaimed, "Heavier than air flying machines are impossible," and, "Radio has no future." Harry Warner, the president of Warner Brothers said, "Who the hell wants to hear actors talk?" and Thomas Watson, the CEO of IBM, said, "I think there is a world market for about five computers."

The stock market and the economy are never easy to predict, and the Crash and the Great Depression were no exceptions. In his final message to Congress, on December 4, 1928, Calvin Coolidge boasted that "no Congress of the Unites States ever assembled, on surveying the state of the Union, has met with a more pleasing prospect than that which appears at the present time." Herbert Hoover took office, and in July 1929 predicted that "the outlook of the world today is for the greatest era of commercial expansion in history." On October 17, 1929, Irving Fisher, the greatest American economist of his day, asserted that stocks had reached "what looks like a permanently high plateau."

The End of the Bull Market The five-year bull market was over, and Fisher could not have been more wrong. After a number of bad days, panic selling hit the market on Thursday, October 24. Terrified investors tried to sell at any price, and market prices plunged, with the panic heightened by the fact that the ticker tape reporting transactions ran hours late, so that investors had no information about current prices. The market finally steadied in the afternoon when six prominent New York bankers put up $40 million apiece to buy stocks. But the market dropped again the following Monday and was hit by panic selling the next day, Black Tuesday, October 29. Again there was an avalanche of sell orders, more than the brokers and ticker tape could process, and, more importantly, dwarfing the scattered buy orders. White Sewing Machine, for instance, had recently traded for $48; on Monday it closed at $11 ⅛. On Black Tuesday, in the complete absence of buy orders, a messenger boy bought shares for $1.[20]

With fits and starts, the market decline continued. By November 13, the Dow had fallen an incredible 48 percent as the prices of America's premier companies collapsed: American Can was down 53 percent, American Telephone 41 percent, General Electric 58 percent, and U.S. Steel 46 percent. Nevertheless, Hoover's optimism persisted. In his December 3, 1929, State of the Union message, he concluded that "the problems with which we are confronted are the problems of growth and progress." In March 1930, both President Hoover and the Secretary of Commerce predicted that business would be normal by May. In early May, Hoover declared that "we have now passed the worst"; in late May, he predicted recovery by the fall.[21] In June, he told a group that had come to Washington to urge increased government spending, "Gentlemen, you have come sixty days too late. The depression is over."[22] The President's cheerleading did not reassure the public. In October, the Republican National Chairman complained that "persons high in Republican circles are beginning to believe that there is some concerted effort on foot to utilize the stock market as a method of discrediting the administration. Every time an administration official gives out an optimistic statement about business conditions, the market immediately drops."[23]

The Dow recovered to nearly 300 in the spring of 1930, but then it began a long, tortuous slide, punctuated by brief, inadequate rallies before finally touching bottom at 42.84 in June 1932—down 89 percent from September 1929. It was not until 1956, twenty-seven years later, that the stock market regained its 1929 peak.

Economic Collapse The Great Depression was more than a stock-market crash. Between 1929 and 1933, the nation's output fell by one-third, while the unemployment rate rose from 3 percent to 25 percent. More than one-third of the nation's banks failed, and household net worth dropped by 30 percent. Behind these aggregate numbers were millions of private tragedies. Approximately 100,000 businesses failed, and 12 million people lost their jobs, and, with them, their income and, in many cases, their self-respect. Many lost their life savings in the stock-market crash and in the tidal wave of bank failures. Without income or savings, people could not buy food, clothing, or proper medical care. Those who could not pay their rents lost their shelter; those who could not make their mortgage payments lost their homes. Farm income fell by two-thirds, and many farms were lost to foreclosure. Desperate people moved into shanty settlements (called Hoovervilles), slept under newspapers (Hoover blankets), and scavenged for food where they could. Edmund Wilson reported that

> *There is not a garbage-dump in Chicago which is not haunted by the hungry. Last summer in the hot weather when the smell was sickening and the flies were thick, there were a hundred people a day coming to one of the dumps.*[24]

The unemployment rate averaged 19 percent during the 1930s and never fell below 14 percent. The Great Depression did not end until the federal government began spending nearly $100 billion a year during World War II.

October 19, 1987

Federal Reserve Board (Fed)

The Federal Reserve Board controls monetary policy in United States.

The **Federal Reserve Board (Fed)** controls monetary policy in the United States. Alarmed by inflation in late 1979, the Fed began a tight money policy that pushed up interest rates and discouraged spending, particularly for houses, factories, and other investment projects. In the spring of 1980, Fed Chairman Paul Volcker said that he would not be satisfied "until the last buzz saw is silenced."[25] By 1982, the economy had been brought to its knees with long-term Treasury-bond rates above 12 percent and the unemployment rate above 10 percent for the first time since the Great Depression. Satisfied that inflation had been brought under control—down to a livable 3.9 percent—and fearing the complete collapse of the economy, the Fed gradually eased its pressure. The subsequent decline in unemployment and interest rates fueled a bull market in stocks.

A Five-Year Bull Market In August 1982, the Dow Jones Industrial Average was at 777. Five years later, it had more than tripled, to 2722. Of course, no one bought at exactly 777 and sold at exactly 2722. But, along the way, a lot of people noticed the runup in stock prices and wanted to hop on for at least part of the ride.

When the Dow surged past 2000 in January 1987, stocks were widely perceived to be overvalued by conventional criteria; yet players stayed in the market, hoping for more profits and believing that they could get out before the bubble burst. *The Wall Street Journal* ran a front-page story titled, "Stock Market's Surge Is Puzzling Investors; When Will It End?"[26] The story began with the exclamation, "Wheee!" and went on to say that "the market madness is as puzzling as it is exhilarating." For a typical view, the newspaper quoted Steven Leuthold, the head of a financial-advisory service: "You have to realize we're in Looney Tunes land and you should stay fairly close to the exits . . . [But] it's a lot of fun, and you could make a lot of money here."

When the Dow topped 2700 in August, stocks were selling for twenty-three times earnings, and divided yields were a mere 2.2 percent, compared to 10 percent interest rates on Treasury bonds. If we add a 5 percent risk premium to the 10 percent Treasury bond yield, then stocks should have had a 15 percent required return. The constant-dividend-growth benchmark model discussed in Chapter 7

$$P = \frac{D}{R - g}$$

implies

$$R = \frac{D}{P} + g$$

With D/P = 2 percent, long-term investors in 1987 needed a 13 percent dividend growth rate to achieve a 15 percent return from holding stock for keeps.

Buyers in 1987 were not planning on holding their stock for keeps, however. There was a lot of wishful thinking, including wildly optimistic forecasts of future earnings and interest rates, and a heavy reliance on the Greater Fool Theory, with U.S. investors hoping that the Japanese were the ultimate bigger fools, with unlimited cash and an eagerness to pay twenty times earnings for U.S. stocks because Japanese stocks were selling for sixty times earnings. *The Wall Street Journal* used this story to illustrate the market's predisposition to believe:

> On June 23, an obscure investment advisor, P. David Herrlinger, announced a $6.8 billion offer for Dayton Hudson Corp. Mr. Herrlinger appeared on his front lawn to tell the Dow Jones News Service that he didn't know whether his bid was a hoax. "It's no more of a hoax than anything else," he said. Later, he was taken to a hospital. Yet the news sent the giant retailer's stock soaring, with 5.5 million shares changing hands in frantic trading.[27]

The Crash   After topping 2700 in late August, the Dow Industrial Average slipped back to 2500 in October. Then the Dow fell by a record 95 points on Wednesday, October 14; dropped by another 58 points on Thursday; and fell an unprecedented 108 points on Friday, to close at 2246.74. The volume of trading on Friday was also the highest ever, with 338 million shares traded, and falling prices outnumbering gainers by a staggering seventeen to one.

Monday's "Abreast of the Market" column in *The Wall Street Journal* suggested that Friday's bloodletting might have been the "selling climax" that many technical analysts believe precedes a bull market. One said that "the peak of intensity of selling pressure has exhausted itself," and another argued that "if we haven't seen the bottom, we're probably very close."[28]

The very day that this article appeared was Black Monday, a frightening market convulsion that participants will never forget. When the market opened, the excess of sell orders was so large that trading was suspended in eight of the thirty Dow industrials for an hour. For the day, an astounding

604 million shares were traded, and the Dow dropped 508 points (23 percent). Losers outnumbered gainers by forty to one, and the aggregate market value of stocks fell by roughly $500 billion.

On the next day, Terrible Tuesday, markets came close to a total collapse. At the opening, many specialists and other market makers quoted prices far above Monday's close and sold heavily. The Dow opened with an extraordinary 200-point gain, but by noon it had fallen back below Monday's close. During the day, trading was temporarily suspended in many of the most well known stocks, including IBM for two hours and Merck for four hours. Several major financial institutions were rumored to be bankrupt and some banks cut off credit to securities firms who, in turn, made urgent margin calls to large traders. Several specialist firms had difficulty raising cash to buy securities, and some of the largest securities firms urged the New York Stock Exchange to shut down completely.

The day was saved when the Federal Reserve began buying bonds (driving interest rates down), issued a promise to supply much needed cash, and pressured banks to lend money. In addition, with vigorous encouragement from investment bankers, several major corporations announced plans to repurchase their stock, and the system held together— if just barely. (For the week, the ten largest New York banks ended up lending an extra $5.5 billion to securities firms.) One market participant said that "Tuesday was the most dangerous day we had in 50 years. I think we came within an hour [of the disintegration of the stock market]."[29] The Dow closed Tuesday up 102 points on 608 million shares and rose another 187 points the next day—ending the short-run crisis.

Tidbits of bad economic news preceded the October 19 crash—congressional discussion of restrictions on corporate takeovers, a larger-than-expected trade deficit, and slightly higher interest rates—but nothing that seems substantial enough to explain the magnitude of the crash. A mail survey of individual and institutional investors found little reason for the collapse in prices other than a widespread belief that prices had been too high and that, once prices started declining, people tried to sell all at once, swamping the will and financial ability of specialists to maintain orderly markets.[30] Recalling the January advice in *The Wall Street Journal* cited earlier that "we're in Looney Tunes land and you should stay fairly close to the exits," it appears that on October 19 too many people tried to squeeze through the exit door at the same time.

The Role of Portfolio Insurance Investors have long used stop-loss orders and less formal rules to try to limit their losses; for example, selling when the price of a stock drops 10 percent from a previous high or when it drops 10 percent below the price paid for the stock. In the 1980s a more flexible procedure for limiting losses was developed, given the appealing label **portfolio insurance,** and tried by a number of pension funds, mutual funds, and other institutional investors. A full description will have to wait for

portfolio insurance
Portfolio insurance is a flexible procedure for limiting losses by selling securities continuously as prices drop.

TABLE 12–2 Portfolio Insurance with Continuous Trading

Market Price of Stock	Stock Investment			Treasury-Bill Investment		Total Portfolio Value
	Number of Shares	Value	Percentage of Total Portfolio	Value	Percentage of Total Portfolio	
$ 75	0.00	$ 0.00	0	$1875.00	100	$1875.00
80	2.35	187.65	10	1688.89	90	1876.54
85	4.45	378.32	20	1513.29	80	1891.61
90	6.39	575.41	30	1342.62	70	1918.03
95	8.23	781.77	40	1172.66	60	1954.43
100	10.00	1000.00	50	1000.00	50	2000.00
105	11.74	1232.70	60	821.74	40	2054.44
110	13.47	1482.16	70	635.65	30	2117.81
115	15.23	1751.38	80	437.84	20	2189.22
120	17.03	2043.24	90	226.70	10	2269.94
125	18.88	2361.11	100	0.00	0	2361.00

Chapter 17's discussion of futures contracts; but the spirit can be illustrated simply.

Stop-loss orders and similar rules have an all-or-nothing characteristic: unless the price drops 10 percent, do nothing; when it drops 10 percent, sell all shares. In contrast, portfolio insurance (at least in theory) involves continuous trading: if the price drops a little, sell a little; if it drops further, sell some more. The system sets rules for trading the other way too: if a stock's price rises, buy more; if the price keeps rising, keep buying.

Table 12–2 gives a detailed example of a simplified kind of portfolio insurance. The initial market price of the stock is $100, and an institution has invested $2,000 (presumably $2,000 million), evenly divided between stocks and Treasury bills. As the stock price drops, the institution follows a rule of continuously selling a sufficient number of shares so that if the price reaches $95, stock will only comprise 40 percent of its portfolio and it will have sold at an average price of $97.5. Similarly, if the stock price falls as low as $90 it will have planned its sales so that stock is now 30 percent of its portfolio and the average selling price is $95. At a price of $75, it is out of the market. On the other hand, if the price rises, the institution increases its holdings as shown in Table 12–2.

There are two main advantages. First, the mechanical selling rules avoid the large capital losses that might occur if an institution held onto a large stock position as prices deteriorated. In fact, when dividends and interest are taken into account, continuous trading, in theory, can insure that the portfolio never loses money. Second, continuous trading avoids the awkward discontinuity of selling everything at one fixed price.

Nonetheless, there are problems with portfolio insurance, analogous to those for stop-loss orders. The assumption of continuous trading was undone by the price discontinuities on October 19. As with stop-loss orders, an intent to sell if the price falls to $95 does not guarantee that, in practice, you will be able to sell at $95. The market price may drop right past $95 to $85, $75 or even lower. In addition, we ignored brokerage fees, which make continuous trading prohibitively expensive. In practice, portfolio insurers only act after the price moves up or down by 3 percent, or some other set rule. If we modify Table 12–2, so that trades are made at $5 intervals, the firm sells 1.79 shares at $95, for a portfolio value of $1950, increasing its loss (not counting brokerage fees) from 2.28 percent to 2.5 percent. With trading at $10 intervals, the loss at a $90 price grows from 4.1 percent to 5 percent. Another drawback to portfolio insurance is that brokerage fees accumulate if the market see saws, forcing the portfolio insurer to sell one day and buy the next.

A Meltdown? In the context of October 19, 1987, portfolio insurance implies a seemingly perverse strategy of buying after prices have risen and selling after a decline. If enough institutional investors follow these mechanical rules, they may destabilize markets. In late 1986 and early 1987, John Phelan, the chairman of the New York Stock Exchange, began publicly warning of a market "meltdown" in which falling prices would provoke portfolio insurers to sell, pushing prices lower and setting off another round of sales.

The Brady commission, a presidential task force, concluded that portfolio insurance was indeed the trigger that precipitated the crash on October 19 and threatened further panic on October 20. It also criticized the actions of some specialists, the presumed buyers of last resort, as "poor by any standard." Trading in many stocks was erratic, with large price movements and trading suspensions. Some 30 percent of the specialists were net sellers on Black Monday, and 82 percent were net sellers on Terrible Tuesday. Countless small investors could not reach brokers or mutual funds, and many of those who did get through did not have their trades executed promptly. The Brady commission's primary policy conclusion was that the three markets for stocks, options, and futures are really one market. On October 19 and 20, these markets became disconnected and went into virtual free falls. To avoid a repeat, the commission recommended that the markets be supervised by a single regulatory authority (such as the Federal Reserve), that the markets be subject to consistent margin requirements, and that trading be halted simultaneously in all three markets during crises to allow time for matching buyers and sellers.

Portfolio insurers sold about $6 billion worth of stock on October 19, by itself not an overwhelming amount. But a lot of people follow less formal policies designed to limit losses by selling when prices fall below predetermined levels. Approximately 40 percent of the individuals and 20 percent of the institutions who sold on October 19 followed some sort of loss-limiting policy, and nearly half of these people had adopted such policies within a month of the crash—indicating that they believed stocks to be overpriced and were fearful of a collapse.[31]

In addition, many institutions knew that portfolio insurers would sell when prices started dropping and attempted to "front-run" portfolio insurers by selling first. Some portfolio insurers delayed mandated sales in early October, hoping to outwit the front-runners. However, the 261-point drop in the Dow on October 14 through 16 forced their hand. Said one member of the Brady commission, "Suddenly with Monday, they not only had to do an enormous amount of selling, they had an enormous holdover, and the front-runners just ate them alive."[32]

Approximately $100 billion was covered by portfolio insurance before the October 19 crash. Within months, its use fell by two-thirds because it did not live up to its advertised "assurance that all the implications and expectations of the selected strategy are known in advance. No unhappy surprises."[33] Many individual investors were also scarred by October 19 and, not wanting any more unhappy surprises, left the stock market, vowing never to return—much like the person burned by a hot stove who vows never to eat cooked food again.

SUMMARY

Investment decisions are usually subjective and often emotional, swayed by dreams of easy riches. An understandable hope for an easy fortune leads many investors to be swindled by the unscrupulous. Chain letters, Ponzi schemes, and pyramids use the money of new participants to pay off investors who joined earlier. Such schemes require an ever expanding group of participants and collapse when new investors cannot be found. A simple Ponzi scheme is a zero-sum game that transfers wealth from late entrants to early ones. More often, the promoters, pretending to be financial wizards, send investors fraudulent financial statements and spend most of the money raised by the scheme on themselves.

Unfounded hopes sometimes lead people to turn their money over to virtual strangers and to invest in schemes that are, at best, long shots. At times, groups of investors are overcome by what, in retrospect, seems a collective euphoria. Seeing asset prices rise, they rush to buy, pushing prices higher still. In a speculative bubble, asset prices lose touch with intrinsic values as people hope to profit not from an asset's cash flow, but from selling the asset at ever-higher prices. When the bubble collapses, buyers cannot be found, and prices fall precipitously.

The 1982–87 bull market was fueled by lower interest rates and a stronger economy. In the summer of 1987, dividend yields had fallen to about 2 percent while Treasury bonds yielded 10 percent, suggesting that only unrealistic expectations could justify prevailing stock prices. On October 19, 1987, prices fell by more than 20 percent in a single day as many investors tried to leave the market at once, including portfolio insurers who automatically sell when prices fall.

EXERCISES

1. In 1948, a distinguished economist pro-claimed that "never in the lifetime of anyone in this room will government two-and-a-halves [2½ percent coupon bonds] sell below par."[34] Was he right?

2. The International Bank of Roseau made this offer: For $300, you can receive a short course on international banking and earn the right to sign up others for this course. If you sign up six people, you receive a $1000 "loan" from the bank that does not have to be repaid. Suppose that you sign up six people, and each of these sign up six people, and so on eight more times. How many people will have taken this course? How much money will the bank have taken in and paid out? Why do you think the Florida attorney general shut down this bank?

3. A security analyst argued that the Great Crash was in 1930–32, not 1929:

> The Dow Jones Industrial average peaked at 381.17 during September 3, 1929. The so-called Great Crash pushed this index down 48% by November 13. But by April 17, 1930, the index rebounded 48% from the November bottom . . . In other words, anyone who bought a diversified portfolio of stocks during September 1929 would have experienced no net change in the value of his portfolio by April of 1930.[35]

Show the error in his conclusion.

4. In late 1983, J. David & Co. sent a memo to a bank stating that J. David's cash-flow prob-lems were temporary, because its investor re-quests for withdrawals could soon be satisfied by the arrival of funds from new investors. Why might such a memo suggest fraud? Why might a legitimate business do the same thing, with no fraud whatsoever? If you were a bank officer, how would you tell the difference be-tween a fraud and a legitimate business?

5. Between August 1982 and August 1987, the Dow Jones Industrial Average rose from 777 to 2722. What was the annual percentage rate of increase?

6. A newspaper columnist wrote that

> More than $500 billion was wiped off stock prices on Oct. 19 . . . Yet there is hope, even a growing belief, that somehow that $500-billion loss doesn't touch the real American economy.
>
> Unfortunately, the hope is false—as you'll see if you think about it. The $500 billion was real enough when it increased corporate cash flow; real enough when investors paid it out for stocks at high prices. Stocks do not rise on air, but on somebody paying real money to buy them.
>
> Where is that real money now? It is gone. It is as if that $500 billion had built 10,000 factories and office buildings and homes and shopping centers and they had all burned down in a single day.[36]

Keeping the columnist's remarks in mind, answer the following questions:

a. Do investors buying stock increase a cor-poration's cash flow?

b. If the market value of a company's stock rises by $1 million, must investors have pur-chased $1 million worth of stock?

c. Where does the money that investors spend on stock go?

d. If you were the president of the United States, would you rather have the stock market fall by $500 billion or have $500 billion worth of factories destroyed by fire?

7. In the aftermath of the October 1987 stock market crash, a prominent economist argued that

> The fundamental cause of the crash was an overvalued market. Historically, the U.S. stock market has never been able to maintain price-to-earnings ratios of more than 20-to-1 for any substantial period. Moreover, in early October,

the price-to-earnings multiple on bonds was 10-to-1. Why would anyone pay over $20 for $1 worth of annual earnings capacity where there was another place, the bond market, where it could be had for less risk for $10?[37]

What does he mean by the "price-to-earnings multiple on bonds"? Under what circumstances would stocks not be overvalued at twenty times earnings even though bonds were only ten times earnings?

8. An institutional investor who had been buying before the market crash on October 19, 1987, said that although he believed stocks were overpriced, "we followed the 'trend is your friend' philosophy."[38] What do you think he meant by this statement? Why is this strategy risky?

9. The fifth edition of Graham and Dodd's classic *Security Analysis* was published in late 1987, updated by three longtime associates.[39] In it, they used the following economic projections from financial institutions to estimate the fundamental value of the S&P 400 Industrial Stock Index:

Dividend = $9.00
Firm profit rate = 14 percent
Dividend payout ratio = 46 percent
Required return = 8.5 percent Aaa
industrial-bond rate
+ 2.75 percent risk
premium

On October 13, 1987, the actual value of the S&P 400 Index was 364. Calculate the book's estimate of fundamental value.

10. One observer of the October 19, 1987, crash said that "all the pros knew the portfolio insurance selling was coming; so, the guys with sneakers cut in front of them and tried to sell first."[40] Expand this comment into a 250-word explanation of this action, suitable for the average newspaper reader.

Risk and Return

CHAPTER 13

Decision Making Under Uncertainty

*The safest way to double your money is to
fold it over once and put in your pocket . . .*
Frank McKinney Hubbard

Our lives are filled with uncertainties, ranging from tomorrow's weather
to the success of a marriage to war and peace. Who will be the next president? What score will you get on your next test? Should you take a job
in another state? Will you get a good meal at a new restaurant? Uncertainty,
with all of the attendant excitement and frustration, is unavoidable. However, we can use probabilities to make rational choices. There will still be
surprises, pleasant and unpleasant, but, on average, we will fare better
if we consider our alternatives and the likely consequences before
we act.

A number of techniques have been developed to help us make rational
decisions in an uncertain world, and these tools can be applied to a wide
variety of choices, including investment decisions. In the next several chapters, we will look at some of these principles and their applications. We
will begin in this chapter by seeing how the uncertainty surrounding investment returns can be quantified by specifying probabilities and calculating two statistical measures—the mean and the standard deviation. You
will learn that these two measures are useful for describing uncertain investment returns, but that the specific assets investors choose depend on
their attitudes towards risk.

USING PROBABILITIES

If there is uncertainty, then a variety of outcomes are possible. **Probabilities** can be used to quantify these uncertainties by describing which outcomes are likely and which are unlikely. When a coin is flipped fairly, the two possible outcomes, heads and tails, are equally likely; so we assign a probability of one-half to each. In the same way, consider an investment with two possible outcomes, a $100 loss and a $200 gain. If we consider these outcomes equally likely, then we can assign a probability of one-half to each. If we believe, instead, that the $100 loss is twice as likely as the $200 gain, then we can express this belief by saying that there is a two-thirds probability of a $100 loss and a one-third probability of a $200 gain. Investment Example 13–1 tells how some doctors use probabilities to clarify their diagnoses. Investment analysts can use probabilities to clarify their forecasts.

Subjective Probabilities

As with coin flips, investment probabilities cannot be negative and must add to one. The essential difference is that with coins, dice, and cards we may be able to determine logically what the probabilities are from the physical characteristics of the experiment, while investment probabilities are inherently subjective. Historical data are useful for estimating some probabilities, such as the 0.51 probability that an unborn baby is male or the 0.53 probability that a twenty-year old female will live to be eighty, and a knowledge of history is useful for investment probabilities too. The frequency of recessions, information about recent Federal Reserve policies, measures of the volatility of stock prices, and estimates of the correlation between corporate profits and inflation are all helpful, but, unfortunately, they are not decisive. The present situation is always unique. There may be some similarities to the past, but there is never an exact match of events and personalities.

For instance, in 1946, the "Wizard of Odds" calculated presidential probabilities as follows:

> *Miss Deanne Skinner of Monrovia, California, asks: Can the Wizard tell me what the odds are of the next President of the United States being a Democrat? . . . Without considering the candidates, the odds would be 2 to 1 in favor of a Republican because since 1861 when that party was founded, there have been 12 Republican Presidents and only 7 Democrats.*[1]

However, it does not make much sense to predict an election winner simply by calculating the relative frequencies with which Republicans and Democrats have been elected President. The electorate, the parties, the candidates, and the nation all evolve as time passes, making the outcome of an election 100 years ago of little relevance today.

PROBABILITIES CLARIFY OUR VIEWS

Some medical diagnoses are definite (as when x-rays reveal a broken bone), but others are uncertain—a patient may or may not have heart disease. One way of handling an uncertain diagnosis is with probabilities. Consider a patient who takes a electrocardiographic stress test and shows some inconclusive symptoms of coronary heart disease. When the patient asks "Do I have heart disease?" a definite answer of either "yes" or "no" is unwarranted because the test is imperfect. The patient should be told that the results suggest the possibility of disease, but words can be misunderstood. When sixteen doctors were asked to assign a numerical probability to the diagnosis "cannot be excluded," the answers ranged from 5 percent probability to 95 percent, with a mean of 47 percent.* When they were asked to interpret "likely," the probabilities ranged from 20 percent to 95 percent, with a mean of 75 percent. Even the phrase "low probability" elicited answers ranging from 0 percent to 80 percent, with a mean of 18 percent. If by "low probability" one doctor means an 80 percent chance and another means no chance at all, then it is better to state the probability that one has in mind than to risk an unfortunate misinterpretation of ambiguous words. The same is true of investments. Instead of saying that the possibility of higher interest rates "cannot be excluded" or that a recession "is likely," analysts should use probablities to ensure that their views are understood.

*George A. Diamond and James S. Forrester, "Metadiagnosis," *The American Journal of Medicine,* July 1983, pp. 129–137.

In 1936, Franklin Roosevelt ran for reelection against Alf Landon. Should the forecasters have assumed that Landon had a 70 percent chance of winning, because Republicans had won 70 percent of the previous contests? Or should they have taken into account that Roosevelt was a popular president running for reelection against the unexciting governor of Kansas, the standard bearer of the party that many voters blamed for the Great Depression? Were the odds the same in 1972 when Richard Nixon ran against the liberal George McGovern as in 1964, when Barry Goldwater ran against the incumbent Lyndon Johnson? Will George Bush's chances in 1992 be identical to 1988? The odds change from election to election, along with the candidates and the state of the nation.

The same is true of investments. The best alternative to a shrug of the shoulders and a sheepish "Who knows?" is to list the possible investment outcomes and to use whatever information is at your disposal to assign probabilities as best you can. Unlike a coin flip, investment probabilities will no doubt vary from person to person, leading some people to believe

TABLE 13–1   One Investment's Probability Distribution

Range of Possible Returns	Probability
$200 to $300	0.10
$100 to $200	0.30
$0 to $100	0.30
− $100 to $0	0.20
− $200 to − $100	0.10

FIGURE 13–1   Investment return probabilities

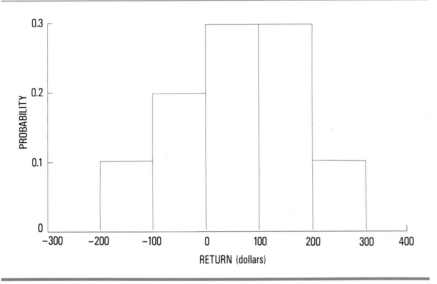

that one investment is very attractive while others think the opposite. This is why there is a stock market, so that the bulls can buy from the bears.

Probability Distributions

Investment outcomes are seldom as simple as the heads/tails possibilities for a coin flip. The infinite variety of possible returns precludes an exhaustive enumeration of them, and, so, instead we specify a **probability distribution**, showing the probabilities for ranges of outcomes. Table 13–1 shows one example. There is a 10 percent chance that the return will be between $200 and $300, a 30 percent chance that it will be between $100 and $200, and so on. Figure 13–1 is a graphical representation of this probability distribution, using the area in each block to show the probability for that range of outcomes. With a graph, we can tell at a glance which

probability distribution

A probability distribution can be used to specify the probabilities for ranges of outcomes.

INTERST-RATE UNCERTAINTY AT MORGAN GUARANTEE

The success of asset/liability decisions made by financial institutions depends critically on future interest rates. When interest rates rise unexpectedly, those who invested long term at a fixed interest rate and those who borrowed short term at a variable interest rate find that they made an expensive mistake. An unexpected drop in interest rates is costly for those who invested short term or borrowed long term. Yet, interest rates are notoriously difficult to forecast.

Up until 1971, the top managers at Morgan Guarantee Trust met regularly to determine the interest-rate forecasts to use in all asset/liability decisions, and for each interest-rate prediction, they would come up with a single number: e.g., "Our best estimate of the Treasury-bill (T-bill) rate three months from now is 6%." Yet, as the senior operations-research officer explained,

Considerable discussion normally preceded the managers' arrival at the single-valued expectation, but there was no formal procedure for quantifying the collective expectations of the participants, and the uncertainty surrounding these expectations.*

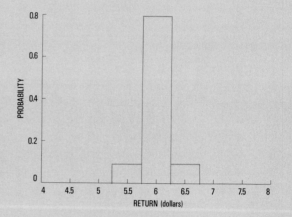

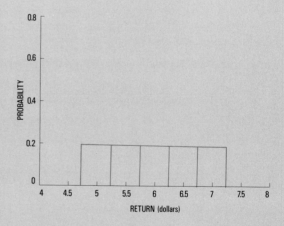

How confident were Morgan Guarantee's managers in their 6 percent forecast? Did they mean 5¾ percent to 6¼ percent or 4 percent to 8 percent? If the T-bill rate is not 6 percent, is it more likely to be somewhat higher or a bit lower? The answers to such questions require probabilities and, so, in 1971,

they began reporting probabilities in place of a single interest-rate forecast.

Twice a month, specialists write down interest-rate probabilities individually and then meet as a group to compare notes. Instead of thinking of the most likely value for the interest rate, perhaps 6 percent, each member of the group thinks of the possible values—5 percent, 5½ percent, 6 percent, and so on—and assigns probabilities to each possibility.

*This quotation and the accompanying discussion is based on Irwin Kabus, "You can bank on uncertainty," *Harvard Business Review*, May-June 1976, pp. 95–105.

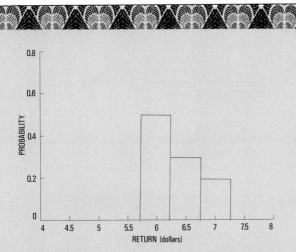

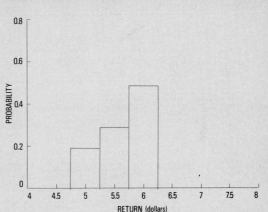

The probability distribution in panel (a) of the accompanying figure reflects a committee member who is pretty confident that the T-bill rate will be 6 percent. The distribution in panel (b) shows considerable uncertainty. In panels (c) and (d), 6 percent is the most likely value; but in one case the person feels that there is a good chance that the T-bill rate will be less than 6 percent, and, in the other, the opposite is true. None of these subtleties are revealed in a 6 percent forecast that is unaccompanied by probabilities. With probabilities, Morgan Guarantee's managers can see not only the most likely value but also the likely range of values and see whether an individual believes that the rate is more likely to be above or below 6 percent.

The senior research officer described the value of probability graphs at a November 13, 1972, group meeting:

It was useful to know why both Griffin and Riefler felt the rate would stay essentially the same, whereas the others felt it would rise; and to find out why Engle felt that there was no chance the rate would drop below 5 ⅛% and felt so strongly that it would rise over 5 ⅝%, when nobody else in the group felt that way.

After discussion, the committee constructs a consensus probability distribution, which then is presented to top management.

The probabilities used by Morgan Guarantee are necessarily subjective, but they accomplish their task of describing the beliefs of committee members:

The only "incorrect" [distribution] is one which does not correctly reflect its creators' expectations. While there is no guarantee that [probability distributions] will give an accurate picture of the future, they will give an accurate picture of an individual's view of the future.

outcomes are considered likely and which are thought unlikely. Investment Example 13–2 on p. 410–411 tells how one financial institution uses probability distributions to help make its investment decisions.

THE EXPECTED VALUE MEASURES
THE AVERAGE RETURN

Probability theory was originally developed in the 1600s by Blaise Pascal, Pierre de Fermet, and other mathematicians interested in games of chance. One of the quesitons that Pascal sought to answer was posed by a French nobleman, the Chevalier de Mere, who asked why, on average, he made money betting that he could roll at least one 6 in four throws of a single dice, but lost money betting that he could roll at least one double-6 in twenty-four throws of a pair of dice. Pascal showed that de Mere, in fact, had a 0.518 probability of winning the first bet but only a 0.491 probability of winning the second bet. With these probabilities, Pascal then calculated de Mere's expected profits.

Calculation of the Expected Value

expected value
The expected value is a weighted average of the possible returns, using probabilities as weights to reflect the likelihood of each outcome.

The **expected value,** usually denoted by $E[x]$, E, or the Greek symbol μ (pronounced "mu"), is a weighted average of the possible returns, using probabilities as weights to reflect the likelihood of each outcome. Suppose, for instance, that there are two outcomes, winning or losing $100, and each is equally likely:

Return x_1	Probability $P[x_1]$
+$100	0.5
−$100	0.5

The expected value uses the probabilities to average these two possibilities:

$$\mu = (+\$100)(0.5) + (-\$100)(0.5) = 0$$

The general formula is

$$\mu = \Sigma \ x_i \ P[x_i] \tag{1}$$

The expected value is a statistical average, not, as in everyday English, the outcome that we expect or consider most likely. Indeed, in the example, there is no chance that you will win $0—you will either win $100 or lose $100. The expected value is the long-run average return if the frequency with which each outcome occurs is in accordance with its probability. If you win $100 half the time and lose $100 the other half, your average winnings are zero.

Similarly, the expected value can be used to measure the amount, on average, that de Mere, in our earlier example, could expect to win or lose in his gambles. If he bets the equivalent of $100 that he can roll one 6 in four throws of a single dice, then his expected value is

$$(+100)(0.518) + (-\$100)(0.482) = \$3.60.$$

On a single wager, he wins or loses $100. However, in the long run, if, as expected, he wins 51.8 percent of his bets, he wins an average of $3.60 per wager. On his second game of chance, betting that he can roll at least one double-6 in twenty-four throws of a pair of dice, the 0.491 chance of winning gives an expected value of

$$(+\$100)(0.491) + (-\$100)(0.509) = -\$1.80$$

so that he can expect his losses to average $1.80 per wager.

Here is a somewhat more complicated problem. Consider a state lottery in which the purchaser of a $1 ticket tries to match five digits randomly selected by the state's computer. A match of all five digits pays $25,000, and a match of any four digits pays $500. The probability of matching all five digits is $(1/10)^5 = 0.00001$, and the probability of matching four digits works out to be 0.00045. The expected value of the payoff is

$$\$25,000(0.00001) + \$500(0.00045) + \$0(0.99954) = \$0.475$$

or about half the cost of the ticket, a payoff typical of state lotteries. The habitual player can expect, in the long run, getting back an average of 47.5 cents for every dollar spent on tickets. The state treasury keeps, on average, 52.5 cents of every dollar wagered. Another use of an expected value calculation is described in Investment Example 13–3.

Should We Choose the Investment With the Highest Expected Value?

Pascal and other early probability theorists used probabilities to calculate the expected value of various games of chance and to determine which were the most profitable. They argued that a rational person should always choose whichever course of action has the highest expected value. An expected-value criterion is very appealing for gambles that are repeated over and over. It makes good sense to consider the long-run average when there is a long run over which to average. Casinos, lotteries, and insurance companies are all keenly interested in the expected returns of the repetitive gambles they offer, realizing that any venture with a negative expected return will almost certainly be unprofitable in the long run.

414

MAXWELL HOUSE'S PRICE OF COFFEE

Maxwell House, the nation's largest coffee producer, acquires coffee beans from coffee-growing nations, grinds and roasts these beans, and sells them— either as ground or instant coffee.* For many years, ground coffee came in a can that had to be opened with a key, like a sardine can. In 1962, a competitor, Folger's, began marketing a coffee can that could be opened quickly without a key, and in 1963, Maxwell House decided that it, too, should sell coffee in a keyless can.

A keyless can would cost Maxwell House an extra 0.7 cents per can, but consumers seemed willing to pay extra for the convenience. The company considered (a) holding the price steady and absorbing the extra cost or (b) raising the price by 2 cents per can to cover the extra cost, and

*This example is from Joseph Newman, *Management Applications of Decision Theory* (New York: Harper & Row, 1971), pp. 32–61.

then some. The accompanying table shows how probabilities were used to gauge the change in profits with each strategy.

If the price is held constant, the expected value of the change in profits is

$$\mu = \$4.1(0.2) - \$0.6(0.5) - \$0.8(0.2) - \$1.2(0.1)$$
$$= 0.24 \text{ million.}$$

The anticipated enthusiastic consumer response more than makes up for the extra cost of making keyless cans.

A higher price of 2 cents a can increases profits on each can, but reduces the number of cans sold. On balance, the expected value of the change in profits works out to be

$$\mu = \$11.9(0.25) + \$6.5(0.25) +$$
$$\$2.9(0.25) - \$1.1(0.25)$$
$$= \$5.05 \text{ million.}$$

Maxwell House decided to raise the price of its coffee by 2 cents a can.

Strategy of Holding Price Constant			Strategy of Increasing Price 2 cents		
Change in Market Share (percent)	Profits (millions of dollars)	Probability	Change in Market Share (percent)	Profits (millions of dollars)	Probability
+2.8	+ $4.1	0.20	+2.5	+ $11.9	0.25
+1.0	− 0.6	0.50	+1.0	+ 6.5	0.25
0.0	− 0.8	0.20	0.0	+ 2.9	0.25
−0.6	− 1.2	0.10	−1.5	− 1.1	0.25

It is equally clear, however, that the expected-return criterion is sometimes inappropriate. State-lottery payoffs are set to give the state a positive expected return and, because their gain is your loss, must offer a negative expected return to the people who buy lottery tickets. People who buy lottery tickets are not maximizing expected return. The same reasoning applies to insurance. Insurance rates are set to give insurance companies a positive expected return and, hence, to give insurance buyers a negative expected return. People who buy insurance must not be maximizing expected return either. Diversified investments provide yet another example. If you want to maximize expected return, you should invest all your money in the single asset with the highest expected return. Why, then, do people instead divide their money among dozens of assets?

We can also construct hypothetical situations to show that expected-return maximization is not always appealing. Suppose that a messenger from a rich recluse bursts into class and announces that you have been chosen to receive a gift of $1 million. She opens a briefcase filled with $100 bills to show you that she is serious; but as you reach for them, she closes her briefcase and asks you to consider another possibility. You can either take the $1 million, or you can flip a coin five times: if you get heads on every flip, you get $40 million; if you get tails on any flip, you get nothing but a good story. Think about it. If like most people you would take the sure million dollars, then you are not maximizing expected return.

RISK AVERSION

The primary inadequacy of expected-return maximization is that it neglects risk—how certain or uncertain a situation is. An expected-return maximizer considers a sure $1 million, a 50 percent chance at $2 million, and a 1 percent chance at $100 million all equally attractive, because each has an expected value of $1 million. If these alternatives were offered over and over, there would be little difference in the very long run, because the payoffs from each alternative would almost certainly average close to $1 million per play. But if you only get one chance at this game, the possible payoffs are very different, a difference ignored by an expected-value calculation. In an expected-return computation, it does not matter that in the first option there is a 100 percent chance of receiving $1 million, and in the third option there is a 99 percent chance of receiving nothing. However, this difference *does* matter to many people.

Much of the uncertainty we face is unique, not repetitive, and the chance that the actual outcome will not equal the expected value does matter. The possible divergence of an actual outcome from the expected value is *risk*, and how people react reflects their risk preferences. In particular,

Risk preferences can be gauged by whether a person prefers to take a gamble or, instead, to receive the expected value of the gamble.

Consider, for example, a gamble with a 50 percent chance of receiving $100 and a 50 percent chance of receiving nothing. Would you rather take this gamble or instead receive $50, which is the gamble's expected value? There is no right or wrong answer: but how you answer reveals your attitude towards risk.

Risk Preferences

risk neutral
A risk-neutral person chooses the alternative with the highest expected return.

There are three broad categories of risk preferences. First, a person can be **risk neutral**—willing to choose the alternative with the highest expected return and, thus, indifferent between a safe $50 and a 50 percent chance at $100. Second, a person can be **risk seeking** ready to take a gamble rather than receive the expected value of the gamble. Third, a person can be **risk averse**—preferring the expected value of a gamble to the gamble itself, the $50 in cash instead of a 50 percent chance to make $100.

risk seeking
A risk-seeking person will sacrifice expected return to increase risk.

While the risk-neutral person maximizes expected return, a risk seeker is willing to give up some expected return to get more risk, and a risk-averse person is willing to give up some expected return to avoid risk. For example, a risk-neutral person does not like insurance or lottery tickets because both have negative expected returns. A risk seeker, in contrast, will definitely buy a lottery ticket if the expected value is zero and may buy one even if the expected return is negative. A risk-averse person will certainly buy insurance if the expected return is zero, and may purchase insurance even with a negative expected return.

risk averse
A risk-averse investor sacrifices expected return to reduce risk.

Risk Bearing

This acknowledged variety in preferences explains why some people accept gambles that others shun and why some people buy insurance that others avoid. A person's response to risk may depend also on the size of gamble. It is not unreasonable to be risk neutral about a wager involving a few dollars and risk averse about a gamble involving all of your wealth. You might flip a coin to see who buys coffee and still buy fire insurance.

One implication is that wealthy people may be willing to take gambles that others shun because these gambles have a smaller percentage effect on their wealth. A person who owns little more than the house he lives in and his human capital buys fire and life insurance, even though the expected return is negative, to avoid the possibility of a catastrophic loss. For someone who is very wealthy, the loss of a house or wages has little effect on personal wealth, and a decision not to purchase insurance is a relatively small gamble with a positive expected return.

In fact, a wealthy person might be willing to sell insurance to a person of more modest means. Consider an individual, named Joe, who owns a $50,000 house and little else. This house is near an earthquake fault, and Joe is afraid that he will lose his house in a quake. Jane, on the other hand, is very rich, and winning or losing $50,000 to her is like Joe flipping a coin to see who pays for beer. If both believe that the probability that the house will be destroyed by an earthquake is 0.001 and Jane is risk neutral about a $50,000 gamble, she may offer to insure Joe against an earthquake for a $100 fee. The expected value of the insurance payoff is

$$0.001(\$50,000) + 0.999 (\$0) = \$50,$$

only half the $100 cost of the policy. A risk neutral person like Jane may be willing to take this gamble, selling for $100 something with an expected value of $50. Joe, on the other hand, may be sufficiently risk averse that he pays $100 to avoid this gamble with its expected loss of $50. If so, there is room for a deal, in that he is willing to buy what she is willing to sell.

An earthquake is a real physical danger, a natural risk that has to be borne by someone. Those people who are the least risk averse are the most willing to bear such risks. Those who are more risk averse can, for a price, use financial contracts to pass such risks on to others. In the same way, stocks and bonds reflect real economic risks—including the possibility of recession and/or high interest rates—and their prices are set so that, considering the risk and the expected return, some investors are willing to hold such assets.

THE STANDARD DEVIATION MEASURES RISK

Drawing on their statistical backgrounds, in the 1950s Harry Markowitz and James Tobin proposed, as a plausible and useful approximation, that investors base their decisions on two factors—the mean and the variance. The *mean* is just another word for the expected value, and, as we have seen, it was long ago argued that expected values influence decisions. The problem with an expected-value criterion, as we also have seen, is that it ignores risk. Markowitz and Tobin suggested extending the expected-value criterion by using the variance to measure risk. The technical details of the mean-variance analysis that they developed are described in the next chapter. But it is useful to consider at this point the assumption that underlies their approach and that is widely used today by financial analysts—that the variance (or its square root, the standard deviation) is a useful measure of risk.

TABLE 13–2 Gauging Three Alternative Investments

Investment	Possible Return	Probability	Expected Return	Variance	Standard Deviation
1	$ 5.00	1.00	$5.00	0	$ 0.00
2	{ 0.00 10.00	0.50 } 0.50 }	5.00	25	5.00
3	{ −15.00 5.00 105.00	0.25 } 0.50 } 0.25 }	5.00	5000	70.71

variance

The statistical variance is the average squared deviation of the outcomes about their mean.

The standard deviation of historical data was introduced in Chapter 1. The standard deviation of a probability distribution is similar, but instead of seeing how often various outcomes appeared in the past, we now weight each possible outcome by its probability. If the possible returns are denoted by X, and the expected value of X is denoted by μ, then the **variance** of a probability distribution is the expected value of $(X - \mu)^2$—that is, the probability-weighted, average squared deviation of the possible outcomes about their mean, or

$$\sigma^2 = \Sigma\ (x_i - \mu)^2\ P[x_i]. \tag{2}$$

standard deviation

The standard deviation is the square root of the variance.

The square root of the variance is the **standard deviation**, σ (pronounced "sigma").

For each possible outcome X, we calculate how far X is from its expected value μ, and then we square this deviation. By squaring, we do two things. First, squaring eliminates the distinction between positive and negative deviations. What matters to a variance calculation is how far the outcome is from μ, not whether it is above or below μ. Second, squaring gives primary importance to large deviations. One deviation of 10 squared will increase the variance as much as four deviations of 5 squared.

After calculating the squared deviations for each possible outcome X, we calculate the average squared deviation using the outcome probabilities as weights. This weighted average of the squared deviations from μ is the variance, and its square root is the standard deviation. Either can be used, but the standard deviation is usually easier to interpret because it has the same units (percent or dollars) as X and μ, while the units for the variance are dollars-squared and percent-squared.

The standard deviation measures uncertainty by considering the probability of returns far from the expected value. Table 13–2 illustrates this principle by showing the mean, variance, and standard deviations for three alternative investments. The first, $5 with certainty, has an expected value of $5 and a standard deviation of $0. For the second, the mean is

$$\mu = \$0(0.5) + \$10(0.5) = \$5,$$

and the variance is

$$\sigma^2 = (0 - 5)^2(0.5) + (10 - 5)^2(0.5) = 25,$$

which implies a standard deviation of

$$\sigma = \sqrt{25} = 5.$$

For the third investment,

$$\mu = -\$95(0.25) + \$5(0.5) + \$105(0.25) = \$5$$
$$\sigma^2 = (-95 - 5)^2(0.25) + (5 - 5)^2(0.5) + (105 - 5)^2(0.25) = 5000$$
$$\sigma = \sqrt{5000} = 70.71$$

Each of the three alternatives has a $5 expected return, indicating that they can be expected, on average, to do equally well in the long run. As one-shot deals, however, they have varying degrees of uncertainty or risk. The first investment has a $0 standard deviation because there is no uncertainty about its return. Its payoff is sure to be $5. The third investment has a larger standard deviation than the second because there is a substantial chance that the payoff will be far from the $5 expected value.

If the standard deviation is an appropriate measure of risk, then a risk-averse person will select the first investment, a risk seeker prefers the third, and a risk-neutral person considers all three equally attractive.

The Normal Distribution

Often it is useful to assume that the possible returns in an uncertain situation can be approximated by a standard probability distribution, such as the bell-shaped Gaussian or **normal distribution** shown in Figure 13–2. Many outcomes are the cumulative consequence of a large number of random events, and the central-limit theoreom, the most important discovery in the long history of probability and statistics, holds that outcomes that are the cumulation of independent, identically distributed random events are approximately normally distributed. In nature, the number of ridges on scallop shells, the number of kernels on ears of corn, the number of leaves on trees, the number of hairs on dogs, the breadths of human skulls, heights, weights, IQ scores, and the motion of molecules and planets all conform to an approximately normal distribution. In financial markets, the efficient-market hypothesis implies that asset returns are the cumulative consequence of independent random events and, so, may be approximately normally distributed, as illustrated by Investment Example 13–4 on pp. 442–423.

normal distribution
The normal distribution is the widely used bell-shaped Gaussian probability distribution.

FIGURE 13–2   The normal distribution

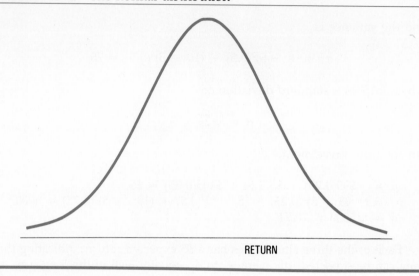

RETURN

Two Rules of Thumb

The center of a normal distribution is determined by its mean. Figure 13–3 illustrates this by showing two distributions with the same standard deviation, but with different means. These distributions describe the percentage returns during the coming year from two investments. One investment has a 10 percent expected return, and the other has a 20 percent expected return, indicating that in the long run the second investment will almost certainly have the higher average return. For the coming year, the equal standard deviations indicate that the two investments are equally risky, in that their returns are equally uncertain. The probability that the actual return will turn out to be, say, more than five percentage points below the expected value is the same for both investments. We can describe these two investments by saying that they have expected returns of 10 percent and 20 percent, respectively, and that we are equally confident of how close the actual return will be to the respective expected values. If offered such a choice, investors would invariably choose the second investment.

Figure 13–4 shows a different situation. Here the expected values are the same, but the standard deviations differ. All three investments should have nearly equal average returns in the long run; but, in a single year, the unequal standard deviations imply that these alternative investments are not equally risky. For the investment with a 2.5 percent standard deviation, we are very confident that the return will turn out to be between

FIGURE 13–3 Two investments with different means but the same standard deviations

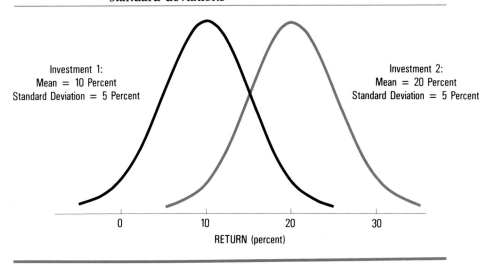

FIGURE 13–4 Three Investments with different standard deviations but the same expected values

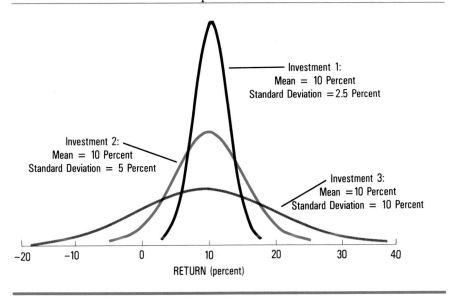

422

ONE YEAR WITH IBM AND SIXTY-FIVE YEARS WITH THE MARKET

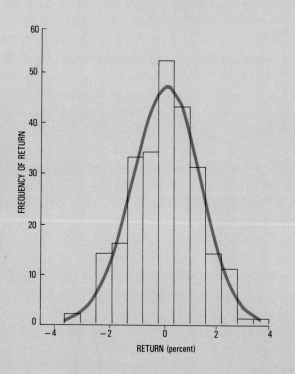

If the daily return on a stock is the cumulation of several independent price changes during the day, then the probability distribution may be approximately normal. The first figure shows that the actual distribution of the daily returns from IBM in 1983 is approximately normal, with a mean of 0.12 percent and a standard deviation of 1.28 percent. According to the one-standard-deviation rule of thumb, approximately 68 percent of the monthly returns should be in the interval 0.12 percent ± 1.28 percent; that is, − 1.16 percent to 1.40 percent. In fact, 69 percent of the returns fall in this range. With a normal distribution, there is a 95 percent probability of a return being within two standard deviations of the mean; 96 percent of the IBM monthly observations are in this range.

5 percent and 15 percent. For the other two investments, there is a substantial chance that the return will be outside this range. Risk-averse investors prefer the investment with the low standard deviation, because it is expected to do as well on average as the others, and its return is more certain.

Some convenient rules of thumb can help us interpret the standard deviation of a normally distributed random variable. There is about a two-thirds probability (more precisely, 0.683) that the value of a normally distributed variable will be within one standard deviation of its mean, and

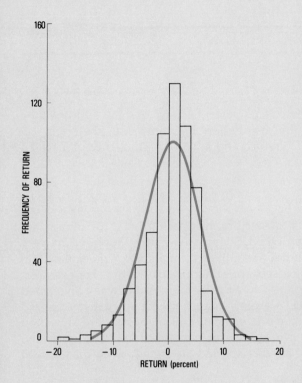

Ibbotson and Sinquefield have assembled data on monthly returns since 1926 for the S&P 500 index.* The second figure shows that the normal distribution with a mean of 0.51 percent and a standard deviation of 4.92 percent provides a reasonable approximation of the actual distribution of these data. As with the IBM daily returns, the actual distribution is not exactly normal, but it is close enough so that the normal distribution can be used as a simplifying approximation.

Despite the apparent success in describing historical returns, we should be cautious in inferring that these figures also describe appropriate probability distributions for the coming year. The expected returns, and perhaps the standard deviation too, vary from year to year along with interest rates; they also vary from person to person with differing assumptions about the economy. The fact that stock returns have averaged about 10 percent a year over the past sixty-five years does not compel us to assume an expected value of 10 percent this year.

*Roger G. Ibbotson and Rex A. Sinquefield, *Stocks, Bonds, Bills and Inflation: 1986 Yearbook* (Chicago: Ibbotson Associates, Inc., 1986).

there is about a 0.95 probability that it will be within two standard deviations. Thus, for the investment in Figure 13–3 with a mean of 10 percent and a standard deviation of 5 percent, the one-standard-deviation rule implies that there is about a two-thirds probability that the return will be between 10 percent − 5 percent and 10 percent + 5 percent; that is, between 5 percent and 15 percent. The two-standard-deviations rule says that there is a 0.95 probability that the return will be between 10 percent − 2(5 percent) and 10 percent + 2(5 percent); that is, between 0

TABLE 13–3 Two Asymmetrical Investments

Investment	Possible Return	Probability	Expected Return	Standard Deviation
1	−\$ 100.00 } 99,900.00 }	0.001 0.999	\$0.00	\$3160.70
2	− 99,900.00 } 100.00 }	0.001 0.999	0.00	3160.70

percent and 20 percent. There is a 5 percent chance that the return will be outside this range. Since the distribution is symmetrical, there is a 2.5 percent chance of a negative return and a 2.5 percent chance of a return above 20 percent.

Long Shots and Skewness

The standard deviation is a satisfactory measure of risk if the returns are approximately normally distributed. Some asset returns, however, are very asymmetrical, and the standard deviation is not an adequate explanation of why investors find these assets appealing or unattractive. For example, why does a risk-averse investor, who buys insurance and owns a diversified portfolio, buy a lottery ticket—a risky long shot with a negative expected return? Similarly, the relatively low mean and high standard deviation cannot explain why a risk-averse investor buys stock in a new company, hoping to catch the start of another spectacular growth stock such as IBM or McDonald's.

The large standard deviation of a long shot shows its riskiness. However, because the squaring of deviations about the mean treats gains and losses symmetrically, it cannot distinguish between one investment that has a large probability of a slightly above average return and a small probability of a catastrophic loss, and another investment that has a large probability of a small loss and a small chance of a bonanza, as illustrated by the two investments in Table 13–3. Both investments have the same expected value and the same standard deviation; yet many people prefer the first asset to the second.

Unlike the normal distribution, both of these investments have very asymmetrical, skewed returns. The first is a positively skewed long shot, with a small chance of a large gain; the second is a negatively skewed long shot, with a small chance of a large loss. Figure 13–5 shows continuous probability distributions with similar positive and negative skewness.

FIGURE 13-5 Skewed probability distributions

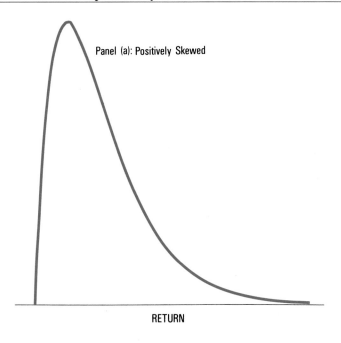

Panel (a): Positively Skewed

RETURN

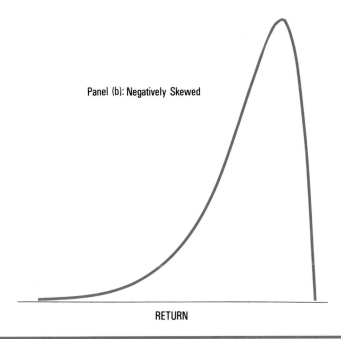

Panel (b): Negatively Skewed

RETURN

The purchase of a lottery ticket is a positively skewed gamble like the first investment in Table 13–3, but with a negative expected return. A decision not to purchase fire insurance is a negatively skewed gamble, similar to the second investment, but with a positive expected return. The use of the standard deviation to measure risk explains why a risk-averse person might buy insurance and spurn lottery tickets, while a risk seeker does the opposite. However, the standard deviation offers no easy explanation for the simultaneous purchase of both lottery tickets and insurance.

Perhaps some otherwise risk-averse people enjoy the mild suspense provided by lottery tickets and consider the purchase inexpensive, if brief, entertainment. Others may have a very mistaken assessment of their chances of winning (what Adam Smith called "absurd presumptions in their own good fortune"[2]). Another possibility is that people care about not only the uncertainty, as gauged by the standard deviation, but also skewness. Long shots offer them the slim chance of changing their lives completely, or as one Pennsylvania woman put it, "My chances of winning a million are better than my chances of earning a million."[3]

The cancellation of fire insurance is a negatively skewed gamble, offering a slim chance of a catastrophic loss, that does not appeal to many. The popularity of lottery tickets and insurance suggests that people prefer positively skewed returns to negatively skewed ones. This preference is also suggested by the overbetting on long shots at horse races and by a number of empirical studies.[4]

These apparent preferences imply that we should be cautious in using the standard deviation alone to gauge risk if the probability distribution for the returns is highly skewed, as with lottery tickets and stock in new companies. In other situations, where the probability distribution is reasonably symmetrical (or, even better, approximately normal), the standard deviation is a very simple and powerful way to measure risk.

DIVERSIFIED PORTFOLIOS

A risk-neutral individual maximizes expected return by investing all funds in the single asset with the highest expected return. A risk-averse person, in contrast, builds a **diversified portfolio**—a group of several dissimilar assets that is owned by a single investor. The prevalence of diversified portfolios suggests that most investors are, in fact, risk averse.

The Advantages of Diversification

The benefits of diversification can be illustrated without excessive arithmetic by considering two risky investments, each hinging on the flip of a fair coin. With the first, the possible percentage rates of return are +50

TABLE 13–4 Four Possible Outcomes of Diversification

Outcome of Investment in First Asset	Outcome of Investment in Second Asset	Outcome of Investment in Both Assets
50 percent ($80,000) = $40,000	130 percent ($20,000) = $26,000	$66,000
	− 70 percent ($20,000) = − $14,000	$26,000
− 50 percent ($80,000) = − $40,000	130 percent ($20,000) = $26,000	− $14,000
	− 70 percent ($20,000) = − $14,000	− $54,000

percent and − 50 percent. For the second, the percentage return will be either + 130 percent or − 70 percent. The expected returns are

$$\mu_1 = (50 \text{ percent})(0.5) + (-50 \text{ percent})(0.5) = 0 \text{ percent}$$
$$\mu_2 = (130 \text{ percent})(0.5) + (-70 \text{ percent})(0.5) = 30 \text{ percent}$$

An expected-return maximizer invests all wealth in the second asset since it has the higher expected return. However, risk-averse persons may resist putting all eggs in a single basket with a 0.50 probability of losing 70 percent of their wealth. The first asset is not much safer. What about diversifying, investing some money in the first asset and the rest in the second?

Table 13–4 shows the four possible outcomes of a $100,000 investment, depending on whether you make a profit on both, lose money on both, make money on the first and lose on the second, or lose money on the first and make money on the second. If the two coin flips are independent, there is a 0.25 chance of the return being $66,000, $26,000, − $14,000, and − $54,000. This compares with a 0.5 probability of gaining or losing $50,000 if the entire $100,000 is invested in the safer asset. Diversification makes it less likely that a lot of money will be lost and less likely that a lot will be gained.

Diversification generally makes the extreme outcomes, good or bad, less likely. If you invest all your money in just one stock, then your return hinges entirely on the success of that stock. If the company goes bankrupt, you will too. If you instead buy twenty stocks, it takes an incredible string of bad luck to break you. It also is hard to get rich, since the chances of finding one stock that quadruples in price are better than the chances of finding twenty that do so. Diversification avoids both ruin and riches. Risk seekers avoid diversification, but the risk averse may find it attractive.

Asset Correlations

The degree of risk reduction provided by diversification depends on the correlations among the returns on the individual investments. In the coin-flip example, the outcomes were assumed to be independent, in that the first outcome had no effect on the chances of gain or loss on the second flip. A large number of independent investments provides very effective diversification. If you bet on 10,000 independent coin flips, you can be very confident of your overall return since you will almost certainly win about half your bets and lose about half. The chances of losing even 51 percent of 10,000 coin flips are very small.

If the returns are not independent, then they may be either positively or negatively correlated. If the returns from two investments are negatively correlated, when one investment does poorly, the other is likely to do well. Because your losses tend to be offset by gains, and your gains offset by losses, a portfolio of negatively correlated assets has little risk of large losses or gains. The extreme case is perfectly negatively correlated returns, in which the outcome of one investment is sure to be the opposite of the other. Perhaps there is only a single coin toss, and you bet heads with one person and tails with the other. You will win one and lose one, no matter how the coin lands. With perfectly negatively correlated returns, you can always construct a perfectly hedged portfolio in which your return is guaranteed. For the payoffs given in our $100,000-investment example, investing two-thirds of your wealth in the first asset and one-third in the second guarantees a $10,000 profit.

In gambling, bookmakers strive for a perfectly hedged portfolio, with an equal volume of wagers on each side of a bet; then they are sure of a profit no matter which team wins. In financial markets, effective hedges can be constructed by using special instruments, such as options, warrants, futures, and convertible bonds. Among ordinary stocks and bonds, there are few negatively correlated returns. A few exceptions, such as liquidation firms or gold-mining companies, sometimes buck the trend; but most stocks and bonds are affected similarly (though to varying degrees) by interest rates and the economy.

If investment returns are positively correlated, there is less potential for risk reduction through diversification. The extreme case is perfect positive correlation, where the outcome of the first investment is always the same as the outcome of the second. In our example, there might be a single coin toss, and you bet heads with two people, guaranteeing that you will either win or lose both bets. Then you cannot benefit from the primary advantage of diversification—the balancing out of gains and losses. Fortunately, although most asset returns are positively correlated, this correlation is far from perfect, and diversification can reduce risk substantially.

Figure 13–6 shows the risk, as measured by the standard deviation of the return, for randomly selected stock portfolios of different sizes.[5] As shown, risk is substantially reduced by diversifying among fifteen to thirty stocks, but the gains from further diversification are slight. Of course, investors need not diversify randomly, as in this figure. A randomly selected portfolio might contain, by the luck of the draw, a dozen savings and loan associations, with highly correlated returns. Such a portfolio would be fine for someone who wants to bet on the health of the S&L

FIGURE 13–6 The effect of a portfolio's size on its standard deviation

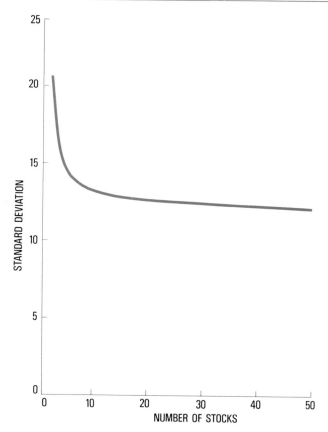

industry, but is inappropriate for a risk-averse investor seeking a diversified portfolio. Such investors should instead deliberately choose securities from a wide range of diverse industries: savings and loans, automobiles, computers, chemical forestry, entertainment, medical, and so on.

Investment returns are necessarily uncertain, because no one can infallibly predict the future course of the economy, interest rates, tax laws, and the fortunes of individual companies. We can confront this uncertainty rationally by estimating the expected returns from various investments and using standard deviations to gauge our uncertainty. While a single asset, in isolation, may be very risky, we can invest in several imperfectly correlated (or, better, negatively correlated) assets, using this diversification to reduce risk. Diversification, counting on asset gains and losses to offset each other, is of no interest to those who are risk neutral or risk seeking, but is very attractive to risk-averse investors.

SUMMARY

We can quantify the uncertainty of investment returns by specifying probabilities, which show the relative likelihood of the possible outcomes. These probabilities are influenced by historical data but are necessarily subjective. The expected value is the long-run average return if the frequency with which each outcome occurs corresponds to its probability. The variance is the average squared deviation of the possible outcomes about the expected value; the standard deviation is the square root of the variance. The standard deviation (or variance) gauges risk by measuring how certain we are that the return will be close to its expected value.

For many assets, the normal distribution is a reasonable approximation that is useful for describing our uncertainty about the return. Two convenient rules of thumb are (a) that there is about a two-thirds probability that a normally distributed return will be within one standard deviation of its mean and (b) that there is about a 95 percent probability that the return will be within two standard deviations. Some asset returns are very asymmetrical and cannot be approximated by a normal distribution—for instance, lottery tickets, stock in new companies, and other long shots. Investors who like positive skewness might buy such assets, even though the expected returns are low and the standard deviations are high.

A risk-neutral person chooses the alternative with the highest expected return, leading to the placement of all eggs in one basket. A risk seeker accepts fair bets and even sacrifices expected return to increase risk. Like the risk-neutral person, the risk seeker shuns diversification. A risk averter sacrifices expected return to reduce risk and selects a diversified portfolio, containing dissimilar assets. Diversification reduces risk most effectively if the asset returns are uncorrelated or, even better, negatively correlated.

EXERCISES

1. Table 13–A shows a firm's anticipated revenues in each of four inflation/unemployment scenarios and the probabilities it assigns to these scenarios. What is the expected value of revenue? Is the expected value also the most likely value?

2. Investment Example 4–2 tells how someone who purchased Duquesne University's prepaid tuition plan in 1985 will receive either $5700 in 1999 if the child does not enroll at Duquesne or four years of tuition if the child does enroll. Assume that there is a 0.5 probability that the child will enroll and, if the child does enroll, the tuition waiver will be worth $52,905 (as estimated by Duquesne). Is the expected value of the payoff from this prepaid tuition plan larger or smaller than the $25,216

that a family could have received in 1999 by purchasing a zero-coupon bond instead? For what probability P of enrolling are the expected values exactly the same?

3. In May 1987, Kidder, Peabody estimated that Prime Computer, then selling for $27 a share, had a "potential price range" over the coming twelve months of $18 to $36.[6] What is the percentage rate of return to someone buying at $27 if the price goes to $18? If the price goes to $36? What is the expected rate of return if each of the nineteen prices from $18 to $36 is considered equally likely? (Assume that all prices are rounded off to the nearest dollar.)

4. A new restaurant will either be successful (and sold after one year for a $2 million profit) or unsuccessful (and liquidated after one year

TABLE 13–A

Scenario	Inflation	Unemployment	Probability	Revenue (millions of dollars)
1	high	high	0.16	$2.0
2	high	low	0.24	4.0
3	low	high	0.36	1.0
4	low	low	0.24	3.0

TABLE 13–B

Warranteed Repair	Cost to Mammoth (dollars)	Probability of Occurrence
None	$ 0	0.20
Minor	500	0.40
Moderate	1000	0.30
Major	3000	0.10

for a $400,000 loss). How high must the probability of success be for this restaurant to have a positive expected value?

5. Mammoth Motors provides a three-year warranty on the cars it sells. The company anticipates the repair probabilities shown in Table 13–B. What is the expected value of the cost of warranteed repairs? What use might Mammoth make of this expected-value calculation?

6. In 1987, with gold selling for $460 an ounce, a mining company offered investors a chance to buy gold at $250 an ounce—but they would have to pay the money immediately and not receive their gold for fifteen months. The company purportedly would use the investor's money to obtain the gold from a mine with uncertain reserves.[7] Say that there is a probability P that you will get the gold and a probability $1 - P$ that you will not. If you are risk neutral and determined to buy gold (and to hold it for at least fifteen months), what is the lowest value of P that will persuade you to accept this company's offer?

7. Many business inventories are perishable—for instance, the raspberries stocked by a grocery or the daily newspapers at a newsstand. Imagine that you are the buyer for a department store, deciding whether or not to order fifty Calvin Keen winter coats, at a price of $100 each. You will price these coats at $200 each, but any that are unsold at the end of the season will be disposed of for $60 apiece. For simplicity, assume there are only two possible outcomes: People will buy all fifty coats, or they will buy none at all. How high does the probability of fifty sales have to be to persuade an expected-value maximizer to order two dozen coats?

8. Extend your analysis of Exercise 7 to consider the options, if coats are unsold, of either disposing of the lot for $60 apiece or reducing the price of each coat to $100. Assume that there is a 0.5 probability that you will be able to sell the half-price coats and that, if unsuccessful, you will be forced to dispose of them for $40 apiece. (Again assume that your customers will either buy all or none of these coats.) Now how high does the probability of fifty sales at $200 apiece have to be to persuade an expected-value maximizer to order two dozen coats?

9. Limited Liability is considering insuring Howard Hardsell's voice for $1,000,000. The company figures that there is only a 0.001 probability that it will have to pay off. If it charges Hardsell $2000 for the insurance, will the policy have a positive expected value for the company? What is the expected value of the policy to Hardsell if he agrees with their probability assessment? If his expected value is negative, why would he even consider buying such a policy?

10. It has been estimated that Activase, which costs $2500 per treatment, has a 70 percent chance of dissolving blood clots in heart-attack patients, while Streptokinase, which costs $250, has a 35 percent chance of success. If we let X be the amount one would pay for a drug that is certain to dissolve clots, then a risk-neutral person would be willing to pay PX for a drug with a probability P of dissolving clots. For what values of X will such a person choose Activase? Choose Streptokinase? Use neither?

11. *Donoghue's Moneyletter* developed a test to differentiate speculators from the risk averse.[8] One of the questions is as follows:

> You are on a TV game show and can choose one of the following. Which would you take?
> a. $1,000 cash.
> b. A 50 percent chance at winning $4,000
> c. A 20 percent chance at winning $10,000
> d. A 5% chance at winning $100,000

Which answer indicates behavior that is risk averse? risk neutral? risk seeking?

12. Here is another test question from *Donoghue's Moneyletter:*

> You inherit your uncle's $100,000 house, free of any mortgage. Although the house is in a

fashionable neighborhood and can be expected to appreciate at a rate faster than inflation, it has deteriorated badly. It would net $1,000 monthly if rented as is; it would net $1,500 per month if renovated. The renovations could be financed by a mortgage on the property. You would:

> a. Sell the house.
> b. Rent it as is.
> c. Make the necessary renovations, and then rent it.

This question does not really give enough information to judge whether a person is risk averse or risk seeking. What else do we need to know?

13. Which would you prefer: (a) $200,000 in cash or (b) a lottery ticket with a 20 percent chance of winning $1,200,000 and an 80 percent chance of losing $50,000? How would you characterize a person who prefers the cash? prefers the lottery ticket? is indifferent between the two?

14. On a football betting card, the bettor picks the winners of n selected games and is paid a specified amount if all n picks win. A point spread is used to equalize the games. For example, if Team A is much better than Team B, the point spread might be 6½ points, meaning that a bet on A only pays off if A wins by 7 or more points; otherwise, a bet on B pays off. We will assume that the point spread exactly equalizes each game so that the bettor must choose between two equally likely winners. You can spend $10 on any of the following three cards and be paid the indicated amount:

a. $60 for correctly picking three of three games.
b. $110 for correctly picking four out of four games.
c. $160 for correctly picking five out of five games.

What is the expected return on each of these cards? What does the structure of payoffs suggest about bettor preferences?

TABLE 13–C

Return (percent)	Probability	
	First Fund	Second Fund
35 to 45	0.00	0.20
25 to 35	0.10	0.20
15 to 25	0.10	0.20
5 to 15	0.60	0.20
− 5 to 5	0.10	0.20
− 15 to − 5	0.10	0.00

15. A computer company must decide whether its new computer, Granny Smith, will have a closed architecture or an open one that allows users to add enhancements. The profits depend on whether potential customers prefer an open or closed architecture, events considered to be equally likely:

Computer Design Used	*Estimated Profits (millions of dollars)*	
	Customers Prefer Open Design	*Customers Prefer Closed Design*
Open	$500	$300
Closed	100	900

(For example, if the company uses an open design, there is a 0.5 probability that its profits will be $500 million and a 0.5 probability that profits will be $300 million.) Which action maximizes expected return? If the company chooses a closed design, how would you characterize its risk preferences?

16. You have been offered $2 for a raffle ticket with a 1 percent chance of winning $100. What can we say about your risk preferences if you decline this offer?

17. Jill owns stock in one company, NEW, which may be taken over by another company, GLOM. If so, her stock will be worth $40 a share; if not, it will be worth $20. She considers the two possible outcomes to be equally likely.
a. What is the expected value of Jill's stock?

b. If Jill accepts $27 a share for her stock, is she acting risk averse or risk seeking?
c. Would anyone pay Jill more than $30 a share for her stock?

18. Ira Betaman is considering investing $100,000 in either Treasury bills, with a guaranteed 5 percent return, or in a Bynight, Incorporated, junk bond, which has a high prospective return if there is no default:

Event	*Estimated Return (percent)*
No default	+ 20
Partial default	− 10
Total default	−100

Historical data for bonds issued by similar companies suggest that 5 percent have a total default and another 20 percent a partial default. If Ira applies these probabilities to the Bynight bond, does the expected value of its return exceed that of Treasury bills? If Ira buys the Bynight bonds, what can we conclude about his risk preferences?

19. Four thousand years ago, Chinese shipowners who were worried about pirates and natural disasters put part of their cargo on each other's ships. How does modern portfolio theory explain this behavior?

20. An investor is considering two mutual funds and assigns probabilities shown in Table C to the possible percentage rates of return.

TABLE 13–D

Relative Strength of Rental Market	Probability	Profit (millions of dollars)	
		One-Story Complex	Two-Story Complex
Strong	0.2	$4	$10
Medium	0.5	2	3
Weak	0.3	−1	−2

a. Graph the two probability distributions, the first on the top half of a sheet of paper and the second on the bottom half.
b. Which fund appears to have the higher expected return and which has the higher standard deviation?
c. Calculate the means and standard deviations, and see if you are right. (Use the interval midpoints for your calculations.)
21. A stock analyst has found the following probability distribution "to be very useful:"[9]

Stock Price Change During Next Six Months	Probability
+40	0.1
+20	0.2
0	0.4
−20	0.2
−40	0.1

What is the expected value? The standard deviation?
22. A business is considering building either a one-story or two-story apartment complex. The value of the completed building will depend on the strength of the rental market when construction is finished. The subjective probability distributions for the net profit with each option are shown in Table D. Use the mean and standard deviation to compare these two alternatives.
23. Consider two alternative investments: (a) stock with a 0.5 probability of a 50 percent gain and a 0.5 probability of a 10 percent loss; or (b)

land with a 0.5 probability of an 80 percent gain and a 0.5 probability of a 20 percent loss. If the outcomes are independent, find the expected value and standard deviation of the percentage return for each of these strategies.

Strategy 1: Invest all of your money in stock.
Strategy 2: Invest 80 percent of your money in stock and 20 percent in land.

(Hint: for Strategy 2, lay out the four possible outcomes.)
24. Program traders simultaneously buy and sell stocks, stock options, and/or stock futures. When the options or futures expire, these traders unwind their position by liquidating their stock holdings. One study looked at the volume of trading on the New York Stock Exchange during the last hour on Friday afternoons, comparing those days when stock-market index options and futures both expired with days when neither expired:[10]

	Share Volume in Last Hour	
	On Expiration Day	On Non-expiration Day
Mean volume	31,156,000	15,959,000
Standard deviation	11,612,000	5,011,000

Based on these data, write a brief paragraph comparing the last hour of trading on expiration and non-expiration Fridays.
25. ABC stock has a 0.5 probability of yielding

a 15 percent return and a 0.5 probability of yielding a 5 percent return. What are the expected value and the standard deviation of its return? CAB stock has a 0.3 probability of yielding a 20 percent return, a 0.5 probability of yielding 10 percent, and a 0.2 probability of yielding 0 percent. What are its expected return and standard deviation? Which is riskier: ABC stock or CAB stock? Which stock is preferred by a risk-neutral investor? By a risk seeker? By a risk-averse investor? Are the returns from ABC and CAB stock positively skewed, negatively skewed, or symmetrical?

26. Identify each of the following probability distributions as positively skewed, negatively skewed, or symmetrical:

a. The normal distribution.

b. A Superfecta bet, in which correctly picking the first four finishers in a horse race wins a large amount of money.

c. The purchase of a junk bond.

27. Why might an insurance company limit the number of homes it insures against loss by fire or flood in a given area, while remaining willing to write such policies in different areas?

28. The second figure shown in Investment Example 13–3 indicates that the monthly returns on the S&P 500 were approximately normally distributed with a mean of 0.51 percent and a standard deviation of 4.92 percent. According to the normal distribution rules of thumb, what range encompasses about 95 percent of the returns?

29. The text says that if you have $100,000 and invest two-thirds of your money in the first asset shown in Table 13–4 and one-third in the second asset, and the asset returns are perfectly negatively correlated, then you have a completely hedged investment. Show that your return does not depend on the investment outcomes.

30. A unit bond trust pools money from thousands of investors and buys a package of bonds. Which of the two opinions reported in the following excerpt from a magazine article do you agree with?

> Many trust sponsors argue that because a trust is diversified, investors can accept the higher risk—and higher income—of lower-rated bonds. "A trust is stronger than any of its parts in the same way that a bundle of pencils is stronger than one pencil," insists Norman Schvey, a Merrill Lynch Vice President. "Not so," says Diana Munder, a New York CPA whose clients often ask her for advice about their investments. "If you would not feel comfortable buying individual issues of obscure revenue bonds or lower-grade utilities," she believes, "there is no reason why you should feel more comfortable buying a whole package of them."[11]

CHAPTER 14

Mean-Variance Analysis

*The idea is there, locked inside. All
you have to do is remove the excess stone . . .*
Michelangelo

In the 1950s, James Tobin and Harry Markowitz introduced mean-variance analysis, a framework for analyzing investment opportunities based on the mean and variance (or standard deviation) of the prospective returns.[1] This framework is easy to use and yields a variety of striking, yet reasonable, conclusions. Mean-variance analysis teaches investors how to choose portfolios and tells us how assets will be priced if investors follow these lessons. Today, both individual and institutional investors routinely measure risk by the standard deviation and are influenced, directly or indirectly, by the implications of mean-variance asset-pricing models.

The preceding chapter introduced the idea that the mean and standard deviation are useful for describing uncertain asset returns. In this chapter, you will see how these two statistical measures can be used to determine the opportunities available to investors and help them make informed investment decisions. We will begin by considering how investor preferences depend on the mean and standard deviation. Then we will see how the mean and standard deviation of a portfolio of assets are related to the means and standard deviations of the assets in the portfolio. You will learn why some portfolios dominate others, and how portfolio managers can use this insight to make investment decisions that are consistent with their preferences and their beliefs about the future.

INVESTOR PREFERENCES

Mean-variance analysis assumes that investor preferences depend on only the mean and variance of asset returns, which is a reasonable simplifying assumption if the returns are approximately normally distributed. The expected return is clearly an important measure of an asset's appeal. The variance (or standard deviation) is a plausible measure of risk. Whether investors find a large standard deviation appealing or not depends, of course, on their risk preferences. The next section will describe a useful technique to clarify these preferences.

The Description of Preferences

A risk-neutral investor cares only about an asset's expected return, not the size of its standard deviation. These preferences are depicted in panel (a) of Figure 14–1. The expected return is on the vertical axis and the standard deviation is on the horizontal axis. Each of the three horizontal lines is an **indifference curve,** a graphical way of showing opportunities that an investor finds equally appealing. A risk-neutral investor is indifferent between Asset 1 and Asset 3 (and all of the other points on this horizontal line) because these assets have the same expected return and the standard deviation is unimportant. Similarly, a risk-neutral investor is indifferent between Asset 2 and any other point on the horizontal line passing through Asset 2. Asset 2 is preferred to Asset 3, and Asset 3 is preferred to Asset 4, because, for a given standard deviation, all investors prefer a large expected return.

> **indifference curve**
> An indifference curve is a graphical device for depicting investment opportunities that an investor finds equally appealing.

Panel (b) shows three indifference curves for a risk-averse investor. Assets 1 and 3 have the same expected return, but the risk-averse investor prefers Asset 1 because it has the lower standard deviation. The upward sloping indifference curve passing through Asset 1 and Asset 2 shows the increase in the expected return that is required for this investor to consider the high-risk investment as attractive as the low-risk one. The indifference curve would be nearly vertical for an investor who is extremely risk averse and almost horizontal for someone who is mildly risk averse. This person, like all investors, prefers Asset 2 to Asset 3, and Asset 3 to Asset 4.

A risk seeker prefers a high standard deviation and, as shown by the downward sloping indifference curves in panel (c), will accept a low expected return to get more risk. This risk seeker is indifferent between Assets 1 and 4 because Asset 4's low expected return is offset by its high risk. Risk means that the return is uncertain, in that there is a substantial chance that it will be either much lower or much higher than its expected value. The chance of an extremely large return is very important to a risk seeker.

Now imagine that only Asset 1 and Asset 3 in Figure 14–1 are available. Which will each investor choose? A risk-neutral investor cares only about the expected return and is indifferent between these two assets. The risk-averse person will not hold a risky asset unless it has a risk premium and, so, chooses Asset 1. The risk seeker chooses Asset 3. Thus, investors with different risk preferences are drawn to different investments. The indifference curves in Figure 14–1 allow us to display an investor's risk preferences graphically and determine the appropriate investment decisions.

FIGURE 14–1 Indifference curves

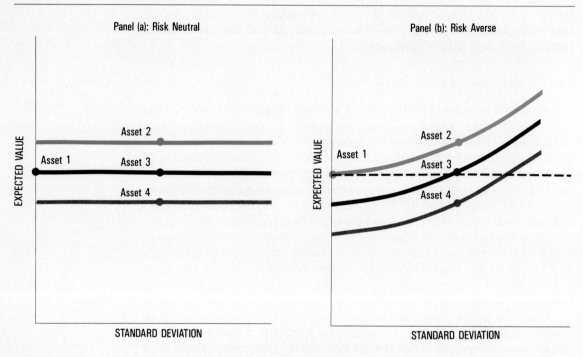

Panel (a): Risk Neutral

Panel (b): Risk Averse

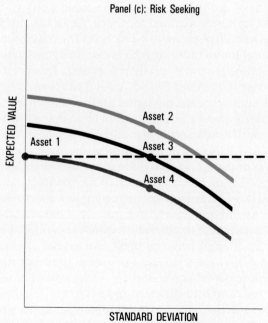

Panel (c): Risk Seeking

Implications for Asset Pricing

This simple model also has implications for the pricing of assets. If all investors are risk neutral, all assets must offer the same expected return (or there must be disagreement about the expected returns). Otherwise, no one will hold the assets with low expected returns, and someone must. If, on the other hand, all investors are risk seeking, then risky assets can be priced to give relatively low expected returns and still find willing owners. In a world filled with risk-averse investors, risky assets must be priced to have high expected returns (risk premiums) to persuade the least risk averse to hold them. The fact that, historically, investments with high standard deviations have had high average returns suggests that most investors are risk averse. However, investment opportunities are more complex than so far depicted, and asset pricing is a bit more subtle, as you will soon see.

PORTFOLIO OPPORTUNITIES

The analysis in Figure 14–1 considered an all-or-nothing choice between two assets. Investors may prefer instead to invest in both assets. To analyze this possibility, consider two assets, with returns R_1 and R_2. The respective expected returns are μ_1 and μ_2; the standard deviations are σ_1 and σ_2. If a fraction a of the wealth is invested in the first asset and a fraction $1 - a$ in the second, then the portfolio return, R, is a weighted average of the returns on the two assets in the portfolio, with the weights a and $1 - a$ reflecting the fractions of wealth invested in each asset:

$$R = aR_1 + (1 - a)R_2 \tag{1}$$

The portfolio's expected return μ is a similar weighted average of the asset expected returns:

$$\mu = a\mu_1 + (1 - a)\mu_2 \tag{2}$$

The portfolio variance is more complicated because it depends on ρ, the correlation coefficient between the two returns:

$$\sigma^2 = a^2\sigma_1^2 + (1 - a)^2\sigma_2^2 + 2a(1 - a)\sigma_1\sigma_2\rho \tag{3}$$

The appendix to this chapter shows the calculation of the correlation coefficient, and examples are given later in this chapter. For now, it is sufficient to note that if the asset returns are uncorrelated, then $\rho = 0$. If the returns are positively correlated, the correlation coefficient is positive, with a maximum value of 1. With negatively correlated returns, the correlation coefficient can be as low as -1.

TABLE 14–1 Portfolio Opportunities with a Safe Asset and a Risky Asset

Portfolio Fraction Invested in Safe Asset, a	Portfolio Fraction Invested in Risky Asset, $1 - a$	Portfolio Expected Return	Portfolio Standard Deviation
1.0	0.0	10	0
0.8	0.2	11	2
0.6	0.4	12	4
0.4	0.6	13	6
0.2	0.8	14	8
0.0	1.0	15	10
−0.2	1.2	16	12
−0.4	1.4	17	14

One Safe Asset and One Risky Asset

We will first consider the case where the one asset is safe ($\sigma_1 = 0$), perhaps a Treasury bill or a bank deposit, with a guaranteed 10 percent return. The second asset is risky, perhaps a stock, with an expected return of 15 percent and a standard deviation of 10 percent. Table 14–1 shows the portfolio expected return and standard deviation, using Equations 1 to 3 for various values of a. As the fraction invested in the risky asset increases, both the expected return and standard deviation increase by a constant amount. As shown in Figure 14–2, the **opportunity locus**—a graphical depiction of the alternatives available to an investor—is a straight line.

opportunity locus
The opportunity locus is a graphical apparatus showing the alternatives available to an investor.

Leverage If a is positive, then a fraction a of wealth is invested in the safe asset. If a is negative, the investor is not buying the safe asset, but selling it—that is, borrowing. For instance, if wealth is $100,000, then $a = -0.4$ means borrowing $40,000; the value of $1 - a$ is 1.4 because now this person can invest $140,000 in the risky asset. The dotted line in Figure 14–2 for $a<0$ and $1 - a>1$ describes the borrowing of funds at a 10 percent interest rate in order to invest more money in the risky asset. This is leverage, and the figure confirms our discussion in earlier chapters of its consequences.

 If the expected return on the risky asset exceeds the interest rate on the borrowed money, the leverage increases the portfolio's expected return. Leverage also increases risk, the chances of making or losing a great deal of money, shown here by the increased portfolio standard deviation as one borrows additional amounts. Investment Example 14–1 on p. 442 explains how investment trusts created enormous leverage in the 1920s.

FIGURE 14-2   Opportunity locus with a safe asset

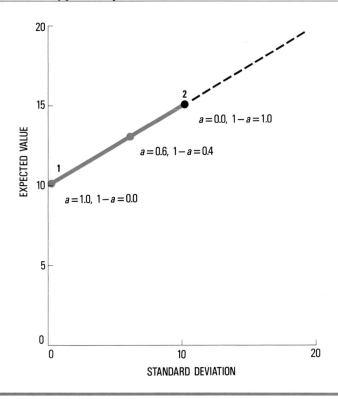

Two Risky Assets

So far, we have considered one safe asset and one risky asset. Now we consider the case of two risky assets. The portfolio standard deviation and the shape of the opportunity locus depend critically on the correlation between the asset returns. Three very different correlations are shown in the scatter diagrams in Figure 14–3 on p. 444.

Asset Correlations Each point in these graphs shows the returns on two assets during a particular period, say, a year; the ten points in each graph record ten years of annual returns. In panel (a), the correlation coefficient is 0 because the returns are uncorrelated. When the return on Asset 1 is unusually high, the return on Asset 2 is as likely to be low as it is high. Knowing that one security had a high return is of no help in predicting the return on the other security.

INVESTMENT EXAMPLE 14-1

PYRAMID TRUSTS

In the 1920s, a series of investment trusts were sometimes used to pyramid leverage. Such trusts, known as pyramid trusts, work as follows: Trust A is established by raising $10 million from shareholders and borrowing $20 million at 6 percent. This $30 million is used to buy all the shares in Trust B, which, in addition to this $30 million in equity, borrows $60 million at 6 percent. Trust B's $90 million is used to buy all of the shares in Trust C, which then borrows another $180 million at 6 percent. Trust C's $270 million is invested in the stock market.

Through this sequence of 3-to-1 leveraging, investors with $10 million are able to borrow a total of $260 million and buy $270 million worth of stock, creating 27-to-1 leverage. Each trust sets $a = 3$ and $1 - a = -2$ by borrowing twice its net worth in order to invest an amount equal to three times its net worth. If we let R be the return on the stock market and let R_A, R_B, and R_C be the respective returns on the three trusts, then the application of Equation 1 gives

$$R_C = 3R - 2(6\%)$$
$$R_B = 3R_C - 2(6\%)$$
$$R_A = 3R_B - 2(6\%)$$

Repeated substitution gives

$$
\begin{aligned}
R_A &= 3R_B - 2(6\%) \\
&= 3[3R_C - 2(6\%)] - 2(6\%) \\
&= 9R_C - 8(6\%) \\
&= 9[3R - 2(6\%)] - 8(6\%) \\
&= 27R - 26(6\%)
\end{aligned}
$$

The accompanying figure shows the relationship among these returns, drawn here on the assumption that the expected return on stocks is larger than 6 percent.

In panel (b), there is a positive correlation coefficient because these returns tend to move up and down together. When the return on Asset 1 is unusually high, the return on Asset 2 tends to be high also. The largest possible value of the correlation coefficient ρ is 1.0; in such a case, all the points lie on a straight line with a positive slope (not necessarily 1.0), indicating that the returns move in the same direction and that if we know the return on one security then we are certain of the return on the other. The 0.9 correlation coefficient in the figure reflects returns that are strongly, but not perfectly, correlated.

In panel (c), the correlation coefficient is negative because these two asset returns usually move in opposite directions. When one return is high, the other tends to be low. The lowest possible value for the correlation

Pyramid trusts offer investors the opportunity to gain or lose substantial amounts. If it turns out that the stocks earn an annual return of exactly 6 percent, then this (6 percent) ($270 million) = $16.2 million will cover the (6 percent) ($260 million) = $15.6 million interest due on debt and leave $0.6 million in profits, a 6 percent return on the original $10 million investment. If the stocks earn 16 percent, a seemingly modest goal in the 1920s, this 10 percent differential over the 6 percent borrowing rate is multiplied twenty-seven fold by leverage, giving shareholders a 6 percent + 27(16 percent − 6 percent) = 276 percent return. [Checking, 16 percent ($270 million) − $15.6 million = $27.6 million.] If, on the other hand, the stocks earn only a modest 1 percent return, this 5 percent shortfall is multiplied twenty-seven fold into a return of 6 percent + 27(1 percent − 6 percent) = −129 percent; the shareholders are bankrupted because the $15.6 million interest owed exhausts both the stock profits of 1 percent ($270 million) = $2.7 million and the investors' initial $10 million investment. These trusts did wonderfully when the market boomed in the 1920s, but were the first to collapse when the market crashed.

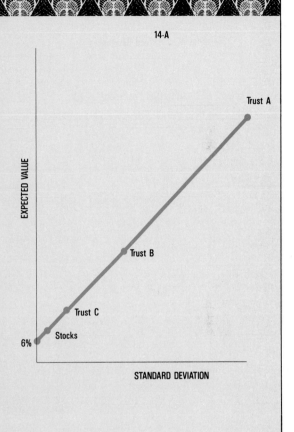

coefficient is $\rho = -1.0$, indicating perfect negative correlation in that the returns all lie on a straight line with a negative slope.

The Opportunity Locus The value of the correlation coefficient determines the shape of the mean-variance opportunity locus. Consider two assets, each with two possible outcomes: one pays $+50\%$ or -50% and the other pays $+130\%$ or -70%. The means are:

$$\mu_1 = 50\%(0.5) - 50\%(0.5) = 0\%$$
$$\mu_2 = 130\%(0.5) - 70\%(0.5) = 30\%$$

The standard deviations work out to be:

FIGURE 14-3 The correlation between asset returns

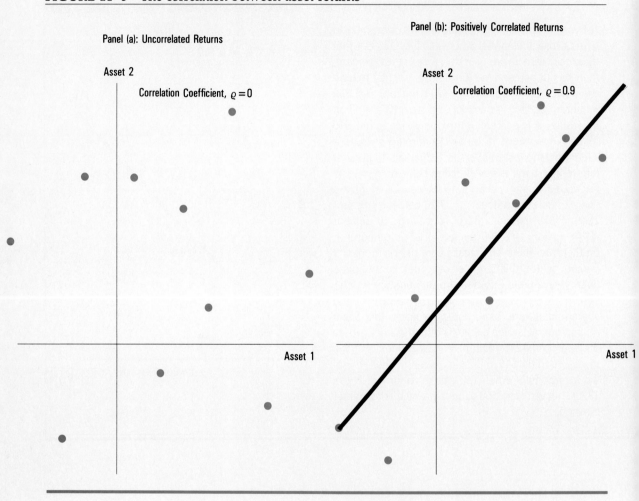

Panel (a): Uncorrelated Returns

Panel (b): Positively Correlated Returns

$$\sigma_1 = 50\%$$
$$\sigma_2 = 100\%$$

Table 14–2 gives the portfolio mean and standard deviation for various values of a, the fraction of wealth invested in the first asset. The standard deviation is calculated for three specific cases: independence ($\rho = 0$); perfect positive correlation ($\rho = 1$), in which either both assets do well or both do poorly; and perfect negative correlation ($\rho = -1$), in which one asset always does well if the other does poorly. Figure 14–4 graphs these three cases.

In general, the shape of an opportunity locus is a hyperbola, like the one drawn for $\rho = 0$, that lies inside the extreme boundaries of $\rho = 1$ and $\rho = -1$. The curvature of the opportunity locus is greater, the smaller is the correlation coefficient. Thus, for any portfolio allocation a, the portfolio

FIGURE 14–3, *cont'd*   The correlation between asset returns

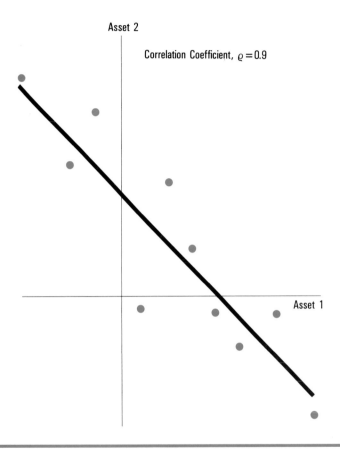

Panel (c): Negatively Correlated Returns

standard deviation is smaller if the correlation coefficient is lower, showing that diversification reduces risk more effectively if the asset returns are uncorrelated or, even better, negatively correlated. At the extreme of perfectly negatively correlated returns, we can construct a perfect hedge—the combination of individually risky assets to give a safe portfolio. Here, the perfect hedge is with $a = 2/3$, $1 - a = 1/3$.

The Minimum-Risk Portfolio   When $\rho = 1$, the safest portfolio contains only the safer asset (Asset 1). But when $\rho = 0$, an even safer portfolio can be obtained by holding some of both assets, as shown in Figure 14–4 by the fact that the opportunity locus curves to the left of Asset 1. Figure 14–5 shows that if $\rho = 0$ the minimum-risk portfolio has 80 percent of wealth in the first asset and 20 percent in the second. In general, some tedious algebra shows that a diversified portfolio can be constructed with

TABLE 14–2   Portfolio Opportunities with Two Risky Assets

Portfolio Fraction Invested in First Asset, a	Portfolio Fraction Invested in Second Asset $1 - a$	Portfolio Expected Return (percent)	Portfolio Standard Deviation (percent)		
			$\rho = -1$	$\rho = 0$	$\rho = 1$
1.0	0.0	0	50	50	50
0.8	0.2	6	20	45	60
2/3	1/3	10	0	47	67
0.6	0.4	12	10	50	70
0.4	0.6	18	40	63	80
0.2	0.8	24	70	80	90
0.0	1.0	30	100	100	100

FIGURE 14–4   The shape of the opportunity locus depends on the correlation coefficient

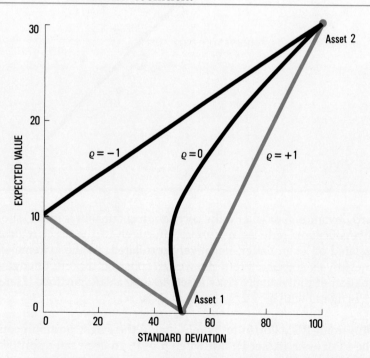

FIGURE 14–5   A minimum-risk portfolio

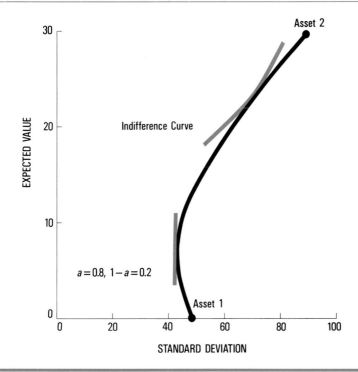

a standard deviation smaller than the standard deviation of the safer asset, say Asset 1, whenever

$$\rho < \sigma_1/\sigma_2$$

This condition is always satisfied if the asset returns are uncorrelated ($\rho = 0$) or negatively correlated ($\rho < 0$), and may hold even if the asset returns are positively correlated.

Of course, only the most risk averse will choose the safest portfolio. Others will compare the available combinations of expected return and standard deviation. The risk neutral or only slightly risk averse will choose Asset 2 alone. The more risk averse will include Asset 1 in their portfolio. No one will hold Asset 1 alone.

TABLE 14–3 Annual Returns for the Stock Market and Three Risky Stocks, 1972–1980

| | Annual Return (percent) | | | |
Year	Market	Consolidated Natural Gas	U.S. Home	Kloof
1970	4.01	23.0	9.6	38.5
1971	14.31	7.1	51.4	6.3
1972	18.98	7.3	−17.2	53.6
1973	−14.66	−13.4	−77.3	107.9
1974	−26.47	−3.7	−48.8	1.1
1975	37.20	25.1	128.0	−38.1
1976	23.84	59.3	56.5	−45.1
1977	−7.18	29.0	−8.8	58.2
1978	6.56	−8.3	22.7	16.2
1979	18.44	15.0	113.1	304.4

TABLE 14—4 Asset Means, Standard Deviations, and Correlation Coefficients for Three Risky Stocks

| Security | Expected Return (percent) | Standard Deviation (percent) | Correlation Coefficient | | |
			Consolidated Natural Gas	U.S. Home	Kloof
Consolidated Natural Gas	14.0	21.4	1.0	0.5	−0.2
U.S. Home	22.9	65.9	0.5	1.0	0.1
Kloof	50.3	100.3	−0.2	0.1	1.0

THE MARKOWITZ FRONTIER

Now we consider the case of more than two risky assets, illustrated by historical data for three risky stocks in Table 14–3. The table shows the annual returns (percent dividends plus capital gains) for three stocks during the period 1972–80, and Table 14–4 shows the calculated means, standard deviatons, and correlation coefficients. (The matrix of correlation coefficients is symmetrical because the correlation of Asset 1 with Asset 2 is the same as the correlation of Asset 2 with Asset 1; there are 1s down the diagonal of this matrix because the correlation of any asset with itself is 1.)

U.S. Home is the nation's largest homebuilder, and its profits are very sensitive to the economy and to interest rates. Consolidated Natural Gas is a regulated utility company, and while its profits are less dependent on

FIGURE 14–6   The Markowitz frontier

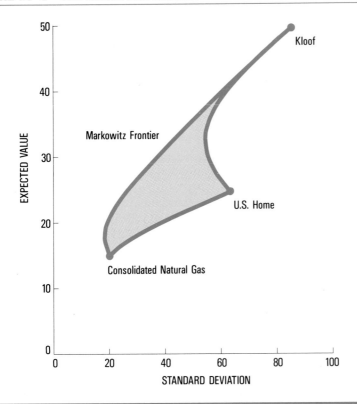

the economy, the value of its stock is, like U.S. Home, buffeted by interest rates. The 0.5 correlation coefficient shows that the stock returns on U.S Home and Consolidated Natural Gas were positively correlated during the period studied, but did not move in lockstep.

Gold is a traditional refuge for frightened investors during periods of political or economic turmoil, perhaps because it has value everywhere and is easy to carry across borders. Kloof is a South African gold-mining stock and during the turbulent 1970s sometimes did well when the U.S. stock market did poorly. This is reflected in the slight negative correlation between Kloof and Consolidated Natural Gas. The 0.1 correlation coefficient between U.S. Home and Kloof indictes that their returns essentially were uncorrelated.

We should be cautious about using historical data, particularly the means, to estimate the opportunities offered by investments, but, nonetheless, do so here for simplicity. The opportunity loci we have discussed so far are single lines, straight or curved. When there are more than two assets, the infinite variety of possible asset combinations gives the shaded region of opportunities shown in Figure 14–6. The dark curve, known as

TABLE 14–5 Some Portfolios on the Markowitz Frontier

Expected Return (percent)	Standard Deviation (percent)	Fraction in Each Stock		
		Consolidated Natural Gas	U.S. Home	Kloof
15	20.4	0.9725	0.0000	0.0275
20	21.8	0.8347	0.0000	0.1653
30	43.0	0.4796	0.1054	0.4149
40	69.2	0.0918	0.2543	0.6539
50	99.3	0.0000	0.0109	0.9891

Markowitz frontier
The Markowitz frontier is the envelope of efficient portfolios, showing the minimum standard deviation attainable for each possible expected return.

an *envelope*, shows the minimum standard deviation attainable for each possible expected return. This envelope of efficient portfolios is called the **Markowitz frontier** in recognition of Harry Markowitz's pioneering work in identifying and calculating such envelopes.

Each point on the Markowitz frontier represents a different portfolio, which combines the underlying assets in varying proportions. Some of these efficient portfolios are shown in Table 14–5. Investors can choose among the efficient portfolios on the Markowitz frontier, depending on their risk preferences. Table 14–5 shows that the more risk averse would put most of their money in Consolidated Natural Gas, settling for a low expected return in order to get a low standard deviation. The less risk averse would invest heavily in Kloof. Notice that, because of Kloof's negative correlation with Consolidated Natural Gas, even the very risk averse find it advantageous to diversify their portfolio by including some shares of Kloof, shares which are very risky in isolation.

Tobin's Separation Theorem

If there is a safe asset with, say, a 10 percent return, it can be combined with any of the risky portfolios in Figure 14–6, based on our earlier observation that the opportunity locus for a safe asset and a risky one is a straight line. The optimal combination is with a portfolio on the Markowitz frontier, in particular with the portfolio shown in Figure 14–7 where a straight line from the safe asset is tangent to the frontier. This opportunity locus dominates all others in that, for any level of risk, the highest attainable expected return is on this straight line tangent to the Markowitz frontier.

The risky portfolio on the Markowitz frontier at the tangency in Figure 14–7 happens to contain the following proportions of the underlying assets:

Consolidated Gas	0.73
U.S. Home	0.01
Kloof	0.26
	1.00

FIGURE 14–7   Tobin's Separation Theorem

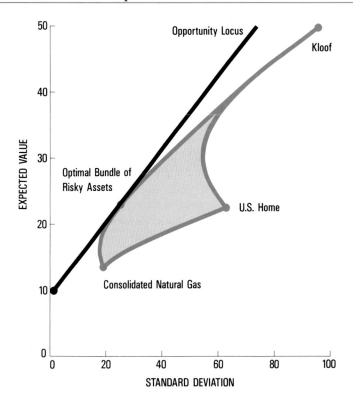

Each point on the optimal opportunity locus in Figure 14–7 represents a combination of the safe asset and this optimal risky portfolio. The extremely risk averse might put all of their wealth in the safe asset. Another possibility, for the less risk averse, is to put 0.5 in the safe asset and 0.5 in the risky portfolio, divided in the proportions given above. Thus, $0.5(0.73) = 0.365$ is invested in Consolidated Gas, $0.5(0.01) = 0.005$ in U.S. Home, and $0.5(0.26) = 0.130$ in Kloof. The more venturesome can put 20 percent in the safe asset and 80 percent in the risky portfolio, with $0.8(0.73) = 0.584$ in Consolidated Gas, $0.8(0.01) = 0.008$ in U.S. Home, and $0.8(0.26) = 0.208$ in Kloof. Others may put 100 percent in the risky portfolio or, by leveraging, more than 100 percent.

As the investor moves along the straight line tangent to the Markowitz frontier in Figure 14–7, there is a change in the division of wealth between the safe asset and the risky portfolio, but not in the composition of the optimal risky portfolio. The optimal bundle of risky assets is deter-

Tobin's Separation Theorem

Tobin's Separation Theorem states that, if there is a safe asset, then the selection of the optimal risky portfolio does not depend on risk preferences.

mined by the tangency and does not depend on risk preferences. This is **James Tobin's Separation Theorem:**

> **The selection of the optimal risky portfolio can be separated from preferences about how much risk to bear.**

According to this theorem, investment decisions can be separated into two distinct parts: first, the use of means, standard deviations, and correlation coefficients together with the safe return to determine the optimal portfolio of risky assets and, second, the use of preferences to determine the division of wealth between the safe asset and this optimal risky portfolio.

These two distinct actions can be performed by different people. An investment-advisory service or portfolio manager can determine the optimal risky porfolio for all clients, and each investor then can decide how much to invest in this portfolio. This conclusion contradicts the traditional investment practice in which different stocks are selected for different clients—the more risk averse choosing safe stocks and the less risk averse selecting riskier ones. Tobin's Separation Theorem suggests that conservative clients may be better off including risky stocks in their portfolio and then reducing risk by putting most of their money in Treasury bills. More aggressive investors may do well borrowing money to buy the very same stocks as the more cautious.

RISK-ADJUSTED PERFORMANCE

In a world full of risk-averse investors, risky portfolios must be priced to have relatively high expected returns. If so, one way to get high average returns is to take above-average risks. It is, therefore, not sufficient to judge investment performance solely by the average return. If an investor has had a high average return but that return has fluctuated greatly, then this riskiness should be taken into account.

Mean-variance analysis provides one way of adjusting the average return for the risks that are taken. Consider two mutual funds: Fund 1, with an average return of 14 percent and a standard deviation of 15 percent, and Fund 2, with an average return of 17 percent and a standard deviation of 25 percent. Fund 2 has the higher average return, but it also has a higher standard deviation. Is the extra risk adequately compensated for by the additional return? If a safe asset yields 5 percent and we use historical performance to gauge the opportunities offered investors, the answer is no.

Figure 14–8 shows the mean and standard deviation for these two mutual funds. The lines drawn to the 5 percent return available on a safe asset show the opportunities offered investors by each fund. Fund 1 dom-

FIGURE 14–8   Risk-adjusted performance of two mutual funds

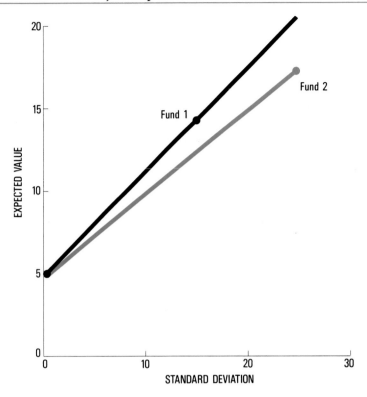

inates Fund 2 in that for any level of risk, the expected return that an investor can get by combining Fund 1 with the safe asset exceeds that available from combining Fund 2 with the safe asset. By this criterion, risk-adjusted performance can be gauged by the slope of the opportunity locus, as follows:

$$\text{risk-adjusted performance} = \frac{\mu - R}{\sigma} \qquad (4)$$

where R is the return on the safe asset, and μ and σ are the fund's average return and standard deviation.

An appealing benchmark for all mutual funds is the risk-adjusted performance of an unmanaged portfolio containing Treasury bills and a stock-market index, such as the Dow Jones Industrial Average or the S&P 500. William Sharpe's seminal study found that, taking management fees into account, the risk-adjusted performance of twenty-three of thirty-four mutual funds studied was inferior to the Dow Jones Industrial Average, as

FIGURE 14–9   Mutual fund performance, 1954–1963

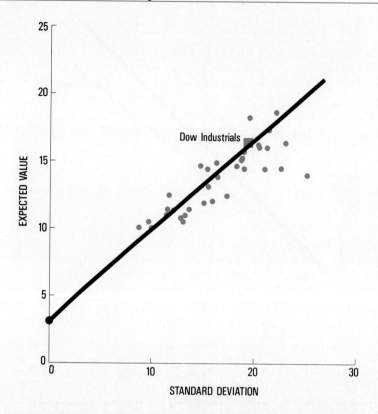

shown in Figure 14–9.[2] If management fees are ignored, nineteen funds did better and fifteen funds worse than the Dow. A number of subsequent studies have come to similar conclusions. Mutual funds and other professionally managed portfolios do as well as or slightly better than unmanaged portfolios, but not well enough to justify their management fees. When their fees are taken into account, their performance is inferior to that of unmanaged portfolios. Mutual funds offer diversifiction for small investors, but not superior stock selection.

PORTFOLIO MANAGEMENT

Some portfolio managers, including Harry Markowitz, use mean-variance analysis in their investment decisions. Typically, historical data are used to estimate the Markowitz frontier and, hence, the perceived opportunities available to investors. The client or the fund manager then considers the combinations of risk and return that are available on the frontier and, taking into account risk preferences, selects one of these optimal portfolios. If there is a safe asset, then Tobin's Separation Theorem implies the existence of an optimal bundle of risky assets, with risk preferences determining how wealth is divided between the safe asset and this optimal bundle.

Some investors use mean-variance analysis to choose an optimal stock portfolio. Others determine an optimal portfolio of bonds of varying coupons and maturities. Some look at bonds and stocks together and perhaps include options contracts, financial futures, commodities, and foreign securities in an effort to find uncorrelated or negatively correlated assets that will reduce risk effectively. Investment Example 14–2 on pp. 456–457 shows how international diversification can be helpful.

The Success of Markowitz Portfolios

There is some evidence that Markowitz portfolios beat the market, in apparent contradiction of the efficient-market hypothesis. For example, Cohen and Pogue used ten years of historical data to estimate the means, standard deviations, and correlation coefficients of widely traded stocks, and from these identified portfolios on the Markowitz frontier.[3] They then calculated the performance of various portfolios in succeeding years and found that Markowitz-frontier portfolios dominated randomly selected portfolios.

The Single-Index Model Markowitz portfolios require a great deal of data and exhaust even large computers. For instance, 1000 securities require nearly 500,000 correlation coefficients and hours of computer time on all but the fastest computers. Following up on a Markowitz suggestion, William Sharpe has extensively analyzed a **single-index model**, which assumes that the return R_i on asset i is linearly related to the return R_M on the overall market basket of assets and to an error term ϵ_i which encompasses other influences specific to this particular asset:

single-index model
The single-index model assumes that an asset's return depends on the market return and idiosyncratic factors.

$$R_i = \alpha_i + \beta_i R_M + \epsilon_i$$

We will discuss the motivation for this model and some applications in the next chapter. All that need be noted at this point is that the assumption that the ϵ_i are independent conveniently simplifies the data and computational burden. Cohen and Pogue found that single-index models performed almost as well as Markowitz portfolios and continued to dominate randomly selected portfolios.

Other Simplifications To avoid the estimation and manipulation of literally millions of correlation coefficients, one investment manager, the Huntington CPI+ Fund, service divides assets into eight major categories:[4]

456

GLOBAL DIVERSIFICATION

Much of the early empirical work on diversified portfolios focused on U.S. stocks. These academic studies demonstrated the advantages to risk-averse investors of selecting a wide variety of dissimilar stocks. Many portfolio managers restricted their attention to the U.S. stock market, too, perhaps reasoning that this is their area of expertise and that, in the long-run, stock returns have averaged above bond returns.

However, a number of studies now suggest that the risk-return opportunities available to an investor can be made more attractive by the inclusion of bonds and foreign securities.[1] Other researchers encourage the inclusion of an even wider range of assets, including commodities and futures contracts. One investment firm that stresses the benefits of international diversification is Huntington Advisers.[2] They argue that there are several persuasive reasons why it is advantageous to supplement a portfolio of New York Stock Exchange stocks with other securities:

Small stocks: Large and small stocks may be affected differently by the economy and interest rates.

Long-term bonds: Stocks are affected by the economy and interest rates, bonds just by interest rates.

Treasury bills: The shape of the term structure changes so that short-term and long-term interest rates are not perfectly correlated.

Foreign bonds: U.S. and foreign interest rates are imperfectly correlated and, more importantly, exchange rate movements cause divergences in the dollar value of foreign and domestic securities.

Foreign stocks: U.S. and foreign economic conditions are not perfectly correlated.

Treasury bills	Small U.S. stocks
Treasury bonds	Small British stocks
Utility stocks	Small Japanese stocks
Energy stocks	Gold boullion

The rationale is that assets within each sector are reasonably similar, but that there are important differences among sectors.

The portfolio managers at Huntington Advisers have made a number of empirical studies buttressing their arguments. One is summarized in the accompanying figure. Using quarterly data from June 1985 through June 1988, they estimated the means, standard deviations, and correlation coefficients among the real returns on the assets described above. The point labeled S&P 500 shows the average return and standard deviation of a portfolio consisting of the S&P 500 stocks. The Markowitz frontier for U.S. securities shows how investor opportunities are improved by the inclusion of other U.S. securities in the portfolio. The Markowitz frontier for global securities shows that the inclusion of foreign securities offers substantial further improvement. Persuaded by this evidence, Huntington Advisers uses global diversification in the portfolios that it advises and manages.

[1] For example, J. Madura, "International Portfolio Construction," *Journal of Business Research*, 1985, pp. 87–95; and Haim Levy and Zvi Lerman, "The Benefits of International Diversification in Bonds," *Financial Analysts Journal*, September-October 1988, pp. 56–64.

[2] Edward C. Franks and Donald Gould, Huntington Advisers, personal correspondence, 1989.

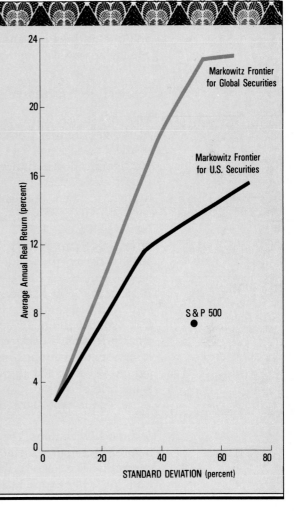

Each quarter, monthly data for the past five years are used to estimate means, standard deviations, and correlation coefficients for all eight sectors and to locate the Markowitz frontier. This firm works with real rates of return, and because the rate of inflation is uncertain, even Treasury bills have an uncertain real return. Since there is no safe asset, Tobin's Separation Theorem is not used. Instead, the firm locates the point on the Markowitz frontier with a 10 percent expected real return. The client's portfolio is then divided into the appropriate proportions among the eight sectors and, within each sector, invested in a diversified basket of securities.

This investment service claims that its average risk-adjusted return is several percentage points better than that of any of the eight sectors alone and one to three percentage points better than that of a portfolio divided equally among the eight sectors.

Subjective Assessments (optional)

This investment firm's approach is a purely mechanical calculation of the Markowitz frontier from historical means, standard deviations, and correlation coefficients. But there is no reason why we should restrict our anticipation of the future to a simple averaging of the past. Markowitz procedures can also be usefully employed to describe our beliefs about the future and, then, to select a portfolio that reflects these beliefs.

Expected Values The fact that, over the last sixty years, long-term bonds have yielded an average of 5 percent and stocks 10 percent is not a persuasive reason for assuming that the expected values of the returns on bonds and stocks during the coming year are, respectively, 5 percent and 10 percent. Perhaps long-term bonds are priced currently to yield 12 percent, and you think that bond prices are equally likely to go up or down. If so, you should use 12 percent, not 5 percent, as the expected return. If stock prices have reached what you consider unreasonable levels relative to dividends, earnings, and corporate assets, you are not compelled to assume an expected 10 percent return on stocks this year. If you expect stock prices to drop, you should express that belief by using a negative value for the expected return.

Standard Deviations The past volatility of bond and stock prices can be helpful in gauging uncertainty but, here too, need not be applied mechanically. The clearest example is Treasury-bill rates. In the Great Depression, these rates were but a fraction of a percent; in the inflationary 1970s, T-bill rates soared to double-digit levels. Over the past sixty years, the average value has been about 3.5 percent, and the standard deviation about this mean has been 3.5 percent. But despite this annual variation in the level of Treasury-bill rates over the past sixty years, there is no uncertainty at all about the return on a one-year Treasury bill over the coming year! If a $10,000 Treasury bill sells for $9400, you are certain to make $600, a percentage return of $600/$9400 = 6.4 percent, and you should use an expected return of 6.4 percent with a standard deviation of 0 percent (not 3.5 percent).

Similarly, the standard deviations for stocks and long-term bonds that are used in mean-variance analysis should reflect our uncertainty, not historical volatility. If the chairman of the Federal Reserve announces that the Fed will maintain orderly financial markets by holding long-term interest rates rock-steady, then the implied constancy of long-term bond prices means that there is virtually no uncertainty about the return on long-term Treasury bonds. A low standard deviation on bond returns reflects our confidence in the success of the Fed's policy. If the Fed chairman instead announces that the Fed intends to ignore interest rates, a large standard deviation should be used to describe our uncertainty about bond prices and about the rate of return to be realized by buying long-term bonds.

If you are willing to assume approximate normality, then you can gauge your uncertainty by remembering the rules of thumb that there is a two-thirds probability that a normally distributed variable will be within one standard deviation of its mean and a 95 percent probability of it being within two standard deviations of its mean. Suppose that long-term bonds are priced to yield 8 percent during the coming year. If you think that bond prices are as likely to go up as down and that it is unlikely (less than a 5 percent probability) that bond prices will rise or fall by more than 10 percent, then the two-standard-deviations rule implies that a 5 percent value for the standard deviation is appropriate. You can check the reasonableness of this assumption by considering the implication of the one-standard-deviation rule that there is only a one-third probability that bond prices will go up or down by more than 5 percent.

Asset Correlations Anticipated correlations among bond and stock returns need not be a mechanical replication of the past either. Bond and stock returns were negatively correlated in the 1960s, but positively correlated in the 1970s. The correlation coefficient used for portfolio management should reflect the sources of our uncertainty. Bond returns depend on interest-rate surprises, while stock returns are affected by surprises in both interest rates and the economy.

The 1960s were a recession-free decade, propelled by increases in private and government spending, and the strong economy increased borrowing and interest rates. Although rising interest rates reduced bond prices, prices generally increased because the negative effects of high interest rates were overwhelmed by the strong economy. This coexistence in the 1960s of higher interest rates with larger corporate profits caused a negative correlation between bond and stock prices.

The 1970s and early 1980s, in contrast, were dominated by the Federal Reserve, which repeatedly used high interest rates to cool the economy and slow inflation, and then used low interest rates to stimulate the economy when it seemed on the verge of collapse. The rise in interest rates during periods of recession caused bond and stock prices to fall together; the decline in interest rates during booms caused bond and stock prices to rise together. Thus, bond and stock prices were positively correlated in the 1970s and early 1980s. The question we need to ask for the future is, "If interest rates rise unexpectedly, do we think it will be because the economy is expanding or because the Fed is using high interest rates to contract the economy?"

FIGURE 14–10   Four portfolios for a risk-averse investor with varying expectations

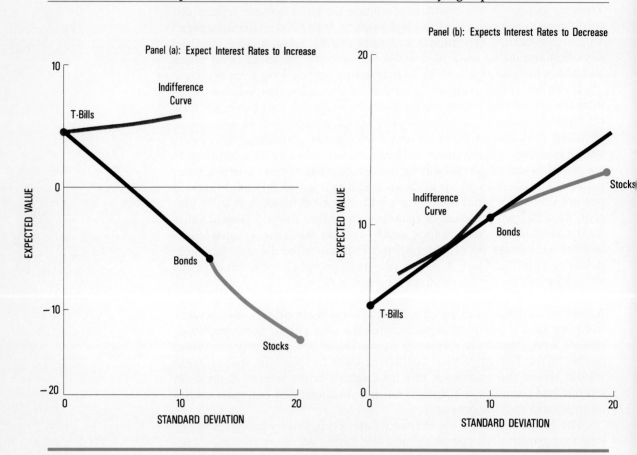

Anticipating the Future The optimal portfolio depends on specific assumptions—on the expected returns from various assets, on our uncertainty as measured by the standard deviations, and on the assumed correlations. The types of recommendations that might result can be illustrated with four examples. The details of each case are less important then the general point that mean-variance analysis can help investors select portfolios consistent with their assumptions.

Figure 14–10 shows four different portfolios chosen by a risk-averse investor under very different circumstances. In panel (a), the investor believes that interest rates will rise (relative to the term structure), causing capital losses for bonds and stocks. The substantial standard deviations show that the investor is far from certain that this will happen; but, none-

FIGURE 14–10, *cont'd*   Four portfolios for a risk-averse investor with varying expectations

Panel (c): Expects a High Positive Correlation Between Bond and Stock Returns   Panel (d): A Negative Correlation Between Bond and Stock Returns

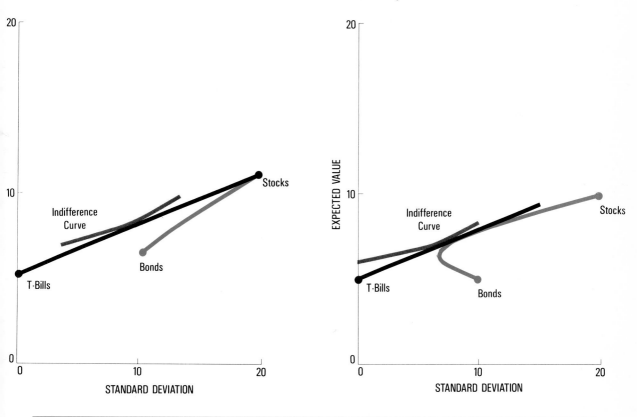

theless, the opportunity locus is such that a 100 percent investment in T-bills is selected.

In panel (b), the investor anticipates (but is not certain of) a decline in interest rates that will benefit bonds nearly as much as stocks. Both stocks and long-term bonds have high expected returns; but because of a high correlation coefficient, there is little curvature in the opportunity locus between bonds and stocks. Given that stocks have considerably more risk and not much higher expected return, this investor chooses to invest only in T-bills and long-term bonds.

In panel (c), bond and stock expected returns are more modest, because a decline in interest rates is not anticipated. There is little uncertainty about the economy, but considerable interest-rate risk, giving a very high correlation coefficient between bond and stock returns. The investor divides the portfolio between T-bills and stocks, excluding long-term bonds because these have a lower expected return than stocks and the high positive correlation with stocks limits their usefulness for diversification.

In panel (d), the correlation coefficient is negative because the investor believes that, as in the 1960s, there is a risk that the economy may either strengthen with interest rates rising or else collapse with interest rates falling. Long-term bonds are included in the portfolio along with stocks and T-bills, because, even though the expected return is no higher than that on safe T-bills, their sensitivity to interest rates makes them an attractive vehicle for diversification.

SUMMARY

The mean and standard deviation can be used to determine the risk and return opportunities available to investors and to help them choose an attractive asset portfolio. The portfolio mean and standard deviation depend on the means and standard deviations of the assets in the portfolio, the correlations among these asset returns, and the allocation of wealth among the assets. Diversification is particularly effective in reducing risk if the asset returns are uncorrelated or negatively correlated.

The Markowitz frontier shows the minimum standard deviation attainable for each possible expected return. If there is a safe asset, then Tobin's Separation Theorem states that there is an optimal portfolio on the Markowitz frontier that can be determined without regard to risk preferences. Those investors who are especially risk averse should put most of their wealth in the safe asset and relatively little in this risky bundle. Those who are less risk averse should invest larger amounts in the risky bundle.

Mean-variance analysis suggests that risk-adjusted performance can be measured by comparing the difference between a portfolio's average return and the return on safe Treasury bills to the standard deviation of the portfolio's return. By this criterion, most mutual funds underperform a market index, such as the Dow Jones Industrial Average or the S&P 500.

When mean-variance analysis is used to select a portfolio, historical data are typically used to estimate asset means, standard deviations, and correlation coefficients. The Markowitz frontier is determined and risk preferences are used to choose one of the portfolios on this frontier. If Tobin's Separation Theorem is invoked, one portfolio on the frontier is identified as optimal and, then, risk preferences determine the appropriate allocation between the optimal risky bundle and the safe asset. Portfolio managers need not rely solely on historical data. The means, standard deviations, and correlation coefficients should reflect their anticipation of the future, with mean-variance analysis used to select a portfolio consistent with their beliefs.

Calculation of the Correlation Coefficient

An asset's return is sometimes above and sometimes below its expected value. The returns from two assets are positively correlated if when one return is above its expected value, the other is likely to be above its expected value too (and when one is below, so is the other). The returns are negatively correlated if one asset return tends to be below its expected value when the other is above. Asset returns are uncorrelated if the chances of being above or below the expected value are unrelated to the other asset's return.

These general principles can be made more precise by the calculation of the statistical covariance:

$$\text{cov}(R_1, R_2) = \Sigma (R_1 - \mu_1)(R_2 - \mu_2) P[R_1, R_2]$$

The covariance is a weighted average of the product of each return's deviation from its mean, using the joint probability of this occurrence as a weight. If the two deviations are either both positive or both negative, then their product is positive; if this is the predominate case, the covariance is positive. If the deviations have opposite signs, the product is negative, leading to a negative covariance. If when one deviation is positive, the other is as likely to be negative as positive, the negative and positive products offset each other, and the covariance is zero.

The accompanying table shows the calculation of the covariance between the returns on Consolidated Natural Gas and U.S. Home, using the annual data in Table 14–3 and the means shown in Table 14–4. First, the products of the deviations about the means are calculated for each of the ten years.

Year	Product of Deviations	Frequency	Product
1970	$(23.0 - 14.0)(9.6 - 22.9) = -119.7$	0.1	-11.97
1971	$(7.1 - 14.0)(51.4 - 22.9) = -196.7$	0.1	-19.67
1972	$(7.3 - 14.0)(-17.2 - 22.9) = 268.7$	0.1	26.87
1973	$(-13.4 - 14.0)(-77.3 - 22.9) = 2745.4$	0.1	274.54
1974	$(-3.7 - 14.0)(-48.8 - 22.9) = 1269.1$	0.1	126.91
1975	$(25.1 - 14.0)(128.0 - 22.9) = 1166.6$	0.1	116.66
1976	$(59.3 - 14.0)(56.5 - 22.9) = 1522.1$	0.1	152.21
1977	$(29.0 - 14.0)(-8.8 - 22.9) = -475.5$	0.1	-47.55
1978	$(-8.3 - 14.0)(22.7 - 22.9) = 4.5$	0.1	0.45
1979	$(15.0 - 14.0)(113.1 - 22.9) = 90.2$	0.1	9.02
			627.47

The preponderance of positive products implies that these two returns are positively related. Next, the products are multiplied by the respective probabilities, here the frequency of these historical data. The summation gives the covariance, 627.47.

We cannot tell whether a covariance is large or small without reference to the standard deviations of the asset returns. This scaling can be accomplished by dividing the covariance by both standard deviations, giving the correlation coefficient:

$$\rho = \frac{\text{cov}(R_1, R_2)}{\sigma_1 \sigma_2}$$

The largest possible value for the correlation coefficient is $+1$; the smallest possible value is -1. For Consolidated Natural Gas and U.S. Home, the standard deviations shown in Table 14–4 give a correlation coefficient of

$$\rho = \frac{627.47}{(21.4)(65.9)} = 0.5.$$

EXERCISES

1. Which of the following portfolios would be chosen by someone who is risk-averse? Risk-neutral? Risk-seeking?
a. 10 percent guaranteed return.
b. 10 percent expected value and a 5 percent standard deviation.
c. 5 percent expected return and a 10 percent standard deviation.
2. You have inherited $100,000 and will invest part in a stock-market-index fund and the rest in Treasury bills. The safe return on T-bills is 5 percent; stocks have an expected return of 15 percent, and a standard deviation of 20 percent. What is your portfolio's expected return for each of the following alternatives?
a. Investing none of your money in stocks.
b. Investing all your money in stocks.
c. Investing half your money in stocks.

Sketch a graph showing your opportunity locus.

3. For the assets described in Exercise 2, how much do you have to invest in stocks to achieve a 10 percent expected return on your portfolio? If you borrow another $100,000 at 5 percent in order to invest $200,000 in stocks, what is your portfolio's expected return?

4. What is your answer to the second question in Exercise 3 if, not being as credit worthy as the U.S. Treasury, you must pay 10 percent when you borrow $100,000? What if you must pay 15 percent? Would any investor borrow at 15 percent to invest in stocks with a 15 percent expected return?

5. A friend with $100,000 to invest is considering the following assets: a savings account paying 10 percent interest; a mutual fund whose return has an expected value of 15 percent and a standard deviation of 15 percent; and borrowing up to $100,000 at a 20 percent interest rate, investing the proceeds in the mutual fund. Graph this investor's opportunity locus in a conventional mean/standard deviation graph. If your friend does borrow $100,000 and invests $200,000 in the mutual fund, what will her personal rate of return be if the return on the mutual fund turns out to be 10 percent? 20 percent? 30 percent?

6. You are considering two tax-exempt assets, one with a guaranteed 0 percent return and the other with a return that is equally likely to be +20 percent or −10 percent. Considering the available risk-return opportunities, you have decided to invest half your wealth in each asset.

a. What is the expected percentage return on the first asset?

b. What is the expected percentage return on the second asset?

c. What is the expected percentage return on your portfolio?

d. What is the first asset's standard deviation?

e. What is the second asset's standard deviation?

f. What is the portfolio's standard deviation?

7. A 50 percent tax has been levied on the investments described in Exercise 6. The first asset continues to yield a 0 percent after-tax return, while the second asset is equally likely to have an after-tax return of +10 percent or −5 percent. (The government gives a tax credit in the case of a loss.) Should you put more or less of your wealth in the risky asset? Use mean-variance analysis, and explain your reasoning carefully.

8. Consider two opportunities A and B. For every dollar you invest in A, you will either win $1 or lose $1, depending on the flip of a coin. For every dollar you invest in B, you either win $2 or lose $1, again depending on a coin flip. You have $100 and will invest a fraction a in A and $1 - a$ in B. Calculate and plot the means and standard deviations for your portfolio return using $a = 0.0, 0.25, 0.5, 0.75,$ and 1.0 in each of the following cases:

a. The coin flips are independent.

b. When you win one flip, you are sure to win the other.

c. When you win one flip, you are certain to lose the other.

9. Using annual data for 1972–80, a portfolio analyst estimated that Merrill Lynch stock has an expected return of 16 percent and a standard deviation of 50 percent, while General Mills stock has an expected return of 9 percent and a standard deviation of 30 percent. The correlation coefficient between the two returns is 0.33. Which return seems the less certain of the two? Which has the larger probability of a 70 percent gain? Since Merrill Lynch has the higher expected return, should we conclude that it is the better investment? Is there any rational explanation in an efficient market for one security having a higher expected return than another?

10. The analyst in Exercise 9 estimated that a portfolio invested 10 percent in Merrill Lynch and 90 percent in General Mills has a standard deviation of 29 percent. How can the portfolio's standard deviation possibly be less than the standard deviation of either stock in the portfolio? What is the expected return on this portfolio?

11. Use the information in Exercises 9 and 10 to calculate a few portfolio means and standard deviations; also, sketch the complete opportunity locus. If a safe asset offers a 10 percent return, what (approximately) is the optimal risky portfolio identified by Tobin's Separation Theorem? Why would anyone invest in a risky asset, such as General Mills, when it has a lower expected return than a safe asset?

12. A certified financial planner wrote:

> Allow me one of Cohen's Laws: It is far better to be very aggressive with your investments and hedge them by diversification than to be conservative and put all your eggs in one supposedly safe basket. You're going to do much better if you buy six or seven aggressive stocks than if you buy one conservative stock. How do you limit your risk? By buying different kinds of stocks, say a mix of electronics, drugs, retailing, computers.[5]

How can a basket of aggressive stocks be safer than a conservative stock? Why would you want to mix a variety of stocks? Isn't it better to find a very profitable investment and stick with it?

13. Write a brief newspaper column explaining why most stock returns are positively correlated with each other. Include one example of two stocks that logically might have negatively correlated returns.

14. In 1981 it was estimated that Continental Illinois Bank had $4 billion (more than 15% of its loan portfolio) in energy loans, mostly to independent oil and gas companies. The bank was confident that these energy loans would be profitable, the senior vice president responsible for oil and gas lending explaining that the recent drop in oil prices was "just a little blip."[6] Why, despite the fact that it consisted of a large

number of loans to independent producers, was this $4 billion loan portfolio not well-diversified?

15. An examination of the annual return on stocks and corporate bonds for the period 1926–78 yielded the following estimates:

	Annual Return (percent)	
	Stocks	Bonds
Average return	11.2	3.4
Standard deviation	22.2	5.7

Assuming these numbers to be the expected return and standard deviation for the coming year, what portfolio of stocks and safe T-bills paying 2.5 percent dominates corporate bonds (in the sense that, although it has the same standard deviation as corporate bonds, it has a higher expected return)? If so, why would any rational investor buy corporate bonds?

16. A computer program identified the following portfolios as being on the Markowitz frontier. Carefully explain why there must be an error in the program.

Portfolio	Expected Return (percent)	Standard Deviation (percent)
1	5	8
2	10	15
3	15	18

17. A mutual fund will divide its money among three groups of assets: T-bills paying 5 percent, a bundle of long-term bonds with an expected return of 8 percent and a standard deviation of 10 percent, and a bundle of stocks with an expected return of 15 percent and a standard deviation of 20 percent. What can you say about the ratio of long-term bonds to stocks that the fund should hold in its portfolio if there is no uncertainty about the economy and considerable uncertainty about interest rates, so that the correlation coefficient between stocks

TABLE 14–A

Mutual Fund	Average Return (percent)	Standard Deviation (percent)
A	10	10
B	15	15
C	20	20

and long-term bonds is 1.0? Would it make any difference if there was considerable uncertainty about the economy?

18. A mutual fund has been established that will invest in U.S. Treasury bills, a diversified basket of U.S. stocks, and a diversified basket of Asian stocks. The fund estimates that the basket of U.S. stocks has an expected return of 10 percent and a standard deviation of 20 percent, while the basket of Asian stocks has an expected return of 20 percent and a standard deviation of 30 percent. Carefully explain why the fund will avoid the U.S. stock market entirely if the two stock markets are perfectly correlated.

19. In fact, the correlation coefficient between the U.S. and Asian stocks discussed in Exercise 18 is 0.30. If the return on safe Treasury bills is 5 percent, Tobin's Separation Theorem implies that the optimal portfolio of risky assets is 35 percent in U.S. stocks and 65 percent in Asian stocks. If the fund has $1 billion, how should it divide its investment among Treasury bills, U.S. stocks, and Asian stocks if it wants a portfolio with an expected return of 15 percent and the lowest possible standard deviation?

20. A widow has all her money invested in Treasury bills paying 10 percent. A financial advisor is trying to persuade her to invest some of her money in one of the three diversified mutual funds shown in Table A. Which should she choose? Explain why her choice does not depend on her risk preferences.

21. You have $100,000 to invest in two assets. The return on Asset 1 has an expected value of 10 percent and a standard deviation of 10 percent, while the return on Asset 2 has an expected value of 20 percent and a standard deviation of 20 percent. The returns on these assets are perfectly negatively correlated. You can also borrow up to $50,000 at 15 percent interest. What is your safest strategy? What is your riskiest strategy? What are the expected returns and standard deviations for these two strategies?

22. Consider three assets, with rates of return R_1, R_2, and R_3. The return on the first asset is certain while the other two are risky with respective means μ_2 and μ_3 and standard deviations σ_2 and σ_3. The returns on the second and third assets are perfectly negatively correlated. How can one construct a portfolio involving the second and third assets that has zero variance? What is the expected return on this portfolio? In an efficient market, what is the relationship between the expected return on the safe asset and the expected return on this zero variance portfolio?

23. In his doctoral dissertation,[7] Shannon Pratt analyzed the following hypothetical situation. At the end of a month, five mutual funds are established with differing attitudes towards risk. The most cautious, Fund A, forms a portfolio consisting of the 20 percent of the New York Stock Exchange (NYSE) stocks which have had the smallest standard deviations in their returns over the preceding three years; Fund B takes the next 20 percent, and so on, down to the most speculative fund, E, which selects the 20 percent of the NYSE stocks which have had the highest standard deviations. Pratt re-

TABLE 14-B

Mutual Fund	Mean, μ (percent)	Standard Deviation, σ (percent)	Return-Variability Ratio, $\frac{(\mu - 3\%)}{\sigma}$
A	9.8	15	0.45
B	11.0	20	0.40
C	11.2	25	0.37
D	11.2	30	0.27
E	10.9	40	0.20

peated this experiment for every month from January 1929 through December 1957, and calculated the returns for each fund during the succeeding year. The mean, standard deviation, and return-variability ratio during these subsequent years are shown in Table B. Give a plausible explanation of why the mean and standard deviation seem to vary from one fund to the next. If the Treasury-bill rate was approximately 3 percent during the period covered in Pratt's research, how do you interpret his findings regarding the return-variability ratio?

24. During the years 1953–81, the correlation coefficient between the real rates of return on stocks (the S&P 500) and a portfolio of commodity futures contracts was −0.21.[8] The standard deviations were 19.48 percent and 17.36 percent, respectively. Sketch the Markowitz frontier using these values; assume a 7 percent expected real return on stocks and a 0 percent expected real return on commodity futures. Make a rough estimate of the minimum-risk portfolio.

25. A study of a portfolio of low-grade junk bonds and high-grade bonds calculated the following means and standard deviations of the monthly returns from January 1977 to December 1986:[9]

Type of Bond	Mean	Standard Deviation
Low grade	0.96	2.86
High grade	0.87	3.87

The low-grade bonds had a higher average return and, surprisingly, a lower standard deviation—perhaps because their high coupons reduce the duration and, hence, the sensitivity to interest-rate fluctuations, which were large during this period. The correlation coefficient between the monthly returns on low-grade and high-grade bonds was 0.77. Using these historical data, calculate the mean and standard deviation of portfolios with a fraction a in low-grade bonds and $1 - a$ in high-grade bonds for $a = 0$, 0.2, 0.4, 0.6, 0.8 and 1.0. Which of these portfolios is the safest (that is, has the lowest standard deviation)? Would anyone ever invest in a portfolio that was not the safest? Sketch the Markowitz frontier, and, assuming the monthly return on safe Treasury bills to be 0.73 percent with a standard deviation of zero, make a rough estimate of the optimal portfolio identified by Tobin's Separation Theorem.

C H A P T E R   1 5

Asset Pricing Models

*We humans are a race of optimists, however much we
protest the contrary. We distrust relationships, but we
fall in love; we are skeptical of institutions, but we get
married; we find the world deteriorating, but we bring
forth children; we regard ourselves as innately unlucky,
but we purchase common stocks . . .*

Louis Rukeyser

Portfolio theory teaches us that risk can be reduced by choosing a portfolio
of imperfectly correlated securities. This lesson has implications for the
pricing of assets. If the market is dominated by risk-averse investors who
hold diversified portfolios, which securities are really risky and which are
safe? The riskiness of an asset that is part of a portfolio depends on how
correlated its return is with other assets in the portfolio. An asset that
invariably does poorly when other assets do poorly is risky, because it
offers no diversification potential. An asset that is independent of other
assets or, even better, does well when others do poorly, reduces portfolio
risk. Thus, the proper gauge of risk for portfolio managers is some measure
of how an asset's return is correlated with the returns on other assets.

In this chapter, we will examine two models that have been developed
to make these general principles more specific. The first, the Capital Asset
Pricing Model, focuses on the correlation between each asset and the overall
market bundle of assets. The second, Arbitrage Pricing Theory, looks at
how asset returns are affected by underlying factors, such as interest rates
and the unemployment rate. We begin with the single-index model, which
aids our understanding of both the Capital Asset Pricing Model and Arbitrage Pricing Theory.

THE SINGLE-INDEX MODEL

First developed by William Sharpe and John Lintner,[1] the Capital Asset Pricing Model is a brilliant extension of mean-variance analysis, with some complicated mathematics leading to a strikingly simple asset pricing equation. The logic is most easily understood by considering the single-index model, which was also developed by William Sharpe.

single-index model
The single-index model assumes that an asset's return depends on the market return and idiosyncratic factors.

The **single-index model** assumes that there is a linear relationship between an asset's percentage return, R_i, and the overall market return on all assets, R_M:

$$R_i = \alpha_i + B_i R_M + \epsilon_i \qquad (1)$$

Figure 15–1 graphs this relationship. The parameter α_i (alpha) is the intercept of the line $R_i = \alpha_i + B_i R_M$. The parameter β_i, the **beta coefficient,** measures the extent to which the return on a particular asset moves with the return on all assets. If the market return increases by 10 percent, the return on this asset tends to increase by more or less than 10 percent, depending on whether its beta coefficient is larger or smaller than 1.

The error term ϵ_i (epsilon) is a random variable, reflecting the fact that, no matter what happens to the market, the return on a particular asset may be pushed up or down by unexpected events, such as technological breakthroughs, the loss of key executives, favorable tax changes, or legal setbacks. The i subscripts indicate that alpha, beta, and the error term vary from asset to asset. The error terms are assumed to be independent of the market return and of each other.

Systematic and Unsystematic Risk

Equation 1 is intended to reflect the fact that all assets are affected by the economy, interest rates and other macroeconomic factors, though in varying degrees, and that each asset return is also affected by idiosyncratic events that affect a particular asset. The variance of R_i can be separated into the following two components:

systematic risk
An asset's systematic risk concerns macroeconomic events that affect all securities and cannot be diversified away.

$$\text{var}[R_i] = \beta_i^2 \, \text{var}[R_M] + \text{var}[\epsilon_i]$$
$$\text{total risk} = \text{macro risk} + \text{micro risk}$$

The **macro risk**, or **systematic risk** (also called market risk and nondiversifiable risk), encompasses macroeconomic events such as unanticipated changes in interest rates, inflation, and the unemployment rate that affect all securities. With macro risk, there is no safety in numbers, in that mere diversification cannot protect investors from recession or high interest rates. The **micro risk**, or **unsystematic risk** (also called idiosyncratic risk and diversifiable risk), arises from events specific to individual companies and can be diversified away by an investor.

unsystematic risk
Unsystematic risk arises from events specific to individual companies and can be diversified away.

FIGURE 15-1   The single-index model

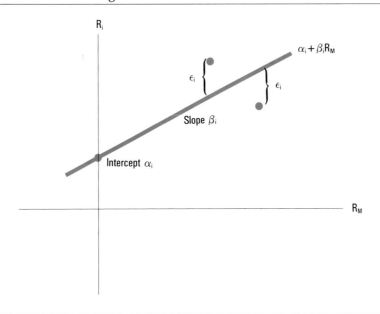

To see this, consider a portfolio of n assets with a fraction a_i of wealth invested in asset i. The overall return on the portfolio is

$$R = a_1 R_1 + a_2 R_2 + \ldots + a_n R_n$$
$$= (a_1 \alpha_1 + \ldots + a_n \alpha_n) + (a_1 \beta_1 + \ldots + a_n \beta_n) R_M$$
$$+ (a_1 \epsilon_1 + \ldots + a_n \epsilon_n)$$
$$= \alpha + \beta R_M + \epsilon.$$

The portfolio intercept α and slope β are weighted averages of the intercepts and slopes of the assets in the portfolio. The portfolio error term ϵ is a weighted average of the underlying error terms. However, to the extent that these individual errors are independent, their weighted sum will almost certainly be close to zero!

Intuitively, we can visualize each ϵ_i as the flip of a coin—heads a pleasant surprise and tails an unpleasant one. With a large number of flips, the average outcome should be close to zero—no surprise at all. In a large, reasonably diversified portfolio, the value of the portfolio ϵ is virtually certain to be small, and its variance is approximately zero too. Thus micro risk can be diversified away, leaving only macro risk,

$$\text{var}[R_i] = \beta_i^2 \, \text{var}[R_M].$$
$$\text{Total risk} = \text{Macro risk}$$

TABLE 15–1 Annual Returns on the Stock Market, Four Stocks, and a
Portfolio Composed of Those Stocks, 1972–1980

			Annual Return (percent)			
Year	Market	Merrill Lynch	AT&T	IBM	General Mills	Portfolio
1972	18.98	−8.0	23.9	21.1	57.4	23.6
1973	−14.66	−55.0	0.5	−21.9	−13.0	−22.5
1974	−26.47	−12.8	−4.5	−29.7	−24.4	−17.9
1975	37.20	37.2	21.6	37.4	50.4	36.7
1976	23.84	79.7	32.3	28.1	17.3	39.4
1977	−7.18	−36.7	1.9	1.3	−9.3	−10.7
1978	6.56	7.5	7.6	13.6	0.7	7.4
1979	18.44	31.2	−5.6	−9.1	−11.8	4.7
1980	32.42	98.3	1.4	10.8	13.1	30.9

The return on a diversified portfolio depends on the portfolio's alpha and beta and on how well the market does. The critical uncertainty is macro risk, what will happen to the overall market (the value of R_M). A portfolio manager cannot do anything about R_M, but can do something about the portfolio's beta, which is what determines how sensitive the portfolio is to market fluctuations. A portfolio with a beta of 1.0 is about as risky as the overall market, in that if the market return turns out to be 10 percent higher or 10 percent lower than expected, then this portfolio should do about 10 percent better or 10 percent worse than expected. A portfolio with a beta larger than 1.0, in contrast, is aggressive, with above-average risk; when the market swings ten percentage points, a portfolio with a beta of 2.0 can be expected to swing twenty percentage points. Finally, a portfolio with a beta less than 1.0 is conservative; when the market fluctuates up or down 10 percent, a portfolio with a beta of 0.5 can be expected to fluctuate by only 5 percent.

Thus, for portfolio managers, beta is the appropriate measure of risk. High-beta securities are risky, because they give high-beta portfolios; low-beta securities are safer, because they create low-beta portfolios. It is not surprising, then, that portfolio managers routinely calculate the betas of their portfolios and also examine the betas of individual securities that they consider including in their portfolios.

Estimated Betas

Table 15–1 shows nine years of annual returns (dividends plus capital gains) on the stock market as measured by the S&P 500, on four individual stocks, and on a portfolio containing equal proportions of these four stocks. Figure

FIGURE 15–2 The returns on Merrill Lynch and the market

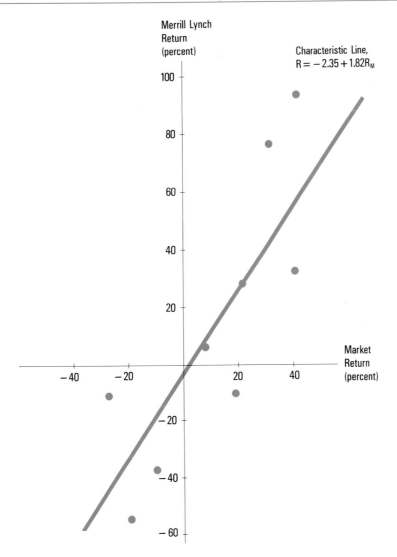

15–2 shows a scatter diagram of the returns on Merrill Lynch and on the overall market, with a line, called the **characteristic line**, fitted to these points. The fit is not done by hand, but by a computer regression program.[2] Here, the equation for the fitted line is

$$R = -2.26 + 1.82 R_M \quad R^2 = 0.61$$

characteristic line
A characteristic line is fit to a scatter diagram of the returns on a security and the returns on the market as a whole.

FIGURE 15–3 A large beta does not imply a high R^2

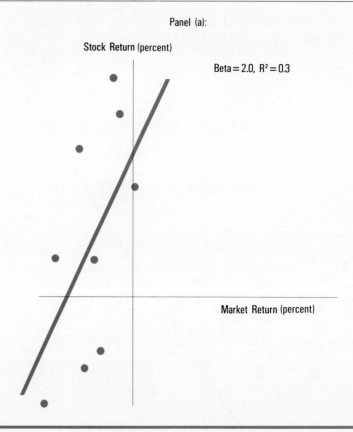

The statistic R^2, **R-squared**, measures the fraction of the variance in the return on a stock (in this case, Merrill Lynch) that can be explained by fluctuations in the overall market. If $R^2 = 1$, there is a perfect fit with all the points lying on a straight line; if $R^2 = 0$, the scatter is random, and the market is of no help in explaining the behavior of Merrill Lynch stock. Here, 61 percent of the variance can be explained by the market, and 39 percent must be attributed to other factors, the omitted influences that comprise the error term ϵ.

It is important that you not confuse beta, the slope of the line, with R^2, the goodness of fit. Figure 15–3 shows that a stock can have a large beta and a small R^2 (a steep slope and a loose fit) or, vice versa, a small beta and a large R^2 (a flat slope and a good fit).

Merrill Lynch, the nation's largest brokerage firm, has a stock that is very sensitive to the overall stock market because, first, it owns a leveraged

FIGURE 15–3, *cont'd*   A large beta does not imply a high R^2

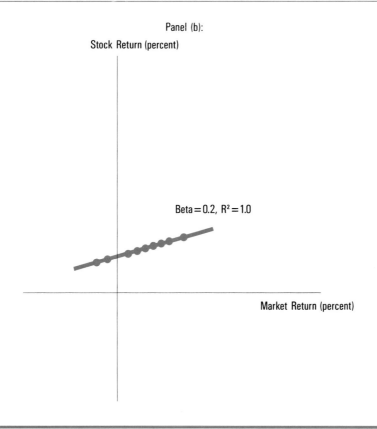

Panel (b):

Stock Return (percent)

Beta = 0.2, R^2 = 1.0

Market Return (percent)

portfolio of securities and, second, customers generally trade more when the market is doing well and sit on the sidelines when it is doing poorly. The 1.82 beta coefficient indicates that, on average, the price of Merrill Lynch stock tends to go up and down almost twice as fast as the market as a whole. This relationship is far from perfect, though. Both the scatter of points in Figure 15–2 and the 0.61 R^2 tell us that, even if we know in advance what is going to happen to the overall stock market, we still do not know for sure how well Merrill Lynch stock will do.

American Telephone (AT&T) was a tightly regulated utility during this period and its profits depended more on the generosity of regulatory commissions than on the overall economy. Figure 15–4 shows the scatter diagram and the fitted line

$$R = 5.34 + 0.35\, R_M \quad R^2 = 0.31$$

FIGURE 15-4   Returns on AT&T and the market

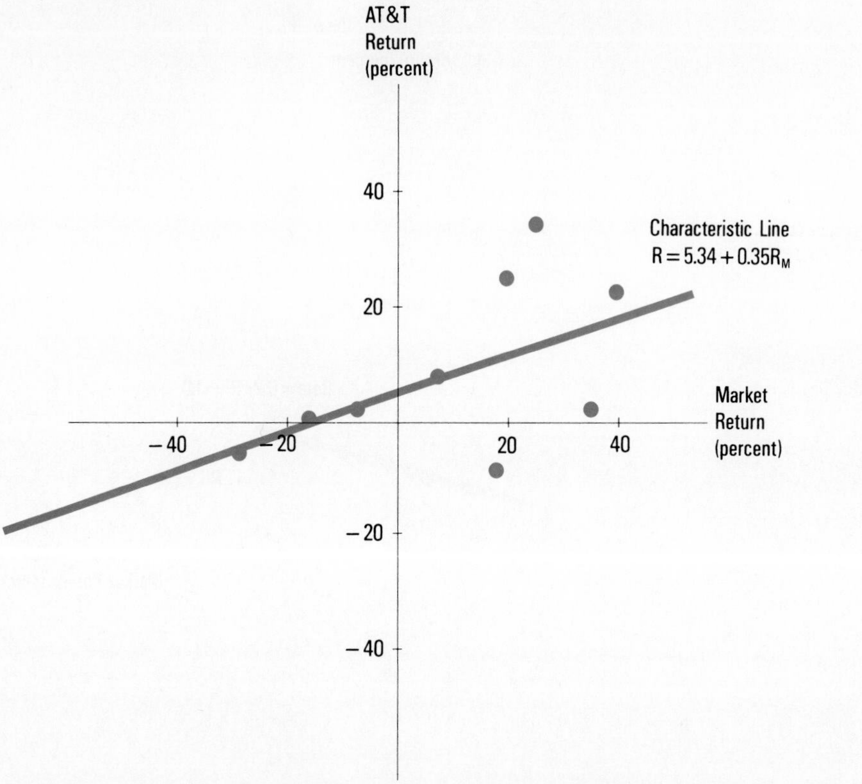

The 0.35 beta coefficient indicates that, on average, AT&T's stock moved only 3.5 percent for every 10 percent move in the market. The 0.31 R^2 shows that most of the fluctuation in AT&T's return cannot be explained by the overall movement of the stock market.

While Merrill Lynch has an unusually high beta and AT&T a low one, IBM and General Mills are more typical companies, with beta values near 1.0, indicating that their stocks tend to go up or down about as fast as the market as a whole. For IBM, the equation for this characteristic line is

$$R = -2.84 + 0.87 \, R_M \quad R^2 = 0.70$$

For General Mills,

$$R = -0.62 + 0.96 \, R_M \quad R^2 = 0.54$$

FIGURE 15–5 A four-stock portfolio

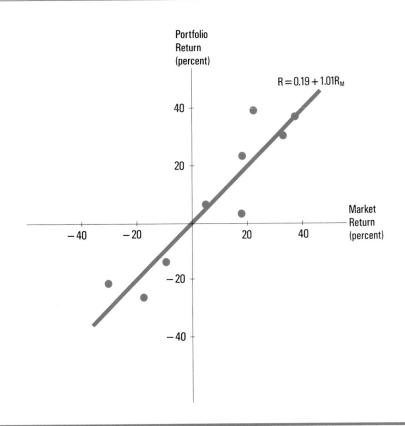

Portfolio Betas

Now consider a portfolio consisting of an equal investment in each of the four stocks. A well-diversified portfolio should have at least twenty or thirty carefully selected securities, but this simple four-stock portfolio illustrates the effects of diversification. The year-by-year portfolio returns are in Table 15–1, and a scatter diagram is shown in Figure 15–5. The fitted line is

$$R = 0.19 + 1.01\ R_M \quad R^2 = 0.87$$

The portfolio's beta is an average of the betas of the securities in the portfolio

$$\beta = a_1\beta_1 + a_2\beta_2 + a_3\beta_3 + a_4\beta_4$$

Here, the portfolio beta happens to be almost exactly 1.0:

$$\beta = 0.25(1.82) + 0.25(0.35) + 0.25(0.87) + 0.25(0.96)$$
$$= 1.01$$

The R^2 for the portfolio is 0.87, higher than any individual stock's R^2. For any given overall movement of the market, the return on the portfolio is more certain than is the return on any of the stocks in the portfolio. This is why betas are important to portfolio managers. While the R^2 for an individual stock is typically in the range 0.30–0.50, a portfolio's R^2 usually exceeds 0.9 after the inclusion of a dozen or so dissimilar securities and approaches 1.0 as the portfolio becomes as diversified as the market itself.

Choosing a Portfolio Beta

A portfolio's beta can be pulled above 1 by including more Merrill Lynch and pulled below 1 by more AT&T. For example, a portfolio that is invested 40 percent in Merrill Lynch and 20 percent in each of the other three securities has a beta of

$$\beta = 0.40(1.82) + 0.20(0.35) + 0.20(0.87) + 0.20(0.96)$$
$$= 1.16,$$

while a portfolio that is 70 percent in AT&T and 10 percent in the other three stocks has a beta of

$$\beta = 0.10(1.82) + 0.70(0.35) + 0.10(0.87) + 0.10(0.96)$$
$$= 0.61.$$

Another way to reduce a portfolio's beta is to invest in a risk-free asset, which has a beta of 0. If a portfolio of risky assets has a beta of 1, then a portfolio that is invested 40 percent in safe Treasury bills and 60 percent in the bundle of risky assets has a beta of 0.6:

$$B = 0.40(0.0) + 0.6(1.0)$$
$$= 0.60$$

Conversely, a portfolio's beta can be increased by leveraging, borrowing money at a fixed rate of interest and investing the proceeds in a bundle of risky assets. Suppose that you have $100,000 in net worth and borrow $50,000, enabling you to invest $150,000 (1.5 times your net worth) in a bundle of stocks with a beta of 1. The fraction invested in the safe asset is -0.50 (since you have borrowed an amount equal to 50 percent of your net worth), and the fraction invested in the bundle of risky assets is 1.5, pushing the beta for your portfolio upward:

$$\beta = 1.50(1.0) + (-0.5)(0.0)$$
$$= 1.50$$

THE CAPITAL-ASSET PRICING MODEL

If beta is the appropriate measure of an asset's contribution to the riskiness of a portfolio, then risk-averse investors will not hold high-beta securities unless the expected returns are high too. The implications of this insight can be made very precise by assuming that investors follow the mean-variance practices described in Chapter 14, and that they all agree about the means, variances, and correlations of asset returns. If so, then it can be shown (a proof is sketched in the appendix to this chapter) that risk premiums have the following very simple structure:

$$E_i - R_0 = \beta_i(E_M - R_0) \qquad (2)$$

where E_i is the expected return on an individual asset, E_M is the expected return on the market as a whole, and R_0 is the return on a risk-free asset.

Although Equation 2 is phrased in terms of an asset's expected return, we know from earlier chapters that it is asset prices that adjust so that the anticipated cash flow gives investors their requisite return. Thus, Equation 2 is really a statement about asset prices and this model is called the **Capital Asset Pricing Model (CAPM).**

> **The Capital Asset Pricing Model states that investors who choose portfolios on the basis of the mean and variance, and agree on the opportunities, price assets so that the expected returns conform to Equation 2.**

Capital Asset Pricing Model (CAPM)
The Capital Asset Pricing Model (CAPM) says that an asset's risk premium depends on its beta coefficient.

Beta, Again

The beta in Equation 2 is the very same beta as in the single-index model, though CAPM makes assumptions about investor preferences, and the single-index model makes assumptions about the error term ϵ. The formal definition of beta in CAPM is the ratio of the covariance between the asset's return and the market return divided by the variance of the market return:

$$\beta_i = \frac{\text{cov}[R_i, R_M]}{\text{var}[R_M]} \qquad (3)$$

This equation is the statistical definition of beta in the single-index model and, empirically, is the formula used to estimate beta by fitting a characteristic line to a scatter diagram. Thus we can interpret beta in Equation 2 as the slope of a characteristic line.

FIGURE 15-6 The security market line

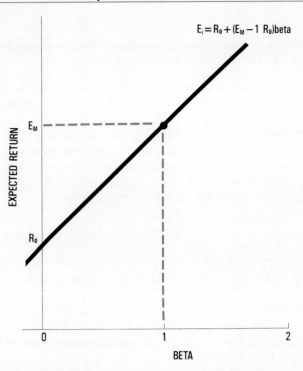

$$E_i = R_0 + (E_M - 1\ R_0)\text{beta}$$

The Structure of Risk Premiums According to Equation 2, the risk premium on an asset is proportional to the risk premium on the market as a whole, with the asset's beta coefficient the proportionality factor. This relationship, sometimes called the **security market line,** is graphed in Figure 15–6 and gives the structure to expected returns that is shown in Table 15–2. Beta is the explanatory variable that determines the appropriate risk premium.

security market line
The security market line shows that an asset's expected return is linearly related to its beta coefficient.

Notice, particularly, that a zero-beta security, which might be very risky in isolation, adds nothing to portfolio risk because all its risk is unique, nonmarket risk that can be diversified away; consequently it requires no risk premium. A negative-beta asset, which reduces portfolio risk because it tends to do well when other investments do poorly, will be held by risk-averse investors even if the expected return is less than the return on a completely safe security. (In practice, very few stocks have negative betas; one study estimated beta coefficients for 4357 stocks and found that only 7 had negative betas.[3])

TABLE 15–2 The Relationship Between an Asset's Beta and Its Expected Return

Type of Asset	Beta Coefficient	Expected Return
Aggressive	$\beta_i > 1$	$E_i > E_M$
Typical	$\beta_i = 1$	$E_i = E_M$
Defensive	$0 < \beta_i < 1$	$R_0 < E_i < E_M$
Uncorrelated	$\beta_i = 0$	$E_i = R_0$
Hedge	$\beta_i < 0$	$E_i < R_0$

Using Betas to Value Securities Earlier chapters emphasized the principle that the required rate of return that is used to discount cash flows should take into account the riskiness of the cash flow, but were vague about the size of the appropriate risk premium. CAPM gives a very specific answer: the risk premium depends on an asset's beta coefficient. If, for example, an investor is calculating the present value of Merrill Lynch stock, the required rate of return used to discount the prospective dividends can use Equation 2 together with an estimate of Merrill Lynch's beta coefficient, the rate of return on the safe asset, and a risk premium for the market as a whole. If safe Treasury bills yield 8 percent, Merrill Lynch's beta is 1.82, and we will settle for a 5 percent risk premium for the market, then Merrill Lynch's required return is as follows:

$$
\begin{aligned}
E_i &= R_0 + \beta_i(E_M - R_0) \\
&= 8\% + 1.82(5\%) \\
&= 17.1\%
\end{aligned}
$$

For AT&T, with a 0.35 beta, the required return is

$$
\begin{aligned}
E_i &= R_0 + \beta_i(E_M - R_0) \\
&= 8\% + 0.35(5\%) \\
&= 9.75\%
\end{aligned}
$$

These required returns determine the prices investors are willing to pay for securities and, hence, market prices. This is why CAPM is called a pricing model, even though Equation 2 is stated in terms of rates of return.

Another application of this equation is in corporate finance, with firms advised to use Equation 2 to estimate their shareholders' required rate of return and, then, as explained in Chapter 8, to use this required return to value investment projects.

TABLE 15–3   Beta Characteristics, April 1986

Beta Range of Stock Group	Number of Stocks in Group	Market-value Weighted Average Beta	Group's Percentage of the S&P 500	Group's Average Dividend Yield (percent)	Group's Projected 1986 Earnings Growth (percent)
0.49 to 0.84	100	0.75	31.3	4.6	7
0.84 to 1.02	100	0.95	24.7	3.9	9
1.02 to 1.13	101	1.07	16.6	2.8	19
1.13 to 1.29	100	1.20	14.4	2.3	40
1.29 to 2.53	99	1.46	13.1	2.2	56

The Distribution of Betas

Merrill Lynch routinely tracks the characteristics of the stocks in the S&P 500. Table 15–3 displays some of their 1986 data, with stocks divided into five groups of approximately 100 each based on the beta coefficients. Figure 15–7 shows the distribution of beta coefficients. More than 60% of the stocks have betas above one. However, the low-beta companies tend to be somewhat larger than high-beta companies: the aggregate market value of the 200 lowest-beta stocks is 56 percent of the total market value of the S&P 500. In a portfolio, stocks are weighted by market value, and when the S&P 500 stocks are weighted by market value, the average beta is 1.

Table 15–3 also shows that high-beta stocks tend to have low dividend yields and high projected earnings growth. These data are consistent with our observations in Chapters 7 and 8 that high-growth stocks are priced to have relatively low dividend yields, and that the prices of growth stocks are very sensitive to interest rates and to the economy. We can characterize the typical high-beta stock as a relatively small company, with rapid earnings growth and a relatively small dividend yield. Low-beta stocks tend to be larger, with modest earnings growth and substantial dividend yields.

The Effect of Corporate Leverage on Beta

Beyond these general characteristics, specific beta values for stocks depend on the nature of a company's business and its leverage. Companies in stock brokerage, construction, transportation, and electronics tend to have high betas, while companies in the food processing, household products, and utilities industries have low betas. Leverage increases any company's beta. Think of a corporation as a portfolio of assets. Just as an individual investor who borrows money to acquire risky assets increases the portfolio's beta,

FIGURE 15-7   Distribution of betas in S&P 500

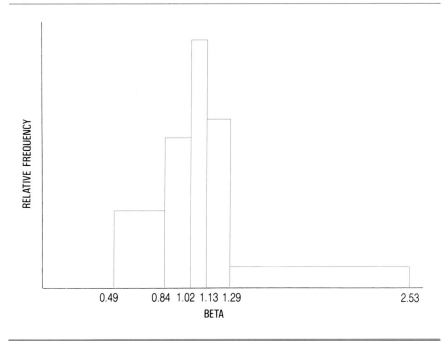

so does a corporation. A company with assets twice the size of its net worth has 2/1 leverage. Its simplified balance sheets might look like this:

Assets		Liabilities	
		Debt	$ 50
Plant and equipment	$100	Shareholders' equity	$ 50
Total assets	**$100**	**Total liabilities**	**$100**

A firm's beta is an average of its asset betas, weighted by the fraction of the company's net worth in these assets. As with an individual investor who has $50,000 and borrows $50,000 in order to buy $100,000 in assets, a firm that has $50 million in net worth and borrows another $50 million to buy $100 million in assets has a fraction 2.0 of net worth invested in risky assets offset by a fraction -1.0 in debt. The firm's beta is

$$\beta = (2.0)\beta_A + (-1.0)(0)$$
$$= 2\beta_A$$

where β_A is the beta of its assets and its debt has a beta of zero. If the firm's assets have a beta of 1.0, then the firm's stock has a beta of 2.0.

INVESTMENT EXAMPLE
15–1

DOES CORPORATE DIVERSIFICATION PAY?

It is sometimes argued that corporations should reduce risk by acquiring businesses in a variety of dissimilar industries. An oil refiner should buy almond groves and banks; a tobacco company should produce personal computers and soup. Best of all is a conglomerate, a smorgasbord of unrelated businesses, acquired not to improve their operations, but just for the sake of diversity.

If we think of a corporation as managing a portfolio of assets, it is clear that risk can be reduced through diversification. A firm can diversify away unsystematic risk, leaving such macro risks as a recession and high interest rates. However, from the investors' perspective, such corporate diversification is of no real advantage to shareholders since they, too, can diversify their portfolios by purchasing stock in a variety of companies. Investors can buy stock in oil companies, almond growers, and banks. Other than possible savings in brokerage fees, there is no inherent advantage to buying stock in a single firm that holds a diversified portfolio of assets over buying stock in the individual assets themselves. If anything, the merger of several companies into one limits shareholder flexibility in choosing an optimal portfolio of assets.

In general, 2/1 leverage doubles beta; 3/1 leverage triples it; and so on, as shown by the following:

$$\text{stock beta} = (\text{leverage})(\text{asset beta}) \tag{4}$$

Corporate leverage is not inherently bad, as investors can always undo the leverage by including appropriate amounts of a safe asset in their portfolios. If a firm owning assets with a beta of 1.0 uses 2/1 leverage to raise the beta of its stock to 2.0, the investor who prefers a 1.0 beta can simply combine this stock with an equal amount of a safe asset:

$$\beta = (0.5)2.0 + (0.5)0 = 1.0$$

Just as corporate leverage is not inherently bad, corporate diversification is not inherently good, as explained by Investment Example 15–1.

Beta Stability

Companies evolve over time and their betas can change as the nature of their business changes. Also, our statistical estimates of beta coefficients can be misled by chance events. If, for example, an otherwise typical com-

TABLE 15–4   The Stability of Portfolio Betas

Number of Stocks in Portfolio	Correlation of Portfolio Betas
1	0.62
2	0.74
4	0.83
10	0.91
20	0.96
50	0.98

Source: Marshall Blume, "On the Assessment of Risk," *Journal of Finance*, March 1971, pp. 1–10.

pany happens to introduce a new product that boosts its profits dramatically during a time when, coincidentally, the economy is slowing and overall corporate profits are declining, the company might appear to have a negative beta. Estimates in other time periods, without such fortuitous timing, will give a beta closer to 1. A key question is whether beta estimates are often revised significantly as time passes.

In one study, the years 1926–68 were divided into six seven-year periods and beta coefficients were estimated during each of these periods to see if the estimates changed much from period to period. Portfolios of different sizes were randomly selected and the portfolio beta coefficients calculated in each of two adjacent seven-year periods. The average correlation coefficients between periods are shown in Table 15–4. While the beta coefficients for individual stocks may be revised substantially as time passes, the betas for portfolios are fairly stable in that high-beta portfolios continue to have high betas and low-beta portfolios continue to have low betas. This finding is comforting because betas are only appropriate for measuring risk if an investor has a large, diversified portfolio.

Adjusted Betas   In another set of calculations, the years 1927–60 were divided into four eight-year periods, and beta coefficients were estimated during each of these periods. At the end of each eight-year period, five hypothetical portfolios were formed by grouping stocks according to their beta coefficients; the portfolio beta in the subsequent eight-year period was then compared with the beta when the portfolio was chosen. The results, averaged over all periods, are in Table 15–5.

Again, the high-beta portfolios continue to have high betas, and the low-beta portfolios have low betas. There is also evidence in these results of regression toward the mean, in that betas below 1 tend to be revised upward while betas above 1 are revised downward. The statistical regression-toward-the-mean explanation is that a security with an estimated beta

TABLE 15–5   Revision of Portfolio Betas After Eight Years

Group	Portfolio β When Formed	Portfolio β During Next Eight Years
1	0.43	0.53
2	0.71	0.80
3	0.93	1.01
4	1.16	1.14
5	1.54	1.43

Source: Marshall Blume, "On the Assessment of Risk," *Journal of Finance,* March 1971, pp. 1–10.

of 1.5 is more likely to be a 1.4-beta security with an unusually high estimate than a 1.6-beta security with an unusually low estimate simply because there are so many more of the former.

Persuaded by such evidence, Merrill Lynch and many other firms routinely adjust their beta estimates for this regression-toward-the-mean phenomena by raising low betas slightly and reducing high betas. Some analysts also make subjective adjustments of beta estimates based on their knowledge of a company and of recent events. If unusual incidents give a stock an estimated beta that is much higher than the betas of other companies in the same industry and with similar leverage, then this estimated beta is adjusted downward.

Betting with Portfolio Betas

A portfolio's beta is a convenient and useful way of gauging its aggressiveness. A portfolio with a high beta can be expected to do well if the market rises rapidly, but to do poorly if the market declines. A portfolio with a low beta is more protected from a market collapse, but can expect only modest gains if the market soars. Betas can thus be used to measure the amount of risk that a portfolio manager is willing to tolerate. Many institutions specify an overall target portfolio beta, which must be maintained by those who select the individual securities in the portfolio. If the fund has a target beta of 0.8, then any securities with betas above 0.8 must be balanced by securities with lower betas.

Beta also can be used by market timers who wish to bet on the direction of the market. Someone who believes that the market is likely to rise can act on this belief by increasing the portfolio's beta—by shifting funds from low-beta securities to high-beta ones, by holding less of the safe asset and more of risky ones, or by borrowing money to leverage the portfolio. Someone who fears a market decline can shift to low-beta stocks, can hold

THE VALUE LINE CONTEST

Value Line, a large investment-advisory service, occasionally runs a well-publicized nationwide investment contest. In the 1972 contest, each entrant picked a hypothetical portfolio of twenty-five stocks. After six months, those entrants with the best-performing portfolios won prizes, while the losers were encouraged to subscribe to Value Line.

Two finance professors decided to collaborate on their entries. One picked the twenty-five stocks with the highest betas, and the other selected the twenty-five stocks with the lowest betas (some negative, many near 0)—reasoning that the first portfolio would do well if the market went up and the second would do well if the market went down.

As it turned out, the stock market declined, and their low-beta portfolio was among the top 2.3 percent of the entries, while the high-beta portfolio was among the bottom 0.6 percent. (The winning entry was a very nondiversified portfolio of twenty-five oil stocks that profited from OPEC's oil embargo.) For its 1985 contest, Value Line changed the rules, using beta coefficients to separate the 1650 eligible stocks into ten categories, each containing 165 stocks, and asked contestants to select a portfolio of 10 stocks, one from each category. By forcing contestants to choose some stocks with high betas and some with low betas, Value Line ensured that all portfolios would have betas near 1, so that the contest would reflect stock selection and not just a bet on the direction of the market.

more Treasury bills, or can borrow less by selling stocks and using the proceeds to repay loans. Investment Example 15–2 tells how two finance professors used these principles to place opposite bets in a stock-market contest.

Risk-Adjusted Performance

According to the Capital Asset Pricing Model, risk-averse investors will not hold assets with high beta coefficients and substantial nondiversifiable risk unless they are compensated with large risk premia. The specific formula is given by Equation 2, repeated here:

$$E_i = R_0 + \beta_i(E_M - R_0)$$

Thus, one way that a portfolio manager can expect to earn above-average returns is to bear above-average systematic risk, by holding a high-beta portfolio.

In Chapter 14, we looked at one risk-adjusted measure of performance, using the portfolio's standard deviation to measure its riskiness. This measure is appropriate if the investor only holds the safe asset and the risky portfolio—which may be true of some mutual-fund investors. However, if the mutual fund is but one of many assets in the investor's portfolio, then the appropriate benchmark is whether the fund's average return exceeds the return E_i that might be expected, given the beta coefficient of its portfolio. (Graphically, the question is whether its average return is above or below the security market line.)

Suppose that over a certain five-year period, a mutual fund has had an average return of 12 percent, while the S&P 500 has averaged only 10 percent. Before concluding that this fund has beaten the market, we should consider the risks it has taken, as measured by its beta coefficient. If its beta is 1.5 and the annual return on Treasury bills is 5 percent, then CAPM implies an expected return of

$$
\begin{aligned}
E_i &= R_0 + \beta_i(E_M - R_0) \\
&= 5\% + 1.5(10\% - 5\%) \\
&= 12.5\%,
\end{aligned}
$$

so that this fund's 12 percent return is actually slightly lower than might be expected, given its riskiness. In Chapter 18, you will see that, by this criterion, most mutual funds do not beat the market.

Is Risk Rewarded? Empirical research has generally been consistent with CAPM's conclusion that because beta is the appropriate measure of risk for diversified portfolios, high-beta stocks are priced to have relatively high expected returns. One influential study divided the years 1931–65 into seven five-year periods; then it used monthly data in each five-year period to estimate beta coefficients and to put stocks into ten groups, ranging from the stocks with the highest beta coefficients to those with the lowest.[4] The researchers calculated the average return on each group of stocks over each subsequent five-year period, thereby tracking the performance of ten hypothetical mutual funds that periodically adjust their portfolios to maintain a level of risk consistent with their preferences. According to CAPM, beta is the appropriate measure of risk, and funds that hold high-beta portfolios should, on average, do better than funds holding low-beta portfolios. Figure 15–8 shows that this was indeed the case.

Another study of actual mutual-fund performance over the period 1960–68 divided 136 funds into three risk classes, depending on their beta coefficients. Table 15–6 shows that the high-beta funds did, in fact, do better on average than low-beta funds.

TABLE 15–6   Mutual-Fund Betas and Returns

Beta Range of Mutual-Fund Group	Group's Average Beta	Group's Average Return (percent)
0.9 to 1.1	0.99	13.5
0.7 to 0.9	0.79	10.6
0.5 to 0.7	0.61	9.1

Source: Irwin Friend, Marshall Blume, and J. Crockett, *Mutual Funds and Other Institutional Investors: A New Perspective* (New York: McGraw-Hill, 1970), p. 150.

FIGURE 15–8   Empirical betas and average returns

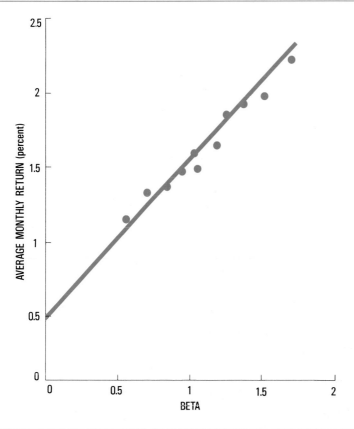

ARBITRAGE PRICING THEORY

CAPM is appealing because it expresses some subtle, yet plausible, ideas in a very simple manner. But, in some ways, the model is too simple. Think of the two primary macroeconomic influences on the stock market: output and interest rates. A booming economy is good for the stock market, and so are low interest rates. Some stocks, such as automobiles and other cyclicals, are very sensitive to the economy, while other stocks, such as savings and loan associations, are more sensitive to interest rates. When the overall stock market rises, do S&Ls go up a lot or a little; that is, how large is their beta coefficient? If the market is booming because of falling interest rates, S&Ls have a high beta coefficient. If the market is being propelled by a strong economy, their beta coefficient is small. It is even possible that if, as in the 1960s, output and interest rates increase together, the overall stock market may rise while S&Ls fall, giving a negative beta coefficient!

This is a specific example of the more general point that there are a variety of reasons for stock market fluctuations, and the correlation of a particular stock with the market (its beta coefficient) may depend on the cause of the market movement. A single beta coefficient cannot capture this variety. Instead, we need a beta coefficient for output, another for interest rates, and possibly more for other macroeconomic events.

Multiple-Factor Models

The single-index model,

$$R = \alpha + \beta R_M + \epsilon,$$

multiple-factor model
The multiple-factor model relates the return on an asset to several explanatory factors, such as output, interest rates, and inflation.

can be extended to include several explanatory factors, thereby becoming a **multiple-factor model.** The general principle can be illustrated with just two factors, F_1 and F_2,

$$R = \alpha + \beta_1 F_1 + \beta_2 F_2 + \epsilon \tag{5}$$

(The parameters vary from security to security, as with the single-index model, but the i subscripts have been omitted here for simplicity.) The first factor, F_1, might be output, the unemployment rate, or some other measure of the strength of the economy; β_1 tells the effect of this factor on this particular security's return. The second factor might be a long-term interest rate, with β_2 giving the effect of the interest rate on this security. Most S&Ls have a relatively large β_2 and a modest β_1, while the reverse is true of automobile companies.

Researchers can include as many factors as they think important—output, interest rates, inflation, oil prices, taxes, and so on. The single-index model is the special case of one factor, the stock market itself. With more than one factor, the beta coefficients cannot be visualized in a scatter diagram but can be estimated by statistical multiple-regression procedures.

The data in Table 15–1 were used to estimate a two-factor model with F_1 being the change in the unemployment rate and F_2 the percentage change in the interest rate on long-term Treasury bonds. For AT&T, the estimated equation is

$$R = 18.9 - 4.8F_1 - 1.0F_2, R^2 = 0.89.$$

For IBM, in contrast,

$$R = 13.8 - 11.1F_1 - 0.6F_2, R^2 = 0.69.$$

The economy has a much larger effect on IBM stock, while interest rates affect AT&T stock more.

Asset Pricing

Stephen Ross has shown how, just as the single-index model provides an intuitive explanation for the Capital Asset Pricing Model, a multiple-factor model leads to an asset pricing model—which he called **Arbitrage Pricing Theory (APT)**.[5] The essential argument for APT is analogous to that for the single-index model, and so is the conclusion. (A formal proof is sketched in the appendix to this chapter.) Equation 5 states that the return on any asset depends on the macro (systematic) factors F_1 and F_2 and on the micro (unsystematic) influences in ϵ. In a large, well-diversified portfolio, the idiosyncratic events in ϵ offset each other, leaving only macro (systematic) risk. Risk-averse investors do not need above-average expected returns to persuade them to hold assets with idiosyncratic risk, because such risk can simply be diversified away. Risk premiums are required for macro risks because these cannot be avoided by diversification.

The crucial divergence from CAPM's conclusion is that APT allows for the possibility that different macro risks may require different risk premiums. For example, in a particular historical period in which there is little chance of interest rates changing, investors do not need to be compensated much for holding assets that are sensitive to interest rates. In general, each asset must be priced to give an expected return that depends on its sensitivity to each factor and on the risk premium for each factor, or mathematically

$$(E - R_0) = (E_1 - R_0)\,\beta_1 + (E_2 - R_0)\,\beta_2 \tag{6}$$

where $(E_1 - R_0)$ is the risk premium for the first factor, and $(E_2 - R_0)$ is the risk premium for the second factor.

Arbitrage Pricing Theory (APT)
Arbitrage Pricing Theory (APT) says that assets have risk premiums for all macro factor risks that cannot be diversified away.

The APT Equation 6 is very similar to the CAPM Equation 2; in fact, if we use the APT model with a single factor, the market return, we obtain Equation 2. However, CAPM and APT are derived from two very different sets of assumptions—one regarding investor preferences and the other, investment opportunities. CAPM assumes that investors use mean-variance analysis and agree about the available opportunities, while APT assumes that the returns can be described by factors and an idiosyncratic term that is independent not only of the factors, but also of idiosyncratic influences on other assets. Empirical tests seem to show that the CAPM and APT models are both generally consistent with available data, but that neither is clearly superior to the other.[6]

Portfolio Management

Factor betas are inherently useful because it is worth knowing the sensitivity of assets and portfolios to individual factors—for example, knowing that a particular asset mix is especially sensitive to interest rates or to the economy, and hence, represents an implicit bet on these factors.

Some strategies have implicit factor betas that investors should be aware of. After the stock-market crash on October 19, 1987, many portfolio managers shifted to stocks with high dividend yields. At the time, many savings and loan (S&L) stocks fell into this category, so that a high-dividend-yield strategy was really an S&L strategy—a bet that interest rates would fall and/or that oil prices would improve and some suspect energy loans would be repaid.

Similarly, a portfolio manager who emphasizes small companies may buy a lot of growth stocks, which are very sensitive to interest rates. A manager who looks for low price-earnings ratios may buy energy stocks when oil prices are depressed (implicitly betting on a strengthening of oil prices), or automobile stocks when a recession is anticipated (implicitly betting that the recession will not materialize), or export firms when the dollar is strong (implicitly betting that the dollar will weaken). The explicit estimation of factor betas can help portfolio managers recognize the macro risks that they are taking.

Factor betas gauge the exposure of a portfolio to interest-rate risk, to output risk, or to other risks. There is no presumption that portfolios should try to minimize these risks; presumably, risk-bearing is compensated by above-average expected returns. Before you can rationally decide which risks to bear, however, you need to identify the risks.

Some money managers may also want to structure their portfolios to meet the needs of their clients; for example, a corporate pension fund might be particularly concerned about output risk, because reduced profits will impair its ability to fund retirement benefits. On the other hand, a life-insurance company is more concerned with interest-rate risk, and a university endowment is more interested in inflation risk. Other portfolio managers may want to know factor betas in order to place bets on interest rates, output, and so on. If the market expects a recession, and you do not, your portfolio can be tilted towards assets with a high output beta. To bet that interest rates will fall, or at least not rise as much as others expect, you can shift your portfolio into assets with large interest-rate betas. APT is more complicated than CAPM, but that is why some find it appealing; it facilitates richer, more subtle portfolio decisions.

SUMMARY

The Capital Asset Pricing Model assumes an efficient market, in which all investors have the same information about expected returns, standard deviations, and correlation coefficients. The beta coefficient of a security gauges the macro, systematic risk that cannot be diversified away; micro, unsystematic risk, which arises from events specific to individual companies, can be diversified away in a large portfolio.

Thus, for portfolio managers, beta is the appropriate measure of risk. Beta coefficients are estimated from the slope of a line, called the characteristic line, fit to a scatter diagram of returns on a security and on a market index. The beta of a portfolio is a weighted average of the betas of the securities in the portfolio, using as weights the fraction of wealth invested in each security. *R*-squared, measuring the fraction of the portfolio's variance that is explained by the market, is close to 1 for a large, well-diversified portfolio.

According to the Capital Asset Pricing Model, risk-averse investors will not hold assets with high beta coefficients and substantial nondiversifiable risk unless they are compensated with large risk premia. The specific formula is

$$E_i - R_0 = \beta_i(E_M - R_0),$$

which can be graphed as a security market line, showing the relationship between a security's beta coefficient and its expected return.

Betas can be used to determine required rates of return and, hence, to value securities. Betas can also be used to gauge a portfolio's sensitivity to the market—either as a measure of its riskiness or as a market-timing tool. A portfolio's beta can be reduced by holding low-beta securities, including the safe asset, and can be increased by holding high-beta securities or by borrowing to create leverage. CAPM suggests that a portfolio's beta coefficient is appropriate for measuring risk-adjusted performance. Hypothetical and real high-beta portfolios have had, on average, higher average returns than low-beta portfolios.

Arbitrage Pricing Theory allows us to take into account the observation that security returns are affected by a variety of diverse factors and, therefore, have a variety of beta coefficients. Assuming that asset returns can be modeled as dependent on factors and an idiosyncratic error term that is independent of the factors and of the idiosyncratic influences on other asset returns, assets will be priced in a manner analogous to CAPM, with risk premiums for macro factor risks that cannot be diversified away.

Factor betas can be used not only to value securities, but also to gauge the sensitivity of a portfolio to various factors, such as unemployment, interest rates, and inflation. A portfolio manager may want to structure the portfolio to reflect his or her beliefs about the future course of these macro factors or, at least, to recognize the risks to which the portfolio is exposed.

A P P E N D I X

Asset Pricing Proofs

Investors are assumed to use mean-variance analysis and to agree on the values of the means, variances, and correlation coefficients. They then agree on the location of the Markowitz frontier and the opportunity locus given by Tobin's Separation Theorem. This locus, called the capital market line, describes the common perception of the risk-return trade-off offered by efficient portfolios. Some investors are drawn to the safe asset and others use leverage; but every investor who holds risky assets holds the relative proportions given by point M, and these must consequently be the market proportions. If every investor holds twice as much IBM as General Electric (GE), then the aggregate market value of IBM must be twice that of GE.

In equilibrium, assets must be priced so that there can be no advantage from increasing or decreasing holdings of any asset. The figure shows two hypothetical opportunity loci for increasing or decreasing holdings of asset i. Neither of these opportunity loci is possible in equilibrium, because each goes above the capital market line, making the market portfolio unattractive. In one case, the opportunity locus is steeper than the capital market line and investors will want to hold slightly less of Asset i; in the other, the opportunity locus is flatter than the capital market line and investors will want to hold slightly more of Asset i. The only possible equilibrium is with the opportunity locus from any asset tangent to the capital market line at point M. The slope is determined by taking the derivative of the opportunity locus. Equating this slope to the slope of the capital market line and manipulating the result yields the CAPM pricing equation given in the text.

If there is no safe asset, then investors need not hold identical portfolios, but (under fairly general assumptions) the market portfolio is an efficient portfolio, lying on the Markowitz frontier. The argument given

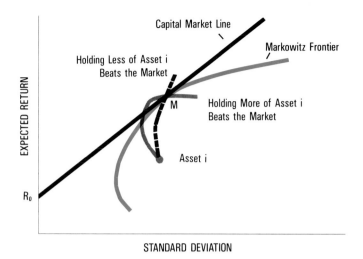

earlier still applies, in that the opportunity locus between any asset and the market portfolio cannot go above the Markowitz frontier, and this condition implies the CAPM pricing equation. The one difference is that R_0 is not the return available on a safe asset, since there is none, but instead R_0 is the expected return on a (perhaps hypothetical) zero-beta portfolio. This zero-beta expected return is the point at which the line tangent to the Markowitz frontier at the market portfolio M crosses the expected-return axis.

Arbitrage Pricing Theory

With two factors, a security's return is given by

$$R = \alpha + \beta_1 F_1 + \beta_2 F_2 + \epsilon$$

where the disturbance term has an expected value of 0 and is assumed to be independent of the factors and of other disturbance terms. Since we are concerned with risk and uncertainty, it is convenient to measure the factors as deviations between actual and expected values, for example,

$$F_1 = \text{actual output} - \text{expected value of output}$$

With this convention, the expected value of each F is 0 and α is the expected value of R, as in the following:

$$R = E + \beta_1 F_1 + \beta_2 F_2 + \epsilon$$

For a portfolio, α and each β are weighted averages of the αs and βs of the assets in the portfolio, with weights equal to the fraction of wealth invested in that asset. The portfolio ϵ is also a weighted average of the asset ϵ, and if the portfolio is large and well-diversified, the average value of ϵ should be close to 0. For such portfolios,

$$R = E + \beta_1 F_1 + \beta_2 F_2$$

With unrestricted short-selling, portfolios can be constructed that depend on only one factor. For example, consider the following diversified portfolios:

$$R_A = E_A + 1.2F_1 + 0.8F_2$$
$$R_B = E_B + 0.8F_1 + 1.6F_2$$

These portfolios can be combined into a portfolio that depends only on F_1,

$$R = 2R_A - 1R_B$$
$$= (2E_A - E_B) + 1.6F_1$$

or into a portfolio that depends only on F_2,

$$R = 3R_B - 2R_A$$
$$= (3E_B - 2E_A) + 3.2F_2.$$

Now consider two well-diversified portfolios that depend only on F_1, one with $\beta_1 = 1$:

$$R_1 = E_1 + 1F_1$$
$$R_C = E_C + \beta_1 F_1$$

The second portfolio can be combined with safe Treasury bills to create a portfolio with $\beta_1 = 1$:

$$R = \left(\frac{1}{\beta_1}\right)R_C + \left(1 - \frac{1}{\beta_1}\right)R_0$$
$$= \frac{(E_C - (1 - \beta_1)R_0)}{\beta_1} + 1F_1$$

In an efficient market with no profitable arbitrage opportunities, these two portfolios, which depend only on the first factor and both have $\beta_1 = 1$, must be priced to give the same return:

$$E_1 + 1F_1 = \frac{E_C - (1 - \beta_1)R_0}{\beta_1} + 1F_1$$

This equation implies

$$E_1 = \frac{E_C - (1 - \beta_1)R_0}{\beta_1}$$

or, rearranged,

$$E_C = R_0 + (E_1 - R_0)\beta_1$$

Analogous arguments yield the APT equation:

$$E = R_0 + (E_1 - R_0)\beta_1 + (E_2 - R_0)\beta_2$$

EXERCISES

1. A researcher has estimated these characteristic lines for two different stocks:

$$R_1 = -6.0 + 1.5R_M \qquad R^2 = 0.35$$
$$R_2 = 3.0 + 0.5R_M \qquad R^2 = 0.50$$

Sketch the characteristic lines for Stock 1 and for Stock 2, identifying the intercept and slope of each line. Which stock has the higher predicted return if $R_M = 10$ percent? If $R_M = -5$ percent?

2. What are the alpha and beta coefficients for the two stocks in Exercise 1? What are the alpha and beta coefficients for a portfolio that is invested one-half in Stock 1 and one-half in Stock 2? What are the alpha and beta coefficients for a portfolio that is invested one-third in Stock 1 and two-thirds in Stock 2?

3. Historical plots of the rates of return on two stocks and on the market as a whole are shown in Figure 15–A. During this period, which of these two firms' returns had the higher

a. average return?
b. standard deviation?
c. beta coefficient?
d. R-squared?

4. A broker has provided the beta coefficients shown in Table 15–A. Calculate the beta co-

FIGURE 15–A

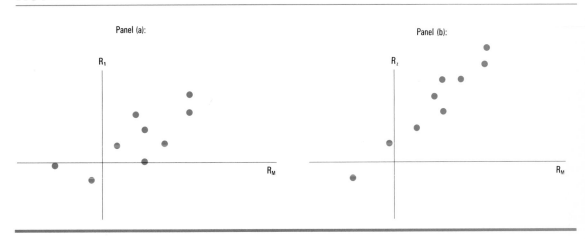

TABLE 15–A

Security	Beta
American Capital Bond Fund	0.55
Battle Mountain Gold	0.55
California Water	0.60
Duke Power	0.70
Salomon	1.60
Texas Air	1.60
U.S. Home	1.70
Vista Chemical	1.80

efficient for each of the following three portfolios:

a. Equal dollar investment in the first four stocks.

b. Equal dollar investment in the last four stocks.

c. Equal dollar investment in all eight stocks.

5. Over the coming year, the return on safe Treasury bills is 11 percent, and your expected return for the stock market as a whole is 15 percent. What does the CAPM predict about the expected returns for the three portfolios specified in Exercise 4? If the market return turns out to be 25 percent, what is CAPM's predicted return for these three portfolios? If the actual returns for these three portfolios turn out to differ from these predictions, can we conclude that the CAPM has been disproved?

6. Explain why the following observation is misleading:

A widely diversified portfolio is not supposed to break downward in value very fast because all its "eggs" won't go bad at once . . . . But this safety mechanism doesn't seem to work particularly well. When steel and motors take a dreadful fall, almost the entire diversified list of securities takes it right along with them.[7]

Be sure to distinguish between systematic and unsystematic risk and to consider whether all securities fall equally.

7. Many investors look at the beta coefficients provided by investment advisors. Explain why the following advice is misleading: "A stock with a low beta is safer than a high-beta stock, because the lower beta is, the less the stock's price fluctuates."

8. Explain why you either agree or disagree with this advice: "If the market was expected to rise, an investor might increase the R-square of the portfolio. If the market was expected to decline, a portfolio with a low R-square would be appropriate."[8]

9. Answer this student question: "Isn't it inconsistent to measure risk by the standard deviation in mean-variance analysis and by the beta coefficient in the Capital Asset Pricing Model?"

10. Explain why you either agree or disagree with this assertion: "According to the Capital Asset Pricing Model, zero-beta stocks have a zero expected return."

11. Is there any portfolio that has a beta of 1 and an R^2 of 1, too?

12. One researcher calculated the annual returns from 1954 through 1978 on an investment in fifteen representative modern art prints and found that these returns were negatively correlated with annual returns from corporate stocks.[9] What does this study tell us about the beta coefficient for modern prints? Why might someone invest in modern prints even if the expected return were very modest?

13. The expected returns and beta coefficients for three firms are shown below. Are these estimates consistent with the Capital-Asset Pricing Model?

Firm	Expected Return (percent)	Beta Coefficient
1	10.0	0.80
2	12.0	1.00
3	15.0	1.50

14. A bank's assets consist mostly of bonds

and loans. Give two examples of macro (systematic) risk and two examples of micro (unsystematic) risk for a bank's asset portfolio.

15. A life-insurance company cannot predict with certainty when its policyholders will die. Give two examples of macro (systematic) risk and two examples of micro (unsystematic) risk for a life insurance company. What inherent risk advantages does a large insurance company have?

16. Value Line, a large private investment-advisory service, recommends that investors who own fewer than fifteen stocks gauge the riskiness of their portfolio by looking at Value Line's "safety ratings" for these stocks, and that investors who own more than fifteen stocks instead calculate the average beta. Why are the safety ratings not identical to the beta coefficients, and why does the appropriate risk measure depend on the number of stocks in the portfolio?

17. In January 1988, Coca-Cola Enterprises announced that it was reducing its ownership of Columbia Pictures from 80% to 49% by distributing 30 million shares of Columbia stock that it owned as a special dividend to Coca-Cola stockholders. At the time, more than half of Coca-Cola's shares were held by institutional investors and a Coke spokesman said that he expected many of these institutions to sell the Columbia shares they would receive, explaining that,

> I think the profile of the kind of institutional shareholder that likes to have a holding in Coca-Cola stock is probably very different than the profile of the shareholder that wants to have a more volatile stock like an entertainment company.[10]

If an institution does not sell its Columbia shares, how does the distribution of these shares by Coca-Cola affect the riskiness of its portfolio, as measured by its standard deviation and beta coefficient?

18. In 1988, *The Wall Street Journal* began a monthly "Investment Dartboard" series in which four experts each select a favorite stock and *The Wall Street Journal* picks four stocks by tossing darts at the financial pages. After the expert portfolio beat the dartboard portfolio three months in a row, a letter to the editor objected that,

> The "random walk" theory suggests that individual investors cannot outperform a randomly selected portfolio. Your procedure pits the random portfolio against the single best choices of different investors, which is an entirely different hypothesis. Since individual stock picks are riskier than diversified portfolios, it is not surprising that the (average) pro's return exceeds that of the dartboard.[11]

Do you agree? Write a letter to the editor supporting or refuting the above letter.

19. Some recent business-school graduates have just incorporated and raised $10 million by selling stock. What will the beta of their stock be if they
a. buy $10 million of assets with a beta of 1.2?
b. buy $8 million of assets with a beta of 1.2 and invest $2 million in Treasury-bills?
c. borrow $4 million and buy $14 million of assets with a beta of 1.2?

20. You have $10,000 in wealth, which you are considering investing in a certain mutual fund whose return during the coming year has an expected value of 15 percent, a standard deviation of 20 percent, and a beta coefficient of 1.5. If you instead borrow $10,000 at 12 percent and invest $20,000 in this fund, what will be the expected value, standard deviation, and beta coefficient for the return on your $10,000 (after paying off the loan)?

21. A study of the determinants of price-earnings ratios asked seventeen professional security analysts for the following data on 178 well-known stocks:[12]

P/E = price/normal earnings, adjusted for temporary events

g = anticipated growth rate

d = anticipated dividends/earnings

β = beta coefficient

After averaging these data, the following equation was estimated to explain the variation in price-earnings ratios among firms in 1963:

$$P/E = 3.47 + 2.57g + 7.17d - 0.84\beta$$

Interpret the coefficients of the three explanatory variables, and identify which, if any, have implausible signs.

22. Using comparable accounting procedures in 1984, the average price-earnings ratio (P/E) for Japanese stocks on the Tokyo stock exchange was about 19.5, as compared to an average P/E of 10 for U.S. stocks on the New York Stock Exchange. Discuss the strengths and weaknesses of the following attempt to compare P/Es:

> [Paul H. Aron says,] "Essentially, the P/E of a stock reflects the premium above the riskless return available in the market. Long-term government bonds have usually served as a proxy for the riskless rate." On Aug. 31, the yield on long-term issues in the secondary market was 7.45% in Japan and 12.69% in the U.S.
>
> Aron adds, "The P/E of a riskless investment is the reciprocal of its yield, or the earnings yield as it is sometimes identified." This is derived from a theory that defines price as the flow of earnings discounted. By this method the P/E of a riskless U.S. stock would be 7.88 [1/.1269] and 13.42 [1/.0745] in Japan. The upshot: "A riskless investment in Japan sold for 1.7 [13.42/7.88] times more than a similar investment in the U.S."
>
> . . . Using the [CAPM] concept that the earnings yield (the reciprocal of P/E) "ought to be in line with the general interest rate

level," Aron divides his Japanese P/E of 19.5 by 1.7, and concludes that "the Japanese P/E should be 11.5 compared to the U.S. P/E of 10."[13]

23. A and B are two companies, identical in all respects, except that A has no debt and B is 50 percent debt financed. For each of the following financial statistics, indicate whether you expect the value of the statistic to be higher for Company A or Company B. *Briefly* (one sentence per statistic), explain your reasoning.

a. Expected return on assets

b. Standard deviation of return on stock

c. Beta coefficient of stock

d. Shareholder's required return on stock

24. In 1987, AT&T announced that it was spending $809 million to repurchase most of its preferred stock, which is like debt in that the dividends are contractually fixed, but which

> has become a relatively expensive form of financing now that interest rates have fallen . . . . Dividends paid on the shares come from after-tax income and, unlike loan payments, are not tax-deductible operating expenses . . . .
>
> AT&T's action comes at a time when many firms are buying back some of their own common stock to help boost the prices of the shares. Analysts said, however, that redeeming preferred shares, stock that carries no voting rights, has no direct effect on the performance of a company's stock.[14]

How would you expect AT&T's repurchase of preferred stock to affect the beta and price per share of its common stock as compared to the alternative action of spending $809 million to repurchase some of its common stock?

25. A firm forms a conglomerate by merging with firms in different industries. To the extent that the merged firms' revenues are uncorrelated, such mergers can reduce the standard deviation of earnings. Is the resulting conglom-

TABLE 15–B

Year	Company Annual Return (percent)	Market Annual Return (percent)
1972	23.9	18.98
1973	0.5	− 14.66
1974	− 4.5	− 26.47
1975	21.6	37.20
1976	32.3	23.84
1977	1.9	− 7.18
1978	7.6	6.56
1979	− 5.6	18.44
1980	1.4	32.42

erate then worth more than the sum of its parts? In particular, consider two very similar firms of equal size, whose earnings are uncorrelated, and assume that the Capital Asset Pricing Model applies. Assume that their earnings have equal expected values, $Y_1 = Y_2$; their market values are equal, $P_1 = P_2$; their beta coefficients are equal, $\beta_1 = \beta_2$; and the expected returns on their stocks can be expressed simply as $E_1 = Y_1/P_1$ and $E_2 = Y_2/P_2$. If the merger has no effect on their earnings, what will be

a. the beta coefficient of the conglomerate?
b. the expected value of its earnings?
c. its expected stock return?
d. its market value?

Explain why the conglomerate is or is not worth more than the sum of its parts.

26. Table 14–3 in Chapter 14 gives the annual percentage returns for the market and for three stocks: U.S. Home, Kloof, and Consolidated Natural Gas. U.S. Home is the nation's largest home builder, and its profits are very sensitive to the state of the economy. A weak economy and high interest rates are bad for the stock market and very bad for U.S. Home. What kind of results do you think we would obtain if we estimated the equation

$$R = \alpha + \beta R_M + \epsilon$$

where R is the return on U.S. Home stock and R_M is the market return? Use the data in the table and a computer regression program to estimate this equation and see if you are right.

27. Kloof is a South African gold-mining stock, and Consolidated Natural Gas is a regulated utility. Use the data in Table 14–3 to estimate their beta coefficients. Interpret your results.

28. For each of the three stocks in Exercises 26 and 27, what is the regression equation's predicted return if the market return is $R_M = 20$ percent? If $R_M = -10$ percent?

29. What is the beta value for a portfolio constructed by investing an equal number of dollars in each of the three stocks in Exercises 26 and 27? How could a portfolio that has a beta value of 0 be constructed using these three stocks? (No short sales are allowed.)

30. The annual returns on a company's stock and on the entire market are given in Table 15–B. Use a computer regression program to estimate the beta coefficient for this company's stock. Now use the CAPM to estimate this stock's expected return if the return on the safe asset is 8 percent and the expected return on the market is 12 percent.

31. The company described in Exercise 30 is considering making a $10 million investment with the cash flow shown below. (Assume that the first year's profits are earned one year from today, the second year's profits two years from today, and so on.)

Year	Sales	Price per Unit	Cost per Unit	Depreciation
1	150,000	$50	$30	$1,500,000
2	200,000	50	30	2,200,000
3	225,000	45	30	2,100,000
4	240,000	40	30	2,100,000
5	250,000	40	30	2,100,000

Assume that after year 5, sales increase by 3 percent a year, while the price and cost per unit are constant and depreciation is 0. Calculate the annual after-tax cash flow [revenue − cost − 0.34(revenue − cost − depreciation)] for this project (assumed to be paid out as dividends), and then use the stock's expected return as the shareholders' required return to calculate the present value of these dividends. Is this present value larger than the $10 million cost? (Hint: remember the constant-growth model of stock prices.)

32. In a two-factor model, which of these assets do you think have relatively high or low output betas and which have high or low interest-rate betas, in each case compared with the output and interest-rate betas of the S&P 500?

a. Short-term Treasury bills.

b. Thirty-year Treasury zeros.

c. Stock in a regulated water company.

d. Stock in a machine-tool company.

e. Stock in a breakfast-food company.

33. Stephen Ross has often used a factor model that includes the following three factors:

F_1 = output

F_2 = long-term bond rate minus short-term rate

F_3 = rate of inflation

What signs would you expect for the three respective beta coefficients of a typical stock? Explain your reasoning.

34. The text reports these estimates of a two-factor model:

$$AT\&T: R_{AT\&T} = 18.9 - 4.8F_1 - 1.0F_2$$
$$IBM: R_{IBM} = 13.8 - 11.1F_1 - 0.6F_2$$

where the first factor is unemployment and the second is interest rates. How could you combine these two securities $R = aR_{AT\&T} + (1 - a)R_{IBM}$ to obtain a portfolio with an unemployment beta of 0? An interest-rate beta of 0?

35. The logic of arbitrage pricing theory can be illustrated with the following single-factor example:

$$R = E + \beta F + \epsilon$$

Consider three assets, with betas of 1, 2, and 3, respectively. How can you combine the second asset with a safe asset, such as Treasury bills, to get a portfolio with a beta of 1? For this portfolio to have the same expected return as the first asset, which also has a beta of 1, what must be true of their risk premia? How can you combine the third asset with the safe asset to get a portfolio with a beta of 1? For this portfolio to have the same expected return as the first asset, what must be true of their risk premia? What is the general relationship illustrated by these two examples?

Other Investments

CHAPTER 16

Options

Options are infinitely attractive to dream about. We all know many stocks which have moved much more than ten points in a month, and more than fifty points in three months. But when a man stops dreaming these transactions and tries doing them, something different always seems to happen . . .

Fred Schwed, Jr.

futures contract
A futures contract is a standardized agreement to deliver a certain item on a specified date at a price agreed to today, but not paid until delivery.

option contract
An option contract gives one of the parties the right, but not the obligation, to buy or sell an item in the future at a price that is specified now.

A **futures contract** is an agreement to trade a designated item at some future date at a price that is specified at the time of the agreement. For example, a mill might agree to pay a farmer $3 a bushel for 100,000 bushels of wheat delivered six months from now—thus, eliminating the mill's uncertainty about the cost of wheat and the farmer's uncertainty about revenue. An **option contract** is an agreement giving one of the parties the right, but not the obligation, to buy or sell an item in the future at a price that is specified now. The mill might pay a farmer $20,000 for an option, giving it the right to buy 100,000 bushels of wheat six months from now at $3 a bushel. If the market price of wheat drops below $3, then the mill will not exercise its option.

Options are considered in this chapter, and futures contracts in the next. You will see how options and futures can be used either for speculation or as insurance. You will learn about the valuation models developed by theorists and see how these models are used by institutional arbitragers. We begin with some historical perspective.

THE DEVELOPMENT OF FUTURES AND OPTIONS TRADING

One of the earliest references to such agreements is in the Old Testament, where Laban agreed to let Jacob marry his youngest daughter, Rachel, in return for seven years of labor. It is not clear whether Jacob could change his mind (that is, whether this was an option or futures contract) but, in any case, after Jacob had worked for seven years, Laban broke the contract and gave Jacob his older daughter, Leah. Jacob persisted, working another seven years so that he could marry Rachel too.

Another early reference is in *Politics,* where Aristotle recounts how Thales became wealthy through an astute use of options. Based on his study of the stars, Thales believed that the next olive crop would be enormous and, for a small fee, purchased options from the local olive-press owners. When the crop did turn out to be large, Thales exercised his options and leased the presses at a considerable profit.

The trading of commodity options and futures began in the United States shortly after the Revolutionary War and were widely used for both commodities and common stock during and after the Civil War. Then, as now, the overwhelming majority of trades were made not by millers, farmers, or other businesses seeking to guarantee the price of a future business transaction, but by speculators hoping to profit from short-term fluctuations in the value of these contracts. In the late 1800s, the progressive movement succeeded in having commodity options classified as a gambling rather than an investment, making them illegal under antigambling statutes. Stock options continued to flourish, particularly in the 1920s, and in the aftermath of the Great Crash attracted the attention of Congress, which considered but did not pass a bill outlawing stock options entirely.

Contributing to the speculative and somewhat unsavory reputation of stock options was the fact that these were not traded on organized exchanges. A loose collection of dealers brought together buyers and sellers through newspaper advertisements, mimeographed price sheets, and telephone calls. Each option was virtually unique in its terms—the number of shares, the exercise price, and the date of expiration. Without standardization, there could be no organized secondary market and little basis for comparing prices.

In 1969, an abundance of agricultural crops brought commodity trading to an almost complete stop, and the Chicago Board of Trade decided to experiment with stock-options trading. After considerable planning, they received approval from Securities and Exchange Commission (SEC), and in 1973 opened the Chicago Board Options Exchange (CBOE). (One of the five SEC Commissioners voted against approval, arguing that this "was essentially a gambling operation. There are enough of those in Las Vegas.")

Stock-option contracts on the CBOE are for 100 shares with uniform exercise prices and identical exercise dates. This standardization makes options interchangeable and allows for a central market with meaningful prices and welcome liquidity. Many investors were attracted to these options and, before long, stock options trading provided much of the Chicago Board's revenue. Other exchanges soon noticed these profits and began trading options in companies not listed on the Chicago Board.

Today, stock-option prices fill a complete page in *The Wall Street Journal*, and there are even options and futures contracts for bond and stock indexes. Stock options and futures are used not only by speculators looking for easy riches, but also by arbitragers, trying to exploit price differentials among similar securities for a virtually risk-free profit, and by institutions trying to insure their portfolios against losses. These portfolio insurers were blamed by many for the market crash on October 19, 1987, and Congress again considered severely restricting trades in what some continue to view as not real assets, but merely speculative flimflam.

We will now look at the specifics of option contracts and how these contracts are used by investors. There are two types of options, put and calls, which can be combined to create a variety of leveraged and hedged portfolios. We'll look first at calls, then puts, and then at some portfolio strategies.

call option
A call option gives the right, but not the obligation, to buy an asset at a fixed price on or before a specified date.

exercise price
An option contract can be exercised at its exercise price.

exercise date
An option contract expires on its exercise date.

European options
A European option can only be exercised on its expiration date.

American options
American options can be exercised before the expiration date.

CALL OPTIONS

A **call option** gives the holder of the option the right, but not the obligation, to buy an asset at a fixed price on or before a specified date. For instance, a call option might give the owner the right to buy a share of ABC stock for $100 any time within the next six months. The fixed price (in this case, $100) is called the **exercise price,** or **striking price,** and the date on which the option contract expires is called the **exercise date. European options** can be exercised only on the expiration date; **American options** can be exercised before expiration, but never are unless there is a large dividend that would be lost by postponement.

An option agreement is between private parties, and, if it is exercised, one person buys stock from another with no change in the total number of shares outstanding. Since it is the seller of the option who makes a commitment that may be exercised at the buyer's discretion, the seller is said to have "written" the option. Before 1973, each option agreement was between two specific parties, and the buyer who decided to exercise an option went to the option writer for fulfillment of the terms. With the trading of standardized contracts on an exchange, there is no need to associate a particular writer with a specific contract. If the buyers exercise their options, the payments are made to the options exchange, which then collects the promised shares from the option writers for distribution, without identifying which particular writer distributed shares to which particular option holder.

In practice, stock options are seldom exercised. Instead, on the expiration date, the option holders sell their options back to the option writers, thereby extinguishing the contract at a price reflecting the value of the contract if it were exercised. The number of outstanding options fluctuates daily, as some investors write new options and others close their positions. Newspapers report the daily volume of trading and also the number of outstanding options, called the **open interest.**

Exercise Value

The value of an option depends on the exercise price and the value of the underlying asset. The right to buy ABC stock for $100 is worth little if ABC stock is currently trading for $10 a share, but it is worth a great deal if ABC stock is trading for $1000. The minimum value of a call option is its **exercise value,** the amount you can save if you purchase the stock by exercising the option. If the stock is selling for $100 or less, an option to buy at $100 saves you nothing; if the stock is selling for $150, the option saves you $50. Thus the exercise value is equal to the difference between the value of the stock P and the option's exercise price E, if the stock's price is higher than the exercise price:

$$\text{exercise value} = P - E \text{ if } P > E$$
$$= 0 \text{ if } P \leq E \qquad (1)$$

This relationship is graphed in Figure 16–1. The value of an option is never negative, because you are not compelled to exercise it. An option that has a positive exercise value is said to be *in the money;* one with no exercise value is *out of the money.*

If we neglect transaction costs, an American option should always sell for at least its exercise value, because it is worth at least this much to investors who want to buy the stock. If an option sells for less than its exercise value, arbitragers can buy the option, exercise it, and sell the stock for an immediate easy profit. Suppose, for instance, that ABC stock is selling for $150, and an option to buy ABC stock for $100 is selling for only $30. An arbitrager can pay $30 for the option, exercise it by paying another $100, and then sell the stock for $150—making a quick $20 profit. The eagerness of arbitragers to exploit such opportunities keeps an option's price from falling below its exercise value.

On the expiration date, the value of an option is equal to its exercise value, because then you have no choice but to exercise it or throw it away. Before expiration, American option prices are invariably above their exercise value, because those who buy options do so in the hope that the price of the underlying stock will rise and make their option more valuable. As Figure 16–1 shows, options are more valuable when there is more time until expiration.

open interest
The open interest is the total amount of outstanding contracts.

exercise value
An option's exercise value is the amount an option holder could save by exercising the option instead of buying or selling the stock at its market price.

FIGURE 16–1 Value of a call option

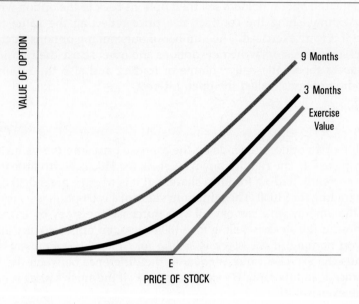

VALUE OF OPTION

9 Months

3 Months

Exercise
Value

E

PRICE OF STOCK

The Lure of Levered Profits

Options provide leverage in that for the price of the option, you earn profits on an asset that is worth much more than the option. Consider again a six-month option on ABC stock with a $100 exercise price, and suppose that the price of the option is $10 while the price of the stock is $100. Table 16–1 shows the percentage profits from buying the stock and from purchasing an option to buy the stock.

If you buy the stock for $100 and its value rises to $110 after six months, you make a 10 percent profit. If you instead buy the option, its value at expiration is its $10 exercise value, just what you paid for it, and your profit is 0 percent. Not very attractive so far! But consider what happens if the price of the stock rises to $120, giving a 20 percent profit to the person who bought stock. The person who bought the option finds its value rising from $10 to $20, for a 100 percent profit. If the price of the stock rises to $130, the option will be worth $30, a 200 percent profit. Because the stock is initially worth ten times as much as the option, there is 10/1 leverage in that each 10-percentage-point increase in the value of the stock brings a 100-percentage-point increase in the value of the option. This leverage is not symmetrical, however, because the value of the option cannot be negative. As the option advisory services say, "The most you can lose is

TABLE 16–1   The Leverage Provided by Options

| Price at Expiration | | Profit (percent) | |
Stock	Option	Stock	Option
$ 80	$ 0	− 20	− 100
90	0	− 10	− 100
100	0	0	− 100
110	10	10	0
120	20	20	100
130	30	30	200

the cost of your option"—a peculiarly cheerful way of noting that if the price of the stock does not go up, your option will be worthless and you will have a 100 percent loss.

It is this chance for enormous leveraged profits that historically has lured investors to options. Some advisory services pander to these hopes by recounting the fortunes that could have been made by timely option purchases: in a four-week period, Allied Products stock went up 29 percent, but the options rose 100 percent; in six weeks, McDonald's stock rose 57 percent, and McDonald's options increased by 395 percent. This opportunity for highly levered profits also makes options attractive to those hoping to profit from inside information. Knowing this, the SEC and the exchanges pay particular attention to suspicious trades in options.

WARRANTS AND EXECUTIVE-COMPENSATION OPTIONS

Many corporations give their top management **executive-compensation options,** which allow them to buy new shares of the company's stock at a set price. These options are a form of executive compensation that once had tax advantages, when capital gains were relatively lightly taxed, and that are intended to focus executive attention on the value of the firm's stock.

Companies also occasionally issue **warrants**—rights to purchase stock that are very similar to call options, except that warrants are issued by the company itself, and, if exercised, the firm issues new shares of common stock. Warrants are sometimes distributed to shareholders in place of a dividend or else in conjunction with the sale of other securities. They are typically traded on the same exchange as the firm's stock, identified by the term *wt* following the company's name.

executive-compensation options
Executive-compensation options give management the right to buy new shares of the company's stock at a set price.

warrants
Warrants are like call options, but are issued by the company itself.

Dilution

Since the exercise of warrants and executive-compensation options creates additional shares of a company's stock, these can dilute the value of existing shares. Suppose that a company has ten million shares of common stock and ten million warrants outstanding. A naive way to estimate the potential dilution is to reason that, like a stock split, a doubling of the number of shares will halve the value of each share. If before the issuance of the warrants, the shares sell for $10 each, then the total market value of the company is $100 million; with 20 million shares, the value of each share is $5.

This estimate is too simple because, unlike a stock split, the company receives money for the new shares that are issued. If the exercise price is $10, then the issuance of ten million new shares raises an additional $100 million—giving this company $200 million in assets and keeping the value of each of the twenty million shares at $10. There is no dilution at all, since the firm receives $10 each for issuing shares worth $10 apiece.

The $5 valuation estimate assumes that the firm receives nothing for the new shares; the $10 valuation assumes that it receives full market value. In practice, the firm does not receive full value when warrants are exercised because the warrant owners do not find it profitable to exercise their warrants unless the exercise price is less than the value of the shares. The new value of the shares will be somewhere between full dilution ($5) and no dilution ($10), with the exact amount dependent on the exercise price of the warrants and the number of warrants issued.

Effect on Share Value

If there are initially m shares outstanding at a price P and n warrants are issued with an exercise price $E < P$, then the aggregate market value after exercise is $mP + nE$, and the per-share value is

$$P' = \frac{mP + nE}{m + n}$$

Table 16–2 shows some illustrative calculations for various values of E, using $P = \$10$ and $m = n = 10$ million.

Similarly the calculation of fully diluted earnings and dividends by dividing current earnings and dividends by the potential number of shares is too simple, because it ignores the fact that the funds received from the sale of warrants will be used to increase earnings and dividends.

put option
A put option gives the owner the right to sell an asset at a fixed price on or before a specified date.

PUT OPTIONS

A **put option** is similar to a call except that the owner has the right to *sell* an asset at a fixed price on or before a specified date. For instance, an American put option might give the owner the right to sell a share of ABC

TABLE 16–2 The Effect of Warrants on Stock Values

Warrant Exercise Price, E	Diluted Value of Stock, P'
$ 0	$ 5
2	6
4	7
6	8
8	9
10	10

FIGURE 16–2 Value of a put option

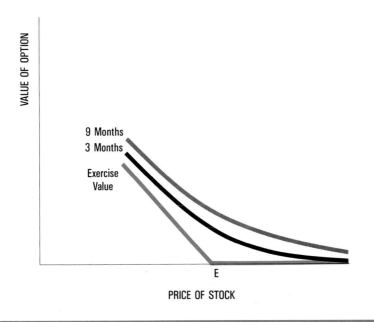

stock for $100 at any time within the next six months. If the price of ABC stock declines, this put option becomes increasingly valuable. Specifically, the exercise value of a put is:

$$\text{exercise value} = E - P \text{ if } P < E$$
$$= 0 \text{ if } P \geq E \tag{2}$$

Figure 16–2 graphs this relationship.

As with a call, the exercise value of an American put is the minimum value that it can sell for without attracting profitable arbitrage. On its exercise date, the market price of a put is equal to its exercise value; before this date, the price of an American put is somewhat higher, as bearish investors buy puts in anticipation of profiting from a drop in the price of the underlying stock.

OPTION STRATEGIES

A put is a bet that the price of a stock will fall; a call is a bet that the stock's price will rise. However, puts and calls need not be purchased in isolation, as all-out bets on the direction of the stock's price. A variety of portfolios can be created by buying or selling various combinations of puts, calls, and the stock itself. The simplest way to analyze the consequences of such combinations is to focus on the profits at expiration, when options sell at exercise value. Figure 16–3 on pp. 514–515 shows the dollar gains from six basic strategies. Once these have been learned, we can use these graphs to analyze compound strategies.

The Basics

Panel (a) shows that if you buy a call at a price P_C, you will lose all of this purchase price unless the price of the stock is above the exercise price on the expiration date. Past the exercise price, every dollar increase in the price of the stock increases the value of the call option by a dollar. Once the stock price reaches $E + P_C$, the exercise value of the call option is equal to what you paid for it six months earlier, and you just break even. Past this point, profits continue to increase, dollar for dollar, with the price of the stock.

Panel (a) also shows that selling a call option gives a profit picture that is the mirror image of buying an option, because, neglecting transaction costs, the purchase and sale of options is a zero-sum game, in that every dollar the buyer makes must be at the expense of the seller, and vice versa. We can confirm the profit graph in panel (a) by thinking through the situation of someone who sells a call option. If the stock price is below the exercise price, the option expires worthless, and the seller pockets the amount initially received for the option. If the stock price is above the exercise price, the option seller's profits decline, dollar for dollar, because he or she must repurchase the option at its exercise value (or, alternatively, buy the stock and deliver it to the buyer, taking a loss equal to the exercise value of the option.)

Panel (b) shows the profits from buying or selling a put option at a price P_P. If the price of the underlying stock on the expiration date is at or above the exercise price, then the option expires worthless—so that the seller gains and the buyer loses the cost of the put. Every dollar the stock's price falls below the exercise price increases the value of the put by a dollar, reducing the seller's profits and increasing those of the buyer.

Panel (c) shows the consequences (neglecting dividends) of buying a stock or selling it short. Every dollar increase in the price of the stock is a dollar profit to the buyer and a dollar loss for the short seller.

We can use these six basic strategies to analyze some of the compound strategies used by investors. We will consider first a conservative strategy followed by many institutional investors, and then discuss a few hedging practices.

Covered Calls

The basic strategy of selling a call option that was depicted in panel (a) of Figure 16–3 is known as selling a **naked call,** because the seller does not own the underlying stock and must either repurchase the call at some point or, else, buy the stock and deliver it to the holder of the call option. If the price of the stock soars, the losses can be devastating—a vulnerability suggested by the label, a naked call.

naked call
A naked call is the sale of a call option without ownership of the underlying asset.

An alternative strategy is a **covered call,** in which the investor simultaneously buys a stock and writes a call option for this stock. Ownership of the stock provides protection against a runup in the price of the stock, since the call writer can simply turn over the stock if it is called. Figure 16–4 on p. 516 shows the profits from this strategy, assuming that the initial purchase price of the stock coincides with the option's exercise price. First, the profits are sketched, as in Figure 16–3, for the appropriate basic strategies: buying the stock and selling a call. Then these profits are added vertically to determine the profits from the combined strategy.

covered call
A covered call is the simultaneous purchase of stock and sale of a call option on this stock.

For this profit addition, look first at the case in which the stock's price on the expiration date is equal to the exercise price. There is no profit on the stock itself and the profit on the call is equal to its initial price, giving a total profit of P_C. As we move to the right, every dollar increase in the price of the stock brings one dollar more profit on the stock and one dollar less profit on the call; these offset each other, leaving the profit constant at P_C. As we move to the left of the exercise price, the stock's profits fall while the option's profits are constant, causing the combined profits to fall steadily.

The complete picture is as shown, and reveals covered-option writing to be a fairly conservative strategy, suitable for those who expect modest increases in stock prices. If a stock's price holds steady or declines, the proceeds from selling a now worthless call provide extra income; the cost is that the stock will be called away if the price increases; thus the profits can never exceed P_C, the price of the call, no matter how much the stock advances. The writer of covered calls trades away the chance for large profits in return for extra income from writing calls. Many college endow-

FIGURE 16–3 Profits from basic strategies

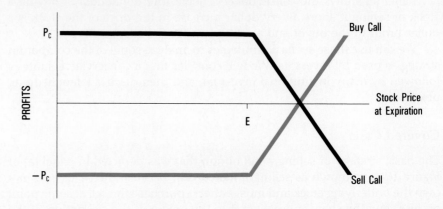

Panel (a) Buying and Selling Call Options

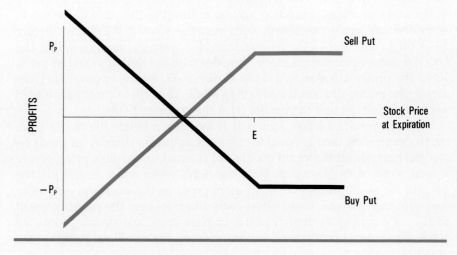

Panel (b) Buying and Selling Put Options

FIGURE 16–3, *cont'd* Profits from basic strategies

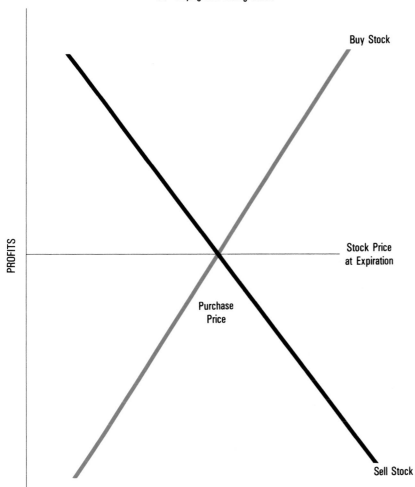

Panel (c): Buying and Selling Stock

FIGURE 16–4   Selling a covered call

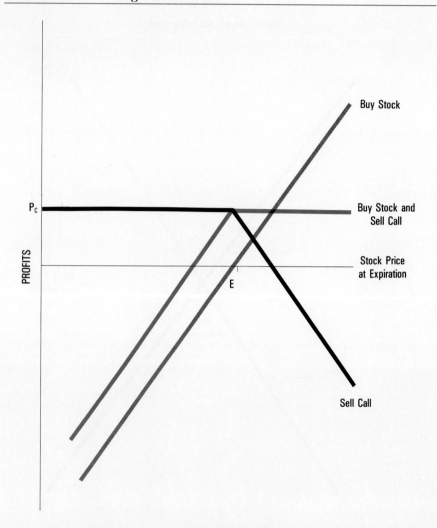

ments and pension funds follow this conservative strategy. Investment Example 16–1 on pp. 518–519 illustrates another use: investors who think that the price of a call is too high relative to the price of the stock can sell the call and buy the stock, thus writing a covered call.

Straddles and Spreads

straddle
A straddle is the simultaneous purchase of a call and put option.

A **straddle** is the simultaneous purchase of a call and a put. While the purchase of a call is a bet that a stock's price will rise and the purchase of a put is a bet that a stock's price will fall, Figure 16–3 shows that the profits

FIGURE 16–5 A straddle

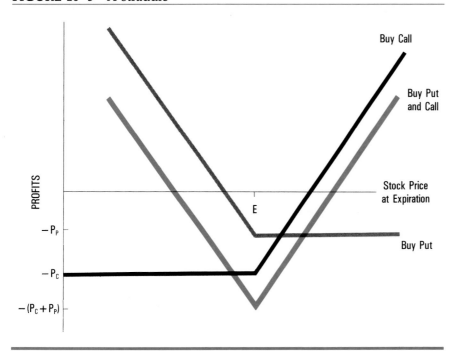

are not symmetrical. Thus the purchase of both a put and a call is not a perfect hedge.

Figure 16–5 shows the profits from a straddle if the put and call have the same exercise price. If the price of the stock on the expiration date is exactly equal to the exercise price, then both options are worthless, and the buyer loses an amount equal to the combined price of both options. Moving to the right of E, the call's value increases dollar for dollar with the price of the stock, pulling up profits; the breakeven point is at $E + (P_C + P_P)$. To the left of E, the increasingly valuable put pulls up profits, with breakeven at $E - (P_C + P_P)$. Thus, a straddle is a symmetrical bet that the price of a stock will either rise or fall, it does not matter which, by an amount equal to the price of the call plus the price of the put.

What about someone who writes a straddle, simultaneously selling a call and a put? This is just the mirror image of Figure 16–5—a symmetrical bet that the price of a stock will not change much, in either direction, during the life of the options. One investor who routinely wrote straddles, betting that stock prices would not change much, built his account up to $120,000 in October 1987. Then the market fell by more than 20 percent

AT&T WARRANTS

In November 1970, with AT&T stock selling at about $50, AT&T distributed 31 million warrants (an amount equal to about 6 percent of its existing 549 million shares of common stock), allowing the purchase of AT&T common stock at a price of $52 up until May 15, 1975. Many brokerage houses recommended these warrants to their customers, suggesting that this was a way to make large profits on AT&T, a stock favored by conservative investors. One predicted before the issuance that the warrant would be very attractive at a price of $15 a share, saying that if AT&T went to $75, the warrant's price should double and that AT&T's price was not likely to drop below $46, making the warrant "an excellent opportunity for purchase even if the common stock does not rise from present levels."*

Of course, if AT&T's price did not rise above $52, the warrants would eventually expire worthless. Panel (a) of the accompanying figure shows the profits from purchasing a warrant at $15 as a function of the price of AT&T on the warrant's expiration date. The price has to rise above $67 for the warrants to be worth $15 at expiration; this is an increase in the stock's price of 34 percent in 4½ years, a plausible, but by no means guaranteed 6.7 percent a year. Even if AT&T's price rises to $75 (9.4 percent a year), the $23 value of the warrant gives a 50 percent profit that just matches the 50 percent profit from buying AT&T common at $50.

As it turned out, AT&T's price sagged and by February 1972 stood at only $43. Yet the price of the warrants was $8, with now only three years until expiration. Panel (b) of the figure shows that AT&T's price now had to rise by 40 percent, to $60 (11.7 percent a year), for the warrants to be worth $8 at expiration. At the time, the warrants seemed temptingly overpriced; yet selling them short carried the risk of substantial losses if AT&T's price did soar.

There was substantial short selling of AT&T warrants in 1972, reportedly by professional traders who simultaneously bought AT&T stock to hedge their position. Panel (c) shows the potential profits from this strategy. If the price is above $52, the profit is $17. At a price below $52, the profit is $8 higher than can be obtained by buying AT&T alone. For more protection on the downside and less on the upside, investors can sell two warrants for every share of common; as panel (d) shows, this strategy is profitable as long as AT&T stays in the fifty-point range, $27 to $77. Selling three warrants for every share of common increases the profit at $P = \$52$ to $32 and tilts the profitable range to $19 to $69. These hedges turned out to be profitable. On May 15, 1975, AT&T closed at $51⅞, and the warrants expired worthless.

*Kidder, Peabody and Co., "AT&T Issue," April 14, 1970.

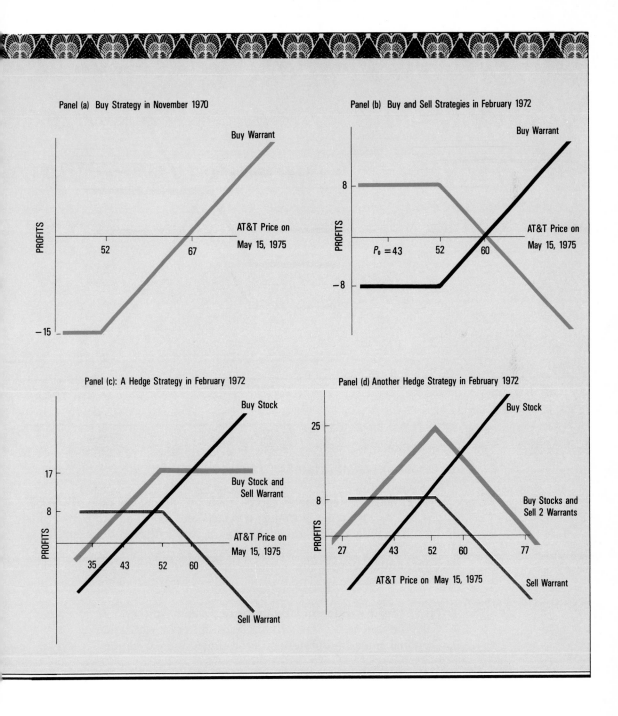

Panel (a) Buy Strategy in November 1970

Buy Warrant

PROFITS

AT&T Price on
May 15, 1975

52   67

−15

Panel (b) Buy and Sell Strategies in February 1972

Buy Warrant

8

PROFITS

$P_0 = 43$ 52   60

AT&T Price on
May 15, 1975

−8

Panel (c): A Hedge Strategy in February 1972

Buy Stock

17

Buy Stock and
Sell Warrant

8

PROFITS

AT&T Price on
May 15, 1975

35   43   52   60

Sell Warrant

Panel (d) Another Hedge Strategy in February 1972

Buy Stock

25

Buy Stocks and
Sell 2 Warrants

8

PROFITS

27   43   52   60   77

AT&T Price on May 15, 1975

Sell Warrant

FIGURE 16–6   IBM spread

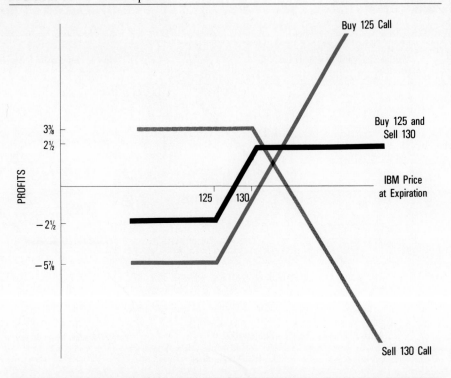

on October 19, and he lost $450,000 in a single day, leaving his account $330,000 in the hole.[1]

Asymmetrical investments can be made by varying the ratio of one call to one put. For example, a *strap* is two calls and a put; a strip is two puts and a call. (These exotic strategies are explored further in the exercises at the end of this chapter.) Another type of strategy is a **spread,** in which an investor simultaneously buys and sells options with different striking prices and/or expiration dates. There are a variety of spread strategies, including:

1. Price spread—different striking prices, same expiration
2. Calendar spread—same striking price, different expiration
3. Diagonal spread—different striking prices and expiration

The easiest to analyze is the price spread, since we can determine the value of both options on the common expiration date. On August 4, 1988, with IBM at 125⅞, an October IBM call with a 125 strike price sold for 5⅞ while an October call with a 130 strike price sold for 3⅜. Figure 16–6 shows the profit possibilities for a bullish price spread, buying the 125 call and selling

FIGURE 16–7 Buying puts as insurance

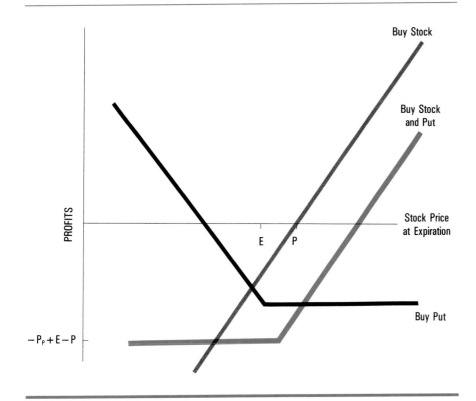

the 130 call. The profit is positive if the stock price exceeds 127½ and negative if below, with a maximum gain or loss of 2½. A bearish price spread would be the reverse, buying the 130 call and selling the 125 call.

Insurance, Hedging, and Synthetic Calls

Insight into the relationship between puts and calls can be gained by interpreting a put as insurance against a decline in the price of a stock, with the cost of this insurance equal to the price of the put. Figure 16–7 shows the combination of buying stock at a price P and paying P_P for a put with an exercise price E. The put provides insurance in that if the price drops below E, the stock can be sold for E, for a maximum loss of $(P - E) - P_P$. If the stock rises, the put will expire unused, with profits diminished by the cost of the put, P_P.

Further examination of Figure 16–7 shows that the combination of buying a stock and a put gives a profit profile that is identical to the purchase of a call option with an exercise price E and a cost $(P - E) + P_P$. Since buying stock and a put creates a synthetic call, it follows that a call

FIGURE 16-8 A synthetic put

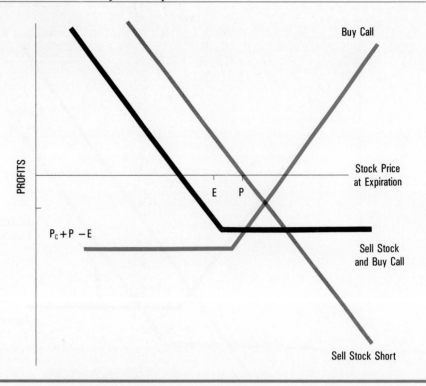

option can be interpreted as equivalent to the purchase of stock plus a put option: call = stock + put.

Further, because the purchase of stock plus a put is equivalent to a call, we might guess that buying a call while selling a stock short creates a synthetic put: put = call − stock. Figure 16–8 shows that this is indeed the case. Finally, the fact that the purchase of stock plus a put is equivalent to a call suggests that the purchase of a stock plus a put, and the sale of a call, may be a perfect hedge: stock + put − call = 0. Figure 16–9 analyzes this strategy of buying a stock while simultaneously buying a put and selling a call that have exercise prices equal to the stock's purchase price. At E, the stock shows no profits, and both options are worthless, giving a profit of $P_C - P_P$. Moving to the right, the stock becomes more valuable and the call less so, holding profits constant. Moving to the left, the stock's losses are offset by the put's gains, and profits again remain constant. This strategy is a perfect hedge, in that the profits are $P_C - P_P$, no matter what happens to the price of the stock. You initially pocket the difference in the two option prices. Then, it does not matter what happens, because the stock will be called away at a price E if the price goes up, and you will

FIGURE 16–9 Arbitrage

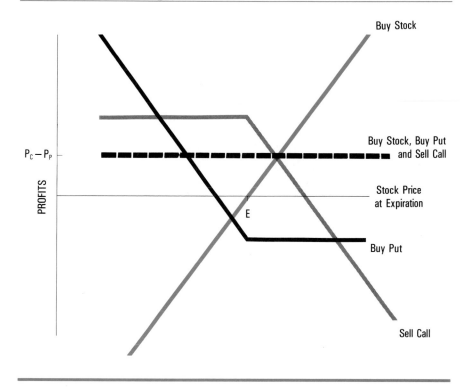

exercise your put and sell the stock at a price E if the price goes down. Years ago, arbitragers reportedly earned 20 percent a year from this strategy, selling call options to speculators hoping to make a big killing, and then hedging their position by buying stock and selling puts.

OPTION VALUATION

The value of a call depends on the characteristics of the underlying stock. A call option is more valuable if

1. the price of the stock is above the striking price,
2. the option has a lengthy period before expiration,
3. the stock is very risky, or
4. interest rates are high.

The first two factors are straightforward. The third reflects the asymmetrical nature of an option. If the price of the stock rises, the price of the call rises too, without bound; but if the stock's price is below the exercise price, the option has no exercise value, no matter how low the stock's price. Thus, a stock that will go up or down a great deal is attractive to option holders.

Consider, for example, the case in which ABC's price is equally likely to be $90 or $130 on the expiration date [an expected value of $90(0.5) + $130(0.5) = $110]. An option with an exercise price of $100 will be worth either $0 or $30, for an expected value of

$$\$0(0.5) + \$30(0.5) = \$15$$

If ABC's price is instead equally likely to be $80 or $140 (still a $110 expected value), the option is worth $0 or $40, and the expected value increases to

$$\$0(0.5) + \$40(0.5) = \$20$$

Increased uncertainty about ABC stock increases the expected value of its call option.

The fourth factor, high interest rates, is also subtle. Consider a one-year option that is likely to be exercised. You can either buy the stock now for a price P, or buy an option and then pay the exercise price E in one year. The value of the option is the difference between the current price of the stock and the present value of the exercise price:

$$\text{value} = P - \frac{E}{(1 + R)}$$

If interest rates are high, the option is more valuable because of the advantages of paying for the stock later.

The Black-Scholes Model

In his Ph.D. thesis, Sheen Kassouf used these explanatory variables to estimate valuation equations for warrants, which, at the time the thesis was written, were more easily traded than options. Together with Edward Thorpe, a mathematician who had earlier shown how to win at blackjack by counting cards, Kassouf published a book in 1967 claiming that investors could beat the warrants market.[2] They argued that speculators hoping for leveraged profits push the prices of warrants to unreasonable heights. As a consequence, selling warrants short is, on average, very profitable.

We have seen that naked options and warrants are also very risky. Kassouf and Thorpe consequently recommended a covered position—buying stock and selling warrants, though not necessarily in a one-to-one ratio. Using Kassouf's empirical equations, they derived hedge ratios of stock to warrants so that any change in a warrant's price will be offset by the accompanying change in the stock's price. If, for example, a $2 change in the price of ABC stock causes a $1 change in the price of an ABC warrant, then buying one share of stock and writing two warrants (a hedge ratio of 1/2) insulates the portfolio.

Kassouf and Thorpe argued that because warrants are overpriced, hedged portfolios can earn a high rate of return with little risk. Two other professors, Fischer Black and Myron Scholes, took Kassouf and Thorpe's procedure a step further by applying efficient market logic.[3] If the hedge strategy is indeed risk free, then its rate of return should just equal the rate of return from risk-free Treasury bills. Black and Scholes then used some advanced mathematics to derive the implied price of a call option. In theory, this **Black-Scholes option model** is an efficient market model of call prices. In practice, if market prices differ from the theoretical values, then risk-free hedges can be constructed that beat the market. Kassouf, Thorpe, Black, and Scholes have all tried to do so. Investment Example 16–2 explains how bond-portfolio managers also can use option pricing models.

Black-Scholes option model
The Black-Scholes option model assumes that riskless hedges can be constructed by continuously maintaining an appropriate hedge ratio between stocks and call options.

The Hedge-Ratio Logic While the mathematics used to derive Black-Scholes model is very complicated, the principle can be illustrated with a simple example. Suppose that a stock's price is equally likely to be $90 or $130 on the exercise date, so that the price of a call option with a $100 striking price is equally likely to be $0 or $30. There is a $40 spread in the possible stock prices and a $30 spread in the possible option prices.

To equalize these spreads, consider buying three shares of stock and selling four options (or other amounts in a 3/4 hedge ratio). The cost of this position is $3P - 4P_C$. If the stock's price turns out to be $90, the option will be worthless, and the position will be worth $3(\$90) = \$270$. If the stock's price instead turns out to be $130, the stock will be worth $3(\$130) = \$390$; but repurchase of the options costs $4(\$30) = \$120$, giving a net position of $\$390 - \$120 = \$270$. Thus an investment that costs $3P - 4P_C$ is certain to be worth $270. In an efficient market, the return on this safe portfolio should equal the rate of return, R, on a safe investment, such as Treasury bills, with the same maturity as the options:

$$(3P - 4P_C)(1 + R) = \$270$$

or

$$P_C = \frac{P - \dfrac{\$90}{(1 + R)}}{\dfrac{4}{3}} \tag{3}$$

Table 16–3 on p. 527 shows the implied values of a six-month call option for different values of the current stock price, assuming the six-month rate

THE CHOICE BETWEEN CALLABLE AND NONCALLABLE BONDS

In analyzing callable bonds, it is helpful to split the security into two parts—a noncallable bond and a call option. An investor who buys a callable bond has implicitly bought a noncallable bond and also sold a call option to the issuer with an exercise price equal to the bond's call price. If the value of the noncallable bond is P and the value of the call option is C, then the value of the callable bond is $V = P - C$. It follows that the difference between the price of a noncallable and otherwise identical callable bond, $P - V = C$, is not constant, but rather varies with the value of the implicit call option.

As with any call option, the value of the call increases as the price of the underlying asset increases. For bonds, this means that a drop in interest rates and accompanying increase in bond prices increases C and widens the gap between the values of noncallable and callable bonds. Further, call options are more valuable if the volatility of the price of the underlying asset increases. Therefore, an increase in interest rate volatility also increases the prices of noncallable bonds relative to callable bonds. Overall, noncallable bonds do relatively well when interest rates are falling and volatility is increasing; callable bonds do relatively well when the reverse is true.

Corporate bonds are normally considered riskier than Treasury bonds and should, on average, have somewhat higher returns. However, Treasury bonds are generally not callable and most corporate bonds are. Over the period 1976 to 1986, interest rates declined slightly and volatility increased substantially, causing noncallable bonds to outperform otherwise equivalent callable bonds.* Thus, as it turned out, bond-portfolio managers who bought Treasury bonds did better than their competitors who bought corporate bonds.

An important aspect of bond-portfolio management is the choice between callable and noncallable bonds—an implicit bet on the level and volatility of interest rates. Those who want to make this bet even more explicit can construct hedged portfolios by buying callable bonds and selling noncallable ones, or vice versa.

*Chris P. Dialynas, "The Active Decisions in the Selection of Passive Management and Performance Bogeys," Pacific Investment Management Company, mimeo, 1988.

of return on Treasury bills is 5 percent (10 percent annually). The put prices are derived later in this chapter.

Equation 3 also indicates that the value of a call, unlike most assets, is positively related to interest rates. For example, with $R = 8$ percent instead of 5 percent, the value of a call at $P = \$100$ rises from $10.71 to $12.50. The reason is that these hedges involve the buying of stock and the selling of options in order to achieve a risk-free return. A large return requires a low cost and, hence, a high price for selling the option.

TABLE 16–3 Option Values When a Safe Investment Has a 5 Percent Return

Current Stock Price	Option Value When Stock's Price will be P = $90 or $130		Option Value When Stock's Price will be P = $80 or $140	
	Call	Put	Call	Put
$ 90	$ 3.12	$8.45	$ 9.21	$14.45
100	10.71	5.95	15.87	11.11
110	18.21	3.45	22.54	7.78

We can also look at the effect of stock volatility on option prices by assuming that the stock's price is equally likely to be $80 or $140 (still an expected value of $110). The option is now worth $0 or $40. The difference in the stock prices is $60, and the difference in the option prices is $40, calling for a $40/$60 = 2/3 hedge ratio—selling three options for every two shares of stock purchased. This position is certain to be worth $160 [the value of the stock alone if the price is $80 or 2($140) − 3($40) = $160 if the price is $140]. The modified Equation 3 then is

$$P_C = \frac{P - \dfrac{\$80}{(1 + R)}}{\dfrac{3}{2}}$$

which implies the call-option values given in Table 16–3, showing, as expected, that a call option is more valuable the riskier is the underlying stock.

The Black-Scholes Equation In practice, there are far more than two possible values for stock prices. However, Black and Scholes showed that the analogous perfect hedges can be constructed if we assume that

1. the percentage changes in stock prices are normally distributed with a constant variance;
2. investors can trade continuously without transaction costs;
3. investors can borrow at a constant risk-free rate;
4. there are no restrictions on short selling; and
5. the stock pays no dividends.

(The relaxation of some of these assumptions leads to modified models.) In an efficient market, an option must be priced so that the rate of return on such a perfect hedge is just equal to the risk-free rate. Using some advanced mathematics, Black and Scholes showed that the implied price of an American or European call option is

$$P_C = P \, N[d_1] - (E/e^{Rt}) \, N[d_2] \tag{4}$$

where

$$d_1 = \frac{\ln\left[\dfrac{P}{E}\right] + Rt + \dfrac{t\sigma^2}{2}}{\sigma\sqrt{t}}$$

$$d_2 = d_1 - \sigma\sqrt{t}$$

and

P = current price of stock
E = exercise price of call option
N = cumulative normal probability
$\ln$ = natural logarithm
e = base of natural logarithms
t = years remaining until expiration
R = continuously compounded annual risk-free rate
σ = standard deviation of continuously compounded annual return on the stock

This formula is daunting, but it need not be memorized or solved by hand. Many financial computer programs, including the disk accompanying this text, contain the Black-Scholes equation. Even some hand calculators include the equation or can be programmed to solve it. We will work through one example here to illustrate the necessary inputs.

The Black-Scholes equation states that the value of an option depends, in a complicated way, on the option's exercise price, the length of time until maturity, the current price of the stock, the riskless rate of return, and the standard deviation of the percentage change in the stock's price. Consider, for instance, a nine-month option with an exercise price of 100 on a stock with a current price of 100. If the annual risk-free rate is 5 percent, and the standard deviation of the stock's return is 30 percent, then

P = 100
E = 100
t = 9/12
R = $\ln[1.05]$ = 0.0488
σ = 0.30

$$d_1 = \frac{\ln\left[\dfrac{100}{100}\right] + 0.0488\left(\dfrac{9}{12}\right) + \left(\dfrac{9}{12}\right)\left(\dfrac{0.3^2}{2}\right)}{0.3\sqrt{\dfrac{9}{12}}}$$

$$= 0.271$$

$$d_2 = 0.271 - 0.3\sqrt{\frac{9}{12}}$$

$$= 0.011$$

A statistical handbook of normal probabilities gives $N[d_1] = 0.607$ and $N[d_2] = 0.504$, so that

$$P_C = 100(0.607) - (100/e^{0.0488(9/12)})(0.504)$$
$$= 12.10.$$

All of the option prices shown in Figure 16–1 early in this chapter were, in fact, calculated by a computer program using the Black-Scholes model for three- and nine-month options with a 5 percent risk-free rate of return and a 30 percent annual standard deviation.

In using the Black-Scholes model, the only difficult input is the standard deviation. Typically, the standard deviation of the historical returns is used, but this estimate may need to be modified if it is anticipated that the future is more or less volatile than the past—perhaps because the corporation has sold off a risky subsidiary, expanded into new fields, or changed its debt-equity ratio. Unfortunately, the value of a call option is very sensitive to the standard deviation. In the preceding example, the nine-month option is worth $8.78 if the standard deviation is 20 percent and $15.43 if the standard deviation is 40 percent. What some professionals do is calculate the standard deviation for which the value of the option is equal to the current market price, and then decide whether they believe the actual standard deviation to be higher than this implied value (suggesting the option is underpriced) or vice versa.

Like Kassouf and Thorpe, Black and Scholes argued that call options have been overpriced historically; but they are more skeptical about the profitability of low-risk hedges, given the relatively large transaction costs.[4] In any case, it is surely more difficult to find bargains today, now that so many institutions are using the Black-Scholes formula to look for mispriced options.

Put Prices

The value of a European put for a stock that does not pay dividends can be derived from out earlier observation that a perfect hedge can be constructed by buying a stock at a price P_0 and simultaneously selling a call and buying a put with the same exercise price E. The net cost of this position is

$$P - P_C + P_P$$

and the value of the position is certain to be E on the exercise date. (Either the stock's price will be E and the options will be worthless or the stock will be sold via one of the options for a price E.) In an efficient market, to prevent arbitragers from earning excessive returns, these assets should be priced so that this safe strategy gives the same rate of return, R, as a safe investment—that is, a Treasury bill that matures on the exercise date. In symbols,

$$(P - P_C + P_P)(1 + R) = E.$$

Rearranging, the price of a put is determined by the put's exercise price, the current price of the underlying stock, the Treasury-bill rate, and the price of a call option with the same exercise price and date, as shown in the following:

$$P_P = \frac{E}{(1 + R)} - P + P_C \tag{5}$$

Modified formulas can be obtained to account for dividends and (approximately) for American puts.

The relationship between put and call prices given in Equation 5 is called **put-call parity**. Written like this

$$P_C - P_P = P - \frac{E}{(1 + R)}$$

we see that the price of a call exceeds the price of a put when a stock is selling at the exercise price ($P = E$). Puts are more expensive than calls only if the stock's price is somewhat below the exercise price.

Table 16–3 shows this to be the case, using the example of ABC stock. This table also shows that an increase in a stock's current price makes a call more valuable and a put less so, while a decrease in the price of a stock has the opposite effects. Both puts and calls are worth more if the stock's price is less certain.

put-call parity
A put-call parity relationship exists between the prices of puts and calls because of the possibility of riskless arbitrage.

INDEX OPTIONS

Options are seldom exercised. As the contract expires, the price of an option equals its exercise value, and any remaining option writers close their position by repurchasing contracts from option holders. Since the reckoning of profits and losses does not depend on actual delivery, contracts can

TABLE 16–4   S&P 500 Index Options, August 10, 1988

September Exercise Price	Option Price	
	Call	Put
260	8⅞	6⅝
265	6¼	8¾
270	4	11¾
275	2⁷⁄₁₆	15¼
280	1½	18

be written on intangible things that cannot be delivered: the Dow Jones Industrial Average, the Consumer Price Index, attendance at Dodger stadium, or the temperature in New York City. All we need to know to settle the contract is a rule for calculating its value at expiration.

An *index option* is an option contract based on the value of an index of asset prices such as the S&P 500 index of stock prices, an index of the prices of oil stocks, or an index of the prices of long-term Treasury bonds. If the striking price is E and the value of the index on the expiration day is P, then

$$\text{value of a call} = \begin{array}{l} P - E \text{ if } P > E \\ 0 \text{ if } P < E \end{array}$$

$$\text{value of a put} = \begin{array}{l} E - P \text{ if } P < E \\ 0 \text{ if } P > E \end{array}$$

In each case, the owner of the option, instead of demanding delivery at the exercise price, sells the option back to an option writer at its theoretical exercise value.

Put and call options now exist for the following indexes and more: the Standard and Poor's 500 stock index (S&P 500), the NYSE composite index, a municipal-bond price index, and an index measuring the foreign-exchange value of the U.S. dollar. We will use the S&P 500 to illustrate the general principles. On August 10, 1988, the S&P 500 index closed at 261.90, and puts and calls expiring in September were available for striking prices ranging from 220 to 300. A few selected prices are shown in Table 16–4.

If you buy a 270 call, you are betting that the value of the S&P 500 index will be above 270 on the September expiration date. If it is at 274 on that date, your option is worth the $4 you paid for it, and you just break even. If it is above 274, you make leveraged profits. If the S&P 500 is below 270, your option expires worthless. (For the S&P 500, the unit of account is 500 times the index; other indexes use other multiples. Thus, each 270 S&P 500 call costs 500($4) = $2000, and if the S&P 500 closes at 285 on the expiration date, it is worth 500($285 − $270) = $7500.)

Index options can be used for speculation or hedging, just like stock options, and all the strategies discussed in this chapter can be applied to index options. The only difference is that the value of an AT&T option depends on the fortunes of AT&T while the value of an S&P 500 option depends on (virtually) the entire stock market.

Those who do not wish to select individual stocks, but think they can predict the overall direction of the market can buy index calls if they are bullish and puts if they are bearish (see Figure 16–3 in this chapter). A pension fund that is willing to trade a chance at large profits for some extra income can write covered calls by buying a diversified portfolio of stocks and writing index calls (see Figure 16–4). A fund that wants to protect itself against a market collapse can buy insurance by purchasing index puts (see Figure 16–7). An arbitrager who thinks that index options are mispriced can create hedges (such as shown in Figure 16–9).

Index options are particularly appropriate for institutions holding large, diversified portfolios, who are skeptical about beating the market by picking undervalued stocks, but would like a risk exposure that cannot be easily obtained simply by buying stocks and Treasury bills. Index options were introduced to give institutions more flexibility, and they have responded enthusiastically to the opportunity. They also use futures contracts for similar purposes, as you will see in the next chapter.

SUMMARY

A call option gives a person the right, but not the obligation, to buy an asset at a fixed price on or before a specified date. A put option gives the holder the right to sell at a specified price. Option agreements are between private parties and, except for transaction costs, are a zero-sum game in that one's gain is the other's loss. The amount of options outstanding fluctuates daily as new options are written and others are covered.

Stock options are seldom exercised. Instead, on the expiration date, the option holders sell their options back to the option writers at a price approximately equal to the option's exercise value—the amount an option holder could save by exercising the option instead of buying or selling the stock at its market price. Since options do not have to be exercised, but merely valued on the expiration date, contracts can be written on intangibles such as the S&P 500 Stock Index.

Warrants and executive-compensation options are like call options, with one important difference: they are issued by the company and dilute the value of shareholders' stock to the extent that the exercise price is less than the market value of the firm's stock.

Traditionally, many investors have been drawn to options because of the leverage, a call being a bet the stock's price will go up, a put a bet that it will go down. However, the combination of puts, calls, and the stock itself makes possible a wide variety of straddles, spreads, and hedging strategies. For instance, a covered call, a popular conservative strategy, is equivalent to selling a put. A call option can be interpreted as the purchase of stock plus the purchase of a put for insurance. Buying stock, selling a call, and buying a put is a riskless strategy.

To the extent that call and stock prices are related, riskless hedges can, in theory, be constructed by continuously maintaining an appropriate hedge ratio between stocks and calls. The observation that the return on a riskless hedge should equal the return on safe Treasury bills, along with some strong assumptions and advanced mathematics, led to the Black-Scholes option-pricing formula. The observation that buying stock, selling a call, and buying a put is a riskless strategy similarly establishes a put-call parity relationship between the prices of puts and calls. Many investors now use these theoretical formulas, looking for mispriced options, an arbitrage activity that has succeeded in eliminating most, if not all, significant mispricing in the option market.

EXERCISES

1. On May 4, 1989, General Electric (GE) common stock closed at 48½, while a GE September 1989 call option with an exercise price of 50 closed at 2. What was the exercise value of this call option on May 4, 1989? What is the exercise value of this call option on the expiration date if GE trades that day for $50? For $55? For $45? Sketch the dollar profit from buying a call option at 2 as a function of the price of GE stock on the exercise date.

2. On May 4, 1989, General Electric (GE) common stock closed at 48½, while a GE September 1989 put option with an exercise price of 50 sold for 2⅝. What was the exercise value of this put option on May 4, 1989? What is the exercise value of this put option on the expiration date if GE trades that day for $50? For $55? For $45? Sketch the dollar profit from buying a put option at 2⅝ as a function of the price of GE stock on the exercise date.

3. Look in the most recent Monday issue of *The Wall Street Journal* and find the Friday closing prices of IBM put and call options with an exercise price that is nearest to the closing price of IBM common stock Friday. (You should identify three calls and three puts, with various exercise dates.) Report the closing prices and exercise values of these six IBM options.

4. Investors who had been following a naked-options strategy touted by brokers as a sure thing lost hundreds of millions of dollars when the Dow dropped 508 points on October 19, 1987. Which of the following strategies were they using? Explain your reasoning.
a. Buying calls.
b. Selling calls.
c. Buying puts.
d. Selling puts.

5. A financial columnist offered several tips to investors who want protection from a bear market, while "allowing yourself room to make money if the bull is still alive":[5]
a. Enter stop-loss orders.
b. Buy put options.
c. Sell stocks that are overvalued.
d. Sell stocks short.
e. Invest in mutual funds with proven track records.
Explain to a novice investor how each action accomplishes the stated objective, and point out each action's drawbacks (if any).

6. On November 23, 1982, Phibro common stock was selling for $51 a share; a January 1983 call option with an exercise price of 50 was selling for $5 a share; and a January 1983 put option with an exercise price of 50 was selling for $4 a share. Graph the dollar gain from each of the following strategies as a function of the price of Phibro stock on the January exercise date:
a. Buy a call option.
b. Buy a put option.
c. Buy a call option and a put option.
d. Buy Phibro common, sell a call option, and buy a put option.

7. When Professor Smith came to Pomona College, he encountered the Economics Club's annual investment contest. Each contestant is given $10,000 in play money to manage over a three-month period; the winner is given a real cash prize. Smith managed the portfolios of two contestants, his secretary and a student. All of his secretary's money was invested in a put option for a certain company's stock; all of the student's money was invested in a call option for the same stock. At the end of three months, the student's portfolio had grown to nearly $50,000—easily winning the contest. Explain Smith's strategy. What kind of stock do you think he selected? What do you think happened to his secretary's portfolio?

8. E.G. Capital Management, an investment-management company buys high-dividend stocks and writes call options against these stocks. The *New York Times* says that this company has done very well in sluggish markets, but "in surging markets . . . will almost always underperform market indexes."[6] Explain why.

9. An advisory service used this argument to show that warrants are less speculative than stock: In 1970, Tenneco sold for 19⅜, and warrants that could be exercised at $24¼ during the next twelve months sold for $3. One hundred shares of stock cost $1937, and 300 warrants cost half that, $900. If the stock doubled to $38¾ (giving a $1937 profit, or 100 percent), the warrants would be worth at least $14½ (for a profit of $3450, or 383 percent). On the downside, if the stock's price is halved to $9⅝, there is a $968 loss; even if the price of the warrant falls all the way to 0, the loss is only $900. Thus, the advisory service claimed

Inescapable Conclusion: Each $1 invested in the Tenneco Warrants *had* to do much better than the same $1 invested in Tenneco common, and could not possibly have done worse on the downside! In November 1970, at 3, the Tenneco Warrants were not only a much better "Buy" than Tenneco common, but actually *less speculative.*[7]

Explain why you agree or disagree with the advisory service's reasoning.

10. A company has 50 million shares of common stock outstanding with a current market price of $20 a share. It decides to distribute a special dividend consisting of 50 million warrants, one for each outstanding share of common stock. The warrants have an exercise price of $20 a share. In theory, what should the value of the common stock be if these warrants are issued and immediately exercised? What should the value of the common stock be if the warrants are issued with an exercise price of $10 and immediately exercised?

11. In 1989 the vice president of options and futures at Alex. Brown & Sons Inc. recommended that investors consider protecting their portfolios by purchasing put options, arguing that "The worst thing that can happen is the value of your portfolio goes up."[8] How do put options protect a portfolio? Why does something bad happen when your portfolio goes up? Is this really the worst possible outcome?

12. Critically evaluate the following October 1986 analysis of IBM call options:

An investor could either buy a share of IBM at $144 (a $14,400 investment) or one IBM January 130 call at $17 (a $1,700 investment). The buyer of stock has the unlimited appreciation potential of IBM, plus dividends—but has $14,400 at risk. The call buyer has the unlimited appreciation of IBM above $147 (the 130 strike price plus 17-point premium) until expiration in January, and no dividend—but is risking only $1,700. IBM is expected to pay $1.10 per share in dividends until the call expiration, but the call buyer can earn approximately $1.75 a share by investing the funds not used to buy IBM at money market rates. In essence, the call buyer has comparable profit potential with less money at risk.[9]

13. Here is an excerpt from a letter to the *New York Times*:

More and more people have become interested in stock options. However, it seems that there has been some uninformed buying by the public.

Under present regulations, stock may be purchased on 50 per cent margin. Six-month call option prices average about 15% of the stock value. Margin buying is usually the better strategy.[10]

Compare these two alternative strategies, each requiring an initial out-of-pocket expense of $3000: (a) buy 60 shares of stock at $100, borrowing $3000 for six months at a 10 percent annual interest rate; or (b) buy 200 options at $15, with a striking price of $100. What are the net profits from each strategy if the price of the stock is $100 when the options expire? If the price is $90? For which values of the stock price, is strategy (b) more profitable than (a)?

14. Critically evaluate the following analysis of covered calls:

Recently, an investor could have purchased Monsanto (MTC) at $75¼ and at the same time written (sold) January 75 calls at $5½. If MTC remains above $75 at expiration, the investor will have to sell the stock at $75, but would still earn $5¼ per share, plus dividends. Even including commissions . . . this would represent a return of 5% in 130 days . . .

Of course, the risk in this transaction is that MTC might decline below $75 by an amount greater than the premium received—but that risk is there is you merely buy the stock, too. These types of transactions [are] always attractive to investors with positive opinions of the stock involved.[11]

15. An investment advisor labels the following argument a fantasy: "The purchase of put options to protect your common stocks against a market decline is like buying insurance and is a prudent tactic for conservative investors." To the contrary, he argues that "As for being prudent, the risk/reward posture is essentially the same as for the speculative purchase of call

options."[12] Do you agree?

16. If a corporation holds a stock for at least 46 days, 85 percent of the dividend it receives is tax free. Some corporations use a dividend-capture strategy, buying a stock approximately 46 days before the dividend record date, and then selling after the record date. To hedge the risk of capital loss during these 46 days, should they buy or sell a call option? Buy or sell a put option? Which of these hedge strategies will do better if the price of the stock rises a lot? Falls a lot?

17. Merton, Scholes, and Gladstein compared the annual returns from 1963 to 1977 for hypothetical investors who followed a strategy of continually writing call options with the annual returns from a strategy of continually writing put options:[13]

	Mean (percent)	Standard Deviation (percent)
Write Calls	7.70	10.50
Write Puts	4.10	5.60

Which strategy is a bet that the stock's price will increase? Based on the above data, write a brief nontechnical summary of the historical returns to these two strategies.

18. Black and Scholes found that call options that are far out of the money tend to be overpriced while those far in the money tend to be underpriced.[14] What spread strategy does this suggest, and how does its profitability depend on the price of the underlying stock on the exercise date?

19. A student recommended selling a stock short and buying two call options whenever the following occurs:

$$P + P_C > E$$
$$P + 4.5 > E + 2 P_C$$

For example, on August 1, 1988, Apple sold for $P = 45$ while a September call with an exercise price of $E = 45$ sold for $P_C = 2⅛$. Use a graph to show the profits from this strategy as a function of the price of Apple when the call option expires. Would you characterize this position as bullish or bearish?

20. One of the ten technical market indicators used by "Wall Street Week" gives a buy signal when the average premium on puts is large relative to that on calls. Give a logical rationale for this indicator, and then explain why, even in a perfectly efficient market, we should expect this ratio to sometimes rise—making it of no use as a buy signal.

21. A *New York Times* financial reporter wrote that "professional stock market traders like [option trading] because it affords them an opportunity to lose money profitably."[15] Give a specific example of how a trader might profitably lose money in options while making an overall profit.

22. In a variable hedge, a stock is hedged by writing more than one call option. For example, you might own a stock worth $50 and, fearing that its price may drop, sell two six-month call options at $5 each with striking prices of $50. Show the dollar profits as a function of the price of the stock on the day the options expire. How would you characterize this strategy?

23. Professional short sellers look for what they consider overvalued stock and then sell it short, anticipating a price decline. Some insure their positions by simultaneously buying call options on the stock they have shorted. Consider someone who sells stock short at $50 and simultaneously buys a call option with a $50 exercise price for $5. Use a graph to show the net profits as a function of the price of the stock on the option's expiration date. (Ignore dividends and interest.) How would you characterize the trader's position?

24. In late January 1975, with Avon at 31¼, Neuberger Securities suggested that those believing that Avon will drop in price should buy one call option and simultaneously sell a call option with a lower striking price; for example,[16] buy an April 30 call at 3⅞, and sell an

April 20 call at 11¼. Show the profits from this spread as a function of the price of Avon when the options expire.

25. One investment advisor recommends this spread strategy:

> You first determine the level of the index— either the S&P 100 Index (OEX) or Major Market Index (XMI)—and then buy the nearest in-the-money option and sell the nearest out-of-the-money option with the same expiration month. If you are bullish, you use call options—and, if you are bearish, you use put options.[17]

He gave an example in September 1986, with the S&P 100 at 237.32, of buying an October 235 call at $7 and selling an October 240 call at $4.50. Graph the profits from this strategy as a function of the value of the index in October 1986. Do the same for buying an October 240 put at 7⅛ and selling an October 235 put at 4⅝.

26. An investment advisor recommended that an investor who is interested in buying stock should consider instead buying a call and selling a put. Assuming the exercise prices are equal to current stock price, compare the potential profits from these two strategies.[18]

27. An investment advisor suggested the following "absurdly easy" way to make money.[19] On July 29, 1988, with the S&P 500 index at 272.02, a December put option on the S&P 500 with a striking price of 260 sold for $8 while a December call option with a 290 striking price sold for $1. Show the dollar gains and losses from selling the put and the call simultaneously, as a function of the value of the S&P 500 index when the options expire in December.

28. Russell Sage, a nineteenth-century New York money broker, was once convicted of lending money to stockbrokers at 8 percent, one percentage point above the state's legal ceiling on interest rates. To avoid this ceiling, Sage came up with the following plan: if someone wanted to borrow money to buy stock, Sage would buy the stock for himself, sell the customer a call option, and buy a put option from the customer. What is the implicit rate of interest on this "loan" if the initial price of the stock is $50, the exercise price of the put and call is $52, the options expire in one year, the price of the call is $4, and the price of the put is $1?

29. On August 1, 1988 gold was selling for $436 an ounce, and February 1989 futures contracts for gold were selling for $453. One could also buy call options on the February gold-futures contracts at the following prices:

Exercise Price	Call Price
400	$55.80
420	40.00
440	25.60
460	15.50

For a "condor" spread,[20] one buys the 400 and 460 calls and sells the 420 and 440 calls. Show the dollar gains or losses from this strategy as a function of the price of the futures contract when the options expire in February.

30. A trust called Americus introduced PRIMEs and SCOREs for AT&T in 1983, for Exxon in 1985, and for other stocks in 1987. We'll use Exxon as an example. With Exxon selling at about $53 a share in 1985, Americus established a trust that accepted ten million shares from current stockholders. These shares were then separated into PRIMEs and SCOREs, which trade separately on the American Stock Exchange and, thus, allow stockholders to hold varying amounts of each. The PRIME units get all the Exxon dividends received by the trust for five years plus the market price of Exxon on September 20, 1990, up to a maximum of $60 a share. Owners of the SCORES receive any excess of the market price over $60. Assume that you are a financial analyst asked to estimate the market price of PRIMEs and

SCOREs before trading begins. How would you use the Black-Scholes model to make your estimates? (Do not make actual estimates; just explain how PRIMEs and SCOREs are equivalent to specific options.)

31. A strap is a combination of two calls and a put; a strip combines two puts and a call. On August 3, 1988, when Sara Lee stock sold at $40 a share, an October call at 40 sold for $1\frac{5}{8}$, and an October 40 put sold for $1\frac{1}{2}$. Show the profit possibilities from buying both a strap and from buying a strip as a function of the price of Sara Lee on the October expiration date.

32. On November 9, 1984, IBM options expiring in July 1985 were selling for the following prices:

Option Type	Striking Price	Option Price
Put	110	$11\frac{13}{16}$
Call	140	$4\frac{1}{2}$
Put	140	17

IBM stock closed at $123\frac{1}{2}$ on this date. Graph the dollar gains from each of these two strategies as a function of the price of IBM stock on the July exercise date: (a) sell one 110 put and sell one 140 call, and (b) sell two 110 puts and buy one 140 put. You may find graph paper helpful, though the graphs need not be drawn precisely to scale. Your graphs, however, must have enough numerical labels to describe the profit function completely.

33. On December 15, 1984, IBM sold for $118\frac{3}{8}$ while seven-month call options (expiring in July 1985) with an exercise price of $120 sold for $9. Show that buying a share of IBM, writing a July 120 call, and buying a July 120 put is a perfect hedge. Ignoring transaction costs and assuming that T-bills yield a safe return of 6 percent over the seven-month period, what do you think the price of a July 120 put should be?

34. In the winter of 1981, Burroughs stock was selling for $90 while July call options with a striking price of $90 were selling for $10 and July call options with a striking price of $100 were selling for $5. Graph the dollar gains for each of the following strategies as a function of the price of Burroughs stock on the July exercise date. (Make sure that your axes have enough labels so that your graph is clear.)

a. Buy a July 90.

b. Sell a naked July 100.

c. Buy a July 90 and sell two July 100s.

35. It is sometimes argued that stock analysts should take into account the possibility that outstanding warrants will dilute a company's earnings. To examine this argument, consider a company with no debt which pays out all of its earnings, earns a rate of return ρ on its assets, and has n shares and m warrants outstanding. If the market price of a share of this firm's stock is set so as to yield a rate of return R, calculate the price per share of the firm's stock before the warrants have been issued and when the warrants have been exercised at a price E and the proceeds used by the firm to purchase assets yielding a rate of return ρ. Compare these prices in general and in the specific case where $\rho = r$.

36. Call options tend to have lower prices if the stock is expected to pay a dividend before the exercise date. Why?

37. Many of those investors using the Black-Scholes formula to value call options estimate the standard deviations from recent data. Were these estimated standard deviations increased or decreased by the 20 percent drop in the stock market on October 19, 1987? Did this change in the standard deviations increase or decrease the value of call options?

38. Use a computer program with the Black-Scholes equation to determine the theoretical value of a six-month call option with an exercise price of 40 if the current price of the underlying stock is 40, the stock does not pay a dividend, the continuously compounded annual risk-free rate is 8 percent, and the standard deviation of the continuously compounded annual return on the stock is 20 percent. Compare this value with the theoretical value as each of the following parameters is changed (keeping the other parameters at their initial values). In each case, explain why the theoretical value increases or decreases.

a. There are nine months until the option expires.

b. The price of the underlying stock is 42.

c. The continuously compounded risk-free rate is 10 percent.

d. The standard deviation of the continuously compounded annual return on the stock is 30 percent.

39. Redo Exercise 38, this time using the Black-Scholes equation and put-call parity to determine the theoretical value of a European put option with an exercise price of 40. Again explain why the value of the put increases or decreases as each of the four parameters is varied.

40. Table 16–4 in the text shows the August 10 prices of S&P 500 index September 1988 puts and calls. Use a graph to show the profits from the following strategies as a function of the value of the S&P 500 on the September exercise date:

a. Buy the 270 call, and sell the 260 call.

b. Sell the 270 call, and sell the 280 put.

c. Buy the stocks in the index at 261.9, and sell two 270 calls.

CHAPTER 17

Futures Contracts

If you bet on a horse, that's gambling.
If you bet you can make three spades, that's
entertainment.

If you bet cotton will go up three points, that's business.
See the difference?
Blackie Sherrod

Futures and **forward contracts** are agreements to deliver a certain item on a specified date at a price agreed upon today, but not paid until delivery. The difference between the two is that futures are standardized contracts traded on organized exchanges, while forward contracts are private agreements with no organized secondary market. The first futures markets in the United States developed in Chicago in the mid-1800s in response to farmers, who had been impoverished by an unexpected collapse in grain prices, and millers, who wanted to ensure deliveries at a known price. If a farmer and miller sign a contract promising the delivery of 5000 bushels of wheat at $3.00 a bushel, then both are protected from fluctuations in the market price, or **spot price,** of wheat for immediate delivery.

This chapter will examine the general nature of futures contracts and consider several varied examples, including wheat, silver, and financial futures. We will discuss what factors influence futures prices and how futures contracts are used for hedging, speculation, and arbitrage. We will pay particular attention to the use of stock-index futures by institutional investors and to program trading, which some people blame for a variety of ills. We begin with some preliminary details on the mechanics of futures trading.

forward contract
A forward contract is a private agreement to deliver a certain item on a specified date at a price agreed to today, but not paid until delivery.

spot price
The spot price is the current market price for immediate delivery.

THE ADVANTAGES OF
STANDARDIZED CONTRACTS

Organized exchanges standardize the terms of futures contracts, enforce their terms, and allow the trading of contracts before delivery. For example, the wheat contracts traded on the Chicago Board of Trade specify the delivery of 5000 bushels of an approved wheat (such as No. 1 Northern Spring or No. 2 Hard Red Winter) to an approved warehouse on a specified date. The miller who takes delivery is sent a receipt from the warehouse certifying that a sufficient quantity of an appropriate wheat has been stored there. Because the exchange's clearinghouse guarantees that the farmer will deliver this wheat and that the miller will pay for it, traders do not have to worry or haggle about the details of the contract.

The trading of standardized contracts on an organized exchange also allows traders to cancel contracts before the delivery date. The farmer who sold wheat futures but will not have enough wheat on the delivery date can repurchase futures contracts; the miller who bought wheat futures and now does not want as much wheat as anticipated earlier can resell futures contracts. The farmer and miller can also use the futures market to protect themselves against fluctuations in the prices of products that are similar but not identical to those specified in the futures contracts. The farmer may grow another type of wheat, or the miller may intend to buy a different kind. Also the approved warehouses may be inconvenient—perhaps it is an Australian farmer or a Belgian miller.

Suppose that a Belgian miller intends to buy 100,000 bushels of a special Australian wheat six months from now, and wants protection against an increase in the spot price. The miller might sign a forward contract with a specific Australian farmer for 100,000 bushels at $3.50 a bushel, but such a agreement is inflexible and may be difficult to enforce. Instead, the miller buys twenty futures contracts on the Chicago Board of Trade for common wheat at $3.00 a bushel. If the world wheat market tightens, the spot price of common wheat may rise to $4.00 a bushel while the price of the exotic Australian wheat rises to $4.50. Shortly before the delivery date, the Belgian miller sells the futures contract at $4.00 to an American miller who intends to take delivery (or perhaps to an Australian farmer who was hedging his position), for a profit of $1.00 a bushel. The $1-per-bushel increase in the spot price that the Belgian miller pays for Australian wheat is offset by a $1-per-bushel profit on the futures contracts, giving a net cost of $3.50 a bushel as intended. The miller may even decide to purchase fewer than 100,000 bushels and pocket some of the profits on these futures contracts.

With a futures market, the miller can make day-to-day adjustments, buying more contracts to lock in the price of larger future deliveries or, at times, becoming a net seller to protect the value of a large wheat inventory. The miller and farmer can also speculate, buying or selling futures contracts to bet on the future price of wheat. Many who are neither millers nor

TABLE 17–1 Contracts Traded on Futures Markets in 1987

Contract Group	Number of Contracts (millions)	Percent of Total Contracts
Bonds	88.0	41.2
Agricultural	39.6	18.6
Stock indexes	26.3	12.3
Energy	20.3	9.5
Foreign currencies	19.9	9.3
Metals	19.4	9.1
Total	213.5	100.0

Source: Paula A. Tosini, "Stock Index Futures and Stock Market Activity in October 1987," *Financial Analysts Journal,* January/February 1988, pp. 28–38.

TABLE 17–2 Most Actively Traded Futures Contracts in 1987

Contract	Number of Contracts Traded (millions)	Exchange
U.S. Treasury bonds	61.1	Chicago Board of Trade (CBT)
S&P 500 stock index	19.9	Chicago Mercantile Exchange (CME)
Eurodollars	17.8	Chicago Mercantile Exchange (CME)
Crude oil	12.8	New York Mercantile Exchange (NYMEX)
Gold	9.8	Commodities Exchange, Inc. (COMEX)
Corn	7.2	Chicago Board of Trade (CBT)

Source: Paula A. Tosini, "Stock Index Futures and Stock Market Activity in October 1987," *Financial Analysts Journal,* January/February 1988, pp. 28–38.

farmers are lured to the futures markets for such speculation, and most lose money doing so.

FUTURES TRANSACTIONS

Futures contracts are traded on several exchanges, with the largest being the Chicago Board of Trade and the Chicago Mercantile Exchange. (See also Investment Example 17–1, on p. 542.) Table 17–1 shows the types of futures contracts traded on all exchanges in 1987, and Table 17–2 shows the most actively traded contracts. While agricultural products are still important, they have been joined in recent years by a wide variety of other real and financial assets. The daily pages of *The Wall Street Journal* and other major newspapers list the specific items and the current prices.

542

THE CHICAGO STING

In January 1989, the federal government revealed a two-year undercover investigation of trading at the Chicago Mercantile Exchange and the Chicago Board of Trade (using the code names Operation Hedgeclipper and Operation Sour Mash). With the cooperation of some colleges and businesses, the Justice Department manufactured phony academic and professional records for several undercover FBI agents (moles). Archer-Daniels-Midland, the world's largest soybean processor, trained the agents in commodities trading. The federal government spent over a million dollars buying seats on the exchanges; spent thousands more for offices, high-rent apartments, luxury automobiles, health club memberships, and other accessories to create an illusion of success for its agents; and spent hundreds of thousands of dollars covering their trading losses.*

Some of the mole's conversations, on and off the

*Scott McMurray and John Koten, "Probe of 2 Exchanges Shows Wild Fraternity Of Traders in Yen Pit," *The Wall Street Journal,* January 26, 1989.

trading floors, were recorded with hidden video cameras or microphones. In addition, at least one legitimate trader was persuaded to join the government investigation and wear a hidden microphone. Several alleged misdeeds were uncovered. Some traders "front ran" large orders, buying or selling for their own accounts before executing large customer orders. Some executed customer orders by making reciprocal trades with each other at noncompetitive prices. Some skimmed money by trading at one price and reporting a different price to their customers, somewhat higher for a buy order and lower for a sell order. One of the government moles told other traders that a private company he owned had large tax losses that could be used to shelter profitable trades. These traders were reportedly persuaded to give some of their profitable trades to the government agent, in return for cash passed in plain envelopes. Despite the widespread negative publicity generated by this sting operation, the exchanges have so far resisted reform proposals, including a ban on dual trading—the practice of trading for both the trader's account and for customer accounts.

Market Prices

As on the stock exchanges, transactions in the futures market are made through traders who own seats on the exchange. But while transactions on the stock exchanges pass through a specialist, members of the futures market trade with each other. Each commodity has a *trading pit*—an oval area with steps leading down to a central floor—where traders buy and sell, either for their own accounts or on behalf of orders from outside the exchange. All offers to buy and sell must be by "open outcry" so that, in theory, all traders in the pit have an opportunity to accept the offer. In practice, the pits are often crowded with people pushing and shoving as they use arcane hand signals and loud shouts to try to communicate with each other. At particularly anxious moments, fights break out and someone on the steps will fall, toppling everyone in front.

A trader signals the number of contracts with a hand touching the face. The price is signaled by the other hand, held away from the body—the palm facing outward for a sale and towards the body for a purchase. Numbers are shown by the fingers on each hand, held vertically for the numbers 1 through 5 and horizontally for 6 through 10. When a trade is made, it is recorded on a small paper card and put in the trader's pocket. Trades are enforced by word of honor: anyone who backs out of a deal is shunned by other traders and unable to continue trading. The story is told of a trader who received an order from off the floor to sell gold contracts and mistakenly bought contracts instead. Gold prices plummeted and he lost $800,000 that day before he realized his mistake. Rather than renege on the deal, he paid his debt by selling his seat on the Chicago Board and leaving the business.[1]

As with options, futures are created by the willingness of people to sell contracts. Those who own contracts are said to be *long*, while those who have written contracts are *short*; and the total amount of outstanding contracts, called the *open interest*, fluctuates daily. Some data on the futures contracts trading on Monday, August 15, 1988, is shown in Table 17–3. We will use wheat to explain this table.

The first line identifies the commodity, the exchange, the size of a contract, and the units in which prices are quoted—thus the reported September 383 price for wheat means $3.83 per bushel. The far left-hand column shows the delivery dates of the available contracts; the next three columns show the opening price and the high and low prices for trades that day. The next column shows the settlement price, which is like a closing price, and will be discussed shortly. The column after that shows the change in the settlement price from the day before. Next are the contract's lifetime highs and lows, the highest and lowest prices at which the contract has traded. Since each contract is traded for a year or less, the wide spread between the lifetime highs and lows accurately reflects the considerable volatility of futures prices. Figure 17–1 shows the daily settlement prices over the entire twelve-month life of the September 1988 wheat contract. The exchanges try to control short-run price fluctuations by imposing **daily limits** on the price changes of many futures contracts. For wheat, the settlement price cannot rise or fall by more than 20 cents in a day.

The last column in Table 17–3 shows the open interest, the number of outstanding contracts. As Figure 17–2 on p. 546 illustrates, the open interest is zero when a contract is first introduced, rises as trading increases, typically reaches a peak a few months before expiration, and then declines to zero on the delivery date. The line at the bottom of the wheat section in

daily limits
Daily limits are used to restrain short-run fluctuations in the prices of some futures contracts.

TABLE 17–3   Selected Futures Prices, August 15, 1988

WHEAT (CBT) 5,000 bu.; cents per bu.

	Open	High	Low	Settle	Change	Lifetime High	Lifetime Low	Open Interest
Sept	383	393	383	392	+ 12¼	421	272	13,187
Dec	396	406½	396	406¼	+ 13¼	431	289	31,240
Mr89	400	409	398	409	+ 14½	432	323	5,328
May	381½	385	376	383¾	+ 9¾	420	330	1,919
July	354	362	354	361	+ 9	395	327	3,815

Est. vol. 17,000; vol. Fri 19,616; open int. 55,489, + 400

HOGS (CME) 30,000 lbs.; cents per lb.

	Open	High	Low	Settle	Change	Lifetime High	Lifetime Low	Open Interest
Aug	47.10	47.40	46.60	47.37	+ .57	53.27	39.60	2,118
Oct	40.50	40.75	39.80	40.65	+ .32	46.40	37.52	8,535
Feb89	45.10	45.60	44.70	45.40	+ .25	52.00	41.80	4,108
Apr	44.30	44.60	44.00	44.45	+ .55	51.65	40.60	2,790
June	48.75	48.95	48.52	48.65	+ .05	56.25	42.50	839

Est. vol. 5,380; vol. Fri 6,130; open int. 26,193, + 111

GOLD (CMX) 100 troy oz.; $ per troy oz.

	Open	High	Low	Settle	Change	Lifetime High	Lifetime Low	Open Interest
Aug	430.70	433.00	430.40	433.00	+ 1.70	527.00	422.00	769
Dec	440.00	443.30	440.00	442.90	+ 1.70	546.00	430.80	68,101
Feb89	446.50	446.60	446.50	448.90	+ 1.70	549.50	440.00	10,036
Dec	475.20	476.90	475.20	479.10	+ 2.00	514.50	469.00	7,018

Est. vol. 20,000; vol. Fri 33,663; open int. 139,982, − 2,304

SILVER (CMX) 5000 troy oz.; cents per troy oz.

	Open	High	Low	Settle	Change	Lifetime High	Lifetime Low	Open Interest
Sept	673.0	679.5	670.0	678.5	+ 4.5	1064.0	588.0	36,561
Dec	690.0	696.0	686.0	694.6	+ 4.6	1082.0	606.0	23,370
Mar89	706.5	712.5	706.5	710.8	+ 4.6	1073.0	660.0	7,448
Dec	755.0	756.0	755.0	761.0	+ 4.6	886.0	722.0	1,419

Est. vol. 15,000; vol. Fri 21,644; open int. 82,912, + 292

TABLE 17–3, *cont'd.*   Selected Futures Prices, August 15, 1988

	Open	High	Low	Settle	Change	Lifetime High	Low	Open Interest
				S&P 500 INDEX (CME) 500 times index				
Sept	262.50	263.20	258.80	259.10	−3.45	343.50	193.00	105,912
Dec	264.50	265.70	261.40	261.65	−3.45	282.10	252.20	9,372
Mar89	267.25	268.10	264.10	264.25	−3.30	283.50	253.90	2,206
			Est. vol. 42,458; vol. Fri 30,259; open int. 117,516, −1.159					

Source: The Wall Street Journal, August 16, 1988.

FIGURE 17–1   Daily settlement prices of September 1988 wheat futures

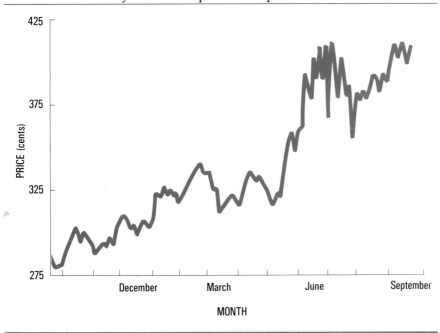

Table 17–3 shows the total trading in five wheat contracts that day and the day before, the total open interest, and the net change in the open interest.

Covering Positions

In each transaction, the buyer of a futures contract agrees to pay the seller the specified futures price F when the item is delivered. In some 97 percent

FIGURE 17–2   Daily open interest, September 1988 wheat futures

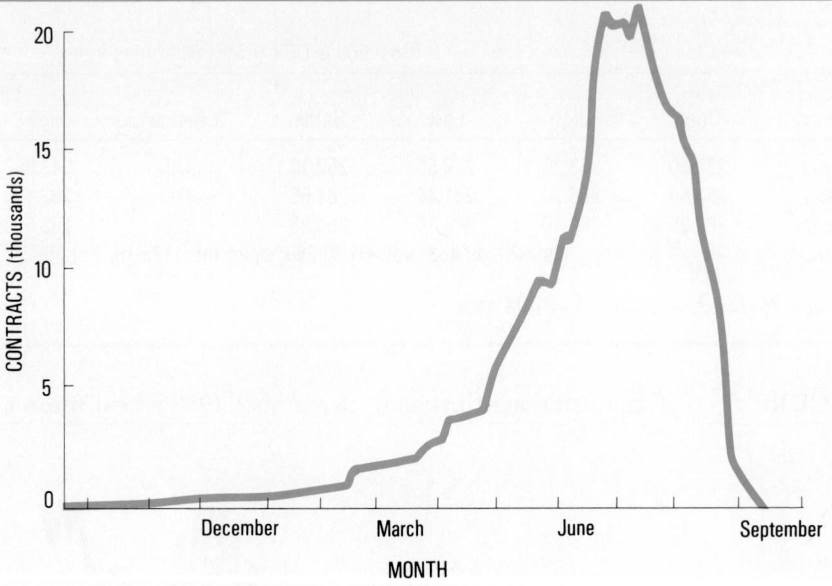

of the cases, however, there turns out to be no delivery, because the shorts repurchase contracts from the longs before the delivery date, an action that is called **covering** or **reversing a position.**

On the delivery date, the price of a futures contract equals the spot price, since both now call for immediate delivery. Say that on the delivery date, the spot price is P. By taking delivery, the holder of a contract can buy for F, the price agreed to when the futures contract was first purchased, and sell for P, a profit of $P - F$, the price agreed to when the futures contract was first purchased, (ignoring the various transaction costs). Except for transaction costs, futures contracts are a zero-sum game, and the writer of the contract must accept F for something worth P, a loss of $P - F$. These same gains and losses can be realized, and usually are, without an actual delivery. Instead of taking delivery, anyone who still owns a futures contract on the delivery date sells it for the current spot price P, realizing a profit of $P - F$, while a contract writer repurchases the contract for P, taking a loss of $P - F$.

In general, if you buy a futures contract for F and later sell a contract for F', then your profit is $F' - F$. Your position is closed even if you do not sell the contract to the same person from whom you purchased it, since your obligation to accept delivery is cancelled by your obligation to make delivery. In practice, virtually all futures trading is by speculators who have no intention of making or taking delivery, or by producers and

covering or reversing a position
The buyer (or seller) of a futures contract can reverse the position by selling (or buying) the contract before the delivery date.

TABLE 17–4 Four Hypothetical Days in the Silver Market

Date	Settlement Price	Contract Value	Daily Profit	Cumulative Profit
October 1	$10.00	$100,000	$0	$0
October 2	9.50	95,000	−5,000	−5,000
October 3	11.00	110,000	15,000	10,000
October 4	10.50	105,000	−5,000	5,000

users who, like the Belgian miller, trade through accustomed channels in the spot market and use the futures market to hedge their position. Any tales of tons of sugar dropped on the front lawn are amusing but untrue. The worst that can happen is that the commodity will be put in a warehouse and the buyer will be billed for the cost of the commodity plus storage charges.

Marking to Market

To ensure the financial integrity of the exchange, the clearinghouse requires a daily settlement of all unrealized profits and losses. At the end of each trading day, the exchange sets a **settlement price** for each contract for the purpose of calculating profits and losses. For actively traded contracts, the settlement price is the closing price (the price of the last transaction). For inactive contracts, the exchange estimates what the price would have been had there been transactions at the close. Settlement prices are used to calculate the change in the value of each trader's position, and those traders with losses in any given day must make cash payments to the brokerage accounts of those traders with profits before the beginning of the next trading day. The daily transfer of funds from losers to winners is called the **daily settlement,** or **marking to market.**

Suppose that you buy two silver futures contracts at $10 an ounce on October 1. Since each contract is for 5,000 ounces, the total value of your position is $100,000. We will assume that the settlement price on October 1 is $10 and that your broker requires a margin deposit of $10,000 to ensure your ability to cover your possible losses. Table 17–4 shows what might happen to your account during the next three days.

On October 2, the settlement price drops to $9.50 and your contracts are worth $95,000—a $5000 loss for the day. Thus, $5000 is deducted from your account and credited to the account of someone who was short silver that day, and your broker will most likely demand that you either put up additional margin or sell your contracts. The price rises to $11 on October 3, and you receive $15,000 from those who were short silver. On October 4, the price dips to $10.50, and you pay $5000.

settlement price
The settlement price, often equal to the closing price, is used at the end of each trading day for calculating each trader's profit or loss.

daily settlement
The daily settlement transfers funds from futures winners to losers.

If you sell on October 4 at $10.50, your position is closed with a cumulative profit of $5000. Your cumulative profit depends on the difference between the $10.50 final price and the $10.00 initial price. But unlike other securities, in which you do not realize your profit until you actually sell the securities, the daily settlement gives you a profit or loss each day. These daily settlements make it very clear that, except for brokerage costs, futures contracts are a zero-sum game.

Margin serves different roles in the stock market and in the futures market. In the stock market, an investor purchases an asset and must pay the seller for it. If the buyer borrows part of the cost from the brokerage firm, the broker holds the stock as collateral and requires the investor to put up *margin*, money that serves as a downpayment to protect the broker in case the value of the stock falls and the borrower defaults on the loan. Since the broker has lent money to finance the purchase, interest is charged on this loan.

The purchase or sale of a futures contract does not involve an immediate payment between buyer and seller. Each party takes a temporary position, hoping to profit from swings in the value of the futures contract. The broker does not charge interest because no money has been lent. The risk to the broker is that the trader will not be able to cover losses resulting from swings in the value of the contract. For protection, brokers (and the exchanges) require margin in excess of the maximum anticipated one-day change in the value of the contract, and the exchange requires that each day's losses be covered by cash payments before the start of the next trading day. Because of this different role of margin in futures trading, both buyers and sellers are subject to margin requirements, and hedgers (who may be long one delivery date and short another) are subject to lower margin requirements than speculators.

Speculation

Futures have a well-deserved reputation for being speculative gambles, a way to make or, more likely, to lose a lot of money in a hurry. David Dreman, a portfolio manager and *Forbes* columnist, wrote that "futures have no place in the portfolio of a conservative investor and should be looked at only by masochists or the wildest of dice players."[2] Investment Example 17–2 on pp. 550–551 tells how one family wagered and lost more than a billion dollars on silver futures.

There are several reasons why futures are risky. There are no dividends, interest, or other cash flow. A futures contract is just a bet on the price of the underlying commodity. The prices of futures contracts are at least as volatile as bond and stock prices, and margin requirements are very low, 15 percent or less, and can typically be met by leaving interest-earning Treasury bills with the broker. This low margin creates powerful leverage, with well-known consequences.

Individual investors are sometimes lured into futures by firms that make phone calls peddling hot tips ("Our computer says that silver is going to double within a month") or that advertise exaggerated claims in newspapers and magazines ("Spectacular new system. $374,566.47 profit in two days!") These are the same kind of people who auction Oriental rugs in motels, push multilevel distribution plans, and sell books on how to profit from the end of the world. A financial reporter for *Barron's* told how she was bombarded by high-pressure phone calls; claiming that "Most of my clients have doubled their money in gold options in the last six or eight weeks, and that's just the beginning. I want to get your $5,000 up to $10,000. I feel the worst we should do is 100 percent in a year . . . but the timing is critical. We really have to make a move by Friday."[3] A 1981 survey found that 40 percent of the readers of *The Wall Street Journal* had similar experiences.[4]

Brokers love commodity markets because the brief contracts with relatively high commissions generate a steady stream of revenue. Those who are tempted to play should remember that, even if there were no brokerage commissions, futures trading would be, at best, a zero-sum game. The only way a player can make a dollar is if another player loses a dollar. The sizable commissions make commodity trading considerably worse than a zero-sum game—more like a high-stakes poker game in which the house confiscates a large part of every pot. Do you really think you can play cocoa prices against Hershey, orange-juice prices against Sunkist, silver prices against Engelhard, and expect to go home a winner? Ask yourself, too, why the brokers who are so confident of their systems are so eager for you to try them. If the system were as successful as they claim, they could make a lot more profits by investing their own money than by fishing around for customers. Clearly, the safest way to make money in the futures market is through brokerage commissions.

It has been estimated that 90 percent of the small investors in commodities lose money, and that the average life span of an individual account is four months.[5] Apparently, most small investors are lured by hopes of a quick profit (maybe after a persuasive phone call, reading about a frost in Florida, or seeing the price of coffee rise in their local supermarket), experience a quick loss and leave, having learned an expensive lesson. A commodities broker quoted in *Forbes* gave even worse odds. Of 1000 small customers he had over a thirteen-year period, every single one lost money.[6] A more formal academic study of the trading records of small speculators found that three-fourths lost money and that their total losses came to $12 million, while the minority who were profitable made only $2 million.[7] The $10 million difference went to brokers and large traders. Another study found that small speculators made $2.6 million in profits before paying $8 million in commissions, giving a net loss of $5.4 million.[8]

In May 1988, an astounding case was brought to court. A Seattle building contractor who belonged to Gamblers Anonymous, an organization for

THE HUNT BROTHERS BUY SILVER

The great East Texas oil fields made H. L. Hunt one of the richest men in America, what a reporter for the London *Sunday Times* called "the archetype of a Texas oil billionaire—arrogant, prejudiced, mean, eccentric, and secretive."[1] Two of his sons, Bunker and Herbert, stayed in the oil business.

Bunker found oil in Libya in the 1960s, enough to give him control over more oil than any single individual in the world. However, Colonel Qaddafi nationalized the Libyan fields in 1973, costing Bunker Hunt some $15 billion in oil reserves. Bunker and Herbert turned to the silver market, ostensibly to protect their wealth against inflation. In late 1973, they bought futures contracts for 35 million ounces of silver and some people suspected they were trying to corner the market.

Normally, almost all futures contracts are liquidated before expiration, with the final price approximately equal to the current spot price. Those who do not sell their contracts, normally industrial users, take delivery from producers who do not close their short positions. But what if the Hunts, or others, decide not to liquidate a large block of futures contracts? The naked shorts, nonproducers betting against a rise in the price of silver, are squeezed, or cornered, in that if they cannot find millions of ounces of silver on short notice, they will be forced to buy the Hunts' futures contracts at whatever price the Hunts demand.

Because the shorts do not intend to actually deliver the commodity, the total number of futures contracts outstanding can far exceed the actual supply of a commodity. Many futures markets guard against corners by restricting the amount that any person or group of persons can buy. There are no limits at all in the silver market.

A growing fear of a silver squeeze pushed the price of March 1974 futures from $2.90 in December 1973 to $4 in January and $6.60 in late February. At this point, the unexpected happened when the Bank of Mexico decided to sell 50 million ounces of silver that it had acquired at less than $2 an ounce, thereby providing the spot market with more than enough silver to meet the Hunt's futures contracts. The Hunts made millions and came close to making much more.

By the end of 1976, the Hunts had accumulated 100 million ounces of silver, and some anticipated an eventual attempt to squeeze the market. The price of December 1979 silver futures was below $18 in September 1979 and expired above $29. In January 1980, the price of March silver futures hit $37.10, with the Hunts and associates controlling nearly 300 million ounces of silver and silver futures, 80 percent of the total amount mined worldwide in 1979. Some 20 to 50 million ounces of silver came onto the market, melted down from coins, jewelry, teapots, and so on; but this was not nearly enough to satisfy the Hunts' buying power.

On January 9, 1980, the Commodity Futures Trading Commission (CFTC) abruptly increased the margin requirements to $75,000 per contract ($15 an ounce) during the delivery month. Still, on January 14, the price of March futures reached an unprecedented $42.50. At this point, the Hunts made a private deal with Engelhard, the world's largest bullion dealer, agreeing to buy 19 million ounces of silver at $35 an ounce on March 31, 1980 (the day that the March futures would expire), thereby canceling 3,800 of Hunt's long and Engelhard's short contracts and relieving the margin pressure on both. Two days later, they agreed to cancel another 2200 contracts by trading 11 million ounces on July 1; as collateral, the Hunts put up 8.5 million ounces of silver. This deal bought time in that margin calls were replaced with a two-month deadline for finding a billion dollars in cash to complete the transaction. It was also a billion-dollar gamble that the price of silver would stay above $35 an ounce.

Bunker still held 8580 March contracts (42.9 million ounces) and his associates held more, enough to squeeze the remaining shorts who, unlike Engelhard, did not own any silver. On January 18, the price of silver topped $50, making the total

market value of the 300 million ounces of silver and silver-futures contracts held by the Hunt group almost $15 billion—ironically, the same amount lost to Colonel Qaddafi. On January 21, the Comex board changed the rules again, raising margin requirements once more and, in an unprecedented move, henceforth allowing trades only for liquidation—the longs could sell to the shorts, but they could not buy any more contracts. The price of March futures promptly dropped to $44, and dropped another $10 the next day, after the Chicago Board of Trade adopted similar rules. Now it was the Hunts who were squeezed. As their profits evaporated, their brokers made urgent margin calls. Every dollar decrease in the futures price cost Bunker $42.9 million in equity; the two-day $16 decline cost a staggering $686 million. In all, during January and February, the Hunts had to borrow $1 billion, and an associated company put up another $0.5 billion, secured by land, oil leases, and 70 million ounces of silver.

On March 14, Federal Reserve Chairman Volcker announced a special credit-restraint program, telling banks to stop lending money to finance speculation in commodities and precious metals. Bunker Hunt hurried to Europe and then to Saudi Arabia to borrow money, without success. The Hunts were slated to pay Engelhard $665 million on March 31, and the margin calls provoked by sagging silver prices were increasingly difficult to meet. On March 25, the price of silver fell to $20.20, and the Bache brokerage firm, which had lent the Hunts $233 million, informed the brothers that they would begin selling silver, silver futures, and other stocks in their accounts to meet margin calls. On March 26, March futures slumped to $15.80, and not only the Hunts were worried.

At 8:00 A.M. on March 27, Herbert Hunt told the CFTC that the Hunts would not sell any of their uncollateralized silver to repay their borrowings and advised the CFTC to close the market and settle all contracts at the previous day's price of $15.80. Bache seconded the motion. The CFTC let the exchange open. Fear of the unknown and Bache's liquidation of the Hunts' futures contracts knocked the price as low as $10.40 that day, dubbed Silver Thursday. On Friday the price rallied to $12, and Bache sold the remaining March futures.

The crisis was not over, for the coming Monday was March 31, the day Engelhard was to be paid $665 million in cash for 19 million ounces of silver that now were worth closer to $200 million. Over the weekend, a deal was struck, giving Engelhard a portion of the Hunts' oil leases.

At this point, the Hunts' total borrowing topped a billion dollars, with their silver holdings worth an approximately equal amount. A consortium of thirteen banks agreed to make a ten-year, $1.1 billion loan (at the prime rate plus 1 percent) to the Placid Oil Company, a Hunt family trust. Placid then lent the Hunts the money so that the brothers could pay off their short-term debt. Among the conditions of the loan was a requirement that the Hunts not speculate in commodities or futures markets for ten years, until 1990, and that they liquidate their silver stockpile in an orderly fashion.

Unfortunately, a worldwide drop in oil prices reduced the market value of Placid Oil's assets, and it filed for bankruptcy in 1986 to protect itself from increasingly worried bankers. It has been estimated that the Hunts lost $1.5 billion in the silver market and that, overall, the market value of their wealth has fallen from $8 billion in 1980 to $0, plus or minus a billion, in 1987. In 1988, a federal jury ruled that the Hunt brothers had conspired to corner the silver market and awarded $130 million to a Peruvian company that had shorted silver in 1979.

[1] Stephen Fay, *Beyond Greed* (New York: Viking Press, 1982). Much of this example is based on this well-researched book.
[2] Fay, p. 78.

helping compulsive gamblers, claimed that he met the manager of a commodity brokerage firm at a dice game in 1979 and soon began trading commodity futures through this firm. Over the next seven years, he traded nearly 11,000 contracts and lost $1.4 million, including $1 million in trading losses and $400,000 in commissions. He subsequently sued the brokerage firm, and in 1988 a federal District Court judged ruled that the firm was indeed negligent in allowing him to trade commodity futures when he was clearly emotionally unfit for it. Losses incurred before February 1984 were excluded because the statute of limitations had expired. While the contractor had to take some responsibility for his actions, the brokerage firm was ordered to reimburse him for half of his losses.[9]

FUTURES PRICES

The most obvious interpretation of a futures price is a bet on the price P of the commodity when the contract matures. If the expected value of the price is $E[P]$, risk-neutral speculators will buy futures contracts at a price F if $F < E[P]$ and sell if $F > E[P]$. The market price of a futures contract therefore provides a market consensus on the anticipated price of the commodity, in the sense that there is a balance between buyers who expect a somewhat higher price and sellers who expect a lower one.

By this interpretation, the wheat futures prices in Table 17–3 imply that traders anticipate an increase in wheat prices in December and March followed by a decline in May and July, which is consistent with the seasonal pattern of wheat growing. Even nonparticipants consequently find it useful to look to futures markets for expert opinion on the course of prices. Farmers who do not buy futures contracts nonetheless look at wheat and soybean futures prices before making their crop plans. Building contractors look at lumber futures before submitting bids, and cattle breeders follow cattle futures.

The Cost of Carry

basis
The basis is the difference between the futures price and the spot price.

spread
Spread strategies involving the simultaneous purchase and sale of options with different striking prices and/or expiration dates.

cost of carry
The cost of carry is the cost of buying a commodity now and holding it until the delivery date of a futures' contract.

There is another explanation of futures prices that is sometimes more appropriate. The **basis,** or **spread,** is the difference between the futures price and the current spot price, or

$$\text{basis} = \text{futures price} - \text{spot price}.$$

For many items, this spread is determined by the fact that a viable alternative to buying a futures contract is to buy the commodity now and hold it until the futures' contract delivery date. The cost of doing so is called the **cost of carry,** and includes the cost of storage, spoilage, insurance, and foregone interest, less any cash flow from the item while it is being held.

The forgone interest arises because buying the item now ties up your money, money that could be earning interest if you instead buy a futures contract and pay for the item later.

Since buying now and buying later are alternative ways of acquiring the same commodity, the net cost should be the same:

$$\text{futures price} = \text{spot price} + \text{cost of carry} \qquad (1)$$

Because the cost of carry is typically positive and increases as time passes, futures prices normally exceed the spot price and increase with the length of the contract. For any given contract, the cost of carry declines as the time horizon shrinks until, on the delivery date itself, the cost of carry is zero and the futures price equals the spot price. In Table 17–3, gold- and silver-futures prices increase steadily as the horizon lengthens and the cost of carry increases. Notice also that the prices of gold and silver contracts change uniformly, presumably with the current spot price and with interest rates. In contrast, the prices of futures contracts for wheat and hogs are affected by anticipated future spot prices, which need not move in lockstep. The short-term supply may be diminishing even while longer-term supplies are increasing.

Equation 1 has the very strong and, for many, counterintuitive impli-cation that the price of a futures contract depends on the current spot price, instead of the anticipated future spot price. The explanation is that because current and future delivery can be arbitraged, the *basis*—or difference between the futures and spot prices—should simply equal the cost of carry:

$$\text{futures price} - \text{spot price} = \text{cost of carry.} \qquad (2)$$

Arbitrage Between the Spot and Futures Markets

Someone who believes futures are mispriced according to Equation 2— that the cost of carry differs significantly from the basis—can arbitrage by buying the commodity and selling a futures contract, or vice versa. Since the arbitragers hope to profit from a change in the basis, they have *basis risk*, which is small if the cost of carry has been estimated accurately. Consider, for instance, a one-year futures contract on a generic commodity with a current spot price of $10. At a 10 percent interest rate, the forgone interest from buying the commodity instead of a futures contract is (10 percent) ($10) = $1. If the annual cost of storage, insurance and so on is $0.50, then the total cost of carry is $1.50, and the price of a futures contract should be $11.50, as shown in the following calculation:

$$
\begin{aligned}
\text{futures price} &= \text{spot price} + \text{cost of carry} \\
&= \$10.00 + \$1.50 \\
&= \$11.50
\end{aligned}
$$

If the futures price exceeds this figure, at say $12, then an arbitrager can buy the commodity for $10 and sell a futures contract for $12. On the delivery date, the arbitrager delivers the commodity for a profit of $2, which, by assumption, exceeds the $1.50 cost of carrying it.

If the futures price is too low, at say $11, then an arbitrager who already owns the commodity can sell it for $10, thereby avoiding the $1.50 carrying costs, and buy a futures contract for $11 so as to recover the commodity in a year's time with a $0.50 profit. An arbitrager who does not own the commodity may be able to borrow it and sell it short for $10, hedging the position with an $11 futures contract; if the $10 proceeds can be invested to earn $1 interest and the person who lent the commodity can be persuaded to pay for the storage costs that would otherwise be incurred, then a $0.50 profit can be realized.

Many commodities, such as butter, potatoes, hogs, and live cattle, are expensive to store and difficult to sell short. The practical impossibility of arbitrage undermines Equations 1 and 2, so that the futures price is not determined by the current spot price and the cost of carry but, instead, largely reflects the expected spot price on the delivery date. Other items are relatively easy to store and to sell short—for example, gold, silver, foreign currencies, Eurodollars, bonds, and stocks—and their futures prices are determined by the cost-of-carry relationship, Equation 1. Even in these cases, however, the existence of transaction costs and restrictions on short sales imply that a futures price can deviate somewhat from the theoretical equilibrium value before arbitrage becomes profitable.

Betting on the Cost of Carry

For items that can be stored and sold short, the cost of carry explains not only the relationship between the current spot price and a futures price, but also between futures prices for delivery on different dates. Consider the application of Equation 1 to futures prices for delivery in both six and twelve months:

  6-month futures price = current spot price + cost of carry for 6 mo.
12-month futures price = current spot price + cost of carry for 12 mo.

These relationships imply that the spread between the twelve-month and six-month futures prices should equal the difference in the cost of carry:

12-month futures price − 6 month futures price
$$= \text{cost of carry for 12 months} - \text{cost of carry for 6 months}$$
$$= \text{cost of carry for extra 6 months.}$$

Since the cost of carry is typically positive, futures prices for items that can be stored and sold short increase with the delivery date. This is true, for example, of the gold and silver contracts in Table 17–3.

To be more specific, consider the August and December 1988 gold futures shown in the table. The difference in the prices,

$$\$442.90 - \$433.00 = \$9.90,$$

should reflect the cost of carry, storage plus interest, during the four months from August to December. The storage charge for gold bullion is about $0.001 per ounce per day, or $0.12 per ounce for these four months. The remainder of the cost of carry is interest costs:

Cost of carry	$9.90
Storage costs	−0.12
Interest costs	$9.78

Converting this figure to a percentage, $9.78/$433.00 = 2.26 percent, or 6.8 percent annualized. The interest rate on comparable Treasury bills at the time was 7 percent, confirming that the spread in the August and December futures prices was determined by the cost of carry.

A comparison of the December 1988 and December 1989 gold futures gives the following estimates:

Cost of carry	$36.20
Storage costs	−0.37
Interest costs	$35.83

The annual percentage is $35.83/$442.90 = 8.1 percent, which again is consistent with the term structure of interest rates on Treasury securities at the time (rates above 8 percent for maturities longer than one year). Financial-market participants expected that interest rates in December 1988 would be above 8 percent, and this anticipated increase is reflected not only in the term structure of interest rates but also in increasing gold spreads on distant gold futures contracts.

Those investors who disagree with the interest-rate expectations imbedded in the term structure and in gold spreads can bet against these expectations with bonds or gold futures. For instance, in August 1988, those who did not think interest rates would increase could sell their Treasury bills and buy long-term bonds. Alternatively, they could buy December 1988 gold futures and sell December 1989 contracts, implicitly betting that the cost of carry will not turn out to be as large as other investors anticipate and that the spread will narrow when others realize their mistake.

A final complication is that the interest cost depends on both the interest rate and the price of gold, as follows:

$$\text{interest cost} = (\text{interest rate})(\text{price of gold})$$

Thus, the spread narrows if interest rates decline *or* if the price of gold falls. Those who believe that both interest rates and gold prices will fall can, as described earlier, buy near contracts and sell distant ones, betting that the spread will narrow as the cost of carry declines. Those who anticipate an increase in interest rates and gold prices can buy distant contracts and sell near ones, expecting the spread to widen as the cost of carry increases.

FINANCIAL FUTURES

Futures contracts now exist for a wide variety of financial assets, including Treasury bonds, foreign currencies, Eurodollars, and British bonds. As with options, the fact that items need not be delivered means that futures contracts can be written on stock indexes and other intangibles that cannot be delivered. Futures contracts are traded for the S&P 500 index, the New York Stock Exchange (NYSE) composite index, an municipal-bond index, and an index gauging the foreign-exchange value of the U.S. dollar.

Financial assets are relatively easy to store and can usually be sold short or, even simpler, sold by investors who already have these assets in their portfolios. Thus, the price of financial futures is determined not by the expected future spot price, but by the cost of carry. For financial assets, insurance, storage, and spoilage are negligible, making lost interest the biggest expense of buying now. Lost interest may be offset to some extent, though, by the fact that many financial assets also yield a cash flow; for example, stocks pay dividends, and bonds pay interest. Thus, for financial assets, the following holds true:

$$\text{cost of carry} = \begin{array}{c} \text{lost interest} \\ \text{from buying now} \end{array} - \begin{array}{c} \text{dividends or interest} \\ \text{from holding the asset} \end{array} \quad (2)$$

We will apply these principles briefly to two important financial futures, foreign currencies and Treasury bonds, and then examine a third, stock-index futures, in more depth.

Foreign Currencies (optional)

There are futures markets for several foreign currencies, including the British pound, West German mark, Japanese yen, and Swiss franc. Since foreign currency can be invested to earn the interest rate prevailing in that country, the cost of carry is (approximately) equal to the difference between domestic and foreign interest rates, or

cost of carry = U.S. interest rate − foreign interest rate

and, thus, according to Equation 1,

$$\text{future price of foreign currency} - \text{spot price of foreign currency} = \text{U.S. interest rate} - \text{foreign interest rate} \quad (4)$$

The exact relationship is shown by the **interest-rate parity equation** as follows:

$$\frac{F}{(1 + R_{US})} = \frac{P}{(1 + R_{for})}$$

where F is the futures price, P the spot price, R_{US} the U.S. interest rate, and R_{for} the foreign rate, because each side is the cost of obtaining one unit of the foreign currency on the delivery date. This equation can be written as

$$\frac{F}{P} = \frac{(1 + R_{US})}{(1 + R_{for})}$$

with Equation 4 an approximation.

For example, on August 16, 1988, the West German mark cost $0.530 U.S. dollars; U.S. Treasury-bill rates were about 8 percent; West German risk-free rates were about 5 percent; and the price of six-month mark futures was $0.538. Mark futures cost more than current marks because those investors who bought marks earned low West German interest rates, while those who bought mark futures could invest their dollars at high U.S. interest rates. Specifically, let us consider an investor at the time who wanted 1000 marks in six months. Since these marks could be invested for six months to earn 5%/2 = 2.5% interest, only 1000/1.025 = 975.6 marks had to be purchased, at a cost of 975.6($0.53) = $517. Alternatively, this person could buy a futures contract for 1,000 marks at a cost of 1,000($0.538) = $538 after six months. The amount of dollars needed at the time to provide $538 in six months was $538/1.04 = $517—the same amount needed with the first strategy.

Thus, in August 1988, the price of marks futures was above the current spot price for marks because West German interest rates were about 3 percent lower than U.S. interest rates. Futures prices for the British pound, in contrast, were below the current exchange rate because British short-term interest rates were around 10 percent, 2 percent higher than U.S. rates. In this case, carrying costs were negative because dollars that were invested while waiting for a futures delivery earned less than British pounds could earn.

Foreign-currency futures can be used for arbitrage by investors who find that Equation 4 is not satisfied or for speculation by investors who want low-money-down bets on the direction of exchange rates (definitely not a recommended gamble). Currency futures can also be used by importers and exporters to hedge against exchange-rate fluctuations. For instance, a U.S. export firm that expects to receive German marks in the future can protect itself against a decline in the value of those marks relative to the dollar by selling a futures contract for delivery of marks at a fixed dollar price. If the value of the mark drops, the diminished value of the marks received is offset by the profit on the futures contract. Similarly, a U.S. importer that anticipates making a marks payment in the futures can hedge this position by buying marks futures; any losses on the marks payment will be offset by profits on the futures.

Treasury Securities (optional)

Futures contracts are traded for a number of Treasury securities. The cost of carry is the difference between the interest lost by purchasing the bonds now instead of somewhat later, minus the coupons that can be earned by owning the bonds now. The cost of carry is close to zero if the term structure is flat and the Treasury-bond coupon rates are approximately equal to current interest rates. (For Treasury bills, which have no coupons, the cost of carry is simply equal to the lost interest between the time of the futures purchase and the time of delivery.) An upward-sloping term structure, with short-term rates lower than long-term rates, reduces the cost of carry and pulls down futures prices relative to spot prices; futures prices have to be low because those investors who buy bonds earn more interest than those who hold Treasury bills and wait for a futures delivery.

As with currency futures, bond futures are used by arbitragers (who try to wring profits out of mispriced futures), speculators (who bet on interest rate movements), and individuals or institutions who want to hedge interest-rate risk. For a given cost of carry, futures prices tend to move up and down with spot prices. Thus, a fall in interest rates, which increases the prices of bonds, also increases the prices of futures contracts for bonds. Those who buy bond futures are making a low-margin bet that interest rates will fall (relative to the expectations already imbedded in the term structure), while those who sell futures are implicitly betting on an interest rate decline.

Speculators place such bets in the hope of large profits. Risk-averse investors can make such bets to offset implicit wagers elsewhere in their portfolios. For example, a savings and loan association that holds long-term, fixed-interest mortgages has made an implicit bet that interest rates will fall; the risk that rates may rise can be hedged by selling bond futures. If an appropriate number of futures contracts are sold, any losses on the mortgage portfolio as interest rates rise are offset by profits on the futures.

Similarly, a corporation that has borrowed a large amount at a long-term, fixed interest rate can hedge against a fall in interest rates by buying bond futures.

Stock Indexes

One of the most heavily traded futures contracts is for the S&P 500 index, and we will use these contracts to illustrate stock-index futures. If an S&P 500 futures contract is bought for F and the value of the index on the expiration day is P, then P is the settlement price, and the profit is $P - F$.

(The value of an S&P 500 contract is actually equal to the index times $500. If you purchase one contract at 300 and the S&P index on the expiration day is at 296, the initial value of your contract is $500(300) = $150,000$, and the final value is $500(296) = $148,000$. Each one-point swing in the index is worth $500; a four-point difference costs you $500(4) = 2000.)

The Cost of Carry Institutional investors can arbitrage the S&P 500 index and S&P futures contracts. The S&P 500 can be stored, simply by purchasing the component stocks. These stocks in the S&P 500 index can also be sold short, or an institution holding a large diversified portfolio can sell some of its shares. This ease of arbitrage implies that the price of S&P futures contracts is determined not by the expected performance of the stock market, but by the cost of carry—the lost interest net of the dividends from the stocks included in the S&P 500 index. Investors can either buy the stocks in the S&P 500 today for P_0 or buy the stocks later for F, the futures price agreed upon today. The advantage of the first strategy is that you receive the dividends D between now and the time of delivery. The advantage of the second strategy is that you earn interest RP_0 by paying later. For both strategies to be equally attractive,

$$\begin{aligned} F &= P_0 + RP_0 - D \\ &= P_0(1 + R - d) \end{aligned} \tag{5}$$

where $d = D/P_0$ is the dividend yield on the S&P 500 stocks. This equation is a specific example of the more general rule that the futures price is equal to the current spot price plus the cost of carry, where the cost of carry for a financial asset is the lost interest minus the cash flow from the asset. In practice, the existence of transactions costs, including brokerage fees and bid-ask spreads, means that futures prices can fluctuate in a range of about 1/2 to 1 percent about Equation 5 without arbitrage being profitable.

Index Arbitrage If futures prices differ significantly from Equation 5, then arbitragers can make excessive risk-free returns. Suppose, for example, that the value of the S&P 500 is 300, the dividend during the next three months is $D = 3$ (1 percent), and the three-month rate of return on Treasury

index arbitrage
Index arbitrage attempts to earn risk-free profits whenever the spread between the price of a stock index futures contract and the index itself differs from the cost of carry.

bills is 2 percent. Equation 5 gives the equilibrium value of a three-month futures contract as

$$F = 300(1 + 0.02 - 0.01) = 303.$$

If F is instead 309 (about 2 percent too high), then arbitragers can buy the stocks in the S&P 500 for 300 and hedge their position by selling S&P 500 futures for 309. The value of the S&P 500 on the delivery date is P, as is the value of the arbitragers' futures contract. At this time, the arbitragers sell the stocks for P and close out their futures position for the same price. No matter what the value of the S&P index, their net profit is as follows:

Dividends	3
S&P 500	$P - 300$
Futures	$309 - P$
Net profit	12

Their profit in three months is $12/300 = 4$ percent, while T-bills only pay 2 percent over this same interval. Because the futures price is two percentage points above the equilibrium value, arbitragers can earn a risk-free return that is two percentage points above the return on risk-free Treasury bills.

What if the futures price is 297, two percentage points below equilibrium? Consider an institution holding the stocks in the S&P 500 index and anticipating a dividend of 3. The institution can increase its rate of return by two percentage points, by selling its stocks for 300, investing the proceeds in T-bills paying 2 percent, and hedging its position by purchasing S&P 500 futures for 297. On the delivery date, the institution will buy back its stocks for P and sell its futures for P, giving the following net profit:

Interest	6
S&P 500	$300 - P$
Futures	$P - 297$
Net profit	9

In comparison with a dividend of 3 on its stock portfolio, this profit of 9 provides an extra, risk-free profit of two percentage points.

Use of Futures Contracts by Indexers Persuaded that it is difficult to pick undervalued stocks, in the mid-1970s many pension funds and other institutional investors converted to indexing. Now, instead of actively managing their portfolios to try to beat the market, they simply buy stocks in amounts proportionate to the stock's weights in an index, such as the S&P 500. Other institutional investors are approximate indexers, using the S&P 500 as their base portfolio and buying somewhat more or less of stock that they especially like or dislike. Another variation is to index some fraction of the institution's portfolio, perhaps two-thirds, and allow the other one-third to be actively managed.

Indexers, complete or approximate, still must decide how much to invest in stocks and how much to invest in Treasury bills and other assets. Index futures are a very inexpensive way to adjust a portfolio's mix between stocks and Treasury bills. An institution that turns bearish can sell index futures instead of selling a few shares of each of the stocks in its portfolio. An institution that receives a large influx of cash need not rush to the market with huge buy orders; instead, it can buy futures temporarily and acquire stocks gradually. Index futures are a very natural tool for institutional indexers and are used extensively by them.

In 1987, the daily volume of trading in S&P futures contracts routinely topped 100,000 contracts, with an aggregate market value of $15 billion—more than the total value of the stock traded daily on the New York Stock Exchange. Another popular futures contract is for the specially constructed Major Market Index, a simple average of the prices of twenty stocks, seventeen of which are in the Dow Jones Industrial Average, giving it a very high correlation with the Dow. There are also futures contracts for the NYSE composite index and the Value Line index of 1400 stocks. Investment Example 17–3 tells of a special futures contract that is traded off this exchange.

Does the Tail Wag the Dog? This extensive use of stock-index futures contracts worries many people. One concern is that the tail wags the dog, so to speak, in that futures prices in Chicago seem to determine spot prices on the New York Stock Exchange, instead of the other way around. Many institutions now respond to macroeconomic news events by buying or selling futures rather than stocks because the transaction costs are lower. This futures trading affects stocks because the no-arbitrage pricing relationship given in Equation 5 implies that, unless the cost of carry has changed, movements in futures prices must be matched by spot prices. Thus, any substantial change in futures prices is soon followed by an equivalent change in stock prices. However, the fact that futures prices precede spot prices does not mean that, if there were no index futures, the stock market would not be affected by news events. If there were no futures market, institutions would go to the stock market directly. There is no evidence that stock prices have become more volatile, in percentage terms, since the introduction of stock-index futures.[10]

Another concern is the flurry of trading activity on the days that index options and futures expire—particularly during the so-called triple witching hour, the last hour of trading on the third Friday of March, June, September, and December. These are the four days each year when stock-index futures, index options, and individual stock options all expire simultaneously. Both the average and the standard deviation of the volume of trading double on such days.[11] There is little reason or evidence, how-

INVESTMENT
EXAMPLE
17–3

BASEBALL FUTURES

There is an unofficial, unsanctioned market in baseball futures involving some 200 investment professionals, who otherwise spend their time trading wheat, silver, and the S&P 500.* Like other intangible futures, there is no actual commodity to be delivered. Instead, the value of the contract at expiration (the end of the baseball season) is determined by the number of games that the specified team wins.

For example, at the start of the 1988 season, the price of New York Yankees futures was 93. If the Yankees ended up winning 103 games, those investors who bought contracts at 93 receive (from

**John Crudele, "Baseball Futures Latest Way to Score on the Street," *Los Angeles Times,* September 18, 1988

those who sold at 93) an amount equal to 103 − 93 = 10 times the agreed value of a game, anywhere from $5 to $500. At $100 a game, there would be a $1000 payment from those who were short Yankees to those who were long. If the Yankees won less than 93 games, the longs would pay the shorts.

As with other futures contracts, there is daily trading at prices reflecting current market conditions. Dedicated participants are short dozens of teams and long dozens of others, making hundreds of trades during the course of the season. One reportedly lost $60,000 in 1987. Yankee futures dipped into the low 80s in September 1988 and finished at 85 when the Yankees won 85 games. The Los Angeles Dodgers, in contrast, opened the 1988 season at 81 and finished at 94. Those who were long Dodgers and short Yankees made money in 1988.

ever, to indicate that this hectic trading has more than a brief effect on prices.

PROGRAM TRADING

program trading
Program trading originally meant the buying or selling of a diversified portfolio of stocks, but is now associated with index futures.

A more serious charge is that the widespread use of index futures has destabilized the stock market and, in particular, was the catalyst for the market collapse on October 19, 1987. **Program trading** is a loosely used term that originally meant the buying or selling of a diversified portfolio of stocks. Although program trading existed before index futures were introduced in 1982, it has been associated with futures contracts ever since because these are the easiest way to trade baskets of stocks. It is helpful to distinguish two very different kinds of program trading—index arbitrage and portfolio insurance—as we will do in the following sections.

Portfolio Insurance

Many investors try to protect their portfolios with stop-loss orders or by an informal rule of selling a stock if its price drops, say, 10 percent. In the late 1970s, two Berkeley finance professors, Hayne Leland and Mark Rubinstein, developed the idea of hedging a portfolio by using formal, computerized rules to buy and sell stocks continuously as prices change—an idea they initially labeled **dynamic hedging,** or **dynamic asset allocation.** Together with John O'Brien, they founded the firm Leland O'Brien Rubinstein (LOR) in 1981 to market their strategy under the appealing label *portfolio insurance.*

A portfolio that is 100 percent invested in Treasury bills never loses money, but it also forgoes the opportunity to earn a substantially higher rate of return by investing in stocks. A portfolio invested entirely in stocks presumably has an expected return that exceeds the T-bill rate, but risks a substantial loss if stock prices decline. Many institutions balance their desire for extra return against their fear of loss by dividing their assets between stocks and Treasury bills, perhaps two-thirds to the former and one-third to the latter. Leland and Rubinstein argued that a more flexible approach can give a higher expected return, while still protecting the portfolio against large losses.

In its original formulation, dynamic asset allocation automatically adjusted the mix of stocks and Treasury bills continuously to ensure a specified minimum return—for example, no more than a 10 percent loss. Suppose that the portfolio is initially two-thirds in stocks and one-third in Treasury bills. If stock prices start to decline, funds are shifted from stocks to T-bills, by selling the portfolio's stocks and using the proceeds to buy T-bills. By the time the stock market has dropped far enough to give the portfolio a 10 percent loss, the portfolio is 100 percent in Treasury bills and protected against further declines. If, on the other hand, stock prices rise, giving the portfolio a profit cushion, then Treasury bills are sold and more stocks are purchased, boosting the portfolio's expected return.

Dynamic asset allocation does not try to time the market by guessing whether prices will rise or fall. Instead, the computer program continuously calculates the appropriate split between T-bills and stocks that is required to prevent losses larger than some preset level. But it is no panacea. Leland and Rubinstein are frank about the potential costs and advertise portfolio insurance as suitable only for those who are especially averse to losses.

If the stock market always has a higher expected return than Treasury bills, then a portfolio that is always fully invested in stocks must have a higher expected return that one that is sometimes partly invested in Treasury bills. This sacrifice of expected return is part of the cost of protection against temporary losses. The claim of dynamic asset allocation is that its flexible protection is cheaper than holding a fixed two thirds-one third split no matter what the market does, because it will, on average, be more fully

dynamic hedging
Dynamic hedging is a flexible procedure for limiting losses by selling securities continuously as prices drop.

dynamic asset allocation
dynamic asset allocation is a flexible procedure for limiting losses by selling securities continuously as prices drop.

invested in stocks. Another cost of dynamic asset allocation is the transactions cost incurred as the portfolio mix is adjusted. A simulation study using historical data for the period 1963–83 estimated that with 0.5 percent transaction costs and floors of 0 percent and −5 percent, portfolio insurance reduces the annual return by 0.8 percent, to 1.7 percent.[12]

In addition, because continuous trading is clearly impractical, the programs only trade when market prices change by a preset percentage, such as 3 percent or 4 percent, which makes the protection less exact than the theoretical model suggests. In a worst case, the market could drop 4 percent (provoking sales), rise 4 percent (causing repurchases), drop 4 percent (prompting sales once again), and so on. In this type of seesaw market, the program is always selling low and buying high, losing 4 percent on each price swing.

With the arrival of stock-index futures in 1982, portfolio insurance was redesigned to use index futures in place of T-bills to hedge a portfolio. Now, a fund can begin fully invested and, by selling futures contracts equal to one-third of its portfolio, be the equivalent of two-thirds invested. If stock prices fall, the computer dictates how many additional futures contracts to sell (an action equivalent to selling stock, but with lower transaction costs). If prices continue to fall, even more futures are sold, until at the preset floor (say, 10 percent losses), the portfolio is fully hedged in that the value of the outstanding futures is equal to the value of the portfolio. The transaction costs for futures are perhaps a tenth of those for trading a comparable basket of stocks, and the transactions can be completed in five to thirty seconds instead of five to forty-five minutes.

Portfolio insurance assumes that index futures can be sold continuously at the equilibrium values given by Equation 5. In the market collapse on October 19, 1987, when the Dow fell 508 points (22 percent) and the S&P 500 dropped 57.6 points (21 percent), the sellers of index futures far outnumbered the buyers, and the few trades that did take place were at prices at least 10 percent below the no-arbitrage equilibrium price. Portfolio insurers were reluctant to sell at these sharp discounts, and those who did decide to sell had difficulty finding buyers.[13] LOR sold 2000 S&P 500 futures contracts (the equivalent of $300 million worth of stock), but the firm needed to sell at least three times this amount to provide the intended level of insurance. Portfolio insurance is supposed to provide protection during a market collapse, but, ironically, this is the time when it is least effective.

index arbitrage
Index arbitrage attempts to earn risk-free profits whenever the spread between the price of a stock index futures contract and the index itself differs from the cost of carry.

Index Arbitrage

Index arbitrage is a very different type of program-trading, with the objective of earning risk-free profits whenever the spread between the index-futures price and the index itself differs from the no-arbitrage equilibrium in Equation 5 by more than the transactions costs that arbitrage entails.

According to Equation 5, the future prices should exceed the index value by an amount equal to the Treasury-bill rate minus the dividend yield on the stocks in the index. As explained earlier, arbitragers buy stocks and sell futures if the futures price is too high, and they do the reverse if the futures price is too low. An arbitrager unwinds, or liquidates, the position either at the expiration of the futures contract or earlier if the spread between the index and the price of index futures narrows before expiration.

Such arbitrage takes considerable resources. Computers are used to monitor prices continuously, to estimate the carrying costs (T-bill rates and anticipated dividends during the life of the contract), and to issue buy and sell orders when the spread makes arbitrage profitable. Timing is critical because if the arbitragers do not get the appropriate stocks at the desired prices, they do not have risk-free profits. At one time, the arbitragers' orders were hand carried to the appropriate specialists by a team of traders. Today, however, arbitrage is made easier by the NYSE's SuperDot system, a computerized order-distribution system that automatically sends orders to the specialists, allowing trades to be executed within five minutes.

To reduce their monitoring and transaction costs, index arbitragers do not buy all 500 stocks in the S&P 500 index. Instead, they try to identify a relatively small group of securities that has historically been highly correlated with the entire S&P 500. Typically, the arbitragers focus on 40 to 50 representative stocks, though some use as many as 250 and others as few as 20. One risk they face is that this correlation will break down. Another is that the futures market's daily settlement system will force them to put up extra cash, cash that they were counting on to earn interest.

It takes a minimum portfolio of $5 million, many say closer to $25 million, for index arbitrage to be profitable. The price differences are so narrow and the transactions cost so large on small trades that smaller portfolios cannot arbitrage profitably. Only some 60 to 100 brokers and institutional investors index arbitrage. The practice is dominated by an even smaller group, some two dozen major players, who follow the S&P 500 or Major Market Index trying to earn a few cents per share, which will add up to thousands of dollars when millions of shares are traded. A risk-free extra 1 to 2 percent annual return gives them around $150 million in annual profits.

Index arbitragers are not the root cause of stock price movements. Instead, they buy in one market and sell in another, so as to keep the price of index futures close to the index itself. Buying or selling pressure that shows up in one market, but not in another, is transmitted to the second market by arbitragers. For example, we have seen how portfolio insurers use futures contracts to protect their portfolios. If the stock market rises, portfolio insurers realize that they need less protection and buy futures. If futures prices consequently rise more than stock prices, index arbitragers sell futures and buy stock until equilibrium is reestablished. It is not the arbitragers who push up stock prices in this case; it is portfolio insurers who buy stocks indirectly through their purchase of futures, exerting a buying power that arbitragers then transmit to the stock market itself. If there were no futures market, or if futures prices were allowed to rise significantly above stock prices, then portfolio insurers would presumably buy stocks instead of futures and have the very same effect on the market. Arbitragers are just the messengers who bring the news to the stock market that portfolio insurers are buying.

The same logic applies to a more worrisome case, that in which portfolio insurers react to a decrease in stock prices by selling index futures. If futures prices drop more than stock prices, arbitragers buy futures and sell stock, transmitting the portfolio insurers' sales to the stock market. Again, the cause of the pressure on stock prices is not the arbitragers, but the portfolio insurers who follow the seemingly destabilizing rule of buying after prices rise and selling after prices fall.

Portfolio insurers appear to have been a catalyst for the collapse of stock prices on October 19, 1987. Index arbitragers played a less prominent role. The Commodity Futures Trading Commission estimated that portfolio insurers accounted for between 12 percent and 24 percent of the trading in S&P 500 index futures on October 19 and that about 9 percent of the NYSE trading that day was associated with index arbitrage. The rest of the year, index arbitrage accounted for as little as 1 percent and as much as 19 percent of NYSE trading.

The prices of stock-index futures are usually somewhat above the index itself, because the cost of carry is positive (interest rates are higher than dividend yields). But, on October 19, 1987, futures traded at an average discount of more than 10 percent from the S&P index. Index arbitrage broke down that day because the market broke down. An astonishing 608 million shares were traded, and, even then, sales could not be completed because buyers could not be found. Trading stopped in many stocks, and the reporting of prices lagged far behind recent trades, let alone the prices at which new trades could be made. Arbitragers could not make risk-free profits because they did not know current prices and were unable to execute offsetting orders simultaneously. In addition, with futures at a discount to the index, arbitrage requires selling stocks and buying futures. However, pure arbitragers had no stocks to sell and were discouraged from short sales by the exchange's uptick rule and margin requirements on short sales. Institutions with large, well-diversified portfolios could have hedged profitably on October 19 by selling some of their stock and buying futures, but they did not—perhaps because of their unfamiliarity with arbitrage or because of the difficulties of making trades amidst the chaos.

Many clients became disenchanted with portfolio insurance, and some institutions reacted to the public distrust of all program trading by voluntarily stopping their index arbitrage. As a result, trading in S&P futures fell by half after the October crash.

To interrupt future meltdowns, the New York Stock Exchange adopted a rule that trading will be automatically restricted for one hour if the Dow falls by 250 points during a single day and for another two hours if the Dow falls by an additional 150 points that day. The futures exchanges also agreed to suspend trading during crises.

SUMMARY

A futures contracts is an agreement to deliver a certain item on a specified date at a price agreed upon today, but not paid until delivery. Futures can be used to hedge a position (for example, a farmer selling wheat futures), to speculate (for instance, a wager on the price of silver); or for arbitrage (as in stock-index arbitrage). Except for transaction costs, futures contracts are a zero-sum game, and contracts are marked to market each trading day by transferring funds between shorts and longs, depending on whether futures prices went up or down that day.

Shorts and longs can cover their positions before the delivery date, and almost all do. On the delivery date, the futures price is approximately equal to the spot price. Before the delivery date, the prices of many futures contracts are influenced by investor expectations of the spot price on the delivery date. For precious metals, financial assets, and other items that can be stored and sold short, the spread between the futures price and the current spot price is determined by the cost of carry—the cost, including forgone interest, of buying the

item now and holding it until the delivery date. Since the cost of carry is usually positive, futures prices are generally above spot prices and increase with the time until delivery.

For stock-index futures, the cost of carry is the difference between the lost interest and the dividends received from buying stocks now instead of later. Many institutional investors use stock-index futures as a fast and inexpensive way of adjusting their portfolio's mix between stocks and Treasury bills. Two kinds of program traders have made headlines. Portfolio insurers sell index futures when stock prices fall in order to keep their losses within a preset limit, a potentially destabilizing response. Index arbitragers buy stock and sell futures, or vice versa, when the basis, or spread, between the index-futures price and the spot price of the index differs significantly from the cost of carry, the Treasury-bill rate minus the dividend yield. When heavy futures selling by portfolio insurers reduces the basis below the cost of carry, index arbitragers buy futures and sell stocks, transmitting the portfolio insurers' selling pressure from the futures market to the stock market.

EXERCISES

1. Use the data on February 1989 hog contracts in Table 17–3 to answer the following questions:
a. What was the opening price on August 15?
b. How many contracts were in existence?
c. If a meat packer took delivery of 1000 contracts, what would be the total cost of the hogs? (Ignore any brokerage fees and other transaction costs.)

d. What was the change between the opening and settlement prices on August 15?
e. What was the change between the settlement price on August 14 and the settlement price on August 15?
2. Answer the same five questions in Exercise 1, this time using the February 1989 gold contracts in Table 17–3.

3. Look in the most recent Friday edition of *The Wall Street Journal* and write a paragraph comparing the current prices of futures contracts for wheat, hogs, gold, silver, and the S&P 500 index with the prices shown in Table 17–3.

4. Why do the settlement prices of gold, silver, and S&P 500 futures contracts all increase as the length of the contract increases, while the same is not true of wheat and hogs?

5. Why might a wheat farmer sell wheat futures contracts even though he doesn't plan on selling his wheat until two weeks after the delivery date?

6. Why might a wheat farmer buy a wheat futures contracts even if he doesn't plan on buying wheat?

7. Write a 250-word essay explaining why margin on futures contracts serves a different purpose than margin on common stock.

8. Investment Example 17–3 tells of a baseball futures market. When the New York Yankees opened the 1988 season at 93, did this futures price reflect expectations or the cost of carry?

9. Rebut this argument by a Kansas congressman in 1890:

> Those who deal in "options" and "futures" contracts, which is mere gambling, no matter by what less offensive name such transactions be designated, neither add to the supply nor increase the demand for consumption, nor do they accomplish any useful purpose by their calling; on the contrary, they speculate in fictitious products [which are never actually delivered]. The wheat they buy and sell is known as "wind wheat" and doubtless for the reason that it is invisible, intangible, and felt or realized only in the terrible force it exerts in destroying the farming industry of the country.[14]

10. Use the data on silver futures in Table 17–3 to estimate the monthly cost of carry. Does this estimate seem reasonable?

11. The cost of storing platinum is $2 per 50 troy ounces per month. If the annual interest rate is 6 percent, what pattern would you expect to find in three-month, six-month, and nine-month futures prices?

12. Carefully explain why someone who expects the price of gold to rise from $400 an ounce now to $450 an ounce a year from now would prefer paying $420 an ounce for a one-year gold-futures contract to paying $400 an ounce for gold today.

13. Carefully explain how someone who owns gold can make a profit selling the gold for $400 an ounce and buying a one-year gold futures contract for $420 an ounce even if the price of gold stays at $400 an ounce.

14. Many savings and loan associations have short-term deposits and long-term mortgages. Will they lose money if interest rates go up or if they go down? Explain which of the following protective actions are appropriate and which are inappropriate:

a. Lengthen the maturity of their assets.
b. Issue more variable-rate mortgages.
c. Buy thirty-year zero-coupon bonds.
d. Buy bond futures.

15. In 1987, many pension funds grew increasingly nervous about their stock portfolios as price-earnings ratios approached all-time highs. Indicate which of the following they could have purchased and which they could have sold to protect themselves from a market crash:

a. Stock-index call options.
b. Stock-index put options.
c. Stock-index futures.

16. The text shows how the observed $36.20 spread in Table 17–3 between December 1988 gold and December 1989 gold can be explained by the cost of carry. How could an arbitrager have made a guaranteed profit if the cost of carry had been $36.20 and the spread in the futures prices had been $41.20? How large is the profit? What if the price spread is $31.20, and you hold gold?

17. On August 16, 1988, the exchange rate for Japanese yen was $0.007488 while the prices of yen futures contracts were $0.007589 for December delivery, $0.007660 for March 1989 delivery, and $0.007741 for June 1989 delivery. Were Japanese interest rates higher or lower than U.S. interest rates? Explain your reasoning.

18. Investment bankers hold inventories of bonds that they have purchased from some clients and intend to sell to others. To hedge their exposure to interest-rate risk, should they buy or sell bond futures? Explain.

19. In November 1984, Professor Stephen Figlewski was quoted in the *New York Times* as saying that stock-index futures are so new and complex that the market is not dominated yet by arbitragers and other professionals, and is consequently not yet efficient. The newspaper reported that

> According to Professor Figlewski, a simple formula tells what the stock index future's price should be, if the market were efficient. Take whatever the index is, say 100, and add the interest rate that an investor would make on his money if it were invested in a money market fund or Treasury bills, say 10 percent. Then subtract the dividend rate, for example, 4 percent. In this case the answer is 106, so if index futures were selling above or below that, then clearly the market is inefficient, Professor Figlewski said.[15]

Clearly explain the logic behind the professor's formula. If, in the above example, the index future were selling for less than 106, how could you make a safe profit larger than that available on Treasury bills?

20. Many of Fidelity's mutual funds are always 100 percent invested in stocks, the firm believing that in a risk-averse world the expected return on stocks must always be larger than the expected return on Treasury bills. Can Fidelity ever be certain of increasing its profits by selling some of its stocks and buying stock-index futures instead? When might this strategy work?

21. A mutual fund that is fully invested in stocks with an average beta of 2.0 is concerned that the stock market may collapse and, yet, because of taxes and transaction costs, does not want to sell any stocks. To hedge its $400 million portfolio completely, should the fund buy or sell S&P 500 index futures with an aggregate value of $200 million, $400 million, or $800 million?

22. On October 19, 1987, stock-index futures sold at a 10 percent discount from the indexes. How could an index arbitrager have exploited this opportunity? Under what conditions would this arbitrage have been profitable?

23. The price of one-year S&P 500 futures is 309; the stock index itself is at 300; the Treasury-bill rate is 5 percent; and the dividend yield on these stocks is 5 percent. An index arbitrager invests $3 million in fifty representative stocks with a dividend yield of 5 percent and sells $3 million worth of futures contracts. What is the net cost of this position? What is the rate of return if the index is at 309 at expiration (and the fifty stocks increase by a comparable amount)? If the index is at 293 (and the fifty stocks fall by a comparable amount)?

24. Carefully explain how the index arbitrager in Exercise 23 may lose money if the S&P is at 309 on the expiration date and the fifty stocks do not increase by a comparable amount.

25. In 1989 Charles Schwab, the president of the discount brokerage firm with that name, argued that "the great white shark of Wall Street—program trading—is back" and urged "policy makers and the securities industry to consider setting a daily limit on the premium or discount that the financial futures can trade above or below the underlying stock [index]— say, a band of 1 percent or 2 percent. If this limit is exceeded, the index futures would stop trading until the next day."[16] Would such a rule eliminate portfolio insurance or index arbitrage? Explain your reasoning.

26. The interest rates on Eurodollars are typically a percentage point above Treasury-bill rates. Under certain circumstances an investment-advisory service recommends a TED spread—buying Treasury-bill futures and selling Eurodollar futures.[17] For this strategy to be profitable, are they counting on the interest-rate differential between Eurodollars and T-bills to widen or narrow? Explain your answer.

27. When stock-market index futures were introduced in 1982, the annual dividend yield on the S&P 500 was about 6 percent, and the annual rate of return on Treasury bills was 10 percent, leading many analysts to predict that the price of an S&P futures contract would be larger than the value of the S&P index. Explain their reasoning. As it turned out, futures prices in 1988 were below the value of the S&P 500. How could an arbitrager have exploited this difference? For simplicity, assume that the length of a futures contract is one year and that it sells at a 1 percent discount to the S&P 500. Estimate the additional risk-free profits that early arbitragers could have made.

28. A 1987 discussion of computerized program trading argued that it would probably worsen a stock-market crash, but that no one knows for sure: "Indeed, one theory suggests that program trading might actually stop a crashing market: the computers would kick in with huge 'buy' orders at the strategic moment."[18] What kind of program trading is being discussed? What event would trigger huge program-trading buy orders and what would they buy?

29. An investment-advisory service argued that,

> The relationship between the price of gold and the price of silver has changed considerably since the days when Menes I [an Egyptian Pharaoh in around 2850 B.C.] could trade three ounces of silver for one ounce of gold. In 1932, for example, in the midst of The Great Depression, it took 20 ounces of silver to buy one ounce of gold. By 1960, the Ratio was 16-to-1. In recent years, however, it has stabilized in the range of 34 to 38 ounces of silver for every ounce of gold . . .
>
> The Ratio has fluctuated widely just in the past seven or eight years, dipping as low as 19-to-1 in 1980 and soaring as high as 52-to-1 in 1982 and 55-to-1 in 1985.
>
> But, as you can also clearly see, it has always—ALWAYS—returned to the range between 34-to-1 and 38-to-1.[19]

The service recommended acting when the Ratio is above 45-to-1 or below 15-to-1. In which case should you buy gold futures and sell silver futures, and in which case should you do the reverse? Is there any risk in the service's strategy?

30. Read the following statement, and then answer the questions that appear after it.

> Twice in the last 15 years, the sugar market has faced crisis. First during the 1973–74 season and again in 1979–80, world inventories sank to less than 30 percent of total [annual] consumption. The impact on the market? In 1980, prices soared to over 45 cents a pound, in '74, sugar skyrocketed beyond the 65-cent mark.[20]

a. Why might inventories be a guide to market conditions and, hence, prices?

b. Why might the sugar industry deliberately reduce its sugar inventory, even when the demand for sugar is weak?

c. Why might a knowledge of inventories, even if an accurate guide to market conditions, be of little use to those willing to bet on the direction of sugar prices?

C H A P T E R   1 8

Investment Companies

*There are two kinds of investors: those who have made
mistakes and those who are liars . . .*

anonymous

An investment company issues shares, like other corporations, but instead
of using the shareholders' money to build factories and office buildings, it
buys a portfolio of securities. About two-thirds of all investment-company
shareholders have less than $10,000 invested.[1] By pooling shareholder
funds, investment companies give many investors access to securities they
could otherwise not afford (for example, $10,000 Treasury bills) and di-
versification that they could otherwise not achieve. In addition, as investment companies emphasize, people who are busy with other things can
have their money managed by professionals.

We will begin this chapter by looking at the general characteristics of
investment companies and at two important distinctions: between open-
end and closed-end companies, and between load-funds and no-load
funds. Then, we will examine the performance of investment companies.

REGULATED INVESTMENT COMPANIES

Almost all investment companies meet the criteria for **regulated
investment companies** established by the Investment Company Act of
1940—a designation that exempts them from corporate taxes. The most
important criteria are:

1. The company must register with the SEC and comply with its disclosure
   requirements.
2. At least 90 percent of its interest and dividend income must be distributed to shareholders as it is received.

**regulated investment
company**
Regulated investment
companies satisfy the
criteria established by
the Investment Company
Act of 1940.

3. At least 75 percent of its portfolio must be diversified. Within this diversified part, it may not invest more than 5 percent of its assets in any one issuer and it may not own more than 10 percent of the voting shares of any company.

The interest and dividends that an investment company earns on its portfolio are passed directly to shareholders, either quarterly or monthly. While the fund pays no taxes on this income, shareholders must. When the fund realizes capital gains, these profits can either be distributed or retained. Shareholders pay taxes on capital gains distributions; for retained capital gains, the process is a bit more complicated, but has essentially the same result: the investment company pays the Internal Revenue Service the maximum capital-gains tax rate, and shareholders then claim a tax refund from the IRS if their tax rate is lower than this maximum. Most investment companies allow shareholders to reinvest interest, dividends, and capital gains automatically, but this reinvestment has no effect on their tax liability.

There are now more than 2000 investment companies, falling into three broad categories:

1. *Money-market funds*—very short-term securities, including Treasury bills and bank certificates of deposit.
2. *Bond funds*—longer-term bonds, with some funds specializing in Treasury bonds, some in high-yield junk bonds, and others in tax-exempt municipal bonds.
3. *Stock funds*—corporate stock, with some funds emphasizing dividend income, others potential capital gains.

There are also investment companies that specialize in commodity options, convertible bonds, covered calls, and other specific types of securities or strategies.

Within these broad categories, there is a tremendous diversity as funds try to establish an appealing identity. There is a fund open only to employees of General Electric, another for baptized Lutherans, one for airline pilots, and another for cemetery owners. One fund only buys aviation stocks; another buys stock in small savings and loan associations. One fund invests in Canadian securities; one in Ohio businesses. Another does not invest in liquor, tobacco, or drug stocks.

Many investment companies are part of a family of funds. Fidelity operates 100 separate funds, and Vanguard has nearly that many. These fund families offer a smorgasbord of funds and allow investors to switch money from one to another with just a telephone call.

Our objective in this chapter is not to catalog funds or to describe the details of each, but to explore some general principles. In that spirit, there are two crucial distinctions: between open-end and closed-end investment companies and, within the open-end category, between load and no-load funds. We begin with open-end funds.

OPEN-END FUNDS

The number of shares issued by an **open-end investment company,** or **mutual fund**, is not fixed, but instead increases as more money is invested in the fund and decreases as money is withdrawn. Each day, or several times a day, the fund calculates the total market value of its portfolio and divides this by the number of outstanding shares to obtain a **net asset value (NAV) per share**, the price at which the investment company will redeem shares or issue new ones.

If a fund has ten million shares outstanding and a portfolio worth $100 million, then each share in the mutual fund is worth $10. Suppose that people now invest another $20 million in the fund. At $10 a share, $20 million will buy two million new shares, bringing the total number of shares to twelve million and increasing the assets of the fund to $120 million; the asset value of each share is still $10. Similarly, if existing shareholders decide to withdraw $20 million, they will redeem two million shares, reducing the fund's assets and shares proportionately, so that the asset value per share stays at $10.

Investors need not buy a round number of shares. If you invest $2356.47 in a fund with a net asset value of $10/share, you will be credited with $2356.47/$10 = 23.5647 shares. As in this example, funds keep track of shares to four decimal places. Fractional shares are necessary because many shareholders automatically reinvest their profits in more shares, and each investor's monthly dividend or interest income will seldom, if ever, buy a round number of shares.

Load Charges

Mutual funds can be bought through a mutual-fund salesperson, through a stockbroker, or directly from the fund itself. No matter which route is used, the fund may levy a sales charge, called a **load fee**. For a *full-load fund* that is purchased through a stockbroker or other financial advisor, the load charge is at least 4 percent and is split between the salesperson and the fund itself. Funds, such as those in the Fidelity group, that sell directly to investors are generally *low-load* with a fee of 3 percent or less, all of which goes to the fund. A fund that charges no load fee at all is called a **no-load fund**.

Load charges are reported in a fund's prospectus, but are typically stated, like Treasury-bill yields, on a discount basis. If you invest $10,000 in a fund with an 8.5 percent load, the load charge is 8.5 percent ($10,000) = $850, and you are credited with a $9150 investment in the

open-end investment company, or mutual fund
An open-end investment company's shares increase as more money is invested in the fund and declines as money is withdrawn.

net asset value (NAV)
Net asset value is the market value of an investment company's portfolio divided by the number of outstanding shares in the investment company.

load fee
A load fee is a sales charge levied by many open-end investment companies.

no-loads
No-load investment companies do not charge load fees.

mutual fund. It is more appropriate to observe that, in order to invest $9150 in the fund, you have to pay an additional $850, which is $850/$9150 = 9.3 percent of your investment.

Load fees can also be calculated from the mutual-fund prices reported in newspapers. The quotations show two prices, sometimes labeled bid and ask, sometimes NAV and Offer. The bid price or NAV is the net asset value of the fund's shares. The ask or offer is the cost of buying a share in a fund, including the load charge. If the bid and ask prices are the same, or if there is an entry "N.L." in place of the ask price, then there is no load charge for buying the fund's shares. If the bid and ask prices differ, then the load can be calculated by comparing the two prices.

Figure 18–1 shows a sampling of price quotations. On the date shown, Merrill Lynch's Basic Value Fund had a NAV of $17.51 and an offer price of $18.73. To purchase one share, worth $17.51, you must pay $18.73, an additional $1.22 over net asset value. The load, therefore, is $1.22/$17.51 = 7.0 percent. (The fund calculates its load fee as $1.22/$18.73 = 6.5 percent.) For Merrill Lynch's California Tax-Exempt Fund, a municipal-bond fund, the offer price is equal to the NAV, because there is no load charge when shares are bought; the "r" immediately after the fund's name indicates that this fund does charge a redemption fee when money is withdrawn. In the next family of funds, Meritor, all three funds have neither a load charge nor a redemption fee.

Since no-load funds have no sales force, investors must find the addresses on their own and then mail in their investment. Some no-loads advertise in newspapers; others are described in such books as Weisenberger's *Investment Companies* and the American Association of Individual Investors' *Guide to No-Loads*.

The maximum load charge allowed by the Securities and Exchange Commission (SEC) is 9.589 percent. Until recently, a 9.3 percent load was standard. In the 1980s, many funds reduced their load charges in response to increased competition from a proliferation of new funds and the recognition by the public of the advantages of small load fees. Unfortunately, these diminished *front-end loads* levied on the initial investment in a fund have been offset by increased annual fees and by the imposition of **back-end loads** charged when money is withdrawn from a fund.

Other Fees

Funds charge annual management fees for their expertise, typically one-half of 1 percent of the fund's asset value for stock funds and somewhat less for bond funds. Since the cost of managing a $2 billion portfolio is not twice that of a $1 billion portfolio, many funds have a sliding percentage fee which declines as the fund's assets increase.

The Tax Reform Act of 1986 requires investment companies to report the fund's income and management fees separately, and for most investors

FIGURE 18–1 A sampling of price quotations for open-end funds. (*Source: The Wall Street Journal,* August 22, 1988.)

```
MUTUAL FUND QUOTATIONS

                 Friday, August 19, 1988
        Price ranges for investment companies, as quoted by the
    National Association of Securities Dealers. NAV stands for
    net asset value per share; the offering includes net asset
    value plus maximum sales charge, if any.


                               Offer NAV
                          NAV  Price Chg.
       Merrill Lynch:
         Basc Val    17.51 18.73+  .03
         CalTxE  r   10.75 10.75−  .01
         Captl Fd    21.46 22.95+  .02
         Corp  Dv     9.85 10.05   ...
         EqBd 1 r    11.55 12.03−  .01
         EuroF  r    p8.38  8.38   ...
         Fed  Sec    p9.13  9.74+  .01
         Fd FT  r   p14.61 14.61−  .05
         GlobCv r     9.82  9.82   ...
         Hi  Incm     7.96  8.29   ...
         Hi QualP    10.85 11.30   ...
         Inst  Int   p9.36  9.36   ...
         Intl Hldg   10.86 11.61   ...
         Inter TP    10.86 11.08   ...
         Muni Ins     7.64  7.96   ...
         Mun HY       9.91 10.32   ...
         NY Mn  r   p10.50 10.50   ...
         Ltd  Mat     9.69  9.76   ...
         MuniI  r    p9.22  9.22   ...
         NatRes r    13.34 13.34+  .06
         Pacific f   17.08 18.27+  .11
         Phoenx      13.27 14.19   ...
         RetBn  r    10.58 10.58   ...
         RetEq  r     9.23  9.23   ...
         RetInc r    p9.21  9.21+  .01
         RetGIB r    p9.85  9.85+  .06
         Sci Tech    10.34 11.06−  .03
         Sp'l Valu   11.60 12.41−  .03
         StrtDv r   p10.59 10.59+  .03
       Meritor  Funds:
         Growth      10.27 N.L.−  .04
         PA    TF    11.71 N.L.+  .01
         US Govt     11.79 N.L.   ...
       MetLife State Street:
         Cap  App  p10.39 10.88+  .03
         Eq    Inc  p8.65  9.06   ...
         Eq   Invs  p9.24  9.68   ...
         Gvt   Inc p11.40 11.40+  .01
         Gv   Sec   p6.68  6.99   ...
         Hi    Inc  p7.24  7.58−  .05
         Tax   Ex   p7.04  7.37   ...
       MFS:
         MIT         11.54 12.44−  .05
         Finl Dev    10.00 10.78−  .01
         Grth Stk     8.30  8.95−  .04
         Cap Dev     11.01 11.87−  .01
         TxFr CA     p4.93  5.18   ...

    d-ex distribution. f-previous
    day quotation. nl-no initial
    load. p-12b-1 plan, distribu-
    tion costs apply. r-redemp-
    tion charge may apply. s-
    stock-split dividend. x-ex-
    dividend. z-quote not availa-
    ble.
```

these management fees are no longer tax deductible. Consider an invest-ment-company shareholder whose shares earn $1000, from which a $200 management fee is subtracted. The shareholder receives $800 and, before the 1986 act, paid taxes on the net income of $800. Now the shareholder must report the full $1000 as income and include the $200 management fee with other investment expenses as a miscellaneous itemized deduction. This $200 expense is not tax-deductible unless the investor itemizes deductions (in place of a standard deduction) and, in addition, the investor's total miscellaneous deductions exceed two percent of adjusted gross income.

turnover

An investment company's turnover is the ratio of its annual sales (or purchases) of securities to its total assets.

Investment companies also incur expenses in buying and selling securities, commissions that may be paid to an affiliated company that handles the transactions. This trading of securities is gauged by a fund's **turnover**, the ratio of its annual sales (or purchases) to its total assets. A fund with a $100 million portfolio that sells $50 million in securities in a year has a turnover of 0.50; many funds have turnovers of nearly 100 percent or even higher. At a cost of 2 to 3 percent per transaction, including both brokerage fees and bid-ask spreads, this turnover can reduce shareholder profits considerably.

In 1980, the SEC issued Rule 12b–1, which allows mutual funds to charge an additional annual fee to cover marketing expenses (including sales commissions). Many funds subsequently reduced their front-end loads and instituted an annual 12b–1 charge equal to 1 percent of assets, or even more. If you invest in a fund for several years, the 12b–1 fees can be even more expensive than a front-end load fee. The exact amount of the 12b–1 fees is often difficult to find in a prospectus, but it invariably is included in the mandatory disclosure of annual expenses to assets. Some funds keep their expenses below 1 percent of assets; others charge more than 2 percent. Two percent may not seem like much, but with the stock market up an average of 10 percent a year, a 2 percent annual fee eats up 20 percent of your profits.

To discourage early redemptions, many funds with substantial 12b–1 fees impose *redemption fees* (back-end load charges). These fees range typically from 4 to 6 percent on withdrawals made during the first year, and then decline to zero on withdrawals after four to six years. This structure ensures that investors either pay several years of 12b–1 fees or else a substantial back-end load.

Since 1988, the SEC has required investment companies to present all charges in a standardized table in the prospectus, including estimates of how these fees affect a $1000 investment (assuming 5 percent annual growth) over periods of one, three, five, and ten years. Unfortunately, it is not mandatory reading. The director of the SEC's investment-management division estimates that fewer than 10 percent of mutual-fund investors ever open the prospectus.[2]

Are More Expensive Funds Worth It?

Numerous studies have found that there is no relationship between a fund's performance (before fees are deducted) and the size of its load charges, management fees, and other expenses. Thus, after such fees are deducted,

TABLE 18–1   Average Five-Year Returns, 1979–1984

Purpose of Fund	Returns on No-Load Funds (percent)	Returns on Load Funds, Including Load (percent)	Average Load (percent)
Maximum capital gains	152.2	128.2	8.2
Long-term growth	114.8	105.2	7.8
Growth and income	98.5	93.1	7.9
Income	78.0	72.2	7.5
Corporate-bond investment	54.8	47.2	7.2
Municipal-bond investment	19.2	14.1	5.4

Source: Gerald W. Perritt, "Is the load too much to bear?" *American Association of Individual Investors Journal,* June 1984, pp. 18–21.

investors do better with inexpensive funds. For instance, a comparison of investor returns from load and no-load mutual funds over the five-year period 1979–84 is given in Table 18–1.[3] Notice that, with one exception, the disadvantage of load funds is approximately equal to the load charge. The one exception is the group of funds aiming for maximum capital gains; these load funds not only charged an 8.5 percent fee, but, even before subtracting the fee, did substantially worse than no-loads.

Despite such evidence, the majority of mutual funds are able to charge investors load fees, and some of the funds with the highest load charges are among the most popular. The reason is that mutual funds are not bought, but sold, in the sense that most people who invest in mutual funds are talked into doing so by persuasive salespeople. The most effective salespeople are drawn to the most lucrative funds, the ones with the highest load charges. Those who represent a variety of funds have a natural self-interest in recommending the ones with the highest load charges. They get no commission for persuading someone to invest in a no-load fund and consequently have no interest in doing so.

CLOSED-END FUNDS

Unlike their open-end relatives, **closed-end funds** have a fixed number of shares outstanding. They do not issue new shares or redeem old ones. If you want to invest in a closed-end fund, you must buy shares from an existing shareholder; those who want to redeem their shares must find someone to buy them. To facilitate these trades, the shares of closed-end funds are traded on the stock exchanges or over the counter, at a market price that need not equal the fund's net asset value.

Closed-end funds have no load fees, since they do not issue new shares; but there is the usual brokerage fee for trading shares of stock. With no load charges, closed-end funds also have no salespeople, and, as a consequence, are overlooked by most investors. The assets of all closed-end funds are less than 1 percent of the assets of open-end funds.

The market prices of closed-end shares are reported each day along with the prices of other corporate stock. The net asset value can be obtained by a phone call to the fund or, once a week, by checking the business section of most newspapers. Many papers report these net asset values on Saturday or Sunday; *The Wall Street Journal*, which is not published on weekends, reports these figures on Monday. Figure 18–2 shows an example. The first fund, Adams Express, is traded on the New York Stock Exchange and had a net asset value of $16.70 per share. The price of Adams Express shares was 15⅝, a 6.44 percent discount from net asset value.

Until the late 1920s, all investment companies were closed-end. The hundreds that flourished in the 1920s were often very speculative and highly leveraged, and most sold at substantial premiums over net asset value. Many of these funds went bankrupt in the Great Crash, and those that survived sold at substantial discounts in the 1930s. Today, as Figure 18–2 illustrates, closed-end funds generally trade at a discount from net asset value, though a few special cases trade at premiums. The Gemini II Income Fund, for instance, is part of a dual-purpose fund, which we will discuss shortly, and pays exceptionally high dividends. The discounts on all closed-end funds ebb and flow with time, increasing when small investors leave the stock market and shrinking when they return. Figure 18–3 shows these annual fluctuations.[4] In the 1970s, discounts of 20 percent to 30 percent were common. Discounts subsequently declined, perhaps because investors became more aware of their existence and advantages.

A Discount is an Advantage

Those who consider buying closed-end shares at a discount from net asset value are sometimes discouraged by the possibility that the discount will persist forever. However, the attractiveness of such shares does not hinge on the eventual disappearance of the discount. Even if the discount never narrows, closed-end funds can be financially advantageous simply because you receive dividends and capital gains on more stock than you actually pay for.

Suppose that a fund has a net asset value of $10 a share. This means that it has a portfolio of securities which would cost $10 per share if purchased directly. If the fund's shares can be acquired for $9, then for your $9 investment you receive the dividends and capital gains on $10 worth of stock. If these annual dividends and capital gains are 10 percent of $10, you receive $1 on a $9 investment—an 11.1 percent return. At a 20 percent discount, a 10 percent return on the fund's portfolio gives a 12.5 percent

FIGURE 18–2 Price quotations for closed-end funds. (*Source: The Wall Street Journal,* August 22, 1988.)

PUBLICLY TRADED FUNDS

Friday, August 19, 1988

Following is a weekly listing of unaudited net asset values of publicly traded investment fund shares, reported by the companies as of Friday's close. Also shown is the closing listed market price or a dealer-to-dealer asked price of each fund's shares, with the percentage of difference.

Fund Name	Stock Exch.	N.A. Value	Stock Price	% Diff.
Diversified Common Stock Funds				
Adams Express	NYSE	16.70	15⅝ −	6.44
Baker Fentress	OTC	25.20	21¼ −	15.67
Blue Chip Value	NYSE	6.99	5⅞ −	15.95
Clemente Global Gro	NYSE	b8.39	7⅜ −	12.10
Gemini II Capital	NYSE	16.12	12⅛ −	24.77
Gemini II Income	NYSE	9.63	12¾ +	32.35
General Amer Invest	NYSE	18.17	15⅛ −	16.76
Global Growth Capital	NYSE	8.35	8⅛ −	2.69
Global Growth Incme	NYSE	9.46	9⅝ +	1.74
Growth Stock Outlook	NYSE	9.74	9⅛ −	6.30
Lehman Corp.	NYSE	13.99	12⅜ −	11.54
Liberty All-Star Eqty	NYSE	8.09	6⅝ −	18.10
Niagara Share Corp.	NYSE	15.66	12¾ −	18.58
Nicholas-Applegate	NYSE	7.91	6⅞ −	13.08
Quest For Value Cap	NYSE	10.51	7½ −	28.64
Quest For Value Inco	NYSE	11.66	10⅛ −	13.16
Royce Value Trust	NYSE	9.53	8⅝ −	9.50
Schafer Value Trust	NYSE	8.64	7 −	18.98
Source Capital	NYSE	a36.77	37½ +	2.00
Tri-Continental Corp.	NYSE	23.98	21⅛ −	11.90
Worldwide Value	NYSE	19.95	16 −	19.79
Zweig Fund	NYSE	9.97	10⅛ +	1.55
Closed End Bond Funds				
CIM High Yield Secs	AMEX	9.64	9¾ +	1.14
Colonial Int High Inco	NYSE	9.29	9⅞ +	6.30
Zenith Income Fund	NYSE	a9.14	9⅞ +	8.04
Flexible Portfolio Funds				
America's All Seasn	OTC	5.61	6½ +	15.86
Specialized Equity and Convertible Funds				
American Capital Conv	NYSE	22.96	23⅛ +	0.7
ASA Ltd	NYSE	bc47.88	36⅝ −	23.50
Asia Pacific	NYSE	z	z	z
Bancroft Convertible	AMEX	22.77	21 −	7.78
BGR Precious Metals	TOR	be13.28	10⅞ −	18.11
Brazil	NYSE	11.71	8¾ −	25.28
CNV Holdings Capital	NYSE	9.13	4¾ −	47.97
CNV Holdings Income	NYSE	9.57	10⅞ +	13.64
Castle Convertible	AMEX	22.17	20⅛ −	9.22
Central Fund Canada	AMEX	b6.20	5¾ −	7.30
Central Securities	AMEX	11.73	9⅞ −	15.81
Claremont Capital	AMEX	51.58	47⅝ −	7.70
Couns Tandem Secs	NYSE	z	z	z
Cypress Fund	AMEX	9.52	7¼ −	23.84
Duff&Phelps Sel Utils	NYSE	7.70	7⅞ +	2.27
Ellsw Conv Gr&Inc	AMEX	8.53	7⅜ −	13.57
Engex	AMEX	11.77	8⅞ −	24.59
Financ'l News Compos	NYSE	15.52	13⅜ −	13.82
1stAustralia	AMEX	11.25	8⅞ −	21.11
First Financial Fund	NYSE	8.71	7⅛ −	18.20
First Iberian	AMEX	9.07	8⅞ −	2.15
France Fund	NYSE	b9.80	9¼ −	5.60
Gabelli Equity Trust	NYSE	10.70	9⅞ −	7.71
Germany Fund	NYSE	7.21	6½ −	9.85
H&Q Healthcare Inv	NYSE	7.81	6 −	23.18
Hampton Utils Tr Cap	AMEX	b9.39	8¼ −	12.14
Hampton Utils Tr Pref	AMEX	b48.68	47⅜ −	2.68
Helvetia Fund	NYSE	10.46	9 −	13.96
Italy Fund	NYSE	b8.95	8⅛ −	8.66
Korea Fund	NYSE	39.14	70¼ +	79.48
Malaysia Fund	NYSE	9.04	8¼ −	8.74
Mexico Fund	NYSE	b7.35	4¾ −	35.40
Morgan Grenf SmCap	NYSE	8.54	8 −	6.30
Petrol & Resources	NYSE	25.57	23½ −	8.10
Pilgrim Regional	NYSE	9.70	8⅛ −	16.24
Regional Fin Shrs Inv	NYSE	7.84	6⅜ −	18.68
Scandinavia Fund	AMEX	8.32	6⅝ −	20.37
Scudder New Asia	NYSE	12.21	9⅝ −	20.76
Spain Fund	NYSE	10.90	10⅛ −	7.11
Taiwan Fund	AMEX	b41.02	37⅛ −	9.50
TCW Convertible Secs	NYSE	b8.22	7⅞ −	4.20
Templeton Em Mkts	AMEX	b9.57	8 −	16.40
Thai Fund	NYSE	11.44	13¾ +	20.19
United Kingdom Fund	NYSE	10.99	9½ −	13.56
Z-Seven	OTC	d14.21	14⅝ +	2.92

a-Ex-dividend. b-As of Thursday's close. c-Translated at Commercial Rand exchange rate. d-NAV reflects $1.96 per share for taxes. e-In Canadian Dollars. z-Not available.

FIGURE 18–3 Discounts from net asset value for closed-end funds

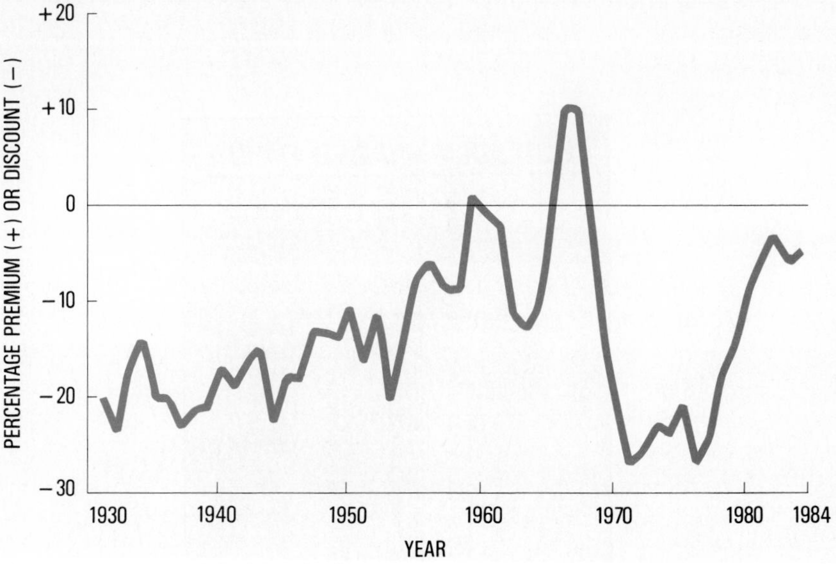

return on your investment; at a 30 percent discount, your return swells to 14.3 percent. Why pay $10 for stock that you can buy for $9 or $8 or $7?

It is true that a fund has annual expenses that you can avoid by buying stock directly. These are typically in the neighborhood of 1 percent a year, which are roughly consistent with about a 10 percent fund discount. (In the preceding example, investors earn 10 percent if they buy stock directly; a fund that earns a 10 percent return and charges 1 percent for expenses will distribute $0.90, a 10 percent return to investors if its shares sell for $9, or 10 percent discount from net asset value.) These annual fees do not explain why funds sell for 20 percent or 30 percent discounts. Nor do they explain the popularity of load funds that charge similar annual fees. Why invest in a load fund, paying a premium over net asset value, when you can buy shares in a closed-end fund at a discount from net asset value? Closed-end funds may not beat the market, but they certainly beat open-end funds.

The explanation that most observers give is, again, that shares in investment companies are not bought, but sold.[5] Large investors prefer to manage their own portfolios, while small investors, the natural audience for investment companies, are not familiar with closed-end funds. They are sold open-end funds with load charges by salespeople who profit from the load.

Share Repurchases

Tobin's q was introduced in Chapter 8 to compare the market value of a firm's stock with the replacement cost of its assets. For a closed-end fund, the replacement cost of a firm's assets is equal to the net asset value of its portfolio, and Tobin's q is as follows:

$$q = \frac{\text{market value of stock}}{\text{replacement cost of assets}} = \frac{\text{market value of fund}}{\text{net asset value}}$$

If the fund sells at a discount from net asset value, then its q is less than 1. Such a firm is worth more dead than alive, in that shareholders would benefit if the firm sold its assets and distributed the proceeds either through special dividends or by repurchasing its stock.

To illustrate this point, consider a closed-end fund with one million shares outstanding and assets with a market value of $10 million. The net asset value is $10. If the fund can repurchase 250,000 shares at $8 a share (a 20 percent discount from NAV), this will cost $2 million, reduce its assets to $8 million and reduce the number of outstanding shares to 750,000. Now the net asset value is

$$\frac{\$8,000,000}{750,000} = \$10.67,$$

and the market price must rise to $8.54 if the fund continues to sell at a 20 percent discount. If the fund buys half its shares at $8, net asset value rises to $12 a share. If it buys all its shares at $8, there is $2,000,000 left over for the last shareholder.

The repurchase of shares at a price less than net asset value must inexorably raise the net asset value of the remaining shares and make all shareholders better off. Those investors who sell do so voluntarily; those who stay enjoy an increase in the net asset value of their shares. If a fund's repurchase plan increases the price of its shares, narrowing the discount, then so much the better.

Why, then, don't all closed-end funds automatically repurchase shares whenever a discount appears? Some are subject to regulatory restrictions that limit the amount of their repurchases. A more typical explanation is simply that management fees depend on the size of a fund's assets, so that while repurchases are good for shareholders, they are not good for management. Sometimes this understandable reluctance is overcome by aggressive investors who buy enough shares to gain control of the fund and liquidate its assets. In the 1930s, Claude Odell made millions by liquidating closed-end funds. Investment Example 18–1 recounts a more recent example.

CONVERSION OF THE JAPAN FUND

In 1987, thirty-year-old T. Boone Pickens, III, the youngest son of the famous corporate raider, announced that he and several partners had acquired a 5.5 percent stake in the Japan Fund, which was then selling at a 20 percent discount from net asset value. With $700 million in assets, this 20 percent discount implied a $140 million gap between the market value of the Japan Fund stock and the liquidation value of its assets.

Fearful that Pickens would force a liquidation, the fund's managers recommended that shareholders approve a resolution converting the company into an open-end fund. This move would eliminate the discount, which would increase the value of the fund's shares and satisfy Pickens and other shareholders, while preserving the managers' jobs. The resolution was overwhelmingly supported by those shareholders who voted, but not enough voted to give it the necessary approval by 51 percent of all outstanding shares. The fund quickly resubmitted the resolution and lobbied even harder for shareholder approval. This time it did pass, and Pickens and his partners had a $10 million profit for their efforts on behalf of all shareholders.

Dual-Purpose Funds

dual-purpose fund
A dual-purpose investment company has two classes of shareholders-income and capital.

Dual-purpose funds have two classes of shareholders—income and capital. The income shareholders receive all the dividends from the stock in the portfolio, while the capital shareholders receive capital gains at the fund's termination date, typically ten to fifteen years after the fund's inception. On the fund's termination date, the income shareholders receive a specified redemption price (usually close to the size of their initial investment), or whatever assets the fund has if it cannot pay the redemption price. The capital shareholders receive any excess of the value of the fund's portfolio over this redemption price.

Consider a fund that starts by selling one million income shares at $10 and one million capital shares at $10, with a termination in fifteen years at a $10 redemption price for the income shareholders. Ignoring any initial sales charges, the fund has $20 million to invest in a portfolio of stocks. Each income share costs $10 and receives the dividends on $20 worth of stock, plus the return of $10 in fifteen years, unless the fund's total portfolio has lost more than 50 percent of its market value. If the stocks initially have a 5 percent dividend yield, then the income shareholders get an initial 10 percent dividend yield, which grows over time as dividends increase.

The value of the capital shares at termination depends critically on the value of the portfolio at that time. The net asset value (NAV) of the capital

TABLE 18–2 Net Asset Value of Capital Shares at Termination

Total Value of Portfolio (millions of dollars)	Aggregate Value of Income Shares (millions of dollars)	Aggregate Value of Capital Shares (millions of dollars)	NAV of Capital Shares
$0	$0	$0	$0
5	5	0	0
10	10	0	0
15	10	5	5
20	10	10	10
25	10	15	15
30	10	20	20

shares is equal to the total value of the fund's portfolio minus the amount due the income shareholders, divided by the number of capital shares. Table 18–2 shows some possible outcomes. (Those who studied Chapter 16 may recognize this as the same profit structure possessed by a call option, and, indeed, the capital shares have an implicit call option on the fund's portfolio with a striking price of $10 million.)

Leverage As long as the capital shares' net asset value is positive, the percentage change in the net asset value that accompanies a 1 percent change in the total value of the fund's portfolio depends on the capital shares' *leverage*, the ratio of the total value of the portfolio to the value of the capital shares,

$$\text{leverage} = \frac{\text{total value}}{\text{capital value}}$$

For instance, at a total value of $20 million, the capital shares are worth $10 million and the leverage is 2/1, implying that each 1 percent change in the value of the total portfolio causes a 2 percent change in the net asset value of the capital shares. If the portfolio increases 25 percent (to $25 million), the net asset value increases 50 percent (to $15); if the portfolio rises 50 percent (to $30 million), the NAV rises 100 percent (to $20).

Catering to Preferences Dual-purpose funds were created to satisfy the differing needs of investors. Corporations who own shares in other corporations are not taxed on 85 percent of the dividends they receive. This tax advantage provides an incentive for buying stocks with high dividends—for example, buying the income shares in a dual-purpose fund. Some tax-exempt institutions may also prefer the larger and stable dividend stream from income shares. For many years, individual investors paid lower taxes on capital gains than on dividends and were consequently drawn to the capital shares of dual-purpose funds. Some investors like the leverage inherent in the capital shares.

Furthermore, no one can be made worse off by splitting the fund's shares into two classes, since investors are free to buy equal amounts of both shares. If you own 1 percent of the income shares and 1 percent of the capital shares, then you receive 1 percent of the profits, no matter how these are divided, just as if the company were an ordinary closed-end fund. But unlike ordinary closed-end funds, investors can vary the proportion of dividends to capital gains.

Before termination, dual-purpose fund typically sell at substantial discounts, like most closed-end funds. The intriguing difference is that the discount must go to zero on the termination date. The prices given in Figure 18–2 show Gemini II's income shares selling at a premium (apparently because of the generous dividend yield), while the capital shares sell at a discount. Together, the combined net asset value of one share of each is

$$\$16.12 + \$9.63 = \$25.75,$$

while the market price of one income share and one capital share is

$$\$12\tfrac{1}{8} + \$12\tfrac{3}{4} = \$24.875,$$

a modest 3.4 percent discount. For the other dual-purpose funds in Figure 18–2, the combined discount is 0.3 percent for Global Growth, 20.5 percent for Quest for Value, and 16.4 percent for CNV Holdings. Counsellors Tandem data were not available by the newspaper's deadline, but later showed a 26 percent discount.

All of these funds were started in the period 1985–87, replacing an earlier group of seven funds that were started in 1967 and since ended. Gemini II is a sequel to Gemini, a very successful dual-purpose fund that terminated on December 31, 1984. Figure 18–4 shows the history of Gemini's discount.

INVESTMENT-COMPANY PERFORMANCE

Many people are drawn to investment companies by their advertised expertise, reasoning that just as they pay a doctor for medical services and a lawyer for legal assistance, so they should pay a professional for investment management. They naturally look at past performance and choose a fund with an outstanding record. If the fund's subsequent performance is disappointing, they switch to a fund that has been more successful.

The Quest for Performance

Since management fees depend on the amount of assets managed, a fund's fees are doubly affected by the fund's performance in that capital losses

FIGURE 18–4   Gemini Capital's discount from net asset value

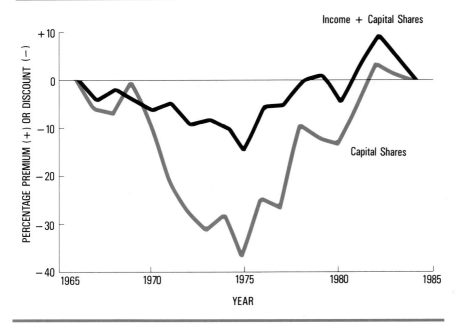

not only reduce the market value of its assets but also incite shareholders to invest elsewhere. Those mutual funds that make large capital gains are swamped by investors looking to share in the success, creating a cult of performance and encouraging funds to trade feverishly, searching for the quick profits that will lure more investors. Funds seeking quick profits become speculators, disdaining patient, long-term investments in order to make guesses about short-term price movements.

In 1967 and 1968, the fastest and quickest fund managers were called "gunslingers" because they were able to spot a concept at 100 paces and pull the trigger (invest heavily) before anyone else. Gerald Tsai's Manhattan Fund was up 40 percent in 1967, while Fred Carr's Enterprise Fund was up 118 percent in 1967 and Fred Mates' Mates Fund was up 158 pecent in 1968. Another fund manager, John Hartwell, disdained diversification, saying, "If you have more than a half dozen positions in an account of, say, $500,000, it only means you are not sharp enough to pick winners".[6]

Some of the fund's profits were artificial, made in thinly traded stock that could not be sold at the market price used to calculate profits; some shares were *letter stock*, shares issued at a discount with the proviso that they not be sold for a specified number of years. Some profits were the result of self-fulfilling crowd psychology, others rushing to follow in the footsteps of the experts, pushing the price upward and confirming the experts' choices. Of course, some profits were due to good fortune, and evaporated when bad luck followed. From 1968–74, the value of Manhattan Fund shares dropped by 80 percent, Enterprise by 70 percent, and Mates by more than 90 percent.

You Cannot See the Future Looking Backward

Many mutual-fund salespeople capitalize on the short-term vagaries of chance by focusing their sales pitch on whichever funds have compiled spectacular records recently, giving the misleading impression that investors are assured of a similarly spectacular performance in the future. Mutual-fund families seemingly play this game too, promoting whichever funds have had recent successes while avoiding mention of disappointments. Fidelity manages about 100 mutual funds, the largest and most successful being Magellan, and spends more than $50 million a year marketing its funds. It introduces new mutual funds at a rate of about one a month, and many in the industry suspect that they do this to ensure that they will have some successes, which are then promoted heavily.[7] An extreme, cynical variation on this strategy is to start two new funds, one which leverages the market while the other sells stocks short. Or one could buy call options while the other buys puts. Whichever does well is advertised widely, while the other is forgotten. Investment Example 18–2 tells of some other deceptive practices.

Several factors caution against investor hopes of getting rich quickly with a mutual fund. First, a properly diversified fund has little chance of gaining or losing a great deal of money, because the gains and losses on individual stocks tend to offset each other. This diversification should, in fact, be the primary attraction of mutual funds. As Paul Samuelson put it, "The prudent way is also the easy way . . . What you lose is the daydream of that one big killing. What you gain is sleep."[8]

Second, the efficient-market hypothesis warns that it is difficult for any fund manager to beat the market consistently. In any given year, some funds do well, and others do poorly, just as some guesses about the outcomes of coin flips turn out to be correct and others incorrect. Past success does not guarantee future success. If anything, the feverish turnover of portfolios by managers trying to beat the market only ensures that transaction costs will drag average investment-company performance below the market averages they are trying to surpass.

Do Mutual Funds Beat the Market?

In 1940, an astute stockbroker wrote that "in actual practice American investment trusts have varied between the disappointing and the catastrophic. The whole subject makes an interesting study of the generous gap between theoretic promise and practical fulfillment."[9] Matters have

INVESTMENT
EXAMPLE
18-2

WHAT YOU SEE ISN'T NECESSARILY WHAT YOU GET

Investment companies have considerable latitude in reporting past results and, understandably, many choose the most favorable method. Some tricks are obvious. If the fund has done relatively well during the past three years and poorly in the years before that, then just report the record over the past three years. If several funds are managed, focus on the ones that have done well. Even if a successful portfolio manager leaves the fund, continue to report the past record as if nothing had changed. Other tricks are more subtle.

If two funds are merged, the manager can choose which of the two performance records to attribute to the combined fund. For instance, if Fund A has earned 10 percent a year and Fund B has lost 10 percent a year, the manager can merge B into A and continue to report the fund's return as 10 percent a year. In this way, embarrassments disappear. The chairman of the Vanguard Group has strongly criticized this practice, observing sarcastically that "We are able to get rid of our poor performing funds by merging them into sister funds with lustrous records, and the record of the 'turkey' simply vanishes into thin air."*

A bond fund can temporarily boost the yield to maturity on its portfolio by buying lots of recently issued junk bonds, since relatively few bonds default in the first year or two after issuance. Another trick is to buy callable bonds which have high yields to maturity—yields that won't last until maturity because the issuers will soon exercise their call rights. Similarly, some funds that hold mortgage portfolios quote attractive yields based on the assumption that none of the borrowers will prepay their mortgages. But if interest rates fall (or have already fallen), homeowners will refinance, and the fund's high quoted yields will never be realized.

While advertisements may be misleading and salespeople deceptive, the Securities and Exchange Commission requires a more complete and accurate disclosure in an investment company's prospectus. One of the best ways to peek behind the hype is to read it carefully.

*James A White, "How a Money Manager Can Pull a Rabbit Out of a Hat," *The Wall Street Journal,* March 16, 1989.

changed little since, as study after study has found that investment companies consistently underperform the market averages.

To gauge the performance of mutual funds, we need to adjust for the riskiness of their portfolios. In a risk-averse world, risky assets are priced to give relatively high expected returns. Thus, the fact that one fund had a higher average return than T-bills, the S&P 500, or another mutual fund may reflect the riskiness of its portfolio, rather than superior management.

If we measure risk by the standard deviation of a fund's return, then,

TABLE 18–3 Mutual-Fund Objectives and Betas, 1962–1972

Investment Objective	Beta Coefficient
Maximum capital gain	1.23
Growth	1.04
Long-term growth and income	1.01
Growth and current income	0.99
Growth, income, and stability	0.90
Income and growth	0.85
Income, growth, and stability	0.86
Income, stability, and growth	0.71
Income	0.71
Stability, income, and growth	0.74

Source: Wiesenberger Services, *Mutual Fund Performance Monthly*, October 1972.

as explained in Chapter 14, an appropriate risk-adjusted measure of performance is

$$\frac{\text{fund's average return } - \text{ return on T-bills}}{\text{standard deviation}}$$

Funds can be compared to each other by this measure or, as a benchmark, to the S&P 500 or another market index. If a fund cannot beat the market index, then its efforts to select undervalued securities and to time the market are in vain. As discussed in Chapter 14, researchers using this criterion have found that, before expenses are deducted, about half the funds do better than market indexes and that, after expenses have been deducted, about two-thirds do worse than market indexes.[10]

The Capital Asset Pricing Model (CAPM) suggests that if the mutual fund is part of an investor's portfolio, then beta may be more appropriate than the standard deviation as a measure of risk. Wiesenberger Services reports regularly on investment companies, grouping funds by the investment objectives stated in each fund's prospectus. Funds that propose to maximize capital gains sound the most aggressive, while those emphasizing growth are a bit less aggressive; and those mentioning both growth and income seem less aggressive still. A fund's beta coefficient is a quantitative measure of a fund's aggressiveness, and Table 18–3 shows that there is a rough correspondence between a fund's stated objectives and the beta of the portfolio it chooses.

If the Capital-Asset Pricing Model is correct, then funds holding high-beta portfolios should, on average, do better than funds with low-beta portfolios. According to CAPM, assets will be priced according to the following equation.

FIGURE 18–5 Mutual-fund risk-adjusted performance, after expenses

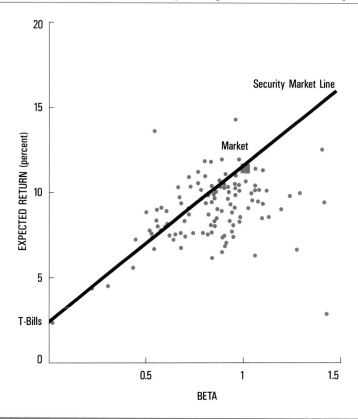

$$\text{asset's expected return} = \text{return on T-bills}$$
$$+ \text{ beta (market's expected return } - \text{ return on T-bills)}$$

If we use the historical average return as a proxy for the expected return, then this equation can be used to compare a fund's actual return with the return predicted by CAPM.

One way to do so is with a graph, as illustrated in Figure 18–5. Funds with average returns above the security market line have beaten the market on a risk-adjusted basis. As shown, most have not. Again empirical studies have consistently found that about half the funds beat the market before expenses, but only one-third do after expenses. The data in Figure 18–5 are from a seminal study by Michael Jenson, who found that, before deducting management fees, 60 of 115 mutual funds did better than the market and 55 did worse. After management fees were deducted, 76 of 115 (about two-thirds) did worse than the market.[11] Their expertise was apparently not worth its cost.

Are Mutual Funds at Least Consistent?

Investors pour money into recently successful mutual funds, paying substantial load fees and other expenses, in the belief that a fund's recent performance ensures future success. While mutual funds, as a whole, do not beat the market, perhaps some consistently do well, and investors need only identify these above-average funds.

Unfortunately, performance seems to be random, in the sense that funds with good records are no more likely than disappointing ones to do well in the future. Chapter 11's discussion of the efficient-market hypothesis has already presented some evidence that there is no correlation between a fund's performance in one period of time and its performance in the next. Here is some more evidence. A study was made of the records of sixty-four mutual funds that, according to the Wiesenberger Service, seek to maximize capital gains.[12] First, each fund's annual percentage return, dividends plus capital gains, was calculated over the five-year period January 1, 1977, to January 1, 1982. This is the performance record that investors might have used to choose a mutual fund in 1982. Then, each fund's annual percentage return was calculated for the subsequent five-year period, from January 1, 1982, to January 1, 1987. This is the five-year return for an investor who bought in 1982 on the basis of each fund's performance over the preceding five years. The resultant scatter diagram is in Figure 18–6, and shows that there is no correlation between fund performance in one five-year period and in the next.

Index Funds

As indicated in earlier chapters, mutual funds are not the only professionally managed portfolios whose performance has been disappointing. Money managers on the whole have found it difficult to beat the market, after paying transaction costs, management fees, and other expenses. As this evidence accumulated in the late 1960s, many realized that if most professionals do worse than the market indexes, then one can compile an above-average record simply by matching these indexes. Instead of trying to pick stocks that will beat the market, an **index fund** buys the stocks in a designated market index, such as the S&P 500, in proportion to the stocks' index weights. For the S&P 500 and other market-value indexes, this strategy implies the purchase of an equal percentage of each company's shares. For the Dow Jones Average, an equal number of shares in each company is appropriate.

An index fund is deliberately passive, seeking to beat other funds with low transaction costs and management fees. Wells Fargo Investment Advisors started an institutional index fund in 1971 and is now the largest single investor in the stock market, managing more than $60 billion in 1987. Wells Fargo employs only about 100 people to manage this $60 billion

index fund
An index fund passively buys stocks in a market index, such as the S&P 500, in proportion to the stocks' index weights.

FIGURE 18–6 Mutual–fund performance, 1982–1987 versus 1977–1982

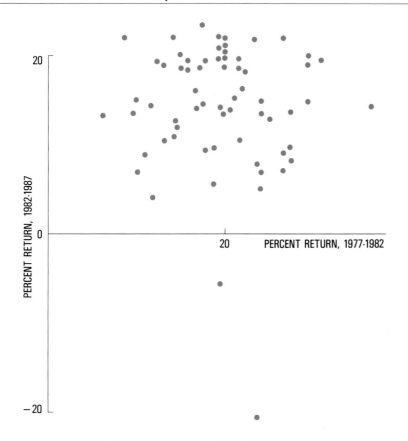

portfolio, and its annual management fees are as low as 0.05 percent. In 1976, Vanguard introduced the first index fund open to small investors, First Index Investment Trust. The total amount of index-fund money was estimated at above $150 billion in 1987.

Index funds routinely beat two-thirds of the managed funds. In addition to their low expenses, another advantage is that they are always virtually 100 percent invested in stocks, which presumably have a higher expected return than T-bills. In bull markets, such as the 1982–87 period, they are bound to look especially good in comparison with funds that, fearing a market downturn, keep a significant part of their assets in cash. The longer-run success of index funds hinges on two assumptions: first, that because investors are risk averse, stocks will do better on average than T-bills; and second, that because the stock market is efficient, efforts to select stocks and time the market are not worth the added expense. Investment Example 18–3 describes the oldest buy-and-hold fund.

592

INVESTMENT
EXAMPLE
18–3

THE ULTIMATE BUY-AND-HOLD FUND

In 1935, in the midst of the Great Depression, the Corporate Leaders Fund was established.* It invested its initial shareholders' money in thirty blue-chip stocks, including American Telephone, Eastman Kodak, Exxon, Sears, and Westinghouse. Fifty-three years later, in 1988, it still held 24 of these 30 stocks. Some of the other six stocks, such as Nabisco, were taken over by other companies. Some, such as International Harvester, were dropped when Corporate Leaders reluctantly decided that these were no longer leading companies.

Although Corporate Leader is an open-end fund, it accepted no new investors for seventeen years, from 1960 to 1987. There is no portfolio manager, because the fund follows a mechanical rule of always owning an equal number of shares in the twenty-four stocks in its portfolio. Any cash that accumulates is automatically reinvested in these twenty-four stocks; if a stock splits, the extra shares

are sold. With this minimal management role, the fund's ratio of annual expenses to total assets is a miniscule 0.08 percent.

Critics argue that the fund has not changed with the economy; it owns no automobile, airline, or computer stocks. A mutual fund advisor said, "Any fund calling itself corporate leader that does not own stock in IBM makes no sense." In its defense, the fund's managers point out that the portfolio evolves as large companies adapt to the changing economy—for example, Westinghouse's expansion into broadcasting and financial services.

How has Corporate Leaders done? In the ten years from 1978 to 1988, its total return was 341 percent, as compared to a 294 percent total return for general equity mutual funds and a 266 percent total return for all mutual funds.

*The information in this example comes from Constance Mitchell, "Trapped in a Time Warp, or Simply Looking Ahead?," *The Wall Street Journal*, November 4, 1988; and Wiesenberger Investment Companies Service, *Investment Companies*, 1987.

SUMMARY

An investment company pools investor funds and buys a portfolio of securities, providing diversification and, the investors hope, superior management. An open-end fund, or mutual fund, has a variable number of shares outstanding, which fluctuates as investors buy more shares or redeem shares, in either case at net asset value. Most open-end funds charge a load fee, part of which may go to the sales-

person who signs up the investor. Some funds also levy load charges on withdrawals, in addition to annual fees for management of the fund and other expenses. Fund performance (before fees are deducted) does not seem to be related to the size of the load charges, management fees, and other expenses.

A closed-end fund has a fixed number of shares, which are traded on the stock exchanges or over the counter at prices that may represent a discount or premium from net asset value. Other things being equal, a closed-end fund selling at a discount seems to be a better choice than an open-end fund selling at a premium (the load charge). Yet the latter are more popular. A closed-end fund selling at a discount has a q less than one and could benefit its shareholders by selling assets and repurchasing shares. Most don't, no doubt influenced by the fact that management fees depend on the size of the fund.

Many fund managers are keenly interested in short-term performance—aware that an impressive record will attract more investors, increasing the size of the fund and the management fee. The evidence is that most funds do not beat the market and that there is little consistency in performance—knowing which funds have done well in the past is of no help in predicting which will do well in the future. Persuaded by this evidence, some have turned to passive index funds which merely try to match a market index, hoping that they can beat most other funds simply by minimizing expenses.

EXERCISES

1. Use a recent Monday issue of *The Wall Street Journal* to determine which of the following investment companies are open-end and which are closed-end, and, among the open-end funds, which are load funds and which are no-load:

> ASA Limited
> Baker, Fentress
> Fidelity Puritan
> Oppenheimer Target
> Vanguard High Yield Stock

2. Go to the library and use Wiesenberger Service's *Investment Companies,* or a comparable publication on investment companies, to research the five companies listed in Exercise 1. Write a 250-word report comparing the objectives of these funds.

3. On August 16, 1988, the newspapers reported that Fidelity's Magellan Fund had a NAV of 45.46 and an offer price of 46.87. In order to buy one share of this fund, what additional percentage must you pay as a sales commission?

4. Use *The Wall Street Journal* or another newspaper to determine the percentage load charge on the following mutual funds. Show your work.

> Dreyfus Leveraged
> Price Rowe New Era
> Putnam Option
> Merrill Lynch California Tax-exempt
> Shearson California Municipal

5. Figure 18–3 shows the average discount on closed-end funds through 1986. Look in the most recent edition of Wiesenberger Service's *Investment Companies* and see whether the average discount has widened or diminished since 1986.

6. The text tells how, in August 19, 1988, the market price of one income share and one capital share of the Gemini II dual-purpose fund was $24.875, a 3.4 percent discount from the combined $25.75 net asset value of these two shares. Redo this calculation, using current data from the most recent Monday edition of *The Wall Street Journal.* Has this discount increased or decreased?

7. An advertisement by the Investment Company Institute boasted that $10,000 invested in mutual funds in 1950, ignoring load charges and assuming the reinvestment of all dividends, would have grown to $113,500 in 1972, twenty-three years later. A finance professor calculated that, over this same time period, an investment in the NYSE composite index, including the reinvestment of dividends, would have grown by 12.54 percent per year.[13] Did the mutual funds do better or worse than the NYSE composite?

8. In late 1987, Fidelity Brokerage announced that it would waive its brokerage fee on stock sales:

> Fidelity Brokerage will usher in the year-end stock trading season with commission-free trading.
>
> This limited-time offer will run through January 15, 1988. It will allow investors to *sell stocks free* when they reinvest the total proceeds of the stock sale in a Fidelity load fund.[14]

How can Fidelity make money on this offer?

9. Why do you suppose that mutual funds strongly encourage shareholders to reinvest their dividends and capital gains in the fund, even if there is no load charge on this reinvestment?

10. In 1986, the Korea Fund, a closed-end investment company that invests in Korean securities, had 5 million shares outstanding with a net asset value of $18 and a market price of $32, a 78 percent premium over NAV. The Korea Fund then sold 1.2 million new shares at $32, raising $38.4 million. Did this sale hurt or help the NAV of existing shareholders? Explain.

11. A market observer wrote that "Frequently, closed-end shares representing $25 in assets will be selling for $20. Such profits may be largely illusory, however, because when the time comes to sell, the discount may persist."[15] Is there any advantage to buying a closed-end fund at a discount if the discount persists?

12. Explain the flaw in this advice: "The problem of picking a mutual fund seems to be simplicity itself: The investor should select whichever fund will give him the largest percentage return, year after year."[16]

13. Ginnie Mae mutual funds buy a pool of residential mortgages that are guaranteed by the Government National Mortgage Association. Investors in these funds receive the monthly mortgage payments, interest and principal, made by homeowners. While investors are protected against default, they can be hurt both by a rise in market interest rates and by a decline. Explain how this is possible.

14. Believing in efficient markets, you have located an index fund, which buys a market portfolio in order to ensure that it does as well as the market averages. What is the beta for such a fund? If you invest one-fourth of your money in T-bills and three-fourths in the fund, what is the beta for your portfolio? How could you use this fund to get a portfolio with a beta of 1.5?

15. Write a 250-word essay arguing against this viewpoint:

> The manager of a fund has a fiduciary obligation to obtain the highest possible return on the money entrusted to his keeping. In an overheated market such as the one that began to build up in the mid-1980s, the fiduciary obligations of the fund managers actually *compelled* them to speculate—and to speculate massively.[17]

16. Exercise 15 in Chapter 1 gives the annual percentage returns for twenty-four randomly selected stock mutual funds.[18] The stock market as a whole fell by 4.8 percent in 1984 and rose by 30.9 percent in 1985. Calculate the average return for these twenty-four mutual funds in 1984 and in 1985. Now make a scatter diagram for these twenty-four funds, putting the percent return in 1984 on the horizontal axis and the percent return in 1985 on the vertical axis. Does there seem to be a close relationship between a fund's performance in 1984 and 1985?

17. If you buy a group of stocks designed to represent the market portfolio, will you have to buy and sell shares every time there are changes in the relative prices of the stocks you hold? Why? If not, when will you have to buy and sell?

18. Explain what is misleading about this analysis of dual-purpose funds:

> Say that Widow A, who has $1000 and wants all the income she can get from it, and Executive B, who also has $1000 and wants all the growth he can get, join forces. The result is $2000, which is duly invested and, in a year's time, has produced a not-unreasonable five percent in dividends and ten percent in capital gains. Five percent of $2000 is $100, and that would go to the widow, who finds that she has received a ten percent return on her $1000 investment. The ten percent in capital gains amounts to $200, and that goes to the executive, who discovers he's blessed with a 20% return. Almost miraculously, both are making twice as much as they would if the fund hadn't brought them together.[19]

19. A phone call from an investment consultant reported that he had identified the top 0.5 percent of all mutual funds, funds that had averaged a 16 percent return over the past five years. Why might you hang up without paying to learn their names?

20. Before the SEC required money-market funds to compute a standard 30-day yield, some funds would, at times, report their shareholder's return over the past year and, at other times, report their shareholder's return over the past week. Which do you suppose they reported when interest rates had fallen during the past year? What about a mutual fund that holds a portfolio of long-term bonds?

21. RJR Nabisco was taken private in a leveraged buyout in 1989, when a private partnership purchased all of RJR's outstanding shares. At the time, RJR was the eleventh largest company in the S&P 500 index. When RJR was removed from the S&P 500 and replaced by a smaller company, what actions were required

of index funds that attempted to match the S&P 500?

22. Dean LeBaron, President of Batterymarch Financial Management, in a February 1986 speech to fellow money managers and corporate financial executives, said:

> In the past, if you [a corporation] thought your stock was too cheap, you held a lunch and told everyone so. Now if you think its cheap, you buy it . . . .
> What we are seeing at the moment are individual securities that are selling like closed-end funds—that is, securities that appear to be selling in the aggregate at a discount from some of the marketable components. To realize the value of these components you must go open end. Institutions won't do that. Individual shareholders won't do it. But public companies will.[20]

Analyze LeBaron's statement by answering the following questions:

a. What is the value of q for such companies?
b. How can corporate stock ever sell at a discount from the liquidation value of its assets?
c. Why might these discounts shrink if the company forgoes expansion to repurchase stock?

23. Comment on the following remark: "A mutual fund has been defined as an outfit which, for a fee, spares investors the trouble of losing their own money. The fund takes over the task for them."[21]

24. A series of unprofitable investments gave one dual-purpose fund, Hemisphere, a net asset value for its capital shares that was often close to zero and sometimes negative. If a dual-purpose fund has two million income shares, two million capital shares, a redemption price for the income shares of $10, and a portfolio of $25 million, what is the net asset value of the capital shares? If the portfolio goes up or down by x percent, what will happen to the net asset value of the capital shares? If this fund's portfolio has a beta of 1.2, what is the beta of the capital share's net asset value?

25. One financial adviser wrote, "For the man who couldn't care less about the intricacies of high finance but still appreciates wealth and all the freedom it implies, mutual funds may be the best investment of all."[22] Acting as an independent financial advisor, what advice would you give a recent college graduate who has inherited $20,000 and wants to buy stock?

26. In 1986, the S&P 500 increased by 22 percent, while the average stock mutual fund gained 16 percent. Why do mutual funds tend to underperform the S&P 500, particularly during bull markets?

27. Wiesenberger Services identified the five best-performing mutual funds for 1986 in each of the twelve fund categories it monitors. In 1987, twenty-seven of these top sixty funds did better than the average fund in their categories, and thirty-three funds were below average.[23] How would you explain this disappointing performance?

28. Some criticize dual-purpose funds because the funds' managers cannot possibly satisfy both classes of shareholders—for example, the purchase of high-dividend, slow-growth stocks benefits the income shareholders at the expense of the capital shareholders. Explain why this claim is refuted by the argument that dividing the fund's shares into two classes cannot make shareholders worse off.

29. A 1989 article in *The Wall Street Journal* noted that after a closed-end fund is set up,

the market price of its shares usually slips to a discount from net asset value. As a consequence, some investors are reluctant to buy the initial offering (and pay a sales fee to the sponsoring brokerage firm), when they can wait a short while and buy the shares at a discount. To overcome this reluctance, some closed-end funds have open-end provisions, guaranteeing that after a specified number of years, shareholders will be allowed to redeem their shares at full net asset value. The article in *The Wall Street Journal* was unenthusiastic about open-end provisions:

> Big deal, specialists say. So you're assured of getting the portfolio's full net asset value. That's often a far cry from getting your original investment back.
>
> What matters is how the markets behave over the years: If stocks or bonds in general slump, so do the values of assets in related portfolios. Open-ending plans "aren't going to insulate you against the marketplace," says Douglas Dent of the Closed-End Fund Digest.[24]

Write a 250-word essay supporting or opposing the argument that open-end provisions are worthless.

30. An author recommends this Superhedge strategy: buying dual-purpose capital shares selling at a discount from net asset value and writing call options on stocks similar to those held by the fund.[25] In what sense is this a hedge?

APPENDIXES

GLOSSARY

REFERENCES

NAME INDEX

SUBJECT INDEX

APPENDIX 1   Future Value of \$1 invested for *n* periods, $F = (1 + R)^n$

Period	1%	2%	3%	4%	5%	6%	7%	8%	9%	10%
1	1.010	1.020	1.030	1.040	1.050	1.060	1.070	1.080	1.090	1.100
2	1.020	1.040	1.061	1.082	1.103	1.124	1.145	1.166	1.188	1.210
3	1.030	1.061	1.093	1.125	1.158	1.191	1.225	1.260	1.295	1.331
4	1.041	1.082	1.126	1.170	1.216	1.262	1.311	1.360	1.412	1.464
5	1.051	1.104	1.159	1.217	1.276	1.338	1.403	1.469	1.539	1.611
6	1.062	1.126	1.194	1.265	1.340	1.419	1.501	1.587	1.677	1.772
7	1.072	1.149	1.230	1.316	1.407	1.504	1.606	1.714	1.828	1.949
8	1.083	1.172	1.267	1.369	1.477	1.594	1.718	1.851	1.993	2.144
9	1.094	1.195	1.305	1.423	1.551	1.689	1.838	1.999	2.172	2.358
10	1.105	1.219	1.344	1.480	1.629	1.791	1.967	2.159	2.367	2.594
11	1.116	1.243	1.384	1.539	1.710	1.898	2.105	2.332	2.580	2.853
12	1.127	1.268	1.426	1.601	1.796	2.012	2.252	2.518	2.813	3.138
13	1.138	1.294	1.469	1.665	1.886	2.133	2.410	2.720	3.066	3.452
14	1.149	1.319	1.513	1.732	1.980	2.261	2.579	2.937	3.342	3.797
15	1.161	1.346	1.558	1.801	2.079	2.397	2.759	3.172	3.642	4.177
16	1.173	1.373	1.605	1.873	2.183	2.540	2.952	3.426	3.970	4.595
17	1.184	1.400	1.653	1.948	2.292	2.693	3.159	3.700	4.328	5.054
18	1.196	1.428	1.702	2.026	2.407	2.854	3.380	3.996	4.717	5.560
19	1.208	1.457	1.754	2.107	2.527	3.026	3.617	4.316	5.142	6.116
20	1.220	1.486	1.806	2.191	2.653	3.207	3.870	4.661	5.604	6.727
21	1.232	1.516	1.860	2.279	2.786	3.400	4.141	5.034	6.109	7.400
22	1.245	1.546	1.916	2.370	2.925	3.604	4.430	5.437	6.659	8.140
23	1.257	1.577	1.974	2.465	3.072	3.820	4.741	5.871	7.258	8.954
24	1.270	1.608	2.033	2.563	3.225	4.049	5.072	6.341	7.911	9.850
25	1.282	1.641	2.094	2.666	3.386	4.292	5.427	6.848	8.623	10.835
30	1.348	1.811	2.427	3.243	4.322	5.743	7.612	10.063	13.268	17.449
40	1.489	2.208	3.262	4.801	7.040	10.286	14.974	21.725	31.409	45.259
50	1.645	2.692	4.384	7.107	11.467	18.420	29.457	46.902	74.358	117.391

12%	14%	16%	18%	20%	22%	24%	26%	28%	30%
1.12	1.14	1.16	1.18	1.20	1.22	1.24	1.26	1.28	1.30
1.25	1.30	1.35	1.39	1.44	1.49	1.54	1.59	1.64	1.69
1.40	1.48	1.56	1.64	1.73	1.82	1.91	2.00	2.10	2.20
1.57	1.69	1.81	1.94	2.07	2.22	2.36	2.52	2.68	2.86
1.76	1.93	2.10	2.29	2.49	2.70	2.93	3.18	3.44	3.71
1.97	2.19	2.44	2.70	2.99	3.30	3.64	4.00	4.40	4.83
2.21	2.50	2.83	3.19	3.58	4.02	4.51	5.04	5.63	6.27
2.48	2.85	3.28	3.76	4.30	4.91	5.59	6.35	7.21	8.16
2.77	3.25	3.80	4.44	5.16	5.99	6.93	8.00	9.22	10.60
3.11	3.71	4.41	5.23	6.19	7.30	8.59	10.09	11.81	13.79
3.48	4.23	5.12	6.18	7.43	8.91	10.66	12.71	15.11	17.92
3.90	4.82	5.94	7.29	8.92	10.87	13.21	16.01	19.34	23.30
4.36	5.49	6.89	8.60	10.70	13.26	16.39	20.18	24.76	30.29
4.89	6.26	7.99	10.15	12.84	16.18	20.32	25.42	31.69	39.37
5.47	7.14	9.27	11.97	15.41	19.74	25.20	32.03	40.56	51.19
6.13	8.14	10.75	14.13	18.49	24.09	31.24	40.36	51.92	66.54
6.87	9.28	12.47	16.67	22.19	29.38	38.74	50.85	66.46	86.50
7.69	10.58	14.46	19.67	26.62	35.85	48.04	64.07	85.07	112.46
8.61	12.06	16.78	23.21	31.95	43.74	59.57	80.73	108.89	146.19
9.65	13.74	19.46	27.39	38.34	53.36	73.86	101.72	139.38	190.05
10.80	15.67	22.57	32.32	46.01	65.10	91.59	128.17	178.41	247.06
12.10	17.86	26.19	38.14	55.21	79.42	113.57	161.49	228.36	321.18
13.55	20.36	30.38	45.01	66.25	96.89	140.83	203.48	292.30	417.54
15.18	23.21	35.24	53.11	79.50	118.21	174.63	256.39	374.14	542.80
17.00	26.46	40.87	62.67	95.40	144.21	216.54	323.05	478.90	705.64
29.96	50.95	85.85	143.37	237.38	390.	635.	1026.	1646.	2620.
93.05	188.88	378.72	750.38	1469.77	2847.	5456.	10347.	19427.	36119.
289.00	700.23	1670.70	3927.36	9100.44	20797.	46890.	104358.	229350.	497929.

APPENDIX 2   Present value of \$1 received after n periods, $P = 1/(1 + R)^n$

Period	1%	2%	3%	4%	5%	6%	7%	8%	9%	10%
1	0.9901	0.9804	0.9709	0.9615	0.9524	0.9434	0.9346	0.9259	0.9174	0.9091
2	0.9803	0.9612	0.9426	0.9246	0.9070	0.8900	0.8734	0.8573	0.8417	0.8264
3	0.9706	0.9423	0.9151	0.8890	0.8638	0.8396	0.8163	0.7938	0.7722	0.7513
4	0.9610	0.9238	0.8885	0.8548	0.8227	0.7921	0.7629	0.7350	0.7084	0.6830
5	0.9515	0.9057	0.8626	0.8219	0.7835	0.7473	0.7130	0.6806	0.6499	0.6209
6	0.9420	0.8880	0.8375	0.7903	0.7462	0.7050	0.6663	0.6302	0.5963	0.5645
7	0.9327	0.8706	0.8131	0.7599	0.7107	0.6651	0.6227	0.5835	0.5470	0.5132
8	0.9235	0.8535	0.7894	0.7307	0.6768	0.6274	0.5820	0.5403	0.5019	0.4665
9	0.9143	0.8368	0.7664	0.7026	0.6446	0.5919	0.5439	0.5002	0.4604	0.4241
10	0.9053	0.8203	0.7441	0.6756	0.6139	0.5584	0.5083	0.4632	0.4224	0.3855
11	0.8963	0.8043	0.7224	0.6496	0.5847	0.5268	0.4751	0.4289	0.3875	0.3505
12	0.8874	0.7885	0.7014	0.6246	0.5568	0.4970	0.4440	0.3971	0.3555	0.3186
13	0.8787	0.7730	0.6810	0.6006	0.5303	0.4688	0.4150	0.3677	0.3262	0.2897
14	0.8700	0.7579	0.6611	0.5775	0.5051	0.4423	0.3878	0.3405	0.2992	0.2633
15	0.8613	0.7430	0.6419	0.5553	0.4810	0.4173	0.3624	0.3152	0.2745	0.2394
16	0.8528	0.7284	0.6232	0.5339	0.4581	0.3936	0.3387	0.2919	0.2519	0.2176
17	0.8444	0.7142	0.6050	0.5134	0.4363	0.3714	0.3166	0.2703	0.2311	0.1978
18	0.8360	0.7002	0.5874	0.4936	0.4155	0.3503	0.2959	0.2502	0.2120	0.1799
19	0.8277	0.6864	0.5703	0.4746	0.3957	0.3305	0.2765	0.2317	0.1945	0.1635
20	0.8195	0.6730	0.5537	0.4564	0.3769	0.3118	0.2584	0.2145	0.1784	0.1486
21	0.8114	0.6598	0.5375	0.4388	0.3589	0.2942	0.2415	0.1987	0.1637	0.1351
22	0.8034	0.6468	0.5219	0.4220	0.3418	0.2775	0.2257	0.1839	0.1502	0.1228
23	0.7954	0.6342	0.5067	0.4057	0.3256	0.2618	0.2109	0.1703	0.1378	0.1117
24	0.7876	0.6217	0.4919	0.3901	0.3101	0.2470	0.1971	0.1577	0.1264	0.1015
25	0.7798	0.6095	0.4776	0.3751	0.2953	0.2330	0.1842	0.1460	0.1160	0.0923
30	0.7419	0.5521	0.4120	0.3083	0.2314	0.1741	0.1314	0.0994	0.0754	0.0573
40	0.6717	0.4529	0.3066	0.2083	0.1420	0.0972	0.0668	0.0460	0.0318	0.0221
50	0.6080	0.3715	0.2281	0.1407	0.0872	0.0543	0.0339	0.0213	0.0134	0.0085

12%	14%	16%	18%	20%	22%	24%	26%	28%	30%
0.8929	0.8772	0.8621	0.8475	0.8333	0.8197	0.8065	0.7937	0.7813	0.7692
0.7972	0.7695	0.7432	0.7182	0.6944	0.6719	0.6504	0.6299	0.6104	0.5917
0.7118	0.6750	0.6407	0.6086	0.5787	0.5507	0.5245	0.4999	0.4768	0.4552
0.6355	0.5921	0.5523	0.5158	0.4823	0.4514	0.4230	0.3968	0.3725	0.3501
0.5674	0.5194	0.4761	0.4371	0.4019	0.3700	0.3411	0.3149	0.2910	0.2693
0.5066	0.4556	0.4104	0.3704	0.3349	0.3033	0.2751	0.2499	0.2274	0.2072
0.4523	0.3996	0.3538	0.3139	0.2791	0.2486	0.2218	0.1983	0.1776	0.1594
0.4039	0.3506	0.3050	0.2660	0.2326	0.2038	0.1789	0.1574	0.1388	0.1226
0.3606	0.3075	0.2630	0.2255	0.1938	0.1670	0.1443	0.1249	0.1084	0.0943
0.3220	0.2697	0.2267	0.1911	0.1615	0.1369	0.1164	0.0992	0.0847	0.0725
0.2875	0.2366	0.1954	0.1619	0.1346	0.1122	0.0938	0.0787	0.0662	0.0558
0.2567	0.2076	0.1685	0.1372	0.1122	0.0920	0.0757	0.0625	0.0517	0.0429
0.2292	0.1821	0.1452	0.1163	0.0935	0.0754	0.0610	0.0496	0.0404	0.0330
0.2046	0.1597	0.1252	0.0985	0.0779	0.0618	0.0492	0.0393	0.0316	0.0254
0.1827	0.1401	0.1079	0.0835	0.0649	0.0507	0.0397	0.0312	0.0247	0.0195
0.1631	0.1229	0.0930	0.0708	0.0541	0.0415	0.0320	0.0248	0.0193	0.0150
0.1456	0.1078	0.0802	0.0600	0.0451	0.0340	0.0258	0.0197	0.0150	0.0116
0.1300	0.0946	0.0691	0.0508	0.0376	0.0279	0.0208	0.0156	0.0118	0.0089
0.1161	0.0829	0.0596	0.0431	0.0313	0.0229	0.0168	0.0124	0.0092	0.0068
0.1037	0.0728	0.0514	0.0365	0.0261	0.0187	0.0135	0.0098	0.0072	0.0053
0.0926	0.0638	0.0443	0.0309	0.0217	0.0154	0.0109	0.0078	0.0056	0.0040
0.0826	0.0560	0.0382	0.0262	0.0181	0.0126	0.0088	0.0062	0.0044	0.0031
0.0738	0.0491	0.0329	0.0222	0.0151	0.0103	0.0071	0.0049	0.0034	0.0024
0.0659	0.0431	0.0284	0.0188	0.0126	0.0085	0.0057	0.0039	0.0027	0.0018
0.0588	0.0378	0.0245	0.0160	0.0105	0.0069	0.0046	0.0031	0.0021	0.0014
0.0334	0.0196	0.0116	0.0070	0.0042	0.0026	0.0016	0.0010	0.0006	0.0004
0.0107	0.0053	0.0026	0.0013	0.0007	0.0004	0.0002	0.0001	0.0001	0.0000
0.0035	0.0014	0.0006	0.0003	0.0001	0.0000	0.0000	0.0000	0.0000	0.0000

APPENDIX 3 Present value of an annuity paying $1 at the end of each period for n periods,

$$P = \sum_{i=1}^{n} 1/(1 + R)^i$$

Period	1%	2%	3%	4%	5%	6%	7%	8%	9%	10%
1	0.9901	0.9804	0.9709	0.9615	0.9524	0.9434	0.9346	0.9259	0.9174	0.9091
2	1.9704	1.9416	1.9135	1.8861	1.8594	1.8334	1.8080	1.7833	1.7591	1.7355
3	2.9410	2.8839	2.8286	2.7751	2.7232	2.6730	2.6243	2.5771	2.5313	2.4869
4	3.9020	3.8077	3.7171	3.6299	3.5460	3.4651	3.3872	3.3121	3.2397	3.1699
5	4.8534	4.7135	4.5797	4.4518	4.3295	4.2124	4.1002	3.9927	3.8897	3.7908
6	5.7955	5.6014	5.4172	5.2421	5.0757	4.9173	4.7665	4.6229	4.4859	4.3553
7	6.7282	6.4720	6.2303	6.0021	5.7864	5.5824	5.3893	5.2064	5.0330	4.8684
8	7.6517	7.3255	7.0197	6.7327	6.4632	6.2098	5.9713	5.7466	5.5348	5.3349
9	8.5660	8.1622	7.7861	7.4353	7.1078	6.8017	6.5152	6.2469	5.9952	5.7590
10	9.4713	8.9826	8.5302	8.1109	7.7217	7.3601	7.0236	6.7101	6.4177	6.1446
11	10.3676	9.7868	9.2526	8.7605	8.3064	7.8869	7.4987	7.1390	6.8052	6.4951
12	11.2551	10.5753	9.9540	9.3851	8.8633	8.3838	7.9427	7.5361	7.1607	6.8137
13	12.1337	11.3484	10.6350	9.9856	9.3936	8.8527	8.3577	7.9038	7.4869	7.1034
14	13.0037	12.1062	11.2961	10.5631	9.8986	9.2950	8.7455	8.2442	7.7862	7.3667
15	13.8651	12.8493	11.9379	11.1184	10.3797	9.7122	9.1079	8.5595	8.0607	7.6061
16	14.7179	13.5777	12.5611	11.6523	10.8378	10.1059	9.4466	8.8514	8.3126	7.8237
17	15.5623	14.2919	13.1661	12.1657	11.2741	10.4773	9.7632	9.1216	8.5436	8.0216
18	16.3983	14.9920	13.7535	12.6593	11.6896	10.8276	10.0591	9.3719	8.7556	8.2014
19	17.2260	15.6785	14.3238	13.1339	12.0853	11.1581	10.3356	9.6036	8.9501	8.3649
20	18.0456	16.3514	14.8775	13.5903	12.4622	11.4699	10.5940	9.8181	9.1285	8.5136
21	18.8570	17.0112	15.4150	14.0292	12.8212	11.7641	10.8355	10.0168	9.2922	8.6487
22	19.6604	17.6580	15.9369	14.4511	13.1630	12.0416	11.0612	10.2007	9.4424	8.7715
23	20.4558	18.2922	16.4436	14.8568	13.4886	12.3034	11.2722	10.3711	9.5802	8.8832
24	21.2434	18.9139	16.9355	15.2470	13.7986	12.5504	11.4693	10.5288	9.7066	8.9847
25	22.0232	19.5235	17.4131	15.6221	14.0939	12.7834	11.6536	10.6748	9.8226	9.0770
30	25.8077	22.3965	19.6004	17.2920	15.3725	13.7648	12.4090	11.2578	10.2737	9.4269
40	32.8347	27.3555	23.1148	19.7928	17.1591	15.0463	13.3317	11.9246	10.7574	9.7791
50	39.1961	31.4236	25.7298	21.4822	18.2559	15.7619	13.8007	12.2335	10.9617	9.9148

12%	14%	16%	18%	20%	22%	24%	26%	28%	30%
0.8929	0.8772	0.8621	0.8475	0.8333	0.8197	0.8065	0.7937	0.7813	0.7692
1.6901	1.6467	1.6052	1.5656	1.5278	1.4915	1.4568	1.4235	1.3916	1.3609
2.4018	2.3216	2.2459	2.1743	2.1065	2.0422	1.9813	1.9234	1.8684	1.8161
3.0373	2.9137	2.7982	2.6901	2.5887	2.4936	2.4043	2.3202	2.2410	2.1662
3.6048	3.4331	3.2743	3.1272	2.9906	2.8636	2.7454	2.6351	2.5320	2.4356
4.1114	3.8887	3.6847	3.4976	3.3255	3.1669	3.0205	2.8850	2.7594	2.6427
4.5638	4.2883	4.0386	3.8115	3.6046	3.4155	3.2423	3.0833	2.9370	2.8021
4.9676	4.6389	4.3436	4.0776	3.8372	3.6193	3.4212	3.2407	3.0758	2.9247
5.3282	4.9464	4.6065	4.3030	4.0310	3.7863	3.5655	3.3657	3.1842	3.0190
5.6502	5.2161	4.8332	4.4941	4.1925	3.9232	3.6819	3.4648	3.2689	3.0915
5.9377	5.4527	5.0286	4.6560	4.3271	4.0354	3.7757	3.5435	3.3351	3.1473
6.1944	5.6603	5.1971	4.7932	4.4392	4.1274	3.8514	3.6059	3.3868	3.1903
6.4235	5.8424	5.3423	4.9095	4.5327	4.2028	3.9124	3.6555	3.4272	3.2233
6.6282	6.0021	5.4675	5.0081	4.6106	4.2646	3.9616	3.6949	3.4587	3.2487
6.8109	6.1422	5.5755	5.0916	4.6755	4.3152	4.0013	3.7261	3.4834	3.2682
6.9740	6.2651	5.6685	5.1624	4.7296	4.3567	4.0333	3.7509	3.5026	3.2832
7.1196	6.3729	5.7487	5.2223	4.7746	4.3908	4.0591	3.7705	3.5177	3.2948
7.2497	6.4674	5.8178	5.2732	4.8122	4.4187	4.0799	3.7861	3.5294	3.3037
7.3658	6.5504	5.8775	5.3162	4.8435	4.4415	4.0967	3.7985	3.5386	3.3105
7.4694	6.6231	5.9288	5.3527	4.8696	4.4603	4.1103	3.8083	3.5458	3.3158
7.5620	6.6870	5.9731	5.3837	4.8913	4.4756	4.1212	3.8161	3.5514	3.3198
7.6446	6.7429	6.0113	5.4099	4.9094	4.4882	4.1300	3.8223	3.5558	3.3230
7.7184	6.7921	6.0442	5.4321	4.9245	4.4985	4.1371	3.8273	3.5592	3.3254
7.7843	6.8351	6.0726	5.4509	4.9371	4.5070	4.1428	3.8312	3.5619	3.3272
7.8431	6.8729	6.0971	5.4669	4.9476	4.5139	4.1474	3.8342	3.5640	3.3286
8.0552	7.0027	6.1772	5.5168	4.9789	4.5338	4.1601	3.8424	3.5693	3.3321
8.2438	7.1050	6.2335	5.5482	4.9966	4.5439	4.1659	3.8458	3.5712	3.3332
8.3045	7.1327	6.2463	5.5541	4.9995	4.5452	4.1666	3.8461	3.5714	3.3333

APPENDIX 4   Future value of an annuity paying $1 at the end of each period for n periods,

$$F = \sum_{i=1}^{n} (1 + R)^{n-i}$$

Period	1%	2%	3%	4%	5%	6%	7%	8%	9%	10%
1	1.000	1.000	1.000	1.000	1.000	1.000	1.000	1.000	1.000	1.000
2	2.010	2.020	2.030	2.040	2.050	2.060	2.070	2.080	2.090	2.100
3	3.030	3.060	3.091	3.122	3.153	3.184	3.215	3.246	3.278	3.310
4	4.060	4.122	4.184	4.246	4.310	4.375	4.440	4.506	4.573	4.641
5	5.101	5.204	5.309	5.416	5.526	5.637	5.751	5.867	5.985	6.105
6	6.152	6.308	6.468	6.633	6.802	6.975	7.153	7.336	7.523	7.716
7	7.214	7.434	7.662	7.898	8.142	8.394	8.654	8.923	9.200	9.487
8	8.286	8.583	8.892	9.214	9.549	9.897	10.260	10.637	11.028	11.436
9	9.369	9.755	10.159	10.583	11.027	11.491	11.978	12.488	13.021	13.579
10	10.462	10.950	11.464	12.006	12.578	13.181	13.816	14.487	15.193	15.937
11	11.567	12.169	12.808	13.486	14.207	14.972	15.784	16.645	17.560	18.531
12	12.683	13.412	14.192	15.026	15.917	16.870	17.888	18.977	20.141	21.384
13	13.809	14.680	15.618	16.627	17.713	18.882	20.141	21.495	22.953	24.523
14	14.947	15.974	17.086	18.292	19.599	21.015	22.550	24.215	26.019	27.975
15	16.097	17.293	18.599	20.024	21.579	23.276	25.129	27.152	29.361	31.772
16	17.258	18.639	20.157	21.825	23.657	25.673	27.888	30.324	33.003	35.950
17	18.430	20.012	21.762	23.698	25.840	28.213	30.840	33.750	36.974	40.545
18	19.615	21.412	23.414	25.645	28.132	30.906	33.999	37.450	41.301	45.599
19	20.811	22.841	25.117	27.671	30.539	33.760	37.379	41.446	46.018	51.159
20	22.019	24.297	26.870	29.778	33.066	36.786	40.995	45.762	51.160	57.275
21	23.239	25.783	28.676	31.969	35.719	39.993	44.865	50.423	56.765	64.002
22	24.472	27.299	30.537	34.248	38.505	43.392	49.006	55.457	62.873	71.403
23	25.716	28.845	32.453	36.618	41.430	46.996	53.436	60.893	69.532	79.543
24	26.973	30.422	34.426	39.083	44.502	50.816	58.177	66.765	76.790	88.497
25	28.243	32.030	36.459	41.646	47.727	54.865	63.249	73.106	84.701	98.347
30	34.785	40.568	47.575	56.085	66.439	79.058	94.461	113.283	136.308	164.494
40	48.886	60.402	75.401	95.026	120.800	154.762	199.635	259.057	337.882	442.593
50	64.463	84.579	112.797	152.667	209.348	290.336	406.529	573.770	815.084	1163.909

12%	14%	16%	18%	20%	22%	24%	26%	28%	30%
1.00	1.00	1.00	1.00	1.00	1.00	1.00	1.00	1.00	1.00
2.12	2.14	2.16	2.18	2.20	2.22	2.24	2.26	2.28	2.30
3.37	3.44	3.51	3.57	3.64	3.71	3.78	3.85	3.92	3.99
4.78	4.92	5.07	5.22	5.37	5.52	5.68	5.85	6.02	6.19
6.35	6.61	6.88	7.15	7.44	7.74	8.05	8.37	8.70	9.04
8.12	8.54	8.98	9.44	9.93	10.44	10.98	11.54	12.14	12.76
10.09	10.73	11.41	12.14	12.92	13.74	14.62	15.55	16.53	17.58
12.30	13.23	14.24	15.33	16.50	17.76	19.12	20.59	22.16	23.86
14.78	16.09	17.52	19.09	20.80	22.67	24.71	26.94	29.37	32.01
17.55	19.34	21.32	23.52	25.96	28.66	31.64	34.94	38.59	42.62
20.65	23.04	25.73	28.76	32.15	35.96	40.24	45.03	50.40	56.41
24.13	27.27	30.85	34.93	39.58	44.87	50.89	57.74	65.51	74.33
28.03	32.09	36.79	42.22	48.50	55.75	64.11	73.75	84.85	97.63
32.39	37.58	43.67	50.82	59.20	69.01	80.50	93.93	109.61	127.91
37.28	43.84	51.66	60.97	72.04	85.19	100.82	119.35	141.30	167.29
42.75	50.98	60.93	72.94	87.44	104.93	126.01	151.38	181.87	218.47
48.88	59.12	71.67	87.07	105.93	129.02	157.25	191.73	233.79	285.01
55.75	68.39	84.14	103.74	128.12	158.40	195.99	242.59	300.25	371.52
63.44	78.97	98.60	123.41	154.74	194.25	244.03	306.66	385.32	483.97
72.05	91.02	115.38	146.63	186.69	237.99	303.60	387.39	494.21	630.17
81.70	104.77	134.84	174.02	225.03	291.35	377.46	489.11	633.59	820.22
92.50	120.44	157.41	206.34	271.03	356.44	469.06	617.28	812.00	1067.28
104.60	138.30	183.60	244.49	326.24	435.86	582.63	778.77	1040.36	1388.46
118.16	158.66	213.98	289.49	392.48	532.75	723.46	982.25	1332.66	1806.00
133.33	181.87	249.21	342.60	471.98	650.96	898.09	1238.64	1706.80	2348.80
241.33	356.79	530.31	790.95	1181.88	1767.	2641.	3942.	5873.	8730.
767.09	1342.03	2360.76	4163.21	7343.86	12937.	22729.	39793.	69377.	120393.
2400.02	4994.52	10435.65	21813.09	45497.19	94525.	195373.	401374.	819103.	1659761.

GLOSSARY

Adjustable-Rate Loan The loan rate rises and falls with market interest rates, protecting lending institutions whose deposit rates move with market interest rates. These flexible-rate loans go by a variety of names: adjustable-rate, variable-rate, re-negotiable-rate, rollover, and so on, and have a variety of terms and conditions. If the monthly payments are fixed while the loan rate fluctuates, there may be negative amortization.

Advance-Decline Index Many technical analysts monitor the number of stocks advancing relative to the number declining. Unlike the Dow Jones Industrial and other market price indexes, such a comparison pays no attention to the value of the stock or to the size of the advance or decline; it simply counts whether most stocks went up or down.

After Taxes An after-tax cash flow is one that has been adjusted for taxes. The required rate of return used to discount an after-tax cash flow should be an after-tax return, reflecting the after-tax rates of return available on alternative investments.

American Options In contrast to European options, American options can be exercised before the expiration date, but never are, unless there is a large dividend that would be lost by postponement.

Amortized Loans The periodic payments on an amortized loan include principal as well as interest so that the loan is paid off gradually rather than with a single balloon payment at the end. The most common amortized loan involves constant monthly payments over the life of the loan, with the n monthly payments X set so that their present value at the stated monthly loan rate R is equal to the amount borrowed $P : X = RP/\{1 - 1/(1 + R)^n\}$.

Arbitrage Pure arbitrage is a virtually riskless exploitation of price discrepancies; for example, simultaneously buying a stock on one exchange for $20 a share and selling it on another for $22 a share until this price discrepancy is eliminated.

Arbitrage Pricing Theory (APT) Assuming that asset returns can be modeled as dependent on factors and on an idiosyncratic error term that is independent of the factors and of the idiosyncratic influences on other asset returns, assets will be priced in a manner analogous to CAPM, with risk premiums for macro factor risks that cannot be diversified away.

Ask Price The ask price is the price at which a specialist or market maker is willing to sell a security; the bid price is the price at which they will buy.

Back-End Loads Some open-end investment companies charge a back-end load fee when money is withdrawn from the fund.

Balloon Loan On a balloon loan, the periodic payments include little or no repayment of the principal and, thus, the last payment (the balloon payment) must be relatively large. Before the great Depression, most home mortgages were 3-to-5-year balloon loans in which only interest was paid until maturity, at which time a balloon payment equal to the size of the loan was due. Now, conventional mortgages are amortized, so that the principal is paid off during the term of the loan.

Basis The basis is the difference between the futures price and the spot price. For precious metals, financial assets, and other items that can be stored and sold short, the basis is determined by the cost of carry—the cost, including foregone interest, of buying the item now and holding it until the delivery date. Since the cost of carry is usually positive, futures prices are generally above spot prices and increase with the time until delivery.

Basis Points Since interest rates generally change by only a fraction of a percent each day, financial market participants use the term basis points to describe hundredths of a percentage point; for example, an increase from 8.50% to 8.58% is 8 basis points.

Bearer Bonds Proof of ownership of a bearer bond is demonstrated by possession of it, in contrast to a registered bond, the owner of which is registered with the trustee and can receive payments by mail without the physical presentation of the certificate.

Before Taxes A before-tax cash flow has not taken taxes into account. Tax rates vary from person to person (because tax brackets rise with income), from institution to institution (e.g., banks, non-financial corporations, and colleges are treated differently), and from asset to asset (e.g., interest on corporate and municipal bonds are taxed differently).

Beta Coefficient An asset's beta coefficient measures the extent to which its return moves with the return on all assets. If the market return increases by 10%, the return on an asset tends to increase by more or less than 10%, depending on whether its beta coefficient is larger or smaller than 1. R-squared gauges the historical reliability of this relationship. The beta coefficient of a security gauges the macro, systematic risk that cannot be diversified away; micro, unsystematic risk, which arises from events specific to individual companies, can be diversified away in a large portfolio.

Bid Price The bid price is the price that a specialist or market maker is willing to pay for a security; the ask price is the price at which they will sell.

Big Board The New York Stock Exchange is sometimes called the "big board" because the stocks traded on this exchange include many of the most prominent U.S. corporations.

Black-Scholes Option Model To the extent that call and stock prices are related, riskless hedges can, in theory, be constructed by continuously maintaining an appropriate hedge ratio between stocks and calls. The observation that the return on a riskless hedge should equal the return on safe Treasury bills, along with some strong assumptions and advanced mathematics, gives the Black-Scholes option pricing formula.

Blue Chip The stocks of large, well-established, financially sound companies are called blue chips. This is an allusion to poker, in which the blue chips are the most valuable.

Boiler Room Boiler room operations involve aggressive sales people using phone calls to persuade gullible investors to invest in very speculative or fraudulent securities.

Book Value A company's book value is its net worth (assets minus liabilities, often calculated on a per share basis), shown on the firm's balance sheets. The market price of the stock may be above or below book value, because investors value a firm for the profitability of its assets while accountants look at depreciated cost.

Buying on Margin An investor who buys stock with borrowed money is said to buy on margin, thus creating leverage that multiplies the gains or losses when the return on the stock is not equal to the interest rate on the loan. The Federal Reserve sets margin requirements (currently 50%), the minimum margin that brokerage firms must require of their customers. With an $x\%$ margin requirement, a stock buyer must pay at least $x\%$ of the cost of the stock, borrowing the rest from the brokerage firm.

Call Option A call option gives the holder of the option the right, but not the obligation, to buy an asset at a fixed price on or before a specified date. For instance, an American call option could give the owner the right to buy a share of a specified stock for $100 any time within the next six months.

Call Provisions Some Treasury bonds and almost all corporate bonds have call provisions that allow the issuer to redeem the bond before maturity at a specified price, typically a small premium over face value, giving the issuer the opportunity to refinance if interest rates fall. An issuer can choose to call all of the bonds issued or randomly selected ones.

Call Rate   The call rate is a brokerage firm's cost of borrowing from banks the money they lend investors, who are then charged the call rate plus a specified percent.

Capital Asset Pricing Model (CAPM)   Investors who choose portfolios on the basis of the mean and variance, and agree on the opportunities, will price assets so that the risk premiums have this simple structure

$$E_i - R_0 = \beta_i(E_M - R_0)$$

where E_i is the expected return on an individual asset, E_M is the expected return on the market as a whole, and R_0 is the return on a risk-free asset.

Capital Gains   The profit made when an asset is sold for more than the purchase price is a capital gain; if the sale price is less than the purchase price, this is a capital loss.

Capital Risk   An unexpected change in interest rates will cause an unanticipated change in the asset's price. The longer an asset's duration, the more sensitive its price to interest rate fluctuations and the larger the capital risk.

Capitalization   A firm's capitalization is the total amount of securities (debt and equity) that it has issued.

Cash flow   When there is more than one future payment, these payments are called a cash flow; the present value of a cash flow is equal to the sum of the present values of the individual payments. A firm's cash flow is the net cash received or paid each period, before accounting adjustments for depreciation, depletion, and so on.

Characteristic Line   A line fitted to a scatter diagram of the returns on one security and the returns on the market as a whole is called its characteristic line. The slope is the asset's beta coefficient; the goodness of fit is measured by R-squared.

Closed-End Funds   Closed-end investment companies have a fixed number of shares outstanding. The shares of closed-end funds are traded on the stock exchanges or over the counter, at a market price that need not equal the fund's net asset value.

Common Stock   The owners of a corporation's common stock are the legal owners of the firm, the name indicating that the shareholders own the firm "in common." Stockholders elect (normally with one vote per share) a board of directors that hires the top executives, supervises their management of the firm, and decides the dividends to be paid to shareholders.

Compound Interest   Describes the earning of interest on interest, a powerful arithmetic that causes seemingly slight differences in annual returns to grow to large differences in wealth after many years. Over short horizons, compound interest—crediting interest monthly, daily, or even continuously—increases the effective return on a bank deposit or other investment, in that you are earning interest on interest. An amount P invested at an annual rate of return R, compounded m times a year, grows to $P(1 + R/m)^m$ after 1 year and to $P(1 + R/m)^{mn}$ after n years.

Conservation of Value   The present value of $(A + B)$ is equal to the present value of A plus the present value of B, implying that nothing is gained or lost by combining two cash flows or by splitting a cash flow in two. Thus corporate mergers, breakups, stock splits, and stock dividends that do not affect the aggregate cash flow do not help or hurt shareholders. Except for tax consequences, shareholders do not gain or lose wealth from the disbursement of cash through a dividend or stock repurchase, or from the raising of funds by cutting dividends or selling additional shares.

Consol   A consol (or perpetuity) pays a perpetual cash flow, which continues period after period, forever. For a required rate of return R, the present value of a consol paying X each period is $P = X/R$.

Constant-Dividend-Growth Model   If the dividend D_1 will grow at a constant rate g and the investor's required return is $R > g$, then the present value of a stock simplifies to this central equation of fundamental analysis, $PV = D_1/(R - g)$.

Continuous Compounding   Continuously compounded interest calculations assume that the frequency of compounding is infinitely large (and the time between compounding infinitesimally small), giving

$$\text{limit } (1 + R/m)^m \rightarrow e^R$$
$$(m \rightarrow \infty)$$

where $e = 2.718 \ldots$ is the base of natural logarithms.

Contrarian Strategy A contrarian strategy is a deliberate attempt to do the opposite of what others are doing, based on a belief that the herd-like instincts of investors cause security prices to go to unwarranted extremes.

Corporate Bonds Corporate bonds are fixed-income securities of various maturities issued by corporations to purchase new plant and equipment, pay current bills, and finance the takeover of other companies.

Cost of Carry The cost of carry is the cost of buying a commodity now and holding it until the delivery date of a futures contract. This cost includes storage, spoilage, insurance, and foregone interest, less any cash flow from the item while it is being held.

Coupon Coupons are the periodic (usually semi-annual) interest payments on a bond, made in addition to a final payment when the bond matures. These are called coupons because, traditionally, they were cut from the bond certificate and redeemed through a local bank or security dealer.

Coupon Rate The coupon rate is the annual coupon as a percentage of a bond's face value; e.g., a bond that pays $1000 at maturity and $45.00 every six months has a 9% coupon rate.

Covered Call A covered call is the simultaneous purchase of stock and sale of a call option on this stock. This conservative strategy is equivalent to selling a put.

Covering a Position See Reversing a Position.

Creative Financing When money is tight and it is difficult to get mortgages from financial institutions, buyers and sellers turn to creative financing, novel ways of financing deals, usually involving a loan from the seller.

Daily Limits To control short-run price fluctuations, exchanges do not allow the settlement prices of some futures contracts to change by more than a specified daily limit.

Daily Settlement The daily transfer of funds from winners to losers required by futures exchanges, using the day-end settlement prices, is called the daily settlement.

Data Mining A data mining expedition is the testing of many theories, searching for a statistically significant result and demonstrating little more than the persistence of the researcher.

Default A borrower defaults when the terms of the debt contract are violated; for example, by not making a scheduled coupon payment on time. A default is not necessarily a complete loss, it may be a temporary suspension of coupon payments or a prelude to a partial payment; in the first month after default, a bond typically trades at about 40% of its face value.

Discount Basis Sometimes, interest rates are calculated on a discount basis, relative to the amount paid back rather than the amount loaned; for example, the calculation of Treasury-bill rates relative to face value rather than purchase price. Banks are no longer allowed to calculate consumer loan rates on a discount basis.

Diversified Portfolio While a single asset may, in isolation, be very risky, a portfolio of several imperfectly correlated (or, better, negatively correlated) assets can be used to reduce risk. Diversification, counting on asset gains and losses to offset each other, is of no interest to those who are risk neutral or risk seeking, but is very attractive to risk-averse investors.

Dividend Yield The ratio of a stock's dividends per share to price, D/P, is its dividend yield. This is an inadequate measure of the shareholders' return, because it neglects the future growth of dividends.

Dow Jones Industrial Average The widely followed Dow Jones Industrial Average is a simple average of the stock prices of thirty prominent blue-chip companies, using a divisor that changes from time to time to offset substitutions and stock splits, thereby maintaining a logically consistent daily index of stock prices. In contrast, market value indexes, such as the S&P 500 and the NYSE index, weight each stock's price by the number of shares outstanding.

Dow Theory Many aspects of technical analysis are derived, in one way or another, from *The Wall Street Journal* editorials written between 1889 and 1929 by Charles Dow and then William Hamilton.

Dual-Purpose Fund A dual-purpose investment company has two classes of shareholders—income and capital. The income shareholders receive all of the dividends from the stock in the portfolio and a specified redemption price at the fund's termination date, typically 10–15 years after the fund's inception. The capital shareholders receive any excess of the value of the fund's portfolio over this redemption price.

Duration   An asset's duration, the present-value weighted average number of years until the cash flow is received, is approximately equal to the percentage change in the asset's present value resulting from a one-percentage-point change in the required return. The duration of a bond with coupons is less than its maturity and is shorter the larger are the coupons. An asset's duration also determines the horizon over which the change in an asset's market price caused by a (small) interest rate change is just offset by the change in the value of the reinvested cash flow, leaving the total future value unaffected.

Dynamic Asset Allocation   See Portfolio Insurance.

Dynamic Hedging   See Portfolio Insurance.

Earnings Yield   A stock's earnings yield is the ratio of the firm's earnings per share to the stock's price per share, E/P. This is only a crude estimate of the shareholders' rate of return on their stock, because not all of the earnings are paid out as dividends, and what is retained may not earn the shareholders' required rate of return.

Efficient Market   In an efficient market there are no obviously mispriced securities and, therefore, no transactions that can be counted on to make abnormally large profits. The efficient market hypothesis does not assume that a stock's price is equal to some objective measure of its intrinsic value, or even that all investors agree on that value—only that investors cannot consistently make unusually large profits trading on information. The weak, semi-strong, and strong forms of the efficient market hypothesis say that abnormal profits cannot be made using information about past stock prices, all public information, and all information.

Equity   In contrast to corporate debt and other fixed-income securities, common stock is equity, a claim on the company's profits after interest and other expenses have been paid and, in the event of liquidation, a claim on the company's assets after its debts have been settled.

Ex-Dividend   To allow for the processing of transactions, the NYSE and most other exchanges stocks use an ex-dividend (excluding dividend) date four business days before the record date used by firms to determine the shareholders entitled to the latest dividend. Those who buy the stock ex-dividend do not receive the dividend. On the ex-dividend date, the market value of the shares should decline by the size of the dividend.

Executive-Compensation Options   Executive-compensation options give a company's management the right to buy new shares of the company's stock at a set price. This practice, which had tax advantages when capital gains were relatively lightly taxed, is intended to focus executive attention on the value of the firm's stock.

Exercise Date   An option contract expires on its exercise date.

Exercise Price   An option contract can be exercised at its exercise price (also called the striking price).

Exercise Value   The minimum value of an option is its exercise value—the amount an option holder could save by exercising the option instead of buying or selling the stock at its market price. The exercise value of a call option is equal to the difference $P - E$ between the value of the stock P and the option's exercise price E if $P > E$ (and zero otherwise). The exercise value of a put is equal to $E - P$ if $P < E$ (and zero otherwise).

Expectations Hypothesis   The Expectations Hypothesis explains the term structure by interest rate expectations—specifically, the Hicks Equation, which assumes that securities are priced so that a strategy of rolling over short-term bonds is expected to do as well as a strategy of holding long-term bonds. When no change in one-year rates is anticipated comparable assets of differing maturities will all be priced to have the same yield. Longer-term rates will be above the current one-year rate if rates are expected to rise in the future and below if rates are expected to decline.

Expected Value   Usually denoted by the Greek symbol μ, the expected value is a weighted average of the possible returns, using probabilities as weights to reflect the likelihood of each outcome, $\mu = \Sigma \, x_i P[x_i]$. The expected value is the long-run average if the frequency with which each outcome occurs corresponds to its probability.

European Options   In contrast to an American option, a European option can only be exercised on the expiration date.

Federal Reserve Board (Fed) This seven-member board is appointed by the President and controls monetary policy in the United States.

Filter System A filter system is a technical strategy: Set some target price change, $x\%$, and then buy after the stock moves up $x\%$ from a previous low and sell after it falls $x\%$ from a previous high. This system implicitly assumes a momemtum in stock prices and has repeatedly been shown to be unprofitable.

Financial Assets Financial assets are paper claims, such as bank deposits, bonds, and stocks. In the United States and other countries with well-developed financial markets, many savers invest in financial assets that are issued by borrowers to raise funds to lend to others or to acquire physical assets.

Financial Markets Financial markets are established means for trading bonds, stocks, and other financial assets. These come in many different forms (such as the New York Stock Exchange and the over-the-counter market) and involve a variety of agents (including brokers and dealers).

Fixed-Income Securities With a fixed-income security, the amount of money to be repaid is specified in the promissory note.

Forward Contract A forward contract is a private agreement to deliver a certain item on a specified date at a price agreed to today, but not paid until delivery. Futures contracts are similar, but standardized and traded on organized exchanges.

Forward Rates Forward rates are the implicit future rates of return embedded in the term structure of interest rates in the sense that these are the future interest rate values for which the strategies of buying longs and rolling over shorts do equally well. An investor whose interest rate expectations are not equal to these implicit forward rates has reason for preferring shorts to longs, or vice versa.

Fundamental Analysis Investors using fundamental analysis compare the price of a security to the present value of the anticipated cash flow. This leads to a study of a firm's dividends, earnings, and assets.

Future Value The future value of an investment is its value after it has earned a specified rate of return for a given number of years. If an amount P earns an annual rate of return R for n years, the investment grows to $F = P(1 + R)^n$.

Futures Contract A futures contract is an agreement to deliver a certain item on a specified date at a price agreed to today, but not paid until delivery; for example, a mill might agree to pay a farmer $3 a bushel for 100,000 bushels of wheat delivered six months from now—thus eliminating the mill's uncertainty about the cost of wheat and the farmer's uncertainty about revenue. Unlike forward contracts, futures contracts are standardized and traded on organized exchanges. Futures can be used to hedge a position (e.g., a farmer can sell wheat futures), to speculate (e.g., a wager on the price of silver), or for arbitrage (e.g., stock index arbitrage).

General Obligation Bonds State and local bonds backed by the issuer's ability to levy taxes to pay the promised coupons and maturation value are known as general obligation bonds, in contrast to revenue bonds, which finance specific projects and are repaid from the project's eventual revenue.

Generally Accepted Accounting Principles (GAAP) The SEC requires that financial statements conform to the principles adopted by the Financial Accounting Standards Board (FASB), an independent group financially supported by the accounting industry, which, from time to time, publishes its opinions on accounting practices that it considers acceptable.

Golden Parachutes Golden parachutes provide lavish severance pay to displaced executives.

Graduated Payment Mortgage In a graduated payment mortgage, the monthly payments are initially low and then increase over time to ease the financial burden on young households who expect nominal income to grow steadily. Ideally, the mortgage payments will be a constant fraction of income, rather than a constant dollar amount.

Greenmail When a company pays a raider to drop a takeover attempt, this is greenmail.

Growth Stock The constant-dividend-growth model shows that a company with a relatively high anticipated growth rate has a higher present value than otherwise similar firms with lower growth rates.

Growth-Stock Paradox In the constant-dividend-growth model, a stock whose dividends will forever grow at a rate g that exceeds shareholders' required return R, has an infinite present value. In practice, such a permanently high long-run growth rate is not plausible.

Hicks Equation In accord with the Expectations Hypothesis, the term structure of interest rates is such that long-term rates are the product of the current and anticipated future short-term rates:

$$(1 + R_n)^n = (1 + R_1)(1 + R_1^{+1})(1 + R_1^{+2}) \ldots (1 + R_1^{n-1})$$

Human Capital Just as a stock yields dividends and a house yields shelter, a person's brains and brawn (human capital) yield income too.

Hypothecation The use of securities as loan collateral; for example, the stocks that a broker holds in street name for a customer who has bought on margin.

Immunized If the holding period of an asset is equal to its duration, the investment is said to be immunized: the future value of the asset and its reinvested cash flow are unaffected by (small) changes in the interest rate.

Income Income encompasses the benefits received while owning an asset. This includes the cash flow generated by the investment (the interest from a bond, dividends from a stock, rent from an apartment building) and the services provided by an asset (transportation from a car, shelter from a house, pleasure from fine art).

Income Risk The future value of the proceeds from an investment depends on the rates of return prevailing when the cash flow is reinvested. Uncertainty about these reinvestment rates of return is income risk. The purchase of long-term assets is profitable if interest rates fall unexpectedly; rolling over short-term assets does well if interest rates rise unexpectedly.

Index Arbitrage Index arbitrage attempts to earn risk-free profits whenever the basis, or spread between the price of a stock index futures contract and the index itself, differs from the cost of carry (the Treasury bill rate minus dividend yield on the stocks in the index) by more than the transactions costs that arbitrage entails. Arbitragers buy stocks and sell futures if the futures price is too high and do the reverse if it is too low.

Index Fund Instead of trying to pick stocks that will beat the market, an index fund buys the stocks in a designated market index, such as the S&P 500, in proportion to the stocks' index weights. An index fund is deliberately passive, seeking to beat other funds with low transaction costs and management fees.

Indexing Persuaded that it is difficult to beat the stock market, many institutions now index at least part of their portfolio, trying merely to replicate the market, rather than outperform it.

Indifference Curve An indifference curve is a graphic device for depicting investment opportunities that an investor finds equally appealing. The investor's choice is determined by combining indifference curves with the opportunity locus.

Inflation Inflation is a persistent, continuing increase in the prices of goods and services, often measured by the change in the Consumer Price Index (CPI), which reflects the price of a standard basket of goods and services.

Inflation Risk The purchasing power of the proceeds from an investment depends on the course of prices. Uncertainty about future prices creates inflation risk. An unexpected increase in the rate of inflation erodes, while an unexpected decrease swells, the purchasing power of fixed nominal cash flows. Although inflation and interest rates do not move in locked step, a strategy of rolling over short-term assets at least offers the likelihood that nominal interest rates will increase if inflation does.

Insider Report A corporation's directors and executives, and those who own more than 10% of its shares, must file an insider report with the SEC whenever they buy or sell the firm's stock.

Interest-Rate Parity For the basis to equal the cost of carry, the difference between the futures and spot dollar price of a foreign currency should approximately equal the difference between U.S. and foreign interest rates.

Intrinsic Value The intrinsic value of a stock is the present value of its prospective cash flow, discounted by the investor's required return, taking into account the returns available on alternative investments, its risk, and other salient considerations. A stock is worth buying if its intrinsic value is larger than its price, but not otherwise.

Institutional Block Ratio The institutional block ratio is a technical indicator that compares the number of trades of 10,000 shares or more at prices higher than the preceding trade with the number at lower prices. A low value shows that big institutions are more interested in selling than buying; a high value shows the opposite.

Investment Company An investment company pools investor funds and buys a portfolio of securities, providing diversification and, it is hoped, superior management. These may be either open-end or closed-end.

Leverage Leverage occurs when a relatively small investment reaps the benefits or losses from a much larger investment; for example, the use of borrowed money to finance an investment. Leverage is said to be a two-edged sword because it multiplies gains and losses. If a fraction x of an investment is your own money, then your degree of leverage is $1/x$. If you pay a rate B on the borrowed money and earn a rate of return R on the total investment, then the rate of return on your own money is $B + (1/x)(R - B)$.

Limit Order A limit order is an order to a broker with a limit on the price—a maximum in the case of a buy order, a minimum for a sell order.

Limited Liability Although stockholders are the legal owners of a corporation, they are not personally responsible for its debts; their potential loss is limited to the amount of money they have invested in the firm's stock.

Liquidity Premium Hypothesis If investors are more concerned with capital risk than income risk, they have a natural preference for short-term assets and will require relatively high returns on long-term bonds—higher than predicted by the simple expectations hypothesis. According to this theory, the term structure is normally upward sloping.

Load Fee A load fee is a sales charge levied by many open-end investment companies and paid to the fund and the salesperson, if any. Funds that don't charge load fees are called no-loads.

Low-Price Activity Ratio Some technical analysts track the volume of trading in low-price (and presumably speculative) stocks relative to the total volume of trading.

Macro Risk See Systematic Risk.

Margin An investor who borrows money from a broker to buy stock ("buying on margin") must put up an initial amount, called margin, that satisfies the broker's margin requirements and must keep the account's equity (market value minus loan) above the broker's maintenance margin requirement.

Margin Call If an investor who buys stock on margin allows the equity—the market value of the stock minus the current loan balance—to fall below a specified "maintenance margin," the investor receives a margin call requesting additional funds to reduce the account's indebtedness (or the deposit of more securities to build up its equity). The stock exchanges require a 25% maintenance margin, but most brokers use a more conservative 30% of market value.

Marginal Tax Rates A person's marginal tax rate is the extra tax levied on an extra dollar of income, and is determined by the person's tax bracket. The Tax Reform Act of 1986 compressed fifteen tax brackets (ranging from 11% to 50%) down to two basic rates, 15% and 28%, with a 5% surcharge on some incomes in the 28% bracket, raising the effective marginal tax rate for these persons to 33%. For comparing and evaluating investment decisions, the marginal tax rate is appropriate (and is generally higher than the average tax rate).

Market Order A market order is an order to a broker to buy or sell a security at the best price currently obtainable—the market price. For an exchange-listed stock, the trade may be at the specialist's bid or ask price. Over the counter, the broker identifies the market maker with the best price and makes the transaction.

Market Segmentation Hypothesis The market segmentation hypothesis holds that investors have diverse preferences and specialize in different maturities. Some investors, such as life insurance companies and pension funds, have long horizons and prefer long-term bonds to minimize income risk, while other investors, particularly those most concerned with real rates of return, consider long-term bonds very risky and prefer to roll over short-term assets. If the market is sharply segmented, then the interest rates on different maturities might depend solely on demand and supply within that segment of the market, allowing very different interest rates on bonds with only slightly different maturities.

Market Timing Market timers attempt to buy stocks at low prices and sell at higher prices, based on technical or fundamental analysis, or both. Many are skeptical of those who claim to be astute enough to jump in and out of the market at the appropriate times.

Marking to Market See Daily Settlement.

Markowitz Frontier In mean-variance analysis, the Markowitz frontier is the envelope of efficient portfolios showing the minimum standard deviation attainable for each possible expected return. Investors can choose among the efficient portfolios on the Markowitz frontier, depending on their risk preferences.

Mean The mean μ of a probability distribution is its expected value, the probability-weighted average of the possible outcomes. The mean $\overline{X}$ of a set of data is the average value of the observations.

Micro Risk See Unsystematic Risk.

Modigliani-Miller Theorem The Modigliani-Miller theorem holds that shareholders are not affected by changes in a firm's debt-equity ratio. Because there is no advantage or disadvantage to corporate leverage, the total market value of a company depends on the profitability of its assets, not on its debt/equity ratio. The most important qualification is that debt is a tax shield that increases the firm's after-tax cash flow.

Money-Market Fund Investment companies that specialize in Treasury bills, certificates of deposit, and other very short-term fixed-income securities are known as money-market funds.

Multiple-Factor Model The multiple-factor model extends the single-index model by relating the return on an asset to several explanatory factors, such as output, interest rates, and inflation.

Mutual Fund See Open-End Investment Company.

Naked Call The sale of a call option without ownership of the underlying asset is called a naked call. The seller must either repurchase the call at some point or buy the stock and deliver it to the holder of the call option. If the price of the stock soars, the loss can be devastating.

Negative Amortization If the monthly loan payment is insufficient to cover the interest charge, the unpaid balance increases: negative amortization. This can occur in many business and personal loans (such as a line of credit from a bank, loans from a stock broker, or credit card balances) where there is no set repayment schedule and with adjustable rate loans if the monthly payment does not increase with interest charges.

Net Asset Value (NAV) The market value of an investment company's portfolio divided by the number of outstanding shares in the investment company is its NAV, the price at which an open-end company will redeem shares or issue new ones.

No-Loads Investment companies that do not charge load fees are called no-load funds. All closed-end funds are no-load.

Nominal Rate of Return The nominal rate of return compares the dollars received from an investment with the dollars invested, without adjusting for the purchasing power of these dollars. The real rate of return measures the percentage increase in purchasing power and is approximately equal to the nominal rate of return minus the rate of inflation.

Normal Distribution The normal distribution is the widely used bell-shaped Gaussian probability distribution. For many assets, this is a reasonable, useful approximation for describing investor uncertainty about the asset's return. A normal distribution is symmetrical about its mean with about a 68% probability of being within one standard deviation of its mean and about a 95% probability of being within two standard deviations.

Odd Lot In contrast to round lots, a trade of a nonstandard size; for example, the sale of 5 shares of AT&T, rather than 100 shares, is an odd lot. Odd-lot trades may be handled by the specialist, as are round lots, or the customer's brokerage firm may simply buy or sell the stock itself. In either case, the customer pays an added cost, called the odd-lot differential, generally an eighth of a point ($0.125 a share) for stocks selling for less than $40 and a quarter point ($0.25 a share) for more expensive stocks.

Open-End Investment Company The number of shares issued by an open-end investment company is not fixed, but increases as more money is invested in the fund and declines as money is withdrawn. Each day, or several times a day, the fund calculates its net asset value (NAV) and stands ready to issue or redeem shares at this price.

Open Interest Option and futures contracts are created by the willingness of people to sell contracts. Those who own contracts are said to be "long" while those who have written these contracts are "short," and the total amount of outstanding contracts, called the open interest, fluctuates daily.

Opportunity Locus The opportunity locus is a graphic apparatus showing the alternatives available to an investor. The choice among these alternatives is determined by the investor's indifference curves.

Option Contract An option contract gives one of the parties the right, but not the obligation, to buy or sell an item in the future at a price that is specified now. The mill might pay a farmer $20,000 for an option giving it the right to buy 100,000 bushels of wheat six months from now at $3 a bushel. If the market price of wheat drops below $3, then the mill will not exercise its option. Since options do not have to be exercised, but merely valued on the expiration date, contracts can be written on intangible things such as the S&P 500 stock index.

Over The Counter Securities that aren't listed on organized exchanges are said to be traded over the counter (OTC), using dealers who make a market by quoting ask and bid prices at which they are willing to buy and sell the security. The prices of many OTC securities are reported on the National Association of Securities Dealers Automatic Quotations system (NASDAQ).

Payout Ratio A firm's payout ratio $d = D/E$ is the fraction of earnings that the firm's board of directors elects to pay out as dividends; the remainder $1 - d$ is the retention ratio, the fraction of earnings plowed back into the firm to finance expansion.

Points A loan with points involves a fee equal to a specified percentage of the loan paid at the time the loan is made; for example, for a $100,000 loan at "12% plus 5 points," the borrower receives $95,000 ($100,000 less the 5% points charge), but pays 12% interest on the full $100,000 loan. Points were originally devised to circumvent usury ceilings, which restrict stated rather than effective interest rates on loans.

Poison Pills Poison pills are anti-takeover provisions that provide for exorbitant cash payments in the event of an unfriendly takeover; for example, a company might specify that if any group acquires more than 20% of the company's stock it will sell new shares to others at bargain prices, in effect giving away assets.

Ponzi Scheme When the money of new investors is used to pay off earlier ones, the investment is a Ponzi scheme. Such schemes require an ever-expanding group of participants and collapse when new people cannot be found.

Portfolio Insurance Portfolio insurance is a flexible procedure for limiting losses by selling securities continuously as prices drop (buying as prices rise). Enough investors following these mechanical rules could destabilize financial markets.

Preferred Stock Preferred stock is similar to a bond in that, unlike common stock, there are often no voting privileges, the shares have a stated liquidation value, and the dividend payments are specified when the stock is first issued—usually a constant dollar amount. If the firm is liquidated, preferred stockholders must be paid a specified value before common stockholders receive anything.

Prepayment Penalties On many loans, the borrower must pay the lender a prepayment penalty if the loan is repaid early. These protect lenders if interest rates fall and the borrower refinances the loan.

Present Value The present value of a cash flow is the amount that an investor is willing to pay for it. This is determined by discounting the cash flow by the investor's required rate of return; for a single payment F after n years and a required rate of return R, the present value is given by $P = F/(1 + R)^n$.

Price-Earnings Ratio A stock's annual earnings divided by its price is its price-earnings ratio, P/E—the inverse of the stock's earnings yield. P/E ratios tend to be high when projected growth rates are high and when shareholder required returns are low.

Primary Market The initial issuance of a security is said to occur in the primary market; for example, a household deposits money in a savings account, the U.S. Treasury raises money by selling bond, a business incorporates by issuing stock. In each case, a financial record of the transaction is created, showing the existence of a debt or of equity. Later trades of these certificates occur in the secondary market.

Private Placement Investment bankers often place a bond privately by arranging for fewer than 35 investors (typically pension funds and life insurance companies) to purchase all of a bond issue at a negotiated price. Bonds acquired through a private placement cannot be resold for at least two years.

Probabilities Probabilities can be used to quantify uncertainty by describing which outcomes are likely and which unlikely. These probabilities cannot be negative and must add up to one. With coins, dice, and cards we may be able to reason the probabilities from the physical characteristics of the experiment; investment probabilities are inherently subjective.

Probability Distribution When there are an infinite number of possible outcomes, a probability distribution can be used to specify the probabilities for ranges of outcomes; for example, a 10% chance that the return will be between $200 and $300, a 30% chance that it will be between $100 and $200, and so on. In a graphic representation of a probability distribution, the area under the curve shows the probability for that range of outcomes.

Program Trading Program trading originally meant the buying or selling of a diversified portfolio of stocks, but is now associated with index futures since these are the easiest way to trade baskets of stocks. Index arbitrage and portfolio insurance are two very different types of program trading.

Put-Call Parity Because buying stock, selling a call, and buying a put is a riskless strategy, there is a no-arbitrage put-call parity relationship between the prices of puts and calls, $P_c - P_p = P_0 - E(1 + R)$, where P_c and P_p are the price of European puts and calls, E is their exercise price, P_0 is the price of the underlying (no-dividend) stock, and R is the return on safe Treasury bills over the life of the options.

Put Option A put option gives the owner the right to sell an asset at a fixed price on or before a specified date. A put option becomes increasingly valuable if the price of the underlying asset declines.

Pyramid Deal A Ponzi scheme, a zero-sum game that transfers wealth from late entrants to early ones (and to the scheme's promoters), is also called a pyramid deal. The image of a pyramid places the initial investors at the top and the latest round on the bottom; the pyramid collapses when the next round doesn't materialize.

R-Squared R-squared is a statistical measure of the fraction of the variance in a stock's return that can be explained by fluctuations in the overall market. If $R^2 = 1$, there is a perfect fit with all of the points lying on a straight line; if $R^2 = 0$, the scatter is random and the market is of no help in explaining the behavior of this stock. A large, well-diversified portfolio has an R^2 close to 1.

Random Walk Hypothesis The weak form of the efficient market hypothesis, also called the random walk hypothesis, says that each change in a stock's price is unrelated to previous changes, much as each flip of a coin is unrelated to previous tosses and each step by a drunkard is unrelated to previous steps.

Real Assets Tangible physical assets, such as land, houses, livestock, and precious metals, are real assets, in contrast to financial assets.

Real Rate of Return An asset's real rate of return measures the percentage increase in purchasing power provided by the investment. This is approximately equal to the nominal (dollar) percentage return minus the percentage rate of inflation. Present value calculations can be done either by discounting a nominal cash flow by a nominal required rate of return or by discounting a real cash flow by a real required return.

Realized Rate of Return The realized rate of return is calculated by comparing the initial cost of an investment with its future value, including the proceeds from the reinvestment of the cash flow.

Registered bonds In contrast to bearer bonds, the owner of a registered bond registers with the bond's trustee and receives coupon payments without the physical presentation of the bond certificate. Since 1983, all Treasury securities have been in registered form.

Regression Towards the Mean The statistical tendency of extreme observations to be followed by more average values is called regression towards the mean. The incorrect conclusion is that all values will soon be average; for example, that all people will soon be the same height or that all firms will earn the same profit rate.

Regulated Investment Company Regulated investment companies satisfy the criteria established by the Investment Company Act of 1940— a designation that exempts them from corporate taxes. Among these criteria, the company must register with the SEC and comply with its disclosure requirements, own a diversified portfolio, and distribute at least 90% of its interest and dividend income as it is received.

Required Rate of Return The required rate of return is used to determine the present value of a cash flow. This required return depends on the returns available on alternative investments and other characteristics (such as the riskiness of the cash flow) that make this investment relatively attractive or unattractive.

Resistance Level In technical analysis, a resistance level is an intermediate high price for a stock, which presumably poses a psychological barrier to further advances. A support level is an intermediate low, which has an analogous psychological interpretation.

Retention Ratio A firm's retention ratio $1 - d = (E - D)/E$ is the fraction of earnings retained by the firm. The fraction $d = D/E$ distributed as dividends is the payout ratio.

Revenue Bonds In contrast to general obligation bonds, revenue bonds are issued by state and local government agencies to finance specific projects, such as a toll road, and are repaid with the income from the completed project. The WPPSS bonds were revenue bonds.

Reversing a Position Instead of taking delivery, the buyer of a futures contract can reverse the position by selling the contract before the delivery date, while a contract writer can reverse this position by repurchasing the contract.

Risk An uncertain situation is risky. The risk of a promised cash flow or anticipated asset return is often gauged by the standard deviation. Risk-averse investors require high expected returns of risky investments.

Risk Averse A risk averter sacrifices expected return to reduce risk and selects a diversified portfolio, containing dissimilar assets. Diversification reduces risk most effectively if the asset returns are uncorrelated or, even better, negatively correlated. A risk-averse person would certainly buy insurance if the expected return were zero, and may purchase insurance with a negative expected return.

Risk Neutral A risk-neutral person chooses the alternative with the highest expected return, leading to the placement of all eggs in one basket. A risk-neutral person does not like insurance or lottery tickets because both have negative expected returns.

Risk Seeker A risk-seeking person accepts fair bets and will even sacrifice expected return to increase risk; for example, buying a lottery ticket if the expected value is zero and maybe buying one with a negative expected return. Like the risk-neutral person, the risk seeker shuns diversification.

Round Lot A round-lot trade involves some multiple of a standard size. For most stocks, 100 shares is the standard size and any multiple of 100 shares is a round lot. For most bonds, the standard size is $1000 of par value. Trades of a nonstandard size are odd lots.

Runs A statistical run is a sequence of uninterrupted above-average or uninterrupted below-average data. Stock prices exhibit few runs if momentum is present and many runs if reaction is important. In fact, the number of runs is close to what would be expected from random coin flips.

Scorched Earth When a company resists an unfriendly takeover by selling its prized assets to make the company less attractive, this is a scorched-earth strategy.

Secondary Market The secondary market describes the trading of assets after their initial issuance in the primary market. For example, after a company issues bonds or stock in the primary market, using the services of an investment banker, these notes and shares may pass from hand to hand in the secondary market, either on an exchange or over the counter.

Security Market Line A graph of the risk-premium structure implied by the Capital Asset Pricing Model, showing that an asset's expected return is linearly related to its beta coefficient, is called the security market line.

Securities And Exchange Commission (SEC) In the aftermath of the stock market crash of 1929 and the subsequent economic depression, Congress passed the Securities Act of 1933 and the Securities Exchange Act of 1934, the latter establishing the SEC as a federal agency to enforce the provisions of these acts. The SEC oversees the public sale of securities in the primary market and trading in the secondary market, with a wide range of powers designed to ensure the fairness and integrity of these markets (for example, prohibiting fraud and compelling the disclosure of pertinent information).

Semi-Strong Form The semi-strong form of the efficient market hypothesis says that abnormal returns cannot be consistently earned using any publicly available information, not only past prices but also such data as interest rates, inflation, and corporate earnings. If so, fundamental analysis cannot beat the market.

Settlement Price At the end of each trading day, a futures exchange sets a settlement price (equal to the closing price for actively traded contracts) for reckoning each trade's profit or loss that day. Those with losses must make cash payments (daily settlements) to the brokerage accounts of those with profits before the beginning of the next trading day.

Shark Repellents Shark repellents are aggressive defenses—including golden parachutes, greenmail, poison pills, and scorched earth—used by target companies to ward off unfriendly takeovers.

Short Interest Many technicians watch short-interest data on the total number of uncovered short sales, looking for signs of pessimism, or the number of shorts who must eventually cover their positions.

Short Sale A short sale is the sale of borrowed securities, which must later be covered by a purchase. A short seller hopes that the price will drop, so that the later purchase price will be lower than the initial sale price. Short sales on the New York and American stock exchanges must satisfy the SEC's uptick rule, which allows a short sale only if the price is higher than for the preceding trade (or at an unchanged price if the most recent price change was upward).

Single-Index Model The single-index model assumes that the return on any asset is linearly related to the return on the overall market basket of assets and to an error term that encompasses other influences specific to the particular asset.

Sinking Funds Many corporate bonds require the issuer to place a certain amount of money into a sinking fund each year to redeem some of its bonds, thereby reducing the firm's indebtedness. These bonds can be called by lottery at a specified premium over face value or repurchased in the secondary market if the market price is lower than the call price.

Small Capitalization Some studies have found that the stocks of firms with a small total market value (debt plus equity)—called small-capitalization or "small cap" stocks—have outperformed the stock market as a whole. Others argue that these stocks do well not because the firms are small but because they have unreasonably low P/E ratios.

Specialist Each stock traded on the NYSE is assigned to a specialist who collects orders and acts as both a broker (an agent trading for others) and a dealer (trading for himself). As a broker, the specialist executes a transaction when someone is willing to buy at a price at which another member is willing to sell. In order to maintain a "fair and orderly" market, specialists also act as dealers by buying or selling, as needed, for their own accounts.

Speculative Bubble Sometimes asset prices lose touch with intrinsic values as people hope to profit not from the asset's cash flow, but from selling the asset at ever-higher prices. During these speculative bubbles, it seems foolish to sit on the sidelines while others become rich; in retrospect, it looks like mass hysteria. When the bubble bursts, buyers cannot be found and prices fall precipitously.

Speculators In contrast to investors who are willing to hold an asset for keeps, speculators buy not for the long-run cash flow, but to sell the asset a short while later for a profit.

Spot Price   The current market price of an item for immediate delivery is its spot price.

Spread   Spread strategies involving the simultaneous purchase and sale of options with different striking prices, expiration dates, or both. The basis of a futures contract is also called a spread.

Standard Deviation   The standard deviation is the square root of the variance. Like the variance, it gauges the spread of a distribution and, thus, gauges risk by measuring how certain we are that the return will be close to its expected value; but the standard deviation has the same units (% or $) as the data, while the units for the variance are dollars-squared or percent-squared.

Stock dividend   The distribution of additional shares of stock as a stock dividend is equivalent to a fractional stock split; for example, a 5% stock dividend increases the number of shares by 5% and, according to the conservation of value principle, reduces the value of each share by 5%.

Stock Market Indexes   Stock market indexes are statistical averages intended to summarize changes in stock prices as time passes. The most well known index is the Dow Jones Industrial Average.

Stock split   A stock split increases the number of shares and reduces the value of each share proportionately. For example, if a company declares a 2-for-1 split, each stockholder's shares are doubled and, if there is no change in the company's actual operations, the conservation of value principle implies that the value of each share should be halved.

Stop-loss Order   A stop-loss order is an order to sell a security if the market price falls below a specified level.

Stop Order   A stop order to a broker is an order to sell if the price falls to a specified level or to buy if the market price rises to a specified level. The most common are sell stop orders, also called stop-loss orders.

Straddle   The simultaneous purchase of a call and a put option is a straddle, a symmetrical bet that the price of the stock will either rise or fall, it doesn't matter which, by an amount equal to the price of the call plus the price of the put.

Street Name   Securities registered in the name of the brokerage firm, rather than the customer, are said to be held in a "street name," a practice that simplifies transactions and that is required of customers who buy stock on margin. The customer still receives dividends, annual reports, and other correspondence from the corporation.

Striking Price   See Exercise Price.

Strong Form   The strong form of the efficient market hypothesis holds that there is no information, public or private, that allows some investors to beat the market consistently. This hypothesis is contradicted by evidence that a few do profit by using information not available to other investors, often in violation of federal laws.

Support Level   In technical analysis, a support level is an intermediate low price for a stock, which is said to provide a psychological cushion against a price decline. A resistance level is an intermediate high, which allegedly poses a psychological barrier to price advances.

Systematic Risk   Also called macro risk, market risk, or nondiversifiable risk, an asset's systematic risk concerns macroeconomic events, such as unanticipated changes in interest rates, inflation, and the unemployment rate, that affect all securities. With macro risk, there is no safety in numbers: mere diversification cannot protect investors from recession or high interest rates.

Tax-Exempt Bonds   The interest on tax-exempt bonds is free of income taxes. The term usually refers to state and local bonds, also called municipals or munis, that are exempt from federal income taxes. A bond that is exempt from both state and federal taxes (such as a California bond held by a Californian) is said to be double tax-exempt. Bonds that are exempt from federal, state, and city taxes are triple tax-exempt.

Tax Shield   Because corporate interest payments are deducted from corporate taxable income, the profits are shielded and reach shareholders without being subjected to corporate income taxes.

Technical Analysis   In contrast to fundamental analysis, which applies present value principles to the valuation of corporate stock, using dividends, earnings, assets, and interest rates to judge whether a stock is really worth its current price, technical analysis tries to gauge the mood of the market by studying changes in market prices, the volume of trading, and other barometers of investors attitudes.

Term Structure of Interest Rates The term structure describes the yields to maturity on zero-coupon bonds that have different maturities but are otherwise identical; a yield curve compares the yields to maturity on coupon bonds of various maturities. The Expectations Hypothesis says that the relationship between short-term and long-term interest rates reflects the anticipated future course of interest rates.

Tobin's *q* James Tobin's *q* is the ratio of the market value of a firm to the replacement cost of its assets. A *q* value larger than 1 indicates that the firm's profit rate exceeds the shareholders' required return on their stock and that the firm will benefit shareholders if it retains additional earnings for expansion. A firm with a *q* less than 1 is worth more dead than alive.

Tobin's Separation Theorem In mean-variance analysis, this theorem states that if there is a safe asset, the selection of the optimal risky portfolio (at the tangency of a line from the safe return to the Markowitz frontier) can be separated from preferences about how much risk to bear.

Treasury Bills T-bills are federal government securities with maturities of less than one year, which are sold to raise money for government expenditures. There are no periodic interest payments; the investor's return is equal to the difference between the bill's purchase price and its face value, which is received when the bill matures. Unlike virtually all other securities, the financial press traditionally calculates T-bill returns on a discount basis, relative to the bill's face value rather than the purchase price, and thereby understates the investor's actual rate of return.

Turnover An investment company's turnover is the ratio of its annual sales (or purchases) of securities to its total assets, a measure of how actively it trades securities (and incurs transaction expenses).

Unsystematic Risk Also called micro risk, idiosyncratic risk, or diversifiable risk, unsystematic risk arises from events specific to individual companies and can be diversified away.

Uptick Rule Short sales on the New York and American stock exchanges are governed by an SEC uptick rule, which allows a short sale to be executed only at a price that is higher than that for the preceding transaction (or at an unchanged price if the most recent price change was upward). The intent is to keep short sales from adding to the momentum of a falling market.

Variance The statistical variance is the average squared deviation of the outcomes about their mean, thus a measure of whether the possible (or actual) values are close to the mean or scattered widely. For a probability distribution, the probabilities are used as weights in calculating this average; for empirical data, the observed frequencies are used. (If the data are a small sample, statisticians usually divide by $n - 1$ rather than n.)

Warrants These are similar to call options, except that warrants are issued by the company itself and, if exercised, the firm issues new shares of common stock, diluting the value of shareholders' stock to the extent that the exercise price is less than the market value of the firm's stock.

Weak Form The weak form of the efficient markets hypothesis holds that past data on stock prices are of no use in predicting future price changes. An immediate implication is that most technical analysis is worthless.

Yield Curve The yield curve is similar to the term structure, but compares the yields to maturity on coupon-paying bonds with different maturities.

Yield to Call A bond's yield to call is calculated like the yield to maturity, but assumes that the bond will be called at the first opportunity.

Yield to Maturity A bond's yield to maturity is that discount rate such that the present value of the bond's coupons and principal is equal to its price. A bond's price is higher than its face value when its yield to maturity is below the coupon rate and is at a discount from face value when its yield is above the coupon rate.

Zero-Coupon Bonds Zeros pay no coupons; as with T-bills, the buyer receives a single, lump-sum payment at maturity. A series of zeros maturing at six-month intervals can be created by stripping away the coupons from conventional bonds. The implicit annual rate of return R on a zero costing P that pays an amount F in n years is given by the compound interest formula $P(1 + R)^n = F$.

REFERENCES

Chapter 1

1. John M. Keynes, *The General Theory of Employment, Interest, and Money,* New York: Macmillan, 1936, pp. 149–150.
2. Mail advertisement from Bob Jennings Confidential Report, Boca Raton, Fla., July 1987.
3. Gerald Krefetz, *How to Read and Profit from Financial News,* New York: Ticknor & Fields, 1984, p. 1.
4. Louis Rukeyser, *How to Make Money in Wall Street,* Garden City, N.Y.: Doubleday, 1974, p. 90.
5. Mail advertisement from Hampton Numismatics, August 1986.
6. Roger G. Ibbotson and Rex A. Sinquefield, *Stocks, Bonds, Bills and Inflation: 1986 Yearbook,* Chicago: Ibbotson Associates, 1986.
7. Michael Laurence, "Playboy's Guide to Mutual Funds," *Playboy,* June 1969, p. 186.

Chapter 2

1. Robert J. Samuelson, "Interest Rates are Lower—Does that Equal 'Right'?" *Los Angeles Times,* March 13, 1986.
2. Stephen C. Leuthold, "Interest Rates, Inflation, and Deflation," *Financial Analysts Journal,* January-February 1981, pp. 28–41.
3. Lawrence H. Summers, "The Non-Adjustment of Nominal Interest Rates: A Study of the Fisher Effect," in James Tobin, ed., *Macroeconomics, Prices, and Quantities: Essays in Memory of Arthur M. Okun,* Washington, D.C.: Brookings Institution, 1983, pp. 201–241.

4. *New Yorker,* September 22, 1986, p. 111.
5. Letter to the Editor, *Barron's,* December 10, 1984.
6. *London Times,* quoted in the *New Yorker,* March 11, 1985, p. 138.
7. "Inflation to Smile About," *Los Angeles Times,* January 11, 1988.
8. Georgette Jason, "Compounding Is Key to Investment Yields," *The Wall Street Journal,* April 20, 1989; Thomas A. Dziadosz, "It Figures," letter to the editor, *The Wall Street Journal,* May 25, 1989.
9. Kenneth T. Rosen, "The Impact of Proposition 13 on House Prices in Northern California: A Test of the Interjurisdictional Capitalization Hypothesis," *Journal of Political Economy,* February 1982, pp. 191–200.
10. Hume Financial Education Services, "Lesson 2: Escape Taxes the Way the Pros Do," *Successful Investing & Money Management,* Atlanta, 1984, p. 2.29.
11. Jane Bryant Quinn, "A Savings Program for College Tuition," *Cape Cod Times,* September 6, 1987.
12. Robert L. Rose, "Retirement Planning Should Begin with Early Look at Social Security," *The Wall Street Journal,* April 30, 1985.
13. William E. Fruhan, Jr., "How Fast Should Your Company Grow?" *Harvard Business Review,* January-February 1984, p. 87.
14. Edward Yardeni, "Money & Business Alert," Prudential-Bache Securities, September 23, 1987.

Chapter 3

1. Dan Dorfman, "Fed Boss Banking on Housing Slump to Nail Down Inflation," *Chicago Tribune*, April 20, 1980.
2. Quoted in Arthur Schlesinger, Jr., "Inflation Symbolism vs. Reality," *The Wall Street Journal*, April 9, 1980.
3. "Housing Squeeze Tightens More Here," *Houston Chronicle*, April 3, 1980.
4. Don G. Campbell, "S&Ls Turn to Mortgage Acceleration to Help Bail Themselves Out," *Los Angeles Times*, September 12, 1982.
5. Andrew Carron, of the Brookings Institution, quoted in "While Congress Fiddles, More Thrifts Burn," *The Economist*, February 27, 1982, p. 73.
6. Dennis Jacobe, director of research at the U.S. League of Savings Associations, quoted in Eric N. Berg, "Fixed-Rate Mortgages Held Threat to Lenders," *New York Times*, March 10, 1986.
7. Franco Modigliani, "Comment," in James Tobin, ed., *Macroeconomics: Prices and Quantities*, Washington, D.C.: Brookings Institution, 1983, p. 243. One example is an April 11, 1987 *The Wall Street Journal* column (David B. Hilder, "ARMs Race On, But Borrowers Face Choices,") in which negative amortization is said to be a "drawback."
8. "Nibbling Down Affordable Mortgages," *Business Week*, March 14, 1983, p. 153.
9. David Henry, "Lender of Last Resort," *Forbes*, May 18, 1987, pp. 73–75.
10. David Pauly, "Bracing for the Great Car Glut," *Newsweek*, September 15, 1986, p. 59.
11. Robin Gross and Jean V. Cullen, *Help! The Basics of Borrowing Money*, New York: Times Books, 1980, p. 45.
12. R.J. Turner, *The Mortgage Maze*, Arlington, Va.: Alexandria House Books, 1982, p. 64.
13. Les Gapay, "Don't Bank on It: Thinking of Refinancing? Read This First," *Barron's*, June 30, 1986.
14. Don G. Campbell, "Early Loan Payoff Gains Popularity," *Los Angeles Times*, October 20, 1985.
15. Douglas R. Sease, "Buying a Car? Here's How to Figure Savings in Latest Offers from GM, Ford, and Chrysler," *The Wall Street Journal*, May 3, 1982.
16. Amal Kumar Naj, "Car Leasing Allure Grows With Tax Act, But Buying May Still Be the Way to Go," *The Wall Street Journal*, December 12, 1986.
17. Turner, pp. 242–3.
18. "How to Save on a Car Loan," *Consumer Reports*, April 1978, pp. 201–202.
19. "Hot Tips," *Sylvia Porter's Personal Finance*, February 1986, p. 18.
20. Turner, p. 228.
21. Irwin T. Vanderhoof, "The Use of Duration in the Dynamic Programming of Investments," in George G. Kaufman, G.O. Bierwag, and Alden Toevs, eds., *Innovations in Bond Portfolio Management: Duration Analysis and Immunization*, Greenwich, Conn.: JAI Press, 1983, p. 46.
22. S.J. Diamond, "Credit or Cash? The Difference Can Add Up," *Los Angeles Times*, September 23, 1985. Also see S.J. Diamond, "Credit Doesn't Always Rate Better Than Cash," *Los Angeles Times*, September 30, 1985.
23. Don G. Campbell, "Biweekly 'Yuppie Mortgages' Interest State Lenders," *Los Angeles Times*, April 26, 1987.
24. Don G. Campbell, "Creating a Market for Biweeklies," *Los Angeles Times*, April 26, 1987.
25. First Federal Savings of the Palm Beaches, letter dated July 11, 1986.

Chapter 4

1. P.A. Hays, M.D. Joehnk, and R.W. Melicher, "Determinants of Risk Premiums in the Public and Private Bond Market," *Journal of Financial Research*, Fall 1979.
2. M. Weinstein, "The Effect of a Rating Change Announcement on Bond Prices," *Journal of Financial Economics*, December 1977, pp. 329–350. G. Hettenhouse and W. Satoris ("An Analysis of the Information Value of Bond-Rating Changes," *Quarterly Review of Economics and Business*, Summer 1976, pp. 65–78) agree, but Louis H. Ederington, Jess B. Yawitz, and Brian E. Roberts ("The Information Content of Bond Ratings," NBER Working Paper No. 1323, April 1984) disagree.
3. Robert N. Anthony, "Games Government Accountants Play," *Harvard Business Review*, September-October 1985, p. 161.
4. Edward I. Altman and Scott A. Nammacher,

"The Default Rate Experience on High Yield Corporate Debt," Morgan Stanley & Co., March 1985.

5. Harold G. Fraine and Robert H. Mills, "The Effect of Defaults and Credit Deterioration on Yields of Corporate Bonds," *Journal of Finance,* September 1961, p. 433.

6. James A. Wilcox, "Tax-Free Bonds," Federal Reserve Bank of San Francisco "Weekly Letter," March 14, 1986.

7. Robert Lamb, professor at New York University, quoted in Elaine Johnson, "To Have and To Hold," *The Wall Street Journal,* December 2, 1985, p. 16D.

8. James A. Wilcox, "Tax-Free Bonds," Federal Reserve Bank of San Francisco "Weekly Letter," March 14, 1986.

9. "Personal Business," *Business Week,* March 10, 1986, p. 136.

10. Gerald Krefetz, *How to Read and Profit from Financial News,* New York: Ticknor & Fields, 1984, p. 43.

11. Krefetz, pp. 44–45.

12. Consumers Digest, *Get Rich Investment Guide,* Vol. 3, No. 4, 1982, p. 84.

13. Debra Whitefield, "Money Talk," *Los Angeles Times,* June 4, 1987.

14. Andrew Tobias, *The Only Investment Guide You'll Ever Need,* New York: Harcourt Brace Jovanovich, 1978, p. 36.

15. John Kenneth Galbraith, "A Classic Case of 'Euphoric Insanity'," *New York Times,* November 23, 1986.

16. Carmella M. Padilla, "It's a. . .a. . .a. . . All-Terrain Vehicle, Yeah, That's It, That's the Ticket," *The Wall Street Journal,* July 17, 1987.

17. Family Real Estate advertisement, *Claremont Courier,* November 1, 1986.

18. Krefetz, p. 56.

19. Krefetz, p. 50.

20. James Flanigan, "Tax reform: Time for logical deductions," *Los Angeles Times,* March 15, 1987.

21. Karen Slater, "Premium Municipal Bonds Touted for Overall Return," *The Wall Street Journal,* June 3, 1988.

22. Michael E. Quint, "Bond Ratings—the Plain and Arcane," *New York Times,* June 19, 1983.

23. Carole Gould, "The Fading Allure of Incorporation," *New York Times,* September 7, 1986.

24. Edward Yardeni, "Money & Business Alert," Prudential-Bache Securities, May 14, 1986.

25. Pomona First Federal Savings, "Interest," Summer 1983.

26. "The Best Places for Your Cash in 1986," *Money,* January 1986.

27. Andrea Rock, "Profiting from the IRA Revolution," *Money Guide/IRA 1986,* published by *Money* magazine.

Chapter 5

1. Robert J. Shiller, "Conventional Valuation and the Term Structure of Interest Rates," National Bureau of Economic Research Working Paper #1610, 1985 (and several references therein).

2. Michael T. Belongia, "Predicting Interest Rates: A Comparison of Professional and Market-Based Forecasts," Federal Reserve Bank of St. Louis *Review,* March 1987, pp. 9–15.

3. Another study found that the standard deviations increased less than proportionately for bonds with durations of one to five years during the period 1950–1979: Jonathan E. Ingersoll, Jr., "Is Immunization Feasible?" in George G. Kaufman, G.O. Bierwag, and Alden Toevs, *Innovations in Bond Portfolio Management: Duration Analysis and Immunization,* JAI Press, 1983, p. 175.

4. For example, B.G. Malkiel, *The Term Structure of Interest Rates,* Princeton, N.J.: Princeton University Press, 1966; C.R. Nelson, *The Term Structure of Interest Rates,* New York: Basic Books, 1972.

5. Gary Smith, *Money and Banking,* Reading, Mass.: Addison-Wesley, 1982, pp. 98–99.

6. Jane Bryant Quinn, "Woman's Day Money Facts," *Woman's Day,* April 27, 1982, p. 29.

7. Bob Edwards, "Bond Analysis: The Concept of Duration," American Association of Individual Investors *Journal,* March 1984, p. 37.

8. Tom Herman and Matthew Winkler, "Curve on Yields Poses Dilemma for Bond Buyer," *The Wall Street Journal,* November 11, 1988.

9. "Personal Investing," *New York Times Financial Planning Guide,* May 19, 1985.

10. Martin Baron, "'Lions,' 'Tigers,' 'Cats,' Await Small Investor," *Los Angeles Times,* November 21, 1982.

11. Edward Yardeni, "Money & Business Alert," November 20, 1985, p. 1.
12. Pomona First Federal Savings, "Interest," Summer, 1983.
13. Jack Clark Francis, *Management of Investments*, 2nd ed., New York: McGraw-Hill, 1988, p. 500.
14. Robert J. Samuelson, "Interest Rates are Lower—Does that Equal 'Right'?" *Los Angeles Times*, March 13, 1986.
15. Karen Slater, "Jumping on the Bondwagon," *The Wall Street Journal*, December 2, 1985.
16. Jonathan Peterson, "The Taming of Inflation: Will It Last?" *Los Angeles Times*, February 4, 1987.
17. Quoted in Steven Mintz, "Strategies," *Investment Management World*, May-June 1986, p. 22.
18. Tom Herman and Edward P. Foldessy, "Bond Prices Dropping in Market's Upheaval," *The Wall Street Journal*, October 29, 1980.
19. David M. Gordon, "Reining In on the Federal Reserve," *Los Angeles Times*, September 30, 1986.
20. Barbara Quint, "Bonds by the Bundle," *Money*, September 1976, pp. 56–64.
21. Paul Watro, "Bank Earnings: Comparing the Extremes," Federal Reserve Bank of Cleveland, 1987.
22. "Business Bulletin," *The Wall Street Journal*, March 13, 1986.
23. Richard W. McEnally, "Rethinking Our Thinking about Interest Rates," *Financial Analysts Journal*, March-April 1986, p. 64.
24. Gerald Krefetz, *How to Read and Profit from Financial News*, New York: Ticknor & Fields, 1984, p. 45.
25. Eric N. Berg, "Fixed-Rate Mortgages Held Threat to Lenders," *New York Times*, March 10, 1986.
26. Alice Priest Shafran, "Streetsmarts for Househunters," *Sylvia Porter's Personal Finance Magazine*, September 1986, p. 37.
27. Lindley H. Clark, Jr., "Interest Rates Likely to Head Higher," *The Wall Street Journal*, April 13, 1987.
28. Krefetz, p. 27.
29. John Markese, "Buying Treasuries from the Factory," *Money*, December 1988, p. 141.
30. Terri Thompson, "Guess what? A Payoff for Playing It Safe," *U.S. News & World Report*, March 6, 1989, p. 64.
31. Thompson, p. 64.

Chapter 6

1. Sanford L. Jacobs, "Taking It to the Street," *The Wall Street Journal*, May 19, 1986.
2. United States House Committee on Interstate and Foreign Commerce, *Securities Industry Study, Report and Hearings*, 92d Congress, 1972, Ch. 12.
3. Editorial, *New York Times*, Janaury 29, 1964.
4. See, for example, *The Wall Street Journal*, May 20, 1969.
5. For an insider's account, see C. David Chase, *Mugged on Wall Street*, New York: Simon and Schuster, 1987.
6. John Train, *Preserving Capital and Making It Grow*, New York, C.N. Potter, 1983, p. 71.
7. Thomas F. Loeb, "Trading Cost: The Critical Link Between Investment Information and Results," *Financial Analysts Journal*, May/June 1983, pp. 41–42.
8. An informative and entertaining variation is Andrew Tobias' article, "The Broker Made Money, the Firm Made Money (and Two Out of Three Ain't Bad)," *New York*, June 28, 1976, pp. 56–59.
9. G.M. Loeb, *The Battle for Investment Survival*, New York: Simon and Schuster, 1965, p. 57.
10. Michael Metz, market analyst, quoted in Paul Richter, "2 Stocks Added, 2 Are Cut from Dow Jones Average," *Los Angeles Times*, October 30, 1985.
11. David Upshaw, of Drexel Burnham Lambert, quoted in Jack Egan, "Dow and the Law of Averages," *New York*, May 21, 1979, p. 12.
12. Gerald Krefetz, *How to Read and Profit from Financial News*, New York: Ticknor & Fields, 1984, p. 10.
13. *The Wall Street Journal*, January 2, 1987.
14. Louis Rukeyser, *How to Make Money in Wall Street*, Garden City, N.Y.: Doubleday, 1974, p. 115.
15. Andrew Tobias, *The Only Investment Guide You'll Ever Need*, New York: Harcourt Brace Jovanovich, 1978, p. 118.
16. Rukeyser, p. 129.
17. Fred Schwed, Jr., *Where Are the Customers' Yachts?* New York: Simon and Schuster, 1940, pp. 128–129.
18. John Brooks, *Once in Golconda*, New York: Harper and Row, 1969, p. 32.

19. "PaineWebber Tax Reform Report," December 9, 1986, p. 1.
20. Jack Egan, "Dow and the Law of Averages," *New York*, May 21, 1979, p. 12.
21. James Fraser, "An Updated Dow Average," *U.S. News & World Report*, July 23, 1979, p. 73.
22. Ian Rodger and Carla Rapoport, "High Tide and Still Rising," *Financial Times*, September 2, 1986, p. 18.
23. "Selling a Stock Short Is a Lot Riskier Than Buying, But the Way It Is Done Can Make It Very Profitable," *The Wall Street Journal*, September 5, 1985.
24. Mitchell C. Lynch, "Corporate Equity Offers Hit Record Pace as Firms Seek to Avoid High Bank Costs," *The Wall Street Journal*, May 30, 1980.
25. Advertisement, *The Wall Street Journal*, February 25, 1988.
26. Vartanig G. Vartan, "Municipal Bond Swaps," *New York Times*, August 18, 1981.

Chapter 7

1. John Burr Williams, *The Theory of Investment Value*, Cambridge, Mass.: Harvard University Press, 1938.
2. Benjamin Graham and David L. Dodd, *Security Analysis*, New York: McGraw-Hill, 1934. Later revisions have incorporated coauthors. Graham also authored several editions of a briefer version for nonprofessionals, *The Intelligent Investor*, New York: Harper, 1954.
3. Williams, pp. 57–58.
4. John Maynard Keynes, *The General Theory of Employment, Interest, and Money*, New York: Macmillan, 1936, p. 154.
5. The Value Line Investment Service, July 25, 1986 and August 15, 1986.
6. See, for example, "Disney: Trouble in Dreamland," *Dun's*, June 1973, pp. 54–57, 112–117; Dan Dorfman, "Heard on the Street," *The Wall Street Journal*, February 2, 1973, p. 29; and Charles J. Elia, "Heard on the Street," *The Wall Street Journal*, April 10, 1974, p. 35 and December 4, 1974, p. 43.
7. J. Peter Williamson, *Investments: New Analytic Techniques*, New York: Praeger, 1974, p. 152.
8. The details of a simlar model are described in Gary Smith, "A Simple Model for Estimating

Intrinsic Value," *Journal of Portfolio Management*, Summer 1982, pp. 46–49.
9. Editorial, *New York Times*, October 29, 1962.
10. Tom Herman and Edward P. Foldessy, "Big Banks Lift Prime Rate ½ Point to 14½; More Boosts Said Likely," *The Wall Street Journal*, October 30, 1980.
11. For some details, see R.J. Fuller, "Programming the Three-Phase Dividend Discount Model," *Journal of Portfolio Management*, Summer 1979, pp. 28–32.
12. Andrew Tobias, *The Only Investment Guide You'll Ever Need*, New York: Harcourt Brace Jovanovich, 1978, p. 37.
13. Vartanig G. Vartan, "Dow Off by 11.44 to 806.91 as Fears on Fed Heighten," *New York Times*, November 2, 1977.
14. Robert Goerner, "Viva Vino," *Performing Arts*, January 1984, p. 15.
15. S.J. Diamond, "The Unfulfilling Task of Selling One's Valuables," *Cape Cod Times*, August 30, 1987.
16. Eugene Carlson, "New Texas Stock Indexes Bode Poorly for the State's Economy," *The Wall Street Journal*, January 13, 1987.
17. Richard Ney, interviewed on the television program "Firing Line," December 10, 1975.
18. Julius Westheimer, interviewed on the television show "Wall Street Week," April 14, 1975.
19. Randall Smith, "Chrysler May Consider a Different Direction in Place of Its Bond-Heavy Pension Strategy," *The Wall Street Journal*, January 21, 1987.
20. Merrill Lynch, "Performance Monitor: Quantitative Analysis," April 1986.
21. Cynthia Crossen, "An Appraisal: Stocks and Bonds Aren't Easy to Choose Between," *The Wall Street Journal*, May 26, 1987.
22. Greg A. Smith, "Welcome To My Nightmare," Prudential-Bache Securities, August 12, 1987, p. 1.
23. Peter L. Bernstein, "A Green Light for Stocks," *New York Times*, February 2, 1975.
24. Allen Parkman, "Using Economic Analysis in Your Practice," *ABA Journal*, February 1, 1987, pp. 54–58.
25. Michael H. Sherman, "Cash Signals a Lack of Confidence," *Investment Management World*, March-April 1986, p. 23.

26. Peter L. Bernstein, "Diversification: Old, New, and Not-So-New," *Financial Analysts Journal*, March-April 1985, pp. 22–24.

27. James Flanigan, "Stock Market Clock May Soon Strike Midnight," *Los Angeles Times*, March 14, 1986.

28. William Baldwin, "All Coins Have Two Sides," *Forbes*, May 28, 1983, p. 189.

29. Ned Davis, interviewed in "No Bum Steers from This Bull," *Barron's*, December 9, 1985, pp. 8–9, 32.

30. Herb Abramson, "Value is value—but good timing can help," *The Hume MoneyLetter*, September 10, 1986, p. 5.

31. Greg A. Smith, "Remember! It's Always Darkest Before The Whatchamacallit," Prudential-Bache *Strategy Weekly*, October 14, 1987.

32. Robert Guenther, "All-Cash Deals May Sacrifice Favorable Effects of Leverage," *The Wall Street Journal*, October 29, 1986.

33. Tobias, p. 68.

34. Michael Kinsley, "Let's Hear It for a Drop in Home Values," *The Wall Street Journal*, June 5, 1986.

35. Martin L. Leibowitz, "Total Portfolio Duration: A New Perspective on Asset Allocation," *Financial Analysts Journal*, September-October 1986, pp. 18–29, 77.

36. Kinsley.

37. Private correspondence with Bob Hockett at Trammell Crow.

38. Gerald Krefetz, *How to Read and Profit from Financial News*, New York: Ticknor & Fields, 1984, p. 142.

Chapter 8

1. Burton Crane, *The Sophisticated Investor*, New York: Simon and Schuster, 1959, p. 89; for a similar sentiment, see George L. Leffler and Loring C. Farwell, *Investments*, New York: Ronald, 1963, p. 498.

2. Crane, p. 92.

3. Benjamin Graham, David L. Dodd, and Sidney Cottle, with Charles Tatham, *Security Analysis: Principles and Techniques*, 4th ed., New York: McGraw-Hill, p. 422. See also pp. 388–389, 396–400, 458.

4. Charles Osterberg, "Unsafe at Zero Speed," *Journal of Irreproducible Results*, September-October 1983, p. 19.

5. Mark Twain, *Life on the Mississippi*, New York: Harper and Brothers, 1874.

6. Christopher Jencks and others, *Inequality*, New York: Basic Books, 1972, p. 59.

7. Harold Hotelling, review of Horace Secrist, "The Triumph of Mediocrity in Business," *Journal of the American Statistical Association*, Vol. 28, 1933, pp. 463–465. Secrist and Hotelling debated this further in the 1934 volume of this journal, pp. 196–199.

8. Dodd and Graham, Ch. 34.

9. Martin J. Whitman and Martin Shubik, *The Aggressive Conservative Investor*, New York: Random House, 1979, p. 184.

10. Whitman and Shubik, pp. 190–194.

11. John Maynard Keynes, *The General Theory of Employment, Interest, and Money*, New York: Macmillan, 1936, p. 151.

12. Adam Smith, *Supermoney*, New York: Random House, 1972, p. 174.

13. John Quirt, "Benjamin Graham: Rediscovered Apostle of Value," *Investing*, April 1974, pp. 16–18.

14. Patricia A. Dreyfus, "Sleeping Dogs That Investors Shouldn't Let Lie," *Money*, July 1976, p. 37.

15. Dreyfus, p. 37.

16. Graham and Dodd, p. 448.

17. Graham and Dodd, pp. 480–481.

18. Graham and Dodd, p. 490.

19. Graham and Dodd, Ch. 30.

20. Milton Moskowitz, "The 'Intelligent Investor' at 80," *New York Times*, May 5, 1974.

21. Dreyfus, pp. 35–38.

22. T. Hogarty, "Profits from Mergers: the Evidence of Fifty Years," *St. Johns Law Review*, Spring 1970, p. 389; Debra K. Dennis and John J. McConnell, "Corporate Mergers and Security Returns," *Journal of Financial Economics*, June 1986, pp. 143–187.

23. "The Man of Steel," *Business Week*, October 20, 1986, p. 52.

24. Shearson Lehman Brothers, "Ten Uncommon Values in Common Stocks 1987–1988," 1987.

25. Mark N. Dodosh, "Splitting 5 for 1, American Telnet Makes 43¾-cent Stock 'Affordable'," *The Wall Street Journal*, August 14, 1980.

26. John Downes and Jordan Elliot Goodman, *Bar-

ron's *Finance and Investment Handbook,* Woodbury, N.Y.: Barron's, 1986, p. 476.

27. Andrew Tobias, *The Only Investment Guide You'll Ever Need,* New York: Harcourt Brace Jovanovich, 1978, pp. 110–111.

28. James Flanigan, "It's Not Enough for IBM to Be Industry Giant," *Los Angeles Times,* January 20, 1988.

29. Edward Yardeni, "Money & Business Alert," Prudential-Bache Securities, September 24, 1986.

30. Graham and Dodd, p. 484.

31. American Association of Individual Investors, "Explanation of Data in the 'Up Tic' Section of the Journal," undated.

32. William H. Pike, *Why Stocks Go Up (and Down),* Homewood, Ill.: Dow Jones-Irwin, 1983, p. 171.

33. Don R. Conlan, "Profits, Rates Still Key to Stocks," *Los Angeles Times,* September 23, 1986.

34. Bill James, "Esquire's 1981 Baseball Forecast," *Esquire,* April 1981, pp. 106–113.

35. Diane Hal Gropper, "How John Neff Does It," *Institutional Investor,* May 1985, p. 88.

36. Frank Cappiello, "A Sure Path to Market Success—Find Companies That Have a 'niche'," *The Hume MoneyLetter,* November 5, 1986, pp. 1–2.

37. Whitman and Shubik, pp. 185–186.

38. This exercise is from Harold Peterson of Boston College.

39. Michael Kinsley, "Let's Hear It for a Drop in Home Values," *The Wall Street Journal,* June 5, 1986.

40. Mitchell C. Lynch, "Corporate Equity Offers Hit Record Pace as Firms Seek to Avoid High Bank Costs," *The Wall Street Journal,* May 30, 1980, p. 48.

41. Gretchen Morgenson, "The New Dynamo That's Supercharging Utility Stocks," *Money,* June 1986, pp. 85–86.

42. William F. Sharpe, *Investments,* 3rd ed., New York: McGraw-Hill, 1985, p. 430.

43. Frederick Rose and Richard B. Schmitt, "Arco Unveils Restructuring Plan that Features Sale of Many Operations, Purchase of $4 billion in Stock," *The Wall Street Journal,* April 30, 1985.

44. Gerald Krefetz, *How to Read and Profit from Financial News,* New York: Ticknor & Fields, 1984, p. 144.

45. William E. Fruhan, Jr., "How Fast Should Your Company Grow?" *Harvard Business Review,* January-February 1984, pp. 84–93.

46. Jack Clark Francis, *Investments,* 4th ed., New York: McGraw-Hill, 1986, p. 31.

47. Christopher Elias, "History Haunts Restless Bankers," *Insight,* April 20, 1987, p. 14.

48. Richard A. Brealey and Stewart C. Myers, *Principles of Corporate Finance,* 3rd ed., New York: McGraw-Hill, 1988, p. 380.

49. L.J. Davis, "The Next Panic," *Harper's Magazine,* May 1987, p. 37.

50. "How to Double Your Shares Without Spending a Dime," *Business Week,* March 9, 1987, p. 122.

51. Consumers Digest, *Get Rich Investment Guide,* Vol. 3, No. 4, 1982, p. 63.

52. Dreman, p. 50.

53. Louis Rukeyser, *How to Make Money in Wall Street,* Garden City, N.Y.: Doubleday, 1974, p. 81.

54. This exercise is based on Thomas Hopkins, "Pennzoil 'Owes' Texaco $700 Million," *The Wall Street Journal,* August 18, 1987.

55. Eugene F. Brigham, *Financial Management,* 4th ed., Chicago: Dryden, 1985, pp. 570–571.

56. Edwin J. Elton and Martin J. Gruber, "Marginal Stockholder Tax Rates and the Clientele Effect," *The Review of Economics and Statistics,* February 1970, pp. 68–74.

57. Quoted in Rukeyser, pp. 143–144.

58. James McNeill Stancill, "Does the Market Know Your Company's Real Worth?" *Harvard Business Review,* September-October 1982, p. 50.

Chapter 9

1. Abraham J. Briloff, *More Debits Than Credits,* New York: Harper and Row, 1976, p. 1.

2. Brilloff, pp. 109–112.

3. Stanley Penn and Kenneth Bacon, "Investigators Think Fraud Was Involved in Stirling Homex Case," *The Wall Street Journal,* November 19, 1974. p. 1.

4. Briloff, pp. 136–139.

5. Briloff, pp. 170–172.

6. Briloff, pp. 139–152.

7. Briloff, pp. 219–226.

8. Newton W. Lamson, "A Skeptical Eye for Earnings," *New York Times,* February 2, 1975.

9. Michael C. Knapp, "Corporations Are Evading SEC Oversight on Profits," *Los Angeles Times*, October 16, 1985.

10. David Dreman, *The New Contrarian Investment Strategy*, New York: Random House, 1982, p. 45.

11. Burton G. Malkiel, "U.S. Equities as an Inflation Hedge," in J. Anthony Boeckh and Richard T. Coghlan, eds., *The Stock Market and Inflation*, Homewood, Ill.: Dow Jones-Irwin, 1982, p. 87.

12. Martin Feldstein and Lawrence Summers, "Is the Rate of Profit Falling?" *Brookings Papers on Economic Activity*, 1977.1, pp. 211–227.

13. Warren Buffett, "You Pay a Very High Price in the Stock Market for a Cheery Consensus," *Forbes*, August 6, 1979, pp. 25–26.

14. Franco Modigliani and Richard A. Cohn, "Inflation and the Stock Market," in Boeckh and Coghlan, pp. 99–117; in particular, see the graph on p. 101.

15. Franco Modigliani and Richard A. Cohn, "Inflation, Rational Valuation, and the Market," *Financial Analysts Journal*, March–April 1979, pp. 24–44.

16. Milton Moskowitz, "The 'Intelligent Investor' at 80," *New York Times*, May 5, 1974.

17. Modigliani and Cohn in Boeckh and Coghlan, pp. 112–113.

18. Richard W. Kopcke, "Stocks Are Not an Inflation Hedge," in Boeckh and Coghlan, pp. 47–57.

19. A. Berle and G. Means, *The Modern Corporation and Private Property*, New York: Macmillan, 1932.

20. R. Larner, "Ownership and Control in the 200 Largest Nonfinancial Corporations, 1929 and 1963," *American Economic Review*, September 1966, pp. 777–787.

21. Adolf Berle (1931) quoted in Michael A. Hiltzik, "Investors Relinquish Key Rights," *Los Angeles Times*, May 18, 1986.

22. For example, John Kenneth Galbraith, *The New Industrial State*, 2nd ed., Boston: Houghton Mifflon, 1971; for contrasting views, see the papers from a conference on the separation of ownership and control published in the *Journal of Law and Economics*, June 1983, pp. 235–496.

23. An early and influential proponent was William Baumol, *Business Behavior, Value and Growth*, New York: Harcourt Brace and World, 1967.

24. R. Monsen, J. Chiu, and D. Cooley, "The Effect of Separation of Ownership and Control on the Performance of the Large Firm," *Quarterly Journal of Economics*, August 1968, pp. 435–451.

25. T. Hogarty, "Profits from Mergers: the Evidence of Fifty Years," *St. Johns Law Review*, Spring 1970, p. 389; Debra K. Dennis and John J. McConnell, "Corporate Mergers and Security Returns," *Journal of Financial Economics*, June 1986, pp. 143–187.

26. Martin J. Whitman and Martin Shubik, *The Aggressive Conservative Investor*, New York: Random House, 1979, pp. 202–203.

27. Laurie Baum, "The Job Nobody Wants," *Business Week*, September 8, 1986, p. 56.

28. Michael A. Hiltzik, "Investors Relinquish Key Rights," *Los Angeles Times*, May 18, 1986.

29. Amanda Bennett, "Peter Drucker Wins Devotion of Top Firms With Eclectic Counsel," *The Wall Street Journal*, July 28, 1987.

30. Baum, p. 56.

31. Baum, p. 59.

32. Baum, p. 56–8.

33. Carl Icahn, quoted in "The Man of Steel," *Newsweek*, October 20, 1986, p. 54.

34. Baum, p. 58.

35. Carl Icahn, quoted in "The Man of Steel," *Newsweek*, October 20, 1986, p. 52.

36. *Barron's* has exposed and opposed such actions time and again; e.g., "Private Fiefdom?—McGraw-Hill Stockholders Are Getting a Raw Deal" (February 5, 1979); "More 'Scorched Earth'—Who is Standing Up for Shareholder Rights?" (May 5, 1980); "Corporation or Fiefdom?—Conflicts Between Shareholders, Management Mount" (July 7, 1980); "One Shareholder, One Vote?—Scholars Challenge Some Widespread Myths About Corporations" (August 24, 1981); and "What Price Stewardship?—Management Keeps Putting Its Interest Ahead of Shareholders" (February 15, 1982).

37. Robert M. Bleiberg, "What Price Stewardship?—Management Keeps Putting Its Interest Ahead of Shareholders," *Barron's*, February 15, 1982, p. 11.

38. Michael C. Jensen, "Takeovers: Folklore and Science," *Harvard Business Review*, November-December 1984, pp. 109–121.

39. Oswald Johnston, "Big Holders Grill GM on Perot Buyout," *Los Angeles Times*, December 18, 1986.

40. Debra Whitefield, "The Ordeal of Takeover Battles," *Los Angeles Times,* November 11, 1984.

41. Debra Whitefield, "Brunswick Is Stronger Than Before It 'Scorched the Earth'," *Los Angeles Times,* November 11, 1984.

42. See, for example, Jenson.

43. Quoted in Hiltzik.

44. Quoted in Hiltzik.

45. Quoted in Hiltzik.

46. George F. Sorter, "Accounting For Baseball: At Best It's a Diamond in the Rough," *Financial Management Collection,* Spring 1987, pp. 1–2, 5, 7.

47. Michael H. Granof and Daniel G. Short, "For Some Companies, FIFO Accounting Makes Sense," *The Wall Street Journal,* August 30, 1982.

48. Subscription letter from *Forbes,* 1986.

49. Jack W. Wilson and Charles P. Jones, "Common Stock Prices and Inflation: 1857–1985," *Financial Analysts Journal,* July-August 1987, pp. 67–71.

50. Dreman, p. 10.

51. "How High is Up?" *Business Week,* March 17, 1986, p. 95.

52. "Computerized Investing," American Association of Individual Investors, December 1983-January 1984.

53. *Newsweek,* August 27, 1984.

54. John F. Lawrence, "Let's Outlaw Abuses Behind Takeover Bids," *Los Angeles Times,* March 15, 1987.

55. A.J. Merrett and Gerald D. Newbould, "CEPS: The Illusion of Corporate Growth," *Journal of Portfolio Management,* Fall 1982, pp. 5–10.

56. "HCA to Spend $350 Million on Stock Buy-Back," *Los Angeles Times,* November 16, 1985.

57. "Honeywell Adopts Additional Provision to Avoid a Takeover," *The Wall Street Journal,* February 19, 1986.

58. Financial Accounting Standards Board, "Disclosures about Oil and Gas Producing Activities," FASB Statement No. 69, November 1982, p. 40.

59. Fred Schwed, Jr., *Where are the Customers' Yachts?* New York: Simon and Schuster, 1940, p. 58.

60. John F. Lawrence, "Congress Must Act to Control Takeover Binge," *Los Angeles Times,* November 11, 1984.

61. John Buttarazzi, "U.S. Should Sell Loans to Meet Deficit Target," *The Wall Street Journal,* July 28, 1987.

62. Goldman, Sachs, & Co., "Portfolio Strategy,"

September 1988, p. 22.

63. Goldman, Sachs, & Co., pp. 24–25.

Chapter 10

1. Robert D. Edwards and John Magee, *Technical Analysis of Stock Trends,* 7th ed., Springfield, Mass: J. Magee, 1967.

2. Charles Dow, editorial, *The Wall Street Journal,* May 14, 1902.

3. R.B. Joynson, L.J. Newson, and D.S. May, "The Limits of Over-constancy," *Quarterly Journal of Experimental Psychology,* 1965, pp. 209–216. For a sampling of other interesting experiments, see S.C. Lichtenstein and Paul Slovic, "Reversals of Preference Between Bids and Choices in Gambling Decisions," *Journal of Experimental Psychology,* 1971, pp. 46–55; S.C. Lichtenstein, B. Fischhoff, and L. Philipps, "Calibration of Probabilities: The State of the Art," in *Decision Making and Change in Human Affairs,* H. Jungermann and G. de Zeeuw, eds., Amsterdam: D. Reidel, 1977.

4. My discussion of the Wall Street Week technical indicators is based on four mimeographed explanations prepared by Robert J. Nurock. Two titled "Wall Street Week Technical Market Index" (undated) and a third mimeo titled "An Explanation of the Wall Street Week Technical Market Index," 2nd revision, February 28, 1980, were distributed by the Maryland Broadcast Corporation. The fourth, titled "An Explanation of the Wall Street Week Technical Market Index," 5th revision, September 6, 1985, was obtained from Investor's Analysis, Nurock's advisory service.

5. Rukeyser, p. 261.

6. For some early and unusual evidence that small investors aren't so dumb, see Terry Robards, "Little Guy: He's Not Odd-Lot Man Out," *New York Times,* July 23, 1972.

7. David Dreman, *The New Contrarian Investment Strategy,* New York: Random House, 1982, p. 25.

8. "Wall St. Watcher Rides the Wave," *USA Today,* March 21, 1986.

9. Quoted in Linda Sandler, "Crash Topples Bullish Analysts' Pedestals; Role May Diminish," *The Wall Street Journal,* November 13, 1987.

10. Quoted in Reginald C. McGrave, *The Panic of 1837,* New York: Russell and Russell, 1965, p. 145.

11. Burton Crane, *The Sophisticated Investor*, New York: Simon and Schuster, 1959, p. 56.

12. John Andrew, "Some of Wall Street's Favorite Stock Theories Failed to Foresee Market's Slight Rise in 1984." *The Wall Street Journal*, January 2, 1985.

13. "Paper Trained," *Money*, May 1976, p. 5.

14. Lawrence Ritter and William Silber, *Principles of Money, Banking, and Financial Markets*, 2nd ed. New York: Basic, 1977, p. 383.

15. Alfred Cowles III, "Can Stock Market Forecasters Forecast?" *Econometrica* 1 (July 1933), p. 315.

16. Robert D. Merritt, *Financial Independence Through Common Stocks*, New York: Simon and Schuster, 1963, p. 363.

17. Burton Crane, The Sophisticated Investor, New York: Simon and Schuster, 1959, p. 236.

18. Quoted in *Personal Investing Newsletter*, August 12, 1987, p. 117.

19. "Margo's Market Monitor," May 1986.

20. Crane, pp. 116–117.

21. Louis Rukeyser, "Good News Amidst Pessimism," *Houston Chronicle*, December 4, 1979.

22. David Upshaw, of Drexel Burnham Lambert, quoted in John Andrew, "Some of Wall Street's Favorite Stock Theories Failed to Foresee Market's Slight Rise in 1984," *The Wall Street Journal*, January 2, 1985.

23. Beatrice E. Garcia, "Will It Be Friday the 13th, Part 6? Study Ties 3 in Year to Recession," *The Wall Street Journal*, November 13, 1987.

24. Fred Schwed, Jr., *Where Are the Customers' Yachts?* New York: Simon and Schuster, 1940, p. 47.

25. For views from some popular advocates see Ira U. Cobleigh's, *Happiness Is a Stock that Doubles in a Year*. New York: Bernard Geis Associates, 1968 and Nicholas Darvas' *How I Made Two Million Dollars in the Stock Market*, New York: American Research Council, 1960. You will probably find these books entertaining but unpersuasive.

26. John H. Allan, "The Winds of January on Wall Street," *New York Times*, January 18, 1976.

27. Beryl Sprinkel, *Money and Stock Prices*, Homewood, Ill: Irwin, 1964, p. 120.

28. *Newsweek*, March 9, 1987, p. 8.

29. JS&A advertisement, *Discoveries*, United Airlines, June 1986.

30. Dick Fabian, "Mutual Fund Profits Made EASY: An Investment for All Seasons," *Telephone Switch Newsletter*, 1985.

31. Letter to the Editor, *Sports Illustrated*, January 30, 1984.

Chapter 11

1. Quoted in T. McCraw, *Prophets of Regulation*, England: Belknap Press, 1984.

2. Edward Yardeni, "Money & Business Alert," Prudential-Bache Securities, October 29, 1986, p. 1.

3. Edward Yardeni, "Money & Business Alert," Prudential-Bache Securities, February 4, 1987, p. 1.

4. David Dreman, "The Madness of Crowds," *Forbes*, September 27, 1982, p. 201.

5. "International Business Machines," *Value Line*, August 13, 1982, p. 1101 and February 6, 1987, p. 1102.

6. Kidder, Peabody & Co., "Current Recommendation Update: International Business Machines," March 24, 1987.

7. Michael C. Jenson and George C. Benington, "Random Walks and Technical Theories. Some Additional Evidence," *Journal of Finance*, May, 1970.

8. Robert A. Levy, "The Predictive Significance of Five Point Chart Patterns," *Journal of Business*, 1971, pp. 316–323.

9. Burton Crane, *The Sophisticated Investor*, New York: Simon and Schuster, 1959, p. 18.

10. Charles Dow, editorial, *The Wall Street Journal*, May 14, 1902.

11. William F. Sharpe, "Likely Gains from Market Timing," *Financial Analysts Journal*, March-April 1975, pp. 60–69; Jeffries, cited in Mark Johnson, *The Random Walk and Beyond*, New York: Wiley, 1988.

12. David Dreman, *The New Contrarian Investment Strategy*, New York: Random House, 1982, p. 54; *Institutional Investor*, March 1976, pp. 277–279; *Journal of Bank Research*, Spring 1976, pp. 22–29.

13. R. Ball and P. Brown, "An Empirical Evaluation of Accounting Income Numbers," *Journal of Accounting Research*, Autumn 1968, pp. 159–178. But see O. Maurice Joy and Charles P. Jones, "Earnings Reports and Market Efficiencies: An

Analysis of Contrary Evidence," *Journal of Financial Research*, 1979, pp. 51–64, and Eugene H. Hawkins, Stanley C. Chamberlin, and Wayne E. David, "Earnings Expectations and Security Prices," *Financial Analysts Journal*, September-October 1984, pp. 24–38.

14. Avner Arbel and Bikki Jaggi, "Market Information Assimilation Related to Extreme Daily Price Jumps," *Financial Analysts Journal*, November-December 1982, pp. 60–66.

15. David Dreman, *The New Contrarian Investment Strategy*, New York: Random House, 1982, pp. 108–113.

16. Mark Hulbert's ratings, cited in Peter Brimelow, "Rating the Advisers," *Barron's*, July 15, 1985, pp. 6–7.

17. Irwin Friend, Marshall Blume, and Jean Crockett, *Mutual Funds and Other Institutional Investors: A New Perspective*, Twentieth Century Fund Study, New York: McGraw-Hill, 1971.

18. Patricia C. Dunn, and Rolf D. Theisen, "How Consistently Do Active Managers Win?" *Journal of Portfolio Management*, Summer 1983, pp. 47–50.

19. Mark Kritzman, "Can Bond Managers Perform Consistently?" *Journal of Portfolio Management*, Summer 1983, pp. 54–56.

20. One of the earliest published studies is James H. Lorie and Victor Niederhoffer, "Predictive and Statistical Properties of Insider Trading," *Journal of Law and Economics*, April 1968, pp. 35–51. Several studies are summarized in the June 21, 1976 issue of *Barron's*.

21. Quoted in Robert E. Dallos, "Companies Get Bullish on Security," *Los Angeles Times*, February 28, 1983.

22. Frank Cross, "The Behavior of Stock Prices on Fridays and Mondays," *Financial Analysts Journal*, November-December 1973, pp. 67–69.

23. Donald Keim, "Size-related Anomalies and Stock Return Seasonality: Further Empirical Evidence," Graduate School of Business, University of Chicago, 1980.

24. Marshall E. Blume and Robert F. Stambaugh, "Biases in Computed Returns: An Application to the Size Effect," *Journal of Financial Economics*, 1983, pp. 387–404; Richard Roll, "Vas ist das?," *Journal of Portfolio Management*, Winter 1983, pp. 18–28; and James B. Thomson, "Errors in Recorded Security Prices and the Turn-of-the-Year Effect," Federal Reserve Bank of Cleveland, working paper 8611, December 1986.

25. For more on Warren Buffett, read John Train, *The Midas Touch*, New York: Harper and Row, 1987.

26. Dreman, p. 151.

27. Thomas J. Peters and Robert H. Waterman, Jr., *In Search of Excellence*, New York: Harper and Row, 1982.

28. Andrew Tobias, *The Only Investment Guide You'll Ever Need*, New York: Harcourt Brace Jovanovich, 1978, p. 74.

29. "The Superstar Analysts," *Financial World*, November 1980.

30. Benjamin Graham, *The Intelligent Investor*, 4th ed., New York: Harper and Row, 1973, p. 80. Similar results were obtained in a study of 189 high-quality stocks over the period 1937–1962 by S. Francis Nicholson ("Price Ratios," *Financial Analysts Journal*, January-February 1968, pp. 105–109).

31. Henry R. Oppenheimer and Gary G. Schlarbaum, "Investing with Ben Graham," *Journal of Financial and Quantitative Analysis*, September 1981, pp. 341–360; Joel M. Greenblatt, Richard Pzena, and Bruce L. Newberg, "How the Small Investor Can Beat the Market," *Journal of Portfolio Management*, Summer 1981, pp. 48–52; Henry R. Oppenheimer, "A Test of Ben Graham's Stock Selection Criteria," *Financial Analysts Journal*, September-October, 1984, pp. 68–74.

32. David Dreman, *The New Contrarian Investment Strategy*, New York: Random House, 1982, pp. 129–135.

33. Sanjoy Basu, "Investment Performance of Common Stocks in Relation to Their Price-Earnings Ratios: A Test of the Efficient Market Hypothesis," *Journal of Finance*, June 1977, pp. 663–682.

34. Rolf Banz, "The Relationship Between Return and Market Value of Common Stocks," and Marc Reinganum, "Misspecification of Capital Asset Pricing: Empirical Anomalies Based on Earnings' Yields and Market Values," both in *Journal of Financial Economics*, March 1981, pp. 3–18, 19–46. Also see Reinganum, "Portfolio Strategies Based on Market Capitalization,"

Journal of Portfolio Management, Winter 1983, pp. 29-36.

35. Dreman, pp. 170–172; John Peavy and David A. Goodman, "The Signifance of P/Es for portfolio returns," *Journal of Portfolio Management,* Winter 1983, pp. 43–47.

36. Paul J. Strebel and Avner Arbel, "Pay Attention to Neglected Firms!" *Journal of Portfolio Management,* Winter 1983, pp. 37–42. For an update, see Barbara Donnelly, "Investors Looking for 'Neglected' Stocks Shouldn't Rule Out Big Issues, Studies Say," *The Wall Street Journal,* January 28, 1987.

37. Burton Crane, *The Sophisticated Investor,* New York: Simon and Schuster, 1959, p. 18.

38. Crane, p. 234.

39. Shearson/American Express advertisement, *Los Angeles Times,* December 12, 1982.

40. Morton Shulman, "The Difference Between Men and Boys Is the Stock Price of Their Toys," *The Hume MoneyLetter,* November 26, 1985, pp. 1–2.

41. Consumers Digest, *Get Rich Investment Guide,* Vol. 3, No. 4, 1982, p. 63.

42. Consumers Digest, p. 63.

43. 1986 advertisement for Penny Stock Advisor, Coral Springs, Fla.

44. Donald R. Sease, "Clues Abound for the Small Investor to Divine Market Direction," *The Wall Street Journal,* January 3, 1989.

45. "Money & Business Alert," Prudential-Bache Securities, November 20, 1985.

46. Michael C. Jensen, "Takeovers: Folklore and Science," *Harvard Business Review,* November-December 1984, p. 113.

47. Louis Rukeyser, *How To Make Money in Wall Street,* Garden City, N.Y.: Doubleday, 1974, p. 93.

48. "Adam Smith," *The Money Game,* New York: Random House, 1967, pp. 157–158.

49. Kenneth L. Fisher, *The Wall Street Waltz,* Chicago: Contemporary Books, 1987, p. 48.

50. "Fitting Victims to the Crime," editorial, *The Wall Street Journal,* April 27, 1987.

51. Kidder, Peabody & Co., "Portfolio Consulting Service," May 20, 1987.

52. Al Frank, in "The Hume MoneyLetter," December 10, 1986.

53. John Fedders, quoted in Julie Kosterlitz, "The

Thomas Reed Affair," *Common Cause,* January-February 1983, p. 17.

54. Quoted in *Business Week,* December 1, 1986, p. 50.

55. Daniel Burstein, "Market Frenzy: Don't Blame Boesky," *Los Angeles Times,* November 20, 1986.

56. John F. Lawrence, "Many to Blame for Trouble in Stock Market," *Los Angeles Times,* November 23, 1986.

57. Editorial, *The Wall Street Journal,* November 18, 1986.

58. Excerpted in "Dean Witter's Market Advice in 1932," *New York Times,* October 13, 1974.

59. Douglas Frantz, "The Unraveling of Dennis Levine," *Esquire,* September 1987, p. 163.

60. John Kenneth Galbraith, "A Classic Case of 'Euphoric Insanity'," *New York Times,* November 23, 1986.

61. Leo Herzel and Leo Katz, "Insider Trading: Who Loses?" *Lloyds Bank Review,* July 1987, pp. 16–17.

Chapter 12

1. A finctionalized account is given in Donald H. Dunn, *Ponzi: the Boston Swindler,* New York: McGraw-Hill, 1975.

2. "Charles Ponzi's Legacy," *Business Week,* June 29, 1974, p. 61.

3. Martha Brannigan, "Pied Piper: How Advisor Charmed Retirees Into Investment Disaster," *The Wall Street Journal,* June 4, 1987.

4. Martha Brannigan, "Too Good to be True," *The Wall Street Journal,* December 1, 1986.

5. Quoted in Rone Tempest, "Swiss Stock Scam Swindled Investors Out of $250 Million," *Los Angeles Times,* September 6, 1988.

6. Fred Schwed, Jr., *Where are the Customers' Yachts?* New York: Simon and Schuster, 1940, p. 20.

7. Nicholas Darvas, *How I Made Two Million Dollars in the Stock Market.* New York: American Research Council, 1960.

8. Phyllis Feinberg, "The New Issue War of Nerves," *Institutional Investor,* December 1980, pp. 47–52.

9. "Tenuous Play in Synthetic Fuels," *Business Week,* July 23, 1979.

10. "Western Oil Shale Corp. Stresses 'Speculative

Nature' of Its Shares," *The Wall Street Journal,* May 5, 1967.

11. Don A. Christensen, president of Greater Washington Investors, Inc., quoted in Louis Rukeyser, *How to Make Money in Wall Street,* Garden City, N.Y.: Doubleday, 1974, p. 92.

12. Dreman, pp. 76–77.

13. S. Schacter and J.E. Singer, "Cognitive, Social, and Psychological Determinants of Emotional States," *Psychological Review* 69 (1962), pp. 379–399.

14. *Black Enterprise* magazine, cited in Andrew Tobias, *The Only Investment Guide You'll Ever need,* New York: Harcourt Brace Jovanovich, 1978, p. 76.

15. For example, see Charles P. Kindleberger, *Manias, Panics, and Crashes,* New York: Basic Books, 1978.

16. John Carswell, *The South Sea Bubble,* London: Cresset Press, 1960, p. 142.

17. Carswell, p. 161.

18. Virginia Cowles, *South Sea: The Greatest Swindle,* London: Crowley feature, 1960.

19. A wonderful account is given by Frederick Lewis Allen, *Only Yesterday,* New York: Harper, 1931.

20. Allen, p. 333.

21. Allen, pp. 340–341.

22. Arthur M. Schlesinger, Jr., *The Crisis of the Old Order,* Boston: Houghton Mifflin, 1957, p. 231.

23. Simeon D. Fess, quoted in *New York World,* October 15, 1930.

24. Edmund Wilson, "Hull-House in 1932: III," *New Republic,* February 1, 1933, p. 320.

25. Dan Dorfman, "Fed Banking on Housing Slump to Nail Down Inflation," *Chicago Tribune,* April 20, 1980.

26. *The Wall Street Journal,* January 19, 1987.

27. James B. Stewart and Daniel Hertzberg, "Speculative Fever Ran High in the 10 Months Prior to Black Monday," *The Wall Street Journal,* December 11, 1987.

28. John Dorfman, "An Appraisal: Enormous Volume Could be a Good sign, Some Say," *The Wall Street Journal,* October 19, 1987.

29. Felix Rohatyn, a general partner in Lazard Freres & Co., quoted in James B. Stewart and Daniel Hertzberg, "How the Stock Market Almost Disintegrated a Day After the Crash," *The Wall Street Journal,* November 20, 1987.

30. Robert J. Shiller, "Investor Behavior in the October 1987 Stock Market Crash: Survey Evidence," Yale University, November 1987. Also see "What Really Ignited the Market's Collapse After Its Long Climb," *The Wall Street Journal,* December 16, 1987.

31. Shiller, pp. 19–20.

32. Robert Kirby, quoted in Randall Smith, "A Few Institutions Dominated Big Market Sell-Off, Report Says," *The Wall Street Journal,* January 11, 1988.

33. "Follies, Foibles, and Fumbles," *The Wall Street Journal,* January 4, 1988.

34. Cited in Dreman, p. 130.

35. Edward Yardeni, "Money & Business Alert," Prudential-Bache Securities, November 11, 1988.

36. James Flanigan, "Wall Street's Disaster Was All Too Real," *Los Angeles Times,* December 13, 1987.

37. Lester C. Thurow, "Brady Group's Answers Miss the Key Questions," *Los Angeles Times,* January 24, 1988.

38. Robert J. Shiller, p. 15.

39. Sidney Cottle, Roger F. Murray, and Frank E. Block, *Graham and Dodd's Security Analysis,* 5th ed., New York: McGraw-Hill, 1988.

40. "What Really Ignited The Market's Collapse After Its Long Climb," *The Wall Street Journal,* December 16, 1987.

Chapter 13

1. Leo Gould, *You Bet Your Life,* Hollywood, Calif.: Macel Rodd, 1946.

2. Adam Smith, *The Wealth of Nations,* 1776, London: Methuen, 1920, Vol. 1, Ch. 10, p. 109.

3. Carmen Brutto, quoted in *New York Times,* February 17, 1976.

4. William S. Peters, "The Psychology of Risk in Consumer Decisions," in George Fisk, ed., *The Frontiers of Management and Psychology,* New York: Harper, 1964, pp. 209–223.

5. J. H. Evans and S. H. Archer, "Diversification and the Reduction of Dispersion: An Empirical Analysis," *Journal of Finance,* December 1968, pp. 761–767.

6. Kidder, Peabody & Co., "Prime Computer," May 15, 1987.

7. John R. Dorfman, "Company Offers Gold at a Big Discount in Phone Solicitations—but with a Catch," *The Wall Street Journal,* October 12, 1987.
8. Alexandra Peers, "Psych 101: Investor Behavior," *The Wall Street Journal,* November 13, 1987.
9. Thomas C. Noddings, *Advanced Investment Strategies,* Homewood, Ill.: Dow Jones-Irwin, 1978, p. 51.
10. Hans R. Stoll and Robert E. Whaley, "Program Trading and Expiration-Day Effects," *Financial Analysts Journal,* March-April 1987, pp. 16–28.
11. Barbara Quint, *Money,* September 1976.

Chapter 14

1. Harry Markowitz's classic book is *Portfolio Selection,* New York: Wiley, 1959; James Tobin applied mean-variance analysis to macroeconomic theory in "Liquidity Preference as Behavior Towards Risk." *Review of Economic Studies,* February 1958, pp. 65–86.
2. William F. Sharpe, "Mutual Fund Performance," *Journal of Business,* 1966, pp. 119–138.
3. Kalman J. Cohen and Jerry A. Pogue, "An Empirical Evaluation of Alternative Portfolio Selection Models," *Journal of Business,* 1967, pp. 166–193.
4. Edward C. Franks and Shannon Clyne, "A Dynamic Asset Allocation Strategy for Achieving Specific Return Objectives with Reliability and Efficiency," (unpublished paper) 1987.
5. Stanley J. Cohen and Robert Wool, *How to Survive on $50,000 to $150,000 a year,* Boston: Houghton Mifflin, 1984, p. 36.
6. Laurel Sorenson, "In the High Flying Field of Energy Finance, Continental Bank is Striking It Rich," *The Wall Street Journal,* September 18, 1981.
7. Shannon P. Pratt, "Relationship Between Variability of Past Returns and Levels of Future Returns for Common Stocks, 1926–1960," in E. Bruce Frederickson, ed., *Frontiers of Investment Management,* rev. ed., Scranton, Pa.: International Textbook, 1971, pp. 338–353
8. Zvi Body, "Commodity Futures as a Hedge Against Inflation," *Journal of Portfolio Management,* Spring 1983, pp. 12–17.
9. Marshall E. Blume and Donald B. Keim, "Lower-Grade Bonds: Their Risks and Returns," *Financial Analysts Journal,* July-August 1987, pp. 26–33; I've merged their data on treasury and high-grade corporate bonds.

Chapter 15

1. William Sharpe, "Capital Asset Prices: A Theory of Market Equilibrium Under Conditions of Risk," *Journal of Finance,* September 1964, pp. 425–552; John Lintner, "The Valuation of Risk Assets and the Selection of Risky Investments in Stock Portfolios and Capital Budgets," *Review of Economics and Statistics,* February 1965, pp. 13–37.
2. See Gary Smith, *Statistical Reasoning,* Allyn & Bacon, 2nd ed., 1988, Ch. 13–14.
3. Marshall Blume, "On The Assessment of Risk," *Journal of Finance,* March 1971, pp. 1–10.
4. Fischer Black, Michael C. Jensen, and Myron S. Scholes, "The Capital Asset Pricing Model: Some Empirical Tests," in Michael Jensen, ed., *Studies in the Theory of Capital Markets,* New York: Praeger, 1972, pp. 79–121. For other evidence, see Michael C. Jensen, "Capital Markets: Theory and Evidence," *Bell Journal of Economics and Management Science,* 1972, pp. 357–398.
5. Stephen A. Ross, "Risk, Return and Arbitrage," in I. Friend and J. Bicksler, eds., *Risk and Return in Finance,* Cambridge, England: Ballinger, 1976, pp. 189–218; "The Arbitrage Theory of Capital Asset Pricing," *Journal of Economic Theory,* December 1976, pp. 341–360.
6. Several studies are referenced in Richard Roll and Stephen A. Ross, "The Arbitrage Pricing Theory Approach to Strategic Portfolio Planning," *Financial Analysts Journal,* May-June 1984, pp. 14–26; for a critique, see Phoebus J. Dhrymes, Irwin Friend, and N. Bulent Gultekin, "A Critical Reexamination of the Empirical Evidence on the Arbitrage Pricing Theory," *Journal of Finance,* June 1984, pp. 323–346.
7. Fred Schwed, Jr., *Where Are the Customers' Yachts?* New York, Simon and Schuster, 1940, p. 91.
8. James B. Cloonan, American Association of Individual Investors.
9. Robert E. Penn, "The Economics of the Market in Modern Prints," *Journal of Portfolio Management,* Fall 1980, pp. 25–31.

10. Laura Landro & Betty Morris, "Coke's Payout of Columbia Pictures Stock Expected to Be Resold by Some Holders," *The Wall Street Journal*, January 12, 1988.

11. Thomas L. Wyrick, letter, *The Wall Street Journal*, March 6, 1989.

12. Burton G. Malkiel and John G. Cragg, "Expectations and the Structure of Share Prices," *American Economic Review*, September 1970, pp. 601–617.

13. Peter C. Du Bois, "A Fresh Look at Japanese Price-Earnings Ratios," *Barron's*, November 5, 1984, p. 97.

14. Bruce Keppel, "AT&T Plans to Redeem Bulk of Preferred Stock," *Los Angeles Times*, March 9, 1987.

Chapter 16

1. Tim Metz and James A. White, "A Year After Its Peak, Stock Market Battles a Pervasive Malaise," *The Wall Street Journal*, August 25, 1988.

2. E.O. Thorpe and S.T. Kassouf, *Beat the Market—A Scientific Market System*, New York: Random House, 1967.

3. Fischer Black and Myron Scholes, "The Pricing of Options and Corporate Liabilities," *Journal of Political Economy*, 1973, pp. 637–654.

4. Fischer Black and Myron Scholes, "The Valuation of Option Contracts and a Test of Market Efficiency," *Journal of Finance*, 1971, pp. 399–417.

5. Bill Sing, "Possibility of a Bear Market Doesn't Mean Investors Have to Hibernate," *Los Angeles Times*, October 10, 1987.

6. Anise C. Wallace, "Chasing Option and Dividend Income," *New York Times*, August 4, 1985.

7. R.H.M. Associates, "The Greatest Stock Market Opportunities in Forty Years," mimeo, 1975.

8. Stanley W. Angrist, "Put Options Can Help Protect Portfolios," *The Wall Street Journal*, February 28, 1989

9. Michael R. Giordano, "The Strategic Investor," *The Hume MoneyLetter*, October 22, 1986, p. 5.

10. Raymond Piccini, letter, *New York Times*, January 19, 1975.

11. Michael R. Giordano, "The Strategic Investor," *The Hume MoneyLetter*, October 22, 1986, p. 5.

12. Thomas C. Noddings, *Advanced Investment Strategies*, Homewood, Ill.: Dow Jones-Irwin, 1978, p. 107.

13. Robert Merton, Myron Scholes, and Mathew Gladstein, "The Returns and Risks of Alternative Put-Option Portfolio Investment Strategies," *Journal of Business*, 1982, pp. 1–55.

14. Fischer Black and Myron Scholes, "The Valuation of Option Contracts and a Test Of Market Efficiency," *Journal of Finance*, 1971, pp. 399-417.

15. H. J. Maidenberg, "Stock Options—Traders' New Game," *New York Times*, Steptember 2, 1973.

16. Neuberger Securities, "Options Wanted," January 27, 1975.

17. Arthur Darack, "The Uncertain Economy," *The Hume MoneyLetter*, September 10, 1986, p. 1.

18. Thomas C. Noddings, *Advanced Investment Strategies*, Homewood, Ill.: Dow Jones-Irwin, 1978, p. 65.

19. Arthur Darack, "The Opportunistic Investor," *The Hume MoneyLetter*, November 5, 1986, pp. 7–8.

20. Eric Kirzner, "The Speculative Investor," *The Hume Moneyletter*, September 24, 1986, pp. 6–7 and November 5, 1986, pp. 5–6.

Chapter 17

1. James Risen, "Code of Honor in the Trading Pit," *Los Angeles Times*, January 28, 1989.

2. David Dreman, *The New Contrarian Investment Strategy*, New York: Random House, 1982, p. 233.

3. Kathryn M. Welling, "Let the Buyer Beware," *Barron's*, November 7, 1977, p. 13.

4. *The Wall Street Journal*, June 17, 1981.

5. Newton Lamson, "A New Way to Ride the Commodity Roller Coaster," *Money*, September 1975, p. 39.

6. John Train, Quoted in *Forbes*, May 1982.

7. R.L. Ross, "Financial Consequences of Trading Commodity Futures Contracts," *Illinois Agricultural Economics*, 1975, pp. 27–31.

8. B. Stewart, "An Analysis of Speculative Trading in Grain Futures," USDA Technical Bulletin No. 1001, 1949.

9. Stanley W. Angrist, "Stop Him Before He Trades Again, Brokers Are Told by Federal Judge," *The Wall Street Journal*, May 5, 1989.

10. Franklin Edwards, "Does Futures Trading Increase Stock Market Volatility?" *Financial Analysts Journal,* January-February 1988, pp. 63–69.
11. Hans R. Stoll and Robert E. Whaley, "Program Trading and Expiration-Day Effects," *Financial Analysts Journal,* March-April 1987, pp. 16–28.
12. C.B. Garcia and F.J. Gould, "An Empirical Study of Portfolio Insurance," *Financial Analysts Journal,* July-August 1987, pp. 44–54.
13. George Anders, "Portfolio Insurance Provided Cold Comfort," *The Wall Street Journal,* October 28, 1987.
14. Quoted in Richard J. Teweles and Frank J. Jones, *The Futures Game,* 2nd ed., New York: McGraw-Hill, 1987, p. 11.
15. Eric N. Berg, "Contrarians on Campus," *New York Times,* November 18, 1984.
16. Charles R. Schwab, "Wall Street's Great White Shark Is Back," *The Wall Street Journal,* April 25, 1989.
17. Hume & Associates, "The TED Spread," 1986.
18. L.J. Davis, "The Next Panic," *Harper's Magazine,* May 1987, p. 39.
19. Hume & Associates, "The GSR Trade," 1986.
20. International Trading Group, Commodity Option Letter, April 1988.

Chapter 18

1. Investment Company Institute, *1987 Mutual Fund Fact Book,* Washington, D.C.: Investment Company Institute, 1987.
2. Kathryn McGrath, quoted in *Money,* September 1986, p. 13.
3. Irwin Friend, Marshall Blume, and Jean Crockett (*Mutual Funds and Other Institutional Investors: A New Perspective,* Twentieth Century Fund Study, New York: McGraw-Hill, 1971) also found that mutual funds as a whole underperformed the market and that investors in load funds did worse than those in no-loads.
4. The data for 1976 to 1986 are from Wiesenberger Investment Companies Service, *Investment Companies,* 1987; earlier years are from William F. Sharpe and Howard B. Sosin, "Closed-End Investment Companies in the United States: Risk and Return," in B. Jacquillat, ed., *Proceedings of the 1974 Meeting of the European Finance Association,* Amsterdam: North-Holland, 1975.
5. An early proponent of this view is Eugene F. Pratt, "Myths Associated with Closed-End Investment Companies," *Financial Analysts Journal,* July-August 1966, pp. 79–82. Some empirical evidence is given by Burton G. Malkiel, "The Valuation of Closed-End Investment-Company Shares," *Journal of Finance,* June 1977, pp. 847–859.
6. Quoted in Gilbert Kaplan and Chris Welles, *The Money Managers,* New York: Ramdom House, 1969.
7. Pamela Sebastian and Jan Wong, "Fidelity is Scrambling to Keep Flying High as Magellan Slows Up," *The Wall Street Journal,* August 15, 1986; Randall Smith, "Some Mutual Funds' Hot Records May Hide Companies' Cool Moves," *The Wall Street Journal,* March 14, 1985.
8. Quoted in Andrew Tobias, *The Only Investment Guide You'll Ever Need,* New York: Harcourt Brace Jovanovich, 1978, p. 133.
9. Fred Schwed, Jr., *Where are the Customers' Yachts?* New York: Simon and Schuster, 1940, p. 87.
10. The seminal study is William F. Sharpe, "Mutual Fund Performance," *Journal of Business,* 1966, pp. 119–138.
11. Michael C. Jensen, "The Performance of Mutual Funds in the Period 1945–64," *Journal of Finance,* May 1968, pp. 389–416.
12. Wiesenberger Investment Companies Service, *Investment Companies,* 1987, pp. 154–157.
13. A. W. Bigus, "Whatever Happened to Mutual Funds?" *Esquire,* December 1973, pp. 48–54.
14. Fidelity Investments, "Investment Vision," November-December 1987, p. 9.
15. Michael Laurence, "Playboy's Guide to Mutual Funds," *Playboy,* June 1969, p. 196.
16. Michael Laurence, p. 186.
17. L. J. Davis, "The Next Panic," *Harper's Magazine,* May 1987, p. 38.
18. The data for the 24 stocks and the market as a whole are from *Forbe's* annual mutual fund issues of August 27, 1984 and September 16, 1985 and, in each case, refer to "the preceding 12 months," which does not coincide with the calendar year.
19. Michael Laurence, p. 197.
20. Dean LaBaron, President of Batterymarch Financial Management, in a February 1986 speech to fellow money managers and corporate finan-

cial executives, quoted in "LeBaron: Institutions Are Losing Their Grip," *Investment Management World*, March-April 1986, p. 5.

21. C. C. Hazard, *Confessions of a Wall Street Insider*, Playboy Paperback, 1972, p. 25.

22. Michael Laurence, p. 152.

23. Wiesenberger Services, "Mutual Funds Investment Report," February 1988, p. 7.

24. Michael Siconolfi, "Closed-End Funds Open to Gimmicks That Lift Prices," *The Wall Street Journal*, April 13, 1989.

25. Thomas C. Noddings, *Advanced Investment Strategies*, Homewood, Ill.: Dow Jones-Irwin, 1978, p. 127.

NAME INDEX

SUBJECT INDEX